Toys in the
Age of Wonder

Toys in the Age of Wonder

Science Fiction, Society and the Symbolism of Play

MARK RICH

McFarland & Company, Inc., Publishers
Jefferson, North Carolina

Also by Mark Rich

*C.M. Kornbluth: The Life and Works
of a Science Fiction Visionary* (McFarland, 2010)

Frontispiece: Drink McLaughlin's Coffee. This advertising lithograph places "The Scientist" beside instruments that had arisen with New Worlds idealism—electric battery, geographical globe, navigational compass, and telescope, among other delights for the nascent philosopher. Large trade card, late 1800s, lithographed in Chicago (author's collection).

Library of Congress Cataloguing-in-Publication Data

Names: Rich, Mark, 1958– author.
Title: Toys in the age of wonder : science fiction, society and the symbolism of play / Mark Rich.
Description: Jefferson, North Carolina : McFarland & Company, Inc., Publishers, 2020. | Includes bibliographical references and index.
Identifiers: LCCN 2020031295 | ISBN 9780786443925 (paperback acid free paper) ∞
ISBN 9781476639789 (ebook)
Subjects: LCSH: Science fiction, American—History and criticism. | American fiction—19th century—History and criticism. | American fiction—20th century—History and criticism. | Toys—United States—History—19th century. | Toys—United States—History—20th century. | Literature and society—United States.
Classification: LCC PS374.S35 R44 2020 | DDC 813/.0876209353—dc23
LC record available at https://lccn.loc.gov/2020031295

British Library cataloguing data are available

ISBN (print) 978-0-7864-4392-5
ISBN (ebook) 978-1-4766-3978-9

© 2020 Mark Rich. All rights reserved

*No part of this book may be reproduced or transmitted in any form
or by any means, electronic or mechanical, including photocopying
or recording, or by any information storage and retrieval system,
without permission in writing from the publisher.*

Front cover: Buck Rogers Rocket Police Patrol toy,
Louis Marx & Company, 1934 (National Air and Space Museum)

Printed in the United States of America

*McFarland & Company, Inc., Publishers
Box 611, Jefferson, North Carolina 28640
www.mcfarlandpub.com*

To Martha,
and my siblings Kenneth Rich
and Barbara Denzler-Rich

Table of Contents

Acknowledgments   ix
Preface   1

One—Excelsior!   3
Two—Marking the Modern Century   19
Three—The Sleep-Journey and the Navigator   29
Four—Tradition and Change in Symbolic Toys   46
Five—Deep Time and the Thinning Veil   64
Six—Early Automata in America   84
Seven—The Moon and the Anti-Hero Clock   94
Eight—The Maelstrom and New Worlds Fatalism   112
Nine—Fogg's Journey   125
Ten—Later Automata and Shrunken Globes   137
Eleven—The Magic City   152
Twelve—The Antigravity Clock and the Moon   168
Thirteen—The Middle Years and the Ripping Veil   179
Fourteen—Mockeries of Mass Production   197
Fifteen—The Tattered Veil   222
Sixteen—Lines of Motion and the Horizontal Rocket   235
Seventeen—Thirteen O'Clock   261

Chapter Notes   283
Bibliography   309
Index   317

Acknowledgments

The various studies that have gone into this book have extended over all my adult life, if not all my life—given the nature of toys, and of stories. For specific but somewhat random bits of encouragement and assistance relating to literary history, science fiction and fantasy, science history, paleontology, philosophy, the history of technics, toy history, toy collecting, and, not least, book collecting, my thanks go to the many, from years early and years recent, who have extended their help and thoughts, large and small, on miscellaneous matters that helped extend my understanding, in pursuing questions directly or indirectly related to this book—especially those whom I have thanked in my early, minor books on toy history and collecting.

For sharing interests in specific areas addressed in this book, in most cases well before I attempted this book, my thanks must go to uncounted numbers of people, many of whom are no longer with us. The list includes, for reasons both great and small, Roxie Alexander, Bud Clarity, and Scot Crom, Beloit College; Richard Bowes; Ken Boyer; David Christenson; David Drake; Albert Goldbarth; Crawford Gribben, Trinity College, Dublin; David Hartwell; Al Herdklotz, of Midgetoy; John Jungck and Robert Irrmann, Beloit College; Mike Levy, University of Wisconsin–Stout; Don Merrill; Richard O'Brien; John Calvin Rezmerski, Gustavus Adolphus College; my siblings Barbara, Elizabeth, and Kenneth Rich; Denise Terrel, University of Nice, France; Lynne Thomas and her staff, Northern Illinois University archives; and Kent Van Zant and Henry Woodard, Beloit College. Any strengths in this book I must share with these and others, while keeping its weaknesses for my own. Thanks, too, to the extraordinarily patient editors and staff at McFarland, especially Mark Durr and David Alff.

I owe Warren Lapine specific and warm thanks for encouraging me to set down early, somewhat chaotic thoughts on this conjunction of interests, which appeared in the pages of *Science Fiction Chronicle* nearly twenty years ago. Some thoughts expressed there had been turning in my mind for years, even then. I owe a debt of gratitude, too, to the Horatio Alger Fellowship for the Study of American Culture, for assistance. It helped make possible research at Northern Illinois, at a point when I was grasping at straws.

I owe overwhelming debts to my parents, Kikue and the late Charles M. Rich. One debt involves having slept for some years in my father's study, back in our Aurora, Colorado, days. There, daily, I saw volumes by Lewis Mumford, spine-out, alongside poetry, philosophy, theology, and science fiction. Although I later left home knowing Mumford's name and hardly at all his works, the image of his books on those shelves—as crystal-clear to me then as it is now—seems to have done its work.

Unending thanks, as always, to Martha Borchardt, companion in a life replete with venerable books and toys, and many times the household mainstay during the long months, scattered over ten years, of working on what she came to call "the damned book." Notes attached here to photos, as to the "author's collection," take a certain liberty as to house-accumulation attributions. Special thanks, too, to our dearly missed Scottiedog girls, Lorna and Sammy, for health-of-mind distractions during earlier stages in the writing, and for their unshakeable philosophies regarding playthings and life in general; and to our current Scotties, Callie and Hutton—the latter's name just so happens to honor one whose long-ago writings helped influence this book's earliest germs—for deepening my understanding of real necessities, which include nosing-about, eating, rest, and play.

Preface

In *Toys in the Age of Wonder: Science Fiction, Society and the Symbolism of Play*, I delve into the histories of wonder tales and children's toys; and I interweave them as best I can, to help bring out their symbolic aspects and their places within a movement's larger story. Prompted by what Lewis Mumford called the New Worlds visions of geographical and mechanical conquest, this movement brought the sphere of human activity, its cultural sphere as a whole, ever-increasingly into self-enclosure. In a culminating act of Modernity, the human world was swallowing itself—in the way that the fox did, perhaps, in Lewis Carroll's *Silvie and Bruno Concluded*. It ate itself, to leave behind only its mouth.

Focusing on the specifically Modern wonder tale, I estimate its boundaries, identify its forms, and show how it developed and changed through the Modern century. In toy history I likewise emphasize the Modern. I see toys as cultural objects having peculiar importance. They reflect and express social attitudes—often the same ones, in this time period, being reflected in wonder tales.

Toys that arose in traditional ways and forms still appeared, in these years. Others arose from new thoughts—inspired, if not by wonder tales, then by the same technical experiments, engineering feats, scientific discoveries, geographical explorations, and socio-philosophical imaginings that helped inspire those tales.

It long has interested me that, in its toys, Modern society expressed ideas about and attitudes toward its ever-more globalized and unified world. Given by adults, toys encouraged children to spend hours imaginatively engaged with symbols of an expanding technical reach. Given a widespread tendency to produce toys promptly in response to experimental results and new ideas, the briefest moments of social and technological change, usually witnessed directly by only a handful of adults, appeared in miniature versions that offered immediate and personal engagement for children in general. They became witnesses not to their times but to the realized ideas of their times. The youngest participated imaginatively, yet in a hands-on manner, in social and technological "progress" by the millions, while their parents read newspapers, or watched newsreels and television. Perhaps children learned little that their parents did, in those moments. Yet adults may never have learned what their children did, who invested the gradgrind facts of adulthood with imaginative life. "To beautify their lives of machinery and reality with those imaginative graces and delights," Dickens puts it, at the end of *Hard Times*. As an unconscious credo, and a subconscious resolution, I believe this wafted in through countless nursery and playroom windows for children to breathe in, throughout these Modern years. Children always have felt the spirit of the times in ways that no mere adults may understand. The fact that we are here today, to ponder past events, owes everything to the children who came before us, including those that we ourselves were, once upon a time.

In a way, this book offers a volume of historical perspective to which my earlier *C.M. Kornbluth: The Life and Works of a Science Fiction Visionary* might stand as a sequel. In that book my focus rests upon the late variant of the wonder tale, which went first under the twin names "scientifiction" and "science fiction," and then the trio of "science fantasy," "science fiction," and "speculative fiction." That book refers to the Age of the Masses, which follows the Modern, beginning around 1957–58. That term I keep for this study, even though the term Global Age now strikes me as at least equally apt.

Just as that book aimed to stimulate new consideration of a neglected but significant writer, so this one aims to bring to light ideas and connections that may lead others in fruitful directions. While I make the attempt to set out many major developments in Western society, science and technics, wonder tales, and toys, I do so well aware that my gaze falls woefully short of the panoptic; and while sometimes I examine and enumerate minutiae to argue certain points, I do so to exercise what I hope is the broadly inclusive grasp of cultural criticism. Where *Kornbluth* explored biography alongside history and criticism—the usual tripartite territory for the cultural critic—this book explores the rise, diffusion, and demise of a literary form alongside industrial history, cultural history, and criticism.

This book follows chronology, to a great degree. In pursuing different thematic strands, however, I have had to backtrack and foreshadow here and there—or perhaps nearly everywhere—to bring relevant elements and events together. The primary concepts and themes especially have called for that. By and large, these make their entrance in the early chapters, through Chapter Eight.

The chronological element plays heavily into the lexicological forays I make, which some readers may take as asides but which I regard as revealing structural fundamentals. We lodge our understanding of our world, our history, and our own achievements, in words. If we fail to acknowledge how words have changed—how their meanings and usages have evolved, in the so-popular and so-misleading sense nurtured by the Moderns—then we fail to understand all that they are telling us. The proud self-assurance that I have encountered in some, who "know" what thing it is that is a "space ship," a "rocket," or "a torpedo," for instance, makes these forays necessary. Such self-assurance effectively raises a false front that conceals our forgetfulness. The throwing-away of "outdated" dictionaries has come to seem to me much the same as the throwing-away of old toys.

As may become apparent to readers, here I am attempting to understand one of humankind's dream-journeys. This particular journey takes Modernity for its name. Those who go on from these opening words and into the early chapters, and who ponder the "marvelous machine" concept, may understand that I explore these issues and stories with no particular enthusiasms concerning our technologically laden times—past, present, and future. Modern wonder tales, in their outward appearances and in their deeper structures, offered cautionary perspectives that should have caused unsettled, sleepless nights over many years and decades, even when they were promising bright possibilities for both society and the individual human soul.

Not without hope do I offer this story of the world that swallowed itself. If we understand the sources for our worst dreams, we then may see how to cultivate our best. If we cultivate our best with a firmer grounding in those "imaginative graces and delights," moreover, then so much the better for us.

ONE

Excelsior!

> A voice from out of the Future cries,
> "Onward!" while o'er the Past
> (Dim gulf!) my spirit hovering lies
> Mute, motionless, aghast!
> —Edgar Allan Poe, in 1834.[1]

This terrible fowl had no head that we could perceive, but was fashioned entirely of belly, which was of a prodigious fatness and roundness, of a soft looking substance, smooth, shining and striped with various colors. In its talons, the monster was bearing away to its eyrie in the heavens, a house from which it had knocked off the roof, and in the interior of which we distinctly saw several human beings, who, beyond doubt, were in a state of frightful despair at the horrible fate which awaited them. We shouted with all our might, in the hope of frightening the bird into letting go its prey; but it merely gave a snort or puff, as if of rage, and then let fall upon our heads a heavy sack which proved to be filled with sand.
—Poe, in 1844.[2]

Toys: Should always be scientific.—Gustave Flaubert, in the 1870s.[3]

It is said that when Robert Fulton's first steamboat ascended the Hudson, it created a consternation and terror such as had never before been known, many believing that it was the harbinger of the final destruction of the world.
—Edward S. Ellis, in 1868.[4]

The Ball

Since the eleventh century, English-speakers have called a spherical plaything a *ball*, or *balle*. However trifling it may seem, the toy has rolled, bounced, and, when thrown, flown since ancient times. Stone, wood, clay, reeds, leaves, hair, leather, and paper: over the millennia, hands have taken and *balled* any such thing. Early Greeks invested balls with philosophy, having their fortune-goddess Tyche juggle them to show the uncertainty of chance. Ancient Romans filled their small *pila* with feathers, and their large *follis*, as suited their oratorical bent, with air. In times nearer ours, besides the word *ball*, *balloon* came into English for these playthings and the games that involved them. *Balloon* came to mean, too, "a primitive explosive bomb or firework, a form of chemical retort or receiver, and an ornamental globe in architecture."[5] *Ball*, too, has carried violent meanings and associations alongside playful and practical ones.

However and whenever the event occurred, when it became a plaything the ball saw birth as cultural object. The appearance of a toy marks that of a symbol. The toy's double rises to mind, so that the plaything and the thought travel thereafter as one, yoked together through recorded and unrecorded history. The true degree to which toys have added to human society remains for us to conjecture, since physically they are ephemeral—and since symbolically, so often, we bury them during our growing up, much as the children literally do in Kenneth Grahame's *Dream Days*. Yet as symbolic objects they have left tracks and trails in tales and rhymes; in games, activities, and ceremonies; in dictionaries; and in cultural provinces ostensibly outside the diversionary—including "natural philosophy," the humanistic field of studies that split into specialized studies that included the "sciences" during the nineteenth century.

Does complexity in a toy increase its symbolic force? The ball offers one answer. While among the simplest of toys, in its symbolic history it grew in power to such an extent that it became, in a real sense, all-encompassing.

This toy proved useful to ancient and Medieval astronomers and navigators, for instance, in offering them a shape that influenced their thinking about celestial orbs, and helped them invent the conceptual *globe*. In those and other ways, the ball served those who pursued the "terrestrial and mechanical New Worlds"—those twin, intoxicating visions that, as social critic and historian Lewis Mumford noted, seized Western thought-processes by the thirteenth century. These waking dreams arose when the West fell under spells cast by the magnetic compass and gunpowder, newly arrived from China.[6] As the West's world picture shifted away from the providential and toward the mechanical, the Earth came to be seen as an *automaton*—one among many *automata* that comprised the celestial mechanism. The ball thus played an essential role in geographic and mechanistic New Worlds idealism, that belief-construct whose presence and influence characterizes the Modern.

In the astronomical revolution prompted by observations and calculations made by Copernicus and Kepler, Earth's fall from primacy led to the Sun's rising to same—a shift in thinking about circles and spheres having symbolic implications.[7] The new celestial model, with the Earth's conceptual globe now orbiting the discernible ball of the Sun, had a stately predictability that stimulated the Western mind. Since the celestial sphere's "movements"—including Earth's relative to Sun—came to find mechanical expression in the clock, another device having had a long Chinese history, the clock took the name that Earth had held and eventually surrendered: *automaton*.

The ball, which was the globe and therefor Earth, and which was the celestial sphere and therefor automaton, now evoked the human-contrived device that reflected the Divine within the mechanical world picture: the clock.

Far from being a symbolic tangle comprehensible only to the most educated, these connections readily unfolded before children. As toy historian Dan Foley noted,

> *A Description of the Geographical Clock* was a real wonder book. It contained the names and locations of the most remarkable places in the world, and it showed "the time of day or night at all those places 'round the globe," as well as "a copious index." Furthermore it was intended for the instruction and

amusement of youth. It was published in Philadelphia in 1792 for Joseph Scott and sold by Francis Bailey and Peter Stewart. Books like this were even more exciting than toys.[8]

In books for children as in books for natural philosophers, Western thinking rolled the ball, the Earth, and the clock into one. Books for children, however, made evident a step in the symbolic process that was being left unacknowledged in books for adults. This step followed in mirror-image manner the way that toys turned into symbols: for in these books, concepts became toys; and these toys, whether they turned out to be intellectual or child's playthings—if the two may be distinguished—gave rise in turn, again, to new symbolic forms.

Aerial Globes and Fire Balloons, Uplifted by Spectacle

The ball's appeal extended to minds contemplating not heavenly but atmospheric motions—so that Albert of Saxony, a fourteenth-century bishop, thought that an enclosed fire would make a lightweight sphere rise. Others floated similar notions about an atmospheric "fluid" that might be found above ground-level air—in the Empyrean, perhaps; and the Jesuit Francis Lana, in 1670, envisioned an open basket being raised by four large copper globes from which all air had been with drawn, to be steered by sail.[9]

In 1782, in Annonay—a town near Lyons, the silk-production center along the Rhône—the brothers Joseph and Jacques Montgolfier, following experiments made by Priestly in England and Lavoisier in their own France, essayed to generate lighter-than-air *gaz*, but failed. Joseph's wife's chemise, on the other hand, filled and lifted, drying above a fire. They abandoned *gaz* and lifted a bag with smoke—an achievement in aerial and, no doubt, emotional transport.[10]

Practical thinking may have helped prompt their efforts, born as they were into a paper-making family. Publicity stunts and new products may have come to mind. In experimenting, however, they were playing, and not only with fire but an item that would fall, one day, into a new manufacturing category—not the later "hot-air toy," since such toys would usually operate when fixed in place over a heat source, but the "aerial toy." They also had made a specific new toy. Their smoke-bags lifted the name "fire balloons" high enough that others grew curious and excited, and flew their own.

The next year the Montgolfiers proved that they had engaged in imaginary transport, too. They had played, in small, at something that in their minds they saw much larger. On June 5 the spectacle unfolded. A linen bag towered thirty feet over the eight men required to keep it under control as it expanded. Its circumference reached one hundred and five feet. Burning bundles of straw, it went a mile and a half in ten minutes.

The bag, inflated, presented to the viewer a shape that recalled a globe, a ball, a *ballon*. Admittedly, the tossed, aerial ball may have existed from the moment the ball itself did; and the Montgolfiers could hardly have been the first to engage in such scientific play as they pursued in 1782. Even so, in 1783 their labors gave birth formally to the *ballon* as means for *aerostatic* flight, or *aerostation*.[11]

Nearly eighty years after this birth in technics, in 1861, on France's opposite side, a Parisian household busied itself with worries over two quite different births. Jules and Honorine Verne were expecting their first child. Meanwhile Jules found himself preoccupied with experimental aeronautics, having conceived a balloon adventure he wanted to write.[12]

Experiments in powered and guided flight since the Montgolfiers' time had proven frustrating and dangerous, but had led to the observation that wind direction and speed could differ, between ground level and the level to which an aerostat might rise. Verne's fictional aeronaut would have such control over ascent and descent that his balloon could travel in different directions simply by changing altitudes. Verne himself was being borne on scientific currents. Two years earlier, in 1859, the British Association for the Advancement of Science undertook a project to study the upper atmospheric "strata," with one object being "to determine the rate and direction of different currents in the atmosphere." Its first flight took place in July 1862.¹³

Verne was echoing his American literary model, as well. In 1849, Edgar Poe had used this notion in "Mellonta Tauta," a satire set in the far future. Poe in his way acknowledged that this particular vision had helped direct the efforts of aeronauts including Blanchard, Sadler, and Pilâtre de Rozier, fifty or more years earlier.¹⁴

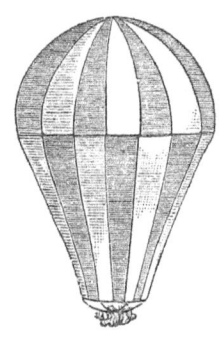

Two Sun Kites and a Montgolfier Balloon.
All given for one new name.

This Kite is the invention of Mr. Crandall, and will delight the boys. It is **self-poising**, is waterproof, and is absolutely perfect.

It can be flown in the lightest summer breeze, or in a strong wind. Ordinary No. 8 white cotton spool thread is strong enough for a very high wind.

By reason of the elastic cord attachment, the Kite poises itself, and thus equalizes the pressure of the wind.

Each Kite is furnished **complete** with tail, etc., all ready for flying, as shown in the cut. The **Montgolfier Balloon** is six feet in circumference, and is made of bright paper.

The Two Kites and Balloon given for one new name. Price of all, 75 cts. Postage and packing, 25 cts., when sent as a premium or purchased.

Aerial playthings, advertised in *Youth's Companion* in the 1880s, arose from a respected name in American toys. Fire-balloon flights remained popular for a century after their first becoming a fad (from Ronald S. Barlow, ed., *The Great American Antique Toy Bazaar 1879–1945*, 1998).

While the 1860s British aerial expeditions were yet in their infancy, Verne learned from Parisian publisher Pierre-Jules Hetzel that his literary child had given birth to the rest of his professional life: for he was to write more such novels regularly for a house that also published Honoré Balzac and George Sand.¹⁵

Around this time Parisian photographer, political cartoonist, and writer Félix Tournachon Nadar set out to construct a gas-balloon able to lift a double-story wicker cabin. He founded the Society for Aerial Location, with Verne as secretary.¹⁶ In the latter's words,

> in 1863, thanks to the efforts of Nadar, a society of "heavier than air" was founded in Paris. There the inventors could experiment with the machines, of which many were patented. Ponton d'Amécourt and his steam helicopter, La Landelle and his system of combining screws with inclined planes and parachutes, Louvrié and his aeroscaph, Esterno and his mechanical bird, Groof and his apparatus with wings worked by levers. The impetus was given, inventors invented, calculators calculated all that could render aerial locomotion practicable.¹⁷

When Verne's novel appeared that year it stirred a public already keenly curious about Nadar's grandiose ambitions.

The Birth of a Form: The Strange Device and the Engineer-Hero

In *Cinq semaines en ballon*, Verne introduces Dr. Samuel Fergusson, who blends the ratiocinative hero—the cogitator extraordinaire in Poe's stories—with the hero of deeds from French melodrama and Charles Dickens novels: for this English aeronautical engineer "belonged to the church militant, not the talking church." Embodying Western technical ambitions to encompass the globe, he has twice, before age twenty-two, circled the world; and "in his travels he was driven rather than drawn, and he went about the world like a locomotive."[18] With that phrase, "like a locomotive," Verne showed that he fully grasped this marvel's symbolism. Having been born in 1828 made him but a year older than the first successful railway locomotive, the *Rocket*.

Dramatically appearing before the Royal Geographical Society of London, Verne's hero halts its prolix proceedings with but a word: "Excelsior!"[19]

Verne uses a singularly apt ejaculation for the anti-hero's advent, in this first example of a new fictional form. That in 1863 the word carried its new connotations more buoyantly in North America than it did in Fergusson's homeland made it no less apt. The Western world could claim *excelsior* for cultural common property, it being the Latin comparative-degree form of *excelsus*, or *high*. Its use on a state seal, adopted in 1778, for instance, had led Americans to call New York "the Excelsior state." Unlike the English word *high*, however, the original Latin *excelsus* sees adjectival use only, not both that and adverbial. The state legislature, though its members had some classical training in preparatory schools and colleges, blundered. Although aiming to express something other than that New York was physically a *higher* state, relative to others, the legislature said this all the same.

When Verne was age thirteen, the Latin adjective gained a yet more powerful adverbial association, thanks to *Ballads and Other Poems*, the 1841 volume that cemented Henry Wadsworth Longfellow's reputation in America.

> The shades of night were falling fast,
> As through an Alpine village passed
> A youth who bore, 'mid snow and ice,
> A banner with the strange device,
>   Excelsior!

Nine stanzas end in the word, seven times cried aloud by the youth or a heavenly voice. The lines convey Romantic idealism pursued to the point of death, if not beyond. Not the meditative Romanticism that saw the sublime in the child, in whom Wordsworth invested a vision of heaven, Longfellow's moves towards positivism. His poem may possibly critique the belief, since in the end a "hand of ice" clutches the banner with the strange device. Yet readers' sympathies for the youth was such, in the 1840s and afterwards, that Longfellow's poem itself became a banner to carry aloft.

Harvard professor though he was, Longfellow wrote his lines without sensing the inaccuracy in the New York state seal. He planted his banner firmly in adverbial territory. It did, indeed, bear a "strange device."

He later recognized the solecism. His poems, however, came to exert such influence that these stanzas fixed in the popular mind the word's new meaning, and inspired a powerful new brand name. Businessmen seized upon the strange device with alacrity. How many new manufacturers took the name Excelsior remains a matter for conjecture; how many established firms used it for individual products, even more so. The word acquired international force within a decade, traveling to the London's Great Exposition in 1851 on Excelsior Soap packages, but more importantly on the lips of American travelers enchanted by the Crystal Palace—since "excelsior" had shifted now from adverb to a fashionable exclamation. American and then British magazines came to deploy the word in their titles.[20] Proving the term's longevity, at least two Excelsior companies exhibited a quarter-century later, at the U.S. Centennial Exposition.[21]

The Latin adjective, having been transformed into American adverb, then a cry of approval, and now proper name, proved pliable yet again in becoming a noun. A widespread usage devolved, in which the word referred to wood shavings for packing material and cheap stuffing. This resulted from the free-for-all that had surrounded Excelsior as a trade name: for an Excelsior machine patented in America in 1868 produced wood shavings.[22] Thus does the higher gyre down to the lowly. By this time, however, "excelsior" had served its purpose in the American vocabulary. The ease to which it sprang to Americans' lips had made it both an invocation and a confirmation of popular positivism's gains over providential faith.

As readers would learn in a later novel, Verne thought the name "rather too much held in honour among the citizens of America."[23]

Heroic aeronaut Fergusson's exclamation, in 1863, reveals him as embodying the Anglo-American energy for, and devotion to, technological advance against any and all obstacles, including grammatical. With this succinct malapropism, Verne gave notice to the reading world that his techniques included a clever economy of literary means. Jaunty and pithy comments from his characters would become a hallmark.

A second adventurer in the novel, Dick Kennedy, speaks of his friend Fergusson in terms belonging to New Worlds idealism: "Why, if I'd let him, he'd be starting for the moon one of these fine days!" Himself no bearer of the Excelsior banner, Kennedy falls prey to a dour meditation of a sort to become common in wonder tales after *Cinq semaines*: "That will very likely be an exceedingly dull epoch when industry will absorb everything for her own benefit. Men will go on inventing machines till they devour them. I sometimes think that the end of the world will come when some immense boiler, heated to three million atmospheres, will blow up the Earth." He pointedly adds, "The Americans are great at that sort of thing." The novel also includes a meditation on the progressive exhaustion of Earth's resources.[24]

A third character in *Cinq semaines*, Fergusson's manservant Joe, possesses a visionary power distinct from those displayed by the engineer or the adventurer, having exceptionally keen eyesight, a quality useful when traveling at an unusual height. While the balloon represents the literal spectacle, Joe serves a symbolic role that is surprising in its nature, in that it represents quite another "spectacle."

In now-obsolete usage, a seeing-glass or telescope was called a spectacle. An irony in ballooning arose in that aeronauts equipped themselves with telescopes; and these they turned downward, at one angle or another, when aloft—to make things appear larger that would have been still larger yet, seen from the ground. The view backwards during a balloon flight, onto the scene of departure, would gradually place that scene within a larger field of view, a larger perspective—which the telescope instantly could negate. The spectacle presented by high elevation above the ground—the spectacular view—fell away completely in the spectacle's view. That a philosophical toy, an optical one, is being used by the aeronaut to look upon what appears to be a toy theater in no way lessens the irony.

The Crisis of Peril was close at hand.

The symbolic view. In Verne's *Five Weeks in a Balloon*, the balloon moves between locations on one world, with the journey between worlds undertaken only in a character's imagination. In later novel *Hector Servadac*, the latter journey takes on fictional "reality." Both balloons end in destruction. Frontispiece in Verne, 1906.

Joe, as one who literally looks after Fergusson and sees to his needs, acts as spectacle-glass, being a spotter during the flight. Yet he also has within him the upturned eyes of the stargazer, and succumbs to a meditation akin to Kennedy's, and imagines the balloon rising straight upwards, and not at all horizontally, from Earth to Moon.[25]

The Dissected Protagonist, Wreckage and Emergence

Verne followed Poe's lead in making an "effort at plausibility in the details of the voyage itself,"[26] especially with regards to Fergusson's marvelous machine. His aerostat *Victoria* has, for her primary innovation, a heated coil lodged within a double-shell balloon. With heat making the contained hydrogen expand, command over the coil gives Fergusson control over his elevation, and thus his direction—making possible his dream to cross Africa from Zanzibar to Senegal aerially.

Through fictional plausibility, *Victoria* advances the New Worlds visions, embodying the space travel that overcomes geographic boundaries. Aerial explorers in the nineteenth century routinely used the word "space" in discussing Earth's atmosphere; and they took the view that Earth's circumference diminished in relation to human reach, when imagining technically enhanced modes for travel. Being a mechanical means for traveling geographically, with both vertical and horizontal distances being covered, balloons rose early in the process that would end with Earth herself coming into human view as a visually graspable and not only conceptual ball. *Cinq semaines* in germ form contains the scene nearly obligatory in later "space novels," in which the manservant, the one subservient to New Worlds idealism, would turn the spectacle-glass backward to view a diminished Earth.

Verne confines his efforts at fictional plausibility to moments when presenting a machine, a landscape, or a natural phenomenon. Those reading *Cinq semaines* who expect the same effort on behalf of his human characters face disappointment. Verne made his characters delightfully vital, paradoxically, by leaving them incomplete. Fergusson, Kennedy, and Joe arise from the page not as three-dimensional personalities but as two-dimensional exaggerations, capering like paper cut-outs on a toy stage. They have specific roles to play: for they represent aspects of a dissected human soul, separated along roughly Platonic lines. Even so, they rise into the reader's understanding in a way not allegorical nor drily instructive, but in a way rather symbolic, satirical, and theatrically diverting.

These sectional humans combine with a further ingredient to the wonder tale being reshaped into its Modern form by Verne's pencil: for the three roles played by Fergusson, Kennedy, and Joe support a fourth character who dominates nearly every scene: the marvelous machine herself. *Victoria* ranks above Fergusson, Kennedy, and Joe insofar as her existence physically encompasses theirs, and her actions involve and often determine theirs. Yet the three adventurers with their marvelous machine make a foursome of interdependency. Together they represent an exploded meta-character. Verne, in employing this structural device, was applying lessons learned from the Parisian stage, where the comedic and melodramatic traditions required stock characters, and where staging often called for "machinery" of a less visible yet similarly marvelous sort.

This unusual novelistic approach draws readers into a super-realism—a *surréalisme*, we might say. Verne's combining of disjunct, incomplete parts into a whole anticipates techniques later developed by self-designated Surrealists. His approach suggests as well as an irreverent name we might apply to what Verne and his successors managed to create: excelsior realism. Realism looms large in a deceptive way, since verisimilitude plays so vital a role; and "excelsior" conveys the New Worlds idealistic attitude that has, at its root, something at which to look askance.

Verne, near the novel's end, adds a further element borrowed from Poe that would become an essential one in the Modern wonder tale: the catastrophe that befalls the marvelous machine.[27] Not simply another spectacle in a spectacle-laden tale, it plays a structural as well as dramatic role. Despite its outward violence, the marvelous machine's destruction offers the symbolic moment when the human soul that is splintered or dissected finds itself entering a new state. The human characters, in surviving the disaster and escaping the wreckage, wake from a technological dream. Their emergence represents not mere survival but the soul's return to cohesion. In other words, the meta-character that had formed around the marvelous machine has disintegrated; and, from a Rousseau-esque perspective, the human entity weakened by technical envelopment has stepped free to the promise of self-realization. Similarly, Mumford might have understood the event as a humanistic return, from distraction by the machine to a respect for the inner life.[28]

These structural elements cohere thanks to an underlying philosophic tension. Many readers have approached this and later novels by Verne as simple positivist entertainment, promoting science and invention with an eye to the future—a misperception that has helped attach the adjective "prophetic" to Verne's name. *Cinq Semaines* as a novel, however, balances, or perhaps juggles, the tensions existing between Positivist "progress" and Rousseau-esque natural humanism; between accepting mechanical advances and distrusting technics' ultimate reach; between Fergusson's technological optimism and Kennedy's pessimism; and between Verne's personal attraction to technological advance and scientific discovery, and his Rousseau-esque fictional structure that ultimately requires that he free his symbolic human characters from the strange device. *Excelsior* must have its splendid day, and then—exposed as inappropriate—its dreadful night.

Often referring to technical innovations and applications, as opposed to the methodology that marks true science as a process, many later tales would assign to "science" the credit and the blame for creating the increasingly claustrophobic envelopment of humankind. In his first novel Verne draws on his experience of human types and activities to illuminate this tension's complex sources; and he conveys an understanding that aims for comprehensive insight, even if couched in melodramatic and even absurdist terms. Verne had enough experience in the world of business, through the *bourse*, the French Stock Exchange, to know toward what ends scientific results tended to be applied, and to know where to place blame should the eventuality occur of a technologically cocooned society—or an exploded one. While he admired the English national spirit that so effectively fostered them, he still pointed to those paired and increasingly influential spheres of business and industry, when seeking the cause for a malaise already evident in the West.

Smashed-Up Locomotive

The story arc that gives to machinery a life-pattern—birth, first success, maturity, and death—from the beginning applied to toys that arose from the technological dream. Countless curious souls, whether childlike or scientific in their pursuits, sent aloft aerial toys that proved their susceptibility to gravitation more often than their affinity for air—especially the helicopter toys, which offered the maple-seed's descent reversed in time to become an ascent. When Ponton d'Amécourt, de la Landelle, and Nadar were pursuing the dream of flight, for instance, they constructed lightweight models with clockwork motors which did sometimes rise ten feet or more into the air. Yet given their fragility, the more successful the trials, the more damaging the falls.[29] Insofar as the experimenters meant these models to fly, and not so much to land, they were designing destruction into their marvelous machines. As a dime-novel character would later put it, "But these new-fangled things generally go well at first, and then, afore yer know it, they bust all to blazes."[30]

Across the Atlantic, around the time *Cinq Semaines* rose into the public arena, a pioneering American toy and game manufacturer hit upon a related insight. Other publishers already issued "dissected maps" or "dissected pictures." In these two toy categories, manufacturers pasted lithographed images onto wooden boards and then cut them by automated jigsaw into a dozen or more pieces. In 1868 Milton Bradley took a boldly entertaining approach in issuing Smashed Up Locomotive, A Mechanical Puzzle for Boys.[31] Its release found a ready market—in part, perhaps, because the public's fancies about what could go wrong with trains was being aggravated by the opening of the first elevated railroad route in New York City.

As a lithographer, Bradley had learned that a print commemorating a railway bridge-construction would barely sell. Another that showed the bridge's end in disaster, however, would find eager buyers. On his new plaything's box, Bradley placed a picture showing "a locomotive so badly wrecked that it must have delighted the destructive instincts of all children who saw it," as toy historians Inez and Marshall McClintock put it.[32] The puzzle-pieces, once assembled, presented to the child an image that failed, however, to match the box-top one. Instead, the pieces assembled into a lithograph depicting the wonder of its time: an immense, steam-powered locomotive on its tracks—miraculous, and not damaged at all. Thanks to the image on the box, the child started with ruin, and moved the pieces, bit by bit, back through imaginative time to the moment before the locomotive's end. To put the puzzle away in its box, the child then destroyed the locomotive again, piece by piece.

Far from being obscure, this plaything, which both depicted and embodied the marvelous machine's destruction, became a long-lived best-seller for Bradley. An item made by W.S. Reed Toy Company of Leominster, Massachusetts, must have had similar appeal: Blown-Up Fort.[33]

The sense that disaster threatened the impressive new buildings and machines being raised and constructed across the country found constant reinforcement in newspapers. Among early steamboats proliferating on rivers in the western United States, for instance, seventy-five ended in spectacle: nine by exploding, nineteen by fire, and forty-seven by sinking.[34] A new steamboat's construction might earn minor notice from the press, at best; its explosion, fiery end, or sinking would rate headlines.

Cities similarly offered opportunity for spectacle. The supply of timber and other construction supplies, readily available thanks to steam transportation, encouraged buildings to appear in clusters that also brought steam boilers, coal furnaces, oil lamps, and gas lighting into close concentration. Large and small communities alike pointed with pride to multistory factories that created products for a national market, and brought wealth to the local population; and large and small alike saw the promise of prosperity vanish in smoke. Fire took out so many toy factories that, among those robust enough to rebuild, few toy manufacturers whose histories began in the 1800s lacked such punctuations in their stories. Their records resembled Cuvier-esque catastrophist prehistories, in which disasters of global proportions periodically wiped clean the slate for each new stage of Earthly Creation.

An iron-casting firm that made toys, bookends, and sadirons, the A.C. Williams Company, eventually opened its catalogs with this litany:

Established at Chagrin Falls, Ohio ... 1844
Destroyed by Fire ... 1889
Rebuilt at Chagrin Falls ... 1890
Destroyed by Fire ... 1892
Rebuilt at Ravenna ... 1893
Incorporated ... 1905

Fire's continuous threat within rapidly expanding Modern society found expression in the fire-fighting equipment made in great abundance, in toy form. Companies frequently weighted their toy-vehicles lines heavily toward horse-drawn ladder trucks, hose wagons, fire patrols, and fire engines.[35] A fire-fighting pumper wagon made by Philadelphia tin-toy

Lion bookends. A.C. Williams Co., late 1800s to early 1900s (photograph by and collection of the author).

firm Francis, Field and Francis, around 1840, may have been the first metal "wheel toy" to have been manufactured in America.[36] In iron versions alone, wheeled and "steam powered" fire-fighting toys must have outnumbered by many thousands their original inspirations, which in reality were spread diffusely among city and town fire-fighting departments.

The toys proliferated for the same reasons that the new mass-circulation newspapers, where bad news was good news for sales, never neglected to cover fires. The excitement produced by fire-wagons rushing through city streets entered all homes, even those far removed from major fires, thanks to the newsprint stories and images that were at least as sensational as they were factual, and to the toys that rushed, day after day, toward conflagrations presumably wholly imaginary.

During this time a meaning-shift was taking place in an old word: *fireman*. As small-shop forges and furnaces began disappearing behind the walls of all-inclusive factory buildings in the early 1800s, the old *fireman*, who *tended* a kiln or forge fire, became less visible in daily life. Even though he held a conspicuous place on coal-fire locomotives, the old-fashioned figure fell away before the highly visible new one who was ascending into the childhood-hero empyrean: the fireman who *damped*—who faced the terror rung out by Poe's "bells, bells, bells ... the clamor and the clangor of the bells," and put it out.

Unknowingly, in playing with toy fire wagons, children internalized both social change and technical innovation: for the new firemen represented an "expansion of labor," in a term soon to be adopted. Improvements in steam-power made possible the pumps that, in turn, made metropolitan fire-fighting conceivable. Toys also represented the incursion of industrial chemicals into everyday life. Children received such playthings as the American Fire Department by Bradley, a "sectional picture" to be assembled to a length of eighty-four inches, showing the "complete modern American Fire Department, consisting of steamer, hose carriage, chemical engine, insurance patrol team, and hook and ladder, on the run to a fire."[37]

Inevitably it occurred that news about such changes and innovations, as well as playthings depicting or embodying them, entered many communities before the changes could

Hose-reel horse-drawn toy. The toy may have been fifty years old by the time this photograph was taken—or brand new, and made during the nostalgia trend that began shortly after World War II. Manufacturers often weighted their lines of small wheeled toys toward emergency vehicles such as this one, from the late 1800s through the 1900s. Photograph marked "11–29–'46" (author's collection).

become actual: for newspapers and magazines responded instantly to changes by disseminating stories; and toy manufacturers, while often operating upon seasonal or yearly schedules rather than daily, weekly, or monthly ones, acted as promptly as possible to take whatever advantage they could from that fleeting phenomenon, the public spectacle. As with spectacle-news and its readers, the spectacle-toy created excitement in children in great part because it represented an element of society that had yet to enter common experience. In other words, toymakers, who traditionally had focused upon those elements that were the most common within society, and most lasting, were shifting their emphasis toward the elements that were the least common and least lasting.

The Champ de Mars, Space Travelers and Public Spectacle

The elements being developed in the Modern wonder tale, and in the Modern toy, had their origins, naturally, in events and developments belonging to their time. Their success arose from technical achievements; the dreams they expressed reflected the dreams being expressed in experiments and trials.

Verne's friend Nadar must have struck many as more dreamer and showman than practical aeronaut. Even so, he enjoyed technical successes, including the launch of his immense *Le Géant*. This extravagant affair had for its car a model cottage in wicker. This offered a self-contained human travel environment of the sort to be found within the marvelous machines that cropped up in Verne's later novels: for it contained a small printing office, a photographic department, a refreshment room, and a lavatory. It offered a compartmentalized human environment. Late in the afternoon of October 4, 1863, a Sunday, the monstrosity rose for its first, brief flight from the Champ de Mars.[38]

The earliest gas-balloon flights had lifted into those same skies. Long before Nadar's, in August 1783, mathematician and physicist Jacques Alexandre César Charles and his new aerostat had inaugurated gas-balloon travel with a factual wonder tale:

> Bulletins were issued daily of the progress of the inflation; and the crowd was so great that on the 26th the balloon was moved secretly by night to the Champ de Mars, a distance of two miles. On the next day an immense concourse of people covered the Champ de Mars, and every spot from which a view could be obtained was crowded. About five o'clock a canon was discharged as the signal for the ascent, and the balloon when liberated rose to the height of about three thousand feet with great rapidity. A shower of rain which began to fall directly after it had left the earth in no way checked its progress; and the excitement was so great, that thousands of well-dressed spectators, many of them ladies, stood exposed, watching it intently the whole time it was in sight, and were drenched to the skin. The balloon, after remaining in the air for about three-quarters of an hour, fell in a field near Gonesse, about fifteen miles off, and terrified the peasantry so much that it was torn into shreds by them.[39]

The month that this marvelous machine met with its destruction, the Montgolfiers launched the first aeronauts: a sheep, a cock, and a duck, who traveled horizontally far faster than had any humans, at two miles in eight minutes. Jean François Pilâtre de Rozier, who curated natural history collections under Louis XVIII, succeeded the farm animals and became the first human to ascend by means of hot-air balloon—the first human space traveler—in October. Jacques Charles himself made ascents in December. Benjamin Franklin observed of one that "the Spectators ... were infinite" and that the ascent offered "a most beautiful Spectacle!"[40] Similar experiments in America by the Philosophical Society at Philadelphia led to carpenter James Wilcox becoming the first American space traveler—in a fittingly symbolic up-rising in a symbolic place, at a time when Great Britain was formally recognizing that America had floated free from its rule.[41] Experiments throughout the West continued into the early 1800s, when Monck Mason, soon to rise into the wonder-tale firmament, became active in aeronautics.

This innovative aerostat may have sprung into existence fully formed, as far as its shape. The aeronautical *ballon* soon came to have, in the public mind, the shape of a spherical bag enshrouded in a net, with the net extending downward to its center of gravity: the basket or passenger cabin. In France, a traditional way to play with a toy *ballon* involved enclosing it in a net. The net allowed the child to swing it in a wide arc, giving it centrifugal force. When released from the hand, its center of "gravity," it went flying.[42]

Although Charles's balloon outperformed the Montgolfiers,' the latter's invention persisted. The fire balloon captured, in small, aerostatic flight's public spectacle. Being easy to construct, it inspired play across the West, became a craze in France and England, and, since it tended to spur less scientific than technical thoughts, fostered the dream of human flight.

These toys continued the tradition of *ball* and *balloon* having destructive alongside playful associations, insofar as fire-balloonists did commit arson, if inadvertently—making yet more complex the relation between the aerial toy and spectacle. Purposeful violence, too, joined itself naturally to the plaything, as when toy-maker Matthew Boulton, in the English Midlands, assembled a fire balloon of paper, about five feet in diameter, equipped with a long-fused firecracker. After rising into the night sky peacefully, in the far distance it exploded, much to the delight of watchers. Boulton's usual "toys" might in America have fallen under the heading of "fancy goods," being metal trifles, trinkets, decorations, and semi-practical items. Birmingham, where he prospered, enjoyed fame for its small metal goods destined for adult use: *toys*. Even so he clearly understood the sense of "toy" that would supplant the one he generally drew upon.[43]

The Earlier Victoria and the Skylark

After the early ascents and before Nadar's, Poe presented with typical humor the spectacle that a balloon presented: "about noon, a slight but remarkable agitation became apparent in the assembly; the clattering of ten thousand tongues succeeded; and, in an instant afterwards, ten thousand faces were upturned toward the heavens, ten thousand pipes descended simultaneously from the corners of ten thousand mouths, and a shout, which could be compared to nothing but the roaring of Niagara, resounded long, loudly and furiously, through all the city and through all the environs of Rotterdam."[44] Poe's 1835 "Hans Phaall—A Tale"—later republished with the hero's name respelled, as "The Unparalleled Adventure of One Hans Pfaall"—offers a wonder tale with a marvelous machine and a narrative style that joined absurdist satire to technical verisimilitude. Among other wonders, Pfaall achieves a scientific first in finding himself, at one point, above the North Pole. The story presents a hoax—played not so much on the reader as on this absurd Rotterdam's populace.

Poe benefited further from public openness to balloon news nine years later, in 1844, when the New York *Sun* published the headline "Astounding News by Express, via Norfolk!" Later republished as "The Balloon-Hoax," the story relates a journey made by "Mr. Monck Mason's Flying Machine" across the Atlantic. The real Monck Mason had made international news in 1836 when he flew from Vauxhall Gardens, London, to near Weilburg, in the duchy of Nassau, traveling about five hundred miles in eighteen hours. Among the passengers, in what came to be dubbed the "Nassau Balloon," was Robert Hollond, M.P., who appears in Poe's hoax as "Robert Holland." Another Nassau Balloon traveler was its builder, Charles Green, who receives mention in relation to the coal gas being used in the balloon.[45]

While "Pfaall" had suggested innovations, "Astounding News by Express" began with a bolder claim: "The great problem is at length solved! The air, as well as the earth and the ocean, has been subdued by science, and will become a common and convenient highway for mankind."[46] The fictional Monck Mason balloon of 1844 is an ellipsoid equipped with an Archimedean screw—emphasizing the propulsive principal that, in fact, Nadar later would announce as inevitable, and that engineer Isambard Brunel would apply to steamships for the first time in 1845.[47] As he had in "Pfaall," Poe describes the balloon and its motive force in detail. Its power derives from "a piece of spring machinery fixed in the car. By the operation of this spring, the screw is made to revolve with great rapidity, communicating a progressive motion to the whole." The spring is of "great power, compared with its dimensions."[48] The description—calling to mind the spring-powered toys not yet common in America, although not uncommon in Europe—includes the note that the ship was first a "model," and only second a full-sized airship.

As does Pfaall's craft, the fictional Monck Mason's dirigible diminishes the Earth in relation to human reach. Mason observes that the Atlantic "becomes a mere lake," and calls it "this small pond."[49]

In both stories, Poe places the marvelous machine in the foreground, as a major character. In "Pfaall," it operates alongside satirically drawn human characters, against a geographical backdrop. While in neither "Pfaall" nor "Astounding News" do the marvelous machines meet their demise, they do endure symbolic destruction, when revealed as hoaxes. "Astounding News" was, in Poe's own phrase, a *jeu d'esprit*—a game of the mind, a play of fancy. In writing afterwards of this *jeu d'esprit*, he mentioned the name of the story's marvelous ship: "if (as some assert) the 'Victoria' did not absolutely accomplish the voyage recorded, it will be difficult to assign a reason why she should not have accomplished it."[50]

Published in 1848, only fifteen years before Verne's novel, Poe's "Mellonta Tauta" offers further satire involving dirigible airships. The narrator is writing "on board balloon 'Skylark,' April 1, 2848." Inventive and perspicacious, the story reiterates issues and concerns voiced by "Pfaall" and "Astounding News" while introducing new ones. It embraces the symbolism of an elevated perspective upon events below, as made possible by aerial travel; and it ties that perspective not only to physical but to temporal distance, so that Pundita, the narrator, speaks to her readers from a future when people are obsessed with traveling everywhere at high speeds but are beset with boredom. Pundita recollects a time when an elongated island, which the reader understands to be Manhattan—albeit a Manhattan still in Poe's future—is dominated by twenty-story buildings inhabited by "the Knickerbocker tribe of savages."

"It is related of them that they were acute in many respects," Pundita notes, "but were oddly afflicted with a monomania for building what, in the ancient Amriccan, was denominated 'churches'—a kind of pagoda instituted for the worship of two idols that went by the names of Wealth and Fashion. In the end, it is said, the island became, nine-tenths of it, church."[51] In his own way, Poe, again in advance of Verne, was pointing a finger at business and industry.

The Technical Life-Order

In his tales Poe offers many elements that become vital ingredients in wonder tales to follow: humankind's globe-spanning reach, with the romance of polar exploration figuring prominently; the technical enclosure, as well as self-enclosure, of the human individual; and technological gigantism. His imaginings would come to be taken as prophetic, as in his description of a "church"-dominated Manhattan, even when the spirit of satire helped give them birth. Moreover, in the cheerful disasters that occur in "Mellonta Tauta," and in the cataclysms elsewhere among his tales, he developed the marvelous machine's destruction as a structural element.

Poe echoed the Deists in expressing appreciation for Nature's interlocking components, and by presenting Earth's "economy" as divine insofar as it reflected mechanical perfection. "Divine creation" served Deists as a term for nature, the Earth, or the universe. They invoked a First Mover or First Cause, rather than an omnipresent deity; and a rational design, or "pre-established harmony," rather than providential order. Yet even Deistic perfection may end in disaster, as it does in Poe's tales of Earthly conflagration. "Disaster" itself states a connection to the celestial sphere, insofar as the word denotes the unfavorable aspect of a star or planet. *Disaster*—a foul star—came as inevitable and perhaps fated, if its influence did derive from a Deistic undesigned design.

"Automaton," the word applied to the Earth and then the timepiece, in the decades before Poe's life came also to denote inventive mechanisms that mimicked nature—on different occasions beautifully, humorously, or satirically, but often mystifyingly. By the time of Poe's birth, in 1809, "automata" had come to refer mainly to these machines that were, above all, marvelous. They evoked wonder for their mechanical perfection; they dazzled audiences, puzzled fellow mechanicians, and frightened not a few. As we will see, Poe recognized that destruction had a role to play, too, in such machines. By bringing focus to the soul surrounded by and imbedded within the machine, he freed that soul.

During Poe's years, a pessimistic realism was ringing more loudly among the notes being sounded by natural philosophers, and being spread by popular accounts. Mary Somerville's *On the Connexion of the Physical Sciences* of 1834, for instance, brought to general notice William Herschel's astronomical observations and his meditations on a catastrophic futurity: "Not only man, but the globe he inhabits—nay the whole system of which it forms so small a part—might be annihilated, and its extinction be unperceived in the immensity of creation."[52] Somerville's book promulged the notion that a non–biblical disaster that might befall Earth, as a planet, without reference to or implications for ethics, morals, or even "progress"—the word which the fashionable public would embrace by the late 1800s as completely as it had the earlier *excelsior*, to much the same effect.

Though Poe's works contained many elements, the definitive form of the Modern wonder tale would await Verne, whose patient pencil and pen drafts married geographical knowledge and technical speculation to a stage experience that Poe, for all that he had been born to actors, never enjoyed. Verne's melodramas would achieve a popularity that would affect balance sheets at publishing houses and public attitudes toward science and technology: for despite their structural humanism they would inspire continuing faith in the paired visions of the geographical and mechanical New Worlds.

Verne, moreover, though writing only a few decades after Poe's death, in those few decades had witnessed considerably more technical change affecting society than had Poe, due to the tempo of that change having increased in the meantime. As a consequence he sensed more clearly what Karl Jaspers would call the "tension between the universal life-apparatus and a truly human world." His stories suggest that he was acquiring an intuitive understanding, that should the "technical life order" or "universal life-apparatus ... effect a definitive conquest of the other, it would thereby instantly destroy itself."[53]

This "other," the "truly human world," has kinship to Mumford's humanistic world that would nourish the "inner life," to Poe's machine-enveloped human individual, and to Verne's dissected-soul protagonists. Yet the "universal life apparatus" has been created by human hands. Both the apparatus without and the soul trapped within are human—as in the enclosed, claustrophobic torture chamber made by the Inquisition in "The Pit and the Pendulum," and its victim; the globe-spanning *Nautilus* in *20,000 Leagues Under the Sea*, and Nemo; and the tin toy in the hands of the child in which a metal shell, perhaps in the shape of a Christmas tree, spins mechanically open to reveal the human figure trapped within, who may be the spirit of Christmas—to be seen only for the briefest, metal-blurred moment.

Two

Marking the Modern Century

> When I dipt into the future far as human eye could see;
> Saw the Vision of the world, and all the wonder that would be.
> —Tennyson, in 1842.[1]

> If development upward is the general law of the race; if we have grown by natural evolution out of the cave-man, and even less human forms of life, we have everything to hope for the future ... we are entering on a new era ... the Revival of Humanity.
> —Oliver Wendell Holmes, in 1872.[2]

> ...the time has come for a series of newer "wonder tales" in which the stereotyped genie, dwarf and fairy are eliminated, together with all the horrible and blood-curdling incident devised by their authors to point a fearsome moral to each tale. Modern education includes morality; therefore the modern child seeks only entertainment in its wonder-tales and gladly dispenses with all disagreeable incident.
> —L. Frank Baum, in 1900.[3]

> We've got a cheek, to say we disbelieve anything in this age of wonders.
> —Buster Brown, in 1910.[4]

"The Modern Universe of Belief"

Peering backwards from the year 1967, a literary critic suggested that the Modern Century commenced with England's Second Reform, Karl Marx's first volume of *Das Kapital*, and the British North America Act that established Canada, a country he regarded as distinctively Modern. The critic, Northrup Frye, saw this commencement in 1867.[5]

Those within the sphere of British influence may, indeed, have felt freshness and difference in the air, just then. Two years had passed since death had claimed Henry John Temple, third Viscount Palmerston, ending an era politically. Across the channel, the 1867 Paris Exposition introduced the Japanese aesthetic sense to a mass public, altering the West's view of an island nation, and its own aesthetic sense, permanently. The French writer who nurtured the Symbolist impulse in literature, and pivotally advanced the wonder tale through his translations, Charles Pierre Baudelaire, in that year died. Baudelaire's literary debtor, Verne, published in that year a boreal adventure in Hetzel's *Le Magasin d'Education et de Récréation*: the enormously popular *Les Aventures du Capitaine Hatteras*. In England, Verne's *Voyage au Centre de la Terre* appeared in translation. In Scotland, poet James Thomson, "B.V.," published "A Lady of Sorrow," in which prehistoric creatures may have made their Symbolist debut. Across the Atlantic, in the realm of the still-nascent American toy industry, Charles M. Crandall obtained his February 5, 1867, patent for what would become the first American plaything to win international favor; and Milton Bradley produced his Zoetrope—or Wheel of Life, a device that animated static images, which he patented but had based upon earlier European diversions that similarly combined automatism and optical effects.[6]

~~~

To some degree, it passes time idly to identify and name time-divisions. What occurs in any period grows from earlier thoughts, events, and accomplishments. The new plant in the garden, that suddenly yields so freshly, sprouts from old seed.

Historians and cultural critics must identify continuities and disjunctions, however. By the middle 1800s, the twin, waking dreams of the geographical and mechanical New Worlds had captivated the West for four centuries already, exerting an increasingly powerful shaping force upon its imagination. Although that shaping force rendered these centuries "modern," an alteration in the current of the times occurred during the middle 1800s that affected daily life, industrial technics, intellectual thought, and the imaginative arts— an alteration so pronounced that Frye felt comfortable in placing, after those "modern" centuries, a Modern Century.

In an earlier year than 1867, as it happens, events both real and symbolic clustered even more unusually thickly. These events would serve in the future as markers indicating a cultural shift, a societal movement-in-place that amounted, in some areas, to revolution in its literal turning-around sense. At the time, political turmoil beset China, India, Austria, France, and the United States, to lasting effect; and yet the new ideas being introduced, pondered, and explored created a less visible turmoil that beset and upset the intellectual arts to equally lasting and perhaps more deeply felt effect. The appearance of these ideas in 1859, in Jacques Barzun's words, opened the "modern universe of belief."[7]

That year of ideas saw publication of John Stewart Mill's *On Liberty* and Karl Marx's *Critique of Political Economy*, and the completion of Wagner's *Tristan and Isolde*, which came to be seen as ushering in post–Romantic music. It saw the death of naturalist Baron von Humboldt, who had helped stir popular curiosity in the vast biological world being discovered and cataloged by Western naturalists. It saw, too, Charles Darwin's monumental publication, in which he built, in part, upon von Humboldt's efforts and vision.

Darwin proposed what came to be called *natural selection* as a mechanism that, over geological timespans, had led to the physical variety observed in the world's plants and animals. His book shook both lofty and lowly souls, for many reasons—much as would *Das Kapital* by Marx, who would praise Darwin's notions as having been essential to his own. In effect unifying the biological world and bringing it into alignment with the geological worldview, *On the Origin of Species* in 1859 changed the tenor of scientific, religious, philosophic, and popular discourse immediately and for decades to follow. As a major development capping others that had fostered a rational and materialist worldview, Darwin's arguments invigorated some sectors within educated society, while plunging others into crises. Darwinism arose as a materialist faith and vision, much as would Wagnerism and Marxism.

By the middle years in the Modern century—if we are to see it as having then lasted roughly a hundred years—language derived from the natural-selection theory would appear with entrenched regularity outside natural science. A book on manufacturing and industry, for instance, would appear then under a title that would seem no longer provocative but merely up to date: *The Industrial Evolution of the United States*. While "development," with its coming-to-maturity sense, had proven itself serviceable in the past, "evolution" now took prominence—all too often to reflect a new, determinist tendency in historical thinking. An "evolutionary" lamp illuminated technological progressivism and social-hierarchical utopianism, so that the *excelsior* fad was flourishing for seemingly good reason. Arguments relating to Darwin's natural selection, and not only the parlor veneer of popular evolutionism, found their way into society and culture—as did, to a lesser degree, Darwin's notions concerning sexual selection and co-evolution. An 1890s literary historian, for instance, would identify in literature "modes or processes of change and development best expressed in the terms that natural science has made familiar,—modification, variation, deviation, persistence, and transformation."[8] Arguments relating to species variation and selection would move into non-biological areas of study—especially sociology, with its ominous phrase, "the survival of the fittest," coming to influence even Darwin. Meanwhile, Darwin's own words and thoughts, within their intended context, were proving enduringly illuminating, even as they yielded enduring misinterpretations.

With both illuminations and misinterpretations swaying the Moderns, the notion that the transition had been made "from Anno Domini to Anno Darwinii" came easily into conversation, almost immediately upon *Origin*'s publication.[9]

The Burnt-Down Bridge

Portents of a changing world appeared, too, in technics. In the 1850s Western society stood poised to step away from a diffuse and slow system for local, regional, and international connection, and toward an integrated system for global travel and communication. The first powered balloon flight had taken place in 1852, in France, under inventor Henri Giffard's guidance; and in 1859 the American Carlincourt Lowe proposed a transatlantic flight on the balloon *The City of New York*—which, however, held true to its name by staying there.[10] Lowe's ambitious programme all the same reflected public hopes. International water travel was expanding, with Western industrial nations successful in opening Chinese and Japanese ports with the second Opium War and Commodore Perry's missions. The builders of the *S.S. Great Eastern*, the largest ship of its time, and the commission responsible for digging the Suez Canal were both pursuing their plans during these years, with work on the latter beginning in 1859. While steam-locomotive engineering was changing cultural norms on several continents, the first railroad bridge joining the split United States and Territories spanned the Mississippi River in Davenport, Iowa, in 1856. Speed and efficiency were becoming their own justifications, in the decade after Poe envisaged a future in which one might prefer "the traveling by the slow train of a hundred miles the hour."[11]

The Mississippi-spanning bridge proved symbolic in being both unifying and divisive. After burning down when a steamboat collided with a piling, steamboat owners filed suit against it as a nuisance. The railroad company, not only joining the continent's halves but forging a link, one of the last in a chain of automated modes for global travel, hired an Illinois lawyer to argue its case. That Abraham Lincoln defended this effort toward technical unification would take on other symbolic overtones, a few years later.

Electrical telegraphy advanced during these years, reaching the point that a transatlantic cable could be conceived, created, and put in place in 1857. Although an innovative, technics-dependent means for communicating, telegraphy met with such rapid acceptance that it provided an important new tool for international diplomats, especially during conflicts in Europe in 1859—the year, too, when the French government honored Samuel F.B. Morse for his part in its development.[12]

The year 1859 would come to be seen as ending the United States' first period of industrial development, which had begun in 1780. The second period then acquired momentum, to be given decisive impetus by a conflict that forced the North's expansion of factory production and the South's about-face from agrarian to industrial economy.[13] In the subsequent Civil War, the North's sustained effort to raise telegraph lines would result in enhanced coordination of military action, and in transformed news reporting. It fed the public's growing sense that electrical communications offered instantaneity, whatever the geographic distances involved. Physiographic barriers between communities, in both practical and figurative terms, would vanish regionally, prefiguring their disappearance around the globe.

Emerging from the financial panic of 1857, the United States as a whole had been shifting its economic base from agriculture to manufacturing, mining, and millwork. Machines that automated the process of sewing already, and radically, had altered possibilities for young women, who now found employment by the thousands in factories making hoopskirts and other garments. Similarly "scientific methods" in agriculture were changing farming, as were developments in machine reapers, whose number included a successful new design by Cyrus McCormick. Chicago by this time had grown into a major center for agricultural distribution: for in 1858, import-export activity in Chicago accounted for one quarter of total U.S. foreign trade. The U.S. economy's center, in other words, was slipping westward from its east-coast origins, anticipating a similar slippage from its existing cultural center. Northern-states economies also saw permanent change due to the drilling of a well for petroleum in August 1859, in Titusville, Pennsylvania. With implications for illumination apprehended almost immediately, petroleum rose to overnight importance in the nation. These changes helped enlarge debts owed by Southern citizens to the merchants and manufacturers of the North, adding to tensions surrounding the slave issue.[14]

Lincoln, the bridge-defender, commanded widespread attention in 1858 appearances as a Senatorial candidate with an outsider's chance against popular seated Senator Stephen A. Douglas. Especially in the old Northwest where non-native-born populations were expanding, Lincoln, though unsuccessful as a candidate, continued drawing audiences and the attentions of newspapers, whose circulations were now eminently Modern. As had Poe, his contemporary, Lincoln appealed to rationality and included the future among his concerns. In 1859 he was addressing the public not as a political candidate but as an independent-minded orator whose "vein of prophecy" held audiences raptly attentive, subtly altering the nature of the nation's public discourse.[15]

In 1859, too, the notion of the equality of human beings found a powerful exponent in John Brown. His doomed raid upon Harpers Ferry, Virginia, and subsequent execution further deepened the gap between North and South.

Lincoln's subsequent ascent to the presidency had a cultural importance internationally that ranked alongside that of the theory by Darwin, yet another contemporary born in 1809.

Not only did Lincoln's insistence on maintaining the Union result in political, economic, and military ascendance for the United States during the Modern years, but his efforts to protect and encourage American manufacturing led quickly to doors being opened for new American firms to find both domestic and overseas markets. Without these initial protections, the development of mass-manufacture in America, already tardy in its development in comparison to England, would have suffered unpredictable and perhaps indefinite delay.

Toy-Making at the Transition

Although the Civil War years would prove difficult ones for toy manufacturers in the northern United States, in the years beforehand signs pointed toward changes in store. In 1858, German immigrant Ludwig Greiner patented a doll head of the new "composition" material, while S.L. Hill of Williamsburg, New York, patented a spelling block which became a reliable best-selling toy in subsequent decades.[16] The paper doll, first made in America in 1854, acquired its most characteristic form in 1859, when first featured in the popular *Godey's Lady's Book*.[17] The year 1859, too, brought patents for important toys including the "shoofly," a safety rocker for infants devised by Jesse Crandall, one of several Crandalls involved in the manufacture of toys in Pennsylvania and New York.[18] In the next year, young Milton Bradley would establish his lithography business with a portrait of the newly announced presidential nominee, Lincoln. Bradley soon afterwards introduced a game of ideals, named The Checkered Game of Life.[19] In 1861, at a school for young ladies in Salem, Massachusetts, another game emerged that would become characteristic of the Modern years. Published by W. & S.B. Ives, and later by many other companies, Authors would help plant among children a salutary literary interest.[20] Also in 1861 came a patent that anticipated countless aerial toys in later decades: the Flying Top, a device for launching upwardly spinning disks.[21]

Gaining influence in these years, an educational philosophy was inspiring toymakers as well as educators to fashion new playthings. In 1856, the year Lyman Frank Baum was born, Mrs. Carl Schurz opened the first kindergarten in the United States, in New York. In 1861, a second opened in Boston under Elizabeth Peabody.[22] As seemed often the case, English trends had anticipated American, with the writer and philanthropist Ellen Julia Hollond having established the first day-nursery in London in 1844—the same year, oddly enough, that Poe mentioned her husband, Robert, in a wonder tale. The degree to which this consciousness had taken root, concerning children and humanistic modes for their upbringing, may be gauged from the youthful characters in Dickens's 1852 *Bleak House* who had grown up without playthings to become self-centered, miserly creatures, and thus perfectly suitable scions of their conniving father, Smallweed.

During the Civil War, northern toymakers often altered their manufacturing emphases, responding to un-playful wartime requirements and opportunities. Some were facing difficulties since, in common with other northern firms, bills were going unpaid by Southern customers.[23] On the other hand, dwindling access to overseas toys caused some importers to shift toward manufacture—as occurred with Adolph Meinecke, who had come to America in 1848 at age seventeen. After working in New York and becoming a traveling salesman, he visited Milwaukee, settled there, and in 1853 opened a shop, for which he first imported but soon manufactured toys.[24]

While toy soldiers long had a place on the playroom floor, in the 1860s toy weaponry took on greater importance. A new invention, the Maynard Tape Primer, opened the door to "paper caps" and the toy firearms to noisily deploy them.[25] In 1859 the first American patent for a toy gun went to J. Johnson of New York City. Also that year a manufacturer of cast-iron toys, J. & E. Stevens, offered Fire Cracker Pistols and cap-firing cannons. As the Civil War began, other companies joined ranks, with their toys including a marble-shooting cannon from Vermont Novelty Works, located in appropriately named Springfield. Johnson's initiative led to numerous other patents for toy guns: thirty-four, within ten years. Their number reflected advances on the warfront, and included a toy breech-loading rifle in 1862.[26]

Protective measures, advocated since Hamilton's time, soon were helping incline the public to buy American over imported baubles. This further encouraged inventors, leading to more toys being produced that reflected their society's changing interests and concerns. As the McClintocks put it, "After the war, the patent records show a continually increasing number of 'mechanical toys,' 'toy automatons,' 'mechanical movements for toys,' and toy steam engines. The war speeded up the mechanical aspects of the industrial revolution considerably, and the toy industry, as usual, followed suit; it even anticipated some events of the adult world."[27]

Child tested. The notion that toys played beneficial roles in child development inevitably led to standards and testing being applied (from McCready Publishing Co., *Playthings Directory*, 1938, p. 10).

Children in the late 1850s and early 1860s already were experiencing childhoods that diverged from their parents' experiences—even though their parents' childhoods had closely resembled that of their grandparents. Velocipedes, first popular in the 1840s, for instance, were becoming typical and expected accessories to childhood.[28] These "wheel toys" usually had three wheels of equal dimensions, a seat, and an axle-pedal arrangement that let children achieve the speed promised by the name. In the related "propellers," also three-wheeled, the sitting child pulled alternately on two levers.

With these and other playthings, children were developing their minds and bodies in a play environment that gave unprecedented emphasis to mechanical swiftness. Mechanical workings and velocity were becoming their own justifications, even in play—even though both elements led to repetitive and often simplified activity.

Wonder Tales at the Transition

Although the American forefather of the Modern wonder tale had died in the decade before, his successors were gaining influence. In 1859, the year Washington Irving followed

Poe to the grave, Fitz-James O'Brien published "The Wondersmith," a Gothic wonder tale involving unpleasant miniature automata. The prior year, he had published "The Diamond Lens," a tale inspired by the optical toy and philosophic instrument, the microscope. In France, Poe's star was rising, with Baudelaire having published his first full volume of translations, *Histoires extraordinaires*, in 1856. This he followed with *Les Nouvelles histoires extraordinaires* in 1857, and *Les Aventures de Gordon Pym*, in 1858.

Verne, one among many fascinated by these books, and at the time pursuing a stockbroker's life, in 1859 went on a summer excursion to England and Scotland, where the evident spirits of industry and commerce astonished him. The under-construction *S.S. Great Eastern*, an impressive example of technological gigantism, left a deep impression. By this time, as a writer, Verne had found minor success in the Parisian theater with plays and in magazines with short stories. One of the latter involved a balloon, while another offered the first of his several answers to Poe's wonderfully absurd clock fantasy, "The Devil in the Belfry."

Many wonder tales to follow these, in the Modern century, would relate to the clock, the automaton, and the Earth's circumference—a trio closely intertwined within the Western mind. The slowed-down and sped-up times in Poe's 1841 "A Succession of Sundays" anticipated standard elements in many such tales. Writers would be envisioning the clock spinning forward to reveal a future that seemed implied by present events, whether intoxicating or horrifying. The entrancing, electrical illumination at the Crystal Palace in London, the American Crystal Palace in New York, and then, to an even greater degree and to greater audiences, the Magic City in Chicago in 1893, seemed to promise ever-continuing, ever-expanding marvels to come—as well as soul-shrinking terrors that the world took longer to apprehend.

Others would be envisioning the clock spun back toward visions of the past, traveling through history or prehistory. The latter would prove a source for Modern imagery that would fuel the imagination of scientists, artists, and writers—thanks, in great part, to geologists who dwelled, in their scientific meditations, upon extinct beings known only from evidence found in stones. In 1854, the year Verne published his own clock-fantasy, the New Crystal Palace near London featured prehistoric-creature models that, writhing, fang-bearing, and irrational, erupted from the outwardly self-possessed Victorian mind. In 1858, the first American example of the type, now named in England *Dinosauria*, came to light in New Jersey. Despite their extinction, prehistoric giants would take commanding places in International Expositions, as they would in wonder tales through to the Modern century's end.

In line with their concern with clocks and Earth's circumference, wonder tales would envision the automaton as taking an increasing part in civilized life—sometimes to the point that the automation of life, which included the "animation" of the inanimate, would become total. Anticipations of this totality also appeared in everyday life, in the increasing amounts of artificial experiences, artificial materials, and artificial goods becoming available to average citizens of industrialized countries by the middle Modern years, to be greeted as not only rational and acceptable but also fashionable and desirable.

Wonder tales would finally envision human grasp extending to include all Earth from East to West and North to South, and from chill oceanic depths to frigid upper reaches. Technology-enabled globe-spanning travel inspired considerable wonder, and remained a source for contemplative hope through the Modern Century, even while reactions against the emerging "globalism" were finding expression—as early as the 1890s, when Yvernés, a fictional violinist whose name evoked that of his creator, despairingly said, "Local colour, what hand has wiped thee from the modern palette?"[29]

Soon after Verne penciled these words, the pessimistic visions of the Romantics, who had imagined the astronomical destruction of Earth, returned with renewed strength to haunt the Moderns—who were beginning to grasp the implications of the Earth being a clock, an automaton, and a single, graspable sphere of human activity.

On "Wonder Tales" and Other Terms

The Romantics applied the name *wonder tales* to mythological, fairy, and Bible stories—a usage that would remain in effect, in a minor way, even after the 1850s. Howard Pyle's *The Wonder Clock, or Four & Twenty Marvelous Tales Being One for Each Hour of the Day*, for instance, appeared in 1887. Despite its clock motif, its "wonder tales" reflect the Romantic sense.[30] Similarly, *Six Wonder Tales for Boys*, published anonymously in 1922, contains short romances based on ancient, biblical, and European historical sources.

In contrast, the Modern wonder tale offered a melodramatic romance influenced by, and often provoked into existence by, New Worlds idealism; and it offered an ambivalent reaction to this idealism, if not outright dismay at its implications, whether expressed explicitly or symbolically. Yet doubt and alarm failed to efface the delight and diversion that arose naturally within the form. During the Modern century, *wonder* consistently denoted an attractive attribute in tales. Typically the word indicated that an imaginative vision was involved. *Wonderland*, for instance, acquired a strongly positive power among readers in 1865, thanks to Lewis Carroll, as did *wonderful* in the middle-Modern years, thanks to L. Frank Baum.

The Modern wonder tale arose not as a "fiction of ideas"—as one middle-period practitioner, Herbert George Wells, viewed it. It arose, instead, from the Symbolist inclination being felt and followed by many writers and artists. In the Modern wonder tale, technical advances and New Worlds idealism itself gave rise to symbolic embodiments; and these symbolic forms, within the fictional framework, appeared as though "real" or "actual." In embracing technical advances for their symbolic power, and in offering them to readers *as though the symbolic incarnations of these advances were material reality*, Modern wonder tales reflected, informed, and irresistibly inspired the "mind" of society. Unlike some other Symbolist expressions, the form enjoyed peculiar popularity.

As a term, *wonder tale*, which came in for use throughout the 1800s and the first half of the 1900s, often in the form *wonder book*, has the great advantage of still conveying its meaning to readers of our day. All the same, the application of any single term to the imaginative tales of the period 1859 to 1958 may seem problematic. Such tales appeared in variety and abundance; and the terms applied to them arrived with similar abandon.

Other terms, therefore, deserve their moment.

Romance of science might seem an ideal one, having been coined around the Modern years' midpoint,[31] with *romance* intended in a literary sense—in Frye's words, "the genre of simplified or black and white characterization."[32] Readers today tend to call to mind the publishing category before the literary one, however; and "romance of science" depends upon an older meaning that may only be conjured now with prompting. It will seem fantastic to many readers today, for instance, that the romance was, in Modern terms, set in opposition to the novel. As put by the literary historian who favored "romance of science," the distinction fell along these lines: "That prose fiction which deals realistically with actual life is called, in criticism and convention, preëminently the novel. That prose-fiction which deals with life in a false or a fantastic manner, or represents it in the setting of strange, improbable, or impossible adventures, or idealizes the virtues and the vices of human nature, is called romance."[33] Since, as Frye noted, the poet imitates the universal not the particular, in the Aristotelian view, the writer of this original "romance" may have had more kinship to the poet than did the novelist.[34]

A greater objection to this term arises from the fact that it fosters the misapprehension that these tales display positive attitudes toward science and technology. We have definite ways, for instance, to take such a phrase as "the romance of travel." Positivist "science stories" did appear during the Modern years, often in educational books about scientific insights for children, or in novels that employed scientific findings without resorting to fantasy, such as Harold M. Sherman's 1931 boys' novel *The Land of Monsters*. Yet wonder tales tended in a direction away from, or at right angles to, positivism.

The *Encyclopaedia Britannica* around those middle years used the term *phantasies*— also employed early in the nineteenth century by Poe, and late in it by James Thomson, "B.V." The *Britannica* also used the apt term "fantastic story" in describing romances in which the newest scientific and technical discoveries were used to advance views on politics and sociology.[35]

In speaking about Verne, the *Britannica* captured the Modern wonder tale's spirit—"delightfully extravagant voyages and adventures to which cleverly prepared scientific and geographical details lent an air of verisimilitude"—and stated that Verne had "struck out a department for himself in the wide literary genre of *voyages imaginaires*."[36] "Imaginary voyages" were also, in France, "*histoires extraordinaires*," the term applied by Baudelaire to Poe's works. The terms "extraordinary stories" and "wonder tales" would seem close kin. Later, by the 1930s, H.G. Wells would use such terms as "fantasies," "fantastic stories," "scientific fantasies," and "fantasias."[37] A wonderfully incisive term appearing in the same period, *superstitions of science*, apparently enjoyed some favor from historians of the English novel.[38] This term reflected sound understanding, insofar as it acknowledged the scientism being exhibited by some writers, whose number included Wells.

One of the most influential writers employing the form in the 1910s and 1920s, Howard R. Garis, used the word "wonder" regularly in the boys' novels he wrote under the Victor Appleton byline. He used it especially when referring to an imaginative attraction in a tale—as in the phrases "land of wonders" and "the Wonder Valley" in one 1925 novel.[39] Boys' novels by others shared this usage.[40]

Around that time other competing phrases were coming into circulation, due especially to editorial predilections at various magazines. In his American pulp magazines, Hugo Gernsback adopted the phrase "scientific fiction" by 1923, and in the following year proposed the title *Scientifiction*.[41] Although that magazine never materialized, he launched his first all-fiction magazine under the title *Amazing Stories* in April 1926—not a "scientific fiction" title, but very much a "wonder tales" one. He apparently decided "amazing" would more powerfully attract readers than would the cerebral "scientifiction." This would find confirmation in 1929 after Gernsback's Experimenter Publishing declared bankruptcy and another publisher obtained *Amazing*. Gernsback rebounded to form Stellar Publishing, which released, in quick succession, not "scientifiction" titles but instead *Science Wonder Stories*, *Air Wonder Stories*, and *Science Wonder Quarterly*—with the first two being combined in 1930 as *Wonder Stories*, and the third being retitled that year as *Wonder Stories*

Quarterly. Even though Gernsback's inclination toward scientism sped the form's decline, his embrace of *wonder* in multiple magazine titles argues for this word's suitability even in discussing the form's late, positivist, "scientifiction" offspring.

Not until early 1938 did a similarly entitled magazine, *Astounding Stories*, become *Astounding Science Fiction*, under new editor John W. Campbell, Jr. The new name's timeliness found confirmation a year later when another magazine took the name *Science Fiction*. The year 1939, in fact, would come to be seen by historians of science fiction as beginning the "golden age of science fiction." The perception is apt, given that "science fiction" as a term barely existed in America before that time. The kind of tale being encouraged by Campbell and others also stood apart from the Modern wonder tale. Just as the positivist Gernsback had encouraged a move toward scientism, Campbell encouraged a move toward "realism" in these tales, and toward a fictional structure diverging sharply from that which had existed in a continuum from Verne to Garis. Because of its combined emphases on positivism and literary realism, Campbellian science fiction in essence stepped away from the wonder tale tradition, even though the wonder tale's contours and structure continued to influence the genre through the 1950s.[42]

To judge from its common occurrence, noted above, it seems possible that before the late 1920s the term "fantastic stories" may have seen more use than did "wonder tales" or "wonder stories." The word "fantastic," however, would come to bear a distinctly non-scientific "fantasy" connotation, among readers who distinguished between stories that reacted *against* the worlds of science and technology, and tended to look backward towards medievalism, and those that reacted *to* those worlds, and thus forward. Insofar as "fantasy" was beginning to denote mainly stories that embraced impossible elements, or supernatural ones, it came to represent stories that, in essence, had more in common with Gothic wonder tales than Modern ones. That the term "science fantasy," favored by James Blish, Judith Merril, and others, failed to take permanent hold in the 1950s was unfortunate, but understandable for this same reason.

Three

The Sleep-Journey and the Navigator

> I have never known a time when it was harder to shake loose the feeling of living in a dream as those first few hours we spent on the Moon.
> —Hugh Lofting, in 1928.[1]

> In a land of wonder that none behold,
> There blooms a rose on the Dreamland Tree
> —Brian Hooker, in 1915[2]

> As time wore on did she think much about the beloved parents she had left behind her? This is a difficult question, because it is quite impossible to say how times does wear on in Neverland, where it is calculated by moons and suns, and there are ever so many more of them than on the mainland.
> —James M. Barrie, in 1911.[3]

> "Give me back my dream," said the Marionette. Then she covered her face with her hands and gave a great sigh.
> —Edith King-Hall, in 1897.[4]

> Over in the corner was a great, tall clock, that had stood there silently with never a tick or a ting since men began to grow too wise for toys and trinkets.
> —Howard Pyle, in 1887.[5]

Gothic Influences

How did the Modern wonder tale arise? And how did Poe's works play their vital role? For the poverty-beset soul rarely leads the middle-class one down the road to fortune. Poe's adult thinness reflected his wherewithal, whereas Verne's abdominal presence, and abdominal ills, reflected his. And how is that that Verne took inspiration no nearer at hand from European authors? Poe himself had taken cues from the Gothic wonder tale that had flourished in England, in its entertainingly disturbing way, from the time of Horace Walpole's *The Castle of Otranto* in 1765. A religious turn, however, may have kept Verne from taking quite the same cues.

Gothic tales do reflect New Worlds idealism. Think of the museum dedicated to natural history and optical illusions, and perhaps, too, of the tower meant for "penetrating the secrets of heaven," in William Beckford's *Vathek*, of 1786. Caliph Vathek, that tale's anti-hero, overweens, aiming "to know everything, even sciences that did not exist"—with "sciences" here referring to knowledge in all fields including the divine.[6] New Worlds idealism played a yet greater role in Mary Shelley's *Frankenstein, or The Modern Prometheus*. It saw print in 1818, when Edgar Poe, nine years old, lived in Stoke Newington, London, as a boarding student. Had he encountered the review that called the book "a tissue of horrible and disgusting absurdity,"[7] he might have striven mightily to obtain it. Shelley's novel reflected natural philosophy, especially chemistry, and polar exploration—in other words, the twin New Worlds visions of mechanical and geographical conquest. As in Walpole's and Beckford's novels, the search for the knowledge that yields power leads the protagonist to the cataclysmic brink, and over it.

Presuming they did encounter that novel, Baudelaire and Verne felt less than the magnetic pull exerted on them by Poe's works. His, besides offering fanciful satire and absurdist humor, revel in obsessive mental effects, including mesmeric impressions. Eyes, teeth, and whole beings appear optically distorted from outer reality, offering keys to inner, disturbed psychological states. His stories take readers on journeys from mystification to explication, and from the surface narrative to the symbolic one—as in "Ms. Found in a Bottle" or "A Descent into the Maelström." In some, the ratiocinative process reveals underlying "truth," in a stepwise fashion that might seem to move away from the subjective realm—and which, one might think, should involve movement away, too, from the symbolic realm. Movement in Poe, however, takes place in the symbolic realm. With respect to Gothic predecessors, Poe accepted their emphasis upon the spectacular and the sublime and rejected their need to seek "rationales" in the supernatural and the providential. Poe wed the spectacular and sublime, instead, to natural philosophy, whose provinces included optics, and the field yet to be named psychology.

Poe

The literary surroundings that Mary Wollstonecraft Godwin enjoyed in her early years may have encouraged her to develop in a thoughtful and reserved direction. Her parents, as social thinkers prominent in intellectual circles, stood at a remove from the effervescent creatures of the boards that were Poe's. Yet even with theatrical parents Mary Godwin might have lacked Poe's mordant humor. The English society in which she matured encouraged earnest attitudes toward the day's issues, molding the reformer Robert Owen as much as it did his audiences. While her Victor Frankenstein indulges in "hilarity," for instance, he never does so directly before the reader. Only his earnestness appears on the page.

Two whose births came twelve years after Mary Godwin's, Darwin and Alfred Tennyson, would rank, as would she, high among thoughtful English writers of the time. The one bent his imagination toward fathoming the condition of organic life within geographical and geological contexts, through natural philosophy; the other, toward fathoming the condition of human life, sometimes in a mythic context, through poetry. That in America matters followed a different course seems suggested by the examples offered by Poe and Lincoln. Of this 1809-born quartet, all seem to have suffered depressive fits. Darwin's hypochondria and solemn water-cures, and Tennyson's melancholia, expressed in the relentless

In Memoriam, seemed to go unbroken by any inner, eruptive sense of the wildly absurd. On the other hand, across the ocean, that he survived his depressions Lincoln credited to humor, at times self-administered with storytelling; while Poe—whose dedication to reason meshed no less well with nineteenth-century materialism than did Darwin's, but who had reasons for melancholy that his wealthy English contemporary never experienced—had such a streak of feverish merriment woven into his being that the most absurd statement to be made about him might be that he lacked a sense of the absurd. Posthumous efforts to paint Poe the man as dismal human wreckage, as well as the tendency fostered by later writers to float his output into the dubious Empyrean of the "horror" story, have failed, fortunately, to efface the mischievous humor prominent in his works. In displaying little inclination to be relentlessly tenebrous, Poe proved himself not America's preeminent terror-tale teller, but its preeminent black humorist. At different times he may have explored the intensities to be discovered in insanity or at the limits of perception; he may have calmly outlined puzzle-solving processes; he may have basked in the serenity to be found in mysteriously beautiful locales. Yet his tendency to erupt into liveliness, into barbed satire, into gay mockery, asserted itself repeatedly. He passed off the ridiculous as the sublime for the inattentive; he dismembered boors with a straight face; he portrayed the nonexistent as reality—while undermining any sense of pseudo-Continental containment and equitable sensibility through extravagance, sensationalism, and irreverent and irrelevant appeals to ancient authors. He hardly kept hidden this bent for serious flippancy, using such story titles as "The Devil in the Belfy: An Extravaganza," or "The Man That Was Used Up: A Tale of the Late Bugaboo and Kickapoo Campaign."

Poe's intellect moved in unpredictable but powerful directions. Contemporary American observers noted his talents without quite knowing where to place him, although some, such as James Russell Lowell and Bayard Taylor, came to appreciate that a bolt of literary lightning had struck and left an indelible mark. Overseas, being removed from the archly contentious American scene, observers proved more able, more speedily, to appreciate what Poe was offering. The Brownings felt a fascination; Dickens, at times, taken aback. Poe's writings more swiftly changed the literary world, however, through French letters than through English or American ones. Baudelaire, twelve years younger than Poe, first read the American's stories in 1847 and "experienced a strange commotion"; similarly Verne, born in 1828, encountered Poe's writings around age twenty, and felt galvanized.[8]

The imaginative contours of the Gothic wonder tale emerged transformed, in Poe. His ratiocinative impulse altered the fictional structure itself. Gothic tales abounded in symbols, often quite powerful ones, that arose from within a supernatural worldview. The irrational, in other words, existed as a given, in the Gothic worldview; likewise, in the Gothic wonder tale. Poe built his fictional realizations with Deistic logic, so that not the irrational but the rational existed as the given. Even so, he retained the irrational, and its powerful symbols, by following, consciously or otherwise, a viewpoint being developed within natural philosophy: that although the irrational does exist, its place lies within the human mind. Poe's moving the irrational from an outer supernatural world to an inner psychological one—itself a rational move—caused the "strange commotion" in France, the home of the Encyclopedists, where rationalism enjoyed robust support and encouragement.

Baudelaire's first translation, "Mesmeric Revelation," appeared in the July 1848 *La Liberté de penser*. In 1852 his essay on Poe, the first outside English, appeared in *Revue de Paris*.[9] His volumes bringing Poe to French readers appeared in the three years before 1859. The astronomical prose-poem *Eureka* followed in 1863; the collection *Histoires grotesques et sérieuses*, in 1865. These offered a living wage to the translator that the originals had denied their author. By the time a complete French edition of Poe saw print in 1869, Baudelaire's first volume had gone through six editions; the second, through four; and his *Pym,* three.[10]

Poe exerted influence not through tales and poetry only but his critical writings as well. As Edmund Wilson noted, these "provided the first scripture of the Symbolist Movement: for he had formulated what amounted to a new literary programme which corrected the Romantic looseness and lopped away the Romantic extravagance, at the same time that it aimed, not at Naturalistic, but at ultra-Romantic effects."[11] French Symbolism subsequently began transforming general literature into forms that would come to be regarded as characteristically Modern. Its innovations gained ground across the channel after a visit by the young William Butler Yeats to Stéphane Mallarmé, and after Charles Algernon Swinburne discovered Baudelaire.

Verne himself published an essay on Poe. After noting that "in the midst of so much that is impossible there is sometimes a verisimilitude that grips the reader's credulity," he identifies "the materialistic side of these tale, in which the intervention of providence never makes itself felt. It would seem, indeed, that Poe rejects the possibility of that intervention and would fain explain all in terms of physical laws."[12] Although disapproving of the positivism he saw in Poe, he himself would lean toward this "materialistic side" in his own work. This practical approach, more than the "mysterious and undying attraction for the ideal"[13] experienced by both Poe and Baudelaire, influenced Verne in constructing novels. This may seem all the more strange insofar as Verne's point of view tended toward Herman Melville's, concerning

> Man disennobled—brutalized
> By popular science—atheised
> Into a smatterer—[14]

All the same, a focus upon the apparently impossible that requires demystification, a reliance upon philosophical and technical verisimilitude, and, to a lesser degree, a rejection of providence, reappeared as characteristic elements in Verne. These elements melded, in his *Voyages extraordinaires*, with the socially conscious human drama taking place within the industrialized world.

Verne tied this symbolic melodrama to a personal geographical ambition—which was to complete his "own vision of the world in novel form."[15] As had Poe's, Verne's primary mode called for deflation before inflation, and diversion before introversion. He favored scientific, geographic, and technical matters over traditional literary concerns—an emphasis that helped the symbolic melodrama to persist after his death as a form that made no more than modest nods toward the Henry Jameses of the world. Because they exerted a peculiar influence upon children and youth, moreover, Verne's works, slowly and invisibly, came to influence countless adult minds: for millions reached maturity only after having absorbed the attitudes and ideas in Verne's novels, in all their memorably vivid and symbolically charged shapes and contours.

Symbolic Melodramas and Toys

Literary Symbolists aspired to Art. Modern wonder-tale writers, on the other hand, won attention by capturing, and responding to, the excitement—the intrinsic spectacle—contained within the New Worlds visions. By capturing it in symbolic terms, they communicated it even to those readers with undeveloped literary, scientific, or technical interests.

A minor Verne biography would, one day, bear the title, *Jules Verne: The Man Who Invented the Future*.[16] While extravagant, the subtitle contains a grain of truth—not the truth of stating the situation, but that of reflecting perception. Writers of Modern wonder tales stood near the beginning of the process in which new ideas found introduction to, then acceptance within, general society—with those ideas finally acquiring the unwarranted sense of having been inevitable. The process made prophets of its participants, without regard for their intentions; and the perception of prophecy made unconscious determinists of the public.

Adults were reading these works, worldwide, and enjoying the "ultra-Romantic effects." Yet they could and did read with the entertained disbelief that adults feel proud to sustain. Such works they easily could dismiss. Youths' manner in reading these tales, voraciously, proved far more important to a distinctly Modern process. In it, society advanced its technical capabilities by advancing, beforehand, its membership's acceptance of, and then desire for, technical and social change.

More easily than adults, youths can stand at no critical remove from their readings. They can immerse themselves in melodramatic entertainment—even if "in over their heads" as far as technical or scientific matters go. They absorb and internalize ideas and rationales as easily, and as unconsciously, as they can ethical implications in plots and character depictions. Sensationalism, moreover, ensures that they embrace symbolic elements to the greatest degree: for the symbols and the wonder-sense in these stories go hand in hand. The motor vehicles, the space craft, the planet-spanning networks, the electrical replacements for labor, the moving sidewalks, the instant and globe-spanning communications, the guided automata of violence and war, the ironclad war machines, the city-structures of massed humankind, and the planet-destroying explosive boilers, rays, and bombs: in the wonder tale, what for adults has *symbolic* reality for young readers has symbolic *reality*. Rather than suspending disbelief, youths were wetting their toes and swimming in rivers flowing with believable visions that opened onto possibility, not impossibility.

Through the Modern years, when convenient toy versions could be devised, these symbolic wonders acquired tactile dimensions. This practice placed physical forms of symbolic realities into the field of vision, and into the hands, of those having the most malleable minds. Many such toys reflected practical achievements, being miniatures of such public-spectacle inventions as the chemical-wagon, the steam shovel, or the locomotive. At other times they appeared as "philosophic toys," in the tradition of the fire-balloons that were the rage in the 1780s. Yet the process would occur time and again in which the functioning model of a working scientific achievement would turn into a simplified and often non-functioning model for youths; and the natural-philosopher's "philosophic toy," which by the late 1800s was being called the "scientific toy," would become a child's toy. Any new, utilitarian mechanism, in other words, yielded a symbolic object—a not-really-functioning equivalent intended for children. This held as true for steam engines and skyscrapers as it did for dial telephones and electrical kitchen eggbeaters.

With the miniatures, the fact that these toys were not exact, working models forced children back on their imaginations; and their imaginations then traveled along natural lines. Thus children who watched fire-balloons, and so witnessed aerostatic transport's uncontrollable nature, later would receive toy "balloons" incapable of any flight except the imaginary. Children then would "fly" them with their own lifting fingers. At the end of that process, from working technics to symbolized technics to played-with toy, there appeared a strangely perfect anticipation of the form to be taken in the future by the working technics. Even in the late 1700s, in the hands of a child, the toy aerostat became nothing less than the toy dirigible—the *aerostat* in form, but the *aeronef* in imaginary function. The toy in the child's hands might have been, in reality, merely a smooth pebble, a balled-up paper sheet, or an eggshell, standing in for a Montgolfier or Charles balloon. Of necessity, the child's play changed the toy. Play itself, as an act, made the toy balloon embody pilot-controlled trips through air that would remain technically unachievable for another century.

Experimental balloonists had no notion that their dreamed-of transition from aerostat to aeronef had been affected symbolically already, in countless playrooms. Only rarely, for that matter, would the children themselves have realized what they were doing.

Yet for impressionable children and youths, the notion grew naturally into a conviction that symbolized ideas could, indeed, acquire reality. The sense of "the impossible" had failed to restrict their play, after all: for in the playroom the "impossible" device encounters no "real" obstacles. In imaginative play, wild fancy gains entry to the realm of the possible.

Melodrama's Transformations

The Modern wonder tale, as a romance provoked into existence by New Worlds idealism, developed within the dramatic tradition of melodrama. The form's name, in its denotation, came to be altered during Modern years for technological reasons. Although "drama" would retain its old sense, its prefix in this context came to drop its original meaning: for "melo" refers to music. This sense remains active in other English words, such as *melody*. The old melodrama, in other words, included songs and musical interludes. Even its dramatic elements aspired to the state of music, in that they aimed likewise to rouse feelings, especially ones attached to ethics and morals. That they are properly "music dramas" found reflection in their eventual name on the American stage: "musicals."

A secondary meaning for "melodrama" arose in the Modern century when it came to be applied to general dramas having a heightened theatricality, with an emphasis on plot and action over character. It was replacing the prior term "romance," in other words. This meaning gained strength with the arrival of film, an immensely influential form that initially featured on-screen printed words to convey dialog and continuity cues. Whatever organ or piano music could be had from local musicians, at whatever theater was giving a showing, compensated for the film's silence: for the "silent movie" as a form included, on a semi-compulsory level, such accompaniment. Even so, that this musical element was improvised weakened the link between the hyper-theatrical play and its musical score, while the name "melodrama" remained in place.

The Modern wonder tale, as melodrama, retains that dependence upon the "score": for the song and orchestral interlude remain structurally important, if in altered form.

A song in melodrama gives play to musical ideas, gathered around a dramatic "aside." In a full song, or *canzone*, a character unveils inner thoughts and emotions; or multiple characters, communal ones. While a song may introduce a plot element upon which subsequent events will turn, it usually fails to advance and even resolutely breaks the action. Since it appeals to the emotions and the aesthetic sense, however, it deepens audience involvement, and redeems plot banalities.

In place of this, wonder tales, whether philosophic, Gothic, or Modern, offer a passage that is a play of ideas. It seems musical insofar as it exerts a similar, absorbing effect upon the reader, diverting attention from the plot and directing it toward a different but stimulating realm. Such asides, the wonder-tale "songs," present imaginative or speculative ideas relevant to the tale, along with explanations that help make these ideas sensible. By means of these ideas, and only by these means, the tale ventures outside ordinary experience. The ideas may relate to an emotional or physical effect, as in the spiritual response to space travel in C.S. Lewis's 1938 *Out of the Silent Planet*; to linguistic points, as in passages about *vril* in Edward Bulwer Lytton's 1871 *The Coming Race*; to an imaginary society whose differences must be established, by arguments political, economic, aesthetic, or otherwise, as in *Gulliver's Travels*; or to a fanciful mechanism, such as Poe's and then Verne's *Victoria*, whose properties or capacities must be made clear. Only by means of these asides can the reader follow the story as it unfolds.

Due to this element's importance—to ignore the symbolic components for a moment—the Modern wonder tale might well deserve the Wellsian thought that it is an idea drama. The *melos* of the idea—the song of the idea—makes the exaggerated, theatrical events in the drama conceivable. The song of the idea halts the action but deepens reader involvement. Often it remains in the reader's memory as a key element for characterizing the whole.

In stage melodrama, the instrumental interlude or *intermezzo* shares some functions with the song. Lacking a sung text, however, it helps establish mood or atmosphere. Moreover, it offers musical scenery—since stage-sets for melodramas typically see reduction to a minimum.

In the wonder tale, the interlude finds its replacement in descriptions relating to travel, and to evocations of setting and landscape. While setting and landscape help convey the sense of the sublime, in Gothic tales, the setting and landscape in Modern wonder tales serve more the function they did in *Robinson Crusoe*, in making clear the difficulties being faced, and in establishing any differences that might exist between the conditions being faced by the fictional character and those being faced by the reader. While such an interlude may overlap with the presentation of ideas, *landscape* in the wonder tale plays an important and separate role from the *idea*. It sometimes imposes itself, as a presence, so strongly as to utterly, and sometimes literally, dwarf the human actors. Thus the immense, self-contained London of the future, in H.G. Wells's 1899 *A Tale of the Days to Come*, embodies an idea; but overwhelmingly it provides the backdrop, the symbolic landscape, before which and within which the tiny, nearly characterless actors play out their roles. Similarly, the vast, enclosed spaces in Verne's 1864 *Journey to the Centre of the Earth* and 1877 *The Black Indies*, and in Lytton's *The Coming Race*, required that many passages be devoted to evocation and description, which greatly affected the novels' moods and tones. By increasing the symbolic depth and weight of the settings, they made sustainable the symbolic journeys being undertaken.

The Melodramatic Platform's Changes

Literary short forms, said Poe, should be designed in such a way as to heighten a single feeling. As Wilson observed, Poe's perspective offered a point of conjunction between Paul-Ambrose Valéry and T.S. Eliot as literary critics, in that they shared the idea "that a work of art is not an oracular outpouring, but an object which has been constructed deliberately with the aim of producing a certain effect."[17] For the Modern wonder tale, the writer would make every effort to create the delight or wonder that is to be engendered by an encounter with the extraordinary. It might be a wonder tinged with mystery and black humor, as in Poe's works; it might be wonder mixed with pessimism, of the sort found in the early Modern century in works by Verne and then Twain; it might be wonder mixed with the poetic and fanciful, of the sort found in the middle years in whimsical works by Baum and Barrie; or it might be wonder turned aside, an embittered anti-wonder, forbidding and tinged with dismay, of the sort found also during those middle years in the works of Wells, who altered the form by reintroducing and emphasizing Gothic wonder-tale tendencies, with the supernatural world-view replaced by an equally irrational scientism.

Where the naturalistic tale lent itself poorly to exploring trends to be observed within a technical culture, or even to exploring the discoveries and speculations of natural philosophy, the melodrama, with its focus on excitement and spectacle, provided a platform both stable and flexible enough to accept nearly any subject matter.

Audiences tend to accept the stage melodrama for being what it is: pure fabrication. It might mimic a contemporary sense of reality, to mock it; it might present a seemingly well-rounded personality, to undermine and expose its pomposity or utter obliviousness to the vital currents of life swirling around-about. In the melodrama, only a flimsy evocation of an individual, a two-dimensional caricature, wins real belief. With such a character, height and breadth are enough: for depth distorts, unless it be emotional. The character must have simple thoughts springing from simple desires, that they might appear to an audience in the verse of a song.

That the melodrama is pure fabrication need not mean that it offers falsehood, nor anything arising from what Sartre called bad faith. The form offers audiences a series of signs pointing toward truth, at the level of the heart.

Hewing as it did to the form, the Modern wonder tale lent itself to the stage, a fact that Verne exploited to advantage. When cinematography arrived in the middle Modern years, its directors and producers immediately

THEY FLEW AWAY TO NEVER-NEVER-LAND

The sleep-journey. The sleep-journey and the journey of childhood fell along parallel lines, in *A Child's Garden of Verses*, *Tommy Trot's Visit to Santa Claus*, and *Peter Pan*, among other works (from James M. Barrie, *The Story of Peter Pan*, 1926).

seized on wonder tales, both Gothic and Modern, for material. Stage-magician Georges Méliès produced *Le Voyage dans la Lune* in 1902, American filmmakers made melodramatic versions of *Frankenstein* in 1910 and 1915, and in 1926 Fritz Lang directed the three-hour *Metropolis*. This last brought to the fore the potential for visual passages to stand in effectively and often quite powerfully for musical intermezzos. In the 1920s the wonder tale made a decisive return to the boards with Karl Čapek's *R.U.R.*, delivering Czech word "robot" to the world.

In a scene in which the female lead, Helena, reflects on mass-produced humanoid workers, Čapek's characters impress the audience by being overly dramatic rather than otherwise—within the collapsed timeframe of rushed Modernity.

HELENA: It's so—so unnatural. One doesn't know whether to be disgusted, or whether to hate them, or perhaps—
DOMAIN: To pity them.
HELENA: That's more like it. No, stop. What did you want to ask about?
DOMAIN: I should like to ask you, Miss Glory, whether you will marry me?
HELENA: What?
DOMAIN: Will you be my wife?
HELENA: No. The idea!
DOMAIN: [*Looking at his watch.*] Another three minutes. If you won't marry me, you'll have to marry one of the other five.
HELENA: But, for Heaven's sake, why should I?
DOMAIN: Because they're all going to ask you in turn.
HELENA: How could they dare to do such a thing?
DOMAIN: I'm very sorry, Miss Glory. I think they've fallen in love with you.
HELENA: Please don't let them do it. I'll—I'll go away at once.
DOMAIN: Helena, you won't be so unkind as to refuse them?
HELENA: But—but, I can't marry all six.
DOMAIN: No, but one, anyhow. If you don't want me, marry Fabry.[18]

Besides being charming in its directness, this efficient exchange reveals what undercurrents exist. Though the emotions being strangled by ideas must be shallow, as befits a strangled inner life, they remain real in their shallowness.

While the Modern wonder tale continued in existence through the Modern century, in the wake of efforts by Wells to inject realism by means of using type characters, rather than stock characters, the form's melodramatic underpinnings began to seem a liability rather than asset. The term "melodrama" itself came into disparaging use, from critics who judged that its presence in a story marked sophistication's absence. Given literary-establishment leanings toward realism and what it called "naturalism," such disparagement came increasingly easily to critics, even though, in general, melodramatic novels enjoyed continuing popularity.

The melodrama as a basic novelistic form, in imaginative stories, however, had begun surrendering its central position before World War II. In the war's aftermath its importance dwindled. The many pulp-magazine readers who began complaining, in the early 1950s, about "the sense of wonder" going missing in the *Astounding*, *Thrilling*, and *Wonder* magazines were responding directly to this change. Later, after Sputnik, the Modern wonder tale gave way almost completely to the two diverging forms that had come to dominate imaginative writing during the 1950s: "serious science fiction," also being called "speculative fiction," and "commercial science fiction," which tended to include adventure romances and thrillers, or what critic P. Schuyler Miller, in the 1950s, recognized as "game" fiction. Since both speculative fiction and "game" fiction avoided stock characters, or sectional characters, sensationalism, and the motif of the marvelous machine, the symbolic melodrama persisted only in diluted form, among new stories and novels, although in film and comic books it retained some power.

The Modern wonder tale began with Verne in a period marked by efforts to rapidly and technologically unify the world; it suffered crises with Wells and World War I; and its days came to a close, as a living literary form, with the globally unifying events of World War II, the atom bomb, and Sputnik.

The Hoax, the Tall-Tale and the "Wonder-Business"

Around the Modern century's opening, the hoax and its American folk form, the tall tale, played a role in shifting "wonder tale," as designation or name, away from stories based on myth, fable, and religion. As noted earlier, Romantic wonder books—such as Nathaniel Hawthorne's 1852 *A Wonder-Book for Boys and Girls* that retold Greek myths "in Gothic or romantic guise"—featured tales about supernatural beings acting within broadly accepted contexts, chiefly Classical or biblical. Such books found a welcoming audience among the young, who knew the tales would contain elements of the marvelous and supernatural, and who resigned themselves—if they thought about it consciously—to the fact that any stated or implied reasoning or explication would take moral or doctrinal form, not empirical or rational.

The tall tale, on the other hand, required that its audience be rooted in the secular realms of "common sense" or "the news." The year before Verne's *Cinq Semaines en Ballon* appeared in France, Samuel Clemens published a few paragraphs entitled "The Petrified Man" in the *San Francisco Bulletin*, playing off the fact that petrifactions, real and spurious, kept appearing in newspapers: "In the fall of 1862, in Nevada and California, the people got to running wild about extraordinary petrifactions and other natural marvels. One could scarcely pick up a paper without finding in it one or two glorified discoveries of this kind. The mania was becoming a little ridiculous."[19] Clemens felt confident that his readers would read his October 15 offering and take it in whole. He intended it as a joke—"burlesque" and "satire" being his terms—and included enough geographic impossibilities within its few paragraphs to let readers know they were ingesting pure fabrication, as a tonic administered to stimulate bemused disbelief.

For a tall-tale to succeed, disbelief plays an essential role—even though commonsense curiosity, and a readiness to believe, must precede its dawning. The amusement comes in part from the audience having been "taken in"—from its having gone along with a "stretcher," in Huck Finn's term. Yet being "taken in" produces no effect, barring wonder, if disbelief fails to follow on its tail. Only disbelief allows humorous appreciation to take full rein.

The form seems to have rooted itself early, and deeply, in American society. Samuel Morse's initial efforts to convince government officials to take seriously his long stretches of telegraph wire, for instance, met with dismissive laughter. His audiences, although they started with commonsense curiosity, moved to disbelief as naturally as do hares, against turtles, to the finish line: for they had been trained in the tall tale.

Clemens's petrifaction tall tale proved more amusing in its failure than in its success. Readers generally missed his cues; and since those readers included the newspaper editors who borrowed and spread it, he found himself addressing an audience that grew into the millions. This minor exercise reached an international readership three years prior to Twain's splash with his "Jumping Frog."

"As a *satire* on the petrifaction mania, or anything else, my Petrified Man was a disheartening failure; for everybody received him in innocent good faith," he later wrote, "and I was stunned to see the creature I had begotten to pull down the wonder-business with, and bring derision upon it, calmly exalted to the grand chief place in the list of the genuine marvels our Nevada had produced."[20]

Clemens, in other words, had planned otherwise than to perpetrate a hoax, yet had done so despite himself. He did admit the power of the miniature narrative: "From beginning to end the 'Petrified Man' squib was a string of roaring absurdities, albeit they were told with an unfair pretense of truth that even imposed upon me to some extent, and I was in some danger of belief in my own fraud."[21] As it happened, his experience with "The Petrified Man" proved repeatable.

His effort may have overachieved due to fast-reading carelessness in newspaper readers; yet his displacement, in the Northrop Frye sense, proved powerful, in his approaching his matter by using the "squib," or newspaper brief, as a form.

In Frye's understanding, mythological underpinnings appear in displaced form, in literature—meaning that the myths giving substance, direction, and depth to narrative appear in guises that are particular to a writer, or to a cultural moment. However brief it was, the squib's underpinnings may be seen as myth in the traditional sense, or as reflective of the still-emerging Modern myths of the post–Medieval Western mind. Here, the surrounding page of truthfully intended stories, and the newspaper-squib form itself, served the function of a rationale arguing for belief—or, at least, in Coleridge's fine turn, for the suspension of its opposite.

Clemens's burlesque, once in print in a multitude of newspapers as "news," became a hoax. As a hoax about the marvelous, it served as a miniature wonder tale. Poe's "Astounding News by Express, *via* Norfolk!," similarly had acquired displacement from its context, being situated among newspaper stories. It took the form of the "feature," however, which required that Poe work consciously at verisimilitude. He applied himself to achieving the "unfair pretense of truth." Verisimilitude serves writers as a means to achieve displacement, to be applied consciously.

"Mark Twain" as Clemens's choice of pen name, incidentally, proved peculiarly fitting: for the cry "mark twain" in riverboat jargon meant "safe waters."

It served well for one who wrote tall tales that turned, of their own accord—thanks to the safe waters around them—into hoaxes.

The Sleep-Journey

When the dual New Worlds visions settled over Western society, promising nearly endless expansions of wealth and power to the privileged, philosophical wonder tales appeared almost immediately. Kepler himself presented visions in an imagination-driven narrative; and his fertile thoughts provided a rich compost for the "science-stimulated fantasies of the seventeenth century" then becoming common.[22] As suggested by Kepler's title of *Somnium*, this wonder tale, despite the mechanistic vision at its heart, offers itself as the outcome of a voyage accomplished while asleep. Sleep figured into fairytales, as well, as in the German folktale of Peter Klaus, or in Charles Perrault's late-1600s "*La Belle au Bois*

Dormante," which appeared in English as "The Sleeping Beauty." Early in the nineteenth century the notion of magical sleep gained new prominence and popularity with a Dutch American retelling of the Peter Klaus tale. The hero in "Rip van Winkle" escapes domestic tyranny by sleeping until a time when, time-etched and bearded, he finds himself a free man, in what amounts to another country. He awakens in the same town and territory under a new government, in his own "future."

Irving's tale appeared in countless American and European editions and became a popular hit in the late 1850s as a play that saw staging across America.[23] At the time, Edward Bellamy was a child. Bellamy at age thirty-eight would offer the world not a short story but a novel predicated upon a journey taken by means of sleep: for the hero of his *Looking Backwards* awakens into a world far in the future from the one into which he had been born. *Looking Backwards* became a national sensation when Edgar Rice Burroughs was a child of thirteen, growing up in the central-northern United States—and when, across the Atlantic, H.G. Wells, who was one year younger than *Alice's Adventures in Wonderland* and now in his early twenties, was graduating with honors from London University after having studied with no less than T.H. Huxley. Wells soon began publishing wonder tales—or tales of pseudo-science, as they were also called, at the time. Publishing as he was in Verne's wake, he came to dislike comparisons to the French writer, saying that he himself intended his works to have the reality of a "good, gripping dream."[24] *When the Sleeper Wakes* took its place among his novels in 1899.

Edwin Arnold in 1905 launched the interplanetary romance as a category, with his *Lieutenant Gulliver Jones, His Vacation*, an adventure on a Mars where Lt. Jones found himself "not greatly surprised … at the novelty of [his] whereabouts"—much like a dreamer who accepts strange and familiar elements with equal ease, in what Lewis Carroll called an unreasoning apathy. Burroughs, at thirty-nine a failure at many occupations but a success at dreaming, may have found his calling in reading Arnold's novel. He wrote a similar one himself, about a man asleep in a desert cave who undergoes mysterious transport across interplanetary space. His *Under the Moons of Mars*, even more remarkably dreamlike than Arnold's, made its magazine debut in 1912. That debut, and its book publication as *A Princess of Mars*, had a revitalizing effect upon the Modern wonder tale. The form had been struggling beneath a ballast of Utopian socialism after Bellamy and Wells, despite the whimsies introduced by Baum—who, in his tales for children, always remembered to have his characters—at least those who could—sleep.

In the year when *Looking Backward* first appeared, when several Verne novels already had established their reign of perennial popularity in America, Philip Nowlan saw the human equivalent of first publication. He was in his early teens when Wells stories were becoming popular, and in his twenties when Burroughs transformed the American popular-literature landscape with *A Princess of Mars* and *Tarzan of the Apes*. In the late 1920s Nowlan published a magazine story that in 1929 became a newspaper comic strip featuring hero Buck Rogers, who dreams his way into the future by sleeping for centuries in a cave.

Youngsters Ray Bradbury and Isaac Asimov, both age nine, felt galvanized by this daily newsprint dose of the futuristic in the comic pages. A boy only six years old when the strip made its debut, however, would write the last of the lasting sleep-journey tales, at a point near the ending of the Modern wonder-tale. Cyril Kornbluth, in "The Marching Morons," would offer an overturned Rip van Winkle who is not a kindly, lazy soul but a slick, self-aggrandizing operator. Not one for charming such boon companions as were found loitering in Irving's bucolic Hudson River village, Kornbluth's tale would offer a discomforting satire at the end of Modernity, skewering a genocidal globalist world that included both a Hitler and a Los Alamos.

Dislocations in space as well as time occur in these tales: for "Rip van Winkle" showed how even one who is stationary may move from one political state to another, via sleep-journey. That this dislocation, an important element in the Modern wonder tale, delighted rather than puzzled readers, seems evident in the success of "Rip" and another tale even more popular, written in the year of Poe's "The Gold-Bug." *A Christmas Carol* by Dickens features a Rip named Scrooge, hen-pecked by his own miserly streak. Scrooge's serial sleep-journeys take him back in time, through space, and forward in time—giving him the opportunity to change the future by altering himself, first. He must remake himself as a fully humane being, with his inner life restored.

A moral melodrama, ghost tale, and Gothic wonder tale, Dickens's tale, too, prefigured much that was to come.

New Worlds Idealism and the Navigator

As Mumford notes, the New Worlds visions owed their existences to Copernicus and Kepler, who corrected Ptolemy's vision of the planetary system by moving the Sun to both physical and symbolic center.

Observations of regular, precise, and seemingly deterministic actions in the heavens made possible the clock and the sextant. In ancient times mariners had consulted the skies, as well, and knew its aspect as a determinate field of motions. With the Western chronometer, the upwards gaze turned into a downwards one: for with that invention, the celestial mechanism saw reduction in size so that it fit first on a clock-tower, then upon a mantle, and then within the hand—becoming in its ultimate form, to no small degree, a philosophical toy.

The clock and sextant when paired with the compass gave authoritative certainty to natural philosophy. Not the explorers themselves but these hand-held examples of technics created the imperative among Europeans to cross the Atlantic: for they needed to bring the nascent mechanical world picture to the New World, and to impose that picture, by nautical "exploration," upon the globe as a whole. In essence the toy globe of the clock needed to encompass the geographic one. The term "circumnavigation" carried the accurate connotation that the navigator was one whose actions were influenced, ordered, and often determined by his chronometric and astronomical tools. For the navigator moved in a circle around the Earth; and since the Earth, in symbolic terms, had become but a minor, shrunken affair within the celestial mechanism, the navigator went around the face of the Earth much as a clock-hand might go around the face of the clock. Navigators themselves became clock-like, increasingly regular and predetermined in their actions as they established fixed trade routes around the globe. As "individuals" they arose out of visions by thinkers such as Descartes who perceived the celestial and earthly mechanisms but also believed in the correctness of authoritarian rule over humans living within and upon those mechanisms. At the helm, the navigator stood in for the divinely chosen Sun King. The great caravels and clippers moved as the churches navigant of knowledge, upon seas of inerrancy.

Curiously, "navigator" came to refer, too, to laborers on land. It applied to those who dug the growing system of canals, and who thus acted as agents of "mechanical uniformity," in Mumford's phrase. They worked, in part, under the dictates of their surveying equipment; and they determined routes for those who would then "navigate" the canals after them: for, as a word, "navigator" was coming to designate anyone who stood at the steering wheel or rudder, who suffered under the illusion of being in command of any vessel, small or large, even when the waterway itself steered their course. The word extended, too, to the skies when the aeronef dream became reality.

The Western world in essence lived within the dreams of mechanical and geographic conquest. The navigators became the ideal for human behavior in the heroic mode—for they, more than almost any others, directly witnessed the waking-dream journey undertaken by the West. They stood at the forefront of the movement that was bringing the human sphere to fall within the machine's.

Gothic Automatism and the Romance of Exploration

During these same centuries, clockmakers, conjurers, and inventors began creating objects that became playthings for kings and those who were kinglike in business and society. As noted, the word *automaton*, which had applied originally to the celestial mechanism, then to the clocks and watches that proliferated to the point of becoming essential to society, now also designated elaborate devices meant for diversion and decoration. Since by the eighteenth century they often took human shape and performed human-like actions, with these devices the clockmakers were depicting symbolically the automatism that was entering daily life. In that century, too, Rousseau and his followers argued that the increasing use of technology was enervating the human being and reducing its chances at reaching its potential, resulting in a weakened society. The tension underlying Modern wonder tales, in other words, explicitly existed in the century before Verne was writing.

Verne's technologically defined, confined, or undermined humans took their bows on a stage that was accustomed to the weight of stock characters, who reflected sub-divisions of the once-rounded human soul. He innovated, however, in presenting beings lacking in inner balance, who nevertheless were bent on extending the outward-reaching grasp of technical human society. They reflected those society leaders who were engineers, scientists, and captains of industry, who exemplified the positivist life rather than the conventional one.[25]

With the intellectual and rational aspects of their human souls enlarged and overemphasized, these individuals required challenges bordering on impossibility, and tests beyond the human norm, to bring them into a more balanced state of being. These tests and adventures needed to be expressed in terms of the melodrama, not only because that form required exaggerated ideas and unusual events, but because melodrama offered audiences the drama of the human soul coming together—in a self-assimilating or self-completing way—against a backdrop of moral or ethical dilemma and tension. Automatism, in creating fractured or, as Baudelaire might have put it, decomposed souls, opened the door for new varieties of human characters whose personal dramas required not that they prove themselves but that they submerge themselves completely in the implications and outcomes of their own ideas, concepts, and dreams, and through both personal perseverance and mechanical disaster achieve self-realization—a result strikingly different from the retributions, deaths, and dooms ending Gothic wonder tales.

The actual explorers and adventurers in Romantic and early Modern years, in contrast, often seemed well-rounded humans, with strengths and weaknesses that may have been outstanding but not impossibly extraordinary. Several major heroes of scientific exploration succeeded as well as they did thanks to their own personal qualities and strengths of character, not their arsenals of scientific gadgets and technological assists. Mungo Park, Scottish explorer of Africa, ranked high among them. Even so, the adventuresome spirit, which most members of Western society preferred to participate in at a remove, went hand-in-hand with an excitement about technical developments that enabled and then propelled that exploration. The public mind coupled the romance of exploration with the romance of industrial advance, with the human dimensions of the one causing the automatism of the other to disappear into the background.

Modern wonder tales brought to the fore this disjunction. In a few instances, as we shall see, they did so by combining automatism and the seemingly individualistic adventurer into one. Since not all these sectional-human figures would rank as navigators, moreover, these stories symbolically presented the subsuming of the human condition, across social levels, into the machine. To a degree, in these stories, all machines became world-machines.

Modern Wonder Tale Characteristics

Since notions and instances presented up to this point suggest much about the wonder tale in its Modern form, some effort at summary may help bring the form more clearly into definition.

The Modern wonder tale's being melodrama suggests that it may rely on coincidence, allow for the absurd, and be extravagant in emotional content. Any or all of these may disappear into "the song of ideas"; but all three—coincidence, the absurd, and emotion—bolster the form's dependence on symbolic characters who reflect aspects of the human soul. These "sectional" actors move around or even within an additional, non-human character—a symbolic construct and circumstance presented as having Being, whose existence depends upon New Worlds idealism. In its nature, this artificial construct may be a journey that takes up the human actors; a setting that enfolds them and unfolds onto situations and encounters; or a machine, vehicular or otherwise. If a machine, it offers a public spectacle, a cause for wonder, that gives emphasis to its nature as an idealistic embodiment; its operation emotionally involves and may physically encompass the human actors; and its existence shapes their actions—making it close kin to a tale's setting. Naturally, these different natures may and perhaps must interweave. The machine may partake in the journey, or the actors or setting may partake in the machine's existence.

In the Modern wonder tale, the sleep-journey dissolves, its ending being an awakening—as in the awakening doubts about prior events that end *Out of the Silent Planet*, or in adulthood's erasing childhood powers in *Peter Pan*. The locale likewise shimmers into disbelief, becomes inaccessible, or succumbs to cataclysm, as with Poe's submarine city "far down within the dim West," and his House of Usher. In the same way, the marvelous machine, confronting the Fates, succumbs to them with drama and violence, much as Frank R. Stockton's "Tricycle of the Future" shoots off a pier to vanish into a lake; as Nemo and his *Nautilus* repose at last in a volcanic tomb; or as John Kendrick Bangs's house-boat is stolen and lost down the Styx, in the end. These irresistible ends have permanence, within the framework of the tale itself. "Try as I like to find the way," as in R.L. Stevenson's "The Land of Nod," "I never can get back by day."

The thematic element of having a character be pointedly "awake" in a tale, as in *When the Sleeper Wakes* or Olaf Stapledon's *Odd John*, rather than offering exceptions to this, suggests that such tales fall nearer the Gothic wonder tale than the Modern. The story whose gyre ends with the dreamer's defeat and death, as does Verne's *Paris in the Twentieth Century*, similarly maintains the Gothic form rather than advancing the Modern—which latter form Verne had solidified in his just-prior novel, *Cinq Semaines*. The shape taken by the Modern wonder tale may owe its unusual distinctness to Hetzel, who brought out *Cinq Semaines* and rejected *Paris*, which then languished unpublished.

In the continuity of serial novels, as in the Van Dyne *Flying Girl* novels of the 1910s or the Appleton *Tom Swift* series of the 1930s, the destruction of the marvelous machine suffers dilution, sometimes existing as a "literal" element within a story only in the case of a villain's invention. The symbolism of the destruction itself, however, becomes a symbolic structure common to the series novels as a whole, in that each new marvel must fall into eclipse in the next novel, being outshone by the marvel in the sequel. Even when an earlier main attraction comes into play in a later sequel, it serves as a routine element that may fail or suffer sabotage, as does the Electric Runabout in the later Tom Swift novel about his aerial warship.

In the Modern wonder tale, a tension underlies the journey—between dream and non-dream; between its fictional reality and our consensus one; or between New Worlds idealism and its difficult co-partner, Modern humanism. Thomas Page Nelson's 1891 "Tommy Trot's Visit to Santa Claus" gives a fine example of this byplay in a sleep-journey, with its mildly erupting reminders of Tommy's daily life. Similarly, Edith King-Hall's 1897 *Adventures in Toyland* contrasts the world of toys wakeful at night with that of children wakeful by day. The most striking example, however, may appear in the occasionally conjoining dreaming and waking episodes in Carroll's 1889 *Silvie and Bruno*. In a machine-laden dream-journey, as in *Cinq Semaines*, the tension may arise between technological optimism and pessimism.

Divisions between the sectional characters reflect this tension, so that an ending to dream, setting, or imaginary construct brings an end to these divisions, symbolically or in a stated manner. Even in a later work such as Baum/Van Dyne's 1911 *The Flying Girl*—in which the central "wonderful machine" brings an archetypal family, and not a sectional soul, together, and not through surrender to but triumph over nemesis—a story-within-the-story does state the thematic element of redemption through wreckage, with a criminal putatively made into honest man.

The Modern wonder tale reflects a shift in underlying assumptions, from the providential to the rational, although the situation may be more accurately described in Barzun's terms, as a shifting in orthodoxies or dispensations, with materialist scientism ranking high among the successors to the religious worldview. While the sense of mystery may pervade the Modern wonder tale, it does so to lend force to the tale's rational underpinnings. The sense helps intensify the songs of ideas that make its events passingly credible. To some degree, too, biblical Providence gives way to authorial providence. This appears in perhaps its most naked form in the second Tom Swift series, at the end of the Modern century.

The Modern wonder tale may gather so much capital from childhood as to become emblematic of it, much as the poem "The Land of Nod" may be read as depicting childhood itself. Along with others in the 1885 *A Child's Garden of Verses*, the expansive but small "Nod" arose from the yearning, youthful spirit still resident in Stevenson's soul even after arduous travels, experiences, and illnesses. Stevenson's ability to retain the child must have been in the air for other responsive writers to grasp and release, to judge from Edward Lear's slightly earlier "The Owl and the Pussy-Cat," which reflects true childhood ambitions regarding a wide and unfathomable world that might avail itself not to navigation but to an impulsive and imaginative pursuit of life. Lear's verse embodies a child's dream to go away completely—away from common sense and from adulthood with its harsh, Copernican sun, and to dance, then, by the light of the Moon.

In Owl and Pussycat, or Duck and Kangaroo in another Lear verse, a child finds imaginary companions who enjoy freedom from growing up—much as, in Stevenson, the pirate in *Treasure Island* enjoys freedom from retribution, even authorial. That Stevenson's pirate exists the way that a skylark does suggests why such imaginative visions so captivated the Modern reader, whether wistful child or system-ensnared adult.

Four

Tradition and Change in Symbolic Toys

[T]he search for information about the earliest toys known to man brings us face to face with a plethora of details about the very beginnings of civilization, and verifies the old truism that toys reflect in miniature the progress of man.
—Dan Foley, in 1962.[1]

Then she began looking about, and noticed that what could be seen from the old room was quite common and uninteresting, but that all the rest was as different as possible. For instance, the pictures on the wall next the fire seemed to be all alive, and the very clock on the chimney-piece (you know you can only see the back of it in the Looking-glass) had got the face of a little old man, and grinned at her.
—Lewis Carroll, in 1871.[2]

Chinese Shades and Animated Pictures

The routines of daily work and social life have appeared often in amusements for children, youth, and adults, with the mechanical element having become a notable ingredient in Europe during and after the 1700s. Once they had their day in the European capitols, attractions major and minor made their ways to American cities. One such, the *Théâtre Pictoresque & Méchanique,* came in 1808 to New York City, billed as "a kind of amusement entirely unknown in this country.... Fontoccini or Artificial Comedians.... Arabesk Fires, Small Chinese Shades, & Animated Pictures."[3]

As this small announcement reveals, many ingredients that later were to become important in the American toy trade made their appearances, in imported form, before the birth of Poe. The Fontoccini, or *fantoccini,* were dolls, puppets, or marionettes. Artificial Comedians may have been French automata—realistic-looking figures that worked by the winding-up and then release of clockwork mechanisms, or that worked with gravity-power, using poured sand or water. Chinese Shades, also known as shadowgraphs, offered entertainment that combined puppetry and optical diversion, with the puppets being cut-out figures held near thin white cloth or paper, and brightly illuminated from behind, so that the audience, from the other side, would see shadow-figures moving across the white surface. Such cut-outs might have been projected by Magic Lantern, as well.[4] Animated Pictures tended to be flat tableaus with elements that moved, with their being "animated" suggesting spring or falling-sand power, although some doubtless relied upon simple hand-power.

Another automaton likely to have reached American shores by this time from England took the form of a clockwork model illustrating relative movements within the Solar System. The device had been introduced in 1700 by "mechanician" George Graham. In the 1710s, manufacturer John Rowley dubbed it the "orrery" to honor Charles Boyle, fourth Earl of Orrery.[5] Although John Herschel, son of William, in 1733 had called them "very childish toys," they still inspired wonder, even in older souls. Over time they would come in for manufacture as standard educational items.[6]

While offering less amusement than mechanical theaters, orreries shared their pre-determined motions. Subtly, these entertainments and other "philosophical toys" nurtured a determinist sense, much as Deist thought did among those willing to face the theological implications.

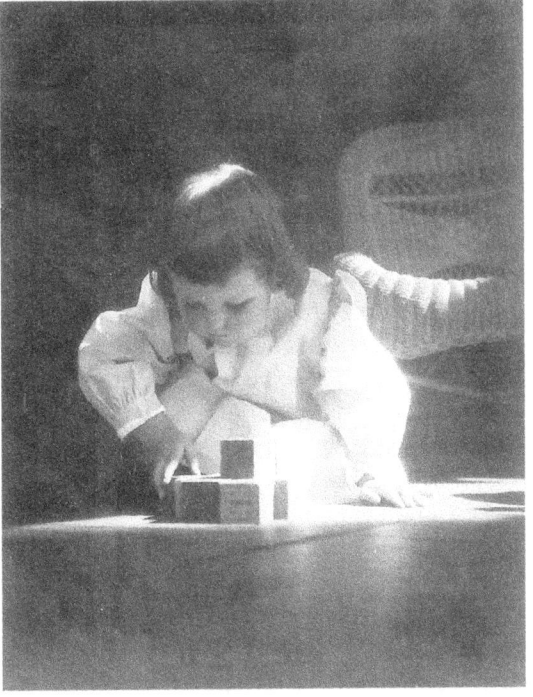

An educational value in toys, no doubt apparent to parents from prehistoric times, gained formal recognition in Modern years. Besides teaching letters, numbers, and spatial relations, blocks came to have a geographical aspect in depicting exotic animals, as well as a story-telling aspect in evoking fairy tales and, later, cartoon characters. Photograph marked "1910" (author's collection).

Toy Theaters

While the Modern wonder tale was developing from the stage melodrama and the literary "phantasie" or "extravaganza," manufacturing processes were developing in such a way that toymakers could more quickly respond to news, fashion, and society's changing focus.

Among more significant developments, the toy theater gained popularity in England in the 1810s.[7] These involved miniature stages and sometimes curtains, cut and assembled from board and paper. The "actors" often came printed six to a sheet. These a child could cut out and deploy to re-enact current dramas or stories. Accompanying pamphlets provided dialog, to help shape the child's play. Since the actual theater was home to spectacle and melodrama, these elements inevitably influenced how children played with their tabletop versions, as well.

As toy theaters developed as a manufacturing category, publishers offered ever more options to the child who wished to recreate a full story. They made available individual characters in different postures and costumes, rather than only one figure for each character; likewise, changes in scenery. More followed: "Elaborate proscenium fronts were brought out—some of which were actually drawn from existing theaters—lighting equipment (for burning colza oil), drop curtains with idyllic scenes of considerable fantasy, and wire 'slides' for pushing on the characters and pulling them off while the dialogue was spoken."[8]

Having started in England around 1808–11 with printers William West and J.K. Green, toy-theater manufacture flourished by the 1830s, with important publishers including J.H. Jameson, the Dyer family, Robert Lloyd, Hodgson & Co., Orlando Hodgson, B. Pollock, and the Skelt family. Hodgson's productions offered "extraordinary plays, the characters of which seem to hover on the very brink of demonic possession. Even in repose they have the air of inmates posturing on some lunatic asylum lawn, their dark-pupilled eyes staring out an an inexplicable and alien world, their elaborate costumes heavily encrusted with pattern and overwrought fringing," as one toy historian observed.[9] In 1857 John Redington took over J.K. Green's business, with B. Pollock then succeeding Redington. In their hands, Dickens's *Oliver Twist* became an important toy-theatrical, encouraging sympathy for the downtrodden among countless children. The new generation taking pleasure in these toys included at least one who would become a spirited and imaginative writer himself: for Robert Louis Stevenson as a boy thrived upon such hours of play and dwelled upon new figures and backdrops in a shop window with "giddy joy."[10]

These theaters led directly to another toy. Less expensive to produce and easier to promote to children of all classes, the paper doll quickly found favor. Even if one-sided and two-dimensional, these figures amply stimulated children's imaginations. They frequently depicted fictional characters and came in for their own "paper-doll dramas."[11]

At the same time, other playthings were arriving from quite a different stage. With the new "chemistry" being popularized by Humphry Davy and others who embraced the name "chemists," and who made public stage-spectacles of their discoveries, manufacturers began issuing such philosophic toys as Portable Chemical Sets, which they made available by the 1810s.[12] These toymakers already knew to seize upon wonder-provoking philosophical

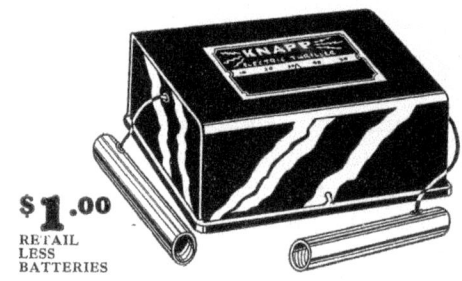

Something New *from* America's Pioneer Makers of Electric Toys

$1.00 RETAIL LESS BATTERIES

The KNAPP Electric Thriller

Here's a toy, with play value and eye appeal, that affords endless fun for children and grown-ups. It's a shocking machine with current supplied by two flashlight batteries. As the handles are pulled the current is increased. The Knapp Electric Thriller is mechanically and electrically perfect. You'll find it "a sure-fire hit"— and a real profit maker. List price $1.00 less batteries.

An old idea remains shocking—when a diversion that inflicts electrical surprise is the one being reintroduced. Knapp Electric, of Indianapolis, began making electrical toys in 1894, the year after Lewis Carroll described a stage show that included battery shocks, in *Sylvie and Bruno Concluded*. The Electric Questioner quiz game, a long-lived favorite, appeared in Knapp's line from the start. The Electric Thriller came forty years later, unencumbered by any educational baggage beyond teaching the limits of one's endurance. Electrical shocks as weapons had entered wonder tales by at least 1870, in Verne's *20,000 Leagues Under the Sea*. Advertisement from magazine *Playthings*, September 1934.

stage-demonstrations: for in the 1700s, when the public flocked to see electric marvels that astonished and sometimes literally galvanized them, enterprising manufacturers produced various devices for producing shocks, for novelty and amusement.[13] Such devices acquired and retained an odd popularity, even being offered at the first world's fair—as the "galvanic walking-stick, which gave you a slight shock if you held it in one hand, and a severe shock if you held it with both."[14] While this might strike our contemporary senses as extreme, in having no purpose besides causing startlement and pain, child-size devices having this nature would become standard, mass-produced playthings during the Modern century.

American Toy Manufacturing in First Blossom

Toy manufacturing was gaining a foothold in America around the time toy theaters were coming into vogue overseas. Previously, in the States, wood turners, silversmiths, and tinsmiths made playthings in limited numbers for local customers, while woodcarvers, seamstresses, and tailors made dolls and doll clothing. Stores with "fancy goods," on the other hand, offered baubles from abroad, particularly Germany. "Toys" as a word still had broad application, though small items of domestic utility were less often than before were being called such. Yet they still included items of decorative appeal. Having begun with blurred boundaries, "toys" as a term remained more inclusive than exclusive well into the Modern century.[15]

A few early American manufacturers, such as New York City's Charles Shipman, clearly emphasized children's toys: for in the late 1760s he was making cups and balls, alphabet cubes, and pieces for chess and backgammon.[16] New England's Newton and Thomson, founded in 1800 to manufacture pill boxes, may have been the first in the States to produce toys in large quantities.[17] By the 1820s, members of the Crandall family of Hokington, Rhode Island, seem to have been producing items for children. Benjamin Potter Crandall, born around 1800, reportedly offered the public the first baby-carriage manufactured in America, when he was in his twenties. After moving the business to New York City in 1841, his four sons all took toy-making vocations.[18] A relative, Asa Crandall, started a wood-working and furniture factory in Covington, Pennsylvania, also in the 1820s, with wooden blocks and children's furniture apparently among his offerings. Gideon Cox of Philadelphia was making hobbyhorses by 1825; and in Gardner, Massachusetts, the Heywood Brothers company began making toy furniture in 1826. Others active in the 1820s included F. & R. Lockwood of New York City, making games and puzzles.

The true early blossoming of American toy-making took place in the 1830s and 1840s, however. Bevin Brothers of East Hampton, Connecticut, began making bells and bell toys in 1836, followed by the East Hampton Bell Company in 1837—starting a long-lived association between that town and the making of bells, bell toys, and mechanical toys. William S. Tower of South Hingham, Massachusetts, began making wooden toys and doll furniture in the 1830s. Around 1840, Francis, Field & Francis established their tin-toy business in Philadelphia. The firm's side-wheel riverboat steamer would rank among the earliest American mechanical tin toys to see commercial production. It anticipated later boat-toys in being a wheeled vehicle for rolling on table or floor.[19]

Two who would rise to prominence in iron toys in the later 1800s founded their joint business in 1843, in Cromwell, Connecticut. Originally making hardware, J. & E. Stevens & Company soon would be making wheel toys, doll furniture, penny toys, and mechanical banks. The following year another iron-toy firm began operations: A.C. Williams, noted earlier for its fire-punctuated story.

S.O. Barnum & Son set up business in Toledo, Ohio, in 1845, with a line including toys; R. Bliss & Co. of Providence began making wood toys in 1845; and William Langdon of New Orleans first issued games around 1846. The year 1847 saw two businesses start in Philadelphia: E.W. Bushnell, who made hobby horses among other children's items, and Ludwig Greiner. In that year, too, E.B. Estes in New York City and Leonard Snow of Marlborough, New Hampshire, entered the wooden-toy business.

In 1848, metal toy production increased again with Peter Pia of New York producing pewter toys, and Benjamin T. Roney of Attleborough, Pennsylvania, tin drums.

Charles M. Crandall, born in 1833, took over the Covington woodworking factory after the death of his father in 1849. By more strongly emphasizing toy production he came to rank among the foremost American toymakers. In Massachusetts, Hadley's Dickinson & Thayer started their business in carriages and wagons in 1849, and Worthington's E.T. Ring, likewise. In Connecticut, E. Henderson & Company, in New Hartford, and L. Robinson in Bristol started similar businesses. In the same year Robert Hattersley began a toy business in Albany, and Newark India Rubber Manufacturing Company began making India-rubber toys and balls.

Others beginning in the 1840s included James H. Hawes Manufacturing Company in Towanda, Pennsylvania, with wooden toys; Joseph H. Hersey and also Joseph Jacob of South Hingham, Massachusetts, with wooden toys; and W. & S.B. Ives of Salem, Massachusetts, with games and toy books.[20]

This early blossoming, which continued into the 1850s, came about, in part, from changes in techniques available to manufacturers. Factory methods sped wooden-toy and carriage output, while entirely new processes allowed cast-iron and even steel toys to be produced. The India-rubber revolution affected most playthings categories, leading to introductions of all-rubber toy dolls, animals, balls, and rattles during the 1850s. A new item, the rubber squeak-toy, gradually supplanted the traditional squeak toy made with wood, fabric, and a spring.

The blossoming came about, too, because changes in society, transportation, communication, and industry opened opportunities for alert manufacturers, especially Pennsylvania tin-toy makers and Connecticut, Pennsylvania, and Ohio iron-toy firms. Though engaged in a traditional trade, New York and Massachusetts carriage makers, too, were responding to urbanization, urban fashions, growth in personal-vehicle traffic, and technical innovations.

This responsiveness to social change, and eagerness to embody that change in children's toys, constituted a departure for a manufacturing category previously bound by tradition. By and large, however, the U.S. toy-manufacturing scene prior to the 1850s revolved primarily around established patterns in toy-making, playthings, and play, thus putting in place securely the foundation that allowed the new expressions to thrive and proliferate during and after the Civil War. That this foundation so well reflected the growing primacy in daily life of the secular spheres of business, industry, and the marketplace made it an especially solid one.

Sunday Toys

Although a toy's debut marks a symbol's appearance, what a toy physically represents may stand apart from what it symbolizes. Pertinent examples of this seemingly discordant situation found their way into Calvinist households well before the Modern century, in a form that came to be called the "Sunday toy." Even well into Romantic years the traditional concept of the Sabbath as a day of devotion had held considerable sway. It being a day not for labor, Calvinists regarded it as being also not for play—even if, in the wake of Locke's thoughts but especially of the more popular Froebel's, almost all toys had been opened to being viewed as heuristic. The fact that doctrinaires sometimes permitted religiously edifying objects to hold adults' attention on a Sunday, however, opened a door just large enough to admit children and their seemingly small needs. Diminutive diversions appropriate to the day, as a consequence, found their ways into unquestionably welcoming hands.

The tale of Noah and the Flood had long proven popular, especially when presented as a mystery play or a puppet drama at a saint's-day festival. While violent and catastrophic in nature, it contained elements that lent themselves to simple representation in paper or wood. Inundating rains and the Flood may have lacked toy equivalents; and, among some Calvinists, teachings against idolatry sometimes played against dolls being made of Noah and his family. Yet the ark with its paired animals offered a great opportunity to toymakers.

The toy ark may have appeared alongside early passion plays being performed across Europe, whether performed by traveling mummers or local tradesman guilds. Historians, however, tend to place its beginnings in Germany's center for both wooden-toy production and religious observance, Oberammergau. Wherever its origins, the toy seems to have become popular in the centuries when the twin New Worlds visions were spreading through the lettered as well as the unlettered public. German toymakers' choice of animals clearly reflected this vision, insofar as a Noah's ark might include paired zebras, leopards, giraffes, camels, impalas, tigers, hippopotami, and elephants—sometimes without any familiar European farmyard animals beyond the essential dogs. Toymakers seized upon the growing interest with the wider globe in this way, and designed the toy, which concerned itself with a transition being made between worlds, to reflect a global perspective.[21]

The Sunday Alphabet of Animals, written by an "Aunt Katie" sometime in the 1800s, offered an equivalent in book form. It illustrated and described animals, adding helpful moral

Noah's Ark. Illustration by Alice B. Woodward, 1897 (from Edith M. King-Hall, *Adventures in Toyland*, ca. 1910).

sidelights, such as the one found in the tale of Elisha's bears ripping children to pieces. "A-ss, B-ear, C-at, D-og, E-lk, F-ox, G-nu, H-edgehog, I-bex, J-erboa, K-angaroo, L-ion, M-ouse, N-autilus, O-possum, P-eccary, Q-uagga, R-abbit, S-quirrel, T-iger, U-nicorn, V-iper, W-alrus, X-iphias, Y-ak, Z-ebu"—with a rhinoceros standing in for the unicorn. That it has geographically expansive reach the book demonstrates from the start. The first letter offers not "The Ass" but "the *Wild* Ass, taller and much handsomer than the common one"; and the second, not "The Bear" but "The Polar Bear." While it would seem unlikely that any among Aunt Katie's readers would ever encounter a wild ass, it would seem nearly impossible that any saw a polar bear without becoming a polar explorer. None would have seen the nautilus, at least in the fanciful form it took here: "It *is* beautiful, truly; and floating upon the water looks like a sort of fairy-ship, with its sails spread and its oars dipped to guide it."[22] As attractive etchings, however, these exotic creatures became familiar companions through childhood.

While secular authorities were pursuing mechanical and geographical visions, in other words, religious authorities were encouraging toys and toy books that inculcated in children a sense of global inclusion.

Although designed for play on a day free from labor, the Noah's Ark lent itself particularly well to early factory production. By early Modern years, toy-making practices called for cutting grooves into a board or a lathed ring of wood, so that, in cross-section, it suggested an animal's outline. After sawing the grooved wood into uniform sections, workers gave matching detail to each piece with knife and paintbrush. By such means, manufactories produced toy animals in multiples to be sold with the arks, which ranged from simple painted boxes to carved boats.[23] By at least the Modern century, Noah's arks fell within a toy category that included, as well, the box filled with toy soldiers or farm animals: the *box toy*. By late-Modern times the toy industry would prefer the term *play set*.

For the child who received Sunday toys, this biblical story came more vividly to life than did others. The Ark gave reality to a tale that floated between the literal and the symbolic. The tale relates a world's destruction by a universal, supernatural force, followed by the transport of the chosen few to a second world. These elements—a first world that is followed by a second, with the two divided by disaster but linked by the ark filled with people and animals—became actual to children as settings, characters, and events. Having been externalized as toys helped the stories and mystery plays to be internalized.

In child's play as in the tale itself, insofar as the second world offers an improvement over the first, the first comes to stand in for the primitive human state, replete with violence and discord. In that survival and safety depend upon Noah's tools and woodworking abilities, moreover, the ark itself represents the acme in human technics—the ultimate in material achievement in that first world. Without it, humankind would have met with extinction, being unable to travel to the second world.

Whether or not it fostered piety, on a weekly basis the toy reinforced the notion that the world might face disaster. The all-inclusive globe might face a universal end. History, children learned, could include cataclysm. A deluge might swallow humankind with no more difficulty than a whale might swallow Jonah.

Animals, moreover, took their place in the child's imagination as innocent beings: for by making it clear that they were worth rescuing, the tale suggests that a primordial goodness exists in the natural world, despite the appearances of antediluvian violence. Animals took their place in imagination, too, as obedient beings: for the tale suggested that subservience, too, is to be found in nature. Although the ark biblically contained all animals, it logically contained only those who followed given orders, and who boarded the ark without succumbing to any urges to follow their own instincts or minds. These presumably would have led them, were they actual animals and not illusory or play-animals, to shy well away. This element established grounding in children's minds for the notion that the chosen few needed absolute uniformity, in not feelings nor thoughts, but in obedience, to reach the second world.

With this symbolic reality impressed upon them, society's most malleable minds could readily accept other narratives sharing similar elements. In the late eighteenth and early nineteenth centuries, these other narratives often displayed outwardly doctrinal aspects. Yet the Romantics, who tended toward materialist thoughts, similarly nursed cataclysmic visions that had their basis in astronomical insight; and Lord Byron, the Shelleys, and Poe approached the idea of the end of the human world from different directions—with Poe seeming to anticipate the prophecy novels of a century later by starting one such cataclysmic tale with the words, "Born again."[24]

In Poe's youth, the Noah story had gained new popularity in transformed guise, in Johann Rudolf Wyss's *Der Schweizerische Robinson*, or *The Swiss Family Robinson*, first published in two volumes in the 1810s. Combining the desert-island tale with Noah's, Wyss has the novel's clergyman-hero and his family emerge from shipwreck along with domesticated animals. This ship puts into literal terms the ark's symbolic element of its having been designed for colonists, since in Wyss the animals and supplies were placed aboard for that explicit purpose, albeit not for that particular destination; and the ship's destruction, in the story's opening storm, shifts emphasis from the ark's construction to its being rendered useless upon reaching the second world. That second world appears as an island in the Wyss tale, as in the biblical one. Given that the book appeared not long after the Luddite uprisings, its essential elements—the colonizing ship's destruction and the survivors' subsequent adventure in basic existence, in isolation from Western civilization—capture a shift becoming evident in the West, away from New Worlds triumphalism and toward a state of doubt and confusion concerning industrial technics.

Noah's arks undoubtedly gave children means for recreating the vastly popular and also quite pious *Swiss Family Robinson*, since the toy provided, or at least suggested, a boat, family, and animals. Some sets even included snakes that might stand in for the novel's malevolent "boa." Where earlier this box-toy had helped confirm religious tradition, it now could help nourish the colonizing impulse—which would seize Western nations with unprecedented strength, as it happened, once the first children to have read *Swiss Family Robinson* matured and reached their seniority in society. Similarly, it may have helped some among them later to understand and embrace Marx's "Bible of the working class," with its "antagonisms which will swallow the present and spew up an automatically improved future."[25]

The arks gave a means for grappling with other transitions, as in the 1895 *A House-Boat on the Styx*. Bangs has Charon, the Ferryman, reflect, "It's a great thing to be the go-between between two states of being," on the novel's first page; and describes the house-boat itself, on which Charon is soon hired to be janitor, in terms that suggest the ark. In a later chapter, the shades of Noah and Barnum argue over the former's having not brought Megalosaurus and other ancient reptiles along on the ark. Such literary play, on the part of Bangs, likely echoed nursery-floor play from the time of the New Crystal Palace, forty years earlier.

A second type of Sunday toy, rather than reinforcing traditional beliefs, surprisingly reflected social change. By the 1800s a better-off family might own a dressed-up doll such as a "Bartholomew baby" tricked up in ribbons and lace, purchased at the famous Smithfield fair. When the Sunday Doll appeared to the child, the parent required that mere admiration supplant play. Outwardly a toy with religious significance, being designated for Sundays, she held primarily a secular meaning, being dressed not to show Puritan restraint but to win approval within a social circle. It reflected an ongoing shift in emphasis—away from the Sabbath for strict religious observance, and toward the Sabbath for attending church for social reasons alongside the religious. As in Mary Wilkins Freeman's 1887 story "An Independent Thinker," to abandon Sunday conventions threatened an individual not with damnation but local ostracism, in a purely temporal society. The doll encouraged children to focus on the day's less forbidding aspects, while helping speed the day's departure from exclusively religious observance.

Toys that incorporated Sunday-toy elements likewise encouraged play that had little Sabbath connection. N.N. Hill Brass Company, for instance, made a wheeled, mechanical, cast-iron bell toy in which, with each wheel-turn, a bell dinged and a whale swallowed and eructed Jonah. As noted, wonder books often included Bible stories; and while their fantastic elements may have fostered religious edification, their non-religious entertainment value may have had greater force. Hill, in making the toy in the later 1800s, probably banked more on the subject's popularity than its religious character. As a consequence the toy had less in common with a Noah's Ark than with Cinderella's Chariot and Chime, made by the Gong Bell Manufacturing Company, Hill's competitor and neighbor in East Hampton. "Wonder-book toy," as a descriptive term, might aptly describe either.[26]

Even in the later 1800s, however, diversions clearly designed to suit the Sabbath appeared. Parker Brothers plainly meant "A Game of Christian Endeavor," first issued in 1890, to appeal to the game-buying parent of a particular type.[27] Although that type survived into the 1900s, the ardent high-mindedness of Wyss faded into quaintness and genial custom, as in Baum's 1911 novel in which a socially adroit but not religiously motivated girl urges her brother not to test his new flying machine on a Sunday.[28]

The Steam Rocket

Far from encouraging play-reenactments of cataclysm, most traditional toys reinforced family, workplace, and community activities, and rendered, in small, things to be found in home, farm, or town. While common across class-boundaries in their homemade forms, in their manufactured forms these toys rarely appeared outside households that were financially better off, before the 1800s. With the rise of the middle class, however, the market for quality as well as uniform playthings grew steadily. Thanks to an already maturing industrial scene, in England a "golden age of toys" was opening by 1820, to extend until around 1860, when America's golden age stood poised in the wings.[29] An average family's increasing access to toys marked these golden ages. So, too, did a revolution in toy types, brought about, in part, by advances in printing and other technical arts. The very nature of toys was changing, moreover, with playthings appearing that would have been impossible only decades earlier.

Notable changes reflected advances in the steam engine, for instance, which had ranked as a curiosity since ancient times. In the mid–1700s, however, Glasgow mathematician and chemist John Robison, intrigued by it, urged a local instrument-maker to try his hand at making one with wheels. That instrument-maker, James Watt, seems to have dabbled in toy-making beforehand.³⁰ Although the pair's ambitions failed in this effort, Watt's continuing work advanced the technology to such a degree that his design improvements moved steam engines outside the realm of the philosophic toy.³¹ Since Watt had progressed by no means along a straight line toward steam-engine perfection, models and toys undoubtedly remained a part of the scene even after his productive but challenging partnership with Matthew Boulton began to flourish, in the English Midlands. Watt apparently continued working on ideas concerning wheeled steam engines; and since his wide-coverage patent on steam power stifled competition from practical engineers, he may have encouraged an inadvertent flourishing in privately produced philosophical toys: for the inventive spirit continued in others than Watt, even though they may have felt dissuaded or were even being held back legally from manufacturing items that might be considered practical.³²

William Murdoch offers an example. A Scottish engineer, in 1779 he became an assistant to Watt, soon Watt's most trusted, in the steam-mill business. In the 1780s, in Cornwall, Murdoch took pleasure in running a wheeled steam-engine around his living room in Redruth. Down a street in Truro he sent another wheeled engine that must have fascinated spectators, in a firecracker sort of way. Further work in this direction might have tempted him, had Watt not been standing in the way.³³

Decades later in northern England, George Stephenson, born in 1781, and son Robert, born 1803, tested a "travelling engine" christened *My Lord*. This 1814 success led to the elder Stephenson's becoming engineer of the first railway that operated without animal power. Passengers and goods traveled by means of "locomotive" on "the Stockton and Darlington," which opened in 1825. In 1829 his locomotive *The Rocket* won a competition sponsored by the Liverpool & Manchester railway, helping confirm the feasibility of steam travel and haulage on rails, as well as the desirability of the locomotive over the stationary engine that might be located at one or both ends of a rail line.³⁴ If any one technical victory may be held responsible, this may have been the one to have whetted the public's taste for mechanical speed.

Being a public spectacle, *The Rocket* seems to have transformed playroom activities overnight, or at least in what passed for "overnight" in factory terms, in the 1800s. In manufactured form, the new *locomotive* became common on the playroom floor—not as a philosophic but a floor toy that in its makeup was little different from a horse-and-wagon or goat-cart toy: for the "locomotives" given to children were toys to be pushed or pulled. Yet while they lacked working steam power, society's growing "railway mania" ensured that these floor toys came fully empowered by the wonder sparked by Stephenson's engine.³⁵

The Rocket established the basic design for the massive machines that would alter the face of the Western world within fifty years—and, too, for toys appearing in England and other countries. While relatively few people saw the actual machine in action, children on at least two and likely three continents regularly acted as *Rocket* engineers during playtime.³⁶ Toy railways and locomotives, large and small, spread before the actual ones, as proved the case, too, in Philadelphia.

There, Matthias W. Baldwin, born in 1795, expressed his interest in toy-making in the 1830s by building a small stationary steam engine, some six inches square at the base. Franklin Peale, son of artist Charles Willson Peale, grew fascinated to the point of asking Baldwin to build a working miniature locomotive for the Peale Museum. Baldwin responded with a machine capable of pulling eight people around a circular track—a great attraction that drew, among others, the owners of the horse-powered railway that stretched for six miles out from the city. Having proven himself with diversionary engineering, Baldwin now constructed one of the earliest practical locomotives in America, Old Ironsides.[37] In Pennsylvania, too, toy locomotives would find a manufacturing center.

Stephenson's *Rocket* exerted a continuing pull upon public imagination, partly because it broke a speed record while aiming to achieve a relatively egalitarian goal. It rolled along rails as a technological wonder, not to move an engineer from place to place, but to move passengers. They might be anyone at all, privileged or otherwise. Along its route, people who might have taken the stagecoach now might ride a steam-drawn car. As a consequence, "rocket" as a word began budging from old associations. The rapid up-shooting motion, or the "red glare" of the patriotic song in the States, no longer fixed the word. It began to suggest the sense of achieving not airborne speeds but land-based and horizontal ones, for the public's convenience. How powerfully symbolic the Stephenson *Rocket* became for the American public became clear when American toy manufacturing was gaining its first real foothold—decades later, in the 1860s and 1870s—and seized upon it as an inspiration for toys, even at that late date.[38]

As the Modern years dawned, the locomotive offered a powerful symbol for scientific advance. The company of Elisha Stevens and George W. Brown, New York City toymakers, made this clear in the 1870s, when it issued a tin steam locomotive with a fully appropriate name stenciled upon its sides: *PROGRESS*.[39]

The Signal-Man

That the elder Stephenson should have been born in 1781 seems fitting, in that the changes that he would help usher in changed the relationship between the public and automation. At the time of his birth, mob violence vented mass anger against mechanical mills—which were labor-stealing mills, from the workers' point of view, and not labor-saving, as the landowning class regarded them. In contrast, on the tracks between towns there then appeared the "fire mills," as locomotives were called; and this event initiated a process that democratized technology. Even though financial benefits continued flowing to owners and makers, tangible benefits accrued to passengers—and to individuals and small businesses now more easily visited from afar. Mass-transit would prove an experience of continuing discomfort to some but of significant convenience to many. Even though the poorest could ill afford passage, all could stand at railside and see that a mix of populace looked out the windows, as passengers: for not all were landowners or business owners. All, moreover, favored the goods being brought from what was formerly a distance away.

The nature of the masses, even of the mob, was changing as society was. Stephenson's *Rocket* operated roughly a quarter-century after the attacks upon Arkwright's mills—and about a quarter-century before the major attraction appeared in London that gathered together the mechanical contrivances of the nations of the globe—an attraction that drew not just the landowning class but also the masses, who came not to loot and pillage but to wonder and learn. Society's expanding middle tiers were acquiring a modicum of respect and representation. They were becoming the "lively, little-cultivated, impecunious masses of the urban population"[40] so attractive to Dickens.

With steam power's close embrace by society came alterations in social positioning and class boundaries. For the first time, a quarter-century after the *Rocket*, an educated man could fall subject completely to the needs of machinery and to the time-tables of the over-arching machine that was beginning to determine urban existence. As the middle classes claimed a larger share of social benefits, the possession of "an education" became more common—as did, too, the phenomenon of being "educated above one's station." Dickens embodied the situation in a character who "observed that instances of slight incongruity in such wise would rarely be found wanting among large bodies of men; that he had heard it was so in workhouses, in the police force, even in that last desperate resource, the army; and that he knew it was so, more or less, in any railway staff."[41] As Keats had said, "Highmindedness.... Dwells here and there with people of no name,/ In noisome alley, and in pathless wood."

This particular character, the Signal-Man, had been "a student of natural philosophy, and had attended lectures," but now accepted his position, at least outwardly, and "had no complaint to offer about that. He had made his bed, and he lay upon it. It was far too late to make another." He was, in other words, the figure in Thomas Gray's elegy, upon whom fair Science had frowned not, and whom Melancholy had marked for her own.

The working class that had produced the anti-mill rioters had changed in its nature, too, due to the ultimate success of those stationary mills that predated the mobile "fire mills." The new middle class that was consolidating during the late Romantic and early Modern years knew this new shadow, however: for that portion of it that overlapped with the upper lower class often ended up working, in an educated way, within strict parameters dictated by society's and industry's machinery. The disgruntlements and anxieties about the new life would find no answer nor relief, neither in that generation nor the next few.

All the same, the comforts and pleasures to be found in mass society were beginning to be felt; and with few or no qualms, the parents, even if kin to the Signal-Man, felt pleased when placing in their children's hands symbols of the changing times, at a birthday or other special occasion: that shiny tin *Rocket*, the new equivalent to that painted wooden toy canal-boat made generations prior in Europe.

Optical Toys by Brewster and Wheatstone

As with steam power, engineers and experimenters exploring optics developed philosophical toys. David Brewster, a Scottish natural philosopher whose work considerably influenced Poe, studied light refraction and reflection, with his practical work in optics leading to lighthouse improvements. In 1815 he rediscovered and developed the kaleidoscope, which gave him greater immediate public fame than the fact that he was elected to the Royal Society and honored with the Copley medal in that year.[42]

As an empirical experimenter he likely engaged in many diversionary pastimes. The spirit of play cannot have stood divorced from a scene in which glass lenses large and small fell into the hands of so curiosity-driven a soul. With the kaleidoscope, he sensed he had something that would appeal to many; and at the fourth meeting of the organization that he and Charles Babbage had launched, the British Association for the Advancement of Science, he spoke about the kaleidoscope in a program that included William Buckland, who happened to be turning "fossil reptiles," which were the as-yet-unnamed *dinosauria*, into objects for comic amusement. This meeting fell in October of the year when the term "scientist" began to replace "natural philosopher," which was 1834.[43] As noted earlier, natural philosophers interested in chemistry and electricity long had offered popular demonstrations, which had led directly to new amusements for children and adults. The public was learning now that lenses and fossils, too, could enlighten and enliven. Brewster's optical device captured fancies in England and America and became common in 19th-century parlors.

Brewster played a role in developing a second instrument that likewise led to a household diversion. In 1710 Cambridge botanist Richard Bradley had invented an optical oddity that created the impression of three-dimensional viewing, based upon pairs of two-dimensional images: the stereoscope.[44] Charles Wheatstone much later discovered the optical principle behind the toy, and built his first "cumbrous but effective instrument" in 1838. The stereoscope combined binocular pictures by means of mirrors. Brewster suggested using lenses to unite the images, leading to the lenticular stereoscopes that entered the social realm around 1850. It ranked among the dominant means for individual optical entertainment even after electrical service became commonplace and brought in its trail electrically enhanced optical diversions.[45]

Wheatstone's interest lay mainly in acoustics, leading him to such inventions as the "acoucryptophone," a ceiling-suspended lyre that appeared to play itself. Since it "played" music actually being performed upon a piano on the floor above, it represented an early remote-control device.[46] Wheatstone's sense of play, and taste for mystifying audiences, found other outlet: for he created "ghosts" with stereoscopes, using glass slides.[47] His fecund spirit of invention led to other diversions, including the concertina, the "kaleidophone," and a cryptographic machine. Cryptography fascinated him to such a degree he acquired, for deciphering, a reputation similar to Poe's in America.

Vibrating wires would bind Wheatstone's life even after his departure from musical-instrument-making for a King's College professorship: for his discovery of the speed of electric discharge in conductors led to his patenting, in 1837, with William Fothergill Cooke, the long-anticipated electric telegraph.[48] This discovery, together with his instrument-making skills, led then to the automatic telegraph of 1868, considered to be his masterwork. By then, the telegraph had already moved into the realm of playful diversions, as with "Smith's Comic Electric Telegraph" shown at the Crystal Palace, which apparently involved an automaton face "speaking."[49]

In the meantime, before the 1860s, several experimenters had demonstrated that the easiest method for creating the stereoscopic effect involved superimposed images in two different colors, viewed with a differently colored glass over each eye[50]—another discovery that would make possible startling mass-entertainments by the end of the Modern century.

Thaumotropes and Zoetropes

When John Ayrton Paris invented a device to demonstrate the "persistence of vision" in 1825, he drew upon the Greek for "wonder" in naming it the Thaumotrope. This simple device consisted of a disk with an image on each side. One that showed, for instance, an empty bird cage on one side, showed a perched parrot on the other. The disk had a hole near opposite edges, on a horizontal plane with the images. Strings threaded through these holes and held to each side could then be wound, so that when the strings were pulled to unwind them, the disk swiftly whirled.

Persistence of vision explains how it is that the eye combines images that exist, in reality, on opposites sides of the disk. In viewing a Thaumotrope, an empty cage acquires a parrot; a prancing horse gains a rider; a gallows obtains its dangling victim. These very images came in for manufacture almost immediately, with the Thaumatropical Amusement—Seeing an Object which Is Out of Sight being introduced in 1826.[51]

Studies being undertaken around 1820 by Peter Mark Roget and Michael Faraday had led to understanding the persistence of vision. Roget himself apparently created a device involving a disk that, once spun around its center, "animated" stationary images when a portion of it was viewed through a constricted aperture. Toys that capitalized on Roget's and Faraday's insights, however, came from other hands. The spinning-disk toy appeared in Belgium as the Phenakistiscope, made by physicist Joseph Plateau, and in Austria as the Stroboscopic Disc, by mathematician Simon von Stampfer. Another name, Magic Disc, captured the wonder created by these playthings, all of which offered moving images that were repetitive yet hypnotically fascinating to gaze upon. The spinning disk might be set behind a second, stationary disk that had an opening cut into it, so that the animated figure would be seen "moving" behind that window. In a like wise, the stationary disk with the images might be set behind a spinning disk that had a window, so that the "moving" image would be seen as traveling around the circle.

A similar toy from around the same time required that the viewer look through slits cut into a spinning drum—a device invented in the 1830s, with an early example being English mathematician William George Horner's Daedalum of 1833, but which seems to have enjoyed greatest popularity with its reappearance as the Zoetrope, or Wheel of Life, issued by Milton Bradley in the 1860s. The images, printed on a strip placed within the drum, became "animated" once the drum was spun and viewed from outside. The slits in the drum revealed the animated figure through what appeared to be but a single, stationary slit, to the viewer. Multiple viewers might look in from around the drum, to enjoy a uniform experience. Other versions appeared, such as the Praxinoscope introduced by Emile Reynaud in France, which employed a mirror.[52]

Interestingly, the Gothic wonder tale anticipated these illusions of wholes, or of life, assembled from component parts. In a fanciful and satirical mode of illustration in children's books, figures would appear who were composed from inanimate items—such as the image of the bird-seller whose body consists entirely of bird cages, in a *London Cries* from around 1800.[53] Shelley's *Frankenstein*, however, depended entirely upon a process that began with inanimate parts, mixed-and-matched and apparently bloodless pieces of cadavers, and ended with the captivating appearance of life—in "the Being," as Percy Shelley referred to his wife's literary creation. As a contemporary reviewer perceived, the Being had a nature suggesting a toy: a "stupendous fantoccino"—a jointed, put-together marionette, brought to life by manipulated strings of narrative.[54] The sense that the optical toys "brought to life" static images led to the Zoetrope-type toy to be called Animateur, in France, by around 1900.[55] They offered to their viewers a "life" not real but artificial, which was "created" by intelligent means.

By this time, Zoetrope-type toys had come to include some that projected images onto a wall or a screen, in a darkened room, using oil or spirit lamps for illumination. In other words, the early persistence-of-vision toys were combining with the magic lantern, a device whose origins were ancient but whose popularity as a source for household entertainment dated from the 1840s, when the lanterns and the glass slides for projection were beginning to be produced by factory methods. Slides intended to educate or entertain proliferated, especially by the 1890s, when German makers issued "dollar lanterns" that met with widespread success. These lanterns typically looked like metal boxes with a chimney located above the light source hidden within, which burned oil or other liquid fuel. Reflective surfaces behind the light source intensified the glow, which passed first through a black-and-white or colored slide made of isinglass or glass, and then through the projector's "focusing tube." Better lanterns used horizontal "sliders" to support the long, rectangular slides, or had "lever action" mechanisms that held circular slides. The 1901 "Little Buckeye magic lantern" offered the option to use either gas or electricity. In that year, too, the Mirrorscope, which could project images off opaque paper, made its debut.[56] Although the name Magic Camera may have applied to other lanterns, it undoubtedly could have been applied to those of the Mirrorscope type that took a *camera-lucida* approach.

Slides depicted any and all subjects, including wonder-book ones, such as the "12 assorted long slipping slides of Comic, Nursery and Fairy Tales &c.," advertised in the 1880s by a New York importer. The religious element appeared in such sets as a Bunyan's Pilgrims Progress and Miracles of Our Lord, while the natural-philosophy element appeared in Cosmic Natural History and Natural History Slides.[57]

Alongside toymakers' efforts to utilize the persistence of vision principle, magic-lantern makers pursued other means to create motion effects, often by using multiple slides at once. The Chromatrope, or Eidotrope, took a particularly effective approach, using geometrical forms painted in different colors on pairs of circular slides, which, when projected together, turned in opposite directions. Altering light-source strengths contributed to their hypnotic effects. Although enjoying considerable popularity before 1900, these efforts fell away as persistence-of-vision diversions acquired increasing influence—as well as electricity—and further transformed the West's diversionary landscape.

The Zoetrope, in fact, played a distinct role in cinematic development. "Prof. Muybridge's Pictures for the Zoetrope" featured "the startling instantaneous photographs made by Prof. Muybridge of San Francisco, showing the attitudes of animals in motion. ... The illusion is perfect when placed in the Zoetrope, or 'Wheel of Life,' and there is the exact appearance of various motions, such as running, trotting, leaping hurdles, etc."[58]

Decomposed Actions

In many optical toys, the images found on the stationary disk, or the paper loop within a Zoetrope, shared an element with Bradley's Smashed-Up Locomotive. Baudelaire aptly called the paper loops' stationary visual elements "decomposed" movements.

"Imagine some movement or other, for example a dancer's or a juggler's performance, divided up and decomposed into a certain number of movements.... The twenty little figures, representing the decomposed movement of a single figure, are reflected in a mirror placed in front of you.... The speed of the rotation transforms the twenty openings into a single circular opening through which you watch twenty dancing figures reflected in the glass—all exactly the same and executing the same movements with a fantastic precision."[59]

While he was writing about the French Praxinoscope, his way of seeing the actions as "decomposed" suggests that he was seeing not just the toy in his mind's eye, but the society behind the toy, as well. By Baudelaire's time, industrial modes for production had become well entrenched in Western society. "Divided up and decomposed" might accurately describe the artfully drawn figures upon the Praxinoscope loop of paper—or the drawn-from-life figures employed in factories who were increasingly taken away from full participation in manufacturing—a word that was losing its root meaning as "producing by hand"—and taken towards labors that literally were "divided up." The interchangeable-parts concept had facilitated the manufacture of weaponry before becoming commonplace in all other areas of production. Inevitably workers, too, became interchangeable parts. That these "parts" were entire humans offered the industrial process no real obstacle.

In the Praxinoscope loop, as with other "animating" devices that relied upon the persistence-of-vision principle, the image of the seemingly whole individual—a man or woman, or some creature that might stand in for a man or woman—was itself a "decomposed" part, and not a whole. While the toy presented what seemed "life," it did so by showing an endlessly repeated action—not unlike the endlessly repeated actions to be seen in factories, and not unlike the mechanically repeated actions required of the Signal-Man.

With these toys, witnessing the reduction of life to elements that might endlessly repeat became a common social experience. The clown or ballerina trapped within the repeating loop elicited wonder and delight from the viewer, which gave way to acceptance and boredom—and which prompted a desire for new loops—for new, interchangeable parts. Easily and cheaply obtained automations-on-demand became part of the child's everyday experience long before they became an acceptable routine within industry.

Did such children grow to be adults who, upon entering the workplace, more easily accepted being reduced to a component? The Signal-Man, who came to literary life in the year H.G. Wells was born, 1866, would have belonged to one the first generations to be raised in a society that was steadily increasing its embrace of automatic, repetitive entertainments. Although quite intelligent, the Signal-Man finds himself reduced to functioning as a gear within larger workings.

"I'm a cog, you're a cog! Let's do our cog work," Verne's character Quinsonnas had said only three years before.

The Signal-Man resigns himself to his mechanical fate because he must "earn a living," even when such "living" threatens his life and ends up taking it.[60]

How important "decomposure" had become, symbolically, appeared in Shepherd's electric clock at the 1851 Crystal Palace. This decomposed clock had its pendulum swinging in the main gallery. The mechanism resided at the building's south end. Its dials moved through their positions on the east and west ends, and on the high, main arch facing south. The entire building, in a real sense, had become an immense, public clock; and thus the clock contained, as if swallowed into itself, everything else to be seen—at a fair that attempted to represent the world.[61]

Modern Symbolic Toy Characteristics

As with Modern wonder tale characteristics, it may help us to gather together the observations and surmises made in these opening chapters concerning Modern toys.

Arising in response to New Worlds idealism, the Modern symbolic toy represents, for children, an alteration in the cultural fabric, material or otherwise, that reflects the spirits of geographical and mechanical conquest. In contrast, a traditional toy reinforces established folkways and beliefs, to influence a child's mind in time-proven directions. Although gradations exist between traditional and Modern toys, the latter's strong ties to factory production often give it distinct character. By late in the Modern century, even "household toys"—a category that included toy brooms, sadirons, and kitchenware—came to represent social change, insofar as factories produced versions that overtly reflected adult fashions, cartoon characters, television shows, and the "branding" of names, as well as technical development.

In a second characteristic, in representing cultural change, the Modern symbolic toy may become common within society, as a physical object, prior to the actual model or inspiration for the toy becoming common. It thus may represent a thing never to become common. By extension, this means it also may represent something outside consensus reality or actual, communal experience.

The toy fire-fighting wagon exemplifies both categories. The toy aerostatic balloon hovers between them, as well, since actual hot-air or gas balloons became popular objects for contemplation while remaining uncommon themselves. Mainly into the second category falls the toy dinosaur. While it reflected an experience that became "common" for fair goers, as we will see, it represented an experience actually impossible. Its symbolic nature, even more strongly than usual, outweighed its material one.

The Buck Rogers toys that enjoyed extraordinary proliferation in the middle and later 1930s also primarily exemplify the second category. The same might be said of the popular "concept car" toys in the decade before Sputnik.

The Modern symbolic toy contains some element inspiring interest and excitement, in the child, which sits apart from the toy's intrinsic play value. This third characteristic arises from the second.

The Modern symbolic toy contains the potential for being outmoded, outdated, or rendered obsolete—a fourth characteristic that arises from the third.

Toys as a word, in its eighteenth-century sense, reflects the fact that around 1750 this fourth characteristic became an important one: for it covered all "novelties." Anything considered a novelty, once seen as old or common, loses that quality. The 1750s factories, or mills, produced goods that endured through time to less a degree than they succumbed to wear and wasting, breakage and disposal. This set a standard met easily by the factories operating in succeeding centuries, and met eagerly by them, by the time the 1950s arrived. Whether sound or fragile of make, factory methods ensured a uniformity of novel experience, in children.

Fifth, the toy may reflect a world-view particular to a dream for society—commercial, literary, or technological—without diminishing its potential as a society-wide toy. In other words, if only some part of society shares the worldview that gave rise to it, the toy tends to remain acceptable even to those children whose parents take other worldviews. Although this may have less importance than other characteristics, it reflects the toy's structural history. The Modern symbolic toy reflects New Worlds idealism, which results from a rationalist worldview; and the possibility of a toy being made that reflects idealism as opposed to realism seems to have been introduced through religious idealism, with the Noah's ark. The ark, no doubt, proved an acceptable toy even for children whose parents leaned heavily toward a materialist outlook—and who, perhaps, let them read *Swiss Family Robinson* even on a Sunday.

To give a different example, the stereoscope, an optical toy reflecting materialist thoughts about human vision, offered relatively little threat to religiously strict households: for stereoscopic viewing-cards might depict churches, stages in a pilgrimage, or religious-story re-enactments—just as easily as they might depict any object or scene that might fall subject to the secular art of photography. Whether or not an individual accepted materialism, the wonder created by the toy itself remained in effect.

The Modern symbolic toy shares with all toys the potential to affect the individual for life. Parents gave children traditional toys—such as toy brooms, axes, teapots, knives, carriages, or wheelbarrows—with exactly this result in mind. That this result holds for Modern toys seems evident in the story of the Wright brothers, who as children played with the powered flying toys that, by the middle Modern years, had become somewhat widely available. All toys inspire imaginative play; and something in the act of imagining yields the enduring. Thanks to the characteristic listed first above, Modern symbolic toys thus contain the potential to spur technical thoughts, to whet curiosity as to technical possibilities, and to create an ambition to expand the globe-encompassing technological network. Such toys, in other words, may generate thoughts having no prior existence.

In thematic terms, many Modern symbolic toys embrace technical progression, technical enclosure, social uniformity, and, often, the social or human regression resulting from enclosure or uniformity.

By placing Modern symbolic toys in children's hands, the Western world was engaging in a process of encasing itself, technologically. Having created automated systems for globally interconnected living, it was encouraging youthful minds to see these systems in a positive light, as worth preserving and furthering. The Western world, in essence, was ensuring that self-enclosure would remain an ongoing process.

We might think, from these characteristics, that the Western world was dismissing the ancient tale of Noah's ark, and leaving behind the toy itself as old-fashioned.

Yet the Western world's toymakers still made and disseminated it. Whether or not it occurred consciously to their minds, the toy suited the prophetic hopes of the evolutionists, Marxists, and other believers in historical materialism, who preached a single future that would emerge from the wreckage of the divided and divisive present. An all-embracing, world-encompassing sphere would carry the world's children away from an outmoded past and into the bright future. The positivist and the Calvinist unknowingly stood together in this, like paired animals obediently lined up before the savior technics.

Five

Deep Time and the Thinning Veil

> 1851 was the very crest of the wave which carried steam-power from the domestic use of collieries to the command of the land and sea ... the steam-engine, in a bare twenty years, had come to be the outstanding factor of British life. Giants like Brunel and Stephenson were still carving their great tunnels and throwing bridges and viaducts across the face of England. Brunel was even now designing the *Great Eastern* steamship. Fortunes were being made, the face of England was being transformed, the lives of millions were being made wider and brighter by the railway. Steam was a living thing, a wild romance. There seemed no limits to its power.
> —Christopher Hobhouse, in 1937.[1]

> When will you freely and gladly own the truth that whatever is born in Time must decay and perish in Time? As your race studies fossil relics of plant and shell and gigantic animal, so shall future existences (to you in their kind inconceivable) study fossil relics of your race. For every kind has its own aeon, and when its aeon is fulfilled becomes extinct: while your earth is by many signs so young in its aeon; and you by your pruriency, your unbounded self-esteem, your pugnacity, your brutality, your ignorance, your weakness, are so plainly among the less noble thoughts and imaginations of its youth (closely succeeding the wild childish extravagances of mammoth, pterodactyl, ichthyosaurus, and the convulsive infant rages of flood and fire); that many much higher races than yours must surely be brought forth ere it reaches its prime and commences to decay.
> —James Thomson (B.V.), in 1867.[2]

Fairings

In centuries long past, a child said to the parent, "Bring me a fairing!"—meaning, "Bring me a toy from the fair!"[3] From twelfth century to nineteenth, across northern Asia and Europe, people gathered on religious feast days. Fairs from their beginning honored St. James, St. Denis, or St. Bartholomew in England, or St. Germaine in France. Becoming centers for commerce, they drew young and old alike for food, festivities, trade, and entertainment, as well as religious observance. Unlike later Sunday toys that resulted from Puritan restraint, the goods and novelties at fairs fell into all categories, with hobbyhorses, toy acrobats, dolls, "penny woodens," jumping jacks, tops, whistles, drums, boats, and merry-go-rounds among their number. A particularly important toy-making material saw widespread use at fairs, for the most ephemeral of playthings. Bakers made gingerbread into any shape that might, for a moment, please a child or adult.

> Smiling girls, rosy boys,
> Come and buy my little toys,
> Monkeys made of gingerbread,
> And sugar horses painted red.[4]

Through the 1800s, fairs were changing in nature. Although the most famous, Bartholomew, had been held at Smithfield, London, since 1133, in 1840 it moved to Islington, only to be closed in 1855—suffering from the ailment Washington Irving saw in the world in general: it had become more "worldly. There is more of dissipation and less of enjoyment."[5] A new type of fair that was secular and serious in nature, in the meantime, had gained in favor, and soon largely supplanted the religious type. In particular, National Exhibitions attracted enormous crowds to displays featuring agricultural products, traditional crafts, and ever-increasing number of inventions and manufactured goods.

As had religious fairs, these drew merchants, peddlers, and criers with novelties to sell for farthings or pennies. As larger exhibitions began remaining open for weeks and even months, and industrial spectacles and attractions grew grandiose in scale, merchants with "brands" to sell began to promote them with giveaway baubles and trinkets. These novelties sometimes took a form that evoked a business or product, but increasingly one that reflected some major sensation at the fair itself. Such items proliferated. As a fair-related novelty, an advertisement's chances for being taken home to the family increased dramatically.

That Americans engaged in this promotional proclivity to a superlative degree inspired Verne to burlesque.[6] In his story "The Humbug," in the late 1860s, an extravagant character, Augustus Hopkins, announces that he is building what will amount to a new World's Fair on grounds in Albany, New York. During excavations for its construction he makes a fabulous discovery: the remains of a great prehistoric creature. Verne refers to the example offered by the "Swedish Nightingale" introduced to America by P.T. Barnum in 1850–52.

> When Jenny Lind was making her debut in England, a Mr. Lumley offered to give the soap manufacturers free moulds, depicting the portrait of the eminent prima donna. The offer was accepted and produced excellent results, since people were now using the famous singer's face to wash their hands. Hopkins employed a similar method. He contracted with cloth manufacturers to have them produce material for clothing that would appeal to the good taste of customers by displaying an illustration of his prehistoric creature. It was printed on the inside of hats, and even plates were decorated with the outline of the amazing phenomenon! And so on, and so on. It was impossible to escape it. You could not get dressed, put on a hat, or eat dinner, except in this interesting company.[7]

In the States, through the earlier 1800s, regional fair displays were becoming heavily weighted toward items produced by industrial and factory methods, as well as toward displays of the impressive machines that made possible these methods. Organized by institutes of mechanics and technology, yearly exhibitions by manufacturers and inventors opened in cities including New York, Philadelphia, and Baltimore, with the first American National Fair of industrial products opening in Washington in 1846.[8]

In Europe, National Expositions featuring displays of "machinery and mechanical devices" began with the London National Exposition of 1761 and the National Exposition in Paris in 1798.[9] Others followed in swift succession during the early 1800s, in London and Paris, joined in 1820 by a National Exposition in Vienna and, in 1822, in Berlin. Switzerland, Belgium, Russia, Portugal, Sardinia, and Spain joined in the practice before 1849, the year that the last great national exhibition in the United Kingdom opened in the industrial center of Birmingham. The pace then slowed due to plans being hatched in London for the first International Exhibition.

Setting a new standard, Queen Victoria's Diamond Jubilee and Great Exhibition, the Industrial Exhibition, opened in 1851. Often called simply "The Great," popularly it came to be called the Crystal Palace Exhibition after a writer in *Punch* coined the name to reflect the elaborate structure raised in Hyde Park to house its many exhibits. While engineers Robert Stephenson and Isambard Brunel both served on the executive committee, an extraordinary architect, Joseph Paxton, designed and oversaw construction of this innovative structure made from prefabricated sections of glass, iron, and laminated wood. Flanked by two towers, the Palace measured 1,848 feet long and 408 feet wide and covered a million square feet.[10] It represented a new kind of enclosure—a hugely expansive elaboration upon the enclosed "arcade," and upon, too, the conservatories becoming popular in England and Europe. Its scale overawed visitors, who flocked even during construction. From outside, it offered reflective faces evoking the crystal, while within its walls the majestic enclosure, aglow with all-pervasive natural illumination, gave visitors the sense of the "sublime" that had become so significant an element in aesthetic pleasure. At night, visitors might admire its gaslit radiance from within or without.

Some fourteen thousand exhibitors, about half representing England herself, created the Great's displays. U.S. productions occupied relatively little space, but included Samuel Colt's revolver, which created a sensation among military visitors, and Cyrus McCormick's reaper.[11] In another sense, however, the Americas filled the fair. The wealth that had resulted from conquest and colonizing made possible most if not all the industrial activity being put on display; and it would have seemed only natural, to observers of the time, if all the enormous resources put at Paxton's disposal, during his rise from gardener to architect, producing wonders along his course, derived from a wealth based upon a system of exploitation that was growing to have global dimensions. One particular exhibit made this clear, even while leaving unstated the large shipping industry's involvement in, and the large British profits from, a particular trade in human beings: "Also from Birmingham was a selection of shackles, leg-irons, manacles, fetters, and handcuffs made for export to the Southern States of America."[12]

SMITH'S COMIC ELECTRIC TELEGRAPH.

Smith's Comic Electric Telegraph at the Crystal Palace offered an early blend of automatism and remote control (from Christopher Hobhouse, *1851 and the Crystal Palace*, 1950).

Besides technology, the Great Exhibition offered attractions based upon the natural sciences, among them Alford Lloyd's glass-enclosed tanks—"marine vivaria." These allowed viewers to imagine themselves underwater themselves. In person they were witnessing the biological wonders of the sea being popularized by such books as 1844's *The Ocean*, by Philip Henry Gosse. Interest in the underwater realm had been gaining steam, sometimes literally. Robert Fulton, an American studying art in England, had found his attention turning toward engineering under James Watt's influence. He worked in France beginning in 1796, and there, in 1801, introduced his *Nautilus*, a steam-powered "diving boat" that descended twenty-five feet.

The Exhibition also featured such literary attractions as a weekly published as an industrial demonstration project. Embracing the geographical theme becoming common in educational books, *The Parlour Magazine of the Literature of All Nations* had for its editor the young Irish writer Fitz-James O'Brien, afterwards an emigrant to New York.[13]

Within the Palace, visitors experienced, in small, the already-shrunken Earth, with different continents' productions within strolling distance. In his "May-Day Ode," W.M. Thackeray made much of this:

> A peaceful place it was but now,
> And lo! within its shining streets
> A multitude of nations meets;
> A countless throng!
> I see beneath the crystal bow,
> And Gaul and German, Russ and Turk,
> Each with his native handiwork
> And busy tongue.

Thackeray envisioned a "brotherhood of nations" within the glass and steel structure, "in England's ark assembled."[14] Visitors, moreover, gained a taste of being encased within an artificial enclosure run on coal and horse-power—that was, as noted earlier, an immense electric clock. The twelve-pane, glass-and-iron semicircular arch that served for the main face of this clock, and that loomed over the public entrance, announced the automated realm within.

Paxton came to be portrayed with this arch behind him. Symbolically this presented the master gardener and conservatory-builder as, too, a master clockmaker.

"Wild Childish Extravagances"

At the Great's closing, the Crystal Palace underwent Baudelairian "decomposure," only to rise a second time in Sydenham Park south of London, in 1854, to house exhibits both permanent and temporary. Lloyd's exhibit of living marine life made the move with the building, and continued drawing the curious. Paintings, sculpture, and live performance attracted others to the "New Crystal Palace."

In 1854, too, Gosse's new book *Aquarium* introduced the popular name for marine vivaria. These quickly became, as son Edmund Gosse recalled, "the fashionable toy of the moment." A dedicated zoologist and a pioneering student of oceanic life, the naturalist had perfected and used aquaria in his daily studies. In the autobiographical novel *Father and Son*, the younger Gosse would recall them in the family house: "There were two, and sometimes three aquaria in the room, tanks of sea-water, with glass sides, inside which all sorts of creatures crawled and swam; these were sources of endless pleasure to me." As a boy he soon was given "the occasional task of watching and afterwards reporting the habits of animals." Despite the elder Gosse's religious conservatism, he allowed such philosophic work, and pleasure, even on Sundays.[15]

Philosophic benefit helped make the activity attractive to both parents and children. As a term for such items as these aquaria, "scientific toy" was gaining in pertinence outside

Ichthyosaurus og Plesiosaurus i Kamp.

The Sydenham menagerie. In countless illustrations the Ichthyosaurus and Plesiosaurus engaged in the same ferocious conflict, even decades after being set in concrete in a lagoon at the New Crystal Palace. An illustration in Verne's *A Journey to the Centre of the Earth* closely resembles this one published decades later. The smoldering volcano in the background signifies the primordial or "pre–Adamite" realm in many such depictions (from Henry Davenport Northrop, *Jord, Hav og Himmel*, 1890, p. 85).

FIVE—*Deep Time and the Thinning Veil* 69

the realms of academy and laboratory. Production of science kits, or "outfits," was enlarging as a province of toy manufacture, in both England and America.

Besides Lloyd's, a second watery exhibit created a sensation, and proved as enduring in its impact. Sculptor Benjamin Waterhouse Hawkins created full-scale reconstructions modeled on extinct animals, which he arranged around the edges and basin of a lagoon in Sydenham whose levels rose and fell with the tide. Dominating the group stood "gigantic monsters," as another naturalist, Charles Kingsley, called them.[16] Hawkins had designed his models in conjunction with the one who had coined the name *dinosauria*, Richard Owen.

Half a year before the park opened, Hawkins invited Owen and twenty other scientists to a celebration by sending them prehistoric novelties, quite possibly the first. He had printed invitations on "Pterodactyl wings."[17] The dinner took place within the shell of the recumbent iron Iguanodon, being reconstructed with its belly to the ground and its tail wrapped to one side. With only its lower portion in place, its cavity became a small room offering a low wall around the diners, that evening of December 31, 1853.[18]

Interest in prehistoric wonders had sharpened, by this time. The annals of antiquity had enjoyed substantial stretching, in the late 1780s, by Scottish gentleman-farmer James Hutton, who developed a rational framework for the interpretation of strata, and mathematician John Playfair, who popularized Hutton's ideas. Hutton's thoughts ran counter to prevailing catastrophist notions and gave rise to a gradualist or "uniformitarian" view. Charles Lyell expanded on Hutton's insights in the multi-volume *Principles of Geology*, the first volume of which appeared in 1830 in London. Lyell compelled the educated public

Iguanodon. The Hawkins-Owen reconstructions of ancient life locked certain images into place, in the public mind, despite paleontology's still-ongoing attempts to improve its understanding of the fossil record. This engraving, published in Chicago forty years after the New Crystal Palace opened, shows Iguanodons in the same poses as in Sydenham. Similarly, another engraving shows Megalosaurus having an all-fours, mammal-like stance (from Henry Davenport Northrop, *Jord, Hav og Himmel*, 1890, p. 85).

to examine the ever-more-substantial evidence that Earth's history stretched back almost inconceivably far.

Once the Sydenham grounds were dedicated by the Queen on June 10, 1854, the Hawkins prehistoria proved potent public draws. Thanks to Owen's involvement, they credibly represented the latest thinking about ancient amphibia, reptiles, and mammals.

Owen, born in 1804, shared a background with many contemporary English natural philosophers, having first studied medicine in Edinburgh. Knowledge concerning ancient amphibians and reptiles had already rapidly expanded during his childhood and youth: for Mary Anning had discovered a fish-like reptile skeleton in 1811, and then the first plesiosaur and first pterodactyl skeletons. Scientific papers describing *Ichthyosaurus* and *Plesiosaurus* appeared in 1821, and *Mosasaurus* in 1822. The first-described carnivorous dinosaur, *Megalosaurus*, reared before readers two years later. The work bringing to light the ancient amphibians of the Permian Coal Measures had taken place around 1829–30. *Iguanodon*'s discovery would come later, in 1848. During his years as Hunterian professor at the Royal College of Surgeons, in the early 1840s, Owen worked on Permian fossils, and named *Labyrinthodont* for its unusual teeth. In 1849, when he became the Royal College's Hunterian-collection conservator, he saw the first volume of his *History of British Fossil Reptiles* into print. Within the scientific community Owen seemed natural successor to the famous French comparative anatomist Baron Georges Cuvier.

The Hawkins and Owen reconstructions daily attracted and edified curiosity-seekers. Engravings depicting the reconstructions, moreover, appeared in newspapers and books around the Western hemisphere. Undoubtedly, too, "fairings" redolent of antiquity appeared—especially since the New Crystal Palace remained an on-going exhibition hall, with special events such as balloon launches helping draw crowds.

If nothing else, traders in baubles could recycle old mystery-play fairings. St. George's dragon, in gingerbread, paper, clay, or wood, might just as well be a Hawkins pre–Adamite reptile.

The Sydenham Monsters

The Sydenham lagoon became a public spectacle at a time when, in toy making, paper and card stock were coming into widespread use.

In the later 1700s, in France and America, jointed cardboard toy figures had been sold as "*pantins*" or "protean figures," often with changes of paper clothing.[19] "Toy books" followed in the early 1800s, with London publisher S. and J. Fuller issuing many in the period from 1810 to 1835. These books offered children a figure accompanied by numerous costumes, to be cut out for play. New York's William Charles printed versions of the English toys not as books but in individual sheets, during this time, while J. Belcher of Boston may have produced the first American toy book with 1812's *The History and Adventures of Little Henry*.[20] During the 1840s paper dolls began appearing in greater numbers across Europe, and as imports in America. A pivotal moment in America occurred when in 1850 P.T. Barnum extravagantly presented a coloratura soprano to U.S. audiences from Sweden and imported not Jenny Lind soap but paper dolls colorfully lithographed in Germany.[21] Barnum's ploy raised playing with paper dolls to a widespread phenomenon, in the States. American-published paper dolls appeared in 1854, from the Boston firm of Crosby, Nichols and Company. By 1857 American game publisher McLoughlin Brothers introduced paper dolls to its lists; and, as noted, in 1859 *Godey's Lady's Book* became the first to feature paper dolls in magazine pages.[22] *Godey's* had the distinction, as it happened, of having been the first high-circulation magazine to bring Poe's fiction before the American public, a quarter-century earlier.

Despite there being ever more families of moderate means, items at "toys and fancy goods" shops remained beyond many's reach. Parents continued making toys by hand, as did children. Books in the 1850s related stories of children who were creating their own paper dolls, for pleasure and profit, which spurred others to do likewise. With juvenile toymakers active, the paper figures played with in that decade grew astronomical in number.[23] Images that appeared in news sheets, catalogs, and children's books came in for cutting-out and imaginative play: for the act of making "cut-outs" had become a form of play that would last through the Modern years.[24]

Inevitably, the Hawkins creatures appeared on playroom floors and tables, if in forms drawn by hand or clipped from papers. That some appeared as printed toys remains conjectural. They may have appeared as "conversation cards" or other educational diversions, in the tradition of the "game of balloons" that so fascinated an early Verne aeronaut.[25] In whatever form, they ranked as philosophic toys to a minor degree, compared to the playthings that appeared in response to that other Sydenham natural-history attraction, the aquarium; and their effect on public imagination took a different turn.

The Sydenham restorations expressed the scientific understanding of the moment—a relatively early moment, at that, given that the name "palaeontology" had been coined only some twenty years before. However accurate the models were, Hawkins literally made concrete the conceptions of the early 1850s, fixing them into place as though they represented the finished result of mature scientific inquiry. As park attractions their immutability placed them in a good stead; yet their being unresponsive to change meant that they persevered in presenting the public with the view of the early 1850s, even as new scientific discoveries came to light and new insights altered scientific understanding.

Their very popularity, as park statuary and as subjects for engravings, insured that the unchanging face they gave to prehistoric life came to be known almost universally.[26]

Wonder-Omens

At the time, natural philosophers received their trainings within the framework of a devout society, often as clerics. The elder Gosse, for instance, studied New World insects and Atlantic hydrozoa while adhering to Brethren beliefs, including Scriptural literalism. Although on friendly terms with Darwin, whom he met in 1855, Gosse gave expression to his religious interpretation of the natural world in two 1857 books. *Life* and *Omphalos* portrayed the origin of higher life-forms as having been spontaneous. While the larger scientific community gave these books a chill reception, the ideas remained bedrock for Gosse as a systematist. He perfected marine aquaria as philosophic toys, in part, to broaden appreciation for the wonders of God's Creation.

Likewise, the systematist Owen, the preeminent comparative anatomist of his day, built his career upon carefully drawn delineations between hundreds of vertebrate and invertebrate species. Developing and regularizing morphological terms, he helped paleontology take rapid strides towards becoming an international field for specialized study. Investigating the forms and structures of fossil creatures alongside living ones, he developed a picture of life that stretched across the spans of time now being called geological. He identified and placed before the public successions of species, representing different geologic eras, whose relation to one another he regarded as obvious.

Even so, for Owen these successions remained no more than just that: successions. He compartmentalized, as a systematist, and resisted the idea that successions of similar biological forms might reflect continuous and unbroken development through time. Labyrinthodonts, dinosaurs, pterosaurs, and extinct mammals, in themselves, offered no contradiction to Cuvier's catastrophism. They seemed, in fact, to validate it. For Owen, prehistoric antiquity remained Antediluvian.

Any existing playthings based upon the Sydenham menagerie, as a result, had equivalence to Noah's Ark toys. In symbolic terms, the Anglican clergyman-naturalist Kingsley spoke truly in calling the Owen-Hawkins reconstructions "gigantic monsters,"[27] since the word "monster" cleaved to its roots in Latin. Verb *monstrare* meant "to show," while noun *monstrum* meant "omen" or "warning"—and also, appropriately, "marvel" or "wonder." For literalist Bible readers, *dinosauria* seemed signs of ancient dispensation, and, as such, omens or promises of Christ's second coming. Viewing prehistoric creatures as "monsters" fit into the worldview that regarded "prehistory" as a series of stages upon which life first thrived and then ended in catastrophe.

Paxton's Crystal Palace and successor New Crystal Palace introduced two great spheres of interest that widened popular understanding of the natural world. Compelling images of oceanic and ancient life became common, together with the unusual and exotic names and terms used in marine zoology and paleontology.

Both, however, arrived shackled to a belief system to be outmoded, in scientific terms, within years.

A Revolution in Perspective

With the publication of Darwin's theory of natural selection—not the first such theory, but the first to take root and create a widespread stir with its historical materialism—ancient amphibians, reptiles, birds, and mammals took new places in an alternate, competing narrative to the one offered by the church and defended by Cuvier's intellectual heirs.

Darwin's narrative concerned "species," a word borrowed from the Greek for "form." Form, in the traditional belief-system of the Roman church, is immutable. Western philosophy and its offspring, natural philosophy, had developed from a Platonist focus upon ideals, placed in an abstract realm apart from the physical one. Without this idealism, the instinct to classify the objects of the natural world, including living objects, might have arisen differently, or not at all. Darwin, himself emerging from this idealism, argued that Platonic fixity was illusory in the slowly changing biological world. Biological form arose thanks to its mutability. As a philosophical judge, with a materialist law behind him that meshed perfectly with the temper of the times, Darwin oversaw the civil divorce of form from immutability—a divorce distasteful to the Church, which, because it early had adopted and built upon Aristotle's thought, considered this marriage to fall beneath its supreme jurisdiction.

In the revised story of the Earth, "gigantic monsters" served as portents pointing toward a new understanding. Geological and biological history, brought together in paleontology, now had recourse to Darwin's theory in tying together life's diversity into a dauntingly complicated but still essentially single narrative.

Had Darwin not delayed publication of On the Origin of Species, the catastrophism attached by Owen to *dinosauria* might still have adhered, if perhaps with less tenacity. As it was, however, by the time Darwin's book saw print, *dinosauria* existed in the public mind without any suggestive link to the notion that species could change over time. The church, moreover, took a stance, post–*Origin*, that gave credence to paleontological findings without any attached heretical views. It did so, in part, by arguing against an ingredient bolstering the notion of evolution by natural selection: extinction. Immutable forms were imperishable. Applied to ancient creatures, the mere fact that geologists had uncovered bones offered no necessary argument for the extinction of the creatures that had left them to be fossilized. Somewhere, in some hidden locale, those same creatures might still exist, having survived the catastrophic divisions in divine chronology; and their continuing, unaltered existence would disprove that their forms could have changed, through natural selection or any other mechanism for biological evolution.

Despite the conundrum it created with regard to catastrophism, the argument had impact in halls other than religious. The search by biologists for still-existing creatures that were considered extinct by paleontologists would extend beyond the Modern century's end. While this search by no means lacked scientific interest, in symbolic terms it represented the religious worldview's tenacious grip.

To the Center

Five years after On the Origin of Species saw English publication, Hetzel published Verne's *Voyage au Centre de la Terre*, an adventure story that is at once delightful, engrossing, and absurd: a journey into the Earth's depths undertaken by a monomaniacal scientist, his nephew Axel, and their staunchly faithful assistant, Hans.

Verne's Professor Liedenbrock, or "Hardwigg" as he appeared in the first English translation, in 1872, resembled no serious-minded student of mineralogy, being a ridiculously vainglorious academic single-mindedly obsessed with achievement. His perceptions of the subterranean world, together with those of his nephew and Man Friday, Axel, offer slapdash porridges of mineralogical and paleontological nomenclature, given some incipient coherence by a few nods to the Geologic Ages but with hardly a whisper from stratigraphic sense. Hard-headed Liedenbrock fails in his obsessive aim to reach Earth's center; yet he succeeds admirably in displaying the foibles of the limited-vision scientist whose grasp of his own society is as shaky as his apprehension of physical danger. Insanely inventive and maddeningly mistaken about countless matters involving the world and its processes, he appears exactly as Verne intended him: for the Earth through which Liedenbrock descends is sand being tossed into the face of heretical theory.

When the trio penetrate the Earth's crust, they find an inner cavern where giant, ancient mammals still roam the shore; and they go sailing upon an inner sea whose waves break to reveal ferocious prehistoric reptiles. Verne, whose Catholic tendencies went on display in his early "Master Zacharius," in this novel leaves Darwin unmentioned, closely though he followed contemporary scientific developments, while mentioning catastrophism's outspoken defender, Cuvier. Leaving out Darwin and natural selection hardly meant Verne lacked means to attack Darwinian ideas. Yet he more effectively presented a roadblock to the theory by dramatically depicting a situation that the church would have liked to be true. His novel shows a world in which forms are permanent.

In designing his novel, Verne adopted the geological rule of thumb that the descending layers of the earth reflect an increasing depth of time—not always a valid assumption, as Hutton had made clear. In the Paris basin, however, steady deposition over a long sequence did, indeed, give the impression that a one-to-one relation existed between depth and age. Although in *Voyage* the layers turn out to be a hodgepodge of geological whatnots, probably reflecting the still-youthful nature of stratigraphy as much as Verne's incomplete understanding, those layered whatnots offer decorative signs to the reader of the transition being effected. In the novel, the geological rule of thumb takes a transitionary journey into symbolism, with the physical descent by the adventurers representing a descent into past time.

That the "prehistoric" creatures encountered by the adventurers comprise relict populations becomes evident, since they so neatly and immediately fit within the professor's powers to identify and classify. Verne ties these populations symbolically to the Noachic Flood, since they exist around and within the great, rolling sea found in this inner region. Providence has held extinction in abeyance; primordial creation remains intact and on display, if isolated much as were the Owen-Hawkins creatures on their island in the Sydenham lagoon. Verne gives his creatures actions, moreover, that bring to life the set-in-concrete contortions displayed by the Sydenham monsters. Even the underground sea itself fit within the providential worldview. Earth contained bodies of subterraneans waters that had been released for the Noachic deluge, according to geologists, including America's Benjamin Silliman, who had sought to align biblical and geological history.[28]

The travelers reach a core of belief concerning the catastrophic history of Earth and its life. However weighty, controversial, and influential Darwin's book was, Verne's symbolic narrative undoubtedly found sympathetic readers in greater numbers, initially and perhaps over the long run, as well.

Axel's Panorama

Readers in England and America encountering *Journey to the Centre of the Earth*, in 1872, must have felt deeply impressed by a visionary reverie to which Liedenbrock's nephew falls subject. After conjuring within his mind such prehistoric creatures as the Mastodon, the Megatherium, and the Pterodactyl, Axel goes further into an "extraordinary dream" that owes a considerable debt to the elder Herschel:

> I thought, such was the effect of my imagination, that I saw this whole tribe of antediluvian creatures. I carried myself back to far ages, long before man existed—when, in fact, the earth was in too imperfect a state for him to live upon it.
>
> My dream was of countless ages before the existence of man. The mammifers first disappeared, then the mighty birds, then the reptiles of the secondary period, presently the fish, the crustacea, the molluscs, and finally the vertebrata. The zoophytes of the period of transition in their turn sank into annihilation.
>
> The whole panorama of the world's life before the historic period, seemed to be born over again, and mine was the only human heart that beat in this unpeopled world! There were no more seasons; there were no more climates; the natural heat of the world increased unceasingly, and neutralised that of the great radiant Sun.
>
> Vegetation was exaggerated in an extraordinary manner. I passed like a shadow in the midst of brushwood as lofty as the giant trees of California, and trod underfoot the moist and humid soil, reeking with a rank and varied vegetation.
>
> I leaned against the huge column-like trunks of giant trees, to which those of Canada were as ferns. Whole ages passed, hundreds upon hundreds of years were concentrated into a single day.

FIVE—Deep Time and the Thinning Veil

Next, unrolled before me like a panorama, came the great and wondrous series of terrestrial transformations. Plants disappeared; the granitic rocks lost all trace of solidity; the liquid state was suddenly substituted for that which had before existed. This was caused by intense heat acting on the organic matter of the earth. The waters flowed over the whole surface of the globe; they boiled; they were volatilised, or turned into vapour; a kind of steam-cloud wrapped the whole earth, the globe itself becoming at last nothing but one huge sphere of gas, indescribable in colour, between white heat and red, as big and as brilliant as the sun.

In the very center of this prodigious mass, fourteen hundred thousand times as large as our globe, I was whirled round in space, and brought into close conjunction with the planets. My body was subtilised, or rather became volatile, and commingled in a state of atomic vapour, with the prodigious clouds, which rushed forward like a mighty comet into infinite space![29]

The phrase "panorama of the world's life" had a particular meaning, in the 1870s. Our words "panorama" and "phantasmagoria" began as names for optical entertainments in the later Romantic years, whose popularity continued to some degree into the Modern.

Panoramas involved enormous pictures painted upon the interiors of cylinders measuring from sixty to over a hundred feet in diameter. A viewer at center experienced an illusion of reality, being completely surrounded by a cohesive scene. Edinburgh artist Robert Barker introduced the form in 1788, with one showing his city as though viewed from a rooftop. He followed this with a second that offered a view of London, with glimpses of Napoleonic War sea battles, thus introducing an almost necessary ingredient to this public spectacle: the gaze into the past. The panorama crossed the Channel, with Robert Fulton introducing it to France in 1796.[30]

The word's use in Axel's vision showed how Barker's name of panorama, for a painting presenting a 360-degree imitation of reality, changed as it moved into daily speech as a word. Here a fictional character looks upon an optical wonder that seems reality itself. The objects in Axel's panorama, however, derived from scientific investigation, reasoning, and

Optical entertainments abounded before the coming of cinema. The panorama was one that traveled city to city. While historical subjects may have won the most favor, those with natural attractions drew crowds as well. Advertising card, roughly 3 inches by 4 inches (author's collection).

imagination. The imitation of reality perceived by Axel, in other words, is an imitation of an interpretation of reality. In Axel's vision, moreover, the panorama moves beyond the static impression captured by Barker. Seemingly real objects suffer dissolution in a backwards plunge through time. This second metaphoric descent into Earth's past transfigures Axel. He emerges as an ethereal mind occupying nebular space, akin to Poe's ethereal creatures—Monos and Una, and Eiros and Charmion—who achieve their transcendent states as disembodied intelligences during the future destruction of Earth.

As a word, "panorama" made the transition into the realm of the children's toy at the same time it was acquiring its new, somewhat poetic force in conjuring imaginary scenes. Makers of magic lanterns introduced "panorama slides," which were fourteen inches long in one case, meant for drawing slowly through the projector, to simulate the experience of panning one's vision across a landscape. Some sets featured double slides to be projected simultaneously, so that certain elements, such as ships in a harbor, might move independently within the shifting landscape.[31]

In America, in 1868, to his optical diversions Milton Bradley added the Historoscope—Panorama and History of America from Columbus to the Civil War, with its images designed to be viewed within a box, akin to a toy theater.[32] As the name indicates, Bradley's panorama pictured not a single moment's "reality" but rather a sequence of events that offered, again, an illusion of linearity. In one sense Bradley offered real linearity: for he printed the historical pictures on a long strip of paper, wound around hidden spools. As the child cranked the rollers, images came into view, in forward-through-time movement. The scenes rolled backward, as well, so that the child might enjoy reversed sequences much as did Axel.

If toymakers in Europe had not already participated in the process of term-modification, they would do so later—at least in France, where toy theaters with *nombreuses vues* would come to be called "panoramas."[33]

Bradley followed the Historoscope with a smaller version, again a miniature theater, called the Myriopticon, showing historical images of the Civil War.[34] Both toys benefited from an undercurrent of interest in automata: for these were, in essence, toy history-clocks made of board and paper, placed under the child's control.

Phantasmagoria and Diorama

"Phantasmagoria" underwent a similar change in meaning. Coined in 1802, it referred to a magic-lantern exhibition with the projector being behind the screen, in shadowgraph or "Chinese shades" manner. Projectionist M. Phillipthal perfected projection techniques that allowed him to make images rapidly grow or shrink in size, and to have them seem to transform, one into another. This he accomplished by having different shapes fade into and away from focus, and by moving the glass "sliders" when the change would go unnoticed by the audience, thereby presenting dissolving views in a continuous series.[35]

The new word easily lent itself to any circumstance involving changing views. The fantastic characters being projected onto screens by Phillipthal and others also influenced its developing meanings, so that it came to suggest any strange or uncanny vision. In his 1839 "The Fall of the House of Usher," Poe used "phantasmagoric" once in reference to a physical object, and a second time to a painting by Roderick Usher—with the word's appearance helping deepen the story's appearance as, itself, an optical extravaganza.[36] James Thomson

(B.V.), writing in 1867, evoked a similar effect:

> The earth's time passed over me unperceived, unregarded; but the true time, which is change, wrought within me. The natural world refused to be wholly shut out; and its countless objects, besieging persistently the gateways of the senses, began gradually to penetrate into my soul. But still I perceived them merely as phantasmagoria, fleeting bubbles and cloud-shadows on the hurrying river of time.[37]

The word's use to refer to "any rapidly or strikingly changing scene, and especially to a disordered or fantastic scene or picture of the imagination"[38] easily outlasted its use as a name for an optical entertainment. Karl Marx assisted in this change, using it in a derogatory sense to mean "what goes on in people's minds about the basic material reality," with some equivalence to "ideology."[39] Although the name fell away and the term persisted, the entertainment itself lasted into the middle Modern years. "But as if a magic lantern threw the nerves in patterns on a screen," in Eliot's 1917 "The Love Song of J. Alfred Prufrock," suggests the experience of a Phantasmagoria or Chromatrope show.

Similarly, the name for another optical diversion would undergo changes of meaning. C.M. Bouton and Louis

Magic lantern. Magic lanterns, ancient in their lineage, became household diversions before the Modern century's middle years, thanks in part to post–Bismarck Germany's efforts to outsell Britain in factory-produced goods. German "dollar lanterns," of simple and flimsy make, sufficed for family entertainment. The magic lantern fell from favor once outshone by electrical diversions bearing the prosaic name of "projector" (photograph by and collection of the author).

Jacques Daguerre, himself a panoramist, opened their first Diorama in 1822, in Paris, and later a second in London. As "panorama" referred to "all-seeing," this new term referred to "through-seeing," or "double seeing." Visitors viewed through apertures an enclosed scene. Parts that were painted on glass helped simulate depth in the visual field. Images on the side walls merged with those on the rear wall, adding to the sense of three-dimensional reality. Bouton and Daguerre controlled light through the ceiling, to imitate light-changes experienced in nature. The diorama, in other words, necessarily mimicked time's passage but at an accelerated pace.

These larger-scale diversions gave rise to portable versions—such as the one in a tale by Hawthorne, carried around by a man from Nuremburg. The German toy-town apparently made these using lenticular viewing apertures.[40]

In both fixed and portable forms, the exhibitor's control over light offered the diversionary technique that Northrop Frye, in discussing poetry and fiction, would call the foreshortening of time—the altering of time's passage to hold the audience's attention.

Verneian Diversions

As does Poe's "House of Usher," Verne's 1864 novel as a whole offers a literary optical extravaganza. The reader gazes into Earth's enclosed spaces. Scenes emerge from utter darkness. Lanterns reveal sharpening and fading visions. Axel's vision swirls toward the primordial.

When the novel appeared in English in 1872, scientific developments gave the downward search for ancient life a feeling of the immediate. In December that year a British expedition set out from Portsmouth on the steamship H.M.S. *Challenger*. In its quest to expand knowledge of the oceans, it planned to bring specimens to the surface from previously untouched regions. Scientists entertained the particular hope that in dredging the sea floor the *Challenger* might bring up a creature considered extinct—not a reptilian one, in this case, but an arthropod that thrived in and sometimes dominated the benthic realm prior to the Mesozoic: the Trilobite.[41]

The link between travel and revelations of antiquity would remain strong. Travel in a forward direction often seemed travel backwards. In early globe-spanning nautical journeys, Westerners encountered societies they regarded as primitive, and discovered creatures inhabiting jungle, river, and sea that seemed revenants from antediluvian times: the crocodile, the lungfish, and the pearly nautilus.

Explorer James Cook returned from Tahiti with a native named Omai, who despite being "primitive" adapted himself intelligently to late-1700s England. Omai's example, together with accounts brought back to England by Cook, Joseph Banks, and other travelers, gave deeper meaning to the idea that the "primitive" human lives in "a state of nature ... a creature of almost pure sensation."[42] His being taken aboard Cook's vessel of science had a symbolic ring to it, as did Omai's subsequent adoption of English modes of thought: for he enacted the process identified by chemist Humphry Davy, of science waking the mind from its primitive mental slumber. Omai's story involved his mental movement quickly forward through conceptual time, as well as his physical travel around the geographical clock. A London pantomime in 1785 captured in its title this combination of primitivism and Earth's shrinkage by technology: "Omai, or a Trip Round the World."[43]

However excellently well treated, Omai served as Cook's toy; and, as the pantomime indicated, he became a bit of fancy goods for English society. "Tahitan" topless grass-skirt entertainments in bawdy burlesques arrived as an early next step, reducing a distant culture in status to an adult toy.

Prehistoric Family Robinson

Although it bore no outward trappings to indicate the fact, *Voyage* reflected Verne's long-abiding admiration for *Swiss Family Robinson*. Wyss's clergyman-hero, with his wife and their four sons, survive being castaways thanks in large part to the clergyman's knowledge concerning new zoological and botanical findings from around the globe, and his similar acquaintance with technical matters, some of which relate to manufacturing. The clergyman acknowledges providence, which at times appears as the Aesopian providence of the put-your-shoulder-to-wagon-wheel variety, but more often as authorial providence—so that Wyss's clergyman, much like Verne's Earth-penetrating professor, encounters only botanical and zoological specimens already familiar to him from his studies. These discoveries all, by providence, prove useful to the family in their efforts to survive.

These have the pasted-together quality echoed in the geological hodgepodge that Verne describes with such enthusiasm, in his 1864 novel. The pell-mell appearances by biological wonders gives zest and a sense of invention to Wyss's story, which retained its popularity and its readability through the Modern years, as a tale true not realistically but symbolically. Verne's seemingly more esoteric story actually contained, for his time, an equivalent mix of wonderful "facts" and authorial providence; and it, too, retained its popularity well after its underlying ideas had proven dead ends for natural science.

America's Crystal Palace

The Great Exhibition's cultural, scientific, and industrial displays had influence immediately across the Atlantic. Not only did news about it appear in newspapers, but an American version arose in New York City, opened by President Franklin Pierce on July 12, 1853.[44] Imitating the Great on a smaller scale, the New York Crystal Palace had an area of 173,000 square feet. The iron-and-glass building inspired a young Samuel Clemens to enthuse that it offered "a perfect fairy palace—beautiful beyond description."[45]

Sydenham's concrete menagerie likewise inspired Central Park's commissioners, who in 1868 asked Hawkins to recreate the "animated races" of antiquity once again, with focus turned upon New World prehistory. Hawkins arrived in America soon afterwards and by 1870 had made significant progress on his models.[46]

At the time, thanks to Charles Willson Peale's influence, Philadelphia held a central place in American paleontological efforts. By the 1860s, alongside Peale's mastodons, the first New World dinosaur had found its home in that city. Having been discovered in Haddonfield, New Jersey, by Joseph Leidy, and excavated in the year before Darwin's *Origin* saw publication, *Hadrosaurus* shared with *Iguanodon* and other European "monsters" in having an aura around it not quite scientific in nature. Calling these creatures "pre–Adamite" more accurately expressed the American public's general attitude than did calling them prehistoric.

By 1865, when he published his *Cretaceous Reptiles of the United States*, Leidy had been chairing the Board of Curators at the Philadelphia Academy of Natural Sciences for some eighteen years. He had grown up in that city breathing deeply of the local legacy, heavy with Peale's influence; and in 1847 he had launched his own paleontological expeditions into western America. Another paleontologist associated with the Academy, Edward Drinker Cope, had been named a curator in 1865.[47] He would begin contributing to American paleontology in the year Hawkins was invited to New York, and would make his name not only with dinosaur discoveries but also a neo-Lamarckian evolutionary theory.

From these Academy naturalists, Hawkins received the guidance and direction in America he had received in England from Owen. The Central Park prehistoric display was to feature not only herbivorous *Hadrosaurus* but another American dinosaur, *Laelaps*, considered to have been an energetically leaping carnivore. In Hawkins's reconstruction, one *Laelaps* would be attacking a *Hadrosaurus*, while nearby two other *Laelaps* would be feasting on fresh kill. Hawkins would fill out the display with ancient mammals: giant armadillos, mastodons, giant sloths, and a giant elk.[48] These choices undoubtedly reflected

Leidy's influence, who in 1869 published his *Extinct Mammalian Fauna of Dakota and Nebraska*.

The Darwinian revolution in scientific thought began, however, in the time between the first *Hadrosaurus* excavation and Hawkins's work on his New York reconstructions. That a backlash against the revolution was being felt may have been reflected in the sudden involvement of William "Boss" Tweed and his political henchmen in 1870, after the foundation for the prehistoric display had been laid near West Sixty-Third street in Central Park. Tweed, at the height of his power, forced the Central Park Commission to close the project. When Hawkins continued his work, Tweed's agents willfully demolished and buried the models already completed.[49]

Cast in Iron

The Tammany Hall gang's actions likely slowed the American public's growth in interest in creatures from past eras. The Hawkins models would have appeared in endless publications, and might have inspired an American Verne to write a *Voyage*. At the time of the Tweed ring's destruction, however, a small share of retribution took shape in the toy world, in the form of an automatic coin bank.

Some among the most distinctive toys of the later 1800s issued from the J. & E. Stevens Company of Cromwell, Connecticut, a manufacturer of iron toys as well as household hardware and tools. Among its earliest and most popular cast-iron toys, the Tammany Bank shows a well-fed gentleman in a chair who pockets any coin placed in his hand while bowing politely to the donor. Stevens kept the bank in production for nearly half a century.[50]

Had the Central Park prehistoric exhibit come about without interference, Hawkins's models would have inspired toys, particularly from the cast-iron companies now clustering as thickly in Pennsylvania as they had previously in the New England states. Makers of both mechanical banks and of bell-toys favored designs leaning toward the fanciful or extravagant. Hawkins' ancient mammals and reptiles might well have suited their needs and helped bring these emblems of time's depths into the playroom sooner than did occur.

Thanks to Tweed's vandalism, American science and popular culture both lost an opportunity. The fairings, paper toys, toy books, educational games, and Vernesque wonder tales of discovery would arrive in America all the same, but only after a delay of decades.

Minikins and Giants

Just as the diorama presented scenery in forced perspective, to allow the viewer "to see into the distance" by looking into a box, many toys stimulated thoughts about scale, perspective, distance, and relative sizes.

As the casting in molds of such materials as rubber, lead alloy, and iron became common in industry, inexpensive toys came to evoke "reality" in a different way than they had previously. Toys animals and human figures carved from wood, especially those produced in large numbers, offered their subjects in simplified and idealized versions, in contrast to the quite realistic wooden-toy versions of such items as brooms, chairs, tables, hammers, and wheelbarrows. Tin toys similarly offered simplified and idealized versions of animals and people, with painted and, later, lithographed details—even though, again, domestic and workplace toys such as dustpans, dishes, coal scuttles, rakes, and carts closely evoked domestic reality.

Molded toys being sold by the 1850s and 1860s, however, included increasing numbers of quite small but relatively realistic figures. These included the cast-metal toy soldiers featured in London's Crystal Palace in the exhibit mounted by Berlin's manufacturers.

Passages in "Hans Pfaall" suggested that Poe's imagination had been stirred by the relative proportions of adults and toys, as when Hans Pfaall is "rapidly ascending" in his balloon: "Immediately beneath me in the ocean, lay a small black object, slightly oblong in shape, seemingly about the size of a domino, and in every respect bearing a great resemblance to one of those toys. Bringing my telescope to bear upon it, I plainly discerned it to be a British ninety-four gun ship, close-hauled, and pitching heavily in the sea with her head to the W.S.W."[51] In a similar way, Verne would convey the sense of flying in a massive but high-speed aeronef. A character "points out a sort of Nuremburg toy planted on a hill top. This toy with its polychrome architecture resembled the Houses of Parliament in London…"[52] Crossing the Nebraskan Badlands, the aerial travelers take in a view of "a chaos of ochre-coloured hills, of mountainous fragments fallen on the soil and broken in their fall," looking like an "enormous game of knucklebones."[53]

Due to their scale, toys meant to be realistic came in for a natural amount of imaginative play based on early wonder tales, in which diminutive or gigantic people did appear. As noted, the entertainment called the phantasmagoria used shapes that grew or shrank in size to enchant viewers. The Crystal

If Mars is inhabited, its people can comfortably support bodies fourteen feet tall

"As a Martian might appear." Voltaire's linking a being's size to the size of its home planet, in his story "Micromegas," found a reversal in Modern imaginings relating it inversely to the home planet's gravitational force. Either rationale gave rise to oppositions of minikins and giants—as in a conversation in a 1954 Tom Swift, Jr., novel: "'Isn't Mars in that direction?' he asked, pointing. 'Bet you a bunch of scientific gnomes are sitting up there on the other planet laughing their heads off at us.' 'You could be right,' Tom agreed. 'But some professors think Martians are giants'" (illustration by John Dukes McKee in Elena Fontany's *Other Worlds Than This*, first published in 1930; quotation from Victor Appleton II, *Tom Swift and His Flying Lab*, 1954).

Palace itself played with scale, being a gardener's conservatory so proportioned that it rose up and around a large tree preexisting in the park—making it appropriate that the Great Exhibition awarded a medal to "Count Dunin's expanding figure of a man, which changed by turning a handle from life-size into gigantic proportions."[54]

The year that Verne's subterranean giants found a place on English shelves happened to witness an American-made toy for the first time enjoying international distribution. Reflecting this fascination with relative physical scale, the toy appeared thanks to an 1840s development in children's blocks: the "picture block." More elaborate decorations appeared upon their faces than previously: for traditional blocks had featured designs printed directly onto the wood. The new blocks featured lithographed images glued to their faces, prompting toymakers quickly to use sectional images in their block sets, after the fashion of dissected maps and pictures.[55]

Blocks in the 1800s held an important place among toys. Charles M. Crandall, in Montrose, Pennsylvania, in essence established toy-manufacturing as an important sector in the American economy by producing wooden construction block-sets. Though made from unembellished wood, they proved striking enough to win a place in P.T. Barnum's museum in New York City—and in Henry Morton Stanley's luggage on his voyage into the Congo. Stanley thought they would make good gifts for natives.[56] In 1872, Crandall offered the toy that won favor overseas: new alphabet blocks named Expression Blocks, made from wooden squares rather than cubes, with alphabet letters on one side. On the other side, children found a dissected image. Assembled, the blocks showed a face looking startled at having miniature people bracing ladders against and crawling over him, evoking the popular episode among the Lilliputians in *Gulliver's Travels*.[57]

By this time, Gulliver had proven himself an enduringly attractive figure. Swift's satire, first published in 1726, came to be seen as suitable youthful fare by at least 1787, when *The Adventures of Captain Gulliver, in a Voyage to the Islands of Lilliput and Brobdingnag*, a version abridged for children, appeared in Philadelphia.[58] In abridged form the story's fantastic elements outweighed its satirical ones, especially among the young who might have missed the satire in any case; and it led to the public's easily adopting Swift's terms. With children knowing what it meant to be Lilliputian, toy sellers used the name for any small, charming figures—as in the advertisement in *The Independent Gazette* of Philadelphia, in the 1780s, touting the toy offerings at John Mason's Upholsterer Store: "drest dolls, naked ditto—Lilliputian dolls."[59] At least one store selling toys and fancy-goods would rely on Swift's popularity to attract crowds to its display window, which featured a mannikin of Lemuel Gulliver tied down by the Lilliputian horde, with some crawling across his face and body.[60]

Gulliver among the Lilliputians offered an imaginary scenario for children that seemed empowering, in that it reversed the fairy-tale situation in which brutal giants threaten little Jack. Yet the image of Gulliver overrun by toylike figures—as in the Crandall set of blocks and in the store window—showed the irony of the situation: for people loved seeing the normal-sized "giant" overpowered by minikins. Gulliver stood in for the adult overcome by the minutiae of life, far smaller even than children.

The delightfully odd or frightfully strange seemed the paired options that would continue to be expressed in terms of minikins and giants. Travel into space would represent society's sense of its own flight into futurity, and also into dwarfing immensity; while fictional or playtime encounters with minikins and even microscopic beings would represent the growing sense that humankind was gaining mastery over the "pitiful globe called the earth."[61]

Equivalent encounters with giants, on the other hand, would sometimes serve in representing an inability to grasp, or to deal with, the new culture being created by industrial mastery over the world. While fairytale encounters with giants provided a literary touchstone for the situation, paleontology's perspective was gaining in influence.

Edward Roth, who "translated" Verne in America, offered Verne's stories with colloquialisms and original elements. In a passage in which Verne makes reference to Gulliver's encounters with giants, Roth wrote, "The old myth of the Giants realized! Perhaps the Titans that played such famous parts in the prehistoric period of our Earth, were adventurers like ourselves, casually arrived from some great planet!"[62]

The second sentence, Roth's own 1874 invention, expresses the fascination with prehistoric gigantism that must have appeared in uncountable and fleeting forms in the 1870s and afterwards. Here it found some permanence by being attributed to the famous French writer. The association between the "old myth of the Giants" and the "Titans that played such famous parts in the prehistoric period" came from a writer who was appropriately placed, geographically, given his association with Broad Street Academy in Philadelphia, the city that was a center for paleontological studies and displays.[63]

Despite the intervention of Tammany Hall in the erecting of concrete emblems in Central Park, the notions and thoughts represented by and associated with *dinosauria* were finding rich soil in the country that was becoming a technological and industrial juggernaut, in the late nineteenth century.

Six

Early Automata in America

The most daring idea that a mechanician has ever ventured to conceive was that of a machine which would imitate, in some way more than the face and movement, the master work of Creation. Von Kempelen has not only had the idea, but he has carried it out and his chess-player is, indisputably, the most astonishing automaton that has ever existed.
—Chrètien de Mechel, in 1783.[1]

Every urchin has had the little gilt toy-watch that is always at half past seven o'clock.
—*The New York Ledger,* on January 2, 1864.[2]

It formed a curious picture, the small fire burning in the valley, motionless forms stretched out before it, the huge steam man silent and grim standing near, the dwarfed boy, pacing slowly back and forth, and, above all, the moon shining down upon the silent prairie.
—Edward S. Ellis, in 1868.[3]

Maelzel's Chess-Player

The clock reflected the visible universe's motions, and thus celestial order. In toys, clock workings led to new developments in mechanical figures, which long had existed as marionettes and other jointed dolls. Automatic animation became the *anima* or soul of their charm. State-of-art achievements by European clockmakers in the 1700s reached America by report before they arrived as theatrical curiosities, items for production, or objects for Poe to demystify in an artistic manner.

In his essay "Maelzel's Chess-Player," Poe mentions the figural automata that Sir David Brewster described in his 1831 *Letters on Natural Magic.* These included a horse-drawn carriage, made by French conjuror Comus; The Magician, by Maillardet; and The Duck, by Jacques de Vaucanson. He also mentions the calculating machine of Charles Babbage as impressive, but ranking second to the "pure machine" that was the true automaton—which Maelzel's Chess-Player ostensibly was, as a humanlike mechanism that played chess against human opponents. Although many automata had won attention through the eighteenth century, Baron von Kempelen's Chess-Player overshadowed them as a public attraction in the 1770s and later decades.[4] The device left for America in the care of Leonard Maelzel, "mechanician" to the Austrian court. His skill making trumpet-playing automata gave cachet to these late appearances by von Kempelen's masterpiece.

After attending a performance, Poe noted, "It is quite certain that the operations of the Automaton are regulated by mind, and by nothing else."[5] From that starting point, in his "Maelzel's Chess-Player," Poe analyzes the workings of "the Automaton." While not the first to see its deceptive character, he offered readers a narrative that symbolically links the machine, the hoax, and the human soul enclosed by technics. In appearance a clockwork mechanism, Chess-Player lacked actual workings within itself, with its base being a control box. Within it only a dwarf or child might fit. The dwarf who did inhabit the mechanism enjoyed freedom on the chessboard, being able to choose game movements. In every other way he fell subject to the machinery's requirements. If the machine needed to perform actions, the dwarf had to make the machine do so. If the machine's "workings" were to be shown, the dwarf needed to hide himself behind cleverly arranged partitions and mirrors, much as a puppeteer traditionally hid behind a curtain. Since the mechanism operated by deceit, maintaining its operation required maintaining the deceit.

Except within the game itself, in other words, the machine deprived the dwarf of independent action. Although his was the mind that "regulated," the machine's performances regulated him, making him slave rather than master. The "automaton" entombed a human who was buried alive—a fate faced by other unfortunate souls in Poe stories.

Poe's examination held added symbolism due to the Hobbesian association, in philosophy, between the "artificial man" and society itself. Brewster, in 1831, underlined this connection in describing technological ruses used by rulers to control the ignorant. Tyrants who were unwilling to gain their subjects' allegiance by appealing to their better natures instead ruled by creating a "dark conspiracy" of "the prince, the priest, and the sage," which ensured submission. A national system of deception, as an instrument for governance, called for contrivances in a variety calculated to astonish beholders, confound their judgments, dazzle their senses, and give dominating influence to the peculiar imposture that the tyrant thought necessary to maintain.[6]

Poe's ratiocinative analysis follows wonder-tale structure to a degree, its subject being sensational and its narrative movement being that of mystification yielding to explication. Chess-Player, a marvelous machine, appears before a doubting world, threatens convention by performing its wonders, and challenges rational understanding concerning limits to mechanical achievement. Thanks to the narrator, rational analysis then destroys the machine.

With the illusion's collapse, moreover, the one "dwarfed" within the machine finds symbolic freedom from confinement and subjugation. The narrator pulls away the deception—the mask that has dehumanized its wearer, who now can resume being simply human.

A work of ratiocinative imagination, "Maelzel's Chess-Player" as an essay embodies the question Poe posed the year before—"How long shall mind succumb to the grossest materiality?"[7]—with the answer that demystification, the analytical process that ends with the destruction of the marvelous machine, may end the mind's debasement and servitude.

After Poe's death, the Chess-Player itself suffered actual destruction in an 1854 Philadelphia fire. Another pseudo-automaton of its sort reappeared soon thereafter. Under the name Ajeeb it became an attraction at the Sydenham Crystal Palace.[8] That mechanism, or another like it, would still be performing in the late 1800s at Eden Musée in New York.[9]

Thirteen O'Clock

Three years after "Maelzel's Chess-Player," Poe further analyzed the automaton in his 1839 story "The Devil in the Belfry: an Extravaganza," a fanciful concoction that presents "the Dutch borough of Vondervotteimitiss."[10] The borough appears to be a great clock face nestled face-upwards in a circular valley, with inhabitants whose existences center around their timepieces. The "good woman of the house" tends the pot of sauerkraut and pork, with a "little heavy Dutch watch" in her hand. Beside her, a tabby cat has a toy watch on its tail, tied there by the three boys in the garden, each of whom "has a pipe in his mouth, and a dumpy little watch in his right hand. He takes a puff and a look, and then a look and a puff." They are watching the pig, to whose tail the boys have also tied a toy watch. The "old man of the house" has a watch, as well, that he leaves in his pocket while fixing his eyes upon the central point of the town, where a tower rises—seven-sided, with a clock on each face, so that all who are in Vondervotteimitiss can keep it in sight.[11]

Into this well-regulated world arrives a mischievous figure who climbs into the belfry, attacks its peaceful old attendant, and causes the noon bell to strike thirteen—destroying the perfect balance of Vondervotteimitiss. Being mischief and irrationality, with a will for disorder, this unnamed imp leaves the borough in disarray. Even individual watches lose their regularity.[12]

In other Poe tales the imp plays an unexpected role. In a seemingly villainous way, the imp works contrary to the narrator's wishes: for the narrator represents the human soul in imbalance. In "The Imp of the Perverse," published in 1845, it stands in for the conscience of society, acting against the "self" when that self is estranged from its own humanity. It represents the inner soul's inability to act against human order, when that order is a reasoned, ethical one. This inner imp reappears in "The Tell-Tale Heart." In the earlier "Devil in the Belfry," externalized as an unkempt character, the imp makes a literally untimely appearance in the exquisitely controlled, perfectly nonsensical Vondervotteimitiss, and by his mischief restores human dimension to its inhabitants. Not themselves automata, the burghers, *hausfraus*, and children have become subsumed within the automaton, being regulated by movements that render unnecessary any other order, including any order based upon reasoned ethics. When the imp enters the circular valley, he exerts himself willfully and capriciously upon the lone soul whose job it is to regulate the central tower's clocks.

Echoing Rousseau, Poe portrays the technologically assisted person as of diminished stature, worthy of amused pity, and fit for satire: for the clock effectively has stripped its subjects of their human character, leaving only their pride in keeping an up-to-the-moment appearance. The "truly human world" then intrudes. Even if motivated by chaotic impulses, the imp represents the human soul in a more natural state.

Poe's "perverse" figure, in other words, stands apart from the selfish or thoughtless mischievous imps that appear in *Pinocchio* or Louisa May Alcott's fairytale "Lily-Bell and Thistledown," who were imps whose misadventures lead them, with some reluctance, to finally acquire conscience. Poe did use the phrase "imp of mischief" for such characters, as well.[13]

In an 1849 story, Poe again thematically linked the imp to the diminutive soul confined within an encompassing machine. In "Hop-Frog: or, the Eight Chained Ourang-Outangs," Hop-Frog, a dwarf, serves as court jester to a "continental power." Besides being himself a source of merriment, he suggests amusing ideas to the King and his seven ministers. In executing his latest absurd entertainment, Hop-Frog escapes from the automaton, which reveals itself to be the original automaton: that of the celestial sphere. For Hop-Frog's shenanigans result in the unpleasant King and his ministers being chained, brought into a circle, lifted into the air, and set afire, in retribution for their inhumanity. Being the Sun and the seven then-known planets, they end in a fiery conflagration—for they are, themselves, the marvelous celestial machine. They represent, again, the clock-regulator and his seven-sided tower, which must topple before the crippled dwarf *animus* and his partner *anima* can escape to freedom.

American Automata in the 1860s

Not all French automata had the life-mimicking appearance possessed by those mentioned in Poe's "Chess-Player." Parisian toymakers and clockmakers also produced simpler, more obviously mechanical entertainments. Yet these mechanicians, keeping in mind the standards set by Vaucanson and others, did aspire to create such evocative life-imitations, or false realities, that viewers might sense "something unearthly about it all," as Ambrose Bierce would put it. In contrast, American automata rarely took such elaborate forms. Toymakers acted as though high aesthetic standards had no pertinence to their trade. Their automata tended to be more hastily built, less carefully outfitted, and simpler in their motions. They conformed to limits set by mass-production factories, moreover—so that they could be placed in middle-class hands, and not be reserved for store-window display.

Although Paris had become the center for making automata by the middle 1800s, Great Britain, Germany, and the United States had their own manufacturers, as well. One toy that did actually bear the name The Automaton—also Der Automate and L'Automata—saw issue in the middle 1800s in Germany. This lithographed and hand-colored male figure appeared

Mechanical toys. Illustration by Alice B. Woodward, 1897 (from Edith M. King-Hall, *Adventures in Toyland*, ca. 1910).

to be standing on a platform. When a child rolled the platform forward, the figure "walked." In essence a mechanical paper doll, the toy came with outfits to vary his appearance.[14]

American toy-making reached a milestone in 1862 when Enoch Rice Morrison patented a doll named Autoperipatetikos. The name, meaning that it was "self-walking-about," would have seemed a reasonable one to at least some. Classical education still prevailed, and the attention given in preparatory schools to Greek philosophy made "peripatetic" a word familiar to many. The small doll, as manufactured by New York City's Joseph Lyon & Company in the 1860s, had a cardboard body that hid its clockwork mechanism.[15]

Lyon apparently made various versions. Porcelain-head ones must have pleased the more well-to-do, while papier-mâché-head dolls came with more popular prices. Skirts concealed wheeled, brass feet that were oversized, of necessity: for the doll had novelty not because she walked, which was becoming a common action in mechanical toys, but because she walked without the supporting balance that might be provided by having a carriage in front or a cart behind.[16]

Morrison and Lyon being not alone in their pursuits, other New York inventors obtained patents involving automated dolls. In 1868, G.H. Hawkins, at 383 Canal Street, began making clockwork dolls based on a patent by William F. Goodwin. A contemporary account called them "some of the most ingenious and interesting mechanical toys that have been invented ... constructed so that they literally walk, taking up the feet by bending the knees in a most life-like manner."[17] They did depend on carriages, however, for stability.

Although these and other mechanical dolls had much simpler operations than store-window French automata, they continued to be recognized as sister productions in their names, which included Automatic Toy and Toy Automaton.[18]

Particularly interesting as symbolic toys, the toy watches that had been common in Poe's time seemed even more widespread in the 1860s. In Rhode Island, two Providence businesses manufactured them: The New England Toy Company and the American Toy Watch Company. Earlier and later, other firms entered this fanciful business. Being automata in appearance only, their popularity suggests that working watches had much more than mere function in their favor, for their owners. Their role in indicating a person's status exercised peculiar power; and children wearing the toy versions physically expressed the wish to reach the age when they might wear cheap watches to keep to schedules set by the owners of gold watches—and to become, as Jarvis Lorry has become in Dickens's 1859 *A Tale of Two Cities*, submerged in a system that lets them "have no time" for themselves.

Tin Men and Clockworks

American "tin men," as they were called, had their beginnings in an immigrant family that included tinsmith Edward Patterson. He arrived in Berlin, Connecticut, in the 1730s, from Ireland—to which he soon returned in order to bring back siblings Anna, Jennie, Noah, and William. Making housewares with imported tinplate, the Pattersons pursued sales and trade in the Connecticut River Valley region, and as far north as Canada. Quite likely they made miniatures of their main wares for children, a practice common among workers in metal and wood.[19]

Berlin and the neighboring New Britain, to the north-northeast, grew to be tinware manufacturing centers, so that in the early 1800s five sizable manufactories and many smaller ones thrived there.[20] Meanwhile another regional industry was developing:

clockmaking. In 1856 George W. Brown and Company combined the two. Brown, born in 1830, began at age fifteen his apprenticeship to a clockmaker in Forestville, located in Hartford County between Bristol and New Britain. Afterwards he established his firm there with Chauncy Goodrich as partner. Forestville offered a propitious site, near both New Britain's hardware manufacture and Bristol's clockmaking.[21]

Brown pursued clockmaking in combination with the tinware and tin-toy trade that had rooted itself just to the east, in New Britain and Berlin. Brown seems to have been first among American toymakers to employ clockwork mechanisms in his toys, which means that he made a trade of doing what others merely dabbled in or experimented with. He produced a variety of toys employing spring-driven mechanisms, such as tin children playing with hoop toys or riding velocipedes. The Automatic Waltzer depicted a couple who danced together. While he invented and patented, Brown remained open to outside ideas. Along with other companies, he seems to have produced the 1860s Automatic Toy of the girl pushing a baby carriage, with the Goodwin-patent legs that bent at the knees.[22]

New York City, meanwhile, was developing into America's Paris in ways that included a growing toy-making sector. In 1869, this cultural capitol drew Brown from Forestville, as well as Elisha Stevens from just southeast of New Britain in Cromwell, where he had been one of the first toymakers to cast in iron, with J. & E. Stevens & Company.[23] Brown and Stevens joined forces to make tin and cast-iron toys, while also distributing toys made by other manufacturers, from then until 1880.

In operation in the same period as the first Brown company and its successor, Stevens and Brown, Merriam Manufacturing Company, located in Durham, Connecticut, from 1856 to the 1900s, also produced tin toys.[24] Merriam's line seems to have been similar to Brown's, in having wind-up toys that included locomotives, walking dolls with carriages, and velocipede riders.[25] A later-starting company, Hull & Wright, later Hull & Stafford, began making tin toys in 1866 east of New Haven, in Clinton, and in the next quarter-century became one of the best-known companies making toy trains, toy animals, and mechanical toys.[26]

Ives

During those years another firm took root nearby. West of clockmaking Bristol, in Litchfield County's town of Plymouth, Edward Riley Ives began making baskets, adding toys by at least 1866—first whistles, then automata that drew their power from stoves, candles, lamps, or gas burners. Toy steam-engines, too, could power them.[27] These hot-air toys featured a figure or two, who operated within a tableau. Propeller blades, situated above, caught the rising air. Though the toys often depicted such figures as washer-women, curtseying couples, or acrobats, fancies appeared, such as animal musicians who sawed at violins and cellos.[28]

In 1869, Ives moved south with his operations to the coastal town where P.T. Barnum had served for a time as mayor, and where the Greatest Show on Earth would be spending its winters. Barnum himself would work with automata, displaying "comic automaton clowns" in the 1870s.[29] Bridgeport had become a center for heavy manufacturing, having easy access to New York City by rail or, via Long Island Sound, by steamboat. In 1872 Ives joined with his brother-in-law, undoubtedly a friend from his Plymouth days, Cornelius Blakeslee, in forming Ives, Blakeslee & Company; and in Bridgeport they seemed vital forces in a flourishing community of toy-inventors. Profiting from Ives's presence, since he offered the means for production, their number included N.S. Warner, who designed a spring-motor velocipede and a rowboat with spring-motor oarsman.³⁰ Joining these automatic-toy inventors, Ives himself obtained five patents in the 1870s.

As a manufacturer, Ives gained a reputation for his workmanship, in part due to a clockwork mechanism he designed, and which the New Haven Clock Company, founded in 1853, manufactured.³¹ In appearances he maintained a high standard, as well. His automated figures included some that were dressed richly enough to rival Parisian productions.³²

Clockwork rowboat. The Spanish toy company Paya, founded in 1902, reissued this wind-up toy using original tooling from the toy made early in the 20th century. Paya's rowboats resembled ones being made by companies elsewhere, including the United States, in the decades yet before. Tin-litho rowboat, 14 inches long, Paya, 1980s (photograph by and collection of the author).

In the Ives-Blakeslee years, clockwork toys became the company's mainstay, although hot-air toys retained their place in the list. By the next decade the firm was exporting to South America and Europe.³³

Others, too, helped make Bridgeport a toy-making center. There, in 1869, C.F. Braitling began making dolls and accessories. Another toymaker, Columbia Instruction Company, may have had an early presence there. Since Braitling and Ives-Blakeslee established companies around the same time, the two must have benefited from proximity. The expertise developed by the doll company may well have contributed to Ives-Blakeslee's finely crafted automata.³⁴

Although Ives and Brown loom large in histories of American toys and automata, the existence of one or two manufacturers of any particular type of toy, in any particular region, often indicates that others in the vicinity were engaged in the trade. Well-developed expertise leads to other companies being founded nearby to produce related, competing, or cooperatively issued playthings. A particular manufacturing climate conduces to making a particular toy-type.

Although in operation when Philadelphia hosted the International Exposition of 1876, Stevens & Brown sponsored no official exhibit. Ives, Blakeslee & Co., on the other hand, did show "mechanical toys and novelties."³⁵ A neighbor to Ives, James B. Secor, also exhibited automata, and won a medal.

Secor had arrived in Bridgeport after having had his sewing-machine manufactory destroyed in Chicago's Great Fire of 1871. In restarting his firm, he pursued an additional interest that may have had its roots, too, beside Lake Michigan: toy automata. Chicago may have been another incipient hotbed of mechanical toy production by this time, before the fire as well as after.³⁶ Secor's interests led him to produce toy birds that "sang," with some standing upon music boxes whose workings aligned with the birds' actions. When sending sewing machines to the Vienna World International Exhibition in 1873 he packed toys, too.[37] While he had intended the diversionary automata to draw people to the utilitarian ones, his business in those machines failed while the toys prospered.

Among his simpler and less expensive devices, The American Songster, a Scientific Novelty, resembled a pipe with an open-beaked bird perched atop its bowl. Jestingly it might have been considered a hot-air toy, with the toy having a rubber hose, to which child placed lips. American Songster represented the whistle in its ultimate form, as a breath-powered automaton.[38]

The Steam Men of Newark

While Stevens and Brown were making tinplate toys, in Newark, New Jersey, the machinists Zadoc P. Dederick and Edward A. Hunt labored over what they dubbed the Steam Man. Powered by a two-cylinder engine, measuring more than seven feet tall, and weighing more than five hundred pounds, it had a frock coat, a top-hat smoke stack, and a painted-on smiling and bewhiskered face.[39] Its debut excursion in January 1868, took it and its towed-along cart around Newark's Military Park to Crump's Garden, a beer hall. There, Dederick lodged it and charged two bits per viewing. He hoped his invention pointed toward inexpensive ground transport. Another Newark inventor, Israel C. Eagles, unveiled a similar mechanism in 1869. Eagles placed the engine in the cart behind the Steam King.[40] Newark would remain a center for steam-engine activity, to judge from the establishment of Dodge & Myer in that city in the 1870s, to produce steam toys.[41]

The steam-man notion arose from both mechanical toys and rail-traveling locomotives; and once proven as a working machine, it acquired fictional potency. Besides the tall tales that could only have arisen overnight in Newark, a dime novel featuring it appeared on stands in August 1868. Its central symbolic figure was a "jumping-jack," as a character calls it. Written by Edward S. Ellis, age twenty-eight and a Red Bank schoolteacher, *The Steam Man of the Prairies* offered melodrama with stock characters, a simplified backdrop of the American West, and villainous Indians. Three of the main characters—a trapper, an Irishman, and a Yankee—came together as a unit after a steamship disaster. They become a foursome with Johnny Brainerd, whose last name indicates his place in their sectional being. He is also "the engineer." A fifth presence commands the novel's title.

That the steam-man notion had widespread currency in 1868 appears in the following exchange between trapper and Brainerd:

> "Wal, you're the smartest feller I ever seen, big or little. Whoever heard of a man going by steam?"
> "I have, often; but I never saw it. I expect when I go back to make steam horses."
> "And birds, I s'pose?"

Similarly, the Yankee had himself had hit on the notion ten years before, although he had lacked a chance to build one.[42]

The novel's innovations mainly lie elsewhere than the steam man. With Brainerd, the new stock character of the boy-inventor takes his bow on the stage. "Wonderful as was the mechanism, yet the boy who had constructed it was still more worthy of wonder," as the narrator notes. That he is the son of a less-brilliant inventor offers a model for a commonplace in later boys' novels. Brainerd seems a scion of Poe's Hop-Frog, as well, being a hunchbacked dwarf. Being so small, moreover, he climbs onto his creation "as another Gulliver."[43]

A second innovation involves the narrative's being placed in a belletristic context. Not only does this reduce the Indians, or "darn skunks," to being ever-present and ever-threatening enemies whose motives seem simply the desire to pursue warfare, it alters the steam-man's nature. No longer merely the "peregrinating locomotive" that the boy intended it to be, it becomes a means for inducing terror and for capricious pursuit. In the end it becomes a weapon: "The shock of the explosion was terrible. It was like the bursting of an immense bomb-shell, the steam man being blown into thousands of fragments, that scattered death and destruction in every direction. Falling in the very center of the crouching Indians, it could but make a terrible destruction of life, while those who escaped unharmed, were beside themselves with consternation." The transition from land transport to weaponry occurs, in symbolic terms, near the novel's beginning, when the Yankee reflects on having conceived his own steam-man notion as a child. The idea came to him while touring Colt's Hartford pistol factory.[44]

Ending its arc as a marvelous machine, the steam man's destruction saves the protagonists' lives, and leaves them free as individuals to pursue fulfillment in society. Impressionable readers in 1868, in the meantime, emerged from that wreckage with a character in mind who might be played with no more costumery than a top-hat and a toy train whistle. Any child thus playing became a "peregrinating locomotive," a steam-machine that triumphs in war against the cardboard enemy of the faceless and heartless aboriginal. The conquest of nature also has a place in the machine's symbolic freight, in that the novel contains scenes involving the "brutal ferocity" of the bison and "a ferocious brute" of a grizzly.

Scientific Factories

A striking conjunction was occurring in the United States in the 1860s. Mechanical toys and toy automata appeared in profusion from New England toymakers; steam-powered automata appeared in roughly human guises; and a new dime-novel category appeared, with boy-commanded mechanical contrivances.

This coalescing focus upon diversionary automatism reflected conjoining social and technological developments. Northern States had embraced the factory system from the early 1800s, when textile factories gained their foothold in Massachusetts and then elsewhere. At first, these employed pieceworkers working in their homes, whose poor pay found some balance in the rewards of domesticity. By 1830, however, the trend to make factories "scientific," by combining under one roof an entire process from raw material to finished good, removed household industry from the scene. The scientific-factory approach spread to non-textile endeavors, and blossomed, as noted earlier, with the Civil War. The factory was taking a leading place as an American work environment.

Working conditions varied greatly from industry to industry, and from factory to factory. Yet a thread that joined this patchwork culture into a whole took the form of a human figure invisibly chained to its labors for half the hours in a day, if not more, and for six days in a week. Thanks to efforts by Horace Mann, children under age twelve received more consideration after 1840, with ten-hour days being the mandated, though not often the observed, maximum. In Massachusetts, the Act of 1866 established that children should work no more than eight hours in a day and banned those under age ten from employment in "any manufactory establishment." The next year the state changed the eight-hour maximum to the sixty-hour week.[45] A commission discovered that factory owners ignored the prohibition against employing children under ten, and generally held to an eleven-hours-per-day standard.[46]

On children the impact of the scientific factory, and of working such hours with respite on a Sunday only, must have been enormous. Even adult workers suffered. Factories called for their continuous application to repetitious tasks, usually involving power-automated machinery. Being little varied in its operations, it required attendance of an unvaried nature. Given this, the mechanical motions overflowed and overwhelmed the natural motions of human beings. For the workday's duration the machines' motion *became* the motions of their attendants. "The music of the iron is a law," Robert Frost would write, after his own mill experience, in his poem "When the Speed Comes." Motion that was rhythmic and repetitive, quick and ceaseless; the whirr, rumble, whine, and thunder of machinery; and restrictions on spontaneous freedom of action: these made workers be flesh-and-blood automatons—wound up by wages, started and stopped by the owners of capitol, and performing tasks without moral involvement or emotional commitment. Automata appeared not as extraordinary elements on the playroom floor or in the popular story, but as entirely typical elements in society, literally and symbolically. While some existed in solitude, in Signal-Man fashion, increasingly the human automata existed as the new masses, whose brightest lights led their existences damped within the lowest tiers of the middle class.

The diversionary automatism in mechanical toys, the Steam Man, and dime novels, in other words, by no means reflected an anticipated future, nor any advance in technical thinking. It reflected and expressed a business culture that had established its reign over society's working class, and a scientific-factory system whose dominance in industry had commenced decades earlier. Materialism reigned to the point of being given to children as a toy with which to play.

Mumford noted, "The degradations undergone by child laborers or women during the early nineteenth century in England's 'satanic mills' and mines only reflected those that took place during the territorial expansion of Western man."[47] If there appeared only rarely a William Blake or a Dickens who might protest and decry these degradations with artistic presence and force, the toys and wonder tales that celebrated and normalized automatism appeared with such frequency, by the 1860s, that they faded into the general cultural background.

Not only were pocket watches among economically successful adults omnipresent, as were toy watches among children, but they were invisible for being everywhere. As in Vondervotteimitiss, the time-keeping pocket watches and their time-kept owners were becoming inseparable, and perhaps indistinguishable.

Seven

The Moon and the Anti-Hero Clock

In "Hans Pfaall" the design is original, inasmuch as regards an attempt at *verisimilitude*, in the application of scientific principles (so far as the whimsical nature of the subject would permit,) to the actual passage between the earth and the moon.
—Poe, in 1835.[1]

Six years ago Verne's wonderful stories, among others his *De la Terre à la Lune*, fairly fascinated me. The boldness of the conceptions, the naturalness of the incidents, the details founded on the strictest practical knowledge, the liveliness of the narrative, the clearness of the thought—all revealing a mind that had sounded the depths of many an intricate scientific problem—were indeed a new revelation. Not only that. The elements usually considered indispensable in the ordinary novel, were totally absent. There was no killing, no betraying, no persecution, no heart breaking, no courtly pageantry, no metaphysical speculations, no mystery, no complicated plot, no thrilling descriptions, no fine writing, no photographic sketches of real life, no turning the human heart inside out, no apotheosis of nastiness—and still the story was profoundly and absorbingly interesting! An ideal story, pure as a sunbeam, less elaborately constructed than Poe's, but like them appealing altogether to the intellect of the reader and his innate love of the marvelous.
—Edward Roth, in 1874.[2]

Symbolic Appropriation

A sense of the absurd can free a mind to engage in associative thinking and allow symbolic meanings that inhere in objects to emerge, develop, and transform. Absurdity as naturally fit with the Modern wonder tale as it did with the nursery tale. Among other consequences, the Moon-trip came within the wonder-tale's purview quickly and easily. The Moon, naturally, had possessed symbolic depth and weight throughout Western history, with its attributes having as much to do with virtue and chastity as they did with distance and removal. Oddly enough, these qualities placed the Moon within the reach of wings.

In a symbolic sense now lost, or largely so, the goose served as a messenger to the realm

SEVEN—*The Moon and the Anti-Hero Clock* 95

Mother Goose and her conveyance. From the *Old Mother Goose*, published by W.B. Conkey in the later 1800s or earliest 1900s.

of virtue. Mother Goose as a name associated with nursery rhymes thus represents not a random fancy but a sensible one. Imagination, to re-envision the messenger as a means for conveyance, made but the smallest leap—which enabled the largest one.

> Jack's mother came in,
> And caught the goose soon,
> And, mounting its back,
> Flew up to the moon.[3]

In the process that led to wonder tales, writers would appropriate symbolic elements from earlier nursery stories, myths, or philosophic tales. These elements they then treated as literal. In other words, literary or cultural objects that originally possessed distinctly metaphoric weight came to have distinctly material weight, within the fictional context. This opened those objects to being judged by material criteria; and, in the Modern century, writers did so, borrowing these criteria from natural philosophy or science.

We might call the process symbolic appropriation, symbolic borrowing, or symbolic literalism. Wonder-tale writers appropriated or borrowed symbolic forms, and in taking them stripped off their symbolic values. Thus writers could pack symbols as "literal" elements in a *pseudo-realism* excelsior.

Symbolic values naturally persisted despite these writers' intents or practices. Frye's term, "displacement," works well within this context: for in Modern wonder tales, through symbolic appropriation, myths reappeared under the guise of rational constructs; and the rationalism itself served as the displacement. This fictional materialism offered a way to view objects as though their symbolic natures no longer existed. It offered a new and deceptive context for myth and symbol.

In reality, wonder-tale writers often obtusely misunderstood earlier writings. It may be that they did so deliberately for rhetorical reasons, or blunderingly, because they suffered a blindness to past understanding—brought on, perhaps, by positivism and the conviction that "progress" had occurred. While acting obtusely, these writers often asserted their own superiority—again, either for show, and to help define a narrator's persona, or because they believed it to be true.

When writers directly revealed that they were engaging in the symbolic-appropriation process by this means, they would describe their predecessors as having fallen short of realism in their natural philosophy, or their science. In other words, they would say that prior writers had fallen short in their pseudo-realism. Such an attitude comes easily to one who chooses to ignore the symbolic values predominating in earlier tales. Thus Poe discussed a moon journey by a Monsieur D'Avisson as a "naive specimen," and another by de Bergerac as "utterly meaningless."[4] Yet Poe's own moon journey rises into the realm of symbols, helped in part by absurdity. Similarly, while expressing his admiration, Verne said that Poe might have tried harder at achieving verisimilitude—forgetting that Poe had been the one to advance verisimilitude, in the first place, as the means whereby to convey a fantastic idea—a symbol-laden idea—to the reader. As noted earlier, moreover, verisimilitude is consciously created displacement.

In the same vein, Wells considered himself more scientific than Verne. Since in his stories Wells included far fewer technical elements than did Verne, and made far fewer efforts at verisimilitude, his attitude arose from his own pronounced positivism. Belief in material progress may have made it impossible for him to think otherwise. Verne, whatever his intention, wrote symbolically charged stories; and his symbols, when seen in literal terms, necessarily seemed outdated and obsolete to the positivist reader.

The literal viewpoint, in itself, extinguishes the symbolic flame, and creates a dull world lacking in living vibrancy and plucked bare of meaning. Poe feared just this result from the peering eyes of knowledge, with science clipping the wings of the poet's heart much as adulthood clouds the soul's eyes, in Wordsworth, who bemoaned the vanished "visionary gleam."

The process involved in symbolic appropriation gave to wonder tales a particular and somewhat paradoxical energy. The writers, by denying a subject's symbolic meaning, in essence insured that the symbolic element would go on unfettered, if in a new form. Their criticizing earlier attempts at pseudo-realism, on the other hand, did become a shackling point of view that would restrict the form. It led to the increasing application of literary-establishment virtues to pseudo-realism, thus making the split inevitable that would occur at the Modern century's end; and this split essentially brought about, if it did not result from, the destruction of the marvelous machine that was the Modern wonder tale itself.

First its positivist offspring, science fiction, would grow to dominance in the 1930s and 1940s. In the 1950s this offspring would develop in two diverging ways, on the one hand yielding game-type fantasy entertainments, and, on the other, literary fantasies. The game-type fantasies inherited the wonder tale's New-Worlds idealistic zest without a proportionate share of symbolic energy, while also, as noted earlier, discarding sectional human characters as unrealistic. The other, more literary "science fantasies," inherited the wonder tale's symbolic content without its idealistic zest. The latter writers tended to consider themselves too worldly to embrace New Worlds idealism openly, while regarding Gothic pessimism as not inimical, and often congenial, to their vauntedly "realistic" pseudo-realism.

By Goose to the Moon

To convey a trip from Earth to Moon, early writers showed literary powers rather than weaknesses in drawing upon older symbols. When Cyrano de Bergerac engaged in symbolic appropriation, it seems likely that he believed that the geese that he used, in lifting Cyrano from Earth, would seem more believable, or at least sensible, to his audiences than the vulture and eagle wings that lifted Menippus to the Moon, in Lucian. However, Cyrano's journey, popular though it was, came to be seen as charming, quaint, and slightly ridiculous—"utterly meaningless"—especially by those of a natural-philosophy persuasion. Natural philosophy, after all, did its utmost to leave little to the imagination.

These doubting readers took Cyrano's geese as actual and literal geese—which, within their fictional context, they were. In their own false-reality, they could be nothing else. Poe, in observing how much more realistic a means his was for reaching the Moon, remained blind, or played at being blind, to the continuity on display in symbolic tales—a continuity in which he participated. To his Moon story he brought natural philosophy and mechanics, both greatly advanced since de Bergerac's day; he believed that he presented the then-impossible in such a way that the reader might think it possible; and he found no meaning in geese going to the moon. This last meant that he failed to see that future readers might find his notion—a balloon going to the Moon—as meaningless. Poe, in other words, in reading de Bergerac, took literally not only the symbolic geese but also Cyrano's symbolic journey. Similarly, more recent readers who scoff at a balloon going to the Moon are taking literally both the symbolic vehicle and the symbolic journey, in "Hans Pfaall." The notion was true to its time, however, as shown in a verse published in the 1830s:

> What's the news of the day,
> Good neighbour, I pray?
> They say the balloon
> Has gone up to the moon.[5]

From before de Bergerac's and through Poe's times, the symbolic goose continued to exert power in the West. If nowhere else, it did so through games. Under such names as The Royal Game of Goose these traveled from Greece to Italy before 1600, to spread through Western Europe early in the Renaissance.[6] They represented a new board-game type soon to be common in Europe, then America: the "spiral game." Players would start at the board's perimeter, to advance to the center. Though spiral games might depart from the avian pictorial theme they remained Games of Goose.

In Poe's days, but in London, Laurie's New and Entertaining Game of the Golden Goose appeared on November 22, 1831, published by Richard Holmes Laurie. With its playing area superimposed upon a goose picture, it shares with other such games the element of having "squares" on which to move, during the player's advance to the center. Should one arrive by luck at a square bearing the image of a small goose, one's marker instantly advanced yet farther ahead.[7]

The game soon saw publication in an American port city, altered in form. European versions must have appeared as imports and gifts from abroad before 1843, the year that

By goose to adulthood. The Shoofly, invented in the 1800s by Jesse Crandall, took innumerable appearances. The goose, however, ranked high among the chosen designs. Here, a goose provides transport beyond the stationary world. Photograph taken in Canada, 1930s (author's collection).

W. & S.B. Ives published theirs. "Mansion of Happiness" lacked a goose image, although an eagle would appear in successor versions. Moral in tone, and attractively lithographed and hand-colored, this spiral game aimed players toward the goal that had proven so elusive in Gothic wonder tales, but not in Modern ones: the goal of Happiness.[8]

That the goose's powers were symbolically feminine, the old tale "Jack and the Beanstalk" suggests—as do the venerable rhymes attributed to Mother Goose. Despite their nonsensical natures these found favor as aids in a child's development, including moral. They had a place not only in Mother Goose's but in the mother's realm. That being the case, the displacement created by Poe's belittling de Bergerac conceals the symbolic element that might have seemed too obviously fairy-tale-like otherwise.

This is that both Pfaall's balloon and his hermetically closed travel-compartment are, in the wake of de Bergerac's geese, simply eggs.

Literal Appropriation

A second tendency that appears in the process that yielded wonder tales, as a mirror-equivalent to symbolic appropriation, might take the name "literal appropriation," or literal borrowing. An actual object—something to be taken literally for what its name says that it is, under normal conditions—would be borrowed for symbolic use. Literal appropriation takes place when the creative spirit lingers not upon a symbolic element found

SEVEN—*The Moon and the Anti-Hero Clock* 99

in prior creative works but seizes upon a material object from the mundane sphere. At some point, for instance, some writer or illustrator took an ordinary north-European sleigh, but pulled by reindeer, to endow with symbolic power by placing it against the sky with Father Christmas or St. Nicholas as driver. In the Modern wonder tale, a writer sometimes found it necessary to seize upon an element from *the world of experience within human culture*, to be deployed in a new context, bolstered with imaginary technical improvements and expanded powers, better to suggest their actual symbolic dimensions within the fictional context.

Although at times this process must have taken place subconsciously, it offered to writers an effective technique: for any common object that calls for transformation already commands attention, and thus lends itself to imaginative belief. The aerostatic balloon in the earlier 1800s, for instance, offered an image grasped by readers readily, even eagerly. To borrow it was to borrow how readers would see it, while reading. When Poe used one in the 1830s to reach the Moon, the element of excitement, of the spectacle, came through to readers—as a borrowing from the mundane. With the literal object, Poe had borrowed the excitement still buoying it. He drew upon the object *for* its existing public symbolism, at least in part. In other words, he borrowed the existing thing and its symbolic power, to enhance both through fiction. The act remained a literal borrowing, even with the borrowed symbolism: for he was borrowing an object to be an object—a physical object to become a fictionally physical one, and not an object-like symbol to become a fictional object. If the act was a conscious one, it may have been prompted by the unconscious sense of continuity with Lucian and de Bergerac.

This technique helped many a wonder tale gain an audience. It also helped many, too, to lose that audience: for new, actual technologies did arrive; and when they did, in many cases they looked nothing like the wonder story's literal-borrowing. That the new inventions and the literal-borrowings might be identical, in their symbolic aspects, literal-minded readers found easy to ignore.

Our moon turns only one side of its face toward the earth—the other is invisible

By monoplane to the moon. An example of literal appropriation (by John Dukes McKee in Elena Fontany, *Other Worlds Than This*, 1934).

Much as symbolic appropriation led writers to issue somewhat inappropriate criticisms, literal borrowing led later writers to feel themselves superior to earlier ones because history had proven "wrong" those earlier writers. Poe chose the aerostatic balloon to visit the Moon, since he imagined an atmospheric continuum to exist between planetary bodies. When technical developments later yielded the Saturn rocket, which looked nothing like Poe's balloon, it gave rise to comments about Poe's naivete. Verne chose the aerostatic balloon to cross Africa, since he imagined those stratified air-currents. Technical developments yielded the dirigible and the airplane, for such guided flight. Scientific and engineering insights placed the imagined and the achieved into disjunction: for science came to see an airless void between planets, and a lack of neat, atmospheric strata around Earth; and engineering found other modes for efficient travel.

The image of Santa aloft involved literal appropriation, at its conception—the borrowing of a commonly known object to place within a symbolic context. The symbolic form is then meant to be taken "literally," within its imaginary context. Cover by Milo Winter, for "Just Right" Authors and Artists, 1927.

SEVEN—The Moon and the Anti-Hero Clock

As we will see, the literal-borrowing process would continue in the same way, toward the same ends, through the Modern century. A toy would depict the new "dirigible" reaching the Moon. A children's book would imagine the new "monoplane" reaching other planets. Similarly, seagoing craft, in pictures, toys, and tales, would appear transformed into aerial vehicles. Although such ideas ended up being "proven wrong" by the technics actually developed, the fact that these toys and stories won instant understanding from children and even adults lies outside the realm of the right, the wrong, the scientific, or the technical. Materialism's point of view, in this area, proves itself immaterial. Once literal appropriation takes in a material object to place in an imaginary context, the object takes on symbolic weight, not material. It becomes a thing available for symbolic appropriation.

Oddly enough, the stories that would focus upon inventions that did seem to offer "accurate predictions," being proven "right" by later events, tended to lose favor among readers—because they tended to be "realistic," in material terms, and thus unmemorable. Even later readers interest themselves in older "wonder" elements; and the merely predictable extrapolation that was "right" excites less wonder than the outrageously "wrong" one. The degree to which a symbolic object is "wrong" may correspond to the degree to which that object is purely symbolic.

To take an example from juvenile novels in the 1910s, the "Motor Boys" went by that name because they embraced everything and anything that had a motor. Their excitement accurately reflected the mood surrounding gasoline-burning motors in the early 1900s. Similarly *Tom Swift and His Motor-Cycle* and *Tom Swift and His Motor-Boat* kicked off a series by Howard Garis that became widely popular. Multitudinous others appeared. Yet by becoming extremely common—by becoming standard elements within people's experience of their own culture—by becoming, in fact, attached to anything and everything—motors lost their glow of being spectacles worthy of either wonder or startled dismay. Actual developments made any motor or motorized thing a commonplace. The spectacle, threat, and dangerous thrill dulled steadily toward becoming humdrum experience with irksome aspects. As a consequence, book three, *Tom Swift and His Airship*, would seem, in retrospect, to mark the entrance of the "real" Tom Swift, because his powered airship, which

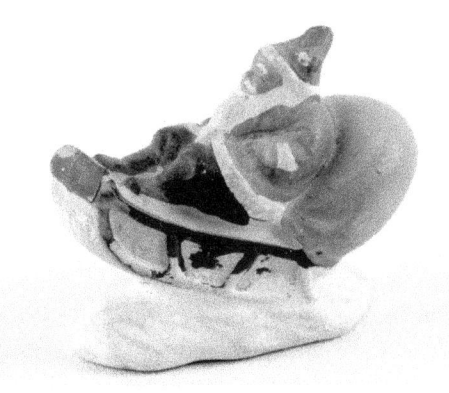

Santa's sleigh rising from the snow. Small composition figure, Japan, 1920s–30s (photograph by and collection of the author).

The rooftop setting. Besides the sleigh, reindeer, and bag of toys, the Santa tale requires the domestic rooftop for a setting. Small composition figure, Japan, 1920s–30s (photograph by and collection of the author).

combined dirigible and tiered-wing aircraft, was proven so "wrong" in the choices it made, in its literal borrowings.

The wonder-sense disappeared from those endless motor books, much as it did from motorized lives and motorized civilization. Having too much about them so much that was "right," they ended up lost to wonder. Among the few remaining passages that recapture that lost sense relates Mr. Toad's ecstatic joy over the automobile, in *The Wind and the Willows*: "The poetry of motion! ... Here to-day—in next week tomorrow! Villages skipped, towns and cities jumped—always somebody else's horizon!"

By Balloon to the Moon

In "Hans Phaall—A Tale," in an 1835 *Southern Literary Messenger*, Rotterdam citizens see in the sky "a queer, heterogeneous, but apparently solid substance, so oddly shaped, so whimsically put together, as not to be in any manner comprehended," which is a "fantastic machine," whose aeronaut is an odd-looking, miniature being.[9]

This first flying machine in "Phaall," or "Pfaall," as later versions have it, gives way to a second. Pfaall constructs a "balloon of extraordinary dimensions" filled with a new gas with a density "about 37.4 times less than that of hydrogen." He further obtains "one of M. Grimm's improvements upon the apparatus for condensation of the atmospheric air," which Pfaall further adapts to his purposes.[10] Pfaall notes: "wishing to live, yet wearied with life, the treatise at the stall of the bookseller, backed by the opportune discovery of my cousin of Nantz, opened a resource to my imagination. I then finally made up my mind. I determined to depart, yet live—to leave the world, yet continue to exist—in short, to drop enigmas, I resolved, let what would ensue, to force a passage, if I could, to the moon."[11] Pfaall calculates the degree to which atmospheric density diminishes away from Earth's surface and ascertains that "with a velocity prodigiously accelerating, I should at length arrive in those distant regions where the force of the earth's attraction should be superseded by that of the moon."[12]

> [M]y object, in the first place, was to surround myself and car entirely with a barricade against the highly rarefied atmosphere in which I was existing, with the intention of introducing within this barricade, by means of my condenser, a quantity of this same atmosphere sufficiently condensed for the purposes of respiration. With this object in view I had prepared a very strong, perfectly air-tight, but flexible gum-elastic bag. In this bag, which was of sufficient dimensions, the entire car was in a manner placed. …. In the sides of the covering thus adjusted round the car, had been inserted three circular panes of thick but clear glass, through which I could see without difficulty around me in every horizontal direction. In that portion of the cloth forming the bottom, was likewise a fourth window, of the same kind.[13]

Couched in these realistic terms, this enclosed car gives symbolic form to the fact that human beings aloft in a balloon depend absolutely upon its operative success. A name for the concept which Pfaall's encapsulated car was introducing would await coinage for a century: for it offered a miniature of the Earth's chemical-biological system—an incipient form of the enclosed, self-sustaining Earth-type environment, or encapsulated ecosystem, that would take the name "ecosphere."[14] The balloon carries not merely a traveller but an entire miniature Earth: for the space traveler cannot live unless Earth herself, or her symbolic equivalent, goes along for the journey.

The story takes the form of a hoax—or rather that of *an account of* a hoax, which places it alongside "Maelzel's Chess-Player," in structural terms. As such, the story's concluding statements necessarily undermine the extraordinary journey's actuality. Poe nevertheless created his fictional vehicle after seriously considering the journey's requirements, based on current philosophic understanding.

The several references in "Pfaall" to a "cousin" and "citizen of Nantz, in France," who was scientifically advanced, may have unsettled his later reader, the Nantes-born Verne.[15]

Verne's Clockwork Villain

Emerging from a youth marked by devotion to the Church, Verne readily perceived that even Poe's seemingly supernatural tales reflected a materialist attitude.[16] Poe, in Verne's estimation, "wrote, thought and dreamed as an American, as a positivist."[17] Yet Verne also absorbed an element in Poe that stood in contrast to the perceived positivism—the sense of who the villain was, who beset and upset society. Poe identified the *monstrum horrendum*, the unprincipled man of brilliance. Verne introduced his own *monstri horrendi* in two *nouvelles* predating *Cinq Semains*, the first being his 1854 "*Maître Zacharius ou l'horloger qui a perdu son âme*," or "Master Zacharius," as it appeared in English decades later. In it, a brilliant clockmaker, having sacrificed his soul to his pride, faces a mysterious being who is both clock and devil.

This extravaganza may well have responded to "The Devil in the Belfry," although not modeled upon it. Verne introduces an elderly Genevan, the inventor of the escapement, who "did not live; he vibrated like the pendulum of his clocks," and who considers life to be "only an ingenious mechanism."[18] Yet now his customers bring back his watches. They are stopping. Even his great cathedral clocks fall still. As his repairs fail, as well, his declining health alarms his daughter Gerande: "it seemed to her as if his existence, so dear to her, having become purely mechanical, no longer moved on its worn-out pivots without effort."[19] Although not himself a mechanical being, on Geneva's streets Zacharius encounters one:

> How old was this singular being? No one could have told. People conjectured that he must have existed for several centuries, and that was all. His big flat head rested upon shoulders the width of which was equal to the height of his body; this was not above three feet. This personage would have made a good figure to support a pendulum, for the dial would have naturally been placed on his face, and the balance-wheel would have oscillated at its ease in his chest. His nose might readily have been taken for the style of a sun-dial, for it was narrow and sharp; his teeth, far apart, resembled the cogs of a wheel, and ground themselves between his lips; his voice had the metallic sound of a bell, and you could hear his heart beat like the tick of a clock. This little man, whose arms moved like the hands on a dial, walked with jerks, without ever turning round. If anyone followed him, it was found that he walked a league an hour, and that his course was nearly circular.[20]

When Zacharius first spots the "little man," he tells Gerande, "Fear nothing, my child; it is not a man, it is a clock!" This clock, who goes by the name Signor Pittonaccio, proves Zacharius's nemesis. Even so, in symbolic terms, being a clock, he is a creation of this Genevan who has made "machines that go all by themselves."[21] Gerande does put her finger to the pride to which her father has succumbed: "that vanity of science which connects everything with itself."[22] In thematic terms the story resonates with Mary Shelley's, whose implacable Being, too, has a connection to clockmaking Geneva, and is another of the "machines that go all by themselves."

As does Poe's "Belfry," Verne's story ends with clock-destruction. The vanities of science—which are the sole clock made by Zacharius still running, and the clock-devil

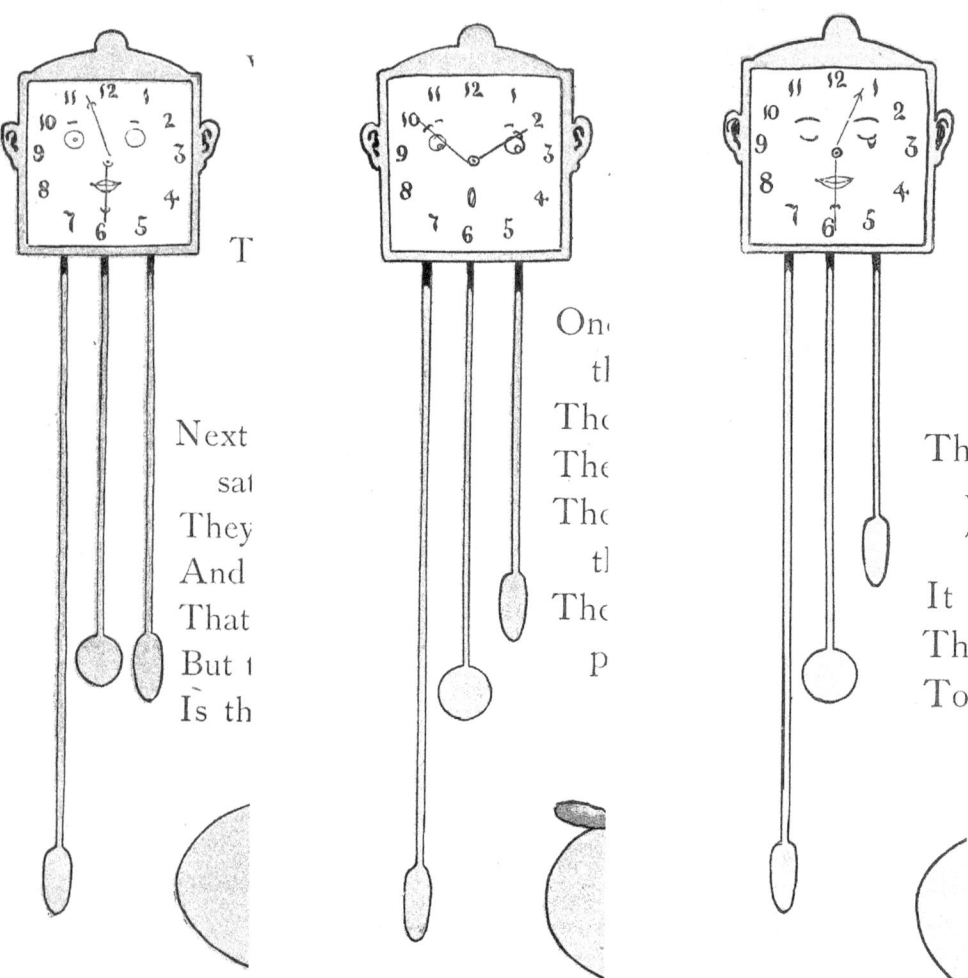

The clock-being became a commonplace in children's book illustrations and stories during the 1800s and early 1900s. These drawings show the "old dutch clock" in Eugene Field's verse "The Duel" (from Alice Harris, *Eugene Field Reader*, 1905, pp. 58–60).

himself—destroy themselves and their maker. Yet Verne's story stands in stark contrast to Poe's, in relying upon the technique whose absence in the latter's works the former bemoaned. Verne thought it necessary that an "intervention of providence" bring about Pittonaccio's end.[23]

While acting autonomously, Pittonaccio remains so much a clock that the hours chime from his heart. Once Verne's career as a novelist commenced—when his sympathy for Catholicism was subsiding, or at least his expressions concerning it became less pronounced and didactic—he would continue exploring the nature of the mechanical being as though compelled to do so. Even in early novels, as an American reader commented in 1874, "Cool heads might consider … his men machines rather than human beings."[24]

Seeing print in Parisian magazine *Musée de Familles*, parents would have read "Zacharius" aloud, or have felt at ease leaving it out for their children, with its moral urging reliance on "the infinite source whence first principles flow."[25] It seems likely, then, that at least a few clocks took their places on the playroom tables of 1854 to stand in for a strange, devilish, and mechanical being, even in religiously inclined households.

The toy clocks abundant in Vondervotteimitiss and in toy boxes across the West, in other words, were undergoing symbolic expansion. Variants upon such play-activity must already have taken place, if a well-established tradition in children's stories gives any indication: for these stories reflected the increasing ease with which writers and artists invested manufactured household goods with human character and animation. Probably a venerable practice already by the 1800s, the tradition gained strength in England and America with the focus in Christmas tales shifting from the religious to the secular. *The Kettle Club: Christmas Tales for Children*, of 1866, by "Cousin Virginia," presumably only charmed children, not alarmed them, with its kettles, teapots, clocks, and saucepans that talk amongst themselves. It would seem natural, when a parent tells a child that an item is not for play, for that item to acquire a life in the child's fancies. As with Sunday dolls, such an admonishment encouraged children to "hold conversations." Clock-fantasies, moreover, had long played a part in the arts, if the sixth preludes in both *Well-Tempered Clavier* volumes by Bach, in the 1700s, are any indication.

Two years after "Zacharius," in 1856, another *nouvelle* reflected a maturing in Verne's thoughts. "*Un Voyage en ballon*," which Hetzel would reprint in 1874 as "*Un Drame dans les Airs*," in English would take the latter title: "A Drama in the Air." Its genius antagonist appears not as a man who, like Zacharius, has lost his soul by abandoning the church, but as one who has lost his senses through a process Verne had observed in Poe's characters: "They must inevitably become mad through abuse of their minds."[26] Verne's narrator, never learning this particular *monstrum horrendum*'s name, refers to him only as "the unknown"—a telling appellation, given how the unknown so attracted Verne. His worries about its maddening dangers may have been justified, insofar as he was losing one of his own senses, which was that predilection for fictional "interventions of providence," along with his qualms about its absence in stories by others. In "*Un Voyage en ballon*," no such intervention occurs. Self-destructive impulses bring an end to the tale—destroying madman and balloon, and nearly the narrator, as well.

This tale revealed another technique Verne was developing as a writer. He deployed lists of historical facts in cascades—in this case, to horrify the narrator while entertaining the reader. The tale displayed, too, his interest in speculative concepts, as when describing a newspaper's satiric engraving:

> It is an immense balloon carrying a ship, strong castles, houses, and so on. The caricaturists did not suspect that their follies would one day become truth. It is complete, this large vessel. On the left is its helm, with the pilot's box; at the prow are pleasure-houses, an immense organ, and a cannon to call the attention of the inhabitants of the earth or the moon; above the poop there are the observatory and the balloon long-boat; in the equatorial circle, the army barrack on the left, the funnel; then the upper galleries for promenading, sails, pinions; below, the cafés and general storehouse. Observe this pompous announcement: "Invented for the happiness of the human race, this globe will depart at once for the ports of the Levant, and on its return the programme of its voyages to the two poles and the extreme west will be announced. No one need furnish himself with anything; everything is foreseen, and all will prosper."[27]

The balloon, as a physical reality, may have provided Verne with the perspective needed to move him away from a settled and churchly devotion. While his predilections would continue leading him to satirize those who felt a blind devotion to science, he accepted technology and felt curious about its implications. His acceptance and curiosity were leading him into a closer alignment with the positivists among his country's philosophers—closer, that is, than simple antagonism. His increasing interest in technical advance, however much it helped him to understand materialism and to adopt its language and ways of thinking as means for achieving verisimilitude, prompted no increase in his faith in scientism, all the same. He had mis-diagnosed Poe as a positivist, and would suffer the same misdiagnosis himself.

After "*Un Voyage en ballon*," Verne's interest in balloon-travel continued—as did his instinct to portray the giantism of industrial society in symbolic terms. Nadar's *Géant* took its name from this giantism, unabashedly; Verne's imaginary *Victoria*, from England's gigantic reach. Subsequently, the fact that Nadar, as a photographer, showed the world how it was to look down upon

"HE KNOCKED THE GROCER FLAT ON HIS BACK."

Granting life to toys. Illustration by Alice B. Woodward, 1897 (from Edith M. King-Hall, *Adventures in Toyland*, ca. 1910).

minikins on the French countryside, while striding across it as a giant, must have helped confirm Verne in his course. Photography—an optical wonder produced by a philosophic toy and artist's device, the camera obscura—reaffirmed that technical change was not to be wiped from society by providence, in the manner of chalk from a slate. The new perspectives had permanency, it seemed. They altered the world with facts that came in "black and white"—a reference to the vastly popular newspapers, and to photographs; and this black-and-white factuality helped bolster, again and again, arguments for materialism.

By Ball to the Moon

After having characters descend into Earth's inner regions to encounter the gigantic, in 1865 Verne had them consider the inevitable and inevitably symbolic toy, the ball, and the ever-increasing connections to be drawn between it and giantism. His new novel bounced Earth and Moon upon the page. His characters, moreover, aimed to fire between the two celestial orbs a cannonball.

The *Cinq Semaines* engineer-antihero, Fergusson, embodies materialism, in that he is prepared to meet danger and difficulty with mental and physical actions unencumbered by emotional reactions or considerations. Verne's third novel for Hetzel, *De la Terre à la Lune*, presents an even more distinctly positivist hero in Impey Barbicane, "a man of forty years of age, calm, cold, austere; of a singularly serious and self-contained demeanor, punctual as a chronometer, of imperturbable temper and immovable character; by no means chivalrous, yet adventurous withal, and always bringing practical ideas to bear upon the very rashest enterprises .... His strongly marked features seemed drawn by square and rule; and if it be true that, in order to judge of a man's character one must look at his profile, Barbicane, so examined, exhibited the most certain indications of energy, audacity, and *sang-froid*."[28] That Verne had incompletely shaken off his youthful attitudes appears in his choice of character name. Since Impey means *Impious*, he recalls Poe's imps less than Verne's own Zacharias.

Impey Barbicane presides over a group of engineers in the city most associated with *Hans Pfaall*'s author. The Baltimore Gun Club exemplifies American materialism and positivism both in its devotion to industrial gigantism and in its embrace of artificial replacements for the real.

The forest of mushrooms. Gigantism, the spectacle, and glimpses into antiquity conjoin in several episodes in the 1864 novel *A Journey to the Centre of the Earth*.

Verne notes with "what energy the tastes for military matters" arose during the Civil War. "But the point in which the Americans singularly distanced the Europeans was in the science of gunnery. ... In point of grazing, plunging, oblique, or enfilading, or point-blank firing, the English, French, and Prussians have nothing to learn; but their cannon, howitzers, and mortars are mere pocket-pistols compared with the formidable engines of the American artillery."[29]

The artificial element, too, gained ground, thanks to the war. The club's members "bore the marks of their indisputable valor" in a conflict that had produced Baudelaire-esque decomposure: "Crutches, wooden legs, artificial arms, steel hooks, caoutchouc jaws, silver craniums, platinum noses, were all to be found in the collection; and it was calculated by the great statistician Pitcairn that throughout the Gun Club there was not quite one arm between four persons, and exactly two legs between six."[30] Ironically, the club member most artificial in his bearing and habits, President Barbicane, survived the war outwardly intact.

To revive the Club's spirits, Barbicane calls a meeting. "Just when the deep-toned clock in the great hall struck eight, Barbicane, as if he had been set in motion by a spring, raised himself up." The President proposes that the Gun Club undertake a "grand experiment worthy of the nineteenth century," and that they take a cue from those who conceived imaginary journeys to the Moon. He presents them with a list ending with Poe—at which point the club responds, "Hurrah for Edgar Poe!" He proposes they create a gun that could send a message to the Selenites, with the message being a cannonball. This proposal fills the Gun Club with an enthusiasm that spreads through the general populace. Against the hope "that some day America would penetrate the deepest secrets of that mysterious orb," however, arises the concern "lest its conquest should not sensibly derange the equilibrium of Europe."[31]

In the chapter "Hymn of the Cannon-ball," Barbicane's friend J.T. Maston succumbs to a rapture:

> The cannon-ball, gentlemen, to my mind, is the most magnificent manifestation of human power. If Providence has created the stars and the planets, man has called the cannon-ball into existence. Let Providence claim the swiftness of electricity and of light, of the stars, the comets, and the planets, of wind and sound—we claim to have invented the swiftness of the cannon-ball, a hundred times superior to that of the swiftest horses or railway train. How glorious will be the moment when, infinitely exceeding all hitherto attained velocities, we shall launch our new projectile with the rapidity of seven miles a second! Shall it not, gentlemen—shall it not be received up there with the honors due to a terrestrial ambassador?[32]

Maston's words, condensed in the version appearing in England, had even more symbolic effect in French, with the words "*balistique*" and "*boulet*" recalling "*balle*" and "*boule*," French words for ball. Maston, moreover, purposely moves the *boulet*, cannonball, into the symbolic realm, in stating, "I leave behind the physical bullet, the bullet that kills, for I envision only the mathematical bullet, the moral bullet." American "translator" Edward Roth may have sensed this symbolic link, consciously or unconsciously, for among his additions to Verne's text he adds a line in which Maston, is not simply leaping from his chair, as Verne has him do, but is instead "bouncing off his chair like an india rubber ball."[33] In making this addition, however, he may have failed to grasp that the Gun Club's cannonball remained a weapon for siege and attack, with the Moon being object for play only in terms of symbolic conquest.

Barbicane, empowered by his being now ranked among the most prominent Americans, enhances the linkage by expanding the Gun Club's effort to a global one. He forms the "Union," a consortium of banks, to help the club collect contributions from around the globe. In the chapter "Urbi et Orbi," or "City and World,"

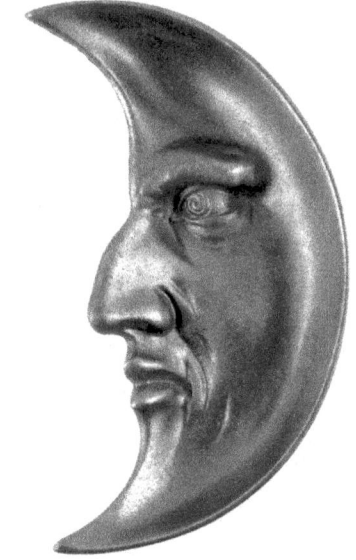

The man in the moon. Fanciful depictions of planetary bodies continued to thrive, even after toy telescopes became available. The "man in the moon" appeared in various guises in wonder tales from authors ranging from Lewis Carroll to Hugh Lofting. Toy dish or dresser tray, 6-inch cast iron, late 1800s or early 1900s.

Verne carefully lists major cities and participating Union banks, thus making a veritable tour of the industrialized world.

A new sense, that the cultural globe had become inseparable from its devices for communicating around it, makes several appearances in the novel, especially in the desire to extend that system of communication beyond it. Verne has his characters invoke a German idea for marking immense, reflective mathematical symbols upon the Siberian steppes, in an attempt to communicate with Selenites.[34] His Americans, moreover, react to the news of the Gun Club's Moon-shot by entertaining ideas about satellite communication, thinking of the Moon "as a polished mirror, by means of which people could see each other from different points of the earth and interchange their thoughts."[35]

When the giant cast-iron cannon, *Columbiad*, nears completion in Florida, Barbicane and his Gun Club hold a noisy, celebratory dinner within it—recalling the celebrated dinner within the Sydenham Park *monstrum*. In these final days, events swiftly change the Moon-shot's nature: for Michel Ardan of France proposes that the hollow aluminum cannonball be changed to a "cylindro-conical projectile"—and that he travel within it to the Moon. In Ardan, impious Barbicane meets another aspect of his soul. Ardan, his name being an anagram for Nadar, offers ebullient contrast to the restrained engineer, and embodies the heart: for "the love of the impossible constituted his ruling passion." He intends to make a tour of the Moon. Barbicane encounters yet a third portion of his splintered soul in an old wartime rival, Captain Nicholl. Again upon Ardan's urging, the Moon-shot alters in its nature once more, becoming a journey to be undertaken by a trio: Ardan, Barbicane, and Nicholl, whom Verne designates Art, Science, and Industry—the dissected soul of Western society.[36] The projectile of the Gun Club's initial plans has become, as it is called in a chapter title, "*Le Wagon-Projectile*," which might be rendered in English as the "Truck-Projectile" or "Carriage-Projectile." In the English edition it appeared as the "Projectile-Vehicle." In the American edition, Roth, in his extravagance, names the chapter "An Improvement on Pullman," and has Michel call the vehicle "the great Air Line Railroad."[37]

The miniature Earth-egg that is Hans Pfaall's balloon-borne enclosure, an incipient ecosphere, finds more vivid realization in Verne's vehicle. Where Pfaall's craft draws in a diffuse atmosphere to be concentrated for breathing, Verne employs chemical means to produce oxygen and remove excess carbonic acid, with the process being made possible, in part, by gas heating.[38]

The symbolic seed that appears in Poe's tale, in the episode in which Puss gives birth to kittens when Pfaall's balloon moves toward the Moon, comes in for stronger evocation in Verne's. Ardan, whom Verne presents as having "a physiognomy essentially feline," proposes to take along representatives of useful species. At this, Barbicane notes that the projectile-vehicle cannot serve as Noah's Ark.[39] All the same, in small, it does.

Verne's 1865 novel ends on an uncertain note. The projectile-vehicle launches according to plan, with the immense cannon *Columbiad* performing its thunderous duty without bursting. Yet an observatory, which the Gun Club has erected upon a mountaintop, sees that things have gone amiss. "The projectile has not arrived at its destination … and it is now pursuing an elliptical orbit round the moon, of which it has become a true satellite."[40]

The trio of Ardan, Barbicane, and Nicholl have moved toward becoming an integrated soul, in undertaking this journey: and they seem to be, as the novel's final chapter title says, "A New Star." While the book's ending suggests a sequel, the novel stood alone for five years. For those years, *From the Earth to the Moon* stood as a completed work unto itself. It followed the symbolic journey taken by a soul toward the presence whom the Gun Club toasts at the bottom of Columbiad's barrel: the celestial Diana, a chaste goddess not to be reached nor touched, around whom the newly cohesive soul circles as an artificial satellite.

Verne constructed his ingenious and entertaining novel from objects easily available, so that even a youth might enjoy the banter, the historical references, and the imagery. These propel it briskly. To participate in the ideas takes no real effort. The cannon, the cannon ball, and the bullet-nosed shell had already reached readers as ideas in newspapers and books, in stories and illustrations about the Civil and other wars; and, as physical objects, they littered the playroom floor. The earth-encased cannon and the Moon-projectile appear in the novel as literal borrowings. Verne also invokes toys, calling Michel Ardan a wooden acrobat that falls always on its feet.[41] The Moon, of course, is always a ball; Earth becomes one. For children as for adults, Verne was initiating the process of making real, in the way fiction can make images real, the Earth as a globe *to be seen*. His efforts toward depicting the diminished dimensions of the globe would continue; but in *From the Earth to the Moon* he was giving his readers new means for imagining the encirclement of the world—and for envisioning its containment. A globe offers a visual circle, to be circled.

Hardly at all had toymakers and manufacturers of educational items awaited such a novel to increase production in the categories of maps, globes, and orreries. Such an increase was occurring already. These manufacturers would have flourished without literary impetus. They did, however, increasingly offer Earth-globes in numbers went far beyond the impressively detailed objects for the library or classroom. For tin-litho penny toys, tin pencil sharpeners, and india-rubber bouncing balls were beginning to appear as if Earths in miniature. The Earth was shrinking to fit in the youngest child's hand.

Around the Moon

By the time Verne published a sequel to his satirical yet serious *From the Earth to the Moon*, half a decade had passed. His 1870 *Around the Moon* makes evident that his ideas and beliefs were undergoing changes. No longer does Verne describe the American scientist-engineer Barbicane as the imperturbable creature of clockwork, heir to clockmaker Zacharias. Verne instead describes him as being of a religious inclination. Always "President Barbicane" or simply "Barbicane" in this second novel, he goes without a first name. Meanwhile his erstwhile opponent and now traveling companion, Nichols, has become the "chronometer" who precisely monitors the time, and who manages calculations "with unparalleled dexterity."[42] This alteration and switching among symbolic attributes suggests Verne's heart may have been less than fully involved in this sequel-novel's composition. Other aspects suggest this, as well—including the forgetfulness of characters about matters they had known perfectly well pre-launch. Yet the change in Nichols, who is Industry, must also have seemed appropriate to Verne.

On the other hand, the imaginative play between the characters offers the reader satisfaction, even if not the spirited entertainment of the first novel. In one episode, the Moon-circlers undergo a hectic trial, due to Ardan having left the oxygen-cock too widely open; and this leads the trio to the fantasy that piped-in oxygen would enliven dull theaters. Verne had expressed a related thought in his 1864 "Edgar Poe," in which he described Poe's characters as "just about feasible: they are eminently human, yet endowed with a highly nervous, supercharged sensibility. They are exceptional individuals, *galvanized* (if I may use that word) like people fed with air that has more oxygen than it should have and whose lives are one long combustion."[43]

Poe's imp, as it happens, has shown itself already in this voyage. Symbolically, once human technics sufficiently diminish the globe in scale, the human instinct to control must extend to it, and around it. In *From the Earth to the Moon*, the Americans reflect this instinct in their gazing "upwards" and wanting to plant their cannonball, then their flag, into the satellite. The scientific Moon-shot, even if it may also be a "mathematical bullet" or "moral bullet," amounts to humans firing a ball from one globe into another. It represents a war between worlds. Delivering the "message" boils down to ballistics. Such a situation, involving a hubris only to be termed monstrous, does require an imp's intervention. In ending the first novel, Verne had it seem that the target has been missed; the projectile-vehicle has become a satellite. The soul within it is human, and not, after all, the spirit of technological conquest and control. In *Around the Moon* this seems confirmed. The figures obtained by the Gun Club from the Cambridge observatory, being in error, made the *boulet* go wide.[44]

Yet due to implacable gravitational forces, the projectile-vehicle ends up not a satellite permanently. Instead it continues following its extended curve away from Earth, then back into her gravitational influence; and the projectile, meant to impact the Moon, impacts Earth. In the end, Impey Barbicane fulfills the promise of his first name: for the symbolic blow he means to strike against another world becomes a blow against his own.

Through Verne, Poe's imp was finding a place in the Modern wonder tale. Clothed in religion, the imp is Pittonaccio. The imp then is the madness suffered by "the unknown," aloft in a balloon. Afterwards, in his novels, Verne humanizes the imp; and in *From the Earth to the Moon*, different characters—different aspects of the splintered soul—serve in the role, in rotation. Impey Barbicane from the outset proves his name's irony: for while impious, he is the clock-regulator in the tower that first all in the club, then in the United States, and finally around the Earth gaze upon—and in this aspect is more Zacharius than Pittonaccio. Then enters Michel Ardan, the imp who will help Impey become a cohesive soul, proposing to insert his utterly human personality into the Moon projectile itself. Succeeding Ardan in the role, Captain Nicholl, a heckling critic of Impey's endeavor, then arrives. In the novel's sequel, the true imp stands revealed—as the simple fact of human fallibility; and this last imp saves from their own actions those whose lives have become encased within their technological pride, who otherwise might have dealt symbolic violence not only to an entire world, but specifically to the "second world" toward which their ark traveled.

Eight

The Maelstrom and New Worlds Fatalism

"Are the valves up to pressure?"
"Six and a half atmospheres."
"Get them up to ten."
This was an American order if there ever was one. It made me feel as if we were in one of those famous races on the Mississippi.
"Conseil," I said to my faithful servant standing next to me, "do you know that we'll probably all be blown sky-high?"
"As Monsieur wishes!" replied Conseil.
—Jules Verne, in 1870.[1]

And sometimes for an hour or so
I watched my leaden soldiers go,
With different uniforms and drills,
Among the bedclothes, through the hills.
—Robert Louis Stevenson, in 1885.[2]

Infallibly Logical Deductions

Maelzel's hoax gave Poe a chance to demonstrate "ratiocination," the process by which intellect rises above the mundane to make telling observations that, if correctly aligned and understood, unravel a puzzle or unveil a deception. Elsewhere, Poe embodied the process in fictional characters. One such, the detective Dupin, solves problems with an analytic prowess elevated to a degree seemingly unnatural. His analyses transcend limits placed on the mind by the senses and normal thought-patterns. The intellect moves, in other words, beyond body and custom in its effort to alter the world, to some degree, for the better. Poe also depicted the aloof intellect in his tales of celestial disaster, in which the mind's transcendence, symbolic in Dupin, becomes fictionally literal.

Although Poe in his celestial-disaster tales depicts the soul that separates itself from the physical realm and rises above the normal, Romantic individualism seems to have held him too strongly for him to feel sympathy for the idea that a machine might emulate the human mind, except as a deception—as an evocation of reality and not a replacement for it. The mechanism that imitates human operations lacks autonomy, being simply a means for extending human control. The Chess-Player houses not an intellect that transcends the body, but an intellect confined by a body confined by a machine. The machine encases the human; it buries the soul alive.

"The Murders in the Rue Morgue," "The Purloined Letter," and "The Gold-Bug" particularly impressed Verne. Of the last, he wrote, "This strange, disturbing story grips us through the use of techniques that no one tried before. It is crammed with observation and infallibly logical deductions."[3] Verne might well have connected these tales with "A Descent into the Maelström." In it, a man's fishing boat, caught in a storm, moves into the whirlpool's grip. He applies observational and reasoning powers, and saves himself despite his terror.

Dupin and William Legrand, the detective in "The Gold Bug," participate to a degree in the superhuman figure, the human-above-nature who makes an appearance in legends, tall tales, fairy stories, myths, and Gothic tales. The student alchemist Victor Frankenstein, for instance, has elements of the supremely cold intellect about him, mixed with superior powers—not least of which seems his ability, in his travels, to tote around quantities of dead women's parts, and do so without exciting suspicion. The prodigious Being in the novel has even greater claim to exemplifying the figure, by impossibly coordinating events in his course of vengeance, again without being detected; by pursuing infallibly, throttling effortlessly, and bounding across the Alps as over so many frosted cupcakes; and by surviving blithely in the wilderness and the desolate Arctic wastes. He moves as does the giant ogre in Charles Perraults "Little Thumb," without needing the ogre's seven-league boots. If considered to be the other half to Victor's divided soul, the Being loses no superhuman standing whatsoever, any more than does William Wilson's omniscient and frighteningly powerful double, in Poe's tale. The superhuman as society's shadowy doppelganger may, indeed, be Gothic fiction's particular gift to the West's industrially shadowed society.

Poe's particular contribution seems to have been that he isolated the intellect to magnify it, in his socially isolated heroes whose power is to command facts and properly order them, even from a distance. Without this magnification, it would seem doubtful that Dickens would have found it within his amply inventive resources to create the figure who might rank as the first Modern superhuman, Mr. Bucket, the detective in *Bleak House* who strides through events in a nearly undetectable and infallible way, and who within himself marries Dupin's inward faculties to the melodramatic stage-hero's physical prowess. The theatrical aspect to Bucket's powers had special impact upon later fictional superhumans: for it would seem a vital attribute that they could physically disguise themselves so well as to move through society undetected.[4]

The Automaton of Human Knowledge

The characters Dupin and Legrand, probably more than Mr. Bucket, influenced Verne in creating the cerebrally inclined but substantially more practical characters populating his novels. He veered slightly in his approach, however, in 1870—in *Vingt Mille Lieues sous les Mers*, which appeared in English three years later as *Twenty Thousand Leagues Under the Seas*.

Unlike Poe's inhabitants of Vondervotteimitiss or Verne's Impey Barbicane, Verne's *mentally* mechanical figure reveals no connection to the machine through clock-fixation or clocklike habit. He comes across instead as an automaton of scientific organization. Conseil, the Belgian assistant to erudite Professor Arronax of the Museum of Paris, amounts to a walking, talking card-file cabinet. Phlegmatic and loyal to the professor, Conseil seems more strongly guided by devotion than reason, and displays little imagination: yet given a question on taxonomic matters, he is, as Verne presents him, an infallible and ever-precise reference machine—an automated index and walking textbook. In a later age he would have been a database.

In a way akin to Milton, who relished the naming of angels in *Paradise Lost*, Verne in *Twenty Thousand Leagues* delves into the richly evocative nomenclature for life forms abounding in his world-spanning and novel-deluging waters, and repeatedly rolls out the harshest and softest namings in Greek and Latin for creatures both common and obscure, by this means washing the reader away from her or his everyday, landlocked, and page-bound existence and into a lexicographic region where taxonomic decorations strike the eye and ear with their mystifying configurations, their musical character, and their indistinct revelations of a living multitude unfamiliar to the typical book-reading, air-breathing creature. The views from the *Nautilus* offer hodgepodges of oceanic life that are kin to the geological porridges in *A Journey*—but ones that celebrate the exuberance and grandeur to be found in Linnaean names and naming. Taxonomy, as any will know who have moved mouselike through some small corner of the vast edifice that it is, may be the greatest science to be regarded as not much of a science at all, by most. Created by systematists who were intelligent, dedicated, patient, multilingual, painstaking, and focused if not obsessed, it stands as an enduring monument to the encyclopedist urge, which made the world seem tantalizingly near to encompassment.

Humbly, in Conseil, the urge has its fictional monument. In marine taxonomy and taxonomic hierarchies, he proves an infallible engine. Not a man of insight nor wisdom, nor of feeling nor ambition, he appears reduced to and yet uplifted by being a pure conduit to knowledge. Conceivably Verne had heard about efforts by William Stanley Jevons in Manchester, England, to perfect a device that could obtain the logical conclusion from any set of premises, mechanically. As it happens, Jevons demonstrated it before the Royal Society in the year *Vingt Milles Lieues* first saw print.[5] For Conseil was a logical machine unable to make astute observations on his own, while being a marvelous machine for handling any offered syllogisms. As Professor Arronax reflects, "In him I had a well-informed specialist in natural-history classification, who could, with an acrobat's ease, rush up and down the ladder of phyla, divisions, classes, sub classes, orders, families, genera, sub genera, species and varieties. But his knowledge ended there. His whole life was classification and he knew nothing else. He was very well read in the theory of classification, but knew little about the practical side, to the point where I don't think he could have told the difference between a sperm whale and an ordinary whale!"[6] Arronax's comment evoked the "ladder toys" often having "acrobats" who swiftly and comically climb down them, if unable to do anything else.[7] As noted, Verne had depicted Michel Ardan, too, as kin to that toy.

The sectional protagonist in *Twenty Thousand Leagues* appears again as a tripartite soul, in this case comprised by Arronax, Conseil, and their hearty Canadian whale-spearing companion, Ned Land. Arronax, possessing both reasoning powers and an enlightened, humanistic impulse, ranks among the most complete individual souls in Verne's stories. His full character arises in part from his role as first-person narrator. Verne's first illustrator, the French artist Riou, took this aspect seriously, and used Verne himself as his model for the professor.[8] Versed in the arts and sciences, and himself an explorer, Arronax contains within himself the elements brought to the fore in his companions. He classifies what he sees, exercises the mnemonic and organizational powers in which Conseil excels to an excessive degree, and displays boldness and strength, if in smaller measure than does the harpooner, who represents robust courage.

While Conseil may appear to be merely overdeveloped memory, his character symbolically resides near the heart, in this dissected Verneian soul. His interest lies in taxonomy—in other words, in the human arrangement of knowledge. He lacks the professor's knowledge of morphology, the observational science that made possible Linnaean classification and that was taxonomy's practical as opposed to theoretical side. Morphological features in organisms are the fixed, observable characteristics that had helped natural philosophers define species. They also had helped observers from ancient Greek times to consider the possibility that change affected biological forms through time—as revealed in the Greek god who lent his name to the observational science: Morpheus, who gives shape to dreams.[9]

Linnaean classification employed a terminology drawn from Classical sources, helping preserve the same Latin that the Church was preserving. It helped, too, to solidify the view of nature as an "arrangement" of imposed creation, which excludes the view of nature as a process of self-developing creation. Conseil, embodying taxonomy and not morphology, reflects unshakeable confidence in a system. Though not the Church herself, he represents an unwavering faith.

Yet, as Arronax observes, Conseil would not give him advice even when asked. Not only unquestioning, he is unanswering.[10]

Captain Nemo

Unlike his prisoners Arronax, Conseil, and Land, Nemo presents a relatively integrated soul. He verges, moreover, upon the superhuman. He has designed and built his own ship, having received the best technical education available in Europe; as an engineer he ranks among the symbolic leaders of positivist Modernity; and he has mastered natural science, philosophy, and literature. He has built both a museum of undersea treasures and a full library. He admires fine paintings and plays the pipe organ installed within the submarine to which he has given a technologically sanctified name. Much as Verne had bowed to Poe in naming his *Cinq Semaines* balloon *Victoria*, so he honored Fulton's 1801 diving boat, the *Nautilus*. As noted earlier, Fulton, being not solely technically minded, had introduced the panorama to France. *Vingt Milles Lieues* presents a literary-visual spectacle that might itself be considered a panoramic tribute to the artist-inventor.

Nemo seems the most credible of all technician anti-heroes. Not only does he exist apart from the ever-enlarging machine of Modern society, he opposes it—not only to maintain personal but to champion general human freedom. Slavery, though a factor in Nemo's reasoning—however maddened and tainted by Modernity his reasoning may be—appears in the novel as an idea, without appearing directly upon the fictional stage. That in a later novel Nemo would end his days on a remote, uncharted island that engineer Cyrus Smith would happen to name Lincoln Island, however, offers a precise reference-point. The journey that brings the narrator of *Twenty Thousand Leagues* into Nemo's company begins aboard an American ship that, too, is named *Abraham Lincoln*.

Nemo's presence finds its full character in his contradictions. He engages in a vengeful vendetta, prompted by humanitarian motives. He devotes himself to freedom, and lives trapped within the technical wonder he has created. He stands as a self-integrated being, while being literally submerged within his own technics. He pursues a global mission while never feeling at liberty to step onto continental land again.

Nemo's complete dependence upon his great *Nautilus*, and his enclosure by the machine, finds expression, too, during his excursions on the sea's floor, in a protective suit topped by copper helmet. Although he and his companions walk freely on the ocean floor without being tethered umbilically to the ship, they can do so only by carrying air-compression mechanisms that are miniatures of the air-compressing *Nautilus* herself.[11] Not only *Nautilus* but also these portable tanks represent what Pfaall's "car" does, in the voyage to the moon: the self-enclosed environment that allows human life to go on within an inimical environment.

Nemo's last words, in *Twenty Thousand Leagues*, emerge from the soul within the machine. They erupt shortly after Aronnax has passed into a dreamlike state. The passage begins with a symbolic marker for an automatic machine's ending:

> I could no longer judge of the time that was passing. The clocks had been stopped on board. It seemed, as in polar countries, that night and day no longer followed their regular course. I felt myself being drawn into that strange region where the foundered imagination of Edgar Poe roamed at will. Like the fabulous Gordon Pym, at every moment I expected to see 'That veiled human figure, of larger proportions than those of any inhabitant of the earth, thrown across the cataract which defends the approach to the pole.' [...] I knew not where we were.[12]

He has reached the turning-point where, in Poe's words, "The hours are breathing faint and low." Aronnax encounters Nemo a last time:

> ...a sigh from Captain Nemo nailed me to the spot. I knew that he was rising. I could even see him, for the light from the library came through to the saloon. He came towards me silently, with his arms crossed, gliding like a spectre rather than walking. His breast was swelling with sobs; and I heard him murmur these words (the last which ever struck my ear)—
> "Almighty God! Enough! Enough!"[13]

Nemo verges on the superhuman but remains an exceptional human being, capable of much yet still dwarfed by, altered, and defeated by the techno-social world that encompasses him just as it is does the world as a whole.

In Poe's "A Descent into the Maelström," an old man called "the guide" survives the maelstrom by logical means, yet emerges from his "six hours of deadly terror" a broken man: "It took less than a single day to change these hairs from a jetty black to white, to weaken my limbs, and to unstring my nerves."[14] Poe begins his story with a reference, not an appeal, to Providence, quoting Joseph Glanvill as to the gap between human conceptions and "the vastness, profundity, and unsearchableness of His works."[15] The old man comes face-to-face with this vastness and profundity; and a part of him vanishes into the vortex, leaving the survivor permanently altered, and barely able to cope with the everyday human life that would have seemed so simple a matter, before. His mind survives, while his heart has succumbed.

The one who survives the maelstrom suffers disintegration, in contrast to the one who, with the marvelous machine's destruction, emerges from disaster as a completed, integrated soul. In Poe's maelstrom tale, the individual suffers, in the end, from anguish and despair. In Verne's, the tripartite soul of Arronax, Conseil, and Ned Land emerges whole, while Nemo and his marvelous *Nautilus* sink into the vortex. Although his hands are crossed upon his breast, in Arronax's last sight of him, his fate remains unknown: for with the *Nautilus* gone, Nemo's realm, which encompasses all the oceans, recedes from normal human perception. The lamp lighting the phantasmagoria has gone out. *Twenty Thousand Leagues* owes its complexity, in part, to this combining of the Modern wonder tale with the maelstrom tale. In common with Poe's, Verne's maelstrom tale makes reference to deity without appealing to providence; and it presents human effort that verges on the superhuman without entering the realm belonging to the actual superhuman—unless one views the unassuming Conseil as superhuman in his lopsided cerebral strengths.

Both tales, moreover, may be read as Gothic wonder tales stripped of that form's most pronounced fairytale elements.

The Fish Pond

Early in their journey, Nemo treats his three prisoners to a spectacle. Solid wall-panels slide aside, in their underwater chamber, to reveal a glass wall through which they see beyond. They gaze "as if through the windows of an immense aquarium."[16] With Axel's vision in *A Journey to the Center of the Earth* this vision shares a symbolic link to the distant past:

> The sea supports the largest known species of mammals, and they perhaps conceal mollusks of incredible size, or terrifying crustaceans such as lobsters a hundred yards long or crabs weighing two tons! Why not? Long ago in geological times earthbound animals, quadrupeds, quadrumans, reptiles and birds, all produced species of gigantic size. The Creator had formed them in a colossal mold which time has reduced little by little. Why could the sea with its unknown depths not have kept some vast specimens of life in another age, since, unlike the earth's shell which is constantly being altered, it is unchanging? Why could it not hide in its bosom the last survivors of titanic species, for whom years are centuries and centuries millennia?[17]

Prizes for fishing. In the Fish Pond game, these cardboard fish, with rings in their snouts, lay unseen within the "pond," into which children dropped hooks and hoped not to haul in the hat. McLoughlin Bros., 1800s (author's collection).

The public continued to be fascinated by the undersea realm, whether inspired by Verne, Gosse, or exposition aquaria. Submergence, the notion that one might descend to inimical regions and emerge unscathed, as a spectacle held many in sway. The urge to be where one could not be, normally, found domestic expression in both aquaria and parlor diversions. The deceptively named Fish Pond games proved especially popular. Presumably publishers issued them in Europe before McLoughlin began issuing them in a variety of formats, including magnetic, by the 1890s. Clark & Sowden also issued Fish Pond in that decade, as did Milton Bradley and Parker Brothers. The designs proved successful enough, in some cases, to stay in production for decades.

Far from evoking the pond of farm or field, this fishing-hole toy was a four-sided cardboard box, open at the top, with sides high enough to prevent players from seeing inside. There, fish of cardboard or metal waited, with rings on their noses, to be hooked. The box's lithographed sides revealed the waters being fished and showed not pan-fish but more exotic creatures. The toys purposefully evoked the experience of being at the Crystal Palace, or other public display. A catalog in the early 1890s describes "Magnetic Fish Pond" as having "a tank or aquarium of cardboard. This is

When the pond is an ocean. Side views of the Fish Pond game, McLoughlin Bros., 1800s (author's collection).

covered on the outside with pictures representing fish swimming in water, as seen through the glass of an aquarium."[18] It offered, in other words, a game that evoked a scientific toy.

In the realm of dolls, any children who felt inspired to play deep-sea diver had only to take a toy figure and place a vase or glass over the head. Toymakers undoubtedly made some such toys in the 1890s. By at least 1900 *Le Scaphandrier*, or The Diver, appeared on shelves in France. A play set, it included a rowboat and a *"bateau sous-marin mécanique,"* or mechanical submarine. The diver's equipment included anchor, axe, and spherical, reinforced-glass helmet. When underwater he moved up and down by remote control, with the control-device being an air-filled bladder in the child's hand.[19]

That such sophisticated and expensive toys appeared in stores serves as a marker that simpler, less expensive toys must have appeared earlier, which themselves must have been anticipated by homemade versions. Newspaper stories probably prompted children to play in this manner and provided images for cut-outs. Among those acquainted with Verne's novel, some may have opted to play at being memory-bank Conseil—for he performs a brave act or two outside the taxonomic realm. More often, though, they would have play-acted Arronax, Ned Land, or the daunting Nemo.

Although they might have enacted scenes above the waves, the story's wonders occurred undersea. The act of "walking" there may have found evocation in the quite simple child's toy of the bubble pipe, or bubble wand. In these toys, the surface tension of soap allowed the creation of bubbles light enough to be suspended in air. Such play must have predated Fulton's *Nautilus*, since its ingredients had household origins—as in the old pipe that Captain Nutter brings downstairs for Tom Bailey to use for blowing soap-bubbles, in *The Story of a Bad Boy*, in an episode that may have taken place around 1850.[20]

If soap bubbles failed to go skyward in a breeze, a child's puffed cheeks could help. While it might have seemed unnecessary to create artificial puffed cheeks, Milton Bradley essentially did so, creating a toy that gave the bubbles the necessary lighter-than-air buoyancy to have more upward lift. Bradley's Patent Soap Bubble Toy offered not only that but the further spectacle of destruction: "With a bit of rubber tube applied to an ordinary gas burner, gas bubbles may be made which can be exploded to the great delight of the juveniles."[21]

To leave a gas-jet uncocked and unlit for play's sake must have seemed, to some, ridiculous. Yet Bradley simply exploited current household technics to their fullest; and that the bubbles might explode appealed to all ages.

Yet another ball—one of gas—conjoined a notion of play with the promise of violence.

The Neo-Gothic Maelstrom

The maelstrom tale made a significant and influential return the next year with the anonymously published *The Coming Race*. Written by Edward Bulwer, Lord Lytton, the 1871 novel combines utopian-tale and Modern-wonder-tale elements, and lodges them within the Gothic wonder-tale form.

Utopian elements include an educational tour of a superior society, and mock learning concerning nonexistent cultural elements, especially language. As often happens in utopian novels, the song of the idea dominates to the near exclusion of action. Its musical equivalent might be an opera whose arias nearly exclude recitatives. Although the utopian ideas include ones that inspire the little action that does transpire, their elevated tone lifts even the action away from the realm of the socio-technological satire, the dissected soul, and the marvelous machine.[22] And while a dream-journey takes place, the ending, as in other maelstrom tales, makes it evident that what has been revealed to the protagonist and the reader amounts to a nightmare, never to fully end. It is the "shadow on the floor" in Poe's "The Raven."

Lytton's Modern wonder-tale borrowings including subterranean dinosaur survivals and remote-controlled automata. The former have their nature stated nakedly. Such a passage as, "the vast reptiles, of some of which antediluvian relics are preserved in our museums, and certain gigantic winged creatures, half bird, half reptile,"[23] makes clear that the creatures are borrowings from older writings that conflated geological and Noachian points of view.

Some readers may take the evolutionary element, stated strongly by Lytton's title, as a distinctly Modern one—which offers us an opportunity to look again at what Verne did, in *A Journey*. There Verne created an underground realm having "extinct" beings living in remnant populations; he invoked Cuvier; and he tossed all geological evidence for a vast, Huttonian, and logical terrestrial history into a stewpot. He accepted the solar system's physical evolution, in Axel's cosmological vision, since astronomical understanding had longer pedigree. Axel witnesses a biological procession—which suggests that Verne accepted biological evolution's appearance, without granting it any more importance than would the average catastrophist: and with these ingredients, in his novel he paints a post-Noachian picture.

Lytton similarly presented an underground realm with remnant populations, and invoked not Cuvier but a popular Harvard professor known for his antagonism to Darwinian thought. Lytton makes his stance with regards to species by quoting Louis Agassiz as to a principle: "Upon it are based not only the higher manifestations of the mind, but the very permanence of the specific differences which characterize every organism. Most of the arguments in favour of the immortality of man apply equally to the permanency of this principle in other living beings."[24] As with the dinosaur description, this departs from Verne mainly in its stating the point of view so baldly. "The very permanence of the specific differences," as a statement, draws a firm line.

Lytton veers sharply from Verne's precedents in presenting the Vril-ya, who are the subterranean superhumans the novel's narrator meets. The Vril-ya represent an evolutionary step "forward" or "upward," as marked by their ability to wield a magical power called *vril* that is attuned to the nervous system, especially in Vril-ya women. The vril-power can heal or destroy; and by its means these superhumans direct their abundant automata, who perform menial tasks. The Vril-ya lodge this power in hand-held rods.

That the Vril-ya themselves represent an evolutionary step within a Providential context means that they represent the next Dispensation. Since they utterly lack remorse about destroying, via vril-power, any lower "race," and fully expect to destroy all those who live on Earth's surface, someday, it seems evident that they will replace humankind. The narrator's exposure to this knowledge is the maelstrom from which, at the end, he emerges. It damages his life and spirit permanently. He is "the guide" from Poe.

The Vril-ya themselves and their vril-power rods arrive as symbolic borrowings. Lytton adapted for his tale the supernatural beings of Faerie, with their wings, powers of flight, and magic; perhaps, too, he called forth those fairytale companions of theirs, who are burrowing and metallurgic. Fays or fairies, with powers beyond human ones, become, in *The Coming Race*, beings who represent the next stage in human catastrophic evolution. In other words, Lytton borrowed symbolic, folk-mythic figures to drape them in rationalist garb—in literary materialism. Moreover, he borrowed the fairytale wand, or perhaps the Promethean reed with its concealed fire, for the vril-power rods.[25]

In each case, the symbolic borrowing moves in a seemingly rational way through Lytton's story. Yet their new symbolic meanings outweigh their pseudo-scholastic bolsterings.

Two elements arrive as literal borrowings. First, among the Vril-ya, females engage in sport and travel by seemingly angelic means, when they strap on powerful, large wings. Vril-power allows them to fly with these, freely. At marriage, however, they give up flight, though they find it pleasurable, to devote themselves to spouse and household. Second, the Vril-ya thrive in their utopian fashion thanks to the labors of uncounted automata, again vril-powered.

These borrowings arrive from the ant colony. Among ants, the females wing aloft to establish colonies, only to dispense with wings on finding suitable locales and mates; and among ants, too, drones perform the endless tasks required in maintaining ant-society, guided by "instinct," a word almost as mysterious as "vril." Lytton, perhaps unconsciously, borrowed such elements to bolster the symbolic tale being told, of a totalitarian, genocidal future.

Verne had written, as his second, unpublished novel for Hetzel, a maelstrom tale which took place in the far future. In the twentieth century, business and industry have taken complete command over society. For those feeling any prognostic curiosity, in Verne's swiftly changing times, the maelstrom-tale, as a form, must have arisen naturally. Since humanistic values were falling victim to the capitalistic, the self-aggrandizing, and the authoritarian, any glance into the future left the artistic soul permanently damaged.

In *The Coming Race*, however, Lytton was writing in the Gothic tradition, at least somewhat consciously: for he was using mesmeric power for vril-power—which in an early draft allowed such marvels as communication with the dead.[26] For Lytton, the pseudo-scientific power and the dispensational superhumans must have nourished some sense that his tale's lineaments arrived from a magical realm, superior to mere human experience and knowledge. Its romantic element, which does turn the utopian novel into an emotional adventure by the final page, won it a wide readership; and it may well have been that the romance more than the maelstrom fears made the novel influential. Imitators would borrow the tale's trappings without always internalizing the cautionary element—if it was, indeed, meant as cautionary in this novel; they would imitate, too, its errors concerning evolution in species; and they would echo its turbulent logic of the superiority of power.

These elements, again, fell into dispensational terms. For while Verne's *Un Voyage* presents a post–Noachic universe, Lord Lytton's amounts to a pre–Noachic one. The rains have yet to arrive. The select few, with lightning in their fingers and with their ship ready to ride high above the drowning, inferior multitude, will bring on the Deluge.

Human civilization, in such a case, is itself the marvelous machine that must in the end face destruction—resulting not in the self-integration but the forced disintegration of the human soul.

Submergence

The political unrest that gave rise to Nemo's *Nautilus* echoed the state of Verne's world. Yet the novel's nods toward the fight against slavery suggest an idealistic point of view, on his part. A nationalistic one engendered by his country's political predicament might have seemed more natural. Since the anti-slavery element plays a structural role, and since Verne depicts Nemo in an ethnically ambiguous light, however, egalitarianism emerges as a palpable theme within the novel.

Other writers in these decades fell more readily into easily held and easily maintained racist positions, which had maelstrom force and effect upon them, especially when they allowed their imaginations to be shaped by Spencerian scientism. Evolutionism—not any particular theory of evolution, but the scientism that embraces the ancient concept—by the 1870s was beginning to exert a pernicious influence. Verne's continuing adherence to the fictional structure that he had devised may have made it inevitable that the egalitarian spirit would breathe itself into his novels. Yet he had arrived at his own Rousseau-esque vision, as well; and this vision must have provided more energies for his imagination than did any mechanistic reliance upon a fictional structure.

His submarine novel appeared against a backdrop of social crisis. Napoleon III had set himself against Prussia, in an ill-fated adventure that brought ignominious defeat to France and an end to Napoleonic dreams for empire. Worse, the Franco-Prussian war brought about the very situation France had hoped to prevent: for it unified the Prussian-German states. For France, the year 1871 came to signify her having lost the Alsatian province and part of Lorraine; and for her conquerors, to signify the German Empire's rise under Prussian domination, with Otto von Bismarck as chancellor, and William I as emperor, as proclaimed in Versailles. France's defeat opened a period of general, outward peace in Europe, which seemed an unusual and remarkable instance of sustained prosperity and cultural advancement. At the same time, the new empire's claim over Alsace would prove an irritant sufficient to undermine the apparent peace.

It dawned upon the West that international power structures had shifted, with France weakened and Germany now ranking among major powers. Bismarck, who had opposed annexing Alsace, soon would exhibit considerable prowess in making the peace lasting: yet in large degree, his policies, in leading his nation to victories over first Austria and then France, had set into motion a process that made the peace lastingly uneasy. He helped maintain stability for nearly twenty years—guiding to prominence an empire that felt ready and even eager, then, to shed his too-well balanced sensibility.

The situation fueled another story, an English one, also published in 1871, that describes England's fall to foreign rule. Although in no sense a Modern wonder tale, "The Battle of Dorking," set in the immediate future, dealt with New Worlds idealism and its consequences; and it decidedly influenced wonder-tale development. Appearing in *Blackwood's Magazine*, George T. Chesney's pared-down style, influenced by journalism, anticipated Kipling and Wells. The story made a stir with its horror-tale approach in depicting England as being lax and wanting in preparedness.[27]

The Franco-Prussian War had shown how quickly, in those ever-accelerating Modern times, new developments could disrupt long-lived international arrangements—in the span of months or weeks, or even days, thanks to hastened communications and travel; and thanks, too, to the factory-produced firearms that gave rise to mass-produced armies. However triumphant England might have felt on the seas, even in the wake of its mismanaged Crimean War, it stood among world powers no less vulnerable to massed technological attack than did France, its Crimean ally. Offering a dim window onto England's future, "The Battle of Dorking" went into pamphlet publication and inspired imitators for decades. Wells's *The War of the Worlds* ranks as only its most visible progeny, with its pedigree reflected in its narrator, its geography, and its fear of outsiders.

Chesney's tale planted a seed for a tradition counter to the one being offered by the Verneian wonder tale. Being set in the future only in political terms, and not up-to-date even in describing military technics, the story offers a horror-thriller. Yet it also offers another Maelstrom tale. Its common-citizen narrator witnesses the fall of his country, and emerges from the experience a changed, estranged man—with Chesney more likely having drawn upon Bulwer-Lytton's novel, than Poe's story, for a model.

The new Maelstrom tale would become the quasi-realistic tale of the future, in coming decades. After the Alsace-Lorraine annexation would bear its bitter fruit, the time would arrive, too, that the Maelstrom tale would prove itself so firmly entered into the Modern wonder-tale tradition that its pessimism, its New Worlds fatalism, would darken even children's stories.

Militarized Toy-Making

The new, expansively militaristic sense of the nation-state—the spirit in which Chesney's Maelstrom tale so deeply participates—had spread swiftly through the West, aided in no small part by the making of small toys in Germany.

Soldiery and the organizing of armies had offered an inspiration for toys in the days of chivalrous jousting and more sanguinary battles between city-states. At the dawn of the nation-state, in the 1600s, German toymakers proved themselves responsive to the times in creating, in substantial numbers, soldiers first in lead, then in tin. The latter proved themselves to be empire-builders, in at least the symbolic realm. In 1760 Andreas Hilpert of Nuremburg developed efficient methods for their production, and enjoyed good fortune in that his toys won favor from the thwarted artist who became king, Prussia's Frederick the Great. Frederick's smile prompted a craze for the toys that infected his immediate region and spread outwards to others.[28] While some toymakers produced these small, solid-cast figures in elaborate and expensive form, others made them simply and cheaply. These latter figures fell largely beneath adult notice, being no more than an inch and a third in height, a measurement that came to be called the Nuremburg scale. All the same, they enjoyed such immense popularity that, during the 1800s, they replaced the wooden toy soldier that had been traditionally made in many parts of Germany. By the early 1800s demand grew such that production spread from Nuremburg and across the nation. In the 1860s "hollow-cast" soldiers appeared: larger, more detailed figures cast from an equal amount, or less, of metal.[29]

Since they reflected a militaristic spirit undeniably present in the adult political world, the toys fostered the same in children; and they, in welcoming war into their play-worlds, grew up regarding war, weapons, and soldiery as having their places within normal experience. Children acquired this perspective despite the fact—or perhaps comfortably reinforced by the fact—that they were growing up in a period marked by scientific, political, and social advance, when prospects for war seemed slight, and when militarism seemed to result mainly in colorful parades.

Neither the open diplomacy nor the behind-scenes machinations of Bismarck, Delcassé, or other diplomats, who worked to avoid war, made appearances on the playroom floor. Only the soldiers did—as baubles that were as indistinguishable from one another as ants, and rendered further uniform in their massed movements. Those lead soldiers "in different uniforms and drills," as Stevenson said, helped mold children into dutiful citizens of their particular nation-state: for this new German toy-making tradition prevailed, to influence young minds across the Western hemisphere. After the U.S. Civil War, a wave of candy-making led, with a seemingly natural ease, to the popularity of sugar soldiers—a consequence that might not have occurred had not the Nuremburg initiative preceded it. By the 1860s and 1870s, matrons and nannies thought it only normal to hand a child, even the youngest, a toy soldier—one made by a confectionary art that perhaps should have yielded candies evocative only of sweetest existence.

However realistic or unrealistic these toys were, upon being produced and distributed they acquired a symbolic power that easily outlasted Bismarck's peace.

NINE

Fogg's Journey

Minds roll in paths like planets.—Oliver Wendell Holmes, in 1872.[1]

"The world is big enough."
"It was once," said Phileas Fogg, in a low tone.
..."What do you mean by 'once'? Has the world grown smaller?"
"Certainly," returned Ralph. "I agree with Mr. Fogg. The world *has* grown smaller, since a man can now go round it ten times more quickly than a hundred years ago."
—Jules Verne, in 1873.[2]

I see no great difference between a man and a watch, except that a man is conscious and a watch isn't, and the man tries to plan things and the watch doesn't. The watch doesn't wind itself and doesn't regulate itself—these things are done exteriorly. Outside influences, outside circumstances, wind the man and regulate him.
—Mark Twain, in 1906.[3]

The Human-Machine

In the years after creating his character Pittonaccio, Verne avoided presenting outwardly mechanical beings, for reasons likely similar to those that influenced the knowledge-cascades that appeared in his stories. They arose from an evident belief in the soul's ultimate freedom. For Verne, the human being, neither in its living fullness nor in its fictional incompleteness, could be a machine. The single human being and tripartite soul can express their identities only through their freedom. Prior to Verne's time, those who found the human-machine idea attractive had included La Mettrie, whose materialist writings forced him from France in 1746, then from Holland after publishing *L'Homme machine* in 1748—to find sanctuary, perhaps appropriately, in Frederick II's Prussia, the land of toy soldiers. Later in the 1700s, Baron d'Holbach, host to the encyclopedists, placed the human-machine notion in a context that blamed the Church for human degradation: "Man has been a mere machine in the hands of tyrants and priests"[4]—strikingly similar to David Brewster's later pointing to the "dark conspiracy" of the prince, the priest, and the sage. The Comte de Saint-Simon's thoughts may have found more favor with Verne. Having given positivism its name, Saint-Simon influenced the socialists who fostered the intellectual atmosphere Verne breathed in deeply, in his youth. Saint-Simon's vision of a society led by industrialists and scientists, but balanced with charity and a non-doctrinaire religion, fed into Verne's own; and his idea that positivism would be the instrument whereby human society would bring itself into balance and harmony recalled the action of a well-regulated timepiece. As Hobbes had maintained long before, society itself was the "artificial man."

One who regulates one's own life by the clock becomes to that degree automated, moreover; and the perfectly methodical person thus moves toward identity with the automaton. Following this chain of thought, Verne created a character who would rank among his most popular. This human-automaton appears in the work that, among his novels, captures most powerfully the New Worlds geographic vision, with no neglect to the mechanical one: *Le Tour du monde en quatre-vingt jours*, published in 1873, or *Around the World in Eighty Days*, as it appeared in English the next year.

Dickens, as earlier noted, prior to his Signal-Man had created a character submerged within a machine. Mr. Jarvis Lorry has surrendered his life completely to that which has encompassed all his adult life. The banking business, as a machine, has reduced him to its own likeness. In this machine of money, he leads an antlike existence. Lorry accepts the situation to such a degree that he takes a further step, and emulates for efficiency's sake even the machine's internal life. He introduces himself as "a man of business. ... don't heed me any more than if I was a speaking machine—truly, I am not much else. ... I have no feelings; I am a mere machine." He expands on this: "Feelings! I have no time for them, no chance of them. I pass my whole life ... in turning an immense pecuniary mangle." This "mere machine" engages in, with other humans, "only business relations."[5] Given the novel's popularity, and Verne's enthusiasm for Dickens, it seems quite possible that Lorry's existence helped make possible the character Phileas Fogg—a centrally important figure in the Modern wonder-tale's development, and perhaps the greatest fictional character by any novelist to utterly lack in character, in the traditional sense.

The Round-the-World Clock

In *Le Tour du monde*, a newly hired domestic servant comments on having seen people at Madame Tussaud's as lively as his new master.[6] In making himself familiar with his place of employment, he scrutinizes his surroundings:

> He suddenly observed, hung over the clock, a card which, upon inspection, proved to be a programme of the daily routine of the house. It comprised all that was required of the servant, from eight in the morning, exactly at which hour Phileas Fogg rose, till half-past eleven, when he left the house for the Reform Club,—all the details of service, the tea and toast at twenty-three minutes past eight, the shaving-water at thirty-seven minutes past nine, and the toilet at twenty minutes before ten. Everything was regulated and foreseen that was to be done from half-past eleven a.m. till midnight, the hour at which the methodical gentleman retired.
> Mr. Fogg's wardrobe was amply supplied and in the best taste. Each pair of trousers, coat, and vest bore a number, indicating the time of year and season at which they were in turn to be laid out for wearing; and the same system was applied to the master's shoes ....
> Having scrutinized the house from top to bottom, he rubbed his hands, a broad smile overspread his features, and he said, joyfully, "This is just what I wanted! Ah, we shall get on together, Mr. Fogg and I! What a domestic and regular gentleman! A real machine; well, I don't mind serving a machine."[7]

As do French-manufactured automata, Jean Passepartout's master maintains perfect composure:

Seen in the various phases of his daily life, he gave the idea of being perfectly well-balanced, as exactly regulated as a Leroy chronometer. Phileas Fogg was, indeed, exactitude personified, and this was betrayed even in the expression of his very hands and feet; for in men, as well as in animals, the limbs themselves are expressive of the passions.

He was so exact that he was never in a hurry, was always ready, and was economical alike of his steps and his motions. He never took one step too many, and always went to his destination by the shortest cut; he made no superfluous gestures, and was never seen to be moved or agitated. He was the most deliberate person in the world, yet always reached his destination at the exact moment.[8]

At the novel's onset, Fogg alters his daily, clocklike routine of customary activity in order to travel around the globe on a wager. The alteration in his routine proves circumstantial and not essential: for he remains the same being, regarded by his companions as, perhaps, eccentric—a term not outside the realm of time-marking regularity, given its meaning in astronomy—but still the self-contained man of the moment who concerns himself with regular habits, regular meals, and games of whist.

During the passage on the Red Sea aboard a steamer, the narrator notes Fogg's level of concern about his enormous wager.

It might be thought that, in his anxiety, he would be constantly watching the changes of the wind, the disorderly raging of the billows—every chance, in short, which might force the "Mongolia" to slacken her speed, and thus interrupt his journey. But if he thought of these possibilities, he did not betray the fact by any outward sign.

Always the same impassible member of the Reform Club, whom no incident could supervise, as unvarying as the ship's chronometers, and seldom having the curiosity even to go upon the deck, he passed through the memorable scenes of the Red Sea with cold indifference…[9]

The world in hand. Tin globes proliferated from the beginning to the end of the Modern century. The larger globe, 4½ inches across, is German, from the late 1930s or early 1940s. The smaller globe upon a stand, also German but probably older, is a pencil sharpener, as is the similarly-sized globe opposite it, made in Japan in the 1950s or 1960s. The smallest, about an inch across, is a penny toy, whose age and country of origin are unknown. Tin-lithographed globes (photograph by and collection of the author).

At Bombay, Fogg finds himself joined by a traveler who had been one of Fogg's whist partners earlier in the trip.

> Sir Francis Cromarty had observed the oddity of his travelling companion [...] and questioned himself whether a human heart really beat beneath this cold exterior, and whether Phileas Fogg had any sense of the beauties of nature. The brigadier-general was free to confess, that, of all the eccentric persons he had ever met, none was comparable to this product of the exact sciences.[10]

Fogg reveals his sympathetic and understanding nature by means of various acts, not least of which is the rescue of an Indian woman from a "suttee," or ritual death. Later in the journey he shows his solicitude toward her well-being, but otherwise seems unchanged from his former self:

> He visited her regularly each day at certain hours, not so much to talk himself as to sit and hear her talk. He treated her with the strictest politeness, but with the precision of an automaton, the movements of which had been arranged for this purpose.[11]

To allay Aouda's worries about her future, Fogg promises that all will be "mathematically arranged" on her behalf.[12]

Verne depicts Fogg in terms of celestial mechanics, that inspiration for the Western Deist and rationalist conceptions of the universe:

> ...Phileas Fogg moved about above them in the most majestic and unconscious indifference. He was passing methodically in his orbit around the world, regardless of the lesser stars which gravitated around him. Yet there was near by what the astronomers would call a disturbing star, which might have produced an agitation in the gentleman's heart. But no! the charms of Aouda failed to act, to Passepartout's great surprise; and the disturbances, if they existed, would have been more difficult to calculate than those of Uranus which led to the discovery of Neptune.[13]

The Whist-Player

With each new technical development, steam power created new and more convenient means for transport and communication. These led to new travel routes and interconnections that led, in turn, to new integrations in systems that were ever more far-reaching. Each stage in this process increased the distances being covered, relative to time. Improving speeds represented progress; regularizing existing systems into ever-greater conformity, likewise. Each stage, in other words, brought the world into greater alignment with a controlling clock. With high-speed mass travel being achieved by steam engines on a system of interconnected canals, fixed ocean routes, and railroads, the world was becoming an integrated system. The Earth, perceived by Poe to be a single, coherent organism, in "The Island of the Fay," was becoming not only a celestial but also a technical automaton.

The systems being created by Western society made the following statement not only believable but one to be taken for granted: "The distance between Suez and Aden is precisely thirteen hundred and ten miles, and the regulations of the company allow the steamers one hundred and thirty-eight hours in which to traverse it."[14]

Verne's *Around the World in Eighty Days* depended upon the vision, a factual one, of automation having become global in scope. "Eighty days" refers not only to the limits of a wager but to the measure of the Earth's girth in time-units. By this measure, the novel's characters see the world as "grown smaller."[15]

Again, in this work, Verne drew upon Poe. The novel involves a trip around the globe on a wager that Fogg apparently loses, by one day. In having traveled westward, however, Fogg has gained one. His valet Passepartout, discovering this, rushes to Fogg with news that the day is Saturday, not Sunday as they thought. Similarly, in Poe's 1841 story, "A Succession of Sundays," also published as "Three Sundays in a Week," confusion arises through the same conundrum of the world-clock. Poe's narrator is speaking to two captains, both of whom have been absent for a year, who have traveled in opposite directions around the globe. To one he says, "Captain Pratt, you must come and spend the evening with us to-morrow—you and Captain Smitherton—you can tell us all about your voyage, and we'll have a game of whist, and—" To this, Captain Pratt replies, "Whist, my dear fellow—you forget yourself. To-morrow will be Sunday. Some other evening—"[16]

Curiously, two years after Verne published his story of whist-playing Fogg, a new incarnation of the trick automaton exemplified by Chess-Player and Ajeeb made its debut. Maskelyne and Cooke in 1875 introduced at London's Egyptian Hall their Psycho, a whist-playing automaton.

In planning *Around the World*, Verne also may have been recalling Poe's "Belfry," which offers a similar picture of a well-regulated system being thrown into turmoil by a figure bent on mischief. In Verne's novel, detective Mr. Fix serves as the imp: for he believes Fogg, beneath his calm demeanor, to be a fleeing bank robber.[17]

Fogg's movements mesh with a world of clocks and watches. In common with the inhabitants of Vondervotteimitis, his valet Passepartout takes pride in his heirloom watch, which he keeps at Greenwich time even when far from that zone. Fogg gauges his travel by hours elapsed and hours available, and lives by ship and train timetables. As a timepiece himself, he circles Earth's clock-tower in his effort

Carriage-making techniques influenced this toy's manufacture, as reflected in the wheel hubs, and the cast-iron central bar and handle support. Note the spool pedals and "welded tires." These velocipedes came in sizes appropriate for boys from three to fifteen years old, in the 1880s. Although such toys fell under the velocipede name, their weight restricted velocity to the imagination, except on downhills. Imaginary qualities in Modern toys, however, were among their most important. "Velocipede" as a name would retain some currency into the 1950s. Photograph by J.B. Howard, Port Washington, Wisconsin, 1880s (author's collection).

to establish that the network of technologically achieved travel—of automated traveling—is in itself a clock: for he depends upon its regularity to such a degree that he has banked his fortune upon it.

Inaccurate timepieces pepper his adventures in various forms. Fogg's plans called for following a course announced as completed: yet when he arrives at a new railway, he finds something else: "It was but too true that the railway came to a termination at this point. The papers were like some watches, which have a way of getting too fast, and had been premature in their announcement of the completion of the line."[18] Fogg proves that he, too, can err, as a clock—and that he is not quite Jarvis Lorry.

> The guide now led the elephant out of the thicket, and leaped upon his neck. Just at the moment that he was about to urge Kiouni forward with a peculiar whistle, Mr. Fogg stopped him, and, turning to Sir Francis Cromarty, said, "Suppose we save this woman."
> "Save the woman, Mr. Fogg!"
> "I have yet twelve hours to spare; I can devote them to that."
> "Why, you are a man of heart!"
> "Sometimes," replied Phileas Fogg, quietly; "when I have the time."[19]

The detective Mr. Fix, even though mistaken about Fogg's guilt, proves correct in his efforts to throw Fogg off schedule. He proves, in other words, his Poesque-imp nature. For Fogg, once thrown in the position of believing he has lost everything, including perhaps his faith in the clock, finds personal happiness. From the clock's symbolic wreckage he emerges more fully integrated as a human soul. The heart within the impassive whist-player stands revealed, without mirrors or trick walls.

A concealed symbolism has made its presence known, in the tale's ending. Passepartout, who discovers the time-travel conundrum, is the equivalent to Kate who, in Poe's tale, brings the conundrum into play, and into focus, in order to win consent for a marriage. The valet's name, moreover, signifies one who "passes anywhere"—or that which is a "master key."

Round-the-Clock Toys

Establishing kindergartens in America created a need for "equipment," including art materials, writing implements, and playthings. Being interested in the movement and also situated near Elizabeth Peabody's Boston school, Milton Bradley undertook to manufacture items expressly for kindergartens, however small a market it was. In 1872 he released his Kinder-Garten Alphabet and Building Blocks, and gradually added other items of school equipment, including a line designed for Sunday schools.[20] As the movement gained ground in the middle 1870s, E. Steiger of New York City became a major source for kindergarten materials and books, perhaps distributing Bradley's line. Increasing concern about the safety of materials being used in toys for young children tended, too, to boost the kindergarten movement. At the Centennial Exposition, "infant schools and kindergartens" fell under the "Education and Science" heading; and the organizers built a structure to be the Exposition's kindergarten.[21]

Around 1885, Bradley introduced an educational device that would become a standard in schools through the remaining Modern-century years.[22] The Toy Clock Dial, in common with Pennsylvania tin locomotives, offered a nonworking toy version of an automaton: a wall-clock's face, with movable dials. It served to help teach children to "read" clocks without waiting for the actual time to change. Being inexpensive, children could also play with them unsupervised. Playing with time, in other words, was becoming common among children, in conjunction with the idea that children could have a set "playtime." The clock, through the kindergarten, was also acquiring a moral dimension, as in the nursery rhyme:

> And may we, like the clock,
> Keep a face clean and bright,
> With hands ever ready,
> to do what is right.

This incursion by clock-time into childhood had significance both practical and symbolic. Dreaming and childhood play had in common the fact that they easily escaped the realm of regularized time, sometimes even day- and nighttime. Fiction shared this trait, with its foreshortening, magnifying, or utter disregard of time. In the Modern wonder tale the trait gained definition. The twelve-hour clock strikes thirteen; the clocks aboard the *Nautilus* stop; the hours breathe faint and low; and for one who is Rip-van-Winkelized, to use Elizabeth Burgoyne Corbett's coinage, even the years disappear. Schooling, however, did what it could to end childhood by inculcating the understanding that life is business. In arithmetic, decimal problems appeared with dollar signs; fraction problems appeared from a shopkeeper's perspective. Teachers had their youngest pupils counting apples, with little talk about what else might be done with such fruit. With Bradley's innovation, children with more uniformity of knowledge could gaze upon the actual schoolroom clock, once that device became commonplace; and they could see, in common, what business they should about, at each hour. With even the play-hour becoming determined, it became inevitable that play should become guided play. Play was acquiring a fixity about it, distancing it further from dreams. Once children firmly acquired, in America, the apothegm about time being money, the doors began shutting on playing and dreaming; and, as Henry Adams observed, "The world, after 1865, became a banker's world."[23] The children in sweatshops long had understood this, in having learned what ten, eleven, or more hours of work meant; they knew to within a tick of the clock exactly how business and industry regarded childhood. The more privileged, who would spend more years in their schoolrooms, moved a step nearer their less fortunate fellows' precocity in this matter, with their being given Bradley's innovation for kindergartens—and with their accepting that word "playtime," a term whose nebulous and undefined nature was being reduced into a universally accepted oxymoron.

Insofar as they helped free the child's mind from "the business of a day," however, toys helped guard children from time's incursions, and helped them develop the resources that would help them grasp and possess the "inner life," the "truly human world." Toys in this manner performed much the same beneficial role that fairytales did.

Dickens, as noted earlier, engaged in what we might call a thought-experiment, in creating that grim Smallweed family in *Bleak House*: "the house of Smallweed ... has strengthened itself in its practical character, has discarded all amusements, discountenanced all story-books, fairy tales, fictions, and fables, and banished all levities whatsoever." In this household, time is money. When the aged Mr. Smallweed says, "Ten minutes," feeble-minded Mrs. Smallweed screeches out what she hears, or at least understands: "Ten ten-pound notes!" Their grandchildren, now young adults and wards of the Smallweeds, have been raised in miserly fashion: "Judy never owned a doll, never heard of Cinderella, never played at any game.... It is very doubtful whether Judy knows how to laugh.... And her twin-brother couldn't wind up a top for his life. He knows no more of Jack the Giant Killer, or of Sinbad the Sailor, than he knows of the people in the stars. He could as soon play at leap-frog, or at cricket, as change into a cricket or a frog himself."[24]

Judy, who has risen from this childhood with a particularly unpleasant streak, does go into the world to find a trade, for a time—making artificial flowers. The irony requires a note, in order to be understood in our time: the note that artificial flowers, as fancy-goods, were toys.

Sky Clippers

"As an ingenious writer of thrilling adventures Jules Verne has no equal," *Youth's Companion* noted in 1887. "He takes his readers with resistless force on the most improbable of journeys. Your mind is filled with thoughts never dreamed before; but all along the way you gather up from his 'Wonderlands' thousands of facts in Science, Natural History and Geography, and so these, as all good books ought, both entertain and instruct. They are charming reading."

Since *Youth's Companion* depended upon its readers to serve as its subscription agents, its premiums reflect society's perceptions of what youths most desired. Those who obtained one new subscriber might choose, for their reward, an instant Verne library containing *Mysterious Island*, *20,000 Leagues Under the Sea*, and *Tour of the World in 80 Days*; or they might choose a single volume, Verne's *Michael Strogoff, The Courier of the Czar*, described as "wonderfully interesting, weird and dramatic."[25] Those who preferred activities over books could choose from philosophical devices including compound microscopes, telescopes, electro-magnetic batteries, photographic outfits, or the Cabinet of Chemical Wonders; mechanical toys including the Vulcan clockwork locomotive, the "Ideal" Magic Lantern and Polyopticon, or a steam engine; or various items for daily use and convenience, such as Griffin's Automatic Rug Machine, Excelsior Self-Inking Press, or Mechanical Organette, an "automatic musical instrument." To obtain any item required energy, dedication, and directed effort—which for many children came to hand more readily than money.

At the time, those who could afford new novels might have picked Verne's 1886 *Robur le Conquérant*, which appeared in English in 1887 as *The Clipper of the Clouds*. Published fifteen years after *Five Weeks in a Balloon*, a scene in *Clipper* makes clear that a lighter-than-air craft still provided spectacle, if to a waning degree.

> We need not stop to describe the excitement, the unaccountable movements, the sudden pushings, which made the mass heave and swell. Nor need we recount the number of cheers which rose from all sides like fireworks when Uncle Prudent and Phil Evans appeared on the platform and hoisted the American colours. Need we say that the majority of the crowd had come from afar not so much to see the *Goahead* as to gaze on these extraordinary men?
> ..."Let's go!" shouted Uncle Prudent; and the *Goahead* rose "majestically"—an adverb consecrated by custom to all aerostatic ascents.[26]

The balloon, named *Goahead*, bears essentially the same name as the tin locomotive, *Progress*. All the same, a second and greater spectacle impresses the crowd that she is rather the *Gonebehind*. Engineer-hero Robur appears to argue that "the future of aerial navigation ... belongs to the aeronef and not the aerostat" and that "the future is for the flying-machine.... There is no progress for your aerostats, my citizen balloonists; progress, is for flying machines. The bird flies, and he is not a balloon, he is a piece of mechanism!" In "the conquest of space by mechanical means," Robur is ascending a new ladder of progress, the rungs of which appear in a Miltonic knowledge-cascade, with Robur himself at the top.[27] His aeronef *Albatross* takes a nautical appearance:

> The Albatross might be called a clipper with thirty-seven masts. But these masts instead of sails bore each two horizontal screws, not very large in spread or diameter, but driven at prodigious speed. ... In fact, the vessel combined the systems of Cossus, La Landelle, and Ponton d'Amécourt, as perfected by Robur. ... Robur had not availed himself of the vapour of water or other liquids, nor compressed air and other elastic gases, nor explosive mixtures capable of producing mechanical motion. He employed electricity, that agent which one day will be the soul of the industrial world.[28]

A craft of lightness and world-conquering speed,

> the Albatross, at full speed, could do her hundred and twenty miles an hour, or 176 feet per second. This speed is that of the storm which tears up trees by the roots. ... In a word, as Robur had said, the Albatross, by using the whole force of her screws, could make the tour of the globe in two hundred hours, or less than eight days.[29]

This literal appropriation of the ocean-going vessel had particular power and longevity. As late as 1913, a boys' novel would refer to a swift airship, named *Wondership*, as a "sky clipper."[30]

Robur's adventures reflect the dream of the aeronef going hand-in-hand with the dream of making geographical boundaries irrelevant to human ambition, and that of rendering political boundaries meaningless. Whereas circumstances had forced Phileas Fogg to rely upon, in a long sequence, a variety of means for up-to-the-minute transportation, Robur makes manifest the same spirit without recourse to any means for transport but his own. The whirling watch-dials become the whirling propeller props that move *Albatross* around the Earth-clock.

Where Fogg is the Everyman submerged within an automated system, Robur is the brilliant, ambitious, and problematic superhuman, the Nemo who takes his system to the skies, the Edisonian intellect unhampered by the heart in wielding corporate power. As Verne made clear in his title, Robur is the conqueror—in a world that seemed to be renewing its call for conquest.

Round-the-World Games

The fact that tours around the world were becoming a possibility for individuals, rather than merely a subject for fancy, did little to dull the romance in the idea. Despite later novels, *Around the World in Eighty Days* remained the world's touchstone—it having won readers around the world, as seemed only fitting. Its example inspired a New York journalist to become, herself, a circumglobal traveler. Taking the name of an 1882 operetta character,[31] Nelly Bly toured the world in 1890 and became a celebrity even among the young, who played "Round the World with Nellie Bly—a novel and fascinating game with plenty of excitement on land and sea," which McLoughlin Brothers released to coincide with her travels. That circumglobal travel and Modern communications were closely allied appeared on the box, which showed "Nellie Bly" standing on a road situated between two wire-laden telegraph poles. Not to be left behind, Bradley also in 1890 issued a Round the World game; Parker Brothers followed in 1891 with Round the World Joe. The Bradley game-box showed an idealized globe nestled unrealistically among clouds—with a steam train, in relative terms an immense one, approaching the viewer from around the globe's edge.[32] The Earth, as a globe nestled among billowy clouds, was gaining popularity as an image, and would be embraced as an emblem by the World's Columbian Exposition only two years later.[33] The globe-encircling train, too, was becoming a fixed, popular image:

> He saw an iron dragon dashing forth
> On pathways East and West and South and North,
> Its bonds uniting in beneficent girth
> Remotest ends of earth.[34]

Nelly Bly became a heroine in Fogg's tradition. Unlike earlier circumnavigators, whether historical Cook or fictional Nemo, Bly went as passenger, and not captain, engineer, or crew member. Such machinery for travel now existed that she could move from her starting point to her identical ending point without stepping "outside" it; and in emulating Fogg's journey she consigned herself to existing within its schedule. The true actor in the process, the machinery itself, achieved the actual circumnavigation. By traveling in this way, encompassed by the machinery that encompassed earth, Bly became the Everywoman—or the Everyone. Parker Brothers expressed this sense of the new world traveler in their long-lived version of the game, in which no famous person circles the globe, but ordinary Joe.[35] In a sense, these travelers followed in the footsteps of Omai, that first Tahitian who, it might be said, discovered England; for Omai lacked control over his fate except insofar as he expressed his willingness to go, via a mechanism of travel that had been imposed upon his world.

The Nelly Bly phenomenon altered the West's perception of the tour around the globe. The sense that such tours had become a game—an amusing one, not a serious one like whist—threatened whatever romance remained in the notion. As had the tin spinning-tops lithographed to be little Earths, McLoughlin and others were helping reduce the planet to a toy. Verne's novels make clear the change occurring. A mere six years after technician anti-hero Robur appeared on the page, a minor character named Weissschnitzeldorfer arrived in 1892's *Claudius Bombarnac*. This German traveler aims to tour the world in thirty-nine days, and provides amusement of the pratfall variety. Verne refers to him at one point as "Monsieur le Baron Tour de Monde."

The round-the-world theme must have played a part, too, in the countless and miscellaneous travel games issued in the 1890s and 1900s, while remaining the main focus elsewhere, as in Parker Brothers' Wide World and a Journey Round It of 1896. Bradley reissued Round the World in a new 1910 version, with competition coming from overseas in the form of A Journey Round the World, an English-language game made in Bavaria. Bradley then released its Game of Voyage Round the World in the 1920s, followed again by a new version in the 1930s. It also reissued the original round-the-world game for the new century, publishing a 1920 edition of Around the World with Nellie Bly.[36] McLaughlin by this time had become a Bradley imprint. All-Fair, another prominent American game-maker, issued The World Flyers Around the World Flight Air Face game in 1927.

Bradley, who had mined the idea most deeply, in 1936 issued a new Around the World: for the phrase "round the world" had shifted back toward "around the world" during the 1910s and 1920s.

Among these games, some continued to present the Earth's globe with oversized vehicles seeming to circle it, pointing toward the "Swirl of Progress" around the Earth in the image used as an emblem by Chicago's Century of Progress Exposition of the 1930s.

The Game of the Clock

Bradley's Toy Clock Dial appeared when American toy-making was coming of age. As Marshall and Inez McClintock observed, "Toys really came into their own by 1885, when Ward's pictured several varieties of roller skates, toy hatchets, sadirons, banks, marbles, toy scales, tool chests, magic lanterns, bell ringers, steam engines with accessories, tin boats, iron stoves with utensils, steamboats, and numerous tin wagons and horses."[37] Such mail-order companies as Ward's, founded in 1872 and advertising toys by 1877, depended upon mass-produced goods in unending supply. Adding to pressure for large production numbers, the "toy department" now occupied floor space in department stores, a practice having begun in 1875 with Macy's.[38] An early marbles-maker, Samuel C. Dyke of South Akron, Ohio, established his business around this time, and to meet demand produced up to thirty thousand clay marbles per day.[39] When Charles M. Crandall's wooden Acrobats became a hit in 1874, he claimed in advertising that he daily shipped out 1,500 boxes. By the 1880s, sales in excess of a hundred thousand units for a single toy were being seen by Ives. Leo Schlesinger Co. of New York City, founded in the same year as Ward's, issued six million tin horses per year from 1875 to 1880. Its line included many mechanical toys.[40] Even the most complex playthings fell subject to mass-production. In effect, every new successful toy created the public sensation of the balloon or the ocean-liner launch, in terms of numbers. Yet each one did so invisibly, since the machinery for distribution spread the spectacle across cities, whole countries, or the world.

Games and toys involving circumglobal travel, clocks, instantaneous communication, and steam power may now seem rarities, to our contemporary perspective. All the same, upon their release they received the same treatment as Dyke's marbles or Crandall's circus figures; and however fleeting their ubiquity may have been, for a time they ranked not as extraordinary productions of their time, but as typical ones, available everywhere.

Although they generated wonder, the wonder itself had become commonplace.

Shades of the Past

Poe's "Three Sundays" exemplifies his ratiocinative approach in a relatively pure form. Lacking the psyche that manifests in other Poe narratives, it moves forward by analyzing and unravelling a seemingly irrational situation. In essence, the story engages in literary play, making a game of the clock, the calendar, and earth's technically induced shrinkage; and through this play it arrives at the surprising result: for his nautical travelers find they have become time-travelers, thanks to advanced maritime technics. One has lost a day, while another has gained one. One, in other words, has moved backwards in time relative to his starting point, while the other has advanced.[41] The one who has remained at home, naturally, is symbolically the reader.

As Earth spins only one direction, so the clock winds down by going forward. Poe's Captain Pratt and Verne's Fogg, who move in space forward to move in time backward, introduce this paradox within what must have been among the first tales to concern themselves with literal, not symbolic, time travel.[42] Symbolic time travel long had existed, in fairy tales especially. Truncations, reversals, and jumps through time occur as a matter of storytelling technique; and they occur in a way almost invisible to auditors or readers. Yet natural philosophers had already perceived that the simultaneity of disjunct "times" has factual basis. Any gaze into the night sky takes in light that represents past times, which otherwise we might have thought lost to us; and a glimpse through a telescope, even a cheaply made toy version, penetrates yet deeper and offers, in the words of John Herschel, "shades of the Past."[43] Any light reveals the factual; and any light from the sky reveals the factual that was, and no longer is. This provides the basis for Poe's *jeu d'esprit* in his "The Thousand-and-Second Tale of Scheherazade," in 1844:

> But the whole nation is, indeed, of so surprising a necromantic ability, that not even their infants, nor their commonest cats and dogs have any difficulty in seeing objects that do not exist at all, or that for twenty thousands years before the birth of the nation itself, had been blotted out from the face of creation.[44]

Poe's three-Sundays story seems to have been the first, or at least first influential, story to turn upon a distorting effect created by a spinning globe. It presented the distorting of time, and the distorting of the time-perception, with the backdrop being the Puritan measure of the week that prohibits whist-playing on the Sabbath.

Had Bradley been making his kindergarten clock-toys decades earlier, canny children might have turned the dials freely, after reading Poe's story; and they might have antagonized their "time-telling" teachers by saying, "This is the time right now—somewhere else." On a symbolic clock, all clock-times might now exist as one.

Ten

Later Automata and Shrunken Globes

He professed the religion of World's Fairs, without which he held education to be a blind impossibility.
— Henry Adams, in 1906.[1]

If Rondaine had been famed for anything at all, it would have been for the number of its clocks. It had many churches … and in the steeple of each of these churches there was a clock. There were town buildings, very old ones, which stood upon the great central square. Each of these had a tower, and in each tower was a clock. Then there were clocks at street corners, and two clocks in the market-place, and clocks over shop doors, a clock at each end of the bridge, and several large clocks a little way out of town. Many of these clocks were fashioned in some quaint and curious way. In one of the largest a stone man came out and struck the hours with a stone hammer, while a stone woman struck the half hours with a stone broom; and in another an iron donkey kicked the hours on a bell behind him. It would be impossible to tell all the odd ways in which the clocks of Rondaine struck; but in one respect they were all alike: they all did strike. The good people of the town would not have tolerated a clock which did not strike.
— Frank R. Stockton, in 1892.[2]

Machinery Hall

Verne noted in Americans "their instinct for the 'big,' their admiration for the 'enormous,'" and imagined its industrial magnates creating an artificial, electrically powered, propeller-driven island with "an area of about twenty-seven million square yards. Of oval form, it measured about four and a half miles long and three broad, and its circuit was about eleven miles." The island has agricultural areas, roads, a moving sidewalk, and a capital, Milliard City, built with artificial stones, glass brick, and aluminum, the "metal of the future."[3] For contemporary readers, Standard Island evoked the juggernaut Standard Oil, and perhaps the new American economy that was siphoning money from the many to the few.[4]

Verne notes this "instinct" again in a short story published in 1875, four years after *Une Ville flottante*. "An Ideal City" relates a sleep-journey to a future France. Toward its end, the "sleeper" attends a "competition" that combines elements from the country fair and the industrial exhibition.

> Then on all sides there were machines of American origin, carried to the last extremes of progress. One was given a live pig, and out of it came two hams, one York and one Westphalian! To another was offered a rabbit, still quivering, and it produced a silk hat! This one absorbed an ordinary fleece and ejected a complete suit of clothes in the best style! That one devoured a three-year-old calf and reproduced it in the twofold form of a smoking blanquette of veal and a pair of newly polished shoes! And so on and so forth.[5]

The next year—the year that a new "great clock" was installed in England's Crystal Palace[6]—Philadelphia honored the United States by celebrating the gigantic and the automatic. To mount the Centennial Exhibition cost five times as much as had the Great, even though the city provided its Fairmount Park site at no cost. That the main hall covered 870,464 square feet made it the largest structure in the world.[7] Gigantism continued in Machinery Hall, covering 504,720 square feet. Its paired steam engines, designed by George Corliss and set in motion on opening day by President Grant and the Emperor of Brazil, stood four stories tall.[8] Its myriad exhibits included the massive rotary presses that were transforming both publishing and reading habits, electroplating, Thomas Edison's "automatic telegraph," and the "speaking telephone" just patented by Boston speech professor Alexander Graham Bell. Automatism filled not only Machinery Hall but elsewhere at the fair. Such everyday items as the "Paragon and automatic umbrella" of E. Charageat, Paris, brought "automatic" to countless lips, countless times, among the thousands viewing displays by the thousands. Entire buildings rose to celebrate specific automatic machines, as did the Singer's Sewing Machines building; and the Automatic Railway provided a popular attraction.[9] Everywhere, moreover, appeared materials and wares produced by automated means, with their mass-produced nature being touted as a selling point—all reflecting the growing interest in all things "artificial."[10]

American Automata at the Centennial

Ives, Blakeslee & Co., as earlier noted, exhibited automatic toys, as did Ives's neighbor James B. Secor, whose "automaton singing birds in cages and vases" included his American Songster.[11] Rather than being grouped with automata and other toys, Secor's appeared among musical instruments, where they won a gold medal. By this time his main business seems to have been in gun and sewing-machine tools, as well as dies. Yet in 1880 he would patent a toy locomotive and a toy pistol, and, being inventive in machining, would devise more elaborate automata, including a mechanical piano player. He would afterwards sell his business to Ives.[12]

Another Connecticut exhibit featured a range of toys that suggested a background comparable to Brown's: W.C. Goodwin, of New Haven, offered "hot-air toys, guns, games, novelties, recording banks."[13]

Connecticut's strength in making automata, whether they were fancily realistic or fanciful, developed naturally alongside other strengths. Ansonia, for instance, possessed both clockmaking and clock-trimming businesses, such as Phelps & Bartholomew, who supplied movements for clocks and toys.[14] To the north of it, Waterbury offered another clockmaking center; and, yet farther north, Thomaston yet one more, with Seth Thomas among its businesses. In the northwest corner, in the Litchfield Hills, sat Winchester, again a center for making clocks and clock trimmings; and Meriden sat on the rail line traveling south from New Britain to New Haven, on the state's southern coastal border. That none from among the many skilled workers in these towns and cities should have created diversionary automata, either to accompany clocks or to stand apart, seems impossible.

From other regions, firms exhibiting self-acting toys at the Centennial included New York City firms Althof, Bergmann & Company, and American Mechanical Toy Company, both of whom displayed "tin and mechanical toys." G.L. Wild & Brother of Washington, D.C., exhibited its "musical dancing toy attachment for piano." An item between household item and toy, the "Fly fan moved by clockwork," appeared in Philadelphia's Fowler Fly Fan Co. display.[15]

The Exposition opened many eyes as to technical developments in diverse areas. Even so, that automata were appearing in such quantities must have made an impression, especially since American companies were competing with overseas ones for attention. Among French "Scientific and Musical Instruments," visitors could

Boy with locomotive. Photograph postcard, 1800s (author's collection).

admire the "clocks, watches, musical boxes, and singing bird" of B. Haas, Jr., & Co. The "mechanical piano" by Debain & Co., the "automatic musical instruments" of C. Gavioli, and the "mechanical harmoniums" of Morand & Tourneur, also appeared.[16] Among the exhibits of toys and dolls, "singing and moving birds" performed at the booth of B. Bontems, while "mechanical toys" appeared in demonstrations at the booth of Truffy.[17]

The full range of displays from the world's toy-making capitol, Nuremburg, remains a matter for conjecture, since many manufacturers appeared in the "Bavarian Collective Exhibit of Toys and Small Wares." Barth & Wagner, based in Rodach near Coburg, however, did bring mechanical toys. The "Collective Exhibit of the Black Forest Clock Manufacturers," too, would have featured automata.[18] Similarly, Swiss watch and clockmakers brought automata, such as "musical boxes," some doubtless having more than casual complexity.[19]

In the Centennial's wake, automation became more common among inexpensive playthings, even among traditionally simpler wooden toys. Morton E. Converse, who founded his toy company in 1878 in Winchendon, Massachusetts, by 1885 was advertising itself as "the first and only concern applying self-acting power to wood toys." Powered by twisted rubber cords, these included Electrical Car. This wooden trolley car had "Edison" on the conductor's booth and "Menlo Park and Berlin" on the roof's signboard. Its child-high "Fandango, or Doll's Swing" featured four brackets that rotated around a horizontal axis, with toy birds attached to two, and with doll swings suspended from the others. Dolls could ride circles up and down in the air without being thrown off.[20]

Aerostatic Articles and Time Globes

In 1876, at a time when other hot-air toys, mainly automata, were popular, fire balloons, too, continued in popularity across the industrialized nations, as seems evident from Centennial Exposition records: for Adalbert Hawsky of Leipzig exhibited "paper balloons" as his sole attraction, while Brodin *fils* of Paris displayed the French equivalent, with his "aerostatic articles." In Machinery Hall, meanwhile, a separate display class centered on "Balloons, flying machines, etc."—a likely area for fairgoers to have found promotional aerial playthings.[21]

Even if it might remain in doubt whether American companies, too, offered balloons in the 1870s, by the 1880s Crandall offered a set of aerial toys that included two kites and a Montgolfier Balloon, an impressive item made from bright paper, measuring six feet around—probably the culmination in a line of toys, rather than a sophomore effort.[22] Balloons as an image associated with playthings continued to provide excitement, partly due to their continuing rarity in daily life; and they came in for both literal and symbolic use. The Parker Brothers' The Game of Speculation of the 1890s, for instance, would feature a high-soaring balloon on its cover.[23]

As with automata, which represented the mechanical New World, diverse attractions reflected a still-deepening interest in the geographical vision. In itself a gathering place for nations, the Centennial followed the intentions reflected in fairs since the Great, and dedicated one department to Earth's being reduced to abstraction: "Botanical, agronomical, and other maps, showing the extent and distribution of men, animals, and terrestrial products. Physical maps. Meteorological maps and bulletins. Telegraphic routes and stations. Railway and route maps. Terrestrial and celestial globes. Relief maps and models of portions of the earth's surface. Profiles of ocean beds and routes of submarine cables."[24] Among American-made "Scientific and Philosophical Instruments" visitors found the "terrestrial and celestial planisphere globe" of Paul Kuhnel of New York City, atlases by S.A. Mitchell of Philadelphia, "terrestrial and celestial globes" by Joseph Schedler of Jersey City Heights, New Jersey, and globes and maps by A.H. Andrews & Co., Chicago. Ernst Schotte & Co. of Berlin likewise showed globes, as did Eloffe & Co. of Paris. Visitors also found "movable planispheres of the heavens," with the planisphere being an "astronomical indicator," displayed by Henry Whitall of Philadelphia; and the "terrestrial orrery," by N.M. Lowe, of Boston.[25]

Similar emphases appeared among U.S. watchmakers, with L.P. Juvet of Glen's Falls, New York, offering a Time Globe. Others offered the "astronomical tower clock," "astronomical clock," "Solar chronometer" and "Lunar clock." One "illuminated clock" bore the name Phantasmagoria.[26]

A major fad in the 1870s took a considerably more mechanical turn than had the one that seized America ten years before the Centennial. In 1866, the nation had embraced the lawn game of croquet. In the late 1870s and into the 1880s bicycling became a nearly compulsory diversion. As with croquet, it attracted people young and old, with riding clubs springing up in the cities. Even the statesmanlike Henry Adams would learn to ride, "solemnly and painfully."[27]

The dream of long-distance communication inspired several to promote new approaches. Besides Bell, Samuel S. White of Philadelphia and Elisha Gray of Chicago, among others, displayed versions of the "electro-harmonic telegraph." William B. Watkins of New York City offered the "automatic fire and burglar telegraph and fire extinguisher," but saw ample competition from fellow Americans in the "burglar telegraph" and what another company called an "automatic thermostat for fire alarm telegraph." Other offerings included the "automatic and duplex telegraphic apparatus" of Atlantic & Pacific Telegraph Co. and the "computing telegraph" of Lockwood, Brooks, & Co. of Boston. A range of products—"Roman letter, etheric, domestic, automatic, and quadruplex telegraph; electromotograph, doubler, and electric pen"—appeared courtesy Edison of Newark.[28]

Other electrical innovations soon would issue from Edison's new research center in Menlo Park. The illusion that single-handedly he was lifting an industry would lead the public to regard him in heroic terms, and as superhuman: the corporate power that appears to be an individual. Never to be dubbed the Electric Man of Newark—the Steam Man of Newark having been forgotten, no doubt—Edison exerted power enough with his own name to begin making appearances in wonder tales.

The Shrinking Political Planet

The Centennial showed that the globe was growing smaller in political terms, insofar as the industrial nations' displays did reflect the "stupendous movement, without parallel in history," as historian Geoffrey Barraclough termed it.[29] Having begun in France and Germany, a new wave of nationalistic colonizing efforts was spreading to Russia, the United States, and England. In the new industrial climate, the strategy was carrying the day that national growth and power would result from acquiring colonies. Colonies first might supply foodstuff and raw goods for production, to then become markets for manufactured goods. The "scramble for colonies" that escalated in the nineteenth century's final quarter would result, by 1900, in European powers controlling one-fifth the planet's land area.[30]

From industrialized societies, technically advanced forces were spreading out to encompass and transform distant locales, while paying little or no respect to indigenous people or their tradition-based institutions. For colonizers, as for the colonized, living conditions were changing rapidly, and in fundamental ways. New powers were arising in the world, as were new tensions and new diplomatic centers of gravity. By late in the nineteenth century it became evident that the revolution in Europe had become a world revolution, and that in no sphere—cultural, technological, political, or scientific—could its impetus be checked or restrained, thanks to the intoxicating wealth being gained through expansive colonization, and through remotely controlled subjugation, enslavement, and pillage.[31]

The boundary-erasing and globe-encompassing spirit had a nationalistic cast that was, in its nature, technological as well as economic: for governmental ministries readily absorbed and accepted what advancing powers in travel and communication implied. Technical experimentation, long considered a possible object for government sponsorship and control, became a necessary object, so that in the later 1800s the balance tilted toward national interests over private ones. By the 1870s, for instance, serious experiments in dirigible balloons were taking place in several countries. Significant successes came in France, however, only after the French War Department took over development efforts in the 1880s. Although similar advances were taking place in Germany, they lagged until Count Ferdinand von Zeppelin began his official work in 1897.

The possibility grew larger, in many imaginations, that Earth's patchwork of cultures might fall within an interconnected whole. Efforts toward a comprehensive network had begun during the globe-spanning days of galleons and clippers, making it a relatively natural symbolic leap—a literal appropriation—that Tennyson made in 1842, to imagine "the heavens fill with commerce, argosies of magic sails," as well as "the nations' airy navies grappling in the central blue." After 1859 that comprehensive network's becoming reality seemed increasingly in view, with the laying of intercontinental cables permitting rapid communication between points distant—especially after automated telegraphy and telephony appeared in the 1870s and 1880s. By 1886 Tennyson was tapping into a common dream, not a personal one, in reflecting doubtfully upon "Earth at last a warless world, a single race, a single tongue."[32]

Even the ironically named microphone, a direct outgrowth from telephony, expressed the "magic of size," and was changing politics by remaking local rallies into spectacles of mass-address that were carried by integrated electrical systems to those at a remove. New powers for magnifying and amplifying, wielded by the privileged, went hand-in-hand with the world's size-reduction. As the centralized speaker's volume grew, the listeners became greater in number, and thus individually smaller—Tennyson's "insects of the hour." For the privileged, the world's general population shrank in importance with each advance in Western self-aggrandizement.

These elements—nationalism, colonizing, all-encompassing communication, technical magnification and amplification, and geographical shrinkage—created pitfalls for creative souls alongside opportunities. As the world's shrinkage became pronounced in the political sphere, the overtly negative aspects yielded by New Worlds idealism, including militant nationalism, social Darwinism, colonialism, racism, eugenics, and mass enslavement, loomed larger.

Since Modern wonder tales dealt with sectional and stock characters, as opposed to complete, realistic, or type characters, these negative elements were finding representation in stock roles and situations, sometimes to be accepted by readers as positive embodiments rather than as forms born from satirical or critical approaches. The characters in melodrama appear with some or all their aspects magnified, since those aspects are relatively few in number; and in this magnification of simplification lay a danger for the literary form uniquely able to grapple with issues surrounding techno-cultural change. While Verne's fictional structure had humanism built into its underpinnings, his tendency to use stock characters gave rise to risk-taking even in humorous portrayal of national types. When his stock characters appeared against the backdrop of worlds markedly shrunken from the norm, the risks that he took grew all the greater.

While we may consider *Around the World* a world-shrinkage novel, and *Twenty Thousand Leagues* as a reaction against the colonialist impulse, *Hector Servadac*, published in 1877, may be Verne's wonder tale to bring geographical shrinkage and colonialism most starkly into the symbolic realm. In that context, it may have been inevitable that the nationalism that always enjoyed some play in Verne novels should come to the fore.

The Foreshortening of Space

In *Hector Servadac*, in a near-solar passage that makes it graze the Earth, a comet scoops up a scattering of physical locations from around the Mediterranean and does so without destroying the inhabitants in these locations—providentially. It carries those places and people, surrounded by likewise-scooped sea waters, around the sun and then into the outer cold regions in the Solar System. The story's dissected character emerges as that of Eurasia herself: for the population turns out to be French, Russian, English, Spanish, and Italian, along with one who proves a difficulty not only for Servadac and his companions but for the reader, as well. This figure generates dislike among his fellows for being Prussian, a single-minded businessperson, a science-denier, and a Jew. The Hardwigg–type intellect upon the comet, the French astronomer who discovered its approach, names it Gallia. The sea on the tiny world becomes the Gallian Sea; and the community, as it gathers its resources to face the comet's wintry season among the outer planetary orbits, becomes a "colony." Servadac, the military officer who had been surveying the French terrestrial colony of Algeria before the comet's strike, acts as governor.

Since the comet appears, at first, to be completely awash in sea waters, and since remnants of both Mediterranean lands and islands become isolated islands scattered upon them, the tale consciously evokes not only Robinson Crusoe but also the Noachic tale. Providence plays a role more overtly than in other Verne novels, as may be appropriate, given the novel's perspective that France has been awarded a divine mandate. This finds representation in the lonely tomb of St. Louis. Taken up by this comet, this tomb, too, has survived intact, even to the point of its oil-lamp having been left burning, undisturbed by the cometary cataclysm.

The winds on the comet's sea fill sails, by providence; a warm home for the deadly winter appears, adjoining a volcano, by providence; and benefits accrue to those scooped up from Catholic or Orthodox nations, while the English and the sole Jew remain out in the cold—even if, perhaps, Verne tells the reader that they choose to be so left.[33]

The comet itself represents literal and symbolic borrowings. The literal, naturally, arrives from astronomy; and the relevant knowledge-cascade, the song of ideas that has to do with comets, arrives early in the second of *Servadac*'s two volumes. The symbolic borrowing appears less obviously: for it arrives in common parlance—as in the conversation in *Around the World* in which "the world *has* grown smaller." This commonplace but symbolic phrase might well describe *Servadac*'s main setting: for the comet Gallia is the phrase taken as though literally meant.

Frye's concept concerning the foreshortening of time, which is a symbolic literary technique, might lead the inquiring mind to consider its

Captain Servadac and Ben Zoof experience low gravity. Title page illustration in Verne's *Hector Servadac*.

other face: that of space—not as a technique in drawing but as in symbolic storytelling. For a foreshortening of time must sometimes appear in spatial terms. Foreshortened time, which brings disparate times into seemingly logical conjunction, in the *story about travel* brings disparate spaces into seemingly logical conjunction. Verne's *Around the World* brings the Earth's girth into the space of that novel's adventures. Without the foreshortening of time, Verne never could have accomplished the task; without the foreshortening of space, likewise. Since *Around the World* is a clock-based tale, however, time always precedes space, as a concern. In *Hector Servadac*'s journey through the Solar System, space as a concern precedes time. Unlike *Around the World*, in which the dream-journey's failed clocks appear near the end, in *Hector Servadac*, clock-time goes awry from nearly the beginning, when Servadac and his companion Ben Zoof awaken after the cataclysmic collision and are being carried off into interplanetary space. Even while watches continue ticking on comet Gallia, the tale's measurements thereafter fall along the lines of planetary orbits; and in Book Two, in terms of distances from Earth. Spatial foreshortening dominates, while the temporal equivalent follows along as it must.

The novel brings to figurative life the toy that is the orrery. That educational diversion vastly distorts spatial relations between Sun and planets, as well as their relative sizes. Although designed to make evident the planets' relative motions, *through time*—although, in other words, it was designed as a foreshortened-time toy—the fact that it shows planets in close proximity, and shows them in a scale comfortable for the human eye, enables that temporal presentation.

The same proves true in the novel. Servadac and Zoof behold Venus, then Mercury. They then sweat through a pass near the Sun—all within a short space of chapters. The "days" on this journey, being accelerated on the small-diameter planetoid, only exacerbate this sense that vast distances are being shrunken, and that the narrative perspective—the perspective of Servadac-Verne—gives witness to the stations along the journey, without respect to whether or not, logically, the narrator would have seen any evidence whatsoever of these stations. In the natural Solar System, the cometary travelers would have seen nothing of Venus and nothing of Mercury, except through some extraordinary rare chance. Since the cometary travelers inhabit a wonder tale, however, they live in a symbolic universe. They travel not in the natural Solar System but in the orrery, and of necessity must see Venus, and then must see Mercury—just as, in moving through the asteroid belt, they must pass near enough one of these minor, diffusely distributed rocks to pick up one for their comet's "moon."

To understand the "Solar System" in the novel as its literal borrowing of a symbolic toy gives it not plausibility but consistency. Perhaps, to develop a thought by Pundita in "Mellonta Tauta," a system's consistency as it approaches perfection must approach truth.

Edison's Talking Doll

In nineteenth century Paris, automata appeared in shop windows to amuse and tempt passersby. Some such devices made their way abroad; and in America the productions of Connecticut clockmakers performed similar service by the 1870s and 1880s. Merchants took these automata westward as they headed toward the Territories. Similarly, wealthier families going west carried toy automata, or ordered them for delivery from the east, for their children. Automata became familiar enough that in the 1890s Ambrose Bierce could effectively describe one's motions as the clue to the reader, in "Moxon's Master." The narrator looks onto a chess game being played by Moxon, an inventor. His opponent the narrator does see, but only from the rear.

> The play was rapid. Moxon hardly glanced at the board before making his moves, and to my unskilled eye seemed to move the piece most convenient to his hand, his motions in doing so being quick, nervous and lacking in precision. The response of his antagonist, while equally prompt in the inception, was made with a slow, uniform, mechanical and, I thought, somewhat theatrical movement of the arm, that was a sore trial to my patience. There was something unearthly about it all, and I caught myself shuddering.[34]

Partaking in the Gothic tradition, the story's events transpire during a storm; and it echoes notes of dismay or repugnance found in E.T.A. Hoffman's tales involving automata.

Around the same time, technicians under Thomas Edison introduced the Edison Talking Doll, the first such to be mass-produced. This attractive and neatly dressed girl-doll recited the nursery rhymes "Jack and Jill" and "Mary Had a Little Lamb," using her internal, miniature record-player. She went on display in the 1890 Wonders of Electricity exhibit at the Lenox Lyceum in New York, despite having a spring-wound mechanism.[35] Although the Edison factory announced its capacity to produce these by the hundreds daily, demand may never have tested the claim. The idea of the doll did move into popular literature, however, to judge from Alice W. Fuller's "A Wife Manufactured to Order," published in 1895, about a man whose wax wife proves an agreeable companion, for a time, thanks to having phonograph cylinders inside.[36]

American toys differed from French automata in many ways, but most of all in being based upon designs reflecting an individualistic spirit. France's clockwork marvels emerged from an elitist social tradition, so that an automaton's verisimilitude held a mirror to upper-class ideals of polished appearance, brilliant style, and exquisite taste. The best French automata mimicked life by mimicking manners—and so, to an American, or at least a non–Bostonian American, mimicked nothing real at all. In contrast, American toymakers took little interest in producing the best of all possible automata; and their productions, with their strongly diversionary element, struck a raw and fresh note, with finery held to a minimum and not mannerisms but emotional body-language erupting. Outside a few centers on the east coast, it remained the case that many Americans had never felt quite tamed by social models and peer expectations—although they knew both well enough to enjoy it when someone, or something, held a mirror to their social lapses.

As with other toys, American automata reflected a capacity for taking pleasure in simple matters. Roughly depicted enjoyments and passions energized clattery spring-driven actions. Early choices for Ives automata took inspiration from everyday sights: a man rowing a boat, a horse drawing a wagon, a Sunday-dressed pair on a teeter-totter, a girl on a swing. A.M. Allen patented a boy riding a velocipede with a twisting-and-turning liveliness to his actions—a toy then manufactured by Ives or some other contemporary, and then imitated by other companies well into the twentieth century and past World War II.[37] New York's Automatic Toy Works, founded around 1870, offered toys that stood at the farthest remove from the French, depicting figures from that city's dynamic social scene, with comic exaggeration. Two that were manufactured in 1875 depicted the Negro Preacher and the Woman's Right Advocate.[38]

The animal energy, religious abandon, and political fervor embodied in these toys stood in contrast to the great clockwork accomplishments by European masters, whose finely perfected motions seemed almost miraculously well-mannered. In part, American firms were pursuing a practical endeavor that involved selling enough units that they might survive in a competitive free-for-all, in which their toys vied against other American concoctions as well as against the daintier, prettier, and often more complicated toys from overseas. Their toys had to catch eyes in the bustling towns that were growing into cities and into centers for international trade.

Yet in their efforts to attract attention by making toys that reflected joys and passions, they created objects that rose to art in a way other than the way works by a Decamps or Lambert did. Parisian automata-makers worked within a culture still clinging to the greatness of a time now past. Many in France savored the satin and gold illusions of royalty, of nationalism, and of early colonial power: and the automata themselves often reflected the fabulous accomplishments of the 17th and early 18th-century automata master-craftsmen. The inward-turning and fantasy-world quality in their creations matched writings rising from the most finely sensitive among the new French writers, the Symbolists, who themselves were inward-turning, self-absorbed, and seemingly obsessed with the creation of interior worlds full of fabrication and delightful deceptions, walling off that exterior world into which locomotives, steam drills, and trams were so noisily intruding.

The rough vigor of American automata, outwardly turned, evoked the practical dynamic prevalent in New England. There, the making of fine mechanical workings had become so established a tradition that cruder workings could be tossed off in idle moments by tradesmen. Those skills were taking root too, in regions westward across the industrial belt, through Pennsylvania and Ohio and on toward Michigan, Illinois, and Wisconsin—where both heavier and lighter industries were attracting technical and mechanical workers to gather into new pools of talent, and where toy companies were springing to life and spreading outward along the rail lines.

Where the French marvels seemed equivalent to the Symbolist writers—who were reaching the conclusion that poetry had no place in the Modern world, or at least no function—the American automata and mechanical toys participated in the mood and the stance adopted by the writers of wonder tales, in which art was not life's imitation but its ebullient replacement, roughly hewn and garbed in invention and satire. No introspective self-questionings nor any pensive social perturbations animated them: for they depicted people possessing few doubts about themselves. The Automatic Toy Negro Preacher preaches with unfaltering fire, the Woman's Right Advocate advocates upon a platform of immovable conviction. The dancers dance for pleasure and not for nicety, and the teeter-totterers simply thrill themselves. That they are artificial constructs no one doubts—seeing their seams, their tin tabs, and their winding keys, and hearing their ratchety, jittery actions. That they are obviously un-lifelike adds to their charm.

Similarly, in the robust and often undignified American wonder tales, mechanism and artifice come to the foreground, undisguised and perhaps more vigorously present to the reader than the supposed human characters. The Steam Men of the dime novels, unlike the beguiling and bedeviling automata women appearing in stories from Europe, fascinated young readers not because they were imitations of life but because they so obviously were not. Their authors understood, as had the organizers for the Centennial Exhibition, the pull that the artificial exerted upon the new Moderns.

The difference between Continental and American visions for the automaton must have been becoming obvious in 1886, for any readers exercising an eclectic taste and taking in widely diverging sorts of literature. In that year, Mathias Villiers de l'Isle-Adams published his symbolist novel *L'Eve Future*, which had first appeared three years before in the popular magazine *La Vie Moderne*.[39] Villiers, as a musician and stage performer, offered audiences "hilarious, grotesque inventions which combined virtuosities on the piano with long, improvised narrations—extravagant and theatrical, yet hypnotically compelling, and funny, sometimes, to the point of tears." A friend to Wagner, and as well to Baudelaire and Mallarmé, his musings led him to deploy a symbolic figure in his novel: Thomas Edison, who creates the physical, material equal to a highly beautiful woman, with a superior soul. This fictional Edison does this for a friend enamored of a real woman, upon whom he models the automaton. This fictional Edison, in other words, assists a friend in constructing for himself a dreamlike, interior world of an artificial perfection that stands in for life. Villiers's novel expresses the Symbolist impulse, as well as the personal and aesthetic loathings he felt for materialism, the world of business, and the idea of progress.[40]

In contrast, also in 1886, Luis P. Senarens presented to his eager readers *The Electric Man*—the latest iteration of the clearly artificial, workaday-useful, cart-pulling Steam Man, with young hero Frank Reade, Jr.[41] Five years later, an adventure series appeared from a competitor publisher, Street and Smith, in its magazines *Good News* and *The Nugget Library*, with a young hero named Tom Edison, Jr.[42]

By this time, the Edward S. Ellis-type boy inventor had become a stock character in stories for boys. The original Ellis story, when republished in 1878 as *The Huge Hunter* in Beadle's Pocket Library, had made a larger mark, then, than it had originally. A competitor publisher noticed it, and hired Harold Cohen, or "Harry Enton," to write the equivalent for his weekly, *The Boys of New York*. This new novel led to two sequels by Cohen and a great many by Senarens, with ever-new technical developments. The novels all seemed to revolve around the automation of individual travel.[43]

The Game of Mass Production

Readers, albeit in diverse parts, in 1886 first saw *Robur the Conqueror*, *L'Eve Future*, and *The Electric Man*. That year apparently saw, too, an assembly line plaything produced. George S. Parker, in a new firm established in 1883 in the city where games pioneer Ives had his start, reissued Ives games that had enjoyed popularity in earlier decades, including the lithographed spiral game Mansion of Happiness. Parker employed "fifteen girls, from seven to eleven years of age, each with a pot of paint containing one color. Each girl dabbed her color in just the right spots, according to a master guide, passed the game along to the next for her color, and so on."[44] With this and other minor means for factory production, later aided by such technical advances as chromolithography, fancier toys and games were spreading more widely through the general population. Poorer families often had fended off the sense of want with a practical philosophy that saw little use in playthings beyond the simplest and the homemade. As a consequence, toymakers needed to cajole them into accepting toys and games as legitimate purchases, with appeals to moral and biblical education being among the most acceptable means, initially—besides, that is, low prices.

On the heels of such lofty diversions as The Checkered Game of Life came new ones that were educational in secular ways. History, language, and geography became common subjects.[45] While Puritan-influenced families in the States were slower to accept this development than had been others, expanding toy and game manufacturing efforts in northern Pennsylvania, and the matching expansions in tin, clockwork, and then iron toys in Connecticut and New York, created such pressure that even religiously conservative families began to accept toys in the marketplace and in the home as being not unusual and perhaps useful, as opposed to frivolous and indulgent. As this shift took place, pioneering playthings, such as had been produced by Charles M. Crandall, came to see more imitation and emulation. While his games and toys might have taught dexterity and creativity, they mainly offered simple enjoyment for those who followed what might be called the Dutch tradition in American play:

The *Clipper of the Clouds*. In the imagination, nautical ships often came in for transformation into aerial ones. In Verne's 1886 novel, *Clipper of the Clouds*, or *Robur the Conqueror*, the masts of sea-going clippers, although already outmoded by steam power, become the supports for a multitude of propellers.

for they existed primarily for the fun to be had. Children received encouragement to think not of deity, duty, or conscience, but of St. Nicholas—"patron saint of Amsterdam and the beloved hero of children in Holland."[46]

Now in Waverly, New York, Crandall was expanding his long-running line of non-moralistic and none-too-educational toys—and proving that they made a better fit than ever with contemporary society: for he found himself with a hit on his hands, in his 1889 Pigs in Clover. The player tilted around a circular tray having concentric tracks with openings for the "pigs," which were marbles, to move them to-

Between high crags, Robur's *Albatross* here appears diminutive, while its propellers evoke the telegraph poles that were altering the West's landscape—a symbolic resemblance, given that Robur, too, aims to encircle the globe.

ward the "pen" at center. As a device for propagating insanity—for so a newspaper termed it—it became the rage in America and abroad.⁴⁷ Attractions that related to it, as with a store-window display that featured a boy's hourly attempts to herd real pigs into a pen, proved crowd-pleasing spectacles—even though the window belonged to Cleveland's Excelsior Clothing House, not a toy shop. Tremendous demand for the toy forced Crandall to expand his Waverly Toy Works and to establish new factories in the City.⁴⁸

Ironically, later in the year, Crandall turned his attention to a backwards-gazing educational game named Growth of a Century, to help the country celebrate the centenary of the Constitution and George Washington's inauguration. Pigs in Clover remained the hit, however, while the centenary came and went.

Consolidation and Trust-Building

The *Albatross* moves in to rescue the beleaguered crew of the *Goahead*, in Verne's *Clipper of the Clouds*.

Around the time Edison's doll made her phonographic debut, and Nelly Bly her round-the-world tour, the process of consolidation and trust-building that was affecting other American economic sectors was making itself felt in the toy industry. Although any profitable or new toy in the marketplace promptly inspired rival versions from other factories—as did Crandall's Pigs—aggressive and sometimes ruthless competition tended to concentrate production in the hands of a few. Noble & Cooley of Granville, Massachusetts, provides an instructive example. Established in 1854 as the earliest and sole American mass-manufacturer of toy drums, it produced a product that, in essence, created its own demand through being inexpensive and available. Although other factories in Massachusetts, having similar equipment and expertise, sprang up to benefit from that new demand, they all failed, with the last one burning to the ground in 1890. The Granville firm bought that firm's assets and subsequently again held sole control. The possibilities for creating regional communities of like-minded toy specialists, as had occurred elsewhere in the country, were diminishing, with other well-established firms increasingly engaging in these consolidations.

Noble & Cooley and other large firms began constructing a "toy trust" by the early 1900s. In response, Morton E. Converse of Winchendon, a specialist now in both wooden and metal toys, took on a "trust-busting" role in the industry. Later he successfully challenged Noble & Cooley's hegemony by applying superior automation to toy-drum making. Sheer numbers seem to have won the day. Converse offered toy jobbers sixty styles of drums, with its daily output being as high as seven thousand drums per day. Around this period, it was producing more than a hundred thousand each Christmas season. Ironically, Converse came to control eighty percent of the market. Yearly production also included one hundred and fifty thousand blackboards and twenty thousand doll trunks.[49]

The New Toy Books

During the 1880s and 1890s, a new paper toy became possible, due to technical advances in printing and die-cutting. These new toy books, printed on card stock, featured mechanical pictures with tabs or strings that children could push or pull to make parts move; or they had folded, cut, and glued-in pieces that opened into a three-dimensional

Fig. 124—Leaves from a transformation scrap-book.

Transformation scrapbook. A popular form of the toy book, the "transformation book" featured pages of characters divided below the head, and sometimes below the waist, as well. This 1910 image shows children how to make their own transformation scrapbook, using trade cards or other pictures (from Lina Beard and Adelia B. Beard, *Little Folks' Handy Book*, 1910).

form when a page was turned. Some among these toy books rivaled toy theaters: for they opened to reveal stages upon which imaginary actions might take place. While at times they invoked everyday childhood activities, such as physical games, more often they invoked fairytales, the circus, or adventure tales that had become childhood favorites, among them the direct predecessors of the Modern wonder tale—such as Daniel Defoe's 1719 novel of the rationally inventive castaway, *The Wonderful Life and Surprising Adventures of that Renowned Hero Robinson Crusoe*, which had appeared in an abridged form aimed at children in 1760 in England, and in 1774 in the United States.[50]

These toy books offered a paper incarnation of the mechanical toy. Historians attribute their invention to Lothar Meggendorfer of Germany, who began designing them in the 1880s after having enjoyed success with wooden mechanical toys, having been a puppeteer.[51] Toy books reflected the full circle being drawn within society by the co-development of the Modern wonder tale and Modern symbolic toy. Besides puppetry, the toy book had arisen from penny dreadfuls, chapbooks, and other inexpensive circulars that featured the horrifying and the spectacular more often than anything staidly reasonable; from toy theaters and paper dolls; and from the books that were "toys" in being doll-size, that contained fairy tales, Bible stories, and alphabets. It had developed into a form that joined children's story-amusement with repetitive play. In common with other Modern symbolic toys, these new toy books encapsulated at child level the symbolic spectacle—a life-representation in a carefully designed, artificial, and exaggerated form.

Eleven

The Magic City

The future! What will it be? Material progress, no doubt, will continue onward with ever-increasing velocity. The wildest dreams scarcely, I believe, foreshadow the realities; nothing need be unexpected. The travelers to the Columbian Exposition a hundred years hence will, perhaps, birdlike, sail through the air, journeying in a half-dozen hours from the Atlantic coast to the city of the Northwest on the banks of the Mississippi. More unlikely would the prophecy of travel by rail, or steam, or electricity have seemed to our forefathers one century ago.
—Archbishop Ireland, in 1893.[1]

For they saw, standing in just the spot the screen had hidden, a little, old man, with a bald head and a wrinkled face, who seemed to be as much surprised as they were....
"I'm supposed to be a Great Wizard."
"And aren't you?" she asked.
"Not a bit of it, my dear; I'm just a common man."
"You're more than that," said the Scarecrow, in a grieved tone; "you're a humbug."
—L. Frank Baum, in 1900.[2]

"Wonders in Every Branch of Thought"

With the Centennial, the first American industrial fair, the public's ability to internalize technical advance reached a turning-point. The machinery, steam engines, lighting, and communication devices provoked observers to proclaim them marvels. Cumulatively, they left in the dust the stage marked by the Crystal Palace, a quarter-century earlier. There, in 1851, a reasonably educated visitor could fathom many if not most the displayed wonders. In the decades prior to the London fair, technical advances had arrived at a swift pace, yet not a hectic one. Non-specialist, intelligent observers could keep themselves informed, and could understand developments to a fair degree, without feeling estranged by their existence, or by their implications. At the Philadelphia Centennial, however, all seemed changed: for inventors, engineers, and manufacturers displayed machines and technical applications that, to be understood, required a scientific or technical background.[3]

This change provoked questions about humankind's ever-extending technical reach, such as Melville voiced in his 1876 "Clarel." Clergyman-geologist George F. Wright, that same year, wondered "whether in our religion there is moral power enough left to control and keep in harness the giant we have awakened."[4]

After a decade passed, and two years after the assembly line helped meet George Parker's concerns for efficiency, convenience, and affordability in game publishing, the automation of daily life found its champion in the bestselling *Looking Backwards*. Edward Bellamy's 1888 socialist-utopian novel transported a then-contemporary man via sleep-journey to a future marked by mechanical accomplishment and social stability. "There is moral power enough," Bellamy, in essence, was replying to George Wright. The next year, Mark Twain's *A Connecticut Yankee in King Arthur's Court* sent a then-contemporary soul into the past rather than future. Twain, too, presented the dichotomy between a human order in the present moment and a mechanized future, with the former being medieval courtly order, and the latter being represented by the crown jewel of New Worlds idealism: the astronomical understanding of the celestial sphere as determinate, whether seen forwards or backwards. The Yankee conceives a hoax, and with New England ingenuity presents celestial mechanics as magic. His being from Connecticut has pertinence: for in essence he gives a clockless society a view of a working clock, albeit a literally dark one.

In but five years, Bellamy's automatic city swept into being. Soon to be ranked among the greatest international fairs, the 1893 World's Columbian Exposition opened in the city where a Floral Globe—a large model of the Earth, with flowers and foliage indicating continents and oceans—was attracting viewers to its Washington Park.[5] In this up-to-date city, not only the Chicago Electric Club but such journals as *Electric Age*, *Electrical Engineer*, *Electrical Review*, and *Railway Age* found their homes.[6] Having re-envisioned and remade itself after the Great Fire of 1871, it seemed a landlocked Standard Island, having "superb hotels, less ornate mansions, shops, public edifices, churches," along with "those monstrosities of skyscrapers."[7]

The Columbian's opening completed "festivities of the four hundredth anniversary of the discovery of America," while the event as a whole celebrated "the golden age of American industry, American progress and American development. Wonders have been achieved in every branch of thought, and in every line of trade."[8]

Automatic Dioramas and Living Panoramas

The Crystal Palace influenced subsequent expositions—in Dublin in May 1853, and in New York that October—in having a main building house its major exhibits. In 1855 the Universal Exposition in Paris, however, featured large buildings in a cluster rather than a central hall. Other, minor buildings rose nearby to accommodate specific areas of manufacture. French planners developed this approach to a further degree for the Paris Exposition of 1867, though organizing it around a large, central building. They created heavily landscaped surroundings, with the whole occupying more than thirty-seven acres in the Champ de Mars. Smaller buildings built by other nations appeared among formal gardens, walkways, and fountains, making it seem that a small but fascinatingly diverse city had sprung into being, with its many elements falling subject to an over-arching aesthetic programme.[9] Although not all subsequent international fairs aspired to so grand a scale, the Philadelphia Centennial did seize upon this initiative in aiming to prove itself the greatest up to that time, with its fair grounds covering 450 acres in Fairmount Park—well more than ten times the space occupied by the 1867 fair.

The Columbian's design aimed similarly high, with its successful execution winning it such names as "the White City" and "the Magic City." Architecturally, the United States stood at a turning point. New Chicago structures pointed in two directions for development: toward the neo-Classical, and toward the utilitarian Modern. In 1892 the latter direction had found its emblem in Chicago, in the culmination of the previous century's upwards-tending buildings. Designed by Daniel Burnham and John Root, the steel-skeleton Masonic Temple rose to the breath-taking twenty stories Poe had imagined for future Manhattan buildings.[10]

The neo-Classical impulse exerted considerable power, however—at least for Burnham and Root, who also designed the Columbian's grounds. Spatial grandeur, found in public architecture in ancient times, offered them ideas for continuing the Crystal Palace tradition that emphasized vast interior spaces, while providing thematic coherence for a miniature city, in the Paris tradition. Each main hall would be, in essence, a new Crystal Palace that would take in visitors and surround them completely with technical and cultural marvels. A dedication to the artificial and fabricated found ample expression in the exposition's early stages—such as in plans for a theater that would transform the wonder tale of the descent into the earth into a paradoxical spectacle. It would have made stops to view a mine shaft, the polar regions, the deepest ocean, and a Calvinist Hell.[11]

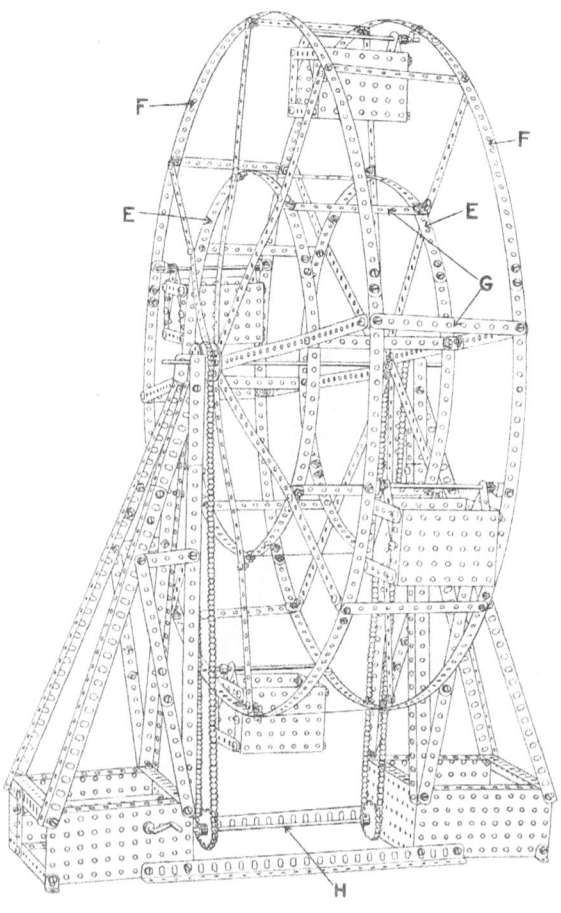

White City Ferris Wheel. Its manufacturers claim that the American Model Builder toy, to be worked by hand or motor, will build "an exact duplicate of the Ferris Wheel used at the Chicago Exposition." From the manual of instructions, 1913, pp. 62–63: American Mechanical Toy Co., Dayton, Ohio.

The account, titled "An Underground Theater," describes a marvelous journey involving a marvelous machine—which is, in the tradition of the chess-player, a machine to create wonder through deceit. To give the sense of descent, canvas walls around the "elevator-car" would roll upwards, while the car itself would shake with "realistic motion." At intervals the openings would give a view of scenes beyond, staged on a large, round, movable stage. Actors would change costumes at the different "levels" to suit the presentation. "A judicious use of mirrors will heighten the effect. In short it will be a living panorama on a large scale."[12] The "concession to orthodoxy" at the lowest level in particular affirmed the attraction's being a wonder tale made actual.

While the Underground Theater seems not to have materialized, another optical attraction did draw viewers along the Midway Plaisance, the fair's avenue of eclectic spectacle. The Electric Scenic Theatre, costing twenty-five cents admission, showed landscapes and various scenes under changing light conditions. These mimicked the changing light seen during the passage of a day, with the "effects being produced by a multitude of various colored electric lights." An automatic diorama, by electricity it showed "to a degree of marvelous faithfulness all the various effects of nature."[13]

Also on the Midway appeared two optical attractions of a nature that now seemed traditional. One panorama showed the volcano Mt. Kilauea; the second, the Alps of Switzerland. The latter, also called a "cyclorama," ranked as "the largest ... ever painted."[14] Chicago hosted other examples, further indicating that the form continued to offer a public spectacle. One evoked a toy: for during the years before and during the Exposition, on the corner of Wabash Avenue and, fittingly, Panorama Place, the old "panorama" toy of Milton Bradley appeared at life scale. The Battle of Gettysburg Panorama put visitors "in the midst of black-browed war with all its attendant horrors and its heroic inspirations." Elsewhere, at Wabash and Hubbard Court, another artificial visual spectacle offered the Panorama of Niagara Falls, fifty feet in height and over four hundred in circumference. Among nearby electrical spectacles, the public could also view "electric contrivances" alongside "natural human and animal freaks" at Epstein's Dime Museum, on Randolph Street.[15]

The Midway Plaisance as a whole offered the public a geographical wonder tale, being "two solid miles of amusement enterprise ... a spot where the lines of longitude and the parallels of latitude were tangled together like a skein of silk after a kitten's play; where the Occident and the Orient were mixed in the most gigantic amusement potpourri the world has ever seen."[16] Here the foreshortening of space, a symbolic feature of international exhibitions since the first, became something to be experienced with all the senses.

As much as any other factor, the Midway Plaisance gave Chicago's Columbian a new feel. While Philadelphia's Centennial had remained an industrial exhibition in the public mind, Chicago's Columbian created a new "World's Fair" atmosphere. Pleasure-seeking and recreation drew crowds equal to or exceeding those drawn by educational opportunities.

A Thrill of Power and Conquest

The Magic City name arose for more than aesthetic and architectural reasons. The exposition as a whole had been planned as "one grand exemplification of the progress that has been made in electricity,"[17] with the "exemplification" beginning on a dramatic note: for at 12:20 o'clock, on May 1, 1893, the U.S. president touched a button to set in motion the fair's opening machinery. "That single touch of Grover Cleveland's finger did a million things.... It transmitted by the magic current of electricity the motion which opened the valve of the greatest of engines and breathed life into the cylinders and wheels of that monster industrial servant. It loosened the throats of a hundred steam whistles, and caused fire and smoke and mighty reverberations to belch from the guns in the harbor. It filled the ivory horizon with 800 flags and streamers from the roofs and towers of the surrounding palaces as if they had all been geared to the same unfurling appliances. It dropped the veil from the beauteous form of the golden statue of the Republic which stood looking at the unparalleled scene. It sent the echoes flying through the great city lying dark and massive in the background, and these in turn were taken up and hurled around the globe to all the nations thereof. It opened the floodgates and permitted the waters to spurt from the fountains in the near foreground, filling the air with a soft mist. It added the silver voices of chimes to the triumphant din.... It sent a thrill of power and conquest through the hearts of the multitude, through all civilization. All this it did—so alert all the local organization, so perfectly instantaneous the means of communication on this our sphere in this day and generation—while the strong, firm hand of President Cleveland still rested upon the ivory key."[18]

Push-button efficiency, the thrill of power and conquest, and the "perfectly instantaneous" communication came into congruence, in that gold and ivory key—a "telegraphic key, the closing of which was to set in motion the massive machinery." George R. Davis, the director-general of the Exposition, himself termed it the "magic key."[19] The vision of communication held such power that associations with the magical became commonplace, as in W.A. Croffut's lines in which "severed friends" are "community fay to fay."[20]

The Magic City operated as a cohesive whole thanks to its electrical system, with power from a 24,000 horse-power steam plant in Machinery Hall conducted along the elevated railroad and through underground tunnels.[21] The electricity being generated and used amounted to ten times that used by the Paris Exhibition of 1889.[22] Far from diminishing the Exposition's architectural impact, electrical marvels enhanced it, especially at night, when crowds arrived to enjoy the purely artificial surroundings more than any specific displays. The towering, colonnaded facades, the ornate domes on the Administration and Horticultural buildings, the Electricity building's imperial grandeur, and the high, Roman-arch windows on the Manufactures and Liberal Arts buildings added to the visual spectacle. The purposefully grandiose found affirmation at the opening ceremonies, in music from Wagner's "Rienzi" with its overtones of Roman restoration.[23] With so many exteriors and statues in white, sunlight could dazzle the eye by day. By night, "artistic effects in illumination" created an optical diversion: "the great structures of the Exposition will be turned into a panoramic view at night by the aid of powerful electric search-lights." These centered around the main court, surrounded by Machinery Hall and the Manufactures, Electricity, Mines, and Agriculture buildings: "At night, this Central court or Main court and its surrounding buildings will blaze and twinkle with electric fire, and the effect will be magnificent. The architectural lines of the buildings will be delineated against the black sky in myriads of electric stars. The shore lines of the basin and its intersecting canal and the architectural lines of the bridges will be outlined in fire, and the spectacular Administration Building with its dome of gold will blaze like a diamond crown. The great Electric Fountain in the center of the court will spout an iridescent deluge and search lights will bathe the marble like unto palaces in ever-changing floods of color."[24]

Within the buildings more light effects waited. Along floor-level aisles, ornamental lampposts held arc lights "shielded [to] present an opalescent glow rather than a fierce sputtering spark."[25] The Electricity building tended to be described in superlatives:

> A more wonderful, magical sight was never seen than that revealed by the marvelous displays of electrical apparatus, machinery and devices made in the Electric building.... Beautiful as was the scene in daytime, the vast theatre of electric wonders was robed with a magical splendor at night, which made it infinitely more gorgeous. It was a hall of marvels, a museum of enchantments, where the eye of curiosity was almost blinded by bewilderment and dazzled by surprises. No pen can ever describe the matchless illumination of that fairy-like exhibition, or fittingly picture the glories of the displays.[26]

This "Aladdin's palace of the Exposition" tended, too, to invite descriptions not in scientific or technical terms but in wonder-tale imagery. "The wonder working genii which find place within its walls have produced marvels undreamed of in the wildest tales of magic and fairy lore," observed one, who also noted language's failure to adequately express the new—for these marvels could hardly be viewed "without something of the old-time awesome fascination which belong to things occult." The building's "strange exhibits" offered a "wonderland exhibition."[27] Even a building whose theme might have called for simplicity of design, the Horticultural building, embraced the Crystal Palace approach with its "illuminated crystal dome."[28] Light came in for celebration, too, in its technological capture—in the Photographic building, as well as in countless photographic publications surrounding the Exposition.

Meanwhile the integrated power system fed into the elevated Electric Intramural Railway. This scaled-down version of the transportation system newly completed in Chicago offered dime circuits of Jackson Park.[29] Electric "pleasure boats" and "electric launches" plied the park's many lagoons and basins, at two bits per round trip.[30] Fifty cents bought fairgoers an elevator ride to the Manufactures roof, and a nickel, access to the "movable sidewalk," an "electrically propelled sidewalk" on the Long Pier in Jackson Park.[31]

Gigantism and the Wheel

As had the Centennial, the Columbian featured the largest single building of its time.

> For vast extent, boldness of conception, wonderful engineering, faultless proportions, and impressive grandeur the Manufactures building is easily the greatest of them all, and the greatest building on earth. This building covers an area of 1,687 × 757 feet, and is, in its main portions, over 200 feet high. It is more than a third of a mile long, and nearly a sixth of a mile wide, and covers over thirty ares of ground. In the center of this space is a court 1,237 × 387 feet in size, the roof of which is supported on gigantic steel trusses, which span the entire width, and are 210 feet high, or fifty feet higher than those of the Machinery Hall at Paris, forming the largest unencumbered court ever constructed. Around this court runs a nave, 107 feet wide, with a gable roof 114 feet high; and around the nave runs a lean-to forty-five feet wide, covering an unenclosed ambulatory.[32]

In continuing the Crystal Palace's work in bringing the world's oceans to public view, the fair's ten large aquaria held from 7,000 to 27,000 gallons of water apiece. Smaller ones held from 750 to 1,500 gallons. Their gigantism in itself offered an attraction: "The glass fronts of the aquaria are in length about 575 feet and have 3,000 square feet of surface. The total water capacity of the Aquaria, exclusive of reservoirs, is 18,725 cubic feet, or 140,000 gallons. This weighs 1,192,425 pounds, or almost 600 tons."[33] Altogether this Fisheries or "Aquarial" building surpassed "the great permanent aquarial exhibitions of the world in size and in the completeness and variety of its specimens."[34]

A scientific theme given even greater prominence at the Columbian emphasized evolution, ethnology, and anthropology, a choice that had political overtones, given that those Christian sects that emphasized literal biblical interpretations were gaining in influence. The Prohibition Party, too, which had Chicago roots in Frances Willard and the Women's Christian Temperance Union, had an avowed interest in merging church and state.[35]

Even the Midway Plaisance, as a living display that let visitors view the human species in its contemporary types, embraced this outwardly scientific emphasis. "The ethnologist might have gone no further than the Columbian Fair to find the races of the world and practically study their characteristics," noted an account published the next year.[36] As an ethnographic walking tour it included, among others, a Javanese Village, a Lapland family and dwelling, a Bedouin encampment, and a street in Cairo. Photographic accounts of the Fair, which were several in number and all popular, gave ample space to these geographical attractions.

In Chicago's Machinery Hall, Philadelphia's found its answer. Measuring 850 by 500 feet, it contained "a marvelous exhibit of the most perfect machinery ever devised by the genius of man, performing work with what seemed to be the highest intelligence, and exciting the amazement of visitors whichever way they turned to make their examinations. There were machines at work turning out needles, pins, buttons, thimbles, and such small articles as are very cheap and common, but which everybody wonders how they are produced."[37] Its alternate name indicated its place in the Magic City: the Palace of Mechanic Arts.[38]

Offering most prominent mechanical spectacle, however, the prodigious Vertical Revolving Wheel rose above the Midway. Although anticipated by such toys as the Converse Fandango, this exercise in gigantism featured two towers, between which a giant wheel slowly turned, carrying viewing rooms high above the lakefront. The pyramidal towers stood 150 feet high, supporting an axle forty-five feet long, in an immense wheel measuring 250 feet in diameter. Its outer margin held thirty-six cars, each twenty-seven feet long and with seating for forty. Powered by a thousand-horse-power engine sunken four feet underground, the wheel turned a full revolution in around ten minutes, with passengers paying fifty cents for two revolutions.[39]

The Columbian's being a "Magic" city had considerable symbolic weight. Its Aladdin aspect loomed large—with its "palaces" seeming to have arisen overnight; with its instantly working genii of electricity; with its exotic cast members along the Midway; and with its fanciful nighttime lighting. Above all, the "city" demonstrated magic in having taken into itself, in shrunken form but whole, the globe.

During the fair, on July 12, 1893, historian Frederick Jackson Turner delivered "The Significance of the Frontier in American History," the paper that announced the frontier's closure.[40] The 1890 census had revealed that, in the States, no region remained so remote as to be uninhabited. His paper reflected the fact that the technologically enhanced reach of human society had its limits. The expansive tendencies displayed by the most powerful Western societies were being indulged within a closed sphere. Earth's immensity was giving ironic meaning to Modern wonders in communication and travel—ironic, since Phileas Fogg's world had become everyone's.

Central to the fair stood the goddess Columbia carrying Earth's weight. The statue held it with her right hand, untaxed by the effort, her frame not bent in Atlas position but erect and effortlessly commanding. She may have been the New Woman, empowered, ennobled, and fixed in an elocutionary poise—the spirit of the times. The sense that the globe was shrinking found ample expression elsewhere, as well—as in the design above The Golden Door of the Transportation Building, with a "virile figure standing upon a globe."[41]

Turner's paper put into academic, self-conscious terms the sense that had been given metaphoric voice in Verne's *From the Earth to the Moon* and in unknown numbers of other wonder tales—and in the attraction at the Moorish Palace on the Midway Plaisance, which featured not only a "chamber of horrors" but also a "trip to the moon."[42] By 1893, however, even the urge upwards, to look down on things in small, was being placed within symbolic limits, as also was seen on the Midway. There, the globe of the Charles-type balloon lifted curious Fair-goers to 1,600 feet on a strict schedule, with two trips per hour at two dollars per person—it being a "captive balloon," the most common remaining form of aerostat.[43] This popular attraction turned a journey of wonder into a routine, and transformed the average woman or man into the new technological adventurer. The Columbian produced new aeronauts with the regularity and dependability of mass production. The words of Christobal Colon at the opening ceremonies, in the imperfect past tense, stated it all too well: "Wonders have been achieved."

The urge to emulate the goddess Columbia naturally found expression at child-level. New, artificial-material playballs appeared in 1893 in "variegated marbleized colors," touted for lightness and toughness. Their designs included Columbus Celluloid Balls, around three inches in diameter and in various colors, that featured the famous Columbus profile as well as the fair's buildings; and the World Celluloid Ball that had "the entire map of the World on its face. It is an exact imitation of a globe, instructive as well as amusing." Columbia Inflated Rubber Balls also appeared on the scene, made by New York Rubber Company, and also showing exposition buildings.[44]

Any child might hold such a globe in but a single hand—just as any child might have pressed the button pushed by Cleveland, even with weak and hesitant fingers, to exactly the same result.

Columbian Fairings

Columbian planners issued a call to children from the U.S. or abroad to form an auxiliary: the International Youths' World's Fair Association. Adults behind the enterprise included Mrs. E.N. Hailman of Indiana, "the well known head of the kindergarten movement."[45] The exposition met children's needs, in part, by dedicating to them a large area on the Woman's Building roof where they could play, or admire a display showing toys "from the rude playthings of Esquimaux children to the wonderful toys which at once instruct and amuse."[46]

Relatively few U.S. toymakers exhibited at the Columbian, however. Chicago stores and concession-stands within the grounds sold their items, freeing them from having to reserve and supervise exhibition space, at least to some degree. The current financial crisis, too, affected toymakers, perhaps more severely than it did hardware and household-goods manufacturers. Yet of the nation's oldest toymakers, two from New York City did exhibit: E.B. Estes & Sons, a firm that since being established in 1847 had grown to include factories in several eastern states; and Peter F. Pia, founded in 1848, a maker of pewter toys. Pia, especially, played to the taste among children and adults for minikins. Barney & Berry of Springfield, Massachusetts, displayed the ice and roller skates it had been manufacturing since 1862. Of newer companies, Converse exhibited wooden toys, presumably including the Fandango; and Parker Brothers, its games. Smaller games companies with exhibits included M.B. Ross of Cambridgeboro, Pennsylvania, and Mrs. A.J. Tabolewski of Denver, with her game, 1893 or Chicagoed.[47]

Only Ives, Blakeslee & Williams Company of New York—formerly Ives, Blakeslee & Company of Bridgeport—showed American mechanical metal toys. Inexpensive spring motors had flourished at the Centennial, being novelties. Though still having charm, by

1893 they had handed the wonder-producing baton to electrical workings. Consolidated Electric Storage Company of Philadelphia exhibited unspecified electric toys, as did American Battery Company of Chicago. Chicago's A.C. Mather exhibited "working models of cars and boats," while Malcolm de la Fere of Minneapolis exhibited a "model electric railroad" and "model electric submarine vessel." While others may have been scattered around the fair the way singing birds and other mechanical diversions seem to have been, at Philadelphia, the non-traditional toys that were featured make it seem that America was taking the lead, in this new industry. Of the many toymakers from Nuremberg and elsewhere in Germany, three—Ernst Plank, Jean Schoenner, and Jean Thaeter—specialized in "optical and mechanical toys." Only one German toymaker, Carl Schillitz of Frankfort, specialized in the new "electrical toys" category.[48]

With the fair itself being the greatest wonder of the day, many new toys and games besides Mrs. Tabolewski's directly borrowed its themes and energies. One tapped into the Midway Wheel's great popularity: a malleable iron and steel Columbian Wheel. New York toy-seller Carl P. Stirn offered it with options: crank, clock, or steam movement.[49] Another, the World's Fair Panorama, offered "correct views in colors" showing Columbian buildings, Columbus's landing, the U.S. Presidents, the capitol at Washington, and Chicago's great wonder, the Masonic temple.[50] The combination-lock Administration Bank presented "a very fair representation" of the fair's Administration Building; and the Columbian Open Horse Car, apparently wooden, imitated the horse-drawn trolleys carrying visitors. Many, such as Columbian Exposition Cubes and World's Columbian Exposition Picture Puzzles, featured the fair's architecture and scenes. As to be expected, board games appeared in multitudes from as many manufacturers.[51]

Beside the Fandango, mechanical toys in stores and catalogs included the Columbus Bank and the Pig and Columbus Egg Bell Toy. Countless miscellaneous playthings appeared

THE PIG AND COLUMBUS EGG BELL TOY.

Half size cut.

The action of the pig in trying to set the egg on end, and at the same time ring the bell, is a very attractive feature.

The Columbus Egg. Mechanical toys appeared in great abundance in the 1890s, ranging from small figures of washerwomen or carpenters to "mechanical show pieces," which were tableaus for window displays featuring a variety of moving parts (from Carl P. Stirn, *Turn-of-the-Century Dolls, Toys and Games: The Complete Illustrated Carl P. Stirn Catalog from 1893*, 1990).

with "Columbia" in their names, including iron pistols and the Columbia Parachute. A new Noah's Ark floated a subtler connection, being sold in 1893 as *The World's Noah's Ark*.[52] Toy designs, names, or decalcomania reflected other thematic connections to the fair, in every category. Toy watches remained popular, with some now having spring movements. In optical toys, kaleidoscopes, zoetropes, and magic lanterns had become common offerings, together with tin wheel toys, tin globes, tin and iron bell toys, mechanical railroads, mechanical velocipede riders, mechanical dancing figures, mechanical pictures, steam engines, and mechanical banks. Toy theaters and "Paper-doll Dramas" remained in vogue.[53]

The Columbian made official allowance for toys, in several "Manufactures" areas. In the rubber-goods area, Class 691 was "Toys of rubber"—a distinctly Modern-century category. In the group "Toys and Fancy Articles," toys fell under Class 693, whose description's first word suggests much about the organizers' perceptions: "Automatic and other toys and games for the amusement and instruction of children." In the Electrical building more appeared. The display group named "Application of Electric Motors" included Class 777: "Toys, novelties, and domestic appliances."[54]

Playthings in their full range, mechanical and otherwise, naturally were appearing elsewhere in Chicago at this time, brought in by crate-loads while the city's population swelled, that summer and fall. Evidence that New Worlds idealism had settled in among the youngest appeared in toy books, as in *By Land and Water*, which offered an around-the-world journey: "This book contains pictures and verses descriptive of the characteristic modes of travel in the United States, Canada, England, Ireland, Australia, India, Egypt, and other lands where strange ways prevail." Another McLoughlin toy book played a role in a childhood saint's move from nursery to wonder tale: *Around the World with Santa Claus*.[55] McLoughlin also issued the *Wonder Story Series*: "The following are the wonderful stories: Rip Van Winkle; Ali Baba, or the Forty Thieves; Jack, the Giant Killer; Aladdin or the Wonderful Lamp; Robin Hood; Robinson Crusoe." Older children could enjoy Pantomime Toy Books, similar to paper dolls or toy theaters, which included "Aladdin" and "Sleeping Beauty," or longer story books of *Robinson Crusoe* and *Swiss Family Robinson*. Those who were yet older could enjoy *A Run Round the World or, Adventures of Three Young Americans*.[56]

Any among the many pamphlets, books, and photo packets showing Columbian buildings, too, participated in New Worlds idealism: for touring the different nations' buildings amounted to touring the world.

The McGinty Surprise Watch. Toy watches and toy clocks remained common in the 1890s in numerous forms. Although silverplate came into use even in toys, manufacturers often used nickel, as in this "watch" which features a man hiding behind the watch face (from Carl P. Stirn, *Turn-of-the-Century Dolls, Toys and Games: The Complete Illustrated Carl P. Stirn Catalog from 1893*, 1990).

Clara Burnham

Since it embodied the wonder-tale vision, the White City inspired writings that partook in that approach. To write about it, even when aiming to create a factual account, required emphasis on aspects that revealed how the fair offered New Worlds idealism in physical form. One effort to capture the experience appeared from Clara Louise Burnham, whose novel *Sweet Clover: A Romance of the White City* appeared in 1894. Although at publication its subject seemed already historical, it took on wonder-tale overtones, with its characters reacting to the marvelous artifice that realized "the possibilities of the Celestial City," that was a "dreamland," "city of enchantment," "city of preternatural loveliness," "mystical city," and "fairy spectacle," and that came to be called Dream City by the novel's end.[57] The Midway Plaisance appeared likewise as a "wonder-world of a street" for its scientific aspect, planned by the Fair's Ethnology department, as well as for its extravagant humbug aspect, in its "Barnumizing the Fair."[58] The Midway, however, had its own celestial aspect, with nightly illumination by "soft arc-moons" and the spectacle of "the great Wheel, slowly revolving in sparkling light as though, sweeping through the heavens, myriad stars had caught thickly along its edges and were borne on to earth."[59] As one character remarks, "it is to be expected that science will do everything possible toward annihilating space."[60] At the same time these attractions of the Midway have their ominous and imposing aspects, the Wheel being also a "monster" and "a gigantic steel web," while the Midway's representative offerings from the greater globe are "some dirty and all barbaric."[61] The fair's vastness in itself offers discomforting perspectives, as during its dedication ceremonies, in which the "largest audience gathered together under one roof" finds itself in circumstances in which "only a Brobdignagian could have felt at ease."[62]

The artificial city, like the philosophical "artificial man" that is society, achieves its own life. Burnham's character Jack Van Tassel observes of the White City before its formal opening that it is like Galatea: "We are waiting to see the breath of life breathed into the statue." Rather than being performed by the Goddess of Love, as in Ovid, this act falls to an elected official. "The music had ceased. The president had begun to speak. It was a solemn moment, a triumphant moment, when at last the electric button was pressed, hitherto motionless machinery suddenly throbbed, and the vast pulses of the stately, statuesque White City began to beat."[63] It seems a complete, complex being; and as another character in the novel, Lovina Berry, notes, "That Midway is just a representation of matter, and this great White City is an emblem of mind."[64] Another notes about the White City after dusk that its proper inhabitants are its statues. "This is a sort of No Man's Land … and when it grows dark here one feels that these marble creatures gain life. See that population on the Peristyle! They belong here. We are only strangers." The inanimate creations achieve symbolic life by the "mystical irradiation" of electricity.[65] Yet this ability to endow the lifeless with life threatens conventional life. Lovina Berry notes, "I wonder how soon electricity'll take the place o' folks. Seems if 't won't take long"; and she feels enchanted by a mechanical operation at the Fair for raising chicks. She takes one home, calling her the "electrical chicken" and naming her Electra.[66]

To Chicagoans and visitors alike, the White City's purpose seems captured in the electric fountain shows twice each evening, in the Court of Honor, dubbed "the illumination."[67] Twin spectacles bring these nightly events into clearer focus. In one, West Point cadets display the "elegant precision of their movements" as they march, seemingly endlessly and seemingly oblivious to their surroundings.[68] Being individual components within a military machine, viewers can distinguish between them neither in their actions nor their inner workings, with an officer commenting, "when you know one, you will know them all. They can talk only on one subject."⁶⁹ A second spectacle offers a different aspect. Early autumn brings the Parliament of Religions—"the congress which, among the many that preceded and followed it, proved, to the general surprise, to be the one of greatest interest to the public." A serious counterpart to the Midway Plaisance, the Parliament succeeds where the "wonder-world of a street" fails, fixing in the public mind that the White City's illumination extended out beyond, and also out *from* beyond, the West.⁷⁰ This glimpse of an integrating world sees symbolic representation in the fascination felt by fairgoers from the "revolving globe of light" in the Electricity Building, and "the various whirling globes and wheels."⁷¹

As a marvelous machine, the White City comes in for comparison to toys and toy-like public spectacles. Fairgoers experience a "constantly stimulating panorama," and when riding the Wheel they see the whole reduced to a "panoramic view."⁷² Similarly, the Midway is "always changin' like one o' these kaleidoscopes," and is busy with "kaleidoscopic life." Its Moorish Palace seems all "tricks and optical illusions," including a labyrinth of mirrors, while nearby camel rides call to mind the games "pitch-and-toss" and "cup-and-ball."⁷³

Symbolically the fair also becomes a museum, a direct descendent of the Philadelphia Peale museum, with the wax figures in the Moorish Palace, the mammoth in the Anthropology Building, and three-dimensional displays meant to convince viewers of their reality.⁷⁴

True to the wonder-tale tradition, too, the miraculous machine ends when the fair does. A cannon gives a "long sullen roar" marking the moment when the magic drains from the Dream City, leaving not ruins but the "corpse of the White City" that later goes up in roaring flame, a Brobdignagian upon a funeral pyre.⁷⁵

The Oz Melodrama

By the late 1800s, literary events were establishing that the crop of writers that had arrived in 1856 was a bumper one. The British Isles in that year had heard H. Rider Haggard, Oscar Wilde, and Bernard Shaw raise their first squalls—with Shaw's undoubtedly pronouncing scathingly upon the world. From obscure Chittenango, New York, meanwhile, came Lyman Frank Baum's answering cries.

Thirty-seven years later Baum visited the Magic City and left it with deep and lasting impressions. Baum's somewhat haphazard experiences beforehand had included writing melodramas and running a store in Aberdeen, North Dakota, with toys among its attractions.⁷⁶ Five years before the fair, in 1888, the year that Bellamy's utopia appeared, Helena Blavatsky's *Isis Revealed: A Master Key*, made an impression upon him; and, the next year, the bestselling *Blue Fairy Book*, edited by Andrew Lang, did likewise.⁷⁷ Baum tried his hand at fairy tales, with considerable success. With W.W. Denslow he then entered into a contract to produce an illustrated book, *The City of Oz*, which became then *The Emerald City*, and which appeared finally as *The Wonderful Wizard of Oz*, in September 1900.⁷⁸ With the reading public primed by Baum's fairy tales, the book became a number-one bestselling book in America for the holiday season.⁷⁹

The Wonderful Wizard of Oz strongly reflects the country of its origin. Wilde and Haggard showed inclinations toward exoticism and the occult—impulses not foreign to Symbolist works; and Shaw pursued a serious social vision that would inspire Wells, in his turn, to nurture his capacities as a social visionary. Baum, on the other hand, created an American fairy tale that built upon world's-fair eclecticism, magic, and humbuggery to create simple delight. The melodrama in *Oz* centers around a lost girl named Dorothy, whose journey brings into conjunction the tale's sectional beings. They embody the soul, partitioned along Platonic lines.

In Plato, the heart represents Courage, the principle of ambition or strength of will—which in *Oz* the Lion aspires to acquire. Baum's character may have been inspired by a Columbian attraction: Hagenbeck's trained animals, put regularly through their paces on the Midway. In Burnham's *Sweet Clover*, the lions seem less than fearsome; and her character Mildred Bryant notes, "I felt for the lions sometimes, too. I didn't like to see them demean themselves. When one had to hold the end of a rope in his teeth and swing it to let a hound jump, it seemed rather small business to demand of the king of the forest."[80]

Baum presents a most unpretentious and likeable Intellect, housing it in his character the Scarecrow. He, too, seeks to acquire what he believes he lacks. Baum joins the Appetites—the desires or "feelings" that must be reined in by intellect—with an apparent mechanism: the Tin Woodman, who has chopped his body completely away with his own ax. Now entirely mechanical, head to toe, he hopes to replace his heart, that again me might have feelings. In the heathy soul, the three principles all participate in one another's qualities, and cannot truly be separated once integrated. Baum's characters each exhibit willpower and intelligence—and all display affection.[81]

A children's novelist concocting a fable based upon Platonism fell within the realm of the normal, in late-1800s American culture—much as the toy name of Autoperipatetikos had, in the early 1860s. Even though Harvard had turned away from the Classical curriculum and toward the Philosophical, causing the rest of the nation—even Yale—to follow suit, vestiges remained in American culture from the Greek and Latin studies that, together with Puritanism, had first shaped American thinking.

A great success as a novel, *The Wonderful Wizard of Oz* soon enjoyed equivalent popularity on the stage, being first presented in a musical extravaganza in June 1901, in Chicago. It opened in a New York City in July 1903, under shortened name: *The Wizard of Oz*, in a production that made actors Dave Montgomery and Fred Stone famous as the Scarecrow and the Tin Woodman. It seems inconceivable that the countless children reading *The Wonderful Wizard of Oz* never concocted costumes and toys to play-act one or more characters; and virtually impossible, that the stage-melodrama lacked its echoes and reiterations during children's playtimes across America, and during adult costume-revelries. Makers of tin, iron, and cloth toys had yet to make it an everyday affair to create toys based upon popular characters from novels, cartoons, or the stage—making it also quite conceivable that no major toymakers around 1900–01 invested in the designs, tooling, and materials necessary for issuing *Oz* character toys. Had they known that the novel and its sequels would have perennial appeal, a toy-making notion might have appeared in their minds. At the time, Baum's story seemed simply another popular novel; and in its stage version, simply another popular musical.

Yet the novel's ideas and characters were nearing mass acceptance. The theatrical productions traveled to California in 1903, making it a coast-to-coast phenomenon. Store windows included Oz characters in displays, as in the Manhattan window with a full-size carriage pulled by the Saw-Horse, driven by the Tin Woodman.[82] In late 1904, a comic drawn by Walt McDougall, *Queer Visitors from the Marvelous Land of Oz*, appeared in Sunday papers; the next summer, giant papier-mâché Oz characters appeared in Chicago.

Besides Baum's further Oz novels, the tales appeared in other media—as in an early radio show in 1908, by the Radio Play Company of America.[83]

Given the circumstances, paper novelties and toys almost undoubtedly appeared that were evocative of the novel or play. It seems likely, too, that many such manufacturers steered away from exactly evoking Baum's characters, to avoid tussles concerning rights with author, publisher, artist, stage-actors, or stage-producers.

What might the toys have been, besides items for costumery? Toy theaters must have appeared, given that the paper dolls would have offered characters whom a child would instantly recognize. As to small games, tricks, and figurines, any small manufacturer could have drummed up such items during the weeks when the play was proving a triumph in Chicago, or elsewhere. Any such company would have hired a street-huckster to vend the toys on sidewalks outside the theater. The theaters themselves, moreover, might have passed out advertising cards with Oz-related images on one side, to be cut out and played with. Theaters, for instance, often gave out toy mirrors backed with advertising. They may have offered toys pulled off the shelf, moreover, that could be painted or otherwise altered slightly to evoke a Dorothy, a Scarecrow, or a Tin Woodman. A lion, long a standard in toy-making, could always be, of course, the Lion.

Other entrepreneurs might have offered balloons painted with a face, or with "Wizard." The Wizard gyroscope top, issued around this time, had no explicit connection, but doubtless benefited from the novel and play, all the same. Some sellers may have offered painted horses, monkeys with wings, or green-tinted spectacles. Funnels would have turned department-store mannikins into Tin Woodmen, while scarecrows borrowed from none-too-distant farmers' fields would have provided simple means for drawing passersby' attention to store windows. Even a heart-shaped item, placed near a mannequin's chest, might have caught the eye, just as heart-shaped items—and, again, pocket watches—must have become toys, during the play's run.

The Wonderful Wizard of Oz seized the public's imagination to a degree that later readers may find hard to grasp. Yet in contrast to daily experience for Americans in later decades, the available entertainments and diversions in the nineteen-aughts remained few; and such was the vaudeville stage's relentless winnowing of the wheat from the chaff, of the truly audience-pleasing from the humdrum, that a national hit stood out starkly. *The Wizard of Oz* rose above mere hit-show success, however. It continued on tour for many years, while being taken up by other companies who found other successes with the same material. More than the thrill of a season, and more than merely an accidental hitting-on-head of the current fashionable nail, it became a cultural event large enough to be discernible even from historical distance. Its ingredients entered its parent culture's texture. It became invisible, due to being so immediately engaging, and so immediately omnipresent.

The Oz story and its characters, rather than being seen as oddities, became typical elements in American culture with the same rapidity achieved by the telegraph or the telephone.

The Tin Woodman

Unlike Lion, Scarecrow, or Dorothy, the Tin Woodman is a laborer. As a woodcutter, his tool and badge of employment, the ax, brings him sorrow: it causes his gradual and eventually total conversion into a machine, making him so much an ultimate, in terms of human-parts replacement, that Baltimore Gun Club members would have found in him a kindred soul and an inspiration. He ranks among true automata not only for being a self-running machine, which finds emphasis late in the novel when he acquires a clock for a heart, but also for being a human rendered machinelike by routine labor. Baum makes the Tin Woodman's nature as a literal automaton no less explicit than his nature as a symbolic one. He moreover depicts the Tin Woodman as an American automaton, based not on carefully fabricated and delicately moving Swiss and French mechanisms but rather on the simple figures made by toy-making "tin men"—with the Steam Man's stovepipe hat replaced with the inverted oil-funnel of the machine shop.

The Tin Woodman embodies the positive attitude toward the automata that prevailed in America, in 1900. "Automatic," as a word, still projected a sense of Modernism to business customers, as is evident in its use in manufacturer-names in 1900. That year in New England, for instance, firms bore such names as the New Haven Automatic Lighting Company, the Gray Automatic Pay Station Company, and Waymouth Lathe and Automatic Machinery.[84] Business and industry took pride in the notion of replacing human or animal labor with mechanical and electrical equivalents: they were, in fact, creating prosthetic devices to enlarge the capacity of human endeavor, although these prosthetics in effect were replacing entire human workers. They served to "take the place o' folks." The Tin Woodman's story, in which he finds himself partially mechanical, then entirely, had become commonplace.[85]

Following the Tin Woodman's debut came that of the second popular mechanical man from Baum's pen: the clockwork character Tik-Tok, introduced in 1907 in *Ozma of Oz*. Baum's play, *The Tik-Tok Man of Oz*, reached the stage in March 1913, followed by the book version, *Tik-Tok of Oz*. As a clockwork being, Tik-Tok emerged from the world of American toys made by northern-states clockmakers and tinsmiths. Baum's characters of the Princess and Betsy find this on Tik-Tok's copper-plated body:

SMITH & TINKER'S
Patent Double-Action, Extra-Responsive, Thought-Creating, Perfect-Talking
MECHANICAL MAN
Fitted with our Special Clockwork Attachment.
Thinks, Speaks, Acts, and Does Everything but Live.

"Isn't he wonderful!" exclaimed the Princess.
"Yes; but here's more," said Betsy, reading from another engraved plate:

DIRECTIONS FOR USING:
For THINKING: Wind the Clockwork Man under his left arm, (marked No. 1).
For SPEAKING: Wind the Clockwork Man under his right arm, (marked No. 2).
For WALKING and ACTION: Wind Clockwork Man in the middle of his back, (marked No. 3).
N.B. This Mechanism is guaranteed to work perfectly for a thousand years.[86]

Poe's ratiocinative dissolution of mystery finds expression in Baum's first Oz book, moreover, in relation to an automaton.[87] Where Poe's subject outwardly seems a mechanical chess-player, Baum's Wizard takes varied appearances, with one being a large, floating head surrounded by flames and smoke, thunderous of voice, and terrifying to those who call upon him in the royal hearing-chamber. Poe's essay reveals the Chess-Player to be a machine designed to impress viewers, with a dwarf inside to pull the levers; and Toto the Scottish terrier pulls aside a curtain to reveal the fearsome Oz to be a device meant to intimidate viewers, with a "little man" behind a screen to pull levers. Tin Man, in other words, has company in the Land of Oz as a machine—although this one in the Emerald City proves to be a false automaton. The re-integrating soul, represented in the Yellow Brick Road travelers, discovers the "magic" of the Wizard to be hum-buggery.

As had Poe, Baum was giving symbolic form to the human being confined within the machine. A fallible human trapped in the Land of Oz, the Wizard lacks the "magic" required to leave a magical land. He has the technical know-how to maintain the illusion of magic, however—and to maintain his rule. While as successful in his illusions as Poe's Chess-Player had been, in playing to audiences, his very success forces him to stay forever behind the curtain, working levers in isolation from any who might crave an audience with him, and who might otherwise have given him human sympathy and comfort.

The floating, thunderous Oz-amplification in the royal hearing chamber falls into the automaton-category that was emerging in wonder tales: the machine that follows the instructions of its controller and does so at a physical remove.

The "remote control" that Lewis Mumford would come to regard as a deeply symbolic hallmark of the Modern century saw expression in the mechanical figures of the wonder tale. While Lytton's remote-controlled automata never became popular figures, Oz and his deceptions did.

As did most toys, early *Oz* toys disappeared as though they never had existed. For children, any toy lion, rag doll, or tin figure served for an *Oz* figure, during play—and so were nearly invisible to adult eyes from the start. The age in toy-manufacturing that belonged to the "official" toy and the "licensed" one had only just opened. The generation being brought up on a child's-novel diet that included Baum's mechanical characters, however, felt comfortable giving their own children toys that expressly represented mechanical humans.

Those children would belong to the first generation to grow up playing with popular, commercially manufactured, and mass-produced "robot" toys, in the 1930s.

Child with cast-iron lion and locomotive. "Barr" studio photograph, San Antonio, Texas: "2 yrs old, 1913" (author's collection).

Twelve

The Antigravity Clock and the Moon

The moon has a face like the clock in the hall...
—Robert Louis Stevenson, in 1885.[1]

But to you, O hypercritical reader, resolute to believe no item of this weird adventure, what need to tell how the mutton was placed on the spit, and slowly unroasted—how the potatoes were wrapped in their skins, and handed over to the gardener to be buried—how, when the mutton had at length attained to rawness, the fire, which had gradually changed from red-heat to a mere blaze, died down so suddenly that the cook had only just time to catch its last flicker on the end of a match—or how the maid, having taken the mutton off the spit, carried it (backwards, of course) out of the house, to meet the butcher, who was coming (also backwards) down the road?
—Lewis Carrol, in 1889.[2]

...he turned at last to the sequence of force; and so it happened that, after ten years' pursuit, he found himself lying in the Gallery of Machines at the Great Exposition of 1900, his historical neck broken by the sudden irruption of forces totally new.
—Henry Adams, in 1906.[3]

Time Machines

Rudimentary workings appeared in some toy watches, so that the hands would rotate. Whether turning stem forward or back, the watch-hands moved on the toy, and also in the imagination, traveling perhaps through mental space but decidedly through mental time. This hand-held time machine might stand at a prior hour, or a later one. Insofar as it had this flexibility, the machine was, in a sense apart from the normal one, "keeping time," rather than being kept by it. While a working clock is regulated, conforming roughly to celestial movements, and checked against a sundial, a play clock goes unregulated, and conforms, if to anything, to fluid and flexible dream time.[4]

> Silently the Professor drew from his pocket a square gold watch, with six or eight hands, and held it out for my inspection. "This," he began, "is an Outlandish Watch—"

Twelve—The Antigravity Clock and the Moon

"So I should have thought."

"—which has the peculiar property that, instead of *its* going with the *time*, the *time* goes with *it*. I trust you understand me now?"

"Hardly," I said.

"Permit me to explain. So long as it is let alone, it takes its own course. Time has *no* effect upon it."

"I have known such watches," I remarked.

"It *goes*, at the usual rate. Only the time has to go *with* it. Hence, if I move the hands, I change the time. To move them *forwards*, in *advance* of the true time, is impossible: but I can move them as much as a month *backwards*—that is the limit. And then you have the events all over again—with any alterations experience may suggest."[5]

The notion that a fixed past, a fixed history, might be accessible to the time-traveler, on the other hand, resonates with materialistic determinism. For in the toy watch's dream time, if not stuck at seven-thirty, movement by the dials to an hour ago is movement to a moment that seems fixed, having been lived through—making it easy to imagine that by moving the dials, then, to an hour hence, one must land in a moment, too, "to be determined." Such a toy appears in H.G. Wells's *The Time Machine*, of 1895. This novelette's protagonist, whom Wells calls "the Time Traveler," has a housekeeper named Mrs. Watchett. In his laboratory, the Time Traveler has made a small model, or a toy, of his Time Machine—"scarcely larger than a small clock."[6] Both this toy and the full-sized version shrink distances between past, present, and future in the way technical communications shrank distances around the globe; and they travel those distances as along a pre-determined route.

An odd simultaneity occurring in backwards and forwards travel plays into any movement along this pre-determined time-route. Poe, as we have noted, had hit upon this understanding, presenting it symbolically in his unusual Sunday *jeu d'esprit*, "A Succession of Sundays." In it, Captain Pratt travels to a point in "time" that is one day behind the "stationary" day. His travel finds its perfect match in that of Captain Smitherton, who lands at a point in "time" one day forward. A conservation of time as a medium for directional travel appears as if symmetrically mirrored. The light of day with which both Pratt and Smitherton began their journeys was the same. That light of day, however, has traveled more quickly with one, and more slowly with the other.

Wells symbolically acknowledges this forwards-and-backwards balance in his chapter "The Palace of Green Porcelain"—named for the building which the Traveler happens upon after his toy clock, his Time Machine, has spun its dials far forward. To him, the Palace's nature becomes evident when he encounters its departments of natural history, geology, and paleontology. He sees on display a Megatherium, an ancient mammal, and then "the huge skeleton barrel of a Brontosaurus. My museum hypothesis was confirmed."[7] Since the Palace has other majestic galleries, some devoted to immense machinery, it seems to have been, on at least a symbolic level, a great international exhibition. With its impractical but impressive architecture, it stands as a memorial to Progress, with displays presenting its evolutionary theme in terms both biological and technological.

Themes that related to evolution and progress, which had figured so largely in Chicago's and other exhibitions, however, appear in altered light, in this future. He comes to "a gallery of simply colossal proportions, but singularly ill-lit, the floor of it running downward at a slight angle from the end at which I entered." Around him he sees the "huge bulks of big machines." Studying these draws him deeper into the gallery, "too intent upon them to notice the gradual diminution of the light."[8] The declined floor and "gradual diminution" point toward the same end. Even though the machinery has rusted into disrepair it sits upon the route that leads to the underground realm ruled by the Morlocks. The Time Traveler awakens to the realization:

> I understood now what all the beauty of the over-world people covered. Very pleasant was their day, as pleasant as the day of the cattle in the field. Like the cattle, they knew of no enemies, and provided against no needs. And their end was the same.
>
> I grieved to think how brief the dream of the human intellect had been. It had committed suicide. It had set itself steadfastly towards comfort and ease, a balanced society with security and permanency as its watchword, it had attained its hopes—to come to this at last.[9]

At least for this tale, Wells allows an element to intrude from Rousseau, who compared society-softened humankind to domesticated animals in the stall: "as he becomes sociable and a slave, he grows weak, timid and servile; his effeminate way of life totally enervates his strength and courage."[10]

The year that the Columbian celebrated the push-button transition from puzzling science to technological magic, Wells had published his first stories. His lengthier imaginative works appeared in a series between 1895 and 1900, the year Baum's *Oz* appeared. He diverged from the Vernesque wonder story, however, and did so in a way that might be called Chesney-esque, or Kiplingesque. Kipling, only a year older than Wells—having been born the year in which Verne's *From the Earth to the Moon* saw print—had blossomed as a writer of short stories and novels in the time before Wells began enjoying success. In the stories few signs appear that Wells gave time to Verne's major influences of Poe, Dickens, and Wyss, even though he noticed Verne himself. Yet he read his contemporaries and gave ample sign that he had absorbed the Gothic impulse. His first novel, *The Island of Doctor Moreau*, in 1896, offered homage to Mary Shelley; and some among his short stories, such as "The Man who Could Work Miracles," reacted to the fairytale tradition.

In Wells, Gothic pessimism runs rampant, if stripped of its moral element to make room for positivism. If he did owe anything to Poe, it may have been the *monstrum horrendum* who first appeared as the narrator in "Ms. Found in a Bottle" and reappeared in later works: the man who adheres to "physical philosophy" to the exclusion of moral philosophy—and who, at least in "Ms. Found," becomes invisible to his fellows. Wells's depressingly self-centered characters in *Moreau*, who do seem horrendous monsters, led to yet more—in *The Invisible Man* in 1897, *The War of the Worlds* in 1898, and *When the Sleeper Wakes* in 1899.

That a more effervescent Modern impulse worked upon his soul, however, did appear from time to time.

The Antigravity Clock and the Moon

The year after Baum's *Oz*, Wells offered readers a character who stood midway between Verne's characters Pittonaccio and Fogg: a flesh-and-blood man whose reduction to machinery seems evident. In *The First Men in the Moon*, Bedford, the narrator, describes this "oddest little figure." He clarifies that toy-invoking adjectival pairing, "oddest little," in terms relating to both clock and play.

> He was a short, round-bodied, thin-legged little man, with a jerky quality in his motions; he had seen fit to clothe his extraordinary mind in a cricket cap, an overcoat, and cycling knickerbockers and stockings. Why he did so I do not know, for he never cycled and he never played cricket. It was a fortuitous concurrence of garments, arising I know not how. He gesticulated with his hands and arms,

and jerked his head about and buzzed. He buzzed like something electric. You never heard such buzzing. And ever and again he cleared his throat with a most extraordinary noise.

There had been rain, and that spasmodic walk of his was enhanced by the extreme slipperiness of the footpath. Exactly as he came against the sun he stopped, pulled out a watch, hesitated. Then with a sort of convulsive gesture he turned and retreated with every manifestation of haste, no longer gesticulating, but going with ample strides that showed the relatively large size of his feet—they were, I remember, grotesquely exaggerated in size by adhesive clay—to the best possible advantage.[11]

The narrator repeatedly notices this man: "next evening the apparition was repeated with remarkable precision, and again the next evening, and indeed every evening when rain was not falling."[12] This man, named Cavor, emerges like a jointed Nuremberg figure from a town's clock-dial at his proper hour; and, as does the Tin Woodman, he avoids the rain.

More in common with Fogg's story than Pittonaccio's, however, Cavor's movement revolves around Earth's globe, as his "round-bodied" form suggests. He does what a pocket-watch does, reducing Earth and its movement to an emblem to be worn fastened to a chain; and he travels to a place where Earth herself appears to be reduced in size, by distance, to a parlor-table terrestrial globe. Cavor embodies the navigator clock, who acquires a perspective so gigantic that his home planet becomes a minikin-object.

In *The Time Machine*, Wells offers characters as nameless types, not as theatrical stock characters, nor as realistic individuals. In *The First Men in the Moon*, in contrast, he gives a stock character a major role, even while the narrator remains a type character. In this hybrid wonder tale, melodrama's stock company has for its representative the buzzing, eccentric Cavor. Since no sectional counterparts make an appearance, Cavor's nature remains indistinct. An absurd dramatic element suitable to melodrama, however, appears in the tale's "scientific" notion: the "antigravity" discovery that allows Cavor to aim his sights Moonward. Cavor, an old-fashioned inventor of the 1700s variety, acts with self-sufficient, self-absorbed confidence, and in such a way that neither the state nor the larger scientific community intrudes. In this, his actions echo those of the solitary alchemist Victor Frankenstein; and, also in this, Wells offers a situation already highly unlikely by 1901.

In offering idealized scientific achievement rather than realistic, the novel diverges from the Verneian wonder tale. Upon this foundation, moreover, Wells builds a quasi-realistic novel. This appears most markedly in the foreground character. Putatively the hero of the tale, the narrator Bedford possesses disagreeable dimensions and qualities in his worrying about winnings and earnings, his becoming violent when threatened, and his regarding science as a tool for exploiting situations. Although this simplified description may paint his colors too strongly, Bedford does embody a stereotypically middle-class type, concerned with the demands of his mid-parts and almost not at all with the needs of his uppermost. Utterly normal in his thoughts, he seems utterly abnormal in the wonder-tale context: for he appears in not satirical but worldly garb; and, once on the Moon, he remains unchanged from what he was on Earth. While he might be seen as a satiric portrayal of the imperialist mindset of the British scientific and industrial establishment of that mid–Modern time, the element goes missing from his portrayal that Poe and Verne injected countless times, in making their satiric moments evident as such. Their barbed spears flew propelled by humor. In Wells, earnestness serves. Bedford, a muscular presence, acts; and if the reader follows him in these rough movements, they do so, as well, as in his example of not laughing. If perhaps he shows as much thickness of head as arm, his presence seems intended to harmonize the fictional experience of the extraordinary journey with the mindset of the somewhat energetic but also somewhat dull beefsteak who might be reading it, to make matters that are marvelous easier for such readers to swallow without much chewing.

Wells was reshaping the wonder tale along the lines of "naturalism," so that the thoughtful, middle-class, self-consciously adult reader of 1901 might nod with sympathetic, if ethically sleepy, acceptance. With Verne, an amused adult reader might glance around surreptitiously, in hopes that no one has noticed the pleasure being taken in such unrealistic goings-on. With the solid and self-assured Wells, readers set aside any qualms about their maturities, since the Wellsian narrator shares in their adult weaknesses and foibles. Through all his more imaginative novels, this character never succumbs to real self-searchings.

Though Cavor ranks among Wells's greatest creations, the author must have felt uncomfortable with him: for he keeps Bedford fore and center, beginning to end, and leaves Cavor imprisoned and then silenced by the Keplerian Selenites. Yet in this lies the novel's symbolic strength. In this Moon journey, an extraterrestrial machine swallows the epitome of the terrestrial human machine—with the Moon being the clock of the future, and Cavor, the clock of the present.

Time's Dissolution

The degree to which a clock-dominated time-sense came to be equated with everyday existence might be measured by how often, in wonder tales, a commonplace phrase appears before the reader as something to be taken literally.

In this commonplace, a person "loses all sense of time." In wonder tales, the phrase appears as a borrowing, insofar as it is taken as representing a literal situation within the context of the fictional flow—as occurs to the hapless survivors aboard the wreckage, in Poe's "Ms. Found in a Bottle." They find themselves in a realm with only night, not day, and without "means of calculating time."[13] Losing the knowledge of time, or losing the time-sense, in the 1800s became a means whereby writers conveyed an escape from normalcy, as well as an escape from the automaton named Earth. In *First Men on the Moon*, Bedford and Cavor, whether in space or on Moon, find they cannot account for their erratic sense of time, as indicated by their only occasional hunger.[14] Variations in the time-sense also find expression in quite other terms, in other stories—as in the juxtaposed sleeping and sleepless characters in Oz:

> The woman now gave Dorothy a bed to sleep on, and Toto lay down beside her, while the Lion guarded the door of her room so she might not be disturbed. The Scarecrow and the Tin Woodman stood up in a corner and kept quiet all night, although of course they could not sleep.[15]

In Baum's story this scene replays itself time and again. Dorothy takes her rest while fabricated beings remain wakeful and waiting, being round-the-clock-ready automata. Similarly, the regimented Selenites of *The First Men in the Moon* remain awake while the humans sleep, and find "sleep" so alien a concept that they quiz the human-clock Cavor concerning it.

In children's tales and poems, the Earth-automaton appeared as always awake, somewhere on its surface.[16] Since an Earth globe like an onionskin marble has bands that are time zones, its inhabitants exhibit a mix of the awake and the asleep.

The Earth-clock time-zones came to enjoy simultaneous existence, in practical terms, once "Earth's electric circle," in the poet James Russell Lowell's words, came into physical existence. An individual might inhabit a Vondervotteimitiss with only one answer in sight, as to the time of day; yet by telephone this individual could be "present" in another time-zone. Callers might be in two times at "the same time." One person might "telephone" someone whose time is tomorrow; another, someone whose time is yesterday.

As noted, these onionskin marble-bands wrap around a second time-structure. James Hutton established that in peering through Earth's layered strata one was looking down into an almost unimaginably deep well of bygone millennia. The geological gaze could take the mind back to more ancient times, or bring it forward to more recent ones. The celestial mechanism, in other words, continues in operation below Earth's surface. Creative logic in the 1800s had only to speculate that this time-sequence might continue beyond Earth's surface—so that the farther one might ascend, the farther one might travel away from the present to see the future.

In Cavor's anti-gravitational departure, he leaves behind the Earth-clock's complex and subjective situation, to enter absolute Lunar conditions. Existence there goes on largely sub-surface, as within a single, great enclosure. It goes on in an orderly manner, as within a "scientific" factory. Its beings go unsleeping about their activities, so that all are pursuing matters simultaneously. Being so much like a manufactured thing himself, it rings symbolically true that once there, Cavor must remain there. He can never leave that which he is, himself, becoming.

Into the World Machine

If Poe's works may be said to have opened the doors to the Modern wonder tale, then the dread of falling into an all-encompassing inner world must be said to have formed an element within the form, at the moment those doors opened. In "Ms. Found in a Bottle," which appeared near the start of Poe's career in fiction, the hapless narrator conceives of himself as hovering "upon the brink of eternity," and then finds that ship is "whirling dizzily, in immense concentric circles, round and round the borders of a gigantic amphitheatre, the summit of whose walls is lost in the darkness and the distance."[17]

The First Men in the Moon presents a celestial body, the Moon, as a location situated symbolically in the future; and it presents the Moon itself as an enclosed, automatous machine, with all the inhabitants dwelling not upon its surface but deeply within it. Wells perhaps echoes Tennyson's "magnetic mockeries" in calling the Selenites "mad mockeries of men" who are also "like the creatures of a dream,"[18] being organic members of a complex society that has so constrained them to their roles that "each is a perfect unit in a world machine." Society has solidified to such a point that each of these perfect units might well be automatic: "In the moon ... every citizen knows his place. He is born to that place, and the elaborate discipline of training and education and surgery he undergoes fits him at last so completely to it that he has neither ideas nor organs for any purpose beyond it."[19] At the same time their appearances reintroduce Kepler's dreamt Moon, with the internal, city-building denizens preying upon the evanescent creatures of the Moon's sun-blasted yet void-frozen surface.

Visions of enclosed worlds beyond Earth's atmosphere had kinship to visions of Earth as an enclosed system; and both of these extended ideas had kinship to Victorian architecture. Two years before *Moon*, in 1899, Wells envisioned a London as seen from the "flying stage" where aircraft landed to drop passengers from Paris. "Their seat looked far over London," Wells wrote of his characters Denton and Elizabeth, of the twenty-second century. "To convey the appearance of it all to a nineteenth-century reader would have been difficult. One would have had to tell him to think of the Crystal Palace, of the new-built 'mammoth' hotels—as those little affairs were called—of the larger railway stations of his time, and to imagine such buildings enlarged to vast proportions and run together and continuous over the whole metropolitan area." Not merely enclosed cities, these complete dwellings house the total population. Wells envisioned not a sprawling metropolitan area that would spread gradually over the entire land of the British Isles but instead cities that would grow upward, and draw into their rising enclosures even the laborers who tended the agricultural regions: "at last in all England only four towns remained, each with many millions of people ... there were left no inhabited houses in all the countryside."[20]

These towers rise in such a way as to echo, or reify, social hierarchies. The privileged occupy the uppermost "head" regions while the poor live in squalor at the feet, reflecting the stratification worsening in Wells's own time, with increasing gaps between economic classes. "In the nineteenth century the lower quarters were still beneath the sky; they were areas of land on clay or other unsuitable soil, liable to floods or exposed to the smoke of more fortunate districts, insufficiently supplied with water, and as insanitary as the great fear of infectious diseases felt by the wealthier classes permitted. In the twenty-second century, however, the growth of the city story above story, and the coalescence of buildings, had led to a different arrangement. The prosperous people lived in a vast series of sumptuous hotels in the upper storeys and halls of the city fabric; the industrial population dwelt beneath in the tremendous ground-floor and basement, so to speak, of the place."[21]

Visitors to the Centennial Exposition, if they were not accomplished technicians nor scientists, felt doubts and confusions in a vague and incipient way. Wonder they did feel, strongly engendered by that widening gap between technical accomplishments and public understanding. Yet now as the doubts and confusions were deepening, the sense of the wonderful was being dulled by the public's ability to take technology for granted, once achieved. Wells in 1899 would have a character of the twenty-second century exclaim, "Nowadays we have almost abolished wonder, we lead lives so trim and orderly that courage, endurance, faith, all the noble virtues seem fading from mankind."[22]

Naturalism and the Superhuman

As noted above, in pursuing naturalism in his stories, Wells for his characters embraced "ordinary types" rather than the sectional humans that Verne and Baum employed so effectively, and that would continue in importance in wonder tales from Appleton and Claudy in later decades. Wells's shift might well have represented a positive one, insofar as it might have led toward a deeper assessment of human potential to adapt to technical and social change. Yet that positive achievement seemed reserved for those having realist bents, such as William Dean Howells, whose *A Traveller from Altruria* in 1894 demonstrated that a writer need not discard realism in characters when approaching the imaginative. Even so, the Wellsian type-character did serve as an answer to a problem that had arisen from the sectional-human character: for satirical excesses in description led naturally, through symbolic borrowing, to the notion of the superman—a Victorian term that, although masculine, applied to either sex. Certainly the supermen in *The Coming Race* seemed mostly female.

Poe's ratiocinative master, the detective Dupin, as noted earlier, offers an early source for the Modern superman—one that differs considerably from the model offered by Shelley's Being. Yet Dupin amounts to an isolated intellect, a mind apart from other portions of his dissected soul, and not an intellect inconceivably enlarged beyond the normal human condition. As noted, too, it seems to have fallen to Dickens to expand Dupin to dimensions that edge ever-so-slightly beyond the normal, in his Mr. Bucket, in the 1852 *Bleak House*— Bucket being a detective possessed of purely rational powers of analysis and deduction, in combination with an inventive approach to situations, a mastery over disguises, and an insight into conditions to surpass the ordinary. The tragedy of Lady Dedlock becomes, in the end, all the greater because even the surpassingly insightful Bucket fails to intervene in time.

Although he seems so much a solitary figure in the novel, in literature Bucket left progeny by the score. The 1890s in literary England would be called "the decade pre-eminently of magazine supermen, drawn with varying degrees of skill, detectives and criminals, sea captains and banditti, vivified mummies and nondescript mystery men, but all alike in their strength and silence, their practical omnipotence, and omniscience in pursuit of ends often the most trivial."[23]

Wells's approach, in altering the Modern wonder tale, oddly enough led to the diminution of the individual, if for no other reason than that naturalism calls for characters

Christmas scene. Alongside the traditional toys—horn, drum, sadiron, carriage, and dolls—this photograph shows nesting blocks, which often included fairytale or wild-animal elements, a Schoenhut Rolly-Dolly, and a friction-powered vehicle toy probably sold under the Hill Climber name, having been made in Dayton, Ohio. These last, which were early motor-vehicle toys, appeared by 1900 and continued in production into the 1910s (author's collection).

either to know or to learn their places—with rude awakenings often used to accomplish the latter. Efforts must end in defeat when the one making them starts out defeated. Attempting to go against the massively integrated system that technological society was becoming, in Wells, amounts to futility: for his type-characters lack the idealism, the transcendental drives, that open the door for self-realization. His 1899 *A Story of the Days to Come* follows a beleaguered couple who are forced into hard employment and grindingly low wages due to being indentured to society's machine. For a solution, Wells has them be named beneficiaries in a will—in other words, to be moved like game pieces into the wealthy class, which grants them the boon of happiness, ease, and power. Having set aside melodrama's sectional human and its inherent possibilities for self-realization, Wells answers the dilemma created by his characters being types, who are locked into the fate that is due to these types, by changing, with authorial providence, those types. Authorial providence makes *A Story of the Days to Come* less depressing than his usual, so that it falls more in line, surprisingly, with Horatio Alger's vision.

That one can effect change in the world does matter in the Verneian tale—if one is to except, as Hetzel did, *Paris in the Twentieth Century*. Even in *Hector Servadac*, the characters exert themselves to the fullest and most inventive degree before emerging from their difficulties through Providence. Verne's lessons from history give backbone to the notion that self-application matters—as he made clear, for instance, in the information-cascades concerning aviation explorers in *The Clipper of the Clouds*. Verne celebrated accomplishments, each one of which confirmed that the individual act has consequence. The narratives themselves exemplify this sense; and they show, too, souls rebuffing a society that cares little for distinct individuals, in preferring types. In this, Verne follows Poe's "Hans Pfaall," in having inventive individuals give society its satirical comeuppance.

Wells, in contrast to Verne, inclined toward the maelstrom tale, as shown especially in *Dr. Moreau*. In this developing form, the individual often confronts the world in the company of others, undergoes an extraordinary trial that destroys those companions, inventively responds to the danger, and survives. He emerges alone; and his loneliness grows to the level of wounding and suffering—because he is disbelieved. The extraordinary nature of his experience has changed him—while society, dismissing his words as lies and empty claims, goes on unchanged.[24]

Toward Pessimism

Wells's quite popular novels set a course followed by many future writers. They would favor efficient description, in semi-literary news-writing prose, above the song of ideas; and they would pursue the naturalistic development of ideas, concepts, and forms even when those ideas, concepts, and forms might be, at heart, more symbolic than naturalistic. The social realism Wells developed in his novels ate away at the predilection he himself felt in his youth for the wonder tale, so that in the end realistic doubt, even despair, supplanted the wonder-sense.

The movement away from valuing the symbol and toward valuing the particular; away from valuing a set of ideals concerning human nature and toward valuing a set of ideas about human society; away from excited explorations of not-yet-possibilities and toward jaundiced explorations of probabilities; and away from aggressive humor and immediacy and toward reactive bitterness and contemplative anguish: these would lead to the imposition of *faux*-realism as the model for wonder tales, by the Modern century's waning days.

Even without Wells, this alteration might have occurred. Symbolist writers and artists wielded influence in relatively small literary circles—while writers taking lessons from Zola in France and Howells in America were becoming bestsellers. In Dickens's time a sense of social consciousness had begun influencing that part of society that considered itself most aware and enlightened. Now it was moving to a place more nearly central to society. In these years, Jane Addams pursued her social work in Chicago while advancing notions of women's suffrage and international peace; and Edwin Markham answered in deed the question that the symbolist poets in France had been asking in a seeming vacuum, as to whether a role remained for poetry in Modern life.[25] In these years, too, in the aftermath of the Columbian Exposition's World Congress of Religions, which encouraged the development of a sense of commonality and social responsibility among churches, a sense of liberal engagement with society began to pervade discussions of congregational and pastoral missions, dismaying conservative preachers who reacted by beginning to advocate a strengthened devotion to Fundamentals.

A concern for social issues, and for the creative role an individual might claim within society, began to be not unusual but usual as a characteristic among intelligent citizens; and

Optical diversion. Besides often serving to record toys and play, the camera itself became a medium for play. Identified as "Mr. Marshall," the man in this photograph appears to be pulling himself in a coaster wagon. In this skillful double-exposure the only "ghostly" element is the wagon's handle, seen both on the sidewalk and in the standing Mr. Marshall's hand, which, too, is a bit ghostly. Photograph, early 20th century (author's collection).

this, among writers and readers, would feed into the careers of such writers as John Steinbeck and Upton Sinclair. This rising concern could not have left the wonder tale, even in its the juvenile versions, untouched. Verne had combined his influences—Poe, French theater, Wyss, and Dickens—to produce fantastic adventures usually replete with liberalism and humanism. Such novels as *The Begum's Fortune* and *The Black Indies* gained strength in their addressing social problems created by Modern scientific and technological progress—doing so in symbolic form, and often with satirical notes. Yet Verne's tales burrow into Earth or veer into strange or distant regions with an eye for fact and detail, for novelty and irony, for self-determination and invention—leaving other aspects to realists and naturalists. His journeys take extraordinary turns, bearing along lives that are likewise extraordinary, and that belong to theater rather than photogravure.

Yet what Wells did, which Verne had not and would not have done in any sense willingly, was to extend the writer's sense of sympathy in a different direction. Wells reached a point at which it made sense for him to place an average man, even a flawed and not necessarily intelligent, likeable, nor amusing man, where he might be viewed as centerpiece in a major and novel-length wonder tale.

Wells came to exert immense influence by publishing thick tomes on science and history, by guiding cinematic content, and by writing novels of contemporary life. Wells and his socially directed activities outshone Verne's aging and dimming star, in England and America. They helped alter the tone of wonder tales from the wittily satiric to the conscientiously pessimistic.

Thirteen

The Middle Years and the Ripping Veil

> But in the New World things make haste:
> Not only men, the state lives fast—
> Fast breeds the pregnant eggs and shells,
> The slumberous combustibles
> Sure to explode. 'Twill come, 'twill come!
> —Herman Melville, in 1876.[1]

> "Mr. Glenn H. Curtiss and Mr. Wilbur Wright ... skillful and clever aviators, pioneers to whom the Art of Flying owes a colossal debt, do not laugh at any suggestion concerning the future of the aëroplane, for they recognize the fact that the discoveries and inventions of the next year may surpass all that have gone before. The world is agog with wonder at what has been accomplished; even now it is anticipating the time when vehicles of the air will be more numerous than are automobiles to-day."
> —"Edith Van Dyne," L. Frank Baum, in 1911.[2]

> "...a time when the future existed, before the anti–Utopias began to appear."
> —Van Wyck Brooks, in 1957.[3]

The Middle Generation

In a time-period's middle generation, noted Van Wyck Brooks, appear the writers who typify their times.

This observation, if as self-evidently true as it seems to be, suggests that the generation born late in the prior time-period must be the one to publish works that open the time-period and help define it.

In that case, the Modern century's early writers who felt some inclination toward wonder tales went through their childhoods and youths when Poe and Mary Shelley were writing: Edward Everett Hale, born 1822; Fitz-James O'Brien and Verne, 1828; Charles Dodgson, 1832; James Thomson and Frank R. Stockton, 1834; Samuels Butler and Clemens, 1835; Edward S. Ellis and Francis Henry Atkins, 1840; Bierce, 1842; and Robert Duncan Milne, 1844. As noted, Verne's first maturity as a writer corresponded roughly with the

Modern century's opening. Bulwer-Lytton, born earlier, in 1803, holds an outsider's place in this group.

From this it follows that middle-generation writers—the ones who typify the Modern century—would have been children during Verne's early and middle career.

To that middle generation we might name Bellamy and Robert Louis Stevenson, born 1850; Garrett P. Serviss, 1851; Harold Cohen, 1854; Baum and Haggard, 1856; Edwin Arnold and Gertrude Atherton, 1857; Arthur Conan Doyle and Kenneth Grahame, 1859; James Barrie, 1860; John Kendrick Bangs and Edward Stratemeyer, 1862; John Jacob Astor, 1864; Kipling and Senarens, 1865; H.G. Wells, 1866; Carolyn Wells, 1869; Garis, 1873; G.K. Chesterton, 1874; Burroughs, Jacques Futrelle, and Arthur Train, 1875; Jack London and Mary Roberts Rinehart, 1876; and George Allan England, 1877. These writers did tend to gain their literary footholds in the middle years, from the later 1890s to the 1910s.

Slightly later writers matured under this early middle generation's influence. To this later-middle generation we might name James Branch Cabell and Carl Claudy, born 1879; Johnny Gruelle, 1880; Justus George Frederick, 1882; Hugo Gernsback and Abraham Merritt, 1884; Austin Hall, 1885; Hugh Lofting and Olaf Stapledon, 1886; Ralph Milne Farley, 1887; Philip Francis Nowlan, 1888; Karl Čapek, Howard Phillips Lovecraft, and Edward Elmer Smith, 1890; Otis Adelbert Kline and Ruth Plumly Thompson, 1891; and Aldous Huxley, 1894.

Brooks's observation appears to hold. In the Modern century, middle-generation writers refined and re-imagined ideas and approaches introduced in the early years, and produced works that influenced late-Modern writers. The utopian and dystopian strands implicit in New Worlds idealism had become, by this time, an explicit dichotomy in Verne's novels. Bellamy, London, and H.G. Wells solidified a focus upon socialism; London, upon naturalism. The sequel-producing tendency nascent in Verne, Clemens, and Dodgson flourished in dime novels and became notable in middle-generation writings, with Baum, Burroughs, Doyle, Garis, Rinehart, Senarens, Stratemeyer, and Carolyn Wells producing series featuring nearly unchanging characters. Bangs, Burroughs, London, Stevenson, and H.G. Wells expanded on the early Modern wonder tale's fascination with prehistory, sometimes celebrating the primitive state that was being eliminated by the world-machine. Burroughs, Doyle, and Haggard developed the superhuman as a continuing, unchanging, and sometimes immortal figure. Stratemeyer and Garis, in the *Tom Swift* series, remade dime-novel wonder tales into a form having more sustained plotting and less pernicious racial stereotyping, more generally acceptable to the more socially conscious readership of their time.[4]

At least in America, in the middle years, the historical novel came to prevail as the leading literary form, as measured by popularity. In separating its narrative from the reader's immediate reference-points, these novels did share aspects with wonder tales that involved dream-trips to past or future times. Light humor, fantasy, and romance also prevailed, as with the Barrie and Bangs bestsellers of 1896 and 1897, and George Barr McCutcheon's *Graustark* of 1901.[5] In 1902, Doyle's *The Hound of the Baskervilles* became the first detective-story bestseller in America, followed in 1909 by the first American-written detective-story bestseller, *The Man in Lower Ten*, by Rinehart.

American bestseller lists gave scant indications that imaginative stories were becoming standard in publishing. Although Verne died in 1905, his most popular titles were selling in numbers never recorded, since reprint and pirate versions appeared from multiple publishers; Baum and Garis were turning out imaginative series for children and young adults, which proved massively popular but beneath the notice of more literary publishers and observers; and the Modern wonder-tale's structural focus upon demystification was finding expression in detective stories, including girl-detective novels by Baum, Stratemeyer, and Carolyn Wells. Technological topics and influences naturally found greater expression through these years, as well. As Alice Payne Hackett observed, in 1905 "novels were beginning to utilize motor cars and wireless telegraphy ... in their plots. ... 'Motormania' hit the nation in a big way and practically all the publicity pictures of authors showed them at the wheels of their 1905 automobiles."[6] Motormania, besides giving rise to the "automobile romance," formed a focus for various youth-novel series of the 1910s, led by the Stratemeyer-Garis Tom Swift books and the Motor Boys books by "Clarence Young," the first two of which Garis wrote.

The Planet Juggler

As we have seen, Wells in *First Men in the Moon* played a variation, probably without so intending, on Poe's human trapped within the machine; and although superficially having nothing in common with *Around the World in Eighty Days*, Wells's book depicted in a similar way a world encompassed by technics, completely encasing a human soul already possessing mechanical character.

From Poe to Verne and then to Wells, the connection between the human-encompassing machine and the global machine grew steadily stronger. For readers, however, to take in the notion that Earth herself might succumb to technical encompassment, in full, required an element that moved beyond "the earth's electric circle" and toward the electric sphere seen spinning at the Columbian Exposition. That element had appeared in positive symbolic form, as in the Earth-ball seen by Moon-travelers; and in negative symbolic form, as in the ultimate explosive in Verne's early imagining: "Men will go on inventing machines till they devour them ... the end of the world will come when some immense boiler, heated to three million atmospheres, will blow up the Earth." The experience, event, or object that would unite Earth as a whole also appeared symbolically in centralized global command, as personified in Wells's Moon-ruling arthropod, the "Grand Lunar." The Grand Lunar's command over the Moon, being centrally placed within, created the effect of simultaneity throughout that sphere.

The technology that had not existed, and that would bring new reality to dreams and fears of world-enclosure, arrived during the years that Wells was writing: for wireless telegraphy made instant global communication seem possible, and the eradication of distance, plausible. In Baum's *The Magic Key* in 1901, a "flat metal box" called the "automatic Record of Events" captures events from around the globe, much as Glinda the Good's magical book does within the Land of Oz's limits, in Oz novels. The 1901 children's novel also includes the "Illimitable Communicator ... a simple electric device which will enable you, wherever you may be, to converse with people in any part of the world, without the use of such crude connections as wires."[7]

The notion found different expression the next year, in a story by a writer who later, from 1910, would edit *The Business World*, and much later, in 1925, release a book, *Masters of Advertising Copy*, that would be regarded as a classic in that trade.[8] Commercial activity and writerly ambition often went hand-in-hand, with Baum having been a shopkeeper and Burroughs soon to be one, and even Henry Adams having been employed by a newspaper called not the *Boston News* but *Daily Advertiser*. Justus George Frederick, the writer who would gain fame in advertising, in 1902, at age twenty, published his *Argosy* story "The Dupe of a Realist," which shares two semi-real characters with countless other fictional stories in the middle Modern years: Edison and Tesla. Frederick's turns upon the instantaneous, universal thought-transmission of an advertisement for "Bascom's biscuits." Although exposed as a hoax, the effort obliquely succeeds—as a disguised test of public susceptibility to mass suggestion.[9]

Instantaneous thought-transmission would take humankind a step nearer global consolidation and integration; and, in linking the notion to advertising, Frederick drew connections between consolidation, integration, and control. He underlined these steps in his

"The Planet Juggler." Although its last chapter bears the title "World-Peace," in this 1908 tale the scientist-hero transforms entire planets into battleships. The "planetary mind," as it was dubbed by Van Wyck Brooks, slipped easily into a planetary militarism (from J. George Frederick, *Famous Fantastic Mysteries*, March 1940).

1908 tale for *All-Story*, "The Planet Juggler," in which the "news" industry receives threatening messages via telegraphy from a planet around the star Canopus. The "Canopian" telegrapher is conducting experiments that require him to draw upon other worlds' resources. The being's plans would raise the most "advanced" species to greater heights, while exploiting and eradicating such less-advanced ones as Earth's humans. "My ambition," says the being, "is to consolidate the numberless solar systems about me into one huge sphere"—a "consolidated civilization scheme [that] is going to systematize the universe." As in any machine state, numberless and faceless Others planned to subjugate the individual self.

Frederick links the means for communication to the Canopian's need for Earth's resources, not through statement but via association: for he has the advanced technology itself, wireless telegraphy, deliver this threat to Earth. Only by this means can the Canopian speak to Earth as a whole, simultaneously. In symbolically representing mass-subjugation, wireless telegraphy represents the sign to the larger civilization that the smaller one stands ripe for culling. Earth's wireless telegraphy points toward a world-machine that, if plucked by alien hands, would contain within it all humankind. In response to the Canopian threat, Earth's political powers assemble a "congress of representatives"—a single global consolidation to pit against the threatening interstellar consolidation.

In the story, "civilized" attitudes on Earth anticipate ones to be held by Western witnesses to the then-upcoming World's War. Noting that the basic techniques and weapons used in that war, which would start in 1914, had been developed before and not during it, a historian would argue that civilization had been saved by its increased technical strength. "War being the ultimate resort of force, then the poet, the dreamer, the scholar, the doctor and the organizer of the arts of peace may succumb to the bully with the square jaw, the low brow and flesh-tearing incisors, unless the civilized man uses his resources and talents to make weapons which are stronger than the bully's fist. This is precisely what civilization does in order to protect itself."[10]

Imaginative writers could do a great deal with ever-increasing strength of weaponry, as did Verne, with his 1897 "fulgurator" in *For the Flag*—which would seem, for much-later readers, uncomfortably near the atomic bomb. Pierre and Marie Curie discovered radium the next year; and as early as 1904, Henry Adams was working on power-increase calculations that would enable him to write, in 1905, that "the assumption of unity, which was the mark of human thought in the Middle Ages, has yielded very slowly to the proofs of complexity. The stupor of science before radium is a proof of it. Yet it is quite sure, according to my score of ratios and curves, that, at the accelerated rate of progression since 1600, it will not need another century or half century to turn thought upside down. Law, in that case, would disappear as theory or *a priori* principle and give place to force. Morality would become police. Explosives would reach cosmic violence. Disintegration would overcome integration."[11] Lewis Mumford noted that Adams "almost alone among his contemporaries, alone not merely among historians but among physicists, immediately understood the revolutionary social potentialities of radium and radioactivity."[12]

In the 1908 "The Planet Juggler," Earth scientists combat the "Napoleon of the universe" from Canopus by tapping into nuclear power. One among them, Elverson, serves as "the civilized man" in Frederick's tale.

> Elverson, stimulated by the great necessity and crisis, was showing positive genius in grappling with problems of a cosmic character. He astonished the electricians of Europe by proving the existence of a hitherto incomprehensible potential force in radium, and showed them how it could be applied in moving great bodies. [...] Not only did this absolutely revolutionize the world's light and power

problems, making it ridiculously cheap, but it also afforded a potentiality which would give the earth a practical independence of the sun for an indefinite number of years.[13]

Frederick, in other words, sensed much what Henry Adams did, if perhaps for other reasons. From Adams's point of view, "man had translated himself into a new universe which had no common scale of measurement with the old."[14]

In Frederick's tale, the "translated" Earth joins with another world threatened by the Canopian. Though described as peopled by artists and writers, planet Mars proposes war as the solution.[15] Elverson, now Earth's technician-ruler, with his "potentiality" turns these two planets into battleships, to threaten other entire worlds with destruction.

This wonder-tale's title reverberates with the understanding that its planets have symbolic weight far beyond their physical mass. Astronomical bodies interconnected through gravitational forces become things to be "juggled." The power to be achieved by exploiting radium, by "grappling with problems of a cosmic character," makes a world fit the palm of a hand. Elverson would appear to be the majestic goddess Columbia but for his violent agenda.

In this appropriation, the story's Earth becomes literally what it is symbolically. It carries violent meanings and associations alongside playful and practical ones, in being a ball. This new Earth, moreover, takes the already familiar images that show a railroad locomotive whirling around the globe, and makes the globe and the locomotive be one and the same. Robert Frost, too, would seize on this notion. Observing the positivist impulse, he noted that people might well "take earth by the pole/ and tired of endless circling in place/ steer straight off after something into space."[16]

The Erupting Primitive

During the Modern century's first half, Western societies took increasing measures to improve life for "the man on the street." In the early 1900s, even so, such a man found himself on a street down which great social accomplishments rarely arrived to increase personal satisfaction.

Perhaps due to his speculating from within a relatively stable Victorian, or American Victorian-esque, social climate, the sense of civilized equanimity so well projected by Bellamy remained elusive. Instead, unremitting progress in science, industry, medicine, and sanitation seemed to enhance chances that a recrudescence of the primitive would occur. In the years before the World's War, such groups as democratically organized labor movements and women's suffrage organizations made spectacles of themselves, engaging in not only ungenteel but unexpectedly violent behavior. In England, as a historian noted, "a universal note of desperation, of hysteria, of pent-up passion" ran through events before 1914.[17] The feelings beneath the unrest had found some embodiment in the 1890s and 1900s in those sensationalist "magazine supermen." Although going largely unleavened by Poesque or Vernesque satire, the stories still gave countless readers diversion from the drudgery of quasi-respectable lower-class and quasi-genteel middle-class existence. Perhaps the man-in-the-street feeling had become contaminated by the notion that to be average, as a citizen, resulted in burial within the increasingly complicated mechanism of society, alongside the Signal-Man. As social options increased, personal options decreased, creating a closing-in box around the individual—one that would require Herculean powers to escape. The average citizen possessed few or no such powers. All, perhaps, felt that such powers must exist, all the same, in some hidden inner recess of the soul, waiting to be unlocked, as in an H. Rider Haggard tale, or in the extremely popular 1903 Jack London tale, *The Call of the Wild*, in which a domesticated dog, following an atavistic call, becomes a ruthless superbeing in a violent land of wolves, human or otherwise.

Among those in the 1910s and 1920s who tapped into this feeling, one American writer's persuasive manner won him an immense readership. Sensational self-importance and the attitude of superiority intrinsic to bearing "the White Man's Burden" still influenced magazine stories, as they had romances and dime novels in the later 1800s. In the early 1900s, they fed into the works of Edgar Rice Burroughs. From 1912 to 1914, he made a lasting impression upon *All-Story* readers with fantastic romances that contained strong motifs, and often controlling motifs, of the recrudescence of the primitive. In his first novel in 1912, *Under the Moons of Mars*, which became *A Princess of Mars*, Earth's John Carter takes a dream-journey to reach a Mars that is a ruin-clogged, war-ravaged desert—the setting for a wild concatenation of exploits among creatures both Earthlike and extraordinary, with Carter's civilized-and-yet-primal vigor bringing justice to situations filled with strange terrors and delights. The low-gravity conditions that allowed diverting scenes in Verne's *Hector Servadac* come in for different play here, allowing Carter, as a military man achieving Martian peace, to perform superhuman feats.

This debut led to a Mars novel-series. Burroughs's next for *All-Story*, *Tarzan of the Apes*, gave rise to a series featuring the primal-and-yet-civilized "ape man." In a novel in which Tarzan encounters the "Pithecanthropus" as well as numerous modern dinosaur descendants, Burroughs penned paragraphs capturing the deliberative mind giving way to superhuman savagery.

> He paused again at the third floor, and here, in spite of the hangings, he saw that the interior was lighted and simultaneously there came to his nostrils from within a scent that stripped from him temporarily any remnant of civilization that might have remained and left him a fierce and terrible bull of the jungles of Kerchak. So sudden and complete was the metamorphosis that there almost broke from the savage lips the hideous challenge of his kind, but the cunning brute-mind saved him this blunder.
>
> And now he heard voices within—the voice of Lu-don he could have sworn, demanding. And haughty and disdainful came the answering words though utter hopelessness spoke in the tones of this other voice which brought Tarzan to the pinnacle of frenzy.
>
> The dome with its possible apertures was forgotten. Every consideration of stealth and quiet was cast aside as the ape-man drew back his mighty fist and struck a single terrific blow upon the bars of the small window before him, a blow that sent the bars and the casing that held them clattering to the floor of the apartment within.[18]

Two years after *Moons of Mars*—in 1914, the year when a recrudescence of primitive savagery might be said to have stricken Europe, bringing decades of outward civility to an end—Burroughs published a third series-beginning novel. *At the Earth's Core* takes place in a region named Pellucidar. A minor literary tradition had sprung up in America, in Poe's day, around the notion that Earth was hollow, and that it contained another world or worlds within. Poe drew upon it, to a degree, in "Ms. Found in a Bottle" and in *Pym*; and this element may have given Verne impetus, consciously felt or otherwise, fictionally to journey "to the center." Burroughs likely embraced both the American tradition and the Vernesque model in *Earth's Core*, in which his adventurers find themselves placed into a realm in which the "primitive" perseveres, and rules, in the way the primitive seemed to need to do.[19]

In the year of *Under the Moons of Mars*, however, Conan Doyle had published his novel *The Lost World*, which follows an expedition inspired by a report that prehistoric creatures survive on a South American plateau. For its first readers, the irascible scientist-hero's name would have evoked the 1870s oceanic scientific survey of the *H.M.S. Challenger*. The professor finds, on the remote plateau, that it plays host to a population gathered piece-meal from across the realm of geologic discovery—a hodgepodge that helps make him another Hardwigg. The novel would stand in contrast to tales by Burroughs, who took a more evolutionary viewpoint, and who introduced creatures into his tales that he extrapolated from, not borrowed directly from, geological writings.

By then, that the world was, indeed, regressing in some fashion did impress itself on many who pondered the Great War, or World's War—so that it might seem reasonable for a historian to embrace a new definition for war: "force, violence, killing."[20] The means by which the West so swiftly retrogressed to the primitive became apparent, as well. The means came with the achievement of technological supremacy through mass-production. Mass-production itself was gaining symbolic force in this context, especially given Henry Adams's observation that "resistance to superior mass is futile and fatal."[21]

That early historian of the World's War, writing in 1916, argued that civilization had been saved by its increased technical strength. Yet he noted, too, the "distinctly less than civilizing" effect of Modern warfare:

> Early in the war, bomb-makers used jam tins and bottles or any handy receptacle that could be filled with an explosive and set off by a fuse. Later, manufacturers appeared for producing a variety of bombs in great quantities. Instances occurred of five thousand being used in a single day over two hundred yards of trench. The bomb had an effect distinctly less than civilizing. A soldier's strategy for the offensive might consist of throwing a bomb from the traverse, having the force follow the explosion by rushing along the traverse and catching the defender with a bayonet while he is *hors de combat* from the effect of the explosion. A historian identified this kind of warfare as an "orgy—characteristic of cave dwellers battling on a precipice in its ferocity."[22]

The Erupting Comical

That dinosaurs might excite the public, early novels by Verne, Bulwer-Lytton, and John Jacob Astor made clear. Burroughs's many adventures that drew upon their presence, and Doyle's one, confirmed this. Deepening the spectacle came a new medium, film, and its new art of "animation." The art form's name broke from an old word's meaning: Thomas Gray's "animated busts" in the churchyard, in the 1700s, were lifelike, not automated. The new name's meaning came to supplant the old word's sense nearly completely.

One early film animator had established himself already in both New York newspaper cartooning and in vaudeville. Cartooning and vaudeville paired themselves comfortably, as suggested by the fact that a cartoonist on the opposite coast, Bud Fisher of San Francisco, also had a vaudeville act.[23] In New York, Winsor McCay's stage-show relied upon the art of drawing. At times he drew pictures of a man and woman "aging" on a large sketch pad before an audience, while a small ensemble provided a musical backdrop. He engaged in what might be called time-lapse illustration—or time-travel illustration, revealing to others the literal face of the future.

That filmmaking had kinship to both cartooning and vaudeville seems apparent in the fact that both McCay and Fisher readily embraced the new form. In the New Yorker's case, the cartoonist himself took a leading role in the work of animating, and succeeded to such a degree that he has come to rank as America's first animator of note.[24]

For his first effort, in 1911, McCay drew characters made famous by *Little Nemo*, his daily strip based on the sleep-journey. The next year he unveiled the cartoon short *How a Mosquito Operates*, and in 1914 moved into amusing prehistory with *Gertie*. This featured a cartoon *Brontosaurus* three years before Willis O'Brien's pioneering stop-action animation appeared in *The Dinosaur and the Missing Link*.

In the late eighteen-hundreds—years that, outwardly, were politically quiet, internationally—newsprint cartooning had risen to prominence as a form to engage adults and win over children, in "comic papers" that combined amusing drawings with captions. Richard Felton Outcault's character *Yellow Kid* appeared in 1895, followed by others; and the adjective "comic" took on new meaning as a noun to indicating the papers themselves. Rudolph Dirks's *Katzenjammer Kids* made first mischief in 1897; Carl E. Schultze's *Foxy Grandpa* and Frederick Burr Opper's *Happy Hooligan* followed in 1900; Buster Brown and his talking dog Tige appeared in *The Yellow Kid*, then re-appeared in a strip of their own in 1902; *The Wizard of Oz* appeared in 1904; and McCay's *Little Nemo in Slumberland* began in 1905. By that year, when light fantasy and upper-class romance were at their height, with Barrie in the theaters and McCutcheon and Bangs in the bookshops, the meaning for the word "comical," like "comic," had expanded beyond its earlier meanings to embrace its new reference to the papers.

Happy Hooligan. Although Albert Schoenhut began as a manufacturer of toy pianos, by the early 1900s his company's line had expanded to include such toys as circus sets and "Rolly-Dolly Toys." Happy Hooligan ranked high among early comic characters embraced by manufacturers for toy licensing. Happy Hooligan Rolly-Dolly, 5 inches tall, A. Schoenhut Co., early 1900s (photograph by and collection of the author).

How great or little an impact this shift had in greater society will likely remain unknown. Its impact in children's society, however, may be measured, to a degree—insofar as American mercantile operations backed away from offering mere "mechanical toys" to entice children and their parents. They emphasized, instead, "comical mechanical toys." New "comical toys" began with Yellow Kid cap bombs, cast-iron vehicles, squeak toys, beach toys, bowling toys, sand toys, and toy-theater figures. Foxy Grandpa, Happy Hooligan, Buster Brown, and others inspired so many licensing deals between cartoonists and toymakers that it seems unlikely that any playthings categories went untouched, or un-comical, in the years before 1914.[25]

However minor a change this might seem, it proved lasting. Toys prior to this had appealed to children along generic lines. Relatively few exceptions crept into the market, reflecting influences from *Robinson Crusoe*, *Gulliver's Travels*, and fairy tales. By 1900 it was seeming increasingly appropriate to encourage children's delight by appealing to their literary and comic-page interests—whether helped or discouraged by the development, in the

1890s, that American publishers were beginning to acknowledge overseas copyrights, to some vanishingly small degree.

Comic-page characters tended to be unrealistic, exaggerated, and fanciful. Yet those very qualities made them ideal subjects for toy makers to depict, emulate, or mimic—so that the generation of children receiving playthings in the 1900s grew up knowing the new sense for the word "comical," and not the one their parents had known. These children knew Yellow Kid, Foxy Grandpa and Old Sport, Little Nemo, Mutt and Jeff, and Little Orphan Annie, among many others; and their reaching for these favorites pointed toward the day when any object, if rendered "comical" by adding a comic-page face to its surface, would fall into the toy category, and into the purview of toy manufacturers.

These comical figures all conveyed elements borrowed from the theatrical, the absurd, and the fantastic. Little Nemo in particular indicated that in the States the wonder tale had become everyday fare—not only for children dazzled by McCay's imagination, but also adults. Even in those who had lost their childhood wonder, McCay's artistry commanded admiration. Each strip offered a condensed wonder tale, with some fantastic incident or adventure unfolding, only to end in the last panel with Nemo's falling from his bed and waking in surprise. The marvelous machine, in McCay, is the dream that ends as must all—day after day.

Wonderland is all about. In a time when materialist evolutionism held sway, idealism persisted in odd corners of society—even in the "funnies." This "Buster Brown" panel appeared in 1905 (from R.F. Outcault, *My Resolutions: Buster Brown*, 1910).

As "comical" applied to general toys, "character" applied to dolls. Thus Dolly Drake and Bobby Blake dolls, around 1911, though comical in appearance, appeared in catalogs as character dolls. This term applied also to more realistic dolls who exhibited some particular aspect, as in the Drake and Blake contemporaries Swat Mulligan in baseball outfit, The Athletic Baby in knitted sweater, The Kimono Baby, or Jack Frost, The North Pole Baby. The last had several claims to being typical for the times: "Unbreakable doll with body of good quality napped plush. Lifelike unbreakable celluloid face. Full polar bonnet to match body. Jointed hips and shoulders. A splendid knockabout doll. Has automatic mechanical voice which sounds by simply tilting the body."[26]

In a change related to the new meaning for "comical," circus toys also arrived, as in Schoenhut's Humpty Dumpty Circus. A shift was taking place in America, affecting the word "circus"—traditionally a circular building, arena, or amphitheater in which such spectacles as fights or horse-races took place. The word was coming to refer to the shows of extravagant entertainment that had become traveling attractions. The word, perhaps, had been "Barnumized." Acrobats, clowns, and trained animals were beginning to take the word as an adjective to connect them not to fixed theaters, traveling tents, nor the "rings" within the tents—in other words, not to the setting and arrangements, but to the show and the spectacle itself.

Air Ships and Space Boats

To the public, travel by means of directional balloons, or dirigibles, continued to offer an exciting prospect. That they might offer transport to regions yet unexplored found expression not only in novels but in games, such as McLoughlin's "To the North Pole by Airship." Its 1897 box shows a spindle-shaped airship hovering above a tableau of man-versus-polar bear violence. The game derived its energy from associating technology not with known but unknown achievements: for it was engaging in literal appropriation and treating the existing air ship as a symbol for the

A New Year's postcard from the 1910s uses literal appropriation in showing a motorboat aloft as an aircraft. Amusingly, the tail of the boat, with its prop, appears as the aircraft's front. Postcard, printed in Germany (author's collection).

future. The game's 1904 edition showed, in the central panel, a cigar-shaped balloon with baskets beneath holding the explorers, and a large propeller to the rear; and, in side panels, icy scenes meant to evoke the North Pole at night—so that the scenes are illuminated by stars, not the sun.[27]

Five years later, in 1909, the first human explorers did arrive at the North Pole; and in 1911, at the South. These achievements hardly dampened the fascination exerted by the Arctic and Antarctic regions: for polar wonder tales continued to appear from the pens of writers. Even less-desolate Alaska continued to offer a compelling subject for wonder tales, from 1911's *Tom Swift in the Caves of Ice* to 1925's *Don Sturdy in the Land of Volcanoes*, both by Garis. In 1926, the year Roald Amundsen crossed the North Pole in the dirigible *Norge*, a wonder tale set in the northern regions and written by George Allan England, *Lost from the Fleet*, appeared in *The Youth's Companion*.

By simile, England made a connection that exerts symbolic force in many such tales—

one that links the polar to the extraterrestrial. Ice fields, England wrote, could "look like miniature mountain chains, with ridges, hills and ravines like those on the surface of the moon, all wondrous ivory tints, blues, emeralds."[28]

At this point in time, polar regions offered a physical frontier. The fact that they could be visited only by technically assisted means, however, separated them from the now-superseded frontier that seemed reduced to a nostalgic element in novels about the Old West. The technological element made it natural that writers should link distant regions symbolically to other worlds, insofar as the linkage helped underline the sense of futurity.

Kites, Boats and Hybrids

Verne's 1886 "clipper of the clouds" had offered early evidence as to an existing association between nautical and air ships, an association that continued to prevail into the middle years: for even though powered, heavier-than-air flight arrived in 1903, toys continued appearing in forms that remained symbolic in the face of the new, realistic options. The 1907 catalog for L.H. Mace & Co., for instance, showed imported toys such as the Mechanical Flying Ships, a carousel toy with four ships dangling from the upper portion. They would spin and "fly" at the spring-motor's release. Rather than looking like the now-factual powered aircraft, these flying ships looked like canoes equipped with propellers.[29]

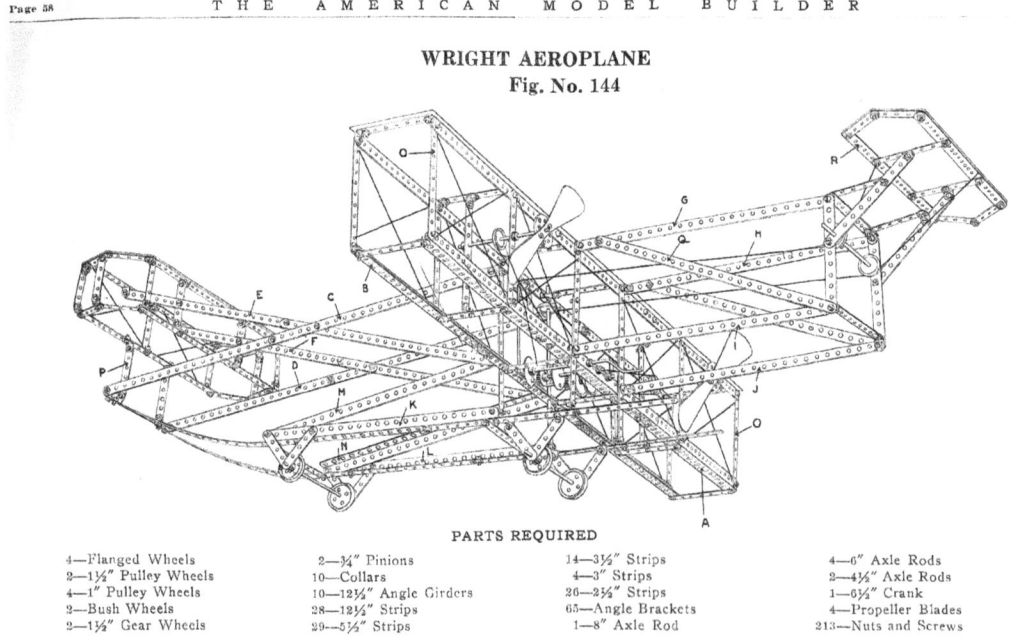

Wright Aeroplane. "Through the courtesy of the Wright Brothers," says the instruction manual for this construction kit, "we are enabled to reproduce an exact Model of their original Aeroplane. This Model stands 36" wide and 43" long when completed, and will give the builder an excellent idea of Aeroplane construction." From the 1913 American Model Builder manual of instructions, pp. 58–59: American Mechanical Toy Co., Dayton, Ohio.

In the earliest 1900s, on the other hand, other toymakers had been producing more birdlike and insect-like aerial toys that involved a basic body, lateral wings, a tail, and propulsion—with that last being the child's throwing arm, or the rubber-band twisting a propeller. While the latter "power" seems to have been slow to develop—the verb *to rubber*, or *to rubberneck*, appeared by 1899, with the twisting-around neck suggesting the twisted rubber band—at least one manufacturer, Penaud in France, had made powered flying toys that anticipated airplanes, selling the lightweight but heavily symbolic toys in Parisian shops around the century's turn. An uncle of Wilbur and Orville Wright purchased one there, and on returning to America gave it to the boys.[30] Several American toy manufacturers followed either the Wright brothers' or Penaud's innovations, relatively quickly. Milton Bradley made "an excellent imitation of the modern machines for navigating the air" by 1905; Sears, Roebuck offered a Mechanical Flying Machine by 1909.[31] The term "flying machine" distinguished these heavier-than-air evocations from the lighter-than. The term flew neck-and-neck, for a time, with "aeroplane." A "biplane" as a toy arrived by 1911.[32] By then, aerial playthings were flourishing to such a degree they required their own category in the toy industry. Specialist firms appeared, such as the Baker Toy Aeroplane Manufacturing Company and H.J. Nice, both established around 1909; and the American Aeroplane Manufacturing Company, around 1911.[33]

Despite the success achieved by the Wrights' design, hybrid aerial vehicles still excited imaginations, often taking the form of dirigibles with vanes and wings. In 1907, for instance, this combination vehicle appeared on postcards offered as confection premiums, drawn by B.E. Moreland.[34] In these drawings, the Cracker Jack Bears travel by airship, its hanging gondola having

STRAIGHT AT THE TOWER RUSHED THE RED CLOUD, AND HIT IT A GLANCING BLOW.
Tom Swift and His Airship.   Page 53.

The Red Cloud. After the depicted accident and the airship's settling on the roof, teachers and students pour out. One of the latter says, "Mayn't we see the airship? It will be useful in our natural philosophy study!" Though the tale's hero, Tom Swift, Jr., has a father within the popular series, in essence he is a renamed Thomas Edison, Jr., who earlier had appeared in wonder tales, after Edison himself ceased appearing in them as the hero (frontispiece in Victor Appleton, *Tom Swift and His Airship*, 1910).

a rear propeller. The balloon is a large box of the confection, with veinous wings protruding from the sides, and a steering rudder or stabilizer, in fish-tail shape, to the rear. The Bears visit vital places—Coney Island, the Statue of Liberty, Niagara Falls, and, of course, the five-story brick edifice of Rueckheim Brothers & Epstein, confectioners, in Chicago. They also land on planet Mars.

Rather than presenting exceptional instances of the imaginative leap, these confection premiums offer images that reflect typical instances. The candy-box aircraft found acceptance among children due to being made up, in part, of real dirigibles and flying machines—as well as the confection box, now transformed through literal appropriation. Evoking the real helped the youthful mind leap to the desirable and the imaginary—to the confection's Chicago factory, then to Mars.

In these middle years a great fluidity in images and concepts empowered the imagination, helped by the great number and variety of inventions that were constantly appearing—many of

Rocket and comet. Boys ride downhill on traditional wooden runner sleds with the typical middle-Modern names of Rocket and Comet, upsetting Santa, from whose bag fall traditional toys: horn, stuffed bear, clown, and ball. Postcard, 1911 (author's collection).

which proved insufficiently useful or failed to work at all, and so disappeared rapidly. Yet the blimps and dirigibles of the late 1800s and early 1900s proved enduring sources for imaginative borrowing. In the 1910 *Tom Swift and His Airship*, Garis offered the *Red Cloud* as the invention of balloonist John Sharp: "primariy an aeroplane, but with a sustaining aluminum container, shaped like a cigar, and filled with a secret gas, made partly of hydrogen, being very light and powerful." In the sequel, Garis refers to it as a "big biplane and dirigible combined."[35] A similar hybrid craft appears as the *Comet*, the "motor ship" operated by the Motor Boys in the 1910 and 1911 books *The Motor Boys in the Clouds* and *The Motor Boys Over the Rockies*—which is similarly described as "a combination of dirigible balloon and aeroplane."[36] Rather than having the enclosed cabin of the Tom Swift vehicle, with landing wheels beneath and propellers fore and aft, the *Comet* has an undercarriage shaped like an open, keeled, wood-slat boat, with a small pilot's cabin to the fore, where twin propellers emerge. Having no wheels underneath, it has kinship to the Mechanical Flying Ships sold by Mace.

A writer of animal tales for children, Edith B. Davidson, understood how such ideas could fall together. In *The Bunnikins-Bunnies and the Moon King* of 1912, Mr. Bunnikins and family join Mr. Gray-Squirrel in a journey aboard his airship. This vehicle-concatenation has, for a body, a cabin-cruiser of the lakes and oceans, with the broad wings and horizontal tail stabilizers of the monoplane. Runner-skids of the sleigh extend underneath, as well as wheels; and a vertical stabilizer appears like a boat rudder, situated above the hull rather than below. From an open platform in the rear, passengers may look out, as they may toward the front, from the cabin, which is commodious and comfortable. In this craft they travel to the Moon, then to Mars. These are simultaneously astronomical bodies and symbolic "islands in space," with the adventurers calling them the Island of the Moon and the Island of Mars. Though their craft is an airship, it makes an astronomical journey. The animals take in the all-important view of Earth as a globe, through the Moon King's "Look-Out Window": "Far, far below they could see the great round earth looking like a little ball, but it made

Sidewalk railway. Most railroad-locomotive toys came as "floor trains," operating without track and propelled by a push or a pull. This unusually large one would have been a wonder for any child. "Bertie, 1920," photograph postcard (author's collection).

them all so dizzy, that they did not look very long." While a journey of exploration—"No Bunnies or Squirrels had ever been seen in the Moon before"—it also offers dream-fancies in which animals can "fall" from one celestial orb to another, as from the Island of the Moon to the Dog Star.[37]

The literal appropriation involved in having the oceans of Earth stand in for the void of outer space—not only the ships but the islands and the immersive experience—would remain common during the Modern century's ending decades.

Through these middle years, a sense of romance also lingered around the aerostatic balloon. Although supplanted by other aircraft in many applications, it retained potency as a symbol of advanced, technologically supported travel through space, in wonder tales such as one in 1909 by Fenton Ash.[38] In toys this potency emerged, too, as in the Aerona Balloon from around 1914. This brightly colored, propeller-topped celluloid balloon could shoot into the air, thanks to the Aerona Revolver. The revolver, also sold separately with sets of three-blade celluloid propellers, apparently set these toys spinning fast enough to achieve lift.[39] Its being

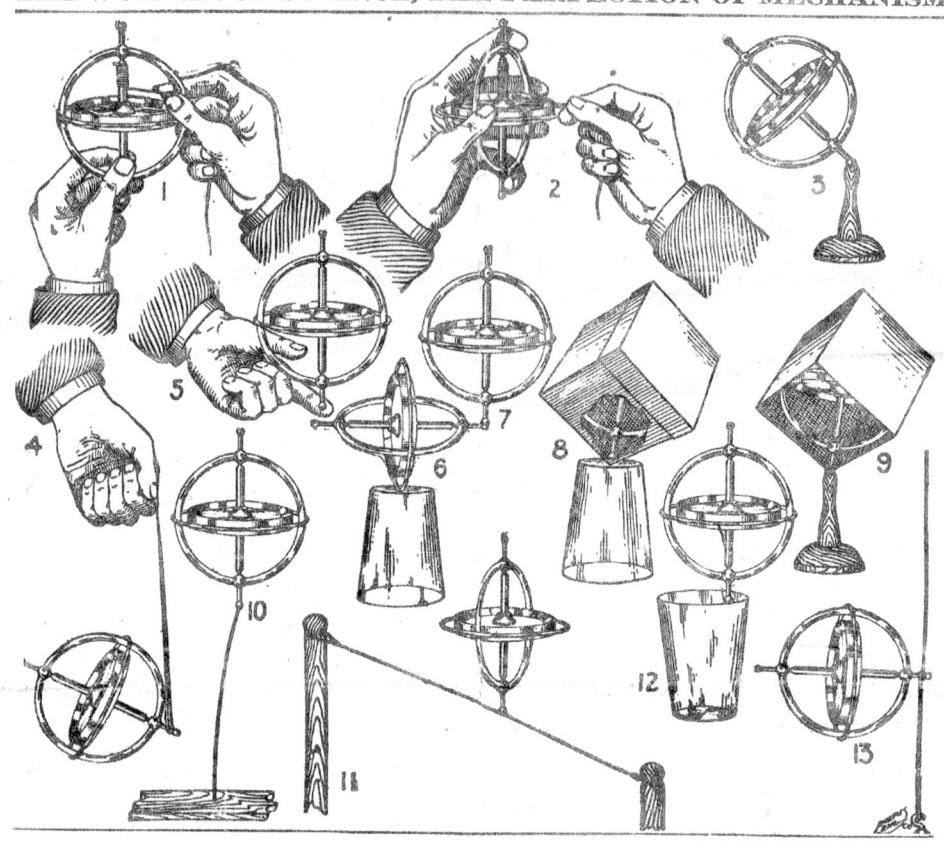

The Wonderful Gyroscope. This instruction sheet likely accompanied the Hurst gyroscope made by Chandler Mfg. Co., Indianapolis. Chandler made them from before the 1920s through the end of the 1950s, and after (author's collection).

a "revolver" may have reflected the militarism being renewed in toys at the time.

This continued symbolic vitality appeared especially in toys issued by Ernst Paul Lehmann, perhaps the most successful German toymaker to supply metal toys for American mail-order catalogs. While lightweight spring-mechanism playthings had been made in Germany since the 1850s, in the 1880s new lithographic processes helped mechanize the color printing of tinplate. Lehmann established his firm in Brandenburg in 1881 and became the most famous German mechanical-toy manufacturer in the period from the 1890s into the 1910s.

Automated horsepower. Abundant motor-related novels, often in series, reflected the intense excitement surrounding the motor car. Toy auto and driver, missing steering rod, 4-inch cast iron, 1900s (photograph by and collection of the author).

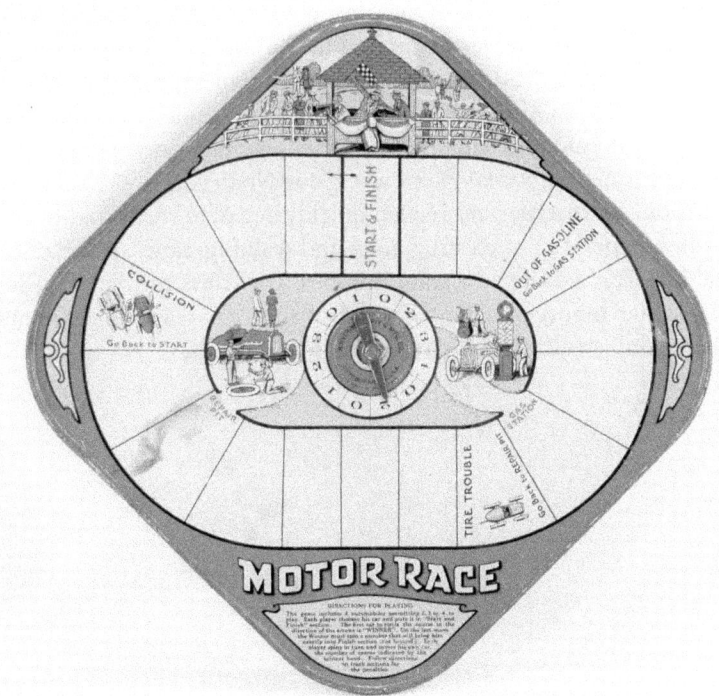

Motor Race. Lithographed steel game, 11 inches square, Wolverine Supply & Mfg. Co., 1920s (photograph by and collection of the author).

Lehman issued toys that realistically embodied the early, framework-fuselage airplanes such as had been pioneered by the Wrights and Bleriot, among others. One such toy bore the mythological name Ikarus, as befit a craft meant to travel what Verne once had termed the "aerial Icarian sea."[40] Yet Lehmann also made balloons of the round-bag, vertical-ascent variety. On one toy-balloon's globe, the company put the name Mars; on another, Jupiter. As sold in America, these were like Uncle Prudent and Phil Evan's rising aerostat, in that they could "hoist the American colours," being equipped by the Lehmann factory with U.S. flags.[41]

Typical to the Modern Century

To apply Brooks's notion to the toy world proves useful: for it leads one to see that the toys that were typically Modern-century ones were nonexistent at the period's beginning, by and large. Achieving popularity around the 1900s and 1910s, an array arrived that included toy automobiles, "automobile caps," motorist's goggles, dirigibles, flying torpedoes, triplanes, biplanes, monoplanes, motorboats, ocean-liners, steel battleships, "circus" toys, character dolls, celluloid toys, typewriters, railroad locomotives and trains, rotary presses, telephones, steel-girder construction sets, walking plush animals, and comical toys.

When these toys arrived in these middle years, they fit easily, on the whole, into existing playthings categories. Mechanical workings, toy "voices," rubber, composition, and artificial fur had become routine ingredients gradually enough to have found ready entry into traditional toy making. These older types, moreover, continued even as new ones arose: for a proliferation and expansion was occurring in the toy world, with little displacement occurring, as of yet, of the old by the new. Animal-drawn toy vehicles continued to appear alongside motor vehicles, tin mechanical animals alongside plush ones, electric trains alongside wind-ups, celluloid amusements alongside wooden ones, character dolls alongside traditional dressy ones, and steamships alongside Noah's arks.

Recently introduced toy types, moreover, quickly began to seem traditional; and theaters, toy books, rifles, paper-cap-exploding guns and walking-canes, mechanical trains, inexpensive magic lanterns, miniature steam engines, tricycles, and velocipedes arrived in even greater variety than before—as did such truly traditional playthings as household toys, tools, wagons, jacks, doll strollers, doll chests, and bisque dolls.

Fourteen

Mockeries of Mass Production

> I rejoice, my dear friend, that we live in an age so enlightened that no such thing as an individual is supposed to exist. It is the mass for which the true Humanity cares.
> —Poe, in 1848.[1]

> "I am not saying anything about that," returned Barnum. "...I haven't advocated the Proterosaurus as a Sunday-afternoon surprise, but as an attraction for a show. I still maintain that a lizard as big as a cow would prove a lodestone, the drawing powers of which the pocket-money of the small boy would be utterly unable to resist. Then there was the Iguanadon. He'd have brought a fortune to the box-office—"
> —John Kendrick Bangs, in 1895.[2]

> [T]he elder woman moved about the shop, setting it in order for the night. It was a labor of love to put the dolls to bed, to lock the glass doors safely on the puffy rabbits and woolly dogs and round-eyed cats, to close the drawers on the tea-sets and Lilliputian kitchens, to shut into boxes the tin soldiers that their queer old customer had craved....
> Yet in the last three years it had been hard to keep up the standard which she had set for herself. Toys were made in Germany, and the men who had made them were in the trenches, the women who had helped were in the fields—the days when the bisque babies had smiled on happy working-households were over. There was death and darkness where once the rollicking clowns and dancing dolls had been set to mechanical music.
> —Temple Bailey, in 1918.[3]

The Toy War

"Lifelike unbreakable celluloid face.... Jointed hips and shoulders. A splendid knockabout doll," read that 1911 advertisement noted earlier. Although describing a polar-adventurer doll, the words "unbreakable" and "knockabout" might have compelled a military leader three years later to place a massive order to replenish his forces. The movement toward a society in which "no such thing as an individual is supposed to exist" was reaching fruition in a war to be dubbed "the World's"—named in the manner of an international fair.

War moved toy production westward from its prior center, somewhere around the region of Germany, France, Holland, and England, and toward the United States, a country that was flirting with isolationism thanks to the oceanic moats around its castle. Yet the States already were fighting a war with Germany, insofar as toys were concerned. Even tin soldiers that were much the same as "Nuremberg flats" were coming to be advertised as being made in the United States. As toy historian Richard O'Brien noted,

> during the early 1900s.... Germany began exporting toys so cheap that many American manufacturers couldn't compete. Imports of toys and games totaled about three million dollars in 1900; by 1908 they topped seven million; by 1912 imports captured 40 percent of the market; and in 1914, they constituted exactly half. The coming of war drastically reduced imports, but when the United States declared war on Germany on April 6, 1917, the toy industry suddenly found itself threatened with restriction of materials. ... The Toy Manufacturers of the United States emerged to cope with the situation. Other toy guilds and trusts had been tried before, but this one took. It became a lobbying group that convinced Congress of the need for a continuing supply of toys to American children, war or no war, and for tariffs against imports that would encourage a native industry.[4]

In those years, when children were first playing at being motorists, aeronauts, ocean-crossers, comical characters, circus performers, skyscraper-builders, and telephone operators, E.P. Lehmann's often-fanciful presence in American shops had first blossomed, only to diminish and then cease. To help fill the gap, a Bavarian-born emigrant in New York, Ferdinand Strauss, left importing for manufacturing, much as had Adolph Meinecke in response to war conditions half a century earlier. Strauss specialized in tinplate mechanical toys. Ohio Art, Unique Art Manufacturing, Walbert Manufacturing, Wolverine, and others in the States also began enjoying success in the field.

When the war that had amounted to "cave dwellers battling on a precipice in its ferocity" ended, the impulses that had been leading technocrats toward international control emerged unscathed. This would have been true no matter which nations should have claimed victory. Despite warnings from Henry Adams and others, a cultural consolidation was taking place on a scale unprecedented in history—a "consolidated civilization scheme." It promised, or threatened, to take the globe into itself, as an entirety. Wonder tales and their anti-wonder counterparts, in the middle years, had already taken a melancholic turn, reflected in such titles as Wells's "A Dream of Armageddon," in 1901, and *The War in the Air*, in 1908; London's *The Iron Heel* in 1907; and England's *The Elixir of Hate* in 1911. Planet Mars had already renewed its association with the Roman war-god, in Wells's 1898 *The War of the Worlds*; in the "march and two step" sheet music of 1901 of "A

Within the machine. The soldier is caught within the military machine, and his actions are limited to emerging from the hatch, and then slipping back within. Louis Marx and Co., postwar (photograph by and collection of the author).

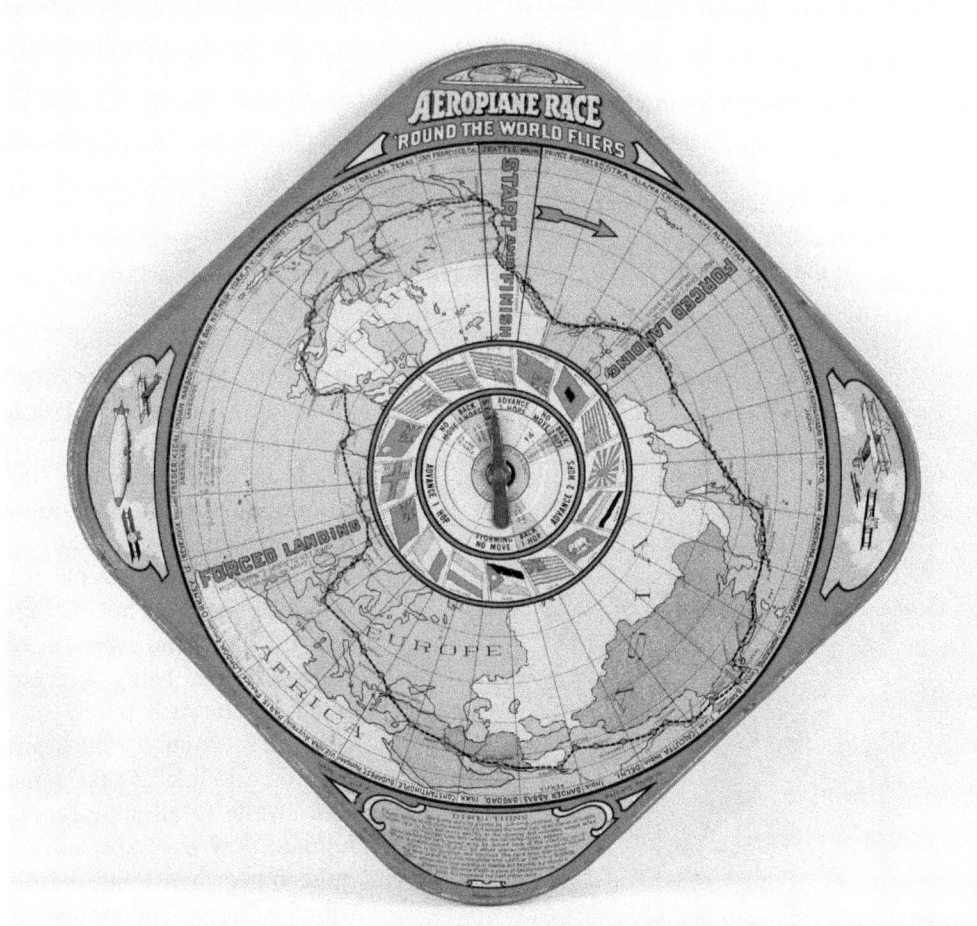

Wolverine, a toy company founded in 1903 in Pittsburgh, made its name with mechanical toys, but also produced topical games such as this Aeroplane Race, 'Round the World Fliers spinner board. The link between air travel and aerial competitions figured large in adventure novels of the same time. Lithographed steel, 11 inches by 11 inches, Wolverine Supply & Mfg. Co., 1920s (photograph by and collection of the author).

Signal from Mars"; in Frederick's "The Planet Juggler"; and in Burroughs's novels in which an ex-Confederate gentleman's dream-journeys center almost entirely around battle and war. His first novel's title might well have been *A Princess of Wars*.

The Mass-Produced Masses

Given the links between stage melodrama and the wonder tale, the success that Verne and Baum enjoyed in moving their novels from page to stage might have been expected to prompt others to create wonder tales for the stage—as did, for instance, Barrie. In these middle years, however, the new medium of film instantly proved itself better suited, and perhaps perfectly suited, to the form. Yet at least one effective stage-play did appear. While works prior to Karl Čapek's *R.U.R.* brought automation and mass-production into conjunction, the Czech playwright did so in such a way that his symbolic stage creations gave a new name to a preexisting symbol in Modern society. Taking place "on a remote island" in an indefinite future, the play also brought new emphasis to the island theme that had attracted readers for centuries already. Čapek's setting echoes with the shipwrecks and social isolations in Shakespeare and Defoe; with island chains, in whose isolations Darwin saw evolutionary significance; and with *Swiss Family Robinson* and Verne's iterations of that providential adventure. It also echoes with the planetary island in the symbolic ocean of the future.

Written in the early 1920s, *R.U.R.* saw staging in English in 1923. Thanks to its success, the term *robot*, or "worker," flourished in England and elsewhere long after its stage currency. The Czech-Polish word "robota" shares roots with words in other languages, including English, that undoubtedly helped its rapid spread.[5]

Lindy Flyers. The spare nature of this pedal toy reflected that of many early aircraft. The nose, apparently tin, evokes the monoplanes of Lindbergh's generation. Photograph, 1920s or '30s (author's collection).

Čapek's play presents the Robot as artificial but biological—a shorthand version of the full human being, and not at all kin to such purely mechanical creations as the Steam Man or Tik-Tok.[6] At the same time, while to all appearances human, they have antecedents quite other than Fogg, Barbicane, or Cavor—and even other than the Being in Shelley: for the Robots are the Masses— the products of industrial processes and conditions when "no such thing as an individual is supposed to exist." Standing in contrast to the "producers," who are engineers and leaders in industry, they have their antecedents in the Signal-Man in Dickens, Nemo's or Robur's crews in Verne, or the Poor in Howells.

That the play has much to say about mass production the stage dressings make evident, when Act I opens within the Rossum's Universal Robots factory. Office-wall placards offer such mottos as "Cheap Labour. Rossum's Robots," and, "Do You Want to Cheapen Your Output? Order Rossum's Robots." From this factory R.U.R. sends its workers around the globe. In every country they replace human labor, becoming indispensable to industrial mass-production in every line. In a later act, the Robots' adaptable utility leads them to deployment in international wars, from which the factory remains aloof, thanks to isolating oceans. In an act yet later, the Robots revolt, somehow finding inner resources despite having been manufactured without any such. The nations of the world fall before an uprising that exterminates humans, leaving only Robots to run the existing networks and systems created for human civilization.

One human individual, however, remains alive on the factory island: Rossum's former clerk, Alquist, who becomes historian at the old world's ending. In this play merge two themes introduced by Mary Shelley: the artificial biological entity, and the Last Man.

Čapek's fabricated drudges represent the working class of the world reduced to the state of machinery by the world's industries and factories; yet their rebellion stands apart from worker-uprisings as envisioned by materialist thinkers such as Marx. Rossum's Robots are Poe's "pure machine" that can operate autonomously, without intervention from human intellect or will. Since they break themselves from their previously necessary connection to humankind, they represent the technical culture that captivated Oswald Spengler, around the time when Čapek was writing: "The unique fact about human technics ... is that it is independent of the life of the human genus. ... Technics in man's life is conscious, arbitrary, alterable, personal, inventive. It is learned and improved. Man has become the creator of his tactics of living—that is his grandeur and his doom. And the inner form of this creativeness we call culture—to be cultured, to cultivate, to suffer from culture. The man's creations are the expression of this being in personal form."[7]

Technical culture that is growing "independent of the life of the human genus" ties into Čapek's vision, in which a single system encompasses the globe, supersedes human labor, and renders humans obsolete. In this, his drama does recapitulate *Frankenstein*, in which the fabricated Being becomes, first, the end to which the fabricator must turn his life, and, second, the end to that life. *R.U.R.* also exhibits symbolic continuity with Poe and Verne, in presenting the enclosure of the human soul within the machine, and of the earth within an integrated, mechanical system.

The technical system swallows the human world first in symbolic terms, and then in fictionally literal terms.

Unification Toward Division

To those who viewed history in a positivist light, the claim made sense, in these middle years, that automation and a machine-based economy offered more a promise than a threat. Even while it was proving true that industrial-based technology was exerting a dehumanizing pressure, positivism acquired a nearly unquestioned and nearly ruling status, in public and private discourse.

The most degrading interpersonal relationship, that of master-slave, had been embraced and perpetuated in the West through the Romantic and early Modern years, providing wealth to a large percentage of the States' landed class, as well as to their equivalents in other countries, and making it possible for them to engage in a life marked by outward gentility and luxury. Although Lincoln's war to maintain the Union would disrupt the bucolic life of the Southern slave-economy's primary beneficiaries, this degraded relationship would continue to reappear around the globe through Modern years. In the West, the most emblematic situation would arise in Germany under Hitler, who transformed the German army into a machine whose human components, its soldiers, were forced to march not with simple military precision but with stiff-legged forward motions and stiff-armed salutes, emulating the jointed toy soldiers of childhood and the mechanical men in dime novels. "When you know one, you will know them all," as in Burnham's novel. In the war that developed from this vision of technological domination over the many by the few, slave labor again came to support an industrial complex that spread the illusion of wealth and gentility among the empowered. Culturally vibrant and outwardly peaceful Dresden displayed gem-brilliant gentility, while hellish Dachau revealed the horror of the free human soul displaced into slavery and reduced to the interchangeable, thus disposable, part.

Even in peacetime, heavy industry reduced workers to mechanisms following time-clock routines. Wells, in *When the Sleeper Wakes* and *A Story of the Days to Come*, presented a megalopolis with exaggerated divisions between the well-to-do and the downtrodden, with the latter's lives dominated by ill-paying drudge-labor. Wells's well-to-do suffer from ennui, much as had the yet-even-more elevated class in Poe's "Mellonta Tauta," for whom there was "nothing to be done but flirt, feast and dance in the magnificent saloons."[8] In *Days to Come*, a pair of individuals accustomed to genteel comforts endure servitude and labor—from which, as noted earlier, Wells saves them by perhaps the only means believable to his middle-class readers—who had some interest in Socialism but more in material betterment: for the heroine and hero return to gentility, but not through personal valor and self-sacrifice, nor through superior labor and virtue. The dehumanized laborers in *The Time Machine*, the underground-dwelling Morlocks, take for their meat the childlike, quite unintellectual innocents, the Eloi, who live aboveground in picturesque ruins. High civilization had produced both the underground laborer-lords and the aboveground pleasure-lords who "flirt, feast and dance."

These stories evoke first a hesitant sympathy for the buried proletariat, then a revulsion against the machine-operating, cannibalistic

On the moon the earth would shine with a light forty times greater than moonlight

Tripping the light fantastic (by John Dukes McKee, in Elena Fontany, *Other Worlds Than This*, 1934).

scions of that buried proletariat. As a critique of a genteel, above-ground society whose colorless sheen of innocence conceals subterranean horrors, the vision presented in *The Time Machine* has great power and efficacy: for the Eloi are, indeed, the children upon whom the sins of the upper-class fathers are visited. They are the enervated offspring of those who, against Rousseau's advice, made society convenient and efficient. Yet even though the power relationship has overturned itself, with the machine operators now ruling the elite, Wells directs his sympathies toward the latter, and his antipathies directed against the literally much-lower class.

Čapek, in contrast, issued a more socialist call for sympathy, invoking not the technological behemoth but the system of production, and imbuing the industrial laborer or serf with symbolic power. His factory-produced biological simulacra provoke conflicting emotions in the audience, being artificial yet human-seeming beings who are kept to a subsistence-level existence by the industrial powers. The latter in essence act as slaveowners who entertain few questions about their own superiority. They feel no more qualms about mass-producing slaves than do the Morlocks, those former sheep that now herd their former shepherds, and who breed them for docility and tenderness.

The Evolutionary Human

From the time Wells published *The First Men in the Moon*, the notion of a "progress" that would be biological and not mechanical went hand-in-hand, in the popular mind, with an emphasis on the head over the heart. Rossum's Robots embody this to a degree, since in being deprived of sexual functions their mental capacities dominate. Wells's cranial wonders among the Selenites embody this, visually. Whether symbolic borrowings from Kepler or literal borrowings from the ant colony, in parallel with Bulwer-Lytton, the Selenites' exaggerated heads make evident what superior intellects were be found in the Moon—when, symbolically, the Moon is the future Earth.

"Human progress," in other words, extends its domain beyond the realm of technical change, and stakes a claim in that of biological change—giving emphasis to those human aspects that might follow the model offered by technical progress.

Rationalism, enhanced by trick mirrors to reflect the "future," thus becomes the rising dome of intelligence—a balloon, perhaps. This somewhat unscientific symbolic form might be called the "evolutionary human," for want of other term. "Evolutionary" has an appropriate ring, since this hyper-cephalic figure would keep appearing in wonder tales as representing the result of "the" evolutionary process. The process being imagined, a uni-directional and teleological re-envisioning of evolutionary theory, has a savor neither quite Lamarckian nor selectionist. It symbolizes the evolution promoted by Scientism, not by science. It arises from the theory envisioned by Spencer and popularized by Fiske, not the theory argued in *On the Origin of Species*.

A relevant concept developed by paleontologists and evolutionary thinkers, including Ernst Haeckel, helped provide the rationale for this vision. The concept of *paedomorphosis* describes the path that variations in physical appearances may take, to be observed in successive species over some vast time scale. It describes features morphologically identifiable in the juvenile or embryonic stage that reappear in magnified or modified form later in an evolutionary lineage. In other words, the juvenile stage of an earlier species may have a salient characteristic not present in its adult stage; yet that salient characteristic may become one that, in a successor or offshoot species, retains its salience into the adult stage.

The enlarged heads presented by the superior Selenite, by the "evolutionary human," or by the space-suited human: all reveal symbolic paedomorphism. The vastly increased intellect—conveyed in the enlarged, internally pressurized cranium—seems genetically linked to small-headed *Homo sapiens* by obvious connection. For the babies of *Homo sapiens* sport hats in large sizes, relative to their clothing. Prior to being babies, as embryos, their heads loom enormously. The brain in the amniotic sac dwarfs the wraithlike, diminutive body.

During these middle years of the Modern century, a graphic technique flourished. It exaggerated head-size over body-size, and offered satirists, caricaturists, and illustrators means for emphasizing recognizable features of head, face, and hair, while de-emphasizing those features that conveyed no less to the viewer by being shrunken. This simple technique produced results in which humor prevails, moreover. Palmer Cox's Brownies, who were fanciful, imp-like figures, enjoyed an often-imitated popularity in these years. Earlier, illustrator John Tenniel's vision of Lewis Carroll's Mad Hatter had enjoyed similar popularity.

Audiences easily accepted the image, graphically or verbally represented, of the person whose normal-sized body appears small beneath an enlarged cranium. Once made common in illustration, moreover, such "forced perspective," as artists might well have called it, easily entered the imagistic vocabulary displayed in wonder tales.

In *The First Men in the Moon*, the hierarchical society in which all inhabitants are perfect units of a World Machine has at its center those Selenites who are defined by their cephalic enlargements.

The novel presents the concept in terms of the Selenite who is to be trained, since "destined," to be a mathematician: "his teachers and trainers set out at once to that end. They check any incipient disposition to other pursuits, they encourage his mathematical bias with a perfect psychological skill. His brain grows, or at least the mathematical faculties of his brain grow, and the rest of him only so much as is necessary to sustain this essential part of him. ... His brain grows continually larger, at least so far as the portions engaging in mathematics are concerned; they bulge ever larger and seem to suck all life and vigour from the rest of his frame. His limbs shrivel, his heart and digestive organs diminish, his insect face is hidden under its bulging contours. His voice becomes a mere stridulation for the stating of formulae; he seems deaf to all but properly enunciated problems."[9]

This forcible channeling of individual development, mental and otherwise, underlies this society's structure. The most paedomorphic Moon-being sits enthroned at the ultimate height, also the womblike center, of Lunar society.

Wells makes plausible this developmental control by describing Selenite anatomy: "These beings with big heads, on whom the intellectual labours fall, form a sort of aristocracy in this strange society, and at the head of them, quintessential of the moon, is that marvellous gigantic ganglion the Grand Lunar. The unlimited development of the minds of the intellectual class is rendered possible by the absence of any bony skull in the lunar anatomy, that strange box of bone that clamps about the developing brain of man, imperiously insisting 'thus far and no farther' to all his possibilities."[10]

A softness in the skull, too, would be a paedomorphic development, in humans.

The Lost World

Early animated films offered but brief entertainment. Willis O'Brien's *The Dinosaur and the Missing Link* lasted all of five minutes. Yet the creative energy and labor put into them—*The Dinosaur and the Missing Link* took several months to "animate"—made them substantial and carefully considered efforts. O'Brien was making himself the leading animator of the wonder tale in America, although his star would tend to disappear behind others. His five-minute dinosaur film won him a place as filmmaker at Edison Company, where he produced additional dinosaur films that would be remembered more as Edison's than O'Brien's.

Works by early animators participated in the wonder-tale tradition not only in their subjects—such as the *Little Nemo* dreamland characters, or prehistoric creatures—but in the medium itself. Besides the fact that films were the descendants of optical diversions and toys, they offered deceptions of the sort practiced upon the inhabitants of Oz by the Wizard, who required, in Baum's first Oz novel, that everyone within the Emerald City's gates wear green spectacles. Movie audiences, who see only what the camera lens reveals, likewise must accept what their eyes see through a single filter. To reject the filter means to leave the Emerald City—or the theater.

Transformation of the ordinary into the extraordinary offered a powerful visual stimulant, as McCay and Fisher were proving on vaudeville stages. McCay and O'Brien went on to confirm the same in theaters, where their films served as fillers before or between lengthier features. McCay practiced the trick of making a black line appear to move on the page of the screen; O'Brien, the trick of making three-dimensional, inert objects seem alive, in their actions. By the late 1910s, O'Brien was beginning his work in placing animated figures in a seemingly interactive relationship, in film scenes, with live actors.[11]

With these techniques in development, O'Brien tackled his first full-length feature, putting fourteen months into the cinematic treatment of Doyle's *The Lost World*. It appeared on the silver screen the year that Baum's *Wonderful Wizard of Oz* first did, in the medium of silent film.[12] Although Verne's Moon-shot and Shelley's Being had established how the wonder tale made a natural fit with film, these 1925 movies explored the medium's potential more fully. Offering mechanized entertainment, they performed, as did most machines, in but a single way. Audience members, moreover, found themselves figuratively dwarfed by the gigantism dwelled upon by O'Brien's films—while finding themselves within a dark room that was, in revived form, the dwarf-containing box of Maelzel's Chess-Player. The box released them only when the machine ceased its actions.

In his animating, O'Brien modeled prehistoric creatures over finely tooled armatures, with internally located but externally controlled air bladders to make the models seem to breathe—a characteristic that gave his creations a powerful sense of life, in certain scenes.[13] This approach to "animating" an inanimate object dated to at least the 1890s, when a wax figure in the Columbian Exposition's Moorish Palace, named Sleeping Beauty, struck viewers as a "marvel." She appeared to be breathing, on her sleep-journey to her dreamy future.[14]

In essence, in O'Brien's films, mechanical toys took starring roles. The screen revealed his automata, powered by electrical motors that turned the film-reels, their every movement having been painstakingly pre-determined, with their lever-pullings curtained by the blank spaces between frames on the celluloid.

More film time, in the finished version, goes to human actors, including a memorably irascible Professor Challenger, than to prehistoria. All the same, the film derives its impact from the life evoked through stop-motion photography, albeit a life-assortment never seen by human eyes. Though he borrowed ideas from Charles R. Knight's museum murals, O'Brien's considerable and consistent modeling skill remained his own. In contrast to many later films involving prehistoric creatures, this one revealed the animator's relentless drive. He showed his creatures in multiples, simultaneously, interacting or moving in a mass; and he orchestrated scenes in which they writhe in, or flee from, flames spreading from a volcanic eruption—in manners more realistic than those displayed by human actors at other moments. Given the silent-film medium, the human actors were communicating with their audience using techniques for exaggeration derived from parlor elocution and performance, and from the stage-melodrama. Occasional breaks for "spoken" words appear in white against a black screen, phrased in manners also melodramatic. Realism lay beyond the realm of possibility, for silent-film actors. This helped deepen the sense of reality being projected by the unreal animations.

As the first major film to embrace stop-motion photography to present such creatures, *The Lost World* influenced the popular view of past time as a single flattened plane—or as a single panoramic optical diversion. The film juxtaposed ancient creatures who were contemporaries only in picture books of prehistoria, or in museum and exposition murals depicting the passage of time by means of the viewer's own foot-passage down their lengths. The film showed the *Allosaurus*, the *Brontosaurus*, the *Triceratops*, the *Styracosaur*, the *Stegosaur*, and the *Pterodactyl* in a single relict population, unchanged for hundreds of millions of years, unaffected by evolutionary processes. Not all were contemporaries, in the scientific understanding of the day. None, moreover, were contemporaries with the primitive human, the fanged Cave Man, who lives with his chimpanzee companion alongside these giant survivals, in the film.[15]

With this movie, dinosaurs moved farther from journal pages, popular magazines, and wonder novels, and into mass consciousness. There, symbolic value triumphed over scientific. They had emerged from cabinets of curiosity and public museums, to rush into the first medium to offer the possibility of nationwide public exposure. Mass audiences now could enjoy nearly the same experiences, roughly simultaneously, even when physically separated by hundreds of miles; and these mass-experiences offered spectacles of gigantism and disaster.

That the prehistoric creatures were automata revealed the film itself to be likewise. An automaton of communal entertainment, it went through its motions, its routines, with the plugging in of an electrical cord, the damping of lights, and the flicking of a switch. The Verne and Burroughs novels placed prehistoric creature on the individual stage deep within the individual mind: their dramas took place as solitary experiences that had as much to do with the personality of the reader as with that of the book. Stop-motion animation, on the other hand, relied upon pre-set, standardized film speed to have the prehistoric creatures "come to life"—or, in the language initially preferred by toy manufacturers, to be "automatic." Given film-standardization, the effect proved marvelous—as a shared encounter with the wonderful, to be experienced in the same way by all who flocked to it. *The Lost World* shared qualities with the printed wonder tale and the stage melodrama, in that the sectional human elements and the exaggerated human dramas appear in the foreground: yet the movie separates itself from them in that the process of enjoyment falls subject completely to the needs of the non-human, of the most machinelike elements that were involved in its composition. The film's type would come to be termed a "monster movie"—a spectacle of gigantism, disaster, biological phobias, and sensational Scientism.

The elaborately fabricated and wonderfully evocative scenes of a Brontosaurus terrorizing London, which in O'Brien's *Lost World* serve for the finale, prefigure the monster films to follow, which were multitudinous even though the decades left remaining to Modernity were few.

O'Brien was restating in 1925 what Jules Verne had affirmed in 1865. Knowledge and the applications of knowledge were leading humankind toward the monstrous, they said; and novelist and animator alike employed an accessible symbol for the monstrous provided by science. To create these monsters—making them unlike the manufactured biological machines of Mary Shelley and Čapek—scientists had merely to see them. They had it in their power, in Poe's words, to alter all things with their peering eyes. The human world could but be changed by being viewed from a balloon; it could but be changed by ideas and images—revelations and omens—relating to prehistory. In Thomas Gray's time, the word "science"—as in the "fair science" in "Elegy in a Country Churchyard"—had equivalence to general knowledge concerning the human sphere and the natural world. In Poe's, human activities that were pushing outward the boundaries of human thought were arising disproportionally from within natural philosophy. The empiricist endeavor, as we have noted, would take over the term almost completely. The word "science" that Poe used was, itself, altered by science; and that science, and that altering, came in part from Mary Anning, who had discovered the monstrous while exploring within the realm of Gray's "fair science."

O'Brien's dinosaurs and Cave Man appeared before the public much as had Verne's center-of-earth creatures—as monsters whose existence had been known before 1859, but who were regarded as of minor world-altering consequence until Darwin's theory of natural selection gained specialists' and then public acceptance. O'Brien's *The Lost World* entertained and edified, moreover, in the same year audiences eagerly awaited news from Tennessee about the Scopes Monkey Trial.[16]

In the film, as the adventurers escape the prehistoric plateau, the most direct threat to one expedition member comes not from a dinosaur—all of which, the herbivores only slightly less than the carnivores, exhibit ferocity—but from the fang-toothed Cave Man. In this scene, the exploring party has mostly descended from the plateau, hurrying down an improvised rope ladder; and in an ironic reversal of the Parades of Progress and the Ladders of Progress being painted by evolutionary advocates, the Cave Man, not the Modern big-game hunter, stands atop the ladder, tugging at it in an effort to drag the Modern man back up to the level of primitive brutality—back to a land so alive that even the extinct are animate.

In newspapers across the country, William Jennings Bryan was emerging the victor in a public battle to steer schools away from acknowledging the existence of a rational evolutionary theory. In movie theaters across the country, an irrational, catastrophist vision fixed O'Brien's dinosaurs and Cave Man in countless viewers' minds, as symbols pointing toward the terrors revealed not by fair science, but by science.

Scientifiction

As dime novels and weeklies gave way to newsstand pulps, wonder tales continued appearing in family, adventure, and children's monthlies. Imaginative, melodramatic pieces also appeared in magazines dedicated to electrical applications. These inevitably favored forward-looking inventions and inventors, none more so than those published by Hugo

Gernsback beginning in 1908. His own short novel, *Ralph 124C 41+: A Romance of the Year 2660*, appeared in installments in his own *Modern Electronics*, in 1911–12. It drew upon melodramatic source-waters that had fed other and earlier wonder tales, with less literary gloss than encountered in adventure magazines.

In his newsstand titles, Gernsback aimed to stimulate interest and further ambitions and abilities in electrical applications, while promoting ideas whose feasibility had yet to be proven. It suited this mission that his wonder tales should put imaginary devices on display, and that his characters should display Elverson-type "positive genius."

Verne had done this, to a degree, yet without making cases for the eventuality of any fictional inventions that arose. He acquired his influence in this area accidentally, to some degree, since cautionary and satirical notes rang as clearly through his fantasies as did the positivist one, even though readers often only heard the latter. Gernsback on the other hand embraced positivism, and in so doing invigorated a specific wonder-tale type. In 1924 he coined "scientifiction"—literally "knowledge fiction" if taken as referring to *scientia*, although he was thinking of the relatively youthful adjective "scientific." The coinage captured well what appeared in his pages: stories impossible to write or read without some knowledge at hand, some openness to technical possibilities, and some belief in progress. Despite his hopes to establish a magazine under that name, as noted earlier, in 1926 he launched *Amazing Stories*.

The form being a robust one, the wonder tale retained much of its compelling quality even when diverted from its core nature. To a degree, this realigned focus depended upon the authority of H.G. Wells, whose positivism had become more pronounced by these years. Gernsback championed and reprinted Wells, Verne, and even Poe—all of whose works began to seem even more positivist than they were, in this context.

The Global Playroom

Along with American manufacturing in general, toy-making was entering a boom period in the decade when *R.U.R.* first played. Toy automata were becoming so common as to be nearly invisible. The words "automata" and "automated" themselves were beginning to disappear, supplanted by words conveying "life" and independent action. "Animate" gained favor, with one new firm calling itself Animate Toy Company. Specializing in small mechanical toys, in 1921 it offered attractively lithographed tin beetles, two inches long, with simple mechanisms, that remained in national distribution for several years.[17]

Another shift in meaning had occurred by 1921, due to the development of a rubber so elastic that it might be made into pockets or bags and easily inflated. While dirigibles continued to be made in toy form, the toy balloon as a model of an aerial craft, or as a paper bag, came to be superseded almost entirely by the "rubber balloon" that rose by air-jet propulsion—unless its open end were to be tied shut, in which case it might be batted upwards, or popped. The new toy offered a return to the original toy-meaning of "balloon," being a playball that was sold deflated. It enjoyed such success that the 1920s came in with some two dozen companies specializing in its manufacture.[18] Balloons further attracted children when made "comical," as in the 1921 Mutt and Jeff Balloon Assortment.[19]

Other new toy materials continued to appear on the market, with Du Pont's Pyralin, a type of celluloid, coming in for increasing use, especially in the realm of the baby's toy.[20] "White rubber" similarly proved attractive in infant-toy manufacture.

Interest in "toy aeroplanes" so flourished that, in 1922, twenty-one U.S. toymakers listed themselves as having that specialty.[21] Mechanical versions ranked high among them, such as the Electric Airplane with electric motor, and uncounted spring-wound examples.[22] Yet automatism in these and other toys had become so prevalent as to be taken for granted, with "mechanical" being the most typical generic word being applied in catalogs—along with such terms as "clever," "just like real" or "very lifelike." These last three phrases appeared on but a single page of toys in the 1921 Sears, Roebuck and Company catalog. One toy only on the page, a "mechanical street car," had its operations described by the term almost fallen from fashion: "automatically."[23] These toy automata were, by this time, in every sense traditional products within the toy industry, although still billed as inspiring wonder in children—as in the 1922 page of toys labeled Wonderful Mechanical Toys.[24] The term "mechanical toys," besides being commonplace, had become a routine industry designation for its category. That children would want mechanical toys, in other words, had become an everyday matter.

Society was continuing to offer toys to children that advanced the sense that civilization was moving toward unitary reach. Games and toys in increasing numbers exalted a panoramic geography and a shrunken globe. McDowell Manufacturing Company of Pittsburgh, apparently new to the field, would establish itself over the next ten years with "mechanical toys, pop guns, sand toys and games."[25] Its 1925 "Aeroplane Race Game," a "combination game," offered checkers on its metal playing surface, on one side. The geographic game, on the other, followed the "actual course of the Round the World Flyers. Beau-

Girl and mother with dirigible. Dirigible toys came into widespread favor just before the Great Depression, and flourished as the hard years waned. Here a girl has an unusual example, with the airship body apparently of fabric. This may have been a wartime toy, when the many zeppelin toys made from steel and other metals no longer could be issued. Photograph, later 1930s or 1940s (author's collection).

tifully lithographed map of the world, flags of many nations."²⁶ Remaining among McDowell's lead items, its appearance fell at a turning point in the transition from round-the-world adventure to round-the-world sport.

A 1926 toy by the rapidly expanding Louis Marx & Company likewise emphasized the globe's shrunken size. Advertised with a stretcher—"the most realistic airplane on the market"—its ten-inch tower supported a thin cross-beam with an aircraft at each end: a prop-plane, and a dirigible. With the spring-motor's release, the "airplane gradually rises until it flies at level near top of tower. As motor dies it glides gracefully to ground." Atop the tower sat a tiny globe of Earth, around which the relatively gargantuan toy vehicles flew.²⁷ 1928 brought another air-race game, The Game of the World Flyers' Around the World Flight, an "All-Fair" game by E.E. Fairchild of Rochester, New York. Rather than airplane, this game's pieces had elongated Zeppelin designs.²⁸

Interest in speed and competition found abundant embodiments. While a Junior Auto Race Game seemed only natural, others offered less likely races. Toonin—A Real Radio Game, for instance, presented an "interesting, thrilling race"—although each playing piece was "a little metal loud speaker representing the six popular sets like Radiola, Crosley, Neutrodyne, etc."²⁹ Not only the geographical New World was moving from daring adventure and spectacle to routine diversion and sport, in other words. The mechanical New World was following suit.

Buck Rogers

In August 1928, Gernsback's *Amazing Stories* published "Armageddon, 2419 A.D.," featuring the hero Anthony Rogers, an accidental time traveler in the tradition of Bellamy's Julian West. This first story by Philip Francis Nowlan gave rise to a sequel, "The Airlords of Han," published the next March.

Between those two stories, thanks to John Flint Dille, president of the National Newspaper Syndicate of America, Nowlan's magazine hero became comics-page hero Buck Rogers, who made his debut on January 7.³⁰ Having been mustered out from Air Service after the World's War, Buck finds employment surveying a cave; a roof collapses, and a strange gas places him in suspended animation; and he revives centuries later. In common with Wells's Time Traveler, Rogers finds a society both advanced beyond and degraded below Modern society—and not the forward-looking, sensibly achieved society Julian West finds. In subsequent installments, much as does the Time Traveler against the Morlocks, he readily wields his fists, or anything else near at hand, against an Asian threat. Much like the Buck in that earlier tale of un-naturalism, *The Call of the Wild*, Rogers exerts an atavistic presence, so that his emergence from a cave seems a fictional gesture similar to canine dog Buck's visions of being the dog companion to a hairy, long-armed man.

Dille's influence helped place *Buck Rogers in the 25th Century* in high-circulation dailies, giving unprecedented exposure to a technically oriented wonder tale. To those who were reading Gernsback's electrical or fiction magazines, notions about ray guns, disintegrator rays, spaceships, truth-telling machines, video communications, and antigravity had become familiar. Within weeks, these quasi-scientific conventions gained general currency among readers having little or no exposure to positivist wonder tales. Through the comic strip, the speculative ideas, their graphic realizations, and their nomenclature became instant public property. Although these ideas, realizations, and nomenclature were imaginative and non-existent, they became daily newsprint reality.[31]

Strangely, a reversal was taking place—a *bouleversement* that must have unsettled some among Gernsback's readers. Before, they had felt that they were taking part in an intellectual revolution: for they were reading articles and stories that suggested that the new coterie of the knowledgeable and the imaginative—the ones who could read and understand elec-

Wireless toy for $1.25. Advertisement, Mandel Toy Co., Chicago: *Literary Digest*, February 2, 1918.

tronics magazines—would be the ones to usher in a new, technically advanced age. January 1929, however, brought a setback to such hopes. Abruptly, ideas concerning future technics appeared before a mass readership in a form that the public could acknowledge as juvenile silliness, hair-brained implausibility, and kid's stuff.

The ideas that had thrilled readers who were young and precocious, or older and yet open to ideas—the ideas that had filled them with a desire to take part in a continuing scientific-technical revolution—were abruptly thrown upon the table in a form that society, or at least the most self-satisfied portion of adult middle-class society, felt comfortable dismissing with a condescending laugh.

The Verne-esque wonder tale had entered the realm of mass entertainment with O'Brien's film *The Lost World*, aimed primarily toward adult viewers. The Wellsian-Gernsbackian form now had followed suit, in a mass-market form that seemed aimed toward children.

By Monoplane to the Moon

As had balloons and zeppelins, the steadily changing aeroplanes, now often "airplanes," appeared in peoples' minds as fact-based shapes and images highly charged with technical and geographical hopes. Within their fuselages writers readily and naturally placed inventive and imaginary thoughts. They offered continually self-renewing objects for appropriation. Once Lindbergh and others in the 1920s had established the monoplane as the aircraft to fly farthest into the future, that relatively simple craft took away responsibility, from the more picturesque biplane or triplane, for transporting minds beyond the ordinary.

Advertisements that manufacturers aimed toward children often drew upon this energy. Toy books produced by the Cracker Jack Company, formerly Rueckheim Brothers & Epstein, in the 1920s, took a typical tack. In one, *Seeing the World with Jackie and His Friends*, the cover shows a scene technically implausible but symbolically accurate. Jackie, or "Sailor Jack," pilots a monoplane whose fuselage is a Cracker Jack Box, with straight wings protruding to each side. Struts emerge from the rear, to connect the body to rear stabilizers. A propeller turns in the front, with lines of motion indicating that the Cracker Jack monoplane is moving quickly toward its destination: a small globe upon which Earth's oceans and continents are visible.[32]

Similar instances appeared elsewhere, as in Elena Fontany's book *Other Worlds Than This*, which enjoyed popularity and went through five or more printings after its first in 1930. It helped children understand planetary characteristics in an imaginative way. One striking chapter, "A Trip to the Moon," discusses distance in terms of speed. For this exercise in conceptualizing, Fontany chose the fastest human-carrying vehicle then known: the monoplane that had won the Schneider Cup Race and held the record at 408 miles per hour. While Fontany pointed out the propeller's unworkability beyond Earth's atmosphere, she used the vehicle all the same, in depicting imaginary interplanetary transport. Illustrator John Dukes McKee embraced the notion, and drew striking images of the up-to-date, high-speed, propeller-driven aircraft's journey. The frontispiece shows the low-gravity aeronauts bounding high among the Moon's crags, while the propeller airplane sits where it landed nearby. The excitement surrounding airplanes added to the wonder experienced by the child, and to the doubting amusement felt by the adult—while the borrowed factuality helped convey the perspectives Fontany wanted to convey to young readers.

In both the Cracker Jack toy book and Fontany's children's book, the monoplane

Bugville. "To wind, draw bug back 2 or 3 feet over flat surface," read the instructions on the underside of these simple but attractive automatic toys. Animate Toy Co., early 1920s (photograph by and collection of the author).

helped children make an imaginative leap concerning travel beyond Earth's atmosphere. Far from being failures of imagination, they represent successful literal appropriation. Similarly, any child's play in which a toy airplane goes to the Moon gained power, in the mind, from the airplane's factuality.

The Torpedo

Streamlined and equipped with a high-energy propulsion system to speed it on its way, an explosive device settled upon its first popular name, "torpedo," along a route strangely circuitous for so direct an object. The name has roots in Latin, with *torpedo* referring to stiffness or numbness. The same roots fed into English words *torpid* and *to torpefy*. The word became the name for an aquatic animal: the electric ray of the Atlantic, which could deliver a substantial shock to the unwary, resulting in stiffness or numbness. Neither shape nor speed influenced the naming. In the late 1700s and 1800s, "torpedoes" entered naval warfare, with the name referring to the fact that these torpedoes, being explosive devices, had a debilitating effect upon any ship encountering them. Much as the unsuspecting sea-wader might step upon an unseen torpedo, and receive a shock, so might a ship strike against an unseen, stationary, and explosive torpedo, shocking its passengers and "numbing" the ship.

The torpedo's history, however, became entangled with that of the submarine. After his 1796 move to France, Robert Fulton attempted to prove his craft's efficacy, in 1801, by using his *Nautilus* to deliver torpedoes to their target. Although he demonstrated this before a commission appointed by Napoleon I, he failed to convince the government that a submarine-delivered torpedo might be effective.[33] As a result the device continued to play a passive deterrent role, as when defending a besieged seaport. Attempts to create "locomotive torpedoes" afterwards threatened to unsettle the stationary word's usage, although early examples played limited role in nautical conflicts. In 1866, however, Englishman Robert Whitehead altered the situation by developing self-propelled torpedoes. These automated, gyroscope-stabilized torpedoes saw development from then to the mid–1880s. Their propulsive power derived from compressed air, steam, or electricity. So much did these self-propelled weapons come to dominate that, by late Modern-century years, "torpedo" would boast a greatly changed definition: "A small, crewless undersea craft, self-propelled and self-steered in both azimuth and depth, carrying an explosive charge that is arranged to detonate in contact with, or in a certain proximity to, its target."[34]

The new craft combined the numbing explosive with fishlike form and mobility. Verne's fictional *Nautilus* symbolically had embodied the idea, in 1870, since Nemo had designed his submarine to ram steamships, putting holes in their hulls that stunned, crippled, or sank them.

The word already had crept into the play-realm, as it happened—in semi-aerial toys. In the days before paper rolls of exploding caps became commonplace toy selections, children made exploding toys by combining fulminating powder and fine gravel. They wrapped this combination in thin paper, tossed the gravel-weighted "torpedo" onto sidewalk or elsewhere, and won noisy gratification.[35] Thanks to this informal usage, the cast-iron "cap bombs" of the middle years, often "comical" and having heads resembling the Yellow Kid or some other, must have taken the "torpedo" name at times. The name thereafter found a place among flying toys, as in the Torpedo Flying Machine advertised in the 1917 John Smyth catalog.[36] Being an enameled metal craft with propellers and "passenger baskets" underneath, the toy showed how the word's meaning had shifted even further, in only five decades. At least in the toy realm, it had become a high-speed vehicle for aerial transport, without explosive associations.

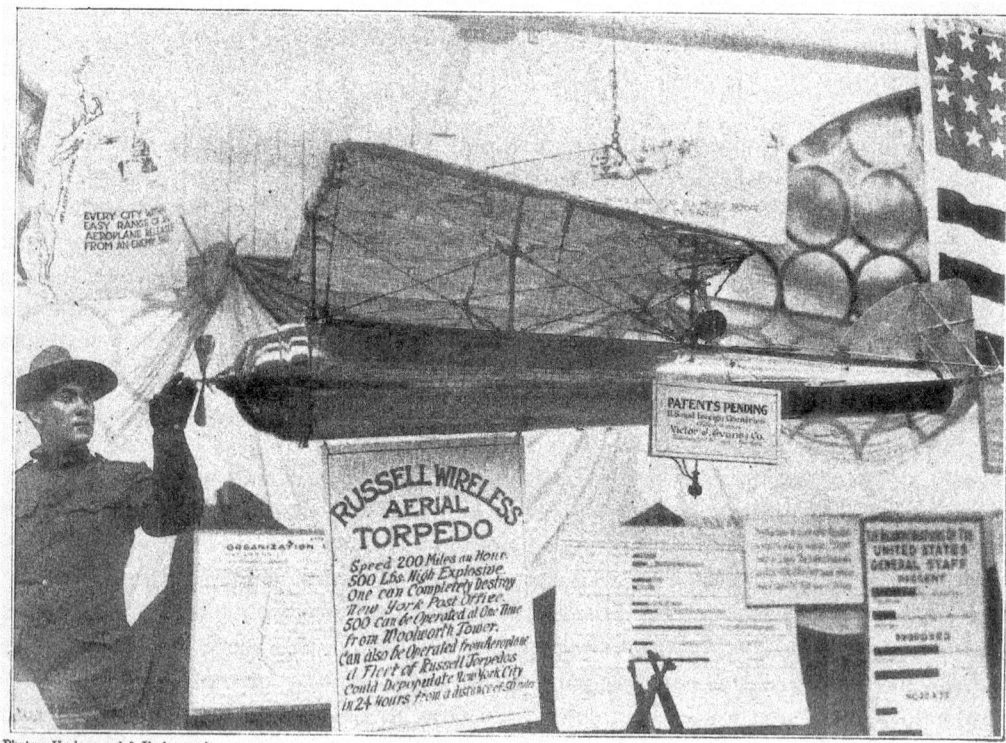

AN AERIAL TORPEDO

Aerial Torpedo. The shift in meaning in the word "torpedo" reached completion in the 1930s, with the original "torpid" sense disappearing before such material examples as this one: "It will carry 500 pounds of high explosive and will travel at 200 miles an hour." From subscription periodical *Progress of the World*, vol. 2, p. 69, ca. 1933.

This toy seems to have anticipated the actual Aerial Torpedo, which would be displayed in 1933 as the Russell Wireless Aerial Torpedo. Looking extremely similar to the snub-nosed Wyandotte steel-toy airplanes of that decade, this aerial torpedo had a nose-cone propeller and monoplane wings and stabilizers: "Speed 200 miles per hour, 500 lbs. high explosive. One can completely destroy New York Post Office. 500 can be operated at one time from Woolworth Tower. Can also be operated from aeroplane. A fleet of Russell Torpedos could depopulate New York City in 24 hours from a distance of 50 miles."[37]

Thanks to these shifts in meaning, *torpedo* by the 1930s would enter the wonder-tale realm not as a torporific or an explosive, but as a powerful craft, sometimes carrying passengers. The year 1934 must have fallen near a pivot-point, in the balance between the word *torpedo* as used in this sense, and the firecracker-denoting word, *rocket*. That year, in *Pirates of Venus*, Burroughs favored *torpedo* in referring to an interplanetary craft. While he introduces it as "a gigantic rocket on Guadalupe Island, off the west coast of Lower California," and refers to "the great torpedolike rocket,"[38] usually he calls it "the torpedo":

> The laying of the track upon which the torpedo was to take off had been the subject of a year of calculation and consultation. ... To allow a sufficient factor of safety I had powered the torpedo to attain a speed of seven miles per second at the end of the runway.... As the torpedo left the earth's surface on a curved tangent.... The enormous torpedo, with its sixty tons, lying there at the end of its mile long track, loomed above me.[39]

As the narrator observes, "The extreme stern compartment is filled with rockets and the intricate mechanical device by which they are fed to the firing chambers by means of the controls in the cabin."[40] At this point in time, *torpedo* tended to be the vehicle, while *rocket* tended to refer to its power source.[41]

The Zeppelin and the Rocket

Germany's gigantic airship, the Zeppelin, rose high among toy inspirations in 1930. Metalcraft Corporation of St. Louis offered the Metalcraft Zeppelin Construction Set in graded sizes, having from nineteen parts in small sets to ninety in the largest, for a toy twenty-eight inches long. Children with these kits assembled specific craft, such as the *Graf Zeppelin* or the *Los Angeles*. Metalcraft also offered retailers a model Lyonsport Airfield with mooring mast, runways, hangars, airships, and monoplanes.[42]

Setting them apart from earlier toys based upon the non-rigid blimp, slender Zeppelins had a relatively pointed nose, tapered tail, and stabilizers evenly arranged around the tail. The prior Marx Flying Zeppelin had only the top and bottom fins in the manner of the much smaller 1928 Dare Devil Flyer, giving it a form somewhat fishlike. The Metalcraft toys, in contrast, had four fins around the tapered tail. These fourfold stabilizers were making an impression upon the public. A Bradley game reissued in the 1930s, Game of Voyage Round the World, showed an immense dirigible from a vantage point emphasizing its tail, with large fins and ailerons near the viewer.[43]

The Zeppelin's tail-finned appearance soon contributed to visions of high-speed aerial and interplanetary travel, with a further ingredient being added in 1933. At A Century of Progress, one attraction symbolized the world's technical advance beyond the Ferris Wheel of forty years before. The Sky-Ride's twin steel towers, 1,850 feet apart and 628 feet tall, supported an aerial-cable transportation system based on the suspension-bridge principle. Any centenarian visitor who attended the Great Exposition of London might have sensed visual continuity between the new, immense attraction and the two towers of the Crystal Palace, or the two towers flanking the 1893 Wheel. Between them, the Sky-Ride presented a bridge for Rocket Car travel.

In bridge travel, a vehicle moves over and above ground-level obstacles in Phileas Fogg manner: "always straight ahead."[44] With girder-and-cable bridges becoming symbols for progress, society as a whole seemed to be traveling above the ordinary, in a single direction. The 1936 Bradley game Around the World would convey this idea, its box showing a skyscraper-filled cityscape, with up-to-date oceangoing vessels in the foreground waters. Above the city, however—even above the clouds that appear in the distance—rise the immense arch and pylons of a bridge: a simultaneously earthbound and high-flying image with which to embody the game's title.[45]

At the time, though as a noun it remained attached to the firework, "rocket" as verb or adverb suggested what a rocket achieved: high speeds. While Burroughs and others considered rocket propulsion a means to make space travel feasible, the name for that propulsion had yet to become the name for the propelled. All the same, as noted earlier, a minor practice already had brought *rocket* closer to public acceptance as a term for human transport: its use in the proper names applied to horizontally moving vehicles. Some among these names achieved widespread household familiarity, thanks to toy versions.

The association between *rocket* and human transportation grew stronger with the Sky-Ride. Exposition attendees rose on the steel towers to ride a Rocket Car at a level two hundred feet above ground. Although flat-sided, the cars had the tapering, spindle-shaped silhouettes of dirigibles. Far from accommodating but a few, they could carry five thousand per hour.[46] Greatly popular, the ride appeared on the box for Parker Brothers' game Petter Coddle at the New World's Fair.

Carl Claudy

Cavor, in *The First Men in the Moon*, in the end embodied the technical mind's surrender to the industrial complex, a theme to find continuing emphasis in wonder tales. A character named Professor Luytens occupies an echoing position, in Carl H. Claudy's *The Mystery Men of Mars*, a 1933 novel that follows the narrative contours of Wells's moon tale. Claudy had ascended in popularity among *American Boy Magazine* readers to the point of being called "the modern boys' Jules Verne."[47] Whether or not a justified comparison, Claudy retained the melodrama's sectional characters for this adventure. Professor Luytens introduces two boy characters to one another in this manner: "Brains—meet Brawn! Alan Kane, Theodore Dolliver." Throughout the novel the two hold their designations as Brain and Brawn.

Kane and Dolliver survive their adventure on Mars, as Bedford does his trip to the Moon. As happened to Cavor, moreover, Professor Luytens is more fascinated with the beings and technologies he encounters than are his travelling companions; and he remains behind—perhaps dead, or perhaps not. Unlike Cavor, he remains behind of his own volition, having bound the boys to the oath that they will return to Earth whether or not he is in their company. After that, he disappears to undergo an operation at the hands of the Martians which the boys find horrifying—considerably more so than the professor does.

In Claudy's Martian society, the individual mind falls wholly subject to the group's needs. The phrase, "for the good of the whole," prevails. The boys hear it from the centrally powerful, disembodied brain that has learned English from them. This Martian ganglion expects them, too, to serve "the whole"—once their brains are removed from their biological bodies and lodged within mechanical ones. Life's automation nears totality, in other words—in a boys' novel published only a year after Huxley's *Brave New World*.

The fear that one's identity and individuality, one's sense of personal being, might be erased to suit the group's needs seemed to be gaining, in the decade when an international exhibition had "Progress" for its thematic central pillar. In that decade, too, a mechanistic state was rising in Germany: a Modern-technocratic empire, with its soldiers jointed only at hips and elbows, bearing weaponry including a Chinese toy—the rocket, which the Germans would turn to the purpose of spreading terror. If viewed as a political, economic, and military machine, this political state validated to a heartrending and horrifying degree Rousseau's argument. The Nazi "social" and military programs dehumanized its citizens along with its victims. Nazism's rise seemed to realize the tenets of materialistic evolutionism. It seemed, too, to realize the recent, apocalyptic imaginings of fundamentalist Christian dispensational millennialists, whose neo-Gothic wonder-tales of Christian rapture had seemed, at times, to echo Poe's tales of a celestial, astronomically informed global disaster; and, to no less degree, to reaffirm the pulp-magazine visions that depended upon a deterministic Fate and mystical oracles, which appeared in other neo-Gothic wonder tales of supernatural horror and "weird fantasy." Many among these fundamentalist and supernatural stories drew upon interracial antagonisms, festering prejudices, and visions of the superhuman.

Yet above all it seemed to realize a toy-soldier dream for automating human society. "The German government did not encourage reasoning," Henry Adams had observed, a quarter-century earlier. "All State education is a sort of dynamo machine for polarizing the popular mind; for turning and holding its line of force in the direction supposed to be most effective for State purposes."[48] In the usual pattern, the toys came first. The communal visions and the reality followed. Stevenson's "leaden soldiers" became steel.

The Mass-Produced Brain

In *The Mystery Men of Mars*, that the mechanical Martians are "robots" marked how, within a decade, the term's meaning had shifted. No longer denoting the ultimate human slave—the biological worker—it referred to the fabricated-metal being. Yet Čapek's *R.U.R.* had innovated in having mass-production be the specter that gives his biological machines their haunting, animistic strength—more than the fact that they should look like humans and should labor in the way factory-owners expected. Everyone witnessing factories might perceive that aspect, without need of a stage. As mass-produced beings, they act as a mass, almost as one, blotting out humankind while easily re-inhabiting an established global civilization: for they are literally everywhere, doing all the work, already. They represent the foe to civilization feared in Poe's time, having "the spirit of the mob," as Čapek's character Dr. Gall frequently says.[49] Claudy's usage, from this perspective, follows Čapek's: the robots are mass-produced beings who act in concert.

Not only are Martian metal bodies mass-produced, but so, too, are the biological brains placed into them. The insect-like rulers clone brains from a few originals that remain after the massacre of upper-level Martians who had come to live underground—"the fleshy, more tender and more able" of the divided Martian race. The boys witness the process at the incubating factory, which generates and splits off new brains. They also witness the gruesome self-sacrifice of a Martian whose head is pulped in "a peculiar apparatus, somewhat suggestive of a cider press."[50] This self-sacrificing Martian views having his head pulped as being "for the good of the whole." From each according to his abilities, and to each according to his needs, perhaps.

Claudy brings together mass-production, life's automation as a totality, and the subjugation of self to state, with gruesome detail for emphasis. Whatever his intent, he tapped into fears gnawing at Western society's heart, and communicated them to the young. Tellingly, on their return to Earth after having travelled interplanetary distances, his boy heroes feel no sense of valorous achievement. They return ravaged by terrible doubts and fears. If *The Mystery Men of Mars* begins with *First Men in the Moon*, it concludes with *The Island of Dr. Moreau*. Brain and Brawn had escaped the maelstrom, physically, only to be marked by it ever after.

Claudy's novel evoked an ambiguous wonder, in depicting future adventures. Youths reading it tasted a bitterness in technical achievement; they learned that, through its application, they might lose innocence, self-confidence, and joy. This ambiguity held, too, for A Century of Progress, the Chicago World Exposition opening its gates that year. Its displays for the massed public depicted technology's reach. State by state, industry by industry, miles of displays set forth to what heights American and world technical society had risen. Progress seemed to be determining history; or, as Henry Adams had put it, "the great word Evolution ... made a new religion of history."[51]

By this time, the scientific-technical-hero exemplar, Thomas Edison, no longer appeared as a hero in new wonder stories, having been supplanted by Tom Edison, Jr. and then Tom Swift. While the public still pictured Edison as a lone man of brilliance, he had become a corporate commander over an army of brilliant and able men and women. Once an individual inventor, Edison had become a multitude. He established with finality the fate of the Modern individual. He lost his individuality as a man, to become a corporation; and all his workers lost theirs, to become part of what he was.

Prehistoric Toys

Whatever forms dinosaur toys took before the 1925 movie release of *The Lost World*, they were fleeting and ephemeral. The 1925 movie, however, made it seem more possible that a toy company could design, produce, and market a toy with clear dinosaur associations, and not be faced with a misunderstanding public. The Twistum wooden toys made in Oakland, California, by the early 1920s, included a jointed, bendable Brontosaurus that may have been produced before 1925, but almost certainly enjoyed popularity afterwards—especially since Bessie Love and Alma Bennett, the female leads in *The Lost World*, appeared in promotional photographs for the toy. Bennett's photo appropriately uses the photographic trick of having her seem to ride the toy. The promotion referred to "her pet dinosaur 'Twistum,'" although the company gave its No. 81 dinosaur entry the name Old Timer, and made room for it in the Twistum Animal Circus.[52]

Slightly later came Dizzy Dino. This 1931 string-puppet appeared among the first toys made by the Fisher-Price Company of East Aurora, New York. The Pop-Up Kritters series, also featuring a cat, a stork, and a giraffe, "took the country by storm," according

Little primitive Annie. Even Little Orphan Annie participated in the move toward the primitive, on the cover to this board game. The cartoon-style dinosaur depiction, though far from the first in the toy realm, ranks early among toy and game depictions that saw factory production and widespread distribution. Little Orphan Annie Travel Game, Milton Bradley, 1930s (photograph by and collection of the author).

to company historians.[53] The company made the Brontosaurus from beads connected by strings, with the latter connecting to finger-rings beneath a hand-held paddle. These enabled a child to "control" the dinosaur that stood atop the paddle—making the sinewy form sway and move its snaking tail and neck. Ironically, the toy-designer's name was Savage.[54]

That in the 1930s dinosaurs were becoming cultural common property found further evidence in the funny pages, where in 1933 Vince Hamlin's strip *Alley Oop* made its debut. Following the example of early novels and movies that reflected anti-evolutionist leanings, these strips presented humans alongside dinosaurs, with the cave people in this strip, Alley Oop and Oola, having a pet named Dinny. On the box cover of Little Orphan Annie Travel Game, a 1930s offering from Milton Bradley, even Annie makes a move toward the primitive. She wears a tiger-skin toga and wields a wooden club, while regarding a "leapin' lizard"—a spiny-backed dinosaur.[55]

The year Dizzy Dino appeared, dinosaurs also formed a focus for boys' novel *The Land of Monsters* by Harold M. Sherman—not a wonder tale, but contemporary adventure involving scientific ambitions and treacheries surrounding dinosaur-bone hunting, with its monsters being purely human.

Ruled by Business

The Modern wonder tale's dissected protagonist had undergone modifications through the decades. In England this wonder-tale aspect had become muted, reflecting the continuing importance of the Chesney-influenced tale—with its near-future approach, its common-citizen and type-character narrator, and its maelstrom-tale structure. This seemed to be the case especially after Wells adopted the approach, in varying degrees, for his short stories and novels. In America, where the Verneian wonder tale persisted with some strength, the dissected-soul character persisted and sometimes thrived. Even so, although Claudy's characters in the 1930s conformed roughly to the Verne model, the most popular wonder tales for boys already had diverged.

In the 1910s, Appleton's Tom Swift books offered characters that owed more to vaudeville conventions than to philosophy, with Tom Swift, the son of an inventor, serving as the ardent, youthful male lead. His surrounding cast included absurd neighbor, Mr. Damon, the faithful fool Eradicate Sampson, and his closest friend, the earnest young bank-employee Ned Newton.

By the 1920s, Tom had inherited his father's mantle as the inventor, while Ned had become Tom's associate, as a business partner. While the two do stand in for Intellect and Volition, to a degree, more strongly they represent a partnership between Science and Industry, with Eradicate serving as a humorous but devoted figure of Labor.

Dark-skinned Eradicate first appeared in the series with his constant companion, a mule named Jupiter. While later readers might object to Eradicate's stereotypical depiction, his appearance in the Stratmeyer-Garis tales marked an improvement, in terms of racial depictions, over earlier dime novels. While Eradicate was a stock character, in this he held exactly the same status as any Caucasian in the Tom Swift novels—all of whom were stock actors to the same degree. References to vaudeville racial depictions even appeared, in these early books. A reader might feel about "Victor Appleton" racial depictions what one does about the depictions in *Peter Pan*, whose first readers had seen the original stage production, or knew of it. They accepted the convention that pale faces were to be found behind the red skins of the "Indians." Rather than racism, a reader in our day who ponders Eradicate might contemplate the similarly thorny issues surrounding the blackface tradition in vaudeville and early film.

With the growing emphasis upon Tom Swift's business operations, once he becomes not only inventor but a manufacturer and government supplier, Eradicate continues as a somewhat side-lined bumbling comic figure. Both old and old-fashioned, he represents devoted but uneducated Labor as much as, if not more than, his race. "Devoted but uneducated" as to science, however, receives frequent reiteration, in reference to all Tom Swift's core companions. Swift acquires a second dark-skinned adherent, the South American giant Koko, whose unquestioning dedication to the Swift cause may help underline his racial symbolism, yet whose superhuman strength points toward the stock character, and, again, toward dedicated Labor.[56]

The Victor Appleton novels were diverging from the Verneian model by depicting not a human's dissected soul but a society's, with upper-class Industry and Business serving as one principle; a faceless but technically educated middle class, made up of "extras," as a second one; and lower-class Labor, as the third. Where, moreover, Baum's dissected human soul tended to give prime powers to feminine aspects—with girls and women, witches and fairies, and princesses and queens always among the lead characters—Appleton's dissected social soul allowed limited onstage time for women. They have roles to play, but primarily offstage.

The Tom Swift series communicated to boys the trends Henry Adams had observed decades earlier. It depicted the rising materialism and the disappearing religious instinct; the growing powers in banking, business, and industry; the replacement by politicians of statesmen; and the change in evolutionary progress from theory to dogma—as the feverishly pulsing evolutionism that replaced the perception of eons-slow, gradual change. As had Baum, Adams came to regard the feminine as a nearly divine principle in the human soul—a principle that he feared was losing strength and failing to hold against the currents that he perceived as gaining in strength, in his lifetime.

Fifteen

The Tattered Veil

[T]he anthropoid apes are now being found more human than they formerly were, at a time when human beings seem more bestial.
—Edmund Wilson, in 1965.[1]

At such a moment the veil of civilization was torn to tatters. Man was reverting to the primeval.
—Austin Hall, in 1919.[2]

Nothing could have been more marked than the transformation of the literary world from the state of mind of a dozen years before when, as Waldo Frank had said, at the time of *The Seven Arts*, "There is a murmur of suppressed excitement in the air." It was, he added, "like that which hovers over a silent crowd before the appearance of a great procession." Had this procession come and gone? Certainly no one in 1930 looked for any such thing to appear in the future, for "a dreadful apathy, unsureness and discouragement is felt to have fallen upon us," Edmund Wilson wrote in the following year. Gertrude Stein said, in fact, that there was no future,—there was "no future any more"; while Paul Rosenfeld, editing *The American Caravan*, noted that after 1930 every contribution to this yearbook was tragic. In the great number of papers that were submitted to it, he said, there was not one cheerful composition....

The writers were generally prepared at least to abandon all interest in the future of the world unless they were Marxists who did not believe in the will and who thought that Utopia was coming by an automatic process; while a series of anti–Utopias in the years to come were to present the future as inevitably dismal.
—Van Wyck Brooks, in 1957.[3]

King Kong

Through the late 1920s, film animator Willis O'Brien refined techniques, including color-filtering, to allow stop-motion and real-motion figures to appear in the same footage. After working on a film named *Creation*, which was canceled by its struggling studio, O'Brien devoted two years to an RKO extravaganza, working on both stop-motion and scenic effects. Although the film's landscapes were miniatures painted on backdrops, he photographed them through glass layers that were painted with "nearer" scenic elements—borrowing diorama techniques for depth-illusions.

As had *The Lost World*, the new film took potshots at evolutionary theory. While the former had juxtaposed dinosaurs anachronistically, not only with each other but with the fanged Cave Man, *King Kong* did the same with a different primate: the fanged gigantic ape. One character's name, moreover, had potent associations: "Ann Darrow," the woman terrorized by Skull Island's monster. Bryan, the man who defended Fundamentalist values in the Scopes trial, might have appreciated this, had he not died shortly after the court case. Clarence Darrow may or may not have felt amused to see a namesake shrieking in the dinosaur-battling gorilla's grip.

The ape-creature exemplified gigantism even more than did the reptilians. The director of *King Kong*, dissatisfied with the height and proportions of the normal African gorilla, insisted on a creature more spectacular—with his size not stable through the film but adjusted to circumstances. Kong's gigantism became another variable for O'Brien and his fellow animators, in creating wonder-effects.

At the time, "primitive" referred to the lower-rungs on evolutionary ladders—to "lower stages." Thanks to Herbert Spencer and others who extended evolutionism beyond the biological realm, human societies outside industrialized zones took the adjective, as well. Even though a burgeoning network was placing the globe within its mesh—within its wreath of winds, railroad locomotives, and airplanes—outside the industrialized zone a great many areas remained where people lived in traditional ways. Despite efforts by Frederick Starr and other anthropologists to counter attitudes concerning Western superiority, from the 1890s onward, Westerners tended to identify the traditional with the primitive.

Ladders that purported to depict progress, and that bore "the great word Evolution," made matters conveniently clear for business and industry: for a hierarchical scheme was solidifying, which tied social rectitude to the needs of capital and the market. The situation in 1933 already contrasted with the one depicted in the 1925 *The Lost World*, in which a visionary Professor Challenger needs to bring back evidence that he had found supposedly extinct dinosaurs—and nearly destroys London in his zeal to prove himself. In *King Kong*, Carl Denham, the Barnum-like hero, evinces little desire to win approbation from his fellow scientists but instead to win fame and wealth from the spectacle offered by the Primitive, chained and displayed before a clamoring Manhattan public.[4]

In figural terms, Denham has captured the "underdeveloped" world, for commercial exploitation—while Kong himself embodies what the historian Barraclough would call the "magic of size," which he would link to the attractiveness of the "new imperialism" among the industrialized nations in the Modern world.[5]

South of the Garden of Comfort

Prehistoric creatures had appeared in fiction, newspaper stories, and scientific journals from the time the New Crystal Palace opened and the Megalosaurus took a bow in *Bleak House*. *King Kong*'s release in April 1933, had such impact that it might seem to have stimulated a deeper interest in prehistoric creatures, in a public that outwardly expressed but a casual curiosity. Yet within the gates to the 1933 Exposition appeared abundant evidence that the film reflected an already deepened public fascination.

The new fair had its roots in a commission formed in January 1928 to plan a Chicago

Second World's Fair Centennial Celebration. In July the next year, it took on the new name: A Century of Progress. Even though the country's sense of progress suffered a severe and shocking setback that October, and despite the Great Depression's onset, the fair's name and theme remained unchanged. It aimed "to bring assurance that the steady march of progress has not … swerved aside, nor even been seriously retarded, that so-called 'recessions' are temporary, like the receding wave that leaves the shore. History holds the evidence that this is true."[6]

In many ways the fair followed in the Columbian's footsteps. Just as the 1893 buildings had constituted a Magic City, so the Century of Progress grounds offered visitors entrance into "a Magic City," or "a dream city."[7] As the Columbian had embraced an evolutionary theme for many exhibits, so the Century of Progress embraced the theme of directional progression, in science and technology. As the Columbian had awakened the semi-torpid aesthetic sense of America with its

The World a Million Years Ago. "The Mesozoic was dominated by reptiles—beasts of strange, bizarre shapes, great in bulk but small in brain." At the World's Fairs, dinosaurs and other prehistoric giants seemed to become ironic emissaries for Progress. The exhibit bearing this name, along with such accompanying publications as this, helped cement a particular vision of ancient life, much as Sydenham sculptures had, eighty years before, at the New Crystal Palace (cover, 1933).

unquestionably grand, Classical presentation, the Century of Progress served to awaken the nation to a new aesthetic ideal embodied by stark but stylish Deco buildings, architectural ornaments, murals, and sculptures. As the 1893 Exposition had introduced many to the spectacle of push-button incandescent lighting, so the 1933 Fair introduced neon lighting as the beacon shining from a Future bright with scientific and technical promise.

To counterbalance its thematic step toward the future, the fair's planners wanted the public to stride back through geological time. In the Hall of Science the immensity of that history, when set against any human scale, found expression in the Clock of the Ages, a display that linked two billion years of the Earth's history to a conventional clock face. Geological images appeared on a screen at center, with automated narration.

Other symbolic manifestations of geological history took similarly giant form, with dinosaurs appearing in both the fair's Hall of Science and the Chicago Museum of Science and Industry in Jackson Park, which was the permanent reconstruction of a temporary Columbian Exposition building. Another top attraction, The World a Million Years Ago, occupied a building based upon the fair's cloud-wreathed Earth logo: for it appeared to be the Earth half-buried in the pavement, wrapped round by a spiral that was the roof covering a descending corridor. An official statement suggests the multiple symbolic roles being played by the ancient creatures inside:

> It is hard for us to conceive of a world inhabited by monsters other than those of industry. But, when we cross the broad plaza at Twenty-third street to a spherical building on the hillside by the lagoon, we see examples of prehistoric creatures that would, in the flesh, terrify the bravest man.
>
> Step onto a platform, in motion, and you will be transported through "The World a Million Years Ago." You are carried past a series of six dioramas displaying the animals of the ice age and "man" before the dawn of history. Then you enter the main arena. Here, gigantic, prehistoric beasts are brought to life—a platybelodon, a huge hairy mammoth, a giant gorilla, saber-tooth tiger, and ground sloth are seen in conflict. Also, the glyptodon, triceratops, pterodactyl, the massive brontosaurus, and the vernops and dimetrodon in a death struggle are represented in their natural habitations—seem to be alive, breathing, uttering cries, and moving.[8]

To wonder-story readers, more than the moving sidewalks might have seemed borrowings from Verne, since the experience involved piercing the Earth's shell to discover living creatures that, in the upper, outer world of humankind, had gone extinct. Fairgoers experienced a moving panorama, similar to Axel's vision; and they enjoyed a spectacle combining animated models and painted backdrops, with sped-time lighting effects deepening the dioramas' impacts.[9] Some or perhaps all these dioramas owed their existence to a firm with roots in the toy industry, which called its main product the Prehistoric Animal Show.[10]

Sinclair Dinosaur Exhibit. "The Dinosaur Exhibit built by the Sinclair Refining Company at the 1933–34 World's Fair in Chicago is the first attempt to recreate out-of-doors a portion of the earth's surface and animal life as they existed 100 million years ago," reads the back of this postcard. "Brontosaurus reproduced life-size is the largest animated animal in the world." Postcard, Sinclair Refining Co., 1933 (author's collection).

Even fairgoers reluctant to pay entrance fees to special exhibits would have struggled to escape dinosaurs. Near the Twenty-Third Street entrance, an outdoors exhibit featured prehistoric creatures large enough to be visible to passengers riding on the Illinois Central Railroad. As the *Official Guide* noted,

> The Sinclair Refining Company has recreated a portion of the earth's surface as it existed a hundred million years ago in the Mesozoic age. The exhibit is located directly south of the Garden of Comfort.
> This little section of prehistoric earth has been populated with strange, grotesque beasts that lived at the time. These monsters, or dinosaurs as they are called, move and breathe and roar just as though they were alive today. Even the trees, shrubs, and rocks have been built as "it might have been."[11]

Being open to all fair-goers, and located near necessary facilities, the exhibit became a common experience for all Fair-goers.

Other exhibits joined The World a Million Years Ago and the Sinclair Prehistoric Exhibit in presenting ancient-life experiences. They included an Embryological and Prehistoric Show on the Midway, mounted by A.M. Dufour, a Chicagoan.[12] Some attractions resonated with *King Kong* viewers in another way: for the "Million Years Ago" dioramas featured not only dinosaurs but the popular Giant Gorilla. Elsewhere, on the Midway, the Gorilla Villa run by G.A. Lintz of Brooklyn, New York, featured two great apes and ten chimpanzees.

Visitors by the millions went home with mementos of various kinds, especially photographic publications with prehistoric-attraction images. Chicago's Kaufmann & Fabry Company sold "official" photographs of the Fair, while R.R. Donnelly & Sons Company offered *Official View Books* and official postcards. Many also carried home mementos explicitly of the dinosaur exhibits. At the Million Years Ago building, for instance, Leon Morgan operated a counter for the sale of publications on prehistoric animals "and miniature reproductions of pre-historic animals."[13] Others undoubtedly appeared in the toy shop run by David S. Schwartz, on "the Children's World's Fair" of Enchanted Island,[14] or in the store selling "children's novelties" in the Hall of Progress, run by J.V. Hood of Racine. Prehistoria

Sinclair dinosaur. This Protoceratops appeared alongside other animated dinosaur reconstructions in the Standard Oil exhibit at the 1933 World's Fair. From the *Official World's Fair Weekly*, "4th Week Ending June 24."

appeared, for instance, in the 1934 World's Fair Playing Cards. The set offered fifty-three views of the Exposition, with the Million Years Ago Giant Gorilla on the Joker card.[15]

Such "fairings" went from Lake Michigan's west shore to homes around the country and around the world. If they had not already in the 1920s, prehistoric creatures were becoming cultural common property, with their images taking on household familiarity.

The Parade of Regress

The fair exhibited Progress by pairing it with the primitive. It celebrated industrial and scientific advance, while a mechanical giant ape drew crowds to the Prehistoric Animal Show and dinosaurs draw viewers in every direction. The juxtaposition reflected connections being made in the public mind—between motions forward and backward, and between progression and regression. In stationary murals and dioramas that showed the passage of time, the viewer could walk forward from the past toward the present—or could reverse direction to symbolically move backwards through time toward the more "primitive" forms of life, or more "primitive" stages in the formation of the Earth, Solar System, Galaxy, or Universe. At A Century of Progress, the Clock of Ages moved only clockwise, just as in A World a Million Years Ago the moving sidewalk took viewers only one direction. Yet the Adler Planetarium and Astronomical Museum, lauded as being the only one of its kind in America, with only one equal in the world, was taking part in the fair, employing "an intricate mechanism called the Zeiss projector."[16] Here, once an hour during the Exposition,

> visitors are admitted to a circular room to sit beneath its domed white ceiling. The light is dimmed. The ceiling becomes a blue sky, sparkling with millions of stars seeming so close and so real that you feel that you can reach up and touch them.
>
> A lecturer tells you about this firmament. His pointer is a beam of light. Beside him is a concealed switchboard, with which he controls the apparatus. You are permitted to look ahead into the future and know where the Pole Star or any other heavenly body will be situated at a particular minute of a particular day decades or centuries hence. You can look back into the past and see the heavens as they appeared when Christ walked on earth or when Galileo studied the stars with the first telescope.[17]

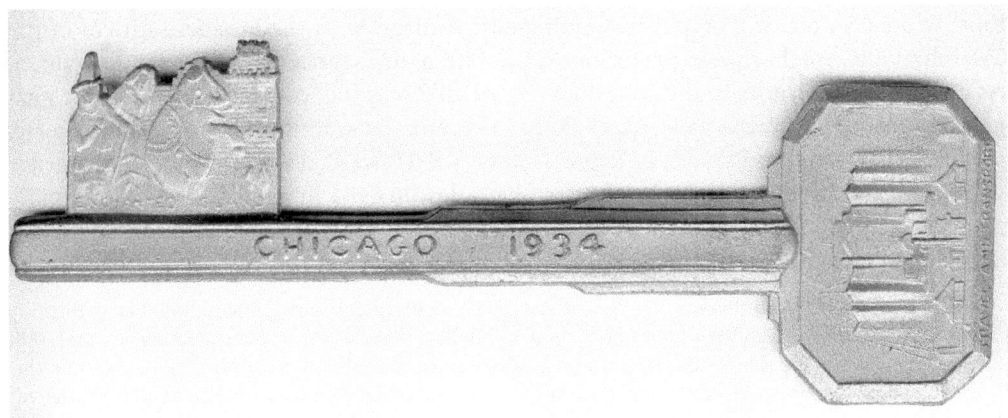

The magic key. This Century of Progress key shows scenes including the Enchanted Island, with the giant Scarecrow of Oz. Metal souvenir key, 8 inches, 1934 (author's collection).

Such legerdemain encouraged thoughts congenial to materialistic determinism, with the view "forward" sharing the inerrancy of the view "backward," and with progression having an inevitable quality, in its unfolding, that matched the implacable process of its refolding.

This sense of determinism appeared in countless, seemingly innocuous ways. The display by Century Homes in the Home and Industrial Arts Group of the Fair featured "a circular glass house, incorporating possible indications of what the future may bring in housing," designed by Chicago architect George Fred Keck and called House of Tomorrow.[18] This inevitably became The House of Tomorrow—a symbolic destination sign that pointed a single direction forward. Although House of Tomorrow would become a past matter, its name would enter common parlance.

Determinism likewise lurked around the stages upon which writers presented wonder stories. In a passage that compared human and machine "imaginations," which had appeared in the August 1932, *Amazing Stories*, John W. Campbell, Jr., imagined how human inventions would "advance" or "march" toward the "correct conclusion":

> Machines had imagination of the ideal sort. They had the ability to construct a necessary future result from a present fact. But men had imagination of a different kind, theirs was the illogical, brilliant imagination that sees the future result vaguely, without knowing the way, nor the how, an imagination that outstrips the machine in its preciseness. Man might reach the conclusion more swiftly, but the machine always reached the conclusion eventually, and it was always the correct conclusion. By leaps and bounds man advanced. By steady, irresistible steps the machine marched forward.
>
> Together, man and the machine were striding through science irresistibly.[19]

While not describing the advances made by humans and machines as pre-determined, the story says they were "irresistible." Campbell's prose propels itself with energy, with ideas pounding a rhythm through these few sentences, emphasized by repetition:

> Machines … imagination … future … men … imagination … imagination … future … imagination … machine … man … conclusion … machine … conclusion … conclusion … irresistible … machine … man … machine … irresistibly.

Campbell was unleashing the rushing-forward word-engine Wells had deployed in *Days to Come*, making conviction and vision go hand in hand—irresistibly.

The Parade of Progress, being so strongly visual, presented linear movement through time, while also offering graphical simultaneity. A diagram in the broadest strokes of the "March of Life" might show a protozoan, a trilobite, a dinosaur, a mammoth, and a human. As did countless visitors to the Fair, the viewer easily sees the "correct conclusion" to such parades. Just as easily, the viewer sees them in reverse, by scanning the images in reverse, and making them into Parades of Regress. Robert E. Howard, a viscerally engaging writer who produced prodigiously, if briefly, for the pulps, in 1934 imagined a scientist experimenting with electricity and animals. In "Valley of the Lost," a scientist draws a visitor's attention to a display.

> "That stuffed ape?" said this scientist to a visitor. "Well, that's what you're going to look like within the hour. Laugh, you ignorant fool! Less than a month ago, that ape was a man, as intelligent and well developed as you are. I have discovered a process of degeneration that retrogrades the human into the beast which was his progenitor. I could go still further, and revert him to the protozoa which fathered us all."[20]

The lobe-finned fish in the shallows precedes the soft-fingered amphibian upon the mud, in the Parade of Life—so why should it not be possible to see the process in reverse, with amphibian preceding lobe-finned fish? Ernst Haeckel's studies led to his memorable concept that ontogeny recapitulates phylogeny—in other words, that a growing organism seems to pass through earlier, ancestral forms during development. The concept suggests that every being within itself retains elements belonging to prior evolutionary types. Why, in that case, should it be inconceivable that the newt might be made to regress to the fish?

Determinist thoughts arrived in homes in forms as attractive as fairings—or as pulp-magazine stories in which machine imagination coincides with human imagination in reaching the correct result, and in which a man is transfigured "backwards" to ape.

Disappearing Automation at the Fair

As had occurred in the toy-realm, the aura that had made the word *automatic* so attractive to business and industry around 1900 was wearing thin, by the 1930s, even though automation had grown so abundantly common. As to be expected, nowhere did its commonness become more apparent than at A Century of Progress—with its nature semi-obscured by terms already proven acceptable by toymakers.

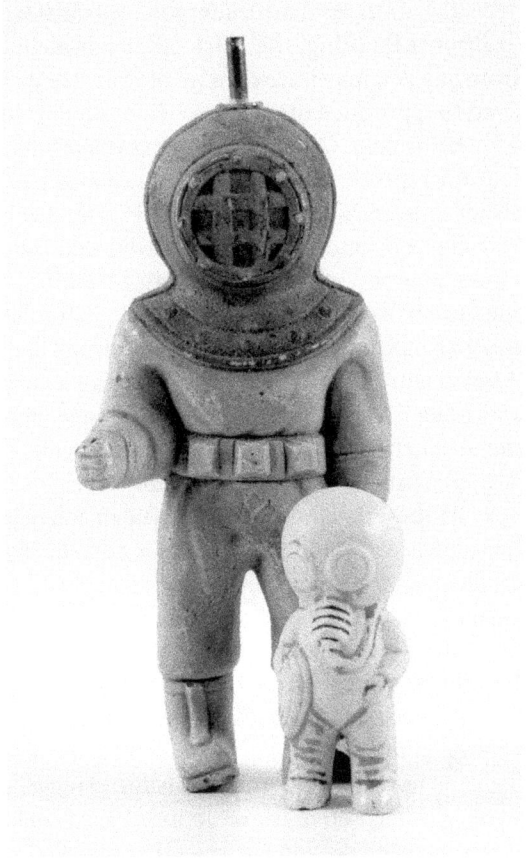

The underwater realm. Sea-diving figures shared with outer-space explorers the environmental suits that encapsulated and sustained the individual within. White-rubber diver, 7½ inches tall, probably 1930s; bisque porcelain aquarium figure, 3 inches tall, made in Occupied Japan, 1940s or early 1950s (photograph by and collection of the author).

The Petroleum Industries Exhibit Committee, for instance, illustrated the history of the petroleum industry by means of "animated models." The Miracul Wax Company showed off its Dri-brite floor wax "with an animated demonstration by a 'Miracle Magician.'"[21] Similarly, a description of an Electrical Building diorama used the noun "life" and verb "to live":

> On the mezzanine, the largest diorama in the world tells you a thrilling, inspiring story. Suddenly the great scene, 90 feet long, leaps into life. Reservoirs in the mountains take the flow from moving rivers, turbines begin to spin, across the plains lights in lonely ranch and farm houses glow in the dusk; the movement races on into a city that takes on life, the streets imbued with activities inspired by great industries, tall sky-scrapers, homes and hospitals, stores and factories, theaters, churches, rushing elevated trains and subways. A steam electric-generating station with switchyards leading into it, and trains running; an airport, and planes *live*.[22]

The diorama had undergone a transformation, with automation. In the Travel and Transport Building, the Fair's official guidebook told visitors, "you see a different diorama from any you may have seen heretofore, for its figures move, and speak." The diorama "is utilized to reproduce the scene of the laying of the corner stone which marked the birth of the railroad system. Quaint figures, in beaver hats, stocks, ruffled shirts, and flaring pantaloons, faithful reproductions of the fashions of the day, carry on conversation, make speeches about this amazing event." Elsewhere, terms that had enjoyed favor since the 1870s, such as "mechanical" and "artificial," showed that they retained their attractiveness alongside such newer ones as "robot." In the Dairy Building, a "mechanical reproduction of a cow shows the animal as a chemical laboratory, manufacturing milk." In the Livestock and Meat Industries building, "you enter into a white-tiled cooler to see how meat is cut and preserved. A retail store next claims you, where a robot indicates the choice cuts of meat, and gives a short talk on each." In the Hall of Science, visitors watched a section of a basswood twig—the "Artificial 'Growing Twig'"—expand with a year's growth in seventy-five seconds, as well as a "dynamic model" of corn-plant cells.[23]

At the Enchanted Island Theater, four times a day, children enjoyed shows based on the antics of remote-control ancestors to automata—marionettes, these being designed by illustrator and puppeteer Tony Sarg, and made by Alexander Doll Company. At other hours, they might ride the Miniature Railroad, or go to the "mechanical zoo."

Many automated experiences evoked "real" life and natural processes, and offered entertainment due to their placing visitors at the junction between the actual and the unreal. They offered, in simulation, daily activities in an industrialized world. They condensed time, enlarged the microscopic, or rendered invisible processes visible. They modeled extinct organisms never beheld directly by human eye, so that the models and their actions were, in essence, interpretive constructions based on scientific understanding. They *realized* a reality that existed only in the scientific mind—in its intellect and imagination.

The human body came in for considerable modeling and animation, with emphasis repeatedly placed upon its mechanical aspects:

> Moving models of the developed human body show the action of various parts of this intricate machine. A life-sized model of a man explains the circulation of the blood, with a magnified heart pumping, showing the action of its valves. A simplified mechanical reproduction of the digestive system will portray the absorption of food elements by the body.[24]

Not all evocations of "this intricate machine" took realistic form. In some, the pictorial innovations of Cubism served to emphasize the machine over the human, as in the Sears, Roebuck Robot, which the *World's Fair Weekly* described as "one-eyed and painted like a clown." The decorations on its "chest," in fact, suggested Picasso Pierrots. Rather than upon legs, it stood fixed to a squared pedestal. Horizontal, chrome-bright strips crossed its "waist." Stylized protrusions, straight on top and wave-edged on bottom, served for arms. The head took its shape from a hat-form with a large, stylized eye lodged in its middle front. In describing it, the *Weekly* uses the "automatic" adjective that remained on people's lips even while largely disappearing from official discourse and advertisements:

> The Robot waves his arms, gives you a little canvass about the Silvertone radio, which plays for you to changing lights. As the music goes on, doors open in the wall and on a glass screen the Clavilux displays its light-patterns, shifting in shape and altering in color as the music carries on its theme. The Robot is a good showman.
>
> He gives you a little more of his line, turns up the lights, opens the doors, and with a final wave of his hand he bids you good-bye. By that time you are sort of used to this automatic business, and you

go out and try one of those automatic drinking fountains that bubble up at you as soon as you bend over."[25]

Besides radio, which was further automating and homogenizing musical and spoken entertainment in American homes, the display featured additional automation in the Clavilux. This "color organ, designed to play with color as musical instruments play with sounds," appeared elsewhere in the fair as well, giving "accompaniment" to a "spectacle" in the Dairy Building, showing dairy history from "cavemen" to "today's organized dairy industry with its scientific" methods.[26] The color organ's equivalent had appeared in Huxley's depressing *Brave New World* only the year before.[27]

The Fair featured its most invisible automata, ironically, in the most visible way: for automated lighting systems pervaded the public spaces. Curtis Lighting set up an elaborate diorama named Alice in Lightland, showing a garden of multi-colored plants made from glass, in the Electrical Building: "The scene is lovely when drenched in white light. It is lovelier still when the lights change and shift, in ruby and emerald and gold, playing here and there over the unreal and dazzling garden."[28] Curtis also provided automated lighting systems for other attractions, including the Sky-Ride, the General Motors building, and The World a Million Years Ago. Other companies undoubtedly became involved, as in the "startling optical illusions" in the Livestock and Meat Industries exhibit that showed "the component parts of a satisfying meat meal, changing suddenly into a healthy child playing." Yet the entire Exposition, from its opening moment, proved to be a massive automation of light to be witnessed as a whole from the observation rooms atop the Sky-Ride towers: "If you stand in one of these observation rooms at night and look down, you gaze upon a magic city that seems to float in a vast pool of light. From the towers, great searchlights sweep the sky, the lake, and over the great city to the west, to clash with other massive beams of light."[29]

Alongside these new achievements in automation organizers placed older delights that still held to their natures as "spectacles," even if in old-fashioned ways—including a panorama that, when shown in Paris for eight years after World War I had attracted more than eight million viewers. As did Axel's vision, this panorama, housed in its own building, aimed to pull the viewer into a former reality: "the battlefields of France and Belgium with a stirring assemblage of 6,000 life-size figures of heroes and leaders in the foreground."[30]

The Shifting "Auto" in Toys

The disappearance of automation into "animation"; the orchestrated machine-performance to make the viewer "believe" the machine to be "alive"[31]; and the ubiquitous special-task automata that disappeared into normalcy: all contributed to the sense that automation and "life" were to be distinguished no longer.

In the toy industry, the word "automatic" continued to shrink in importance, without utterly disappearing. Automatic Rubber Company of Columbia, South Carolina, maker of early-1930s boys' toys including the Zip Zip Shooter, disappeared from the scene by 1937. Automatic Toy Corporation, a maker of mechanical toys situated at 50 Pine Street, New York, seems likewise to have subsided or disappeared in the same time period, although it would reappear after World War II on Staten Island, still making mechanical toys. On the other hand, Chicago's Automatic Recording Safe Company sprang up by 1937, making Mickey Mouse savings banks initially and moving then into non-licensed banks, often in the shape of books. It thrived under that name into the war years.

Perhaps more indicative was the continuing but changing use of "auto" as a prefix. The "self" meaning continued, as in the name of the Autocraft Company, active in the later 1930s. Autocraft model-whittling sets required that young hobbyists make the models; the models presumably failed to make themselves. Others uses seemed to partake in the meaning-erosion of the prefix caused by the ubiquity of the automobile, now often called the *auto* without an ironic sense that it was being called the *self*. As a consequence the Auto-Wheel Coaster Company of North Tonawanda, New York, offered coaster wagons, scooters, pedal cars, and sleds, as opposed to more complexly mechanical wheel-toys; and the Auto-Bike Company of Cincinnati offered bicycles, velocipedes, baby walkers, and coaster wagons, none motorized. Both companies operated in the 1930s, with Auto-Wheel surviving during and after the next War.[32]

In the names of the toys themselves "auto" seemed to increase in usage, with some "automatic" usage—as in the Automatic Bird Target game made by the Hoge Manufacturing, or the Auto Magic picture gun made by Stephens Products. These New York companies introduced the toys in the mid–1930s. Increasingly, however, the prefix evoked its new usage, so that even an obviously "automatic" game made by Electric Game Company of Holyoke, Massachusetts, had a name not at all confusing as to its meaning, in Auto Speedway.[33]

Alley Oop. Anachronistic primitivism, with juxtaposed "cave men" and dinosaurs, appeared daily alongside Buck Rogers in the comic pages, while *Og, Son of Fire* offered the same fare on radio. Although widely popular, in the later 1930s Alley Oop made a major toy appearance only in a game by Roy Toy Co. of Worcester, Mass. While the game enjoyed popularity into the war years, both it and its manufacturer disappeared before war's end (advertisement in McCready Publishing Co., *Playthings Directory*, 1938, p. 11).

The consolidation of life into the industrial complex, a consolidation into automatism, found apt symbol in the skyscraper, the structure that achieved reality in the 1890s, and that became a common element in urban life by the late 1920s. Skyscrapers naturally inspired toys, including the cast-iron banks that had appeared from their beginnings. In 1928 Marx introduced a toy similar to the earlier one that had an airplane and dirigible circling a globe: the Dare Devil Flyer, with the globe replaced by a ten-inch skyscraper.[34] Appropriate for an architectural tendency that had roots in an architect named Root, the A.I. Root Co.

of Medina, Ohio, enjoyed success in the 1930s with its Ski-Scraper building blocks. Root's competitors included the Embossing Company, which issued Sky-Hy building blocks.[35] Although building with blocks formerly meant building any structure that came to mind, it now came freighted with the upwards impulse expressed in the Modern monolith.

The name Excelsior, meanwhile, had lapsed entirely from favor, having gone the way of Classical learning in America.

Into the Interior

While automation was merging into "life," emphases on gigantism and what we might call "interiorism" were gaining in prominence. Fair publications used the words "monstrous," "giant," and "weird" in referring to Mesozoic-reptiles automations, encouraging a focus on their imposing presences—a focus that helped make invisible the machinery surrounding and encompassing them, that was even larger in scale. The simulated ancient world diverted attention from the more impressive feat being accomplished. The machineries that disappeared from the viewer not only filled buildings but in essence were the buildings themselves. The architectural structures making up the fair, interconnected and electrically coordinated, took the visitors in through their doors, and saw to their needs—sometimes even physically ushering them through displays. Underlining this new experience, architects used a design element in major areas of the fair, which they achieved by omission.

> Consider the architecture of the buildings. Wonder, perhaps, that in most of them there are no windows. Note curiously that these structures are for the most part unbroken planes and surfaces of asbestos and gypsum board and plywoods and other such materials on light steel frames, rather than a parade of sculptured ornamentation.[36]

The approach made possible an invariable experience for Fairgoers: "Windowless, these buildings assure, by virtue of the advancement in the science of interior lighting, that on no day of the Fair, no matter how dark and gloomy, can visitors be deprived of the full measure of beauty in interiors and exhibits." The organizers' power over an environment had determining value: "Architects and exhibitors have constant control over both light and ventilation regardless of the kind or time of day." Even the Sears, Roebuck building, an edifice dedicated to a company that sat near the center of the nation's mercantile system, offered a purely interior experience, having no windows, and a "circulating air plant with an air moving capacity equal to that of 1,800 ordinary six-room residences."[37]

Removing windows from buildings made visitors utterly dependent upon technology. They could experience the fair only if fully subsumed within machinery automated to the greatest degree possible. That the Transparent Man brought from Germany was a major emblem for the fair, alongside the "transparent" automobile and the glass demonstration houses, provided ironic concealment for the fact that the surrounding buildings had lost the Crystal Palace's transparency. Instead, despite its hundreds if not thousands of light displays, the fair celebrated the opaque, using mass-enclosures that shut out any natural influences that could be replaced artificially. The fair's opening moment had been triggered by an "electric eye" that caught the "light from Arcturus," which was then amplified to set in motion the full electrical automation of A Century of Progress—an action far removed from a human hand pushing a button.[38] These buildings offered monuments to the enclosed and sometimes regulated environments of Poe, with his ascending, hermetically sealed balloon-cabin and his descending, lightless caskets; to Verne, with his Moon-orbiting shell and his *Nautilus*; and to the interior and enclosed life that was a Symbolist dream.

Late in the Romantic years, the Crystal Palace had anticipated the Modern century. A Century of Progress anticipated the subsequent Age of the Masses, when the sense of being within an enclosed and regulated environment would become the sense of being secured within a society-wide automatous machine—the sense in which the experience of the artificial and the experience of the "real" would become interchangeable, with the globe as a whole, including its lands, waters, atmosphere, orbital regions, and even its Moon, all having been altered by human technics, business, and industry with their products, byproducts, and waste. The human footprint and the human planet would match each other in size.

As the White City had changed for the better the economic depression brought on by the business crises of 1893, at least locally, so A Century of Progress instilled a sense of hope, in the midst of the Great Depression. As the White City's lighting with a single switch had marked a new period for centralization and mass-production, so the automatism implicit in the 1933 fair's "modernity" signaled that both trends were maturing, with a decisive move toward the artificial environment as all-embracing.

Most importantly, the new fair confirmed the Columbian's underlying message. The city itself—not Chicago in particular but the city as it was growing and developing in the Modern mind—realized the progressive Utopian vision of engineers and inventors.

Films captured this by pitting the prehistoric against the up-to-date. Only eight years after a Brontosaurus devastated London, a single New York City skyscraper defeated King Kong.

Sixteen

Lines of Motion and the Horizontal Rocket

The days dragged on, or, I should say, the long night—there were no days, other than the record that I kept of the passing hours. I read a great deal. I made no entries in the log. Why write something that was presently to be plunged into the Sun and consumed.... For thirty days I had been racing alone through space toward absolute annihilation, toward an end that would probably not leave a single nucleus of the atoms that compose me an electron to carry on with...
—Edgar Rice Burroughs, in 1934.[1]

"You don't like noise and bloodshed," he writes to a friend. "No, but you like or admire everything that produces noise and bloodshed. if you worship 'big' things, you will worship 'big' men, who want bigger armies to get bigger nations. The admiration of super-ships, zeppelins and skyscrapers,—that is where the war starts. Or shall we say the war-scuffle that has begun in every mind that likes competitive football on the mass-production scale." Allston thought Americans loved this material grandeur because human grandeur was lacking in their minds.
—Van Wyck Brooks, in 1941.[2]

The Common Superstition

In 1848 Poe imagined people in the future feeling boredom at rail or air speeds below two hundred miles per hour—and yet more bored at higher speeds, with the view being blurred. All the same they traveled for the sake of movement. For those lacking volition, no one destination seems better than any other. Mechanically achieved speed, in other words, renders movement meaningless. The human goes only where the machine goes. If the machine has meaning only in human terms, a quandary results.

As Mumford noted, fast-speeding transportation in effect diminishes "the possibilities of human experience—even the experience of travel." It reaches its climax at ultimate speeds at which the "world has become a static one, in which time and motion work no changes whatever. Not merely space but man shrinks."[3]

Through the late 1800s the railroad—long after those Progress and Rocket locomotives first rolled across the playroom floor—continued to symbolize a linear fast-forward motion for society, and for its technology—as in the 1898 Air Line in Connecticut: not a name for a dirigible route, although such might have been remotely imaginable, but for a division of the New York, New Haven & Hartford Railroad.[4] Yet symbols for speed were separating themselves from any particular mode for transport, due to the constantly changing character of the vehicles themselves. Samuel Clemens, whom readers often associate with waterborne steam travel, and whom they might regard as having been knowledgeable about it, in his later years found himself traveling on ocean-going ships of a quality he had not known existed. "We are the victims of a common superstition—the superstition that we realize the changes that are daily taking place in the world because we read about them and know what they are," he wrote in 1893. "I should not have supposed that the modern ship could be a surprise to me, but it is." The vessel he finds himself aboard, an "ocean greyhound," travels five hundred miles in twenty-four hours: yet within its confines, which Twain thought comparable and in some ways superior to Europe's best hotels, the sense of speed went missing. "A Sabbath stillness and solemnity reigns, in place of the turmoil and racket of the earlier days."[5]

This anomalous Modern experience appeared during the "short and pleasant breathing space" of the period 1880 to 1914,[6] with the transition from "turmoil and racket" to "Sabbath stillness and solemnity" beginning to repeat itself in dirigibles, if not yet on the rails or roads. While public satisfaction grew when this stillness came with speed, excitement and then pleasure fell away before blunted expectancy, and the feeling that a traveler somehow deserves such comfort. The threat then followed: that satisfaction might succumb to the boredom that rules Poe's high-speed and aimless society. While this genteel technological tyranny would suit the needs of a Bellamy-esque society, by creating circumstances in which extravagant privilege becomes the Everyman's edge-dulling condition, this anomaly worked against the interests of a business-oriented society: for if it lacked war to drive demand and maintain consumption at now-possible production levels, stagnation threatened it. It needed a surrogate for war.

Since the Modern mechanical world-picture had for one of its foundation posts the devaluing and destruction of the past—the distancing of itself from prior matters, preferably at an ever-increasing speed—the war-surrogate most easily at hand emerged from the realm of fashion. In transportation, given that people were learning to "travel in style," it took relatively little thought-conditioning to convince those same consumers, no matter their economic or social class, that something called "the outmoded" or "the obsolescent" was real, not artificial; and that new conditions, associated with "the latest in science and technology," had objective reality.[7] "Built-in obsolescence," to which auto-makers would admit by the 1950s, had begun characterizing motor vehicles from that moment in the early 1930s when their makers seized on new style concepts that derived their power by evoking, but not helping achieve, speed.

Speed needed to be evoked even in automobiles, since the sense of stillness was beginning to mark even ground transportation, in the wake of the pneumatic tire. The automobile's split windshield of 1933 had some basis in scientific reasoning concerning efficient achievement of speed, since a split and angled windshield cut through air where the traditional flat windscreen pushed against it. At speeds reached by most autos, however, functions faded before the attractions extended by appearances; and these new stylistic innovations began spreading elsewhere, in similarly nonfunctional directions. Speed, if it might be expressed in a business product, became a value unto itself—so that fixed objects, even building facades, could benefit from its presence: for most if not all the Deco stylings had their origins in "lines of motion."

In vehicles but especially in vehicle toys the ideal for personal land-transport came to approximate the overturned boat, complete with a keel running from front bumper rearwards. This trend began when the United States and other countries were sensing an end to the depression of 1929, in 1933; yet it seems possible that the trend embodied something more than the simple hope of speeding toward the future and away from the past, at the low-friction speeds to be achieved in water travel.

Van Wyck Brooks, who had suffered a nervous breakdown in 1929 for reasons unrelated to the business crash, had absorbed the image that was becoming an intrinsic part of the automobile, but in a quite different manner: for he saw himself in his deeply troubled time as "a capsized ship at night with the passengers drowned underneath and the keel in the air."[8] From an overturned boat all may sink or float away, that had mattered enough to be stowed. Yet the overturned boat, and perhaps even public demoralization, was helping business find its way to recovery.

Lines of Motion

Styling, in other words, came to include an element akin to, but not to be equated with, streamlining. Lines themselves—not functioning outlines in shapes, but lines that had no function beyond striking the eye—proved effective for suggesting movement. Even a stationary thing might convey this sense.

Lines of motion may first have appeared in the panel cartoons and comics that were becoming popular newspaper features in the late 1800s. While these motion-indicators remained absent in 1905 comics by Winsor McCay, they appeared in Bud Fisher's *Mutt and Jeff* cartoons by at least 1911. Fisher embraced the tradition in cartooning that called

Streamlining affected the toys least requiring it, as in this Taylor-Tot type ride-on toy, propelled by the child's kicking-back feet. Originally made without wheel fenders, many such appeared with them in order to display fleet styling, in the 1930s. Photograph, "Wally, 2 yrs 4 mo." (author's collection).

For a period in the 1930s, speed-evocations trumped actual speed in new toys. Western Auto Stores catalog, 1938.

for an informal, sketchy approach, and used a ragamuffin style in depicting everyday folk—not the studied, accomplished, and formal line used by McCay, who was concerned with rendering extraordinary events in the simplest yet most believable fashion possible.

At New York Armory show in 1913, which introduced to America the contemporary French artistic scene, the furor over a painting showing a nude descending a staircase may have erupted due to the shock of the new—or the recognition of unexpected familiarity.

Marcel Duchamp's painting startled an audience that had seen similar visual notions advanced, in a simpler, more amusing form, in "the funnies."

By 1933, whatever surprise had been felt about artistic expression in the 1910s and 1920s had faded. Swirling lines of motion wreathed the emblematic Earth, in the official emblem for A Century of Progress; and they looked normal, appropriate, and even accurate. They communicated a sense to people that they understood and accepted. Where the 1893 World's Columbian had taken an almost anti–Modern stance by impressively reviving Classical architectural ideas, the 1933 fair thoroughly and unabashedly embraced Modernity's sense that new times had arrived and would continue doing so indefinitely. Lines swirling around Earth represented not just motion that existed naturally but the forward motion that had become the implicit necessity of the times: for the times belonged to Fergusson "who went around the world like a locomotive." The fair's attendees shared in it, vicariously, when absorbing technical wonders. Despite the Great Depression, progress loomed as inevitable. The Future not only would but did exist, in the drawing rooms of great industrial corporations. Attendees saw in lines of design its factuality. The artistic movement that helped attach so firm a meaning to these lines could hardly have chosen a more satisfactory name for itself, moreover: Futurism.

The most immediate eruption of this sense of the Future on the playroom floor resulted from the stylistic revolution centering around the now-all-important automobile. Early American cars, essentially buckboards with powered drives, lacked any style but the functional. As they developed into useful commodities for the American Everyman, they appeared at times decorated with elements borrowed from the most elegant horse-drawn vehicles. Most often, though, they remained the Puritanical, squared, and black-enameled boxes, businesslike and lacking fanciful elements, that for decades rolled from Ford Motor Company's assembly lines. Intense competition among automakers helped modify this fairly static picture, and then utterly altered it in the 1930s once stylistic trends made it imperative that autos visibly embody the sense of progress. Design ideas borrowed from Art Deco and Futurism influenced modeling in subtle yet decisive ways, leading manufacturers to introduce the Car of the Future, the prototype machine with extravagant styling—the ideal vehicle for the present moment that was rolling in from next year, where it would be parked beside the House of the Future.

In the year of A Century of

Mystery Plane. Toys made by All-Metal Products Co. of Wyandotte, Michigan, went under the Wyandotte Toys name. Made with relatively simple materials—pressed steel, with white-rubber tires—this late-1930s airplane put the sense of futurity and speed into hands that never touched larger or fancier toys. Dowst Mfg. Co. performed much the same service, through its Tootsietoy line, which included Buck Rogers spacecraft. Mystery Plane, 4½-inch wingspread (photograph by and collection of the author).

Progress, the first guns being fired for advanced styling took a form that would become almost invisible, within a few years. The automobile's flat grille, perpendicular to the road, bent backwards to each side, to make a wedge to split the air. Similarly, as already noted, the flat windshield folded at midpoint. Other elements would follow quickly, with the autos themselves proclaiming, through their model names, their smooth movement not over roads but through air. Crowds flocked to see advanced-style cars in numbers greater than auto-production could match.

All the same, Chicagoan Samuel Dowst had already established that a toy vehicle could be placed in children's hands in numbers even greater. By the 1930s zinc-casting had a long history in America as a workable manufacturing process, having been introduced at least by 1876, when the method was touted by a German firm at the Centennial Exposition, as well as by Philadelphia firm Miller & Krips.[9] At the 1893 Columbian, a new machine for casting type, the Linotype, intrigued Dowst, who at that point was with *National Laundry Journal*. Obtaining one, he adapted it to produce soft-metal collar buttons and promotional miniatures, notably sadirons. Casting the latter brought success. His Dowst Brothers Company of Chicago became Dowst Manufacturing, producing a range of items, especially small die-cast toys, to sell to five-and-tens by the 1920s.[10]

Much as the 1893 Exposition had announced to the world that Chicago had done more than merely recover from its 1871 fire, the 1933–34 Century of Progress announced that the capitol of the North-Central Industrial belt had recovered from the antiquated styles of the past. Dowst's catalog during the fair struck a common note. It showed two children gazing upon a ball that enclosed "1933"—while dressed in elaborate, privileged, and unbusinesslike garb from the century before. Within appeared the harbingers for change. In the previous decade, Dowst had become a leader in making dollhouse furniture and miniature automobiles, under the Tootsietoy name. In 1933, many earlier castings that evoked the prosperous 1920s remained available, as inexpensive toys for Depression-years children. Yet Dowst also released new toys with the streamlined look that was to dominate the American public's dreams about an incoming age of alacritous comfort and ease.[11]

These and similar toys, like the prototype vehicle-designs that inspired them, might begin slicing as efficiently through air as ships cut through water. Children could leave behind driving their toy cars today, to navigate a straight-ahead tomorrow.

Airflow

Promotional models were becoming routine automobile-showroom offerings—sleekly up-to-date, and often made from rubber. New designs moved onto both dime and department store racks, as well, with at least three Airflow toy autos being made by the middle 1930s by Hubley Manufacturing of Lancaster, Pennsylvania; Corcoran Manufacturing of Washington, Indiana; and Kingsbury Manufacturing of Keene, New Hampshire. Around 1937 the Bluebird Air Flow followed from Buffalo Toy & Tool Works. Because the "aero" prefix had a less sleekly up-to-date sound it was losing ground in the toy world, appearing on around fifteen toys at the time of the 1933 exposition, around ten by 1937, and only five, by 1939.

During and after A Century of Progress, product catalogs filled with references to "streamlining." In 1934 the New Improved Scamp Wagon boasted "airplane fenders" and a "modern beavertail back."[12] Among the important debuts that year, Radio Flyer introduced an "all steel streamline coaster wagon" named Streak-O-Lite, with roller bearings pressure-greased for speed and durability. The old-fashioned Irish Mail appeared with a new body as a Stream-Lined Irish Mail.[13] As Sears, Roebuck announced that year, "New Tot's Bike Is Streamlined, Too." Curved-back handlebars and smoothly contoured frames became commonplace on the three-wheeled children's "pedal bikes" that were increasingly being called "tricycles," a term that had seemed in retreat after the late-1800s bicycle fad. Even the traditional mechanical streetcar became an Electric Lighted Streamline Street Car, from Wolverine Supply & Manufacturing of Pittsburgh.[14] Within a few years, Streamline came into its own as a formal toy name, as in the Streamline Motor Tour game by Bradley, Streamliner electric bicycle lamps made by Seiss Manufacturing of Toledo, Streamline roller skates by Kingston Products of Kokomo, Indiana, and Streamliner sleds, velocipedes, and wagons by Garton Toy Company, in Sheboygan.

Gaining new associations from the exposition's emblem, "whirl" became an adjective conveying excitement, as in the Whirl-Glo Christmas tree revolving shades, by Chicago's Sail-Me Company, or the Whirl Ball game by Gotham Pressed Steel.[15] Similarly, Zephyr swept into favor with toy trains in the middle 1930s by Dowst and Buddy L, the Zephyr Crew-zer wagon by American Flyer, and Zephyr roller skates by Chicago Roller Skate Co. The Nic Projector Corporation of New York issued the "Zephyr projector and talkie," while Kingsbury was issuing the Lincoln Zephyr toy based on the existing model.

That all these speed evocations and streamlinings had their answer appeared in a 1936 entry from New York's Samuel Gabriel Sons & Company: the Traffic Jam game.

By the middle 1930s children were playing, too, with railroad toys having the latest swiftness-evoking names, such as the cast-iron Pullman Railplanes by Arcade Manufacturing of Freeport, Illinois; the Playtime Express and Playtime Fast Freight wooden floor trains by Thornecraft of Chicago; or the American Fast Freight wooden floor train by Strombeck-Becker Manufacturing Company of Moline, Illinois.[16] None such, naturally, lived up to their names outside the imagination. In aerial toys, by 1937, the Hi-Flier Manufacturing Company, a kite-maker in Decatur, Illinois, was producing the Strat-O-Flier box kite, possibly the first toy to use that evocative prefix.

In toy vehicles of all types, the molded-in "lines of motion" acquired a prominence they would never have in actual ones. Toys generally exaggerated characteristics being seen as timely and exciting; and some among toy makers seemed able to tap not into the style but the stylistic spirit of an age. As the 1930s closed and the 1940s began, even against the backdrop of the war beginning in 1939, toys were emerging that seemed pure dreams of stationary speed: for they seemed to move at high speeds even while sitting on the shelf.

Automobile toys of the 1930s embodied the speed compulsion in faithfully modeled playthings, moreover, in being inspired by "land speed racers." These technical wonders featured advanced streamlining and horizontal stabilizers to suit salt-flat courses. At times, as with the Bluebird racer, they featured a rear, vertical fin. These developments suited vehicles that aimed for no destination except ahead, into the flat, cultural void of the desert, and that held but one person. That single soul moved for the sake of "beating the clock," and "steered" to go straight, sitting in a cockpit that soon would become a sealed enclosure.

Buck Rogers Stuff

When the first mass-market, newspaper-based futuristic tale became a phenomenon, the phrase "Buck Rogers stuff" arose easily to convey a condescending regard for "inertron jumping belts" and air-cruisers propelled by light rays. The phrase marked a division being created, by this time, between adult and child sensibilities.

Although aware that the comic was popular, adults had little idea to what degree. As late as Christmas, 1933, nearly five years after its debut, manufacturers had yet to release a single toy or accessory enhanced with the comic's name. America had toymakers by the hundreds, all of them accustomed to the benefits and risks involved in licensing deals. Yet by this time, and for a year already, the Buck Rogers story had been reaching another, non-print mass-audience, via a broadcast radio serial sponsored by Kellogg's.

In that year, at the J.L. Hudson Company in Detroit, the department store's toy-merchandising manager Milt Brinkman created a window display with a space-adventure spin, with space creatures and colored lights.[17] Knowing his young customers, Brinkman thought it might catch eyes—especially in that Century of Progress year, with the Earth-awhirl-in-space emblem being seen everywhere.

His toy department's shelves held the latest offerings—mechanical, comical, geographical, aerial—as well as playthings that took children into other times than 1933, or into fairy-tale worlds. He lacked "space toys," however, and lacked even that term to characterize what he was missing. The category had no existence, as yet. Brinkman might well be regarded as visionary, in creating his display, insofar as he was promoting toys in this year that only in the next would exist. All the same, he was taking prompts from the present moment. He knew what children were thinking, at a time when others in the trade knew only what children had thought. The industry that was nothing if not diligent in developing items

Wilma and Buck at Gimbel's. "Buck Rogers and Wilma came to Gimbel's toy department on Saturday, September 29.... They were featured in the department for one week during which time they entertained their little followers with stories about the 25th century and the Martian men ... the crowds were tremendous and ... sales exceeded all expectations." From the magazine *Playthings*, November 1934.

to attract children seemed oblivious to the comic's power. For five years American children had to make their own futuristic toys. Given the strip's steady popularity they undoubtedly did so, and obviously without the nationwide association of "toy men" taking notice.

On the other hand, the toy industry was hewing to the usual order for events. Inventors might create a wonder—the automatic clothes washer, for instance—which, however thrilling as an idea to people, had no potential as a subject for toy-making until it actually appeared in advertisements and stores. It would lack relevance before that point. Once manufactured, however, the new household machine made a toy version desirable and perhaps necessary. Neither inventors nor manufacturers, however, had touched upon an "inertron belt" or "ray-gun." No cultural critic had informed the industry that it should follow the example of Gernsbackian scientifiction and, as a practical approach, to accept as literal what might otherwise be only metaphorical or wishful thinking. The toy industry did possess, of course, good instincts for symbolic appropriation. The industry had begun to understand the notion after having been offered the Yellow Kid, Billiken, the Gumps, and Little Nemo, as characters: yet it failed to see that in the same way fanciful characters might benefit their balance sheets if made into toys, so might fanciful inventions undergo the same transmutation—into both physical objects and profits.

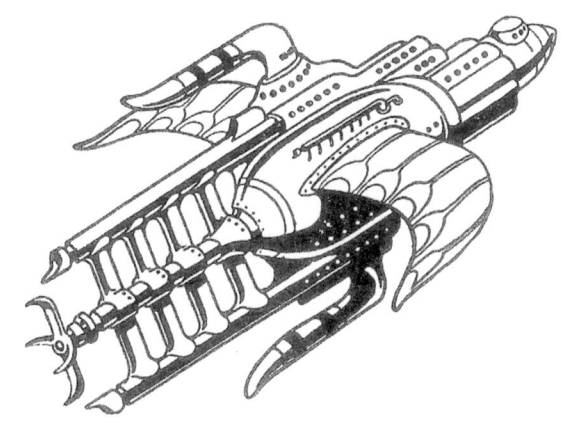

Rubber-Stamp Buck Rogers Spaceship. Superior Type Co. From the magazine *Playthings*, September 1935.

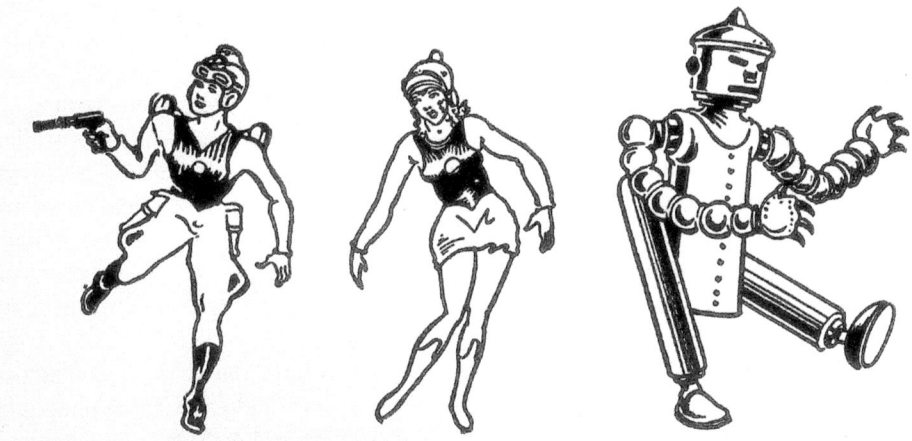

Rubber-Stamp Buck, Wilma, and Robot. A Chicago firm, the Superior Type Co., issued rubber-stamp Buck Rogers sets in 1935. The stamps showed Buck and Wilma in various poses, and a robot. From the magazine *Playthings*, September 1935.

Someone in toy-making, however, did spot Brinkman's cobbled-together Buck Rogers figures. Daisy Manufacturing was situated in Plymouth, an industrial city west of Detroit. Daisy's Cass Hough had enjoyed the daily strip himself, but without having it enter his mind that children might feel similarly and desire related toys. After meeting with Dille, he made an agreement with Nowlan and the strip's artist, Dick Calkins, that the strip would feature a ray-gun design that Daisy could produce. With the promotion, designing, and manufacturing quickly in place, Hough borrowed Brinkman's fanciful figures for the 1934 Toy Fair in New York City. He anticipated enthusiasm from toy merchandisers for his metal gun that went "zap."

The American Toy Fair occurred each spring in Manhattan under Toy Manufacturers of the U.S.A. auspices, with its central locations being the Toy Center, which was the Fifth Avenue Building at Broadway and Fifth, and the official Toy Fair hotel, Hotel McAlpin, at Broadway and 34th. At this point, Daisy was enjoying success in the trade, and had selling agents in two regions, with the Phil B. Bekeart Company in San Francisco, and Louis Williams & Company in Nashville. In New York, the Plymouth firm was not yet maintaining a year-round presence, mounting a display only for the fair.

Standing in his company's show room, however, Hough experienced rejection for two weeks from "toy men"—the industry's name for those involved in and experienced in the business, especially those representing merchandisers and jobbers nationwide. They responded to the price tag of forty-nine cents. Too high, they said. These buyers, confident about what children wanted, turned away.[18]

The Toy Manufacturers of the U.S.A. made suggestions for providing toys to children in different age groups. By these guidelines, children from eight to ten years engaged in "realism in play." Under the heading of this group's toys "for dramatic and imitative play," however, appeared suggestions almost exclusively for toys that evoked wonder, insofar they reflected the technical marvels of the time, and in some cases embraced wonder-tale elements for subject matter and projection: Magic Lantern, Magic Sets, Marionettes, Microphone, Movie Machine, Telegraph Set.[19]

To be fair to the toy men, the idea that Daisy would introduce a "space gun" must have struck then an odd note. The company had made its name by making functional and reliable toys exceptionally well. Flights of fancy, far from being rare in the Daisy line before 1934, had no place in it whatsoever. The company had its roots in practical manufacture, having begun with windmills and only turning to air rifles as promotional items. While the air rifles failed to sell windmills, they sold themselves with such alacrity that the company rethought its business—much as Secor had his, at a similar turning point, in Connecticut. A wheel spinning in air would have captured with some accuracy not only Daisy's main product but its success in the field. Air rifles, however, soon made the company profitable, even against the widespread and aggressive competition that quickly arrived once its success became evident. The company maintained its lead through the late 1800s and early 1900s, introducing innovations and continuing to fine-tune its mechanisms.[20]

As to the air rifles themselves, Daisy produced them as toys, merchandised them as toys, and sold them through toy departments. All the same, they had practical application: for they worked with precision. This would prove itself the case in World War II, when the military attributed American riflery's excellence, in part, to the target-shooting sport popular among boys in prewar years. Seeking to broaden its product line, Daisy did introduce the No. 8 Water Pistol of 1913. Even though clearly intended for entertainment and play, the metal toy's careful engineering made it seem not out of place beside Daisy's level-headed rifles. Since it shot water, moreover, it still did something physically—perhaps even something literary, given Aldous Huxley's memorable line, decades later: "He pointed his water pistol menacingly."[21]

The Buck Rogers 25th Century Rocket Pistol, in contrast, had no conceivable utility. Though rugged and durable, it only clicked and sparked—and not even that, in Toy Fair sales. It seemed to be engineering and manufacturing overkill for what might as well have been a cardboard cutout.

After weeks without success, Hough connected with Bob Wolfe, toy-merchandising manager at the store that had originated the toy department, Macy's. Wolfe mounted a promotion for the oddity that included a window display at the 34th and 6th Avenues corner, in exchange for a one-week exclusive deal with Daisy for New York City. Opening-day's shoppers, as it turned out, crowded around the Macy's block and required police supervision. That day commenced the year's biggest toy event. Buyers from other stores must have felt shocked annoyance at having to scramble to place orders.[22]

Mouse beset by Minikins. The image of Gulliver staked to the ground by Lilliputians, a powerful one for the Moderns, is reenacted here by the hero of animated films who finds himself in the "Land of the Little People" (cover, 1936).

Superhumans: Comical and Comic-Strip

In that watershed year for Buck Rogers in the toy industry, Whitman Publishing of Racine, Wisconsin, obtained rights to issue story books. In activity outfits, Chicago's Rapaport Brothers issued metal-casting kits, and Porter Chemical of Hagerstown, Maryland, well-known for its Chemcraft line, produced a licensed version. A Buck Rogers Game appeared from New York's Lutz & Sheinkman, which may have existed to make that item only. Sackman Brothers of New York issued Buck Rogers play suits. Daisy's pressed-steel toy aside, Louis Marx & Company may have issued the most impressive plaything in its friction toy: Buck Rogers 25th Century Rocket Ship. Movie Jecktor Co. contracted to issue films.[23]

By year's end the John F. Dille Company was assisting with its Buck Rogers Rocket Ship Fleet, presumably the first of its "display pieces for Christmas shows" in toy departments.[24] That such variety appeared in this first year, with all but Daisy's arriving well after the spring Toy Fair, indicates the speed with which the comic was becoming a phenomenon. Once attuned to the adventure strip and its futuristic ingredients, toymakers began enjoying playing with graphic elements that veered from the norm.

Somewhat similarly, children seem to have loved *Popeye*. Perhaps the most popular comic character at the time, toymakers in 1934 were only beginning to sense his vitality, and issued Popeye playthings in that year in significant but not overwhelming numbers. They included a game by the Einson-Freeman of Long Island City; metal and wooden toys by J. Chein; masquerade costumes by E. Simon's Sons; picture puzzles by Saalfield Publishing; and the "Popeyepipe" musical toy by Northwestern Products of St. Louis.[25]

Popeye cut an unusual figure, being more fantastic in appearance than the heroic but quite humanly proportioned Buck Rogers: for the sailor possessed not only salty character but a strength of unguessable proportions, triggered by steamed spinach. As noted, cultural influences around the 1890s had stimulated British writers to create characters who strode with superhuman gait through adventure stories of all stripes. Baum then introduced Rob Joslyn, the technically enhanced child who becomes superhuman in his powers, in his 1901 *The Master Key*; and in the 1910s Burroughs created Tarzan and John Carter, the former having overwhelming primitive powers, and the latter, Earth-gravity muscles on Mars. In the 1930s a new influx of symbolic superhumans arrived, with Popeye perhaps the most amusing yet not least portentous. "Super" itself, as an adjective, came into greater use in the toy world in this decade, being absent around 1934 but beginning to appear in the next few years in such toys as Superjax jackstones by Grey Iron Casting of Mount Joy, Pennsylvania; the Super-Jector movie-projector of Chicago's Trojan; and the Super-Safe toy electric iron by Samson-United, in Rochester.[26] While not firmly indicative of a trend themselves, they marked a tipping toward a new perspective.

The difference in impact between Buck Rogers and Popeye may be seen in the lines of playthings that developed around the characters. By 1937, Buck Rogers toys included a few new prominent numbers, three being from Chicago companies: a cast-metal toy set by Dowst; balloons and rubber toys by Lee-Tex Rubber Products; and a rubber stamping set by Superior Type, a firm that had a minor specialty in cartoon-strip sets. Buck Rogers sporting goods also appeared, made by Edward K. Tryon of Philadelphia. While Porter Chemical had dropped its Buck Rogers license, another company, Gropper Manufacturing of Brooklyn, had picked it up.[27] Marx, too, had dropped its license. Rapaport, Sackman, and Daisy were continuing with their licenses through Dille.

In contrast, by 1937, King Features Syndicate had licensed Popeye rights to at least forty-three different manufacturers of playthings and items for children. In addition, additional licenses went out to toymakers for Popeye's fellow-characters Olive Oyl and Jeep. Popeye items were being made in almost every conceivable form, from banks, flashlights, dolls, felt toys, and paper movies to kites, knives, marble sets, coaster wagons, party favors, and stereoscopic pictures.[28]

Popeye possessed a simple, unmistakable, and comical character. Popeye came unburdened, moreover, by context beyond the idea that there might be a boat, a beach, or a dock involved, given that he was a sailor. To ride coattails on the cartoon's success, a company had actually to portray Popeye or his cohorts. A toy needed to be specifically comical, in the now-well-established sense. Buck Rogers, on the other hand, lacked whimsical character, as a semi-realistic Everyman who becomes a hero within a specific melodramatic context—within, in other words, his particular sleep-journey into a milieu filled with gadgets and wondrous vehicles. In Gernsbackian scientifiction, this context tended to possess more character than did the humans involved, thanks in part to Gernsback's own interest in invention and technical matters, and thanks, too, to the power exerted by magazine-cover artwork, being eye-catchingly colorful, spectacle-oriented, and often violent in its subject-matter.

This being the case, it did sink in, among toy manufacturers, that they might ride coattails on the Buck Rogers phenomenon by issuing toys evoking the context, rather than the characters. They followed Gernsback's lead in having ideas sell the product, with the toy-ideas blending imaginary inventions with "futuristic" styling.

In a real sense, once this practice appeared, the game could go on indefinitely for toymakers without the Buck Rogers name. The industry lost a focal point by this practice, however. In the later 1930s, all the new "space toys" remained Buck Rogers toys, whether or not marketed as such. Yet by helping the melodramatic sleep-journey undertaken by Buck to slip from central place, toymakers were helping the background settings and situations, too, to lose priority in children's minds. The excitement residual from 1934 faded, although the comic strip and its characters retained popular standing through the subsequent decade. The Buck Rogers name, meanwhile, found its place in English as an adjective, often with a derogatory connotation.

Comical superbeings in the Popeye tradition arose naturally in the realms of comics and film animation. In neither form did characters face the limits restricting biological beings. Artists exaggerated qualities in their characters, whether animal or human, to help them rise from their flatness, much as writers using melodramatic forms would exaggerate qualities in characters to help them acquire piquancy and flavor despite their being artificial or incomplete. Whether taking the sectional-soul approach, as in Claudy, or the stock-character one, as in Appleton, the process led to exaggeration; exaggeration, especially by imitators, led to attributes being offered to the reader in concentrated forms; and concentrated aspects pointed toward the "super" effect. An irony devolved from the situation: for writers and artists created superhumans by depicting incomplete humans.

Buck Rogers arose from the tradition employing stock characters, in the Appleton tradition. Being the romantic leading man of melodrama, his attributes see no exaggeration beyond the human norm to any degree greater than had occurred in melodramas belonging to prior centuries. He exhibits verve, bravery, and a duty-sense that fall in line with his predecessors. All the same, he acquires superhuman status by technical means, as had Baum's Rob Joslyn. Superior devices and wondrous machines move him beyond the readers' sense of the norm. He appears before them exaggerated technologically. That he is not an inventor matters not at all. It suits the Everyman role that makes him more kin to Fogg and Nellie Bly than Fergusson or Robur. On the other hand, he brings a natural virility from a time that is less technically developed—a stand-in Noble Savage along the lines of a John Carter or Tarzan, who finds himself thrust into a milieu that juxtaposes advanced technology with a demoralized and even degraded populace, much as the World's Fair during the Great Depression did.

The future had offered a setting used sparingly by Verne, after his early, unpublished *Paris in the Twentieth Century*. His stories almost overwhelmingly took place in times past or in his own decades. His greatest achievements may have been *20,000 Leagues Under the Sea*, which inserted a technologically exaggerated submarine into his own world, and *Around the World in Eighty Days*, whose plot depended upon conditions being just what they were, at the time of its writing. The future served as a setting more often in Wells stories, perhaps due to technical progress having become nearly palpable by the 1890s. Wells, moreover, exhibited substantially more positivism than had Verne; and having been T.H. Huxley's student he accepted Darwin's selectionism as well as an evolutionist scientism. In the 1910s, Burroughs and Appleton emphasized current settings, with sometimes a single technological exaggeration introduced. Current settings dominated not only in terms of the number of separate works, but in terms of audience numbers. *Tarzan of the Apes* proved a bestseller, and the first Tarzan movie, in 1918, a massive hit[29]; the Tom Swift books enjoyed perennially popularity; and three movies—*The Lost World* in 1925, the first sound movie of *Tarzan* in 1930, and *King Kong* in 1933—brought current-setting wonder tales to their largest publics to date.

Another split was occurring in the Modern wonder tale, however. Stories that would be labeled "tales of super-science" had already appeared, such as Frederick's "The Planet Juggler," in 1908, and Gernsback's *Ralph 124 C 41+*, in 1911. Gernsback began *Amazing Stories* in 1926, the year also of Fritz Lang's future-setting movie *Metropolis*. The success in 1930–35 of the Buck Rogers comic strip and Buck Rogers toys, however, marked the real arrival of the new type of wonder tale. Besides fixing in the public mind a visual vocabulary, it played a role in forging an association, in the public mind, between the wonder tale and the distant future—and, to a lesser degree, between outer space and the future.

Rapaport and the Robot

The toymaking firm Rapaport Brothers had offices at 701 West Ohio Street, Chicago, when the Buck Rogers toy phenomenon began. Its reputation rested upon a line of "Craftsman Outfits—Constructive, Educational, Fascinating, Profitable," having become a leader in this category. In the 1930s, the word "outfit" still served where "kit" would later. Usually boxed, one would contain the necessary ingredients for a child or youth to pursue a constructive activity or scientific interest.

Rapaport's particular success arose with metal-casting sets. Children bought their molds for casting, in lead, small toys including horses, soldiers, Indians, and cowboys. Some produced "character" toys, such as the "Rebecca of Sunnybrook Farm" outfit. Others led children to create King Arthur's Knights in Armor, Buffalo Bill, or Captain John Smith with Indians. While a few outfits produced licensed-property figures, Rapaport by and large produced sets based on characters and themes without paying a penny to anyone for the right to do so.

The toy-licensing trend that had been in the making since the 1890s was gathering momentum, with the main engines being comics, animated short films, and the movies. Even though Yellow Kid and Buster Brown toys sold well, licensing costs increased the financial burden on toy companies; and the great increase in comics characters made them unreliable means for moving toys. Yet by the 1930s, even cautious companies were taking second looks at licensing deals, especially when animated characters were involved. Walt Disney animated films were meeting with popular approval; and with the success enjoyed by toy companies that had jumped early onto the Disney bandwagon, industry members were feeling a renewed if cautious enthusiasm. That Disney toys should be meeting with success, however, was eroding self-confidence among established toy men: for they had spent their professional lives seeing their faith in traditional playthings reinforced, season after season. The Disney phenomenon, which commenced just before the Buck Rogers one, fueled worries that a sea-change was taking place.

The rising tide of mass-culture icons portended well for licensed properties in general. With all the mail-order catalogs, newsreels, national magazines, newspapers, movies, and now radio, moreover, a manufacturer's chances seemed better than ever for distinguishing a truly popular entertainment figure from the flash-in-the-pan. Signing licensing agreements, moreover, insured a company that no imitations would immediately appear, if they did enjoy success.

Rapaport Brothers may have been in a better position than others to recognize the promise offered by Buck Rogers, being based in the city where the strip started, and where the buzz among the city's professional men would have made the comic's influence clear. With interest growing in home-casting sets, other companies were entering the field; and Rapaport needed to expand its line to include new molds not being offered by others. The company managed to put together a Buck Rogers Caster set for a test run in Chicago stores, just before Christmas of 1934. It outsold other sets in Rapaport's line three-to-one.[30]

In an unobtrusive way, Rapaport Brothers may have introduced a toy type before any others—as an image, and as a term. Given the popularity of Steam Man, Tin Woodman, Tik-Tok, and other such figures, children in the middle years must have played with toys that allowed them to participate imaginatively in those mechanical figures, by some means or another. Manufacturers since the 1860s also had created countless metal men and women, and metal boys and girls—some as automata, some as banks; some detailed, some crude; and some jointed, some not. When Rapaport signed its license for creating Buck Rogers molds, however, the term that had filtered from the Čapek stage play into general society and then the wonder tale finally became a word in the playroom. One Rapaport mold in the new series made a figure that the company called a robot.

Just as children probably made the first toys representing the Steam Man of the prairies and the Tin Woodman of Oz, using whatever materials they could find at hand, so children melted stray bits of scrounged-up lead to pour into molds to make the first "official" toy robots.

The little toys confirmed and further spread an alteration in the word's shift in meaning, which had become evident in Century of Progress exhibits. No longer the human-looking drudge of monotonous factory work, the robot revealed its fabricated nature in its boxlike contours. The new Rapaport sets also included molds for extraterrestrial creatures, including one with the highly enlarged cranium of superhuman intelligence. These, too, may have been firsts.

Rapaport's home-cast robot had a contemporary in the Robotoy, made by another Illinois toymaker, Buddy "L" Manufacturing Company of East Moline. The boxlike robot appeared only as an image on the side of the truck's cab—with the truck itself being the actual automatic toy.[31] A factory-made robot, also made of lead, appeared in a Buck Rogers group made by Britains, in 1935–6, which made its way to America as a Cream of Wheat premium.[32] By 1937 the term's acceptance in the toy industry seemed confirmed by the fact that the Robotoy survived beyond its introductory year, and by the appearance of additional toys. Cadaco of Oakland, California, a new entrant in the world of game-making, introduced Robotball and Robotennis.[33]

The Horizontal Rocket

Alongside the arrival of "robot," the word "rocket" was undergoing a change in the toy-world. Mainly still seeing conventional use, it appeared in the same context as the words "arrow" or "bullet." These occurred in such race-car and toy names as the Silver Arrow or Golden Arrow.[34] In 1934 and 1935, for instance, higher-profile Rocket toys, included a Rocket Racer pull toy made by a traditional-minded toymaker, Gong Bell, and the Sky Rocket coaster wagon made by American National of Toledo. Sheboygan, Wisconsin, made itself the toy industry's rocket capitol, with another Sky Rocket coaster wagon appearing from Sheboygan Coaster & Wagon Works, and Rocket wagons, from Globe Company. Daisy's Rocket Pistol, however, heralded a change—as did a smaller steel toy. This, which was yet another Rocket Racer, appeared in the Wyandotte Toys line, in the fashion of a Buck Rogers type ship for the 1935 season, but without licensing.[35]

By 1937, while Gong Bell had stopped making its own Rocket Racer, several other wheel-goods companies joined Globe. Atlas Steel & Manufacturing Company of Baltimore, Maryland, was making a Rocket steel coaster wagon, while Garton Toy Company joined its neighbors in Sheboygan by also making a Rocket, which in Garton's case was a "juvenile auto." Sky Rocket appeared as a name for yet again in the toy industry, this time applied by a bagatelle game made by Gotham Pressed Steel Corporation of New York.[36] By 1938 the Rocket Shot game appeared from New York's Lindstrom Tool & Toy Company, who made clear the name's reference by the brightly colorful image of the skyrocket on the bagatelle's board. It proved a long-lived game.

"Rocket ship," on the other hand, was becoming another generally accepted term for an imaginary thing. As with Burroughs's use for "rocket" alongside "torpedo," the rocket ship combined the flying-ship concept with the firework-type propulsion. In contrast to that use, however, the ship's appearance departs from that of the sky rocket. When the new term entered toy-industry vocabulary thanks to Dille and Dowst, their spaceships even more clearly diverged, being ships with a horizontal mode of travel, evoking wildly fanciful maritime craft. Via literal appropriation, Buck Rogers designs also sometimes resembled inverted dirigibles, with the cabin that was below the center of buoyancy in the airship now sitting atop the spindle-shaped spaceship body. The unlicensed Wyandotte toy participated in this approach.

Airships influenced toy vehicles other than space-travel ones. While Marx's Speed King

Rocket Ship No. 1. This "Transcontinental" craft, made with lithographed tin, top and bottom, displays the inverted-dirigible design displayed in Buck Rogers and later spaceships. This toy's black-rubber wheels suggest postwar manufacture. Midgetoy's similar spaceship, of die-cast, first appeared in the late 1940s. Transcontinental Rocket Ship No. 1, manufacturer unknown, 3½ inches, late prewar or early postwar (photograph by and collection of the author).

wind-up had kept to its original design and name through 1934, the Buck Rogers phenomenon may have influenced the name-change reflected in 1935 catalogs, where it appeared as yet another Rocket Racer. Still sixteen inches, with the same rounded nose and body, new lithography replaced the former exhaust pipes with rocket outlets along the sides. In that year, too, Metalcraft Corporation of St. Louis produced a steel ride-on toy with the name Rocket on its sides. Just over two feet long, it had a rounded, conical nose, teardrop fenders over the back wheels, and fins to the rear. It emulated the rocket ships of the Buck Rogers line, despite its overall missile shape. In general, the middle-1930s rocket ship most closely resembled a motorboat, being oriented horizontally and having its cabin on top. Since combination water-and-air craft often appeared in boys' novels, airplanes, too, helped contribute to the rocket ship's visual appearance. Yet as rounded, pointed, and streamlined forms, with rudimentary "fins," the motorboat and the airship had become primary in influence.

A few toys and games did depict vehicles for moving beyond Earth's atmosphere, which in their shapes approached what later viewers might readily call rocket or spaceships. In smaller vehicle toys, a pressed-steel ship made by New York's Automatic Toy resembled a highly stylized, streamlined airplane with greatly reduced wingspan, landing gear underneath, and lateral windows.[37] The art on the Race to the Moon game by Fairchild, in the years 1934–7, showed five rising spacecraft with lateral fins that were reduced to streamlined extensions running most of their lengths. These ships still had the lateral windows of the airplane or the water-going vessel.[38]

In the 1936 game Stratosphere, by Whitman, the cover art transformed the dirigible along airplane lines. The Whitman artist shows cabin windows along a blimp-like body's sides, indicating that passengers, no longer suspended below or positioned above, have been moved inside the fuselage. The spindle still has four fins around its tapered end—which no longer was the dirigible's closed tail but an open outlet for a fiery engine. Although having lateral windows, the spindle itself no longer moves horizontally to the viewer, but upwardly.[39] That such a game showing an Art Deco ship, traveling upwards through atmospheric strata that darken into starry space, should be named Stratosphere, rather than Orbit or Outer Space, struck an appropriate note for its time.

An image being held in common, by now, in the public mind, had contributed to the process that rotated the dirigible to point upwards. The stratospheric balloon, the ultimate Montgolfiers-Charles balloon, had an inverted, attenuated teardrop shape. A protective cover over the balloon draped downward to a finely tapered basal point—making it resemble conventional comet depictions, with spherical body and long tail. The stratospheric balloon appeared to viewers in such a way that any movement horizontally seemed unimportant. It made real the craft envisaged by Dr. Fergusson's manservant Joe, being a balloon directed only upwards.

A game by Parker Brothers reflected public interest in this scientific craft, under the same name that Whitman's took, Stratosphere. Its box-art showed the inverted teardrop's upper curve stark against the outer darkness.[40] The painting offered a symbolic companion to one that appeared on a different game box by Parker Brothers, showing a series of upwardly pointing Modern spires, for 1937's Skyscraper Game.[41] The skyscraper eventually would supplant the oceanliner and zeppelin, as spacecraft models: for in the skyscraper, the horizontal line, marked by the rows of windows that indicates floors, makes a right angle to the line to be drawn from spire to base. Although a new development, this re-oriented the spaceship back to Verne's moon-vessel.

Buck Rogers rocket ships, as noted, did appear in licensed toy form, in Dowst's

Tootsietoy line—with none resembling the traditional skyrocket. In this particular toy-lineage, aircraft design initially predominated. In 1937, Dowst introduced toys modeled on existing aircraft that included the streamlined dirigible *U.S.N. Los Angeles*. This toy's casting included, at the top, a protrusion that housed small pulley-wheels. When a child threaded a string through, and tied the string's ends to chair-backs or wall-hooks, the dirigible "flew" not slowly and majestically, but at whatever speed the child might desire. As toy historians have noted, the streamlined dirigible "forms a link of sorts between these more or less typical aircraft and the fantastic spacecraft issued in the same year."[42]

Among these "fantastic spacecraft" appeared one that was quite dirigible-like, several that were fishlike, and another that was like a double balloon in appearance: the Buck Rogers Rocket Ship Battlecruiser, Buck Rogers Battlecruiser, Buck Rogers Flash Blast Attack Ship, and Buck Rogers Venus Duo-Destroyer, with the last being made in two forms.[43]

Tootsietoy materials being inexpensive, Dowst playthings appeared at modest prices in five-and-dime stores, helping them to spread across America evenly. Households with little cash for nonessentials found them affordable for special occasions. In common with the originating comic, the toys had appeal without respect to economic class divisions.

The Labor-Saving Superhuman

Whatever sense of wonder might greet each Modern invention, each new marvel conformed to the rule that a cutting edge dulls. In the 1930s, when technical progress seemed to speed forward, the wonder-aspect's rate of luster-loss kept pace, like a drab sulky rattling just behind a sleek horse. Surprise gave way to novelty, which gave way to the commonplace, and then to the sense that new mechanical devices and electrical automations were not only appropriate to everyday life but well-deserved by average householders. Invention served society by providing, in the term coined in the 1800s, "the labor-saving device"—among terms for automatism, perhaps the most drab-sulky-like, and the least wonder-evoking.

The hope expressed by upper-class optimists, that technical advance would create "free time" in which people might pursue self-improvement, found its embodiment in the term: for endless innovation turned upon the notion that the individual, especially in the domestic sphere, needed relief from "unnecessary labor." In the household as in the factory, automations made labor redundant, or at least to seem so. That labor might be required to earn money to buy gadgetry seemed an acceptable contradiction—just as it seemed unobjectionable and even unquestionable that simultaneous with the rise in the labor-saving device came the rise in the pursuit of "hobbies," rather than a rise in enthusiasm among the rank-and-file for becoming doctoral candidates. It became commonplace, in sketches of famous personalities, to add color by listing hobbies. William DeBeck, the cartoonist who created *Barney Google*, for instance, pursued ones typical for the time—if only among the well-to-do: golf, bridge, and deep-sea fishing in the Gulf of Mexico.[44]

Hobbyists or not, cartoonists continued to prove themselves alert observers, perhaps none more so than Reuben Lucius Goldberg, in such strips as *Side Show* and *Twisted Tales*. While many "funnies" artists introduced terms and phrases that entered general parlance, his proved particularly long-lived: "the Rube Goldberg device." The fact that his name became an adjective honored his predilection to concoct contrivances that were elaborate and technical but silly in an overwrought way in accomplishing the most minor and

Blondie goes to Leisureland. Westinghouse, with its "Leisure Line of Electric Home Appliances," in the 1930s and '40s published a game printed on a large, linen-paper mat, depicting Blondie's and Dagwood's struggles with domestic mishaps and struggles: "Blondie thinks it ought to be coffee grounds for divorce to have to put up with an old-fashioned coffee pot," says one caption. At game's end, the family live "happily ever after in their all-electric home." Blondie Goes to Leisureland, copyrights 1930, 1934, 1935, and 1940 (author's collection).

pointless tasks. As satires upon Modern American "necessities" they rose to an appropriate level of absurdity.[45] He hardly could be said to have introduced this form of humor, since the smoking-room in Bangs's *Houseboat on the Styx*, in the 1890s, has Goldberg-device earmarks. All the same, and ironically, his illustrative outpouring restored some wonder to now-standard automations that were becoming invisibly common in household life.

As did other technical innovations, the labor-saving device offered a way to "be ahead of the game," especially in social terms. It represented a means to exhibit the "latest" in style or fashion—in this case, the fashion to be expressed in managing one's life: one's "lifestyle." As such, it offered a means for exhibiting superiority. In the wonder tale this often appeared in its association with the inventor—as in Stapledon's 1936 novel *Odd John*, in which an intellectually superhuman child becomes preoccupied with inventing just such items. The young John introduces numerous "small labour-saving devices into the house" and soon afterwards embarks on a career, while still a child, of inventing "gadgets" and "devices" that he patents and sells, as a means to acquire financial power.[46]

The alliance between innovation and style, in the labor-saving device as in other areas, helped create the atmosphere in which American toy manufacturers could create playthings that would seem, in some slight way, to anticipate "the future," and thus to participate in the excitement that was beginning to surround it as an idea, despite a somewhat repressed but steadily increasing association in the general populace's mind having an opposite nature, which linked Modern technology, social advance, and Progress itself to mechanization, regimentation, and mass-control through propaganda, if not coercive measures and terror. The labor-saving device appeared frequently in games evoking daily life in the 1920s and 1930s, the latter decade being the one in which, as noted, toy makers embraced automotive streamlining, year after year, for the "car of tomorrow"—the "car of today" having become the most markedly public item in any middle-class individual's life, and the mechanism invested with the most weight in style-exhibitionism.

Yet even the labor-saving device served to represent the "latest"—followed by that drab sulky of the outmoded.

Remote Control

In the 1930s Buck Rogers comic strip, the robot's remote-control or centralized-control characteristic helped give it a futuristic aspect—just as remote control in a household or shop device indicated its Modernity. Robots, in other words, were remaining true to their factory-drudge models, the loom-running millworkers in Dickens's *Hard Times*, while also hearkening back to the Steam Man, or the Steam Elephant in Verne's *La Maison à Vapeur* of 1881: they acted only upon orders, and upon direction. They were tending away, in other words, from the autonomy possessed by such beings as Pinocchio, Signor Pittonaccio, Tin Woodman, or Tik-Tok.

Given the expense involved in making them, toys with remote-control aspects arrived late, becoming common only after the 1930s—and after World War II. All the same, toymakers in the 1930s, knowing as well as did Nowlan and Calkins that it would attract children, tapped into the notion.

The most prominent instance arrived from a manufacturer in the arena of box toys, or play sets. Through the 1800s, toymakers had produced Noah's Arks, farm sets, and toy soldiers. In the later 1800s and early decades of the 1900s, miniature stores, kitchen sets, and doll houses grew more common in middle-class households, as did toy maritime fleets, auto fleets, and farm miniatures with buildings, equipment, and vehicles. The toy-soldier approach, in which a single figure might be offered in multiples to make an "army," allowed companies to economically produce playthings offering considerably more time-absorption to children than might be offered by the solitary toy. While the solitary toy might have symbolic appeal in a novel such as Bailey's *The Tin Soldier* or children's story *Corporal Keeperupper*, by Katherine Milhous, in which individual bravery or service might need emphasis, the toy army offered children constructive occupations, mainly in set-up and tear-down, which perhaps taught them about power in numbers, and perhaps steered their minds away from the mass-violence being condoned by such activity.

Play sets presented the child with worlds in miniature, with hands-on involvement. Children imagined motorcars in motion, when pushing around wheeled toys; or had people go through their routines, among other figures and furniture. In the imagination, the fingers upon toy cars or figures receded from the visible. Minikins moved on their own, in the child's universe-in-small. In Stevenson's *A Child's Garden of Verses*, the child watches his "leaden soldiers go … across the bedclothes, through the hills." He sees their movement, without seeing his own hands moving them bit-by-bit along their ways. With remote-control, however, on the playroom floor as in the workaday world, the controlling hand's receding from the visible became actual.

The first American remote-control play sets appeared around the time that inexpensive spaceship toys appeared. Their parent company emphasized invisible control even in its own name. The Remotrol Company manufactured play sets that were built upon trays, with the trays being slightly elevated above floor or table thanks to corner legs. In Animals in Motion, the tray featured fixed barn, fences, and trees, with movable cows and horses. In Ships in Motion a shallow metal tank replaced the tray, with docks to each side and a "rock island" in the middle. The child filled the tray with water, to let toy ocean liners float about.

The raised tray rendered the child's hand invisible, since these Remote Control Playthings allowed a child to move toys by "sub-magnetic" means.[47] By moving a magnetic wand underneath, a child led a cow to emerge from the barn, or a steamship to pull away from dock: for these movable parts came equipped with magnets. Remotrol was bringing into mass-production the Factitious Spider—that invention by Charles Darwin's grandfather, Erasmus, in which a spider moved around on a paper sheet, drawn by the magnet held underneath.

Remotrol also offered a Tarzan Jungle set. Not pictured in advertisements, presumably it had jungle accessories and movable figures representing Tarzan, Jane, and African animals. The irony may not have occurred to the Manhattan manufacturers: for they were basing a play set upon the fictional back-to-nature cry of pre-civilized power and vitality, and adding to it the latest appurtenance of Modernism.[48] Had they offered a "robot Tarzan" the irony would have been no less. The Manhattan firm likely gave it no more thought than did other toy companies obtaining across-the-board licenses, capitalizing on the man-ape's popularity. Perhaps children sensed an incongruity, however. The toy disappeared from the line, replaced by a duck-pond set, with a "magic mirror" standing in for the water-tray of Ships in Motion.[49] The company continued developing new miniature environments in which children could exert "remote" control, including, as was appropriate in those Phileas Fogg times, one named World Travel. Horse-racing sets appeared by 1939—a perhaps-wishful application for remote control—and a hockey game by 1940. Ships in Motion and the renamed Magic Farmyard offerings seemed to remain the company's most popular.[50]

Although simple in concept, Remotrol's toys appealed to children, whose demand for them gave the company long-term stability.[51]

Bubbles

The ball that was bounced or thrown into the air had a continuing influence on children's imaginations, wonder stories, and toy manufacturing, thanks to the continuing and expanding associations that conjoined within the toy.

The ball-shaped bathysphere, for transport into ocean depths, joined other forms that became, through literal appropriation, means for transport into outer space. Cavor, in *The First Men in the Moon*, in inventing a spacecraft, hits upon the shape: "Imagine a sphere ... large enough to hold two people and their luggage. It will be made of steel lined with thick glass; it will contain a proper store of solidified air, concentrated food, water-distilling apparatus, and so forth."[52] In the 1930s the shape maintained its hold on the imagination, appearing not only as other imaginary spaceships, as in *The Mystery Men of Mars*, but also as craft for actual exploration. One such, Jean Piccard's *Strato-Balloon*, appeared in the mid–1930s. The balloon itself presented the inverted teardrop common in stratospheric balloons. The gondola, however, Piccard designed as a hermetically sealed chamber to carry two individuals. Although any shape might be lifted by balloon, the gondola was a sphere, with a round air-hatch in submersible-craft style.[53]

Cavor's bathysphere-spacecraft reflected a second literal appropriation, as well. This borrowed symbolism appeared in the spacecraft's behavior, in that it mimicked the bubble dislodged from the tea-kettle bottom that speeds upward through water, without engine or propulsion. Moving upwards through air, Cavor's spacecraft does so by "antigravity."

Illustrations depicting undersea scenes often included air-bubble images, as a graphic convention to suggest a watery realm. In magazine science-fiction illustrations, too, other bubbles appeared. Such illustrations showed multiple planets and moons in the "skies" of far-away worlds, with their apparent diameters or closeness, as well as their numbers, greatly exaggerated from what they would be in reality—as in the orrery. The believable graphic convention conveying the underwater experience offered one of the few elements available to convey the interplanetary void: the ball-shaped planetary body. While the verisimilitude in these depictions was falling short, their symbolic similitude, or symbolic echoing, succeeded well enough that the practice became a convention, especially in comic books.

The two environments, undersea and extraterrestrial, overlapped in their associations in many ways. Near the Modern century's ending, one writer described the Lunar surface: "The rock formations looked like petrified sponges jutting up out of a dried-up sea bottom."[54] H.P. Lovecraft offered alien "horrors" that seemed to be hyper-magnified bryozoa; and countless writers and artists came to depict alien beings with molluscan tentacles and eyestalks, and piscine scales and eyes.

The Glass Helmet

Bubbles reinforced the doubled vision juxtaposing ocean with outer space in other ways, as when rounded helmets used by undersea explorers became bubble helmets for outer-space ones. In both images, the head's enclosure reflects the fact that the light of reason, of intelligence, exists only by being technically enwrapped. The rounded shape, with neck hidden below the head, links Edison's lightbulb to the helmet, with the vacuum of air inside the former being a vacuum of sea water in the diver's headgear; or, in the case of the outer-space explorer, with the vacuum moved from within the lightbulb to outside the helmet, with the air now within. Both seabed-walking and space-walking figures operated at frontiers of human experience, in the Modern years—in the one case doing so literally, and in the other, figuratively.

The environmental suits worn by both have a further feature. While Captain Nemo's crew can walk freely on the bottom of the ocean, they retain the feature necessary to all dives: the tube which acts as an umbilicus to the mother ship, even when the ship is being carried in miniature form on the walkers' backs.

The individual deep-sea diver; the space-walking astronaut; the protectively suited individual walking into any inimical environment, such as an area poisoned by chemicals, gases, or smoke: all exhibit individuality and take individual action, and all exert their personal will, in choosing direction or action to take—at least to appearances. The semblance of independence mutes the potently charged situation embodied in such images: that of the individual's complete dependence upon the machine that must encase them. Individual mobility serves to place an attractive veneer over the reality of the programmed action, the overall course of movement having been determined by the needs, or the programme, belonging to the society that views such actions as being necessary. A society requires the individual to become completely dependent upon an encasing machinery, when the society is the one Mumford termed the "megamachine."

Such a figure, in a placental suit equipped with umbilical cord, presents a symbolic paradox, in that it is an adult who willingly becomes an ambulatory embryo—a social unit that is a desirable one insofar as its individual intelligence fulfills the promise of the encasing technics, and insofar as its actions fall within the parameters set down by the megamachine's needs. Although often we view explorers as individualists, in characterizing a figure as "a diver" or "a spaceman" we are assigning them occupations or roles. They take on these occupations or roles by completely encasing themselves; and although some might be explorers in truth, testing their equipment and not being tested by it, in general such figures are "following suit." Even the individualist explorer, to be successful, must at some point turn back to the society that made exploring possible. Whether a child in a "playsuit" has conscious inklings that might lead them toward such thoughts, they will raise the diving mask knowing they are imaginatively going to be submerged, or lower the spaceman helmet knowing they are heading into the void, which is void of human culture except that which sustains them. At some unguessable level they know, in other words, that they are losing their individual independence, and becoming completely dependent.

Divers. Deep-sea divers remained iconic figures through the end of the Modern century. From the 1950s, the larger figure shown is a salt shaker, while the smaller is aquarium "furniture" in the same mold as the one earlier seen from the 1940s. Porcelain divers, Japan, 4½ and 2½ inches tall (photograph by and collection of the author).

Mumford commented on a psychologist's report about an autistic boy who believed he was run by machines. During the day he carried around what he believed to be a life-support system, and at night rigged his bed with bits of imaginary equipment. These, he thought, kept him alive while asleep:

> But is this just the autistic fantasy of a pathetic little boy? Is it not rather the state that the mass of mankind is fast approaching in actual life, without realizing how pathological it is to be cut off from their own resources for living, and to feel no tie with the outer world unless they are connected with the Power Complex and constantly receive information, direction, stimulation, and sedation from a central external source, via radio, discs, and television, with the minimal opportunity for reciprocal face-to-face contact?[55]

The helmet, globe-shaped or otherwise, took symbolic forms besides ones that suggested bubbles, lightbulbs, or embryonic cranial proportions with mother-connections. Early deep-sea helmets presented a shape not smooth and rounded but angular and faceted, much like a stained-glass window in three dimensions, with the flat panes of glass fitting together into an inverted bowl or bell-jar shape. Windowed-in spaces suggest herbaria or greenhouses, which became characteristic Western constructs in the 1800s as functional conservatories, arcade elements, and tabletop horticultural toys. Popular bell jars and terraria gave expression to the Victorian passion not only for plants but for the world-in-small. They offered an early form of the ecosphere: the self-contained ecosystem, connected to the external, surrounding ecosystem primarily by whatever light and heat may transmit through glass.

The emblematic Crystal Palace, that immense greenhouse, enclosed representative manufacturers belonging not only to Great Britain but to the larger world. That an international audience spent hours and then days within its confines, in touch with the outer realm via glass, helped make it a model of global enclosure that retained its symbolic power through the following Modern years.

Any enclosed system supporting life symbolically acquires the potential lodged within an egg. Such enclosed systems at first floated upon oceans, with their life-support qualities concealed within the main and lower decks, symbolized realistically in the domestic animals and tools rescued from the shipwreck in *Swiss Family Robinson*. In Verne's moon-shot, chickens and seeds help its passengers face the possibility of never returning home; while Konstantin Tsiolkovsky, in his *Beyond the Planet Earth*, published in Russia in 1920, envisioned Earth-colonies in outer space as the seeds for new Earths elsewhere in the universe. By the middle-Modern years Earth as an entirety was becoming known in such a way that it might be recognized, by scientists, as the integrated organic system that Poe had perceived—as an ecosystem itself, as an entirety, and even as an entity. Oliver Wendell Holmes's perception, that Darwinian thought had restored "'Nature' to its place as a true divine manifestation,"[56] to some degree held its own against the countervailing perception that Darwinian thought led necessarily to a reductive, mechanical vision.

Earth is simultaneously the ultimate terrarium and the ultimate egg, a twin symbolism that would be confirmed in the post–Modern photograph of a man in a spacesuit on a Lunar visit, with blue Earth reflected in the curvature of his face-plate's glass.

Bubble Gun. Exelo, KDP Co., Japan, ca. 1960s (photograph by and collection of the author).

The World of Tomorrow

The decade that struggled with the Great Depression and yet that belonged, in some ways, to Mickey Mouse, Popeye, and Buck Rogers, saw the United States hosting not one but two International Expositions, with the second being the New York World's Fair, also named The World of Tomorrow. Much as A Century of Progress opened in the year of *King Kong*, the 1939 fair coincided with another landmark wonder tale in film, the Technicolor movie musical *The Wizard of Oz*. Having entered mass-media tentatively through the comics, Baum's novel had taken a further step in 1938, dramatized for the maturing medium of radio. The new effort to capture it on film premiered in Hollywood on August 15, 1939.[57] Another fantastically imagined satire made the transition to the movie screen that year, when Max Fleischer released *Gulliver's Travels*, an animated work having, as had *King Kong*, a focus on gigantism and the minikin. Fleischer had begun the project once it became clear, in 1938, how great a success Disney was enjoying with fairytale movie *Snow White*.[58]

Parker Brothers had seen continuing sales for *The Wonderful Game of Oz*, first issued in 1921, and still offered it in the year of the Metro-Goldwyn-Mayer release, decorated with character images in the John R. Neill style. Strikingly, in the 1939–40 season that game remained available even while Parker was issuing a new MGM-licensed *Wizard of Oz* board game. Although the game-maker had been alone in offering an Oz plaything for many years, others now joined it. E. Simon's Sons of New Orleans began issuing masquerade costumes; and Dart Board Equipment Company of Philadelphia issued a *Wizard of Oz* game. By 1941 *Wizard of Oz* masks were appearing from Newark Mask Company of Irvington, New Jersey.[59] The game, masks, and playsuits had longevity, and helped keep their parent companies through the war years and beyond.

Ideal Novelty and Toy Company, having had success with Snow White and Dwarves dolls, was issuing a jointed wooden doll related to the Modern wonder tale, this time depicting the comic-book figure Superman.[60] Superman's defining aspect emerged especially in the title of Bradley's 1941 game, Superman Speed Game. The "man of steel" was not only an Edison figure, the sole individual who represented the force and might of an entire industry, but also the epitome of Modernism, being followed frequently by Deco lines of motion.[61] As a figure who made great leaps that followed trajectories like projectiles, he personified the skyrocket, launching himself to deliver the decisive blow at a far distance. In common with the change in the popular conception of rocket ships, in the years beginning World War II, Superman in his leaps at first exhibited a clear horizontal axis, which over time switched to vertical, head-first flight.

The year 1939 also marked the arrival, by one Modern wonder-tale form, at its maturity. Out of the genre characterized in the magazine trade as "pseudo-scientifics," established writer and new editor John W. Campbell, Jr., took over *Astounding Stories of Super Science*. He renamed it *Astounding Science Fiction*, and repositioned it as the home for stories with believable human characters, whose stories happened to take place in the future. These emphases struck a chord with the audience nurtured by the "pseudo-scientifics" editors: for *Astounding*, and science fiction itself, would remain friendly to an outlook guided by scientism and evolutionist materialism. At the same time, these emphases set Gernsbackian science fiction further apart from the Modern wonder tale's tradition. Even though melodramas would still appear in *Astounding*, Campbell's emphasis on believable human characters pointed the way away from the sectional human characters of the Vernesque and from the stock characters of the Appletonian wonder tale. The type characters of the Wellsian wonder tale sat nearer the new standard. The realism implicit in this emphasis eliminated the literal expression of the dream-journey, leaving the symbolic dream-journey muted or absent; and the positivism, which at times did, indeed, amount to scientism, nearly brought the structural criticism of science and technology, as embodied in the wonder-tale's marvelous machine, to its own end.

Previously, the wonder tale had stood outside the technological megamachine being formed by Western society—as an excited but doubting, knowledgeable but questioning, and a lauding-while-ridiculing voice. The world that technology had created, however, now was swallowing this smallest among dissenting voices.

Seventeen

Thirteen O'Clock

It is no age of authentic leaders in the departments of statesmanship or thought: Stalin and Hitler were produced by the swarm, in the manner of queen bees. Nor is it an age of great ideas. There is little left even of Marxism save a mask for a civilization that recalls the hill and the hive, and the remarkable achievements of our periods—the new bombs and the planes that drop them—seem exercises in blind ingenuity turned out by mass production and operated by mass action.
—Edmund Wilson, in 1965.[1]

It was almost normal for people over thirty to be frightened of their own children.
—George Orwell, in 1949.[2]

"Besides ... if our swords fail us we shall have recourse to gunpowder, which will make short work of our enemies."
The Elephant looked at the Officer and his men.
"I don't see it," he said bluntly.
"I didn't suppose you would," said the Officer scornfully. "Don't speak in such a hurry. The powder I'm speaking of is felt but not seen. It's our last improvement, arrived at by slow degrees. Gunpowder,—smokeless gunpowder,—soundless gunpowder,—invisible gunpowder. Thus we may surround an enemy with enough gunpowder to blow up a town, but they neither see it nor hear it. In fact, they know nothing about it until they are blown up."
This time all the Toys nearly expired with fright!
—Edith King-Hall, in 1897.[3]

Is it not truly remarkable that, before the magnificent light shed upon philosophy by Humanity, the world was accustomed to regard War and Pestilence as calamities? Do you know that prayers were actually offered up in the ancient temples to the end that these evils (!) might not be visited upon mankind? Is it not really difficult to comprehend upon what principle of interest our forefathers acted? Were they so blind as not to perceive that the destruction of a myriad of individuals is only so much positive advantage to the mass!
—Poe, in 1848.[4]

Retreating Futures

Although in the 1930s the future's approach had seemed so pronounced and positive, by the early 1940s it seemed in retreat. Even newly issued wonder-evoking toys quickly went into winter hibernation to await a later spring. As war spread across Europe, then engaged the United States, children were receiving fewer toys and books, in any case. Parents found fewer in the stores, with even toy companies retooling for war-related work. Though some did so on their own accord, many were responding to patriotic summons that took the form of directives. The industrial conscription that Britain had fallen back upon, in the World's War, now raised its head in America, making the country's businesses a *de facto* branch of centralized government. Toy-making materials disappeared, requisitioned for government-approved use elsewhere. Steel that had gone into space guns and ships before the war became unavailable for making any playthings, before mid-decade. Other materials, too, fell under rationing. Companies still adhering to toy-making improvised with materials under less stringent control—mainly paper, cardboard, and wood. They filled gaps that opened in the usual categories, and released play sets, dolls, wheel goods, homemaker toys, and toy vehicles. They steered away, however, from the futuristic. Wooden service trucks and Western pistols replaced the now-missing metal ones. No wooden ray-guns nor rocket ships appeared. Stylized aircraft with swept-back wings, such as Wyandotte's Mystery Plane, gave way to blocky, more realistic ones. Streamlining and Deco styling continued appearing to some degree, but only where muted by functional appearances.

In toy trucks, such manufacturers as N.D. Cass, Noma Electric, and Buddy "L" Toys continued making playthings by developing new specialties in wooden and "composition" vehicles. Some among these toys did maintain an appearance of normalcy. Wooden ambulances and milk-delivery trucks kept in the child's mind the notion that domestic life continued, albeit in "civilian" clothing. Alongside these toys, however, new ones appeared that exerted greater pull upon the imaginations of those growing up with radio broadcasts heavy with war news: wooden versions of armored tanks, staff cars, Jeeps, howitzers, troop carriers, and the new searchlight and radar trucks.

While war-related toys had long held a place on the American playroom floor, World War II seemed to call forth a sense, among those on the domestic scene, that everyone, including every child, needed to rally to the Flag and to the war effort. Toy companies swiftly offered means for parents and children to engage in this rallying, and put a wartime spin to even established toys and games. The future for children was becoming the same as for adults, with the sole byword pointing that direction being "Victory."

Early plastic toys issued at the same time as the wooden trucks, oddly enough, looked backward rather than forward. Plastic betokened the future: yet after an auspicious start in the late 1930s, when it broke onto toy shelves with a sleek automobile in Jewels for Playthings, which was Kilgore Manufacturing's line of Modern Plastic Toys, plastic now fell into association with old-fashioned and familiar concepts. Plastic soldiers, ships, planes, dollhouse furniture, and small dolls were taking increasing space in catalog stores and five-and-dimes, winning favor for the new material by embracing tradition. A pioneering company, Bergen Toy and Novelty, produced reassuring toy sets of not only acetate zoo and farm animals, but also cowboys and Indians, those figures arising from the mythic Old West who loomed so large in childhood imaginings through most of the Modern century. Bergen also made acetate soldiers whose garb evoked what was now known as World War I, not II.

It seemed as though the future, which had appeared to be planted in the playroom for good in the 1930s, belonged in the past. This sense had some accuracy: for although Daisy's Rocket Pistol would return after steel-rationing ended, and space toys would enjoy some resurgence in popularity, American fashion by the late 1940s would veer strongly toward nostalgia, bringing the "old fashioned" toy into vogue—as with cast-iron vehicles that reappeared from new companies, sometimes again in iron, and sometimes anew in wartime's all-important aluminum.

Infinite Disaster

To many Americans, the Second World War offered a serial drama marked by unreal, distant events, barely to be understood except as episodes in a fantastic tale having daily newspaper and newsreel installments—German rocket-attacks against London; radar; submarine warfare; British and American air fleets carpet-bombing German cities; flying fortresses; and U.S. atomic explosions over Hiroshima and Nagasaki—followed by revelations concerning death camps, fallout, and radiation sickness. The magnitude of the destructive power released during World War II seemed horrific but justified to participants and observers: for now all might return home who had survived being taken into the global machinery of war. A triumphalist and positivist mood prevailed. The divided global soul stood restored to wholeness by disaster.

Thanks to its sensational nature—a single explosive that might incinerate a city and end global war—the Bomb so dwarfed the drama normally to be found in human interactions, let alone in the mind's emotional and intellectual pursuits, that it presented a nearly imponderable dilemma. All the same, catastrophic visions had been inculcated among Calvinistic and literalist Bible-readers in America, helping prepare the public to take in, perhaps even to accept, the possibility that

Airline Pursuit, a Flexible Flyer runner-sled, embraced the tradition of naming toys in a way to suggest air or space travel. The first "airline" toys may have been toy railway locomotives and cars. Photograph, "Sandra, March 1942" (author's collection).

the Writing on the Wall might be there for a city, a civilization, or even Earth. In a book that would seem anything but apocalyptic, of the help-yourself-to-knowledge sort that children often received as gifts—*How to Know the Birds*—Roger Tory Peterson felt comfortable opening his section on "Crows and Jays" with the statement, "The Corvidae, which is what ornithologists call this family, are probably the most intelligent birds in the world. Someone has predicted that when man, through his ingenuity, has finally destroyed all his neighbors and himself too, there will still be Crows."[5] The statement first saw print in the year when a U.S. guided missile reached 250 miles into the atmosphere, an unprecedented height, and Soviet Russia officially tested its first nuclear weapon. It saw its tenth printing the year Soviet Russia proved by action that it possessed the technical ability to launch an artificial satellite. However morbid its tone in suggesting inevitable human doom, the statement likely provoked few eyebrows to rise. Such was the atmosphere among educated readers that a writer for *The New Yorker* might seem merely waggish and clever, not Chicken Little-ish, to call atomic energy "the world's newest and possibly last industry."[6]

Patsy in her Pursuit Plane. Perhaps in the late 1940s, when materials restrictions would have allowed the making again of large steel toys, a Maurine Joy Triphorn or Tiphorn of Kansas City, Missouri, took this photograph of her daughter (author's collection).

Opposite on the spectrum from Earth's annihilation, a different vision, likewise dispiriting, was arising: that of daily life being reduced to humdrum routine, the logical outcome of automation, which appeared in everyday lives mainly as ever-increasing levels of convenience. Although global disaster had inspired no toys in prewar years, this quieter vision had begun finding expression with items in the middle 1930s that would have seemed unlikely in prior decades—such as Let's Go Shopping, a 1937 board game by Samuel Gabriel; or Toy Town Shopping Center, issued by that year by Minerva Toy of Brooklyn, a specialist in kindergarten toys.[7] Encouraging routine family roles became a greater focus for playthings. Industry and society made efforts to restore family traditions after the disruptions of the 1940s, though in fact these were less actual traditions than late-Modern efforts to encourage conformity, made upon the rationale that this would benefit business, industry, and banking, and thereby society as a whole.

Flying Saucer Rattle. Although the flying saucer phenomenon of the late 1940s and early 1950s fell short of generating society-wide belief in their existence, the fact that companies used "flying saucer" as a name for toddler toys meant that some children grew up attaching the name to a factual item. Celluloid rattle, manufacturer unknown, 1940s or 1950s; and illustration showing rattles made by Stahlwood Toy Mfg. Co., New York City, in *Progressive*, 1953.

Poe saw that speed, once achieved, led to a bored society; and the protective unfolding of automated umbrellas of routine, over previously diversified households and communities, promised a rainproof future filled with a widespread, homogenized hurrying-up of domestic labor, to achieve ease and boredom—"the great objection to utopia," as Brooks observed.[8] Even the Bomb, dreaded for its atmosphere-tainting and planet-destroying potential, lacked power to avert this doom. The West had reached its speed.

Bubble-Tops

Depicting speed, all the same, came again to preoccupy toymakers. Just after the war, streamlining, plastic, and the toy car came together to make toy history. The 1945 hit toy came from a small custom plastics-molding firm in Irvington, New Jersey.[9] Dillon-Beck Manufacturing's toy coupe, three and a half inches long, featured an oval body with a center keel running the hood's length. Its extended, rounded fenders covered both front and rear wheel-wells. Rounded, wrap-around bumpers completed the body's look. In common with Deco-inspired styling in imaginative toy cars during the 1930s, its lines of motion portrayed swiftness, though it barely rolled without help from a hand.

In its most striking feature, the coupe had a rounded, transparent roof that fully revealed the driver and passenger seats inside, and tiny steering wheel. As a bubble-topped

A postwar hit. With its simple lines suggesting speed and futurity, this 3-inch toy auto proved surprisingly popular, just after World War II. Dillon-Beck Mfg. Co., late 1940s (photograph by and collection of the author).

car, it evoked technology from the recently ended war, when bubble-enclosures had appeared atop aerial fortresses.[10] This borrowing from the recent military past, in new context, signified the future.

This particular future arrived in toy departments in time for the 1945 Christmas season. By the time the holiday itself arrived, over a million had sold. Dillon-Beck possessed only a few injection machines to keep running—probably overtime, during that heady season.

That the streamlined, bubble-topped coupe became a hit may have been accidental. Not all America's toy companies had survived the war years; and most of those that did had produced parts for the suddenly immense American military juggernaut. While some of these companies were pulling old tooling from storage, in many cases the necessary raw materials were yet to be derequisitioned. Toys available for this first postwar Christmas came in fewer numbers than consumers may have liked—especially those that had a traditional, prewar appearance. Plastic toys being relatively fresh on the scene, however, they benefited from the luster of representing the latest in manufacturing style.[11]

During that 1945 season, shoppers found two toy cars, no more, made from plastic. The other one proved popular, as well. It captured the times in a different way, representing a vehicle that enjoyed massive popular acceptance. The Willys Jeep had starred in countless newsreels; its sheer utility suggested stalwart determination; and its discomforts remained fresh for returning soldiers. The company making the toy also had its base in New Jersey: Thomas Manufacturing, in Newark.

With only two plastic toy cars to choose from, naturally both proved solid sellers. Yet it remained remarkable about that season that a toy depicting a nonexistent vehicle should succeed so well. It appealed to parents and children alike, perhaps because its apparent reality evoked neither wartime nor postwar situations. After what must have been the single most optimistic Christmas season of the decade, moreover, the fact of its appearance and its success had reverberations, with after-effects being evident in the marketplace for at least a decade. In short order other manufacturers released their own cars of the future. The basic form seemed fixed: a streamlined form, a bubble top, and a driver's seat that seemed often like a cockpit.[12]

By the next Christmas season, the Dillon-Beck automobile in a different way was reflecting "progress." The powers of mass-production and mass-demand, as well as growing potency within the plastics industry, brought the toy's price down from the quarter-dollar of 1945 to the dime of 1946.[13]

Valéry's Vision

During World War II and the period just after, the thought grew in strength that the techno-capitalist machine of Western society was broken. The sentence, "It was a bright cold day in April, and the clocks were striking thirteen," first appeared in 1949. The event that ended peace in Vondervotteimittis commenced George Orwell's *1984*. This anti-futuristic novel features a parody, perhaps an unwitting one, of A Century of Progress: for its Miniluv building has "no windows at all."[14] In the novel's oppressive milieu, even toy-industry techniques become tools for conformity, with Big Brother being depicted in "one of those pictures which are so contrived that the eyes follow you about when you move," and music being "sentimental songs which were composed entirely by mechanical means on a special kind of kaleidoscope known as a versificator." A role-model figure, Comrade Ogilvy, at age three "refused all toys except a drum, a submachine gun, and a model helicopter."[15] Winston Smith, the victim in the novel, and symbolically the Last Man, has entered the world that results from, in Jaspers's words, "the despiritualisation of the world and its subjection to a regime of advanced technology."[16]

Paul Valéry, as clearly as anyone, had seen the end approaching—the end when literature would cease playing a role that had any significance in society's workings. This point may have arrived more rapidly than he expected: for in the 1920s the French poet must have been stirred to his insight, watching as movies and radio made rapid inroads into realms formerly dominated by vaudeville, theater, and the printed page. Television then arrived to join these media that suddenly had become the main stimulants to people's thoughts and emotions.[17]

In live theater, each audience member has a unique seat and sees the stage from a unique perspective—different, even, from a next-seat neighbor. In literature, every reader encounters a unique experience, since each one has a personal rate of reading and comprehension. At a film, in contrast, every viewer sits in the same chair, since a director literally has called the shots and established the view and focus; and all take in the story at the same speed, whatever their individual speeds of comprehension, association, and reflection. Directors in effect exerted remote control over their audiences, regimenting this small portion of daily life among the masses.

The producers and directors behind new electrical entertainments undoubtedly aimed for no such control. Radio and cinema directors instead attempted to offer equivalents to intellectually and emotionally stimulating literature, especially as the 1930s progressed. Television, however, as it developed after World War II, immediately took over many functions previously belonging to melodrama and vaudeville; to some degree movies and radio did likewise, as shows for those media proliferated. Yet television's widespread simultaneity, especially in its sports broadcasting, exerted a special power.

Although, for instance, Hollywood had made earlier attempts to capture *The Wonderful Wizard of Oz* on film, the resulting films at most had caused a decline in stage productions without usurping them altogether. Not until the famous film adaptation of 1939 became a television staple did the process reach completion: for in that medium, the film finally rendered the stage version obsolete. The TV debut came on November 3, 1956, on the CBS *Ford Star Jubilee*. That mass-media had arrived was evident in viewership for *The Wizard of Oz*. The old Kansas showman's balloon had risen permanently, at last—and in exactly the same way, for forty-five million viewers.[18]

Movies and popular writing moved increasingly toward sentimental realism, while the social realism coming to the fore in serious novels led to the perception that earlier symbolist and symbolist-influenced efforts, by writers such as Joyce, Woolf, Yeats, or Hemingway, were decadent, obscure, and obsolete. The Modern wonder tale, too, fell under this pall of obsolescence. Its latest branching, science fiction, turned yet more firmly away from melodrama as its central form, with its practitioners coming to regard that fictional structure as puerile. Writers and editors leaned increasingly toward the naturalism and social realism of literary novels as a model for new novels of a futuristic pseudo-naturalism and pseudo-realism. Satirical speculation and critique suffered, if without ever quite going away. Structural reinforcement to the notion of the tripartite soul's need for integration essentially vanished. The marvelous machine, nevermore destroyed, triumphed. Even a critic within the field, as we have seen, perceived by the 1950s that science fiction had become a genre of "adult game fantasies," in keeping with Valèry's prognostication earlier in the century that literature itself, in a world dominated by radios, movies, and television, would survive primarily as a game.[19]

Globalized Toy Making

As had happened in the 1850s, in the 1950s appeared signs that changes were overtaking American toy manufacturing. In the wake of the Bomb's boom, the baby equivalent stimulated the economy's toy-manufacturing sector, significant in size before World War II, into rapid expansion. This coincided with materials being derequisitioned by the military, new products appearing that were derived from wartime innovations, and an intermittently reviving interest in the futuristic.

That new toy companies by the hundreds entered the field barely tells the full story, however, since these companies were often offering more diverse products than had their equivalents in prewar times, when they had relied more upon tried-and-true and specialized products. Companies that had their beginnings with a single toy—not an unusual circumstance—now would follow that first item with something new or varied, each subsequent toy season. As a result, even minor companies tended to enlarge their product-range, and usually their company size, within years. This movement arose due to a natural desire for growth and expansion, but perhaps equally to a competitive environment in which companies acted in predatory or opportunistic ways when any new ideas appeared.[20]

In the postwar period, American manufacturers, small and large, added a substantially new ingredient: the use of, and reliance upon, overseas facilities, both in advance of demand and to keep up with demand. These American companies, now operating internationally, set up subsidiary operations wherever practical. The firm Louis Marx & Co., founded in 1921, became the world's largest toy manufacturer in the postwar years by establishing factories worldwide. These not only met demand overseas but kept costs low on toys sold in the States.

Due to an overlapping and related development, increasingly in the 1950s American children were playing with toys made in Japan, brought in either by importers or by the manufacturers themselves. These lines were blurring, with some companies calling themselves "manufacturers" that amounted to import offices with packaging facilities.

Toys came to America from Japan well before the 1950s. That they were obtained and displayed during the 1800s when interest in Asian design was at its height seems undoubted. Shikki-shosha of Kiyoto, as Kyoto then was often anglicized, mounted a display at the 1876

Centennial Exposition.[21] Since *shikki* refers to lacquerware, any toys Shikki-shosha exhibited would have been wood-based, lacquered, figural pieces in traditional designs—which means they may well have included some mechanical toys and novelties.[22] That some subsequent toy and doll imports resulted from that Centennial display seems likely. Certainly by the early twentieth century, *Nippon*-marked imports included numerous toy items, notably a range of ceramic and celluloid pieces that sometimes reflected a Japanese sensibility but more often reflected Japanese interest in Western ideas and culture. Lithographed tin toys appeared from Japanese toymakers before World War II, although they were, by that industry's own admission, "cheap makes."[23]

After 1945, toymakers showed remarkable resilience in returning to normal operations, in part because they favored small-shop production over large factories. Often family owned, these shops employed small pools of employees or contract laborers in producing the diverse parts that went into toys; and since these shops tended to cluster together, trading in parts and designs took place. Traditional reliance on the community and on the talents of handworkers, and on neither large facilities nor heavily automated equipment, proved a strength.[24]

German toymakers never fully regained the favorable status they once had enjoyed in the United States, which they lost as a consequence of American feelings against that nation after the First World War. Reactions against German goods intensified during and especially after the second. No such ill feeling seemed to affect re-acceptance for Japanese toys in the 1950s, perhaps because the animosity between the two nations had less duration, and perhaps less depth—even though prejudice in the United States against even its own citizens of Japanese descent had led to displacements from homes, losses of property and business, and mass incarcerations. The U.S. government, whatever its errors on the domestic front, after the war worked to restore to normalcy its international relations. Its assistance in restoring Japan's economy led to that country's revival as an exporter of goods, and eventually to its admittance into the General Agreement on Tariffs and Trade, which came in the latter part of 1955.

Japanese exports of sundry goods, which included bamboo products, musical instruments, imitation pearls, and rubber items, expanded in the early 1950s. Toys, however, showed the most rapid increase, rising in 1954 to a total export value of over eleven million yen. Although Japanese toys were diverse and included paper, wooden, textile, rubber, celluloid, glass, and ceramic forms, metal toys made up nearly half this total, with nearly all being mechanical. Given that mechanical playthings occurred elsewhere, too, scattered among the paper, wooden, and celluloid toys, the middle 1950s might be seen as inaugurating the last, brief efflorescence of Modern-century toy making. Among Japan's largest toymakers, one did, in fact, use for its English name Modern Toys.

Metal toys, the most important mechanical toys in terms of numbers produced and numbers that would survive, saw production primarily in Tokyo, with small numbers also being made in Osaka and Saitama prefectures. In 1955–56, Japan had some three hundred makers of metal toys, most having in the range of fifteen to twenty workers. In these years "power-operated" toys, which were ones employing batteries, came to occupy one-fifth the country's total metal-toy exports.[25]

Acknowledging this sector's growing importance to its economy, the Japanese government sponsored and operated an institute for design research. It also set in place heightened quality inspections of toy exports, to protect Japan's new status as a toy-making country to rival Germany.[26] Japan attempted to improve its image in other areas as well, and responded to U.S. concerns about celluloid's flammability by converting toys to a non-flammable type.

Although Japanese designs resulted in part from observing American consumer culture, its exports reached most parts of the world. In 1954, the U.S. ranked as its largest consumer of sundry goods, followed by U.S. neighbors Canada and Mexico. Countries in Africa, Southeast Asia, South America, and Europe, ranked in that order of descending consumption.[27]

These toys enjoyed success due to how strongly they reflected the ebullient diversity of traditional toy making. While the notion of the "fad" toy had exerted considerable force in the Modern century, beginning with Crandall's Pigs in Clover, such moments of focused mass-popularity had a notable but not determining effect. As the Modern gave way to the succeeding age, however, the "fad" would become increasingly weighty in determining the habits of children, and of parental purchasing patterns—with conformity becoming a watchword for childhood culture. In contrast, in Japanese toys from the period starting in the early 1950s and continuing to some degree into subsequent decades, sheer variety won over obsessive focus upon any passing fad or fixation. While imitation was heavily practiced, this imitation led to a great variety of somewhat similar toys, which often led to inventive variations, rather than to the massive production of closely identical toys. Given their typically small operations, most Japanese toy manufacturers and their employee pools produced a great many colorful, skillfully constructed, and carefully detailed playthings that, although they flooded the world, did so without uniformity.

To the degree that some Japanese companies were able to hold to this approach not only through the 1960s but into the 1970s reflected the fact that not all the globe was being affected as deeply as was America in the move toward the domination of an ever-smaller pool of top brands—which resulted from the successful matching of mass production with mass consumption.

Robots and Prehistoric Play Sets

Japanese toys seemed to retain their Modern character, in part, thanks to Tokyo's distance from the American mass culture's increasingly overwhelming weight. The toymakers emphasized novelty and freshness, employing colors for their own sakes and design elements for variety. They injected humor and absurdity into the designs without merely invoking humor or absurdity by licensing, for instance, a Bozo the Clown or Howdy Doody toy—although, too, they freely imitated popular characters. Japanese toy cars, trucks, tricycle-riding children, cymbal-playing monkeys, and roaring lions had a carefree ebullience of spirit, as if the fact of their being suspended between two different cultures gave them independence from both. In their toy robots especially the Japanese rescued the symbolic toy from the grasp of mass media: for by and large the Japanese robots were generic creations intended simply to amuse and delight, whose forms the child could imaginatively project into almost any scenario or setting. Playing with these toys could continue being constructive and inventive, not derivative and imitative. While their highly constrained actions limited how many years, months, or days the toy might continue absorbing the child's interest, the Toy Manufacturers of America had long known that mechanical toys needed to appeal to children for only so long in their lives—recommending "mechanical novelties" for children ages six to eight: "A Period of Irrepressible Ego."[28]

In America, Louis Marx & Co. held onto a similar toy-making energy, partly because it drew upon Japanese and other shops for its immense and increasingly global line, and partly because its sheer number of manufacturing centers led it toward diversified manufacturing for an eclectic catalog. In its later and last years it would embrace television advertising for toys, the practice inaugurated by A.C. Gilbert that did much to encourage monolithic uniformity in production, and that eventually had the effect of heavily guiding childhood choices and activities. Through the 1950s, however, a seemingly endless variety poured from Marx's many doors, notably in the many variations it played upon the traditional play set. These outfits offered tin, vinyl, and plastic buildings, accessories, vehicles, and figures—generally nicely detailed and attractive, even if the various items were designed to the same scale only by an imaginative stretch.

Marx's early, generic play sets gave way quickly to specific ones. Quality moldings gave Marx the opportunity to offer recognizable characters in its minikins, even when only inches, or an inch, tall. This had some limiting effect on childhood options for imagination and play, in that Marx began offering licensed-character play sets to tap into popular movie and television stars and scenarios. Since its figures were offered in distinct poses, moreover, they lacked the generic flexibility of the old, simple toy animal or doll. These figures lent themselves slightly less to being played with than to being placed within play-set arrangements, to be admired. To some degree, since children needed to draw less upon their own creative and productive resources, this reduced them to bearing witness to Marx's creativity and productivity.

Marx offered ample evidence that various wonder-tale influences continued in vitality into the 1950s. The company helped children move into the human past with Mediaeval, Western-frontier, and World War II sets. As indicated by such titles as The Alamo Play Set, Battle of the Blue and Gray, Battleground, Beachhead Assault Set, Fort Apache Set, and Knights and Vikings, such playroom time-travel often took place to visualize combat and to practice one's belligerence. As to "the" future, the company issued toys and play sets having science-fiction orientations, as with the Tom Corbett sets that contained both realistic human figures and extravagant alien ones borrowed from comics, magazines, and television.

Marx also issued a long-lived series of play sets that arose directly from the Modern wonder-tale tradition: its Prehistoric Times play sets. The plural of Times, in the name, proved appropriate, in that these sets threw together assemblages to delight a Professor Hardwigg, placing the most ancient Triassic reptiles alongside the later Jurassic and more recent Cretaceous giants—and alongside, too, the indispensable "caveman," as well as prehistoric mammals. Multitudinous such sets that juxtaposed prehistoric animals and cavemen appeared in the 1950s, and into the next two decades, made by Marx, Multiple, Tim-Mee, and other plastic-molding companies. They offered children playtime experiences with dinosaurs that seemed guided by scientific achievement and process, while also encouraging play-perspectives contrary to science's findings. They echoed readers' dinosaur-encounters in wonder tales, and prefigured children's acceptance for further such readings as they grew older.

The sense that the Earth had been explored, and that its mysteries had been unveiled, prevailed even in the realm of power and gigantism that dinosaurs represented—a realm large enough to include contrasting and competing appeals to science, scientism, and religious orthodoxy. In science such prehistoric beings form important objects for ongoing study; in scientism they carry symbolic weight in the parade of progress, as emblems of the deservedly extinct; and in religious orthodoxy they inhabit an antediluvian world, fueling desires to find them either still existent within God's world or pre–Noachic. While the Western imagination had largely ceased expecting to find dinosaurs on Earth, it continued placing them within symbolic valleys and plateaus elsewhere—notably on fourth planet Venus, which lent itself to torrid, humid imaginings. Even after astronomers began obtaining stronger clues as to its intense heat and poisonous atmosphere, Venus remained a wonder-tale site for encountering prehistoria.

In the popular imagination, the Venusian surface and the primordial world shared a particular nature. Symbolically, as noted, the distant point in space may stand in for the distant point in time. That point could be distant in the past, as in the 1954 Tom Corbett novel in which a massive creature, "the great king of the Venusian jungle," is identified as being actually a *Tyrannosaurus Rex*, not as a creature merely reminiscent of that dinosaur, to human viewers.[29]

The Round-the-World Clock, Again

Publication of *On the Origin of Species*, in 1859, planted in many minds the sense that a new closure to an ancient question was at hand, opening the way for an all-encompassing, rational understanding about the natural world in which humans live. Earth had lost its central throne, thanks to astronomers; human time had lost its preeminence over history, thanks to geologists; and now humankind had lost its divinity and divine anointment, thanks to biologists—even despite efforts by advocates for evolutionism and scientism to place humans on a teleological pinnacle. *On the Origin of Species* as a society-changing event arrived when others changes were unfolding, especially those related to the globe's consolidation within integrated and automated networks. Reactions to Darwin took such forms as giant-ape and dinosaur fantasies, exposition attractions, and playthings; reactions to the globe's consolidation appeared endlessly, but perhaps most pointedly in the ubiquitous, tin-lithographed, child-sized geographical globes with slits at top for coins. No longer holding mystery, the Earth held only currency.

While a portmanteau "century" designation need not be applied only to neat packages containing one-hundred-year stretches, in the Modern's case, its conclusion arrived in late 1957 and early 1958, when artificial satellites established themselves as feasible and factual. This startling technical and social development affected industry, politics, and public attitudes; it permanently altered the wonder tale's possibilities; and it coincided, as it happens, with a shift in American toy manufacture.

The world fit all too well within Western grasp, in the 1950s. Perhaps the next-to-last world-travel game, Parker Brothers' World Cruise, vanished over the horizon early in the decade. By mid-decade no "around the world" toys or games appeared, although Samuel Gabriel Sons and Company offered a coloring book that might have made Verne's character Yvernés sigh: for it was named World Without Color. Against new wonders, as represented by such items as the Atom Bomb scientific toy, Atom Bomber, Atomic Bomber, Atomic Machine gun, Atomic-Man Kite, and Atomic pistol,[30] not to mention the proliferating "space toys" that vividly but briefly flooded the scene in 1953, a reaction was setting in, so that old-fashioned technological wonders—flintlock guns, steam engines, hot-air balloons, and early automobiles—were acquiring the sheen of romance. The nostalgic tendency led at last, in movies, back to Verne—first with *20,000 Leagues Under the Sea* and then *Around*

Buck Rogers in the 1950s. Sylvania TV advertising flyer, 1953.

the *World in Eighty Days*, the latter leading to the 1957 Transogram travel game, "Michael Todd's *Around the World in 80 Days*" and a Saalfield coloring set.[31] The Modern century's end brought to a full circle, appropriately, the promise of Phileas Fogg. Fogg had pursued single-minded travel around the globe, regarding it as little more than a game, like whist, to be played. An autonomous being with automatic qualities, Fogg confirmed in his actions that the automation of global travel had reached completion. Figuratively he was a satellite

By the 1950s, "space toys" occupied their own niche. This stock photograph for inventory or a catalog shows two that were sold by Minamoto Trading Co., Los Angeles. Spacemen figures in such lines, though often similar in features and movements, tended to have less personality and charm than did the toy robots—as in this pairing. Late 1950s or 1960s (author's collection).

of the Earth, as Verne himself realized: "Phileas Fogg, who was not travelling, but only describing a circumference ... was a solid body, traversing an orbit around the terrestrial globe, according to the laws of rational mechanics." Elsewhere he observed that "Phileas Fogg moved about above them in the most majestic and unconscious indifference. He was passing methodically in his orbit around the world, regardless of the lesser stars which gravitated around him."[32]

In that first decade after World War II, the artificial satellite had emerged as one among the few remaining Modern technological wonders that retained a power that was almost purely symbolic, since it had yet to be achieved. The explosions over Japan had moved a previously powerful symbol—that of atomic destruction—into the realm of fact, making it a subject more suitable, in the 1950s, to the thriller, the horror story, and the postapocalyptic tract than to the wonder tale. German weapons of terror had attached powerful new connotations to the rocket, which helped leach that vehicle of its romance, even though as automatic technology it remained connected to that last unrealized symbol remaining to the consolidating world-machine.[33]

Earlier imaginings that were more feminine in their symbolic nature, and that were visibly influenced by egglike balloons and blimps, still persisted as the Modern century came nearer its closing: for strength remained to the vision of mother Earth giving rise to offspring colonies and ecologies. It became a major source for symbolic power within the future-oriented, positivist form whose name in the 1950s was wavering between sci-

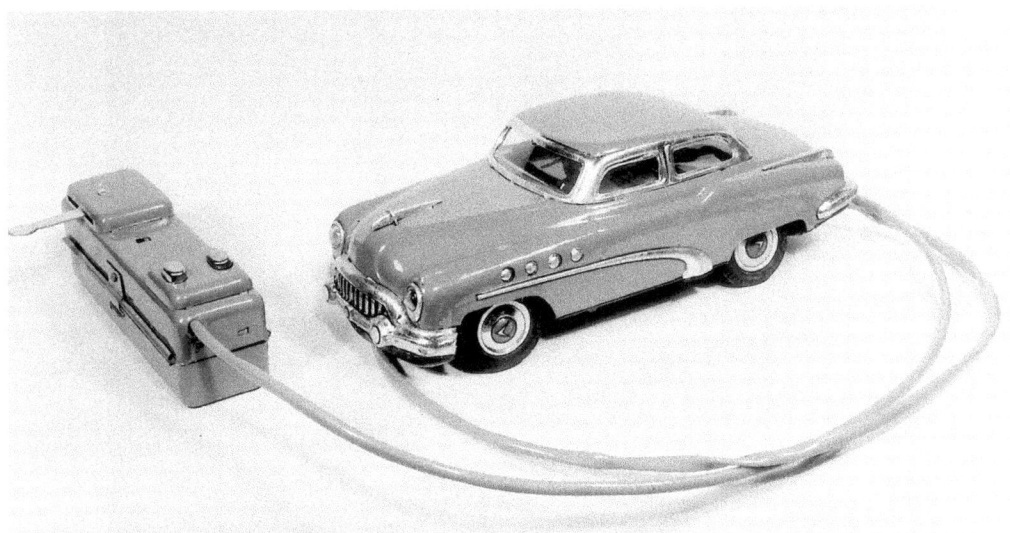

Remote control became a selling point for toys by the 1930s, although already firmly lodged in working technics long before. In the 1950s, toys powered by handheld battery packs became popular. Although the connecting wires were short, the notion still fascinated children. Minamoto Trading Co., Los Angeles, stock photograph (author's collection).

ence fiction and the more apt "science fantasy." The Tsiolkovskian vision helped invigorate stories about humankind's reaching for space, travel into space, and mass-movement into space to seek a Noachian second world; and it helped society respond to, even when it could not cure, the inward demoralization that followed upon the outward technical achievements displayed during 1940s wartime. In that vision, the advanced stratospheric balloons tok the form of generative sperm directed paradoxically outward and away from Mother Earth. These high-altitude balloons lifted scientific instruments to the most rarified reaches of the atmosphere. Photographs that showed technicians assembling the elaborate inner components of high-altitude rockets, moreover, showed

Zoomer. Variations on this battery-operated robot appeared over several decades, under various names. Zoomer the Robot, nearly 10 inches tall with the "radar"; T-N Co., Japan, 1950s (photograph by and collection of the author).

Sputnik. Museum-goers gaze up at a Sputnik model or prototype. Mounted display photograph (author's collection).

them in antiseptic smocks, gloves, and face-masks, as though they were attending nurses at a birth.[34]

Now-common drawings and paintings depicting space stations and extraterrestrial colonies emphasized circles, spheres, and bubbles; and as the scientific process steadily yielded evidence pointing toward the Solar System's regions being devoid of other intelligent beings and perhaps any other life forms, the notion of the "conquest of space"—first raised in relation to the "space" of Earth's atmosphere fictionally conquered by Robur—gave way to the idea of the exploration and exploitation of outer space and of extraterrestrial bodies, making it more akin to the Earth-penetrating activities such as urban reconstruction, tunneling, and mining, all of which held important places among Western industrial efforts. The jetlike, horizontally aligned imaginings for the space rocket continued to give way to the torpedo, the missile, and the German V2-type rocket, in part because the technology's maturation had occurred in that largely masculine arena of military research and development.

Although the Tsiolkovskian dream remained, Sputnik's launch into orbit in late 1957 at last moved the satellite from wonder-tale symbol into the realm of fact. That technology's siren-call, which had given rise to expressions including C.M. Kornbluth's novels *Takeoff* and *Not This August*, became a repetitive beep on home-made radio receivers. In fiction, any future reference to an artificial satellite would offer some combination of symbolic and literal borrowings.

A strange and unexpected result followed those artificial-satellite launches. A wave of nostalgia, as noted, had struck soon after World War II; and such smaller companies as Stanley produced old-fashioned cast-metal toys that depicted horse-drawn wagons and buggies, perhaps less for hopeful children than regretful adults. A similar episode seemed to begin ten years later, after the Russian achievement of Earth-to-orbit transport. Rather than being stimulated into new diversity and vigor, toys related to space exploration barely managed to hold their own on store shelves and in production lines. Far from dominating toy lists at decade's end, they fell to the side while a surge in Old West toys, especially TV-related ones, filled toy aisles and toy catalogs.

Rockets that could launch satellites might have been thought to offer unifying symbols to the "civilized" world that had invented global warfare: for the satellites crossed skies around Earth; and radio kits that were built by the thousands if not millions were tuning in to the beeping announcement of the new enclosure of an already shrunken world.

After this event, the nearest playthings to older wonder-evoking toys that received star treatment hardly evoked wonder at all, in depicting long-distance powers of destruction: for the companies that made toy trucks seemed to sense, as a group, that the time was right to release missile-launching trucks, with atomic-missile launchers prominent among them. As had occurred during World War II, the future again had become the unfortunate present. The potential sign for hope—the satellite that communicated with anyone, anywhere, who cared to listen—lacked the power to distract viewers from the fact that a rocket had lifted it, and had done so during an arms race.

The rocket's combined symbols—for it enabled the globe's ultimate shrinkage and put within technical reach the weapon of remote-control terror—prompted a retreat by the American mind, and perhaps the Westernizing global mind, from the possibilities of the future. It found comfort in adventures set in times that were less than a century past but that were less complicated by several orders of magnitude.

In America, by 1959, television reigned; and it must have struck children with wonder, as it must have at least a few adults, too, that the world had ever offered such possibilities as those that *Paladin*'s or *Gunsmoke*'s Old West seemed to possess—however empire-building, however colonizing, however genocidal those olden days had been.

An End to Modern Symbolic Toys

An appearance by a toy marks a symbol's arrival. Maggie Magnetic's Sputnik reflected in explicit terms technological globalism's arrival, including the political terms that encumbered that arrival. A version of its popular Wheel-O, it featured a heavy parallel-wire track along with a wheel could travel, if equipped with a magnetic axle. In the Sputnik toy, two such wheels traveled a circular track—with one wheel representing the Russian, and the other, the U.S. space effort. In the middle of the circular track sat the Earth. Another toy that closed the 1950s, however, more aptly represented the coming Age of the Masses, in that it overtly represented what Frye already had dubbed "stupid realism"—the embracing of a reality comprised by what art critics were calling kitsch.

Mattel, a California company, though having established a specialty in mechanical, musical toys, in 1959 introduced an all-vinyl doll named Barbie. While fashion dolls with adult woman's figures had become commonplace during the 1950s, the Barbie doll rapidly became the market leader. Based initially on a German doll that depicted a panel-cartoon character defined by her sexual powers, the Barbie doll glorified the notion that personal fulfillment was to be achieved by conformist consumption; and by merging style with sexuality she rendered previous fashion dolls nearly obsolete. The Barbie would also prove herself self-obsolescent, insofar as she would change in her appearance through the years, unlike earlier fashion dolls who were manufactured from the same molds year in and year out, and who even looked much the same from one manufacturer's catalog to the next. The Barbie, a vinyl paean to consumerism, became a focal object for adult buyers. She ranked among the first toys to achieve such desirability that domestic manufacture proved hugely insufficient, forcing the parent company to establish overseas factories not only suited to large-scale mass-production but also profit-making.

The Barbie doll's self-obsolescence became her most compulsory accessory: for once the manufacturing system reached such proportions, it needed to maintain consumer

Dual steering wheels reflect the unity of experience, for children entering the post–Modern age. Permanent amusement parks offered such enticements as "autos" that moved on rail systems, with nonworking "steering." Photograph marked "July 1962" (author's collection).

demand at a level high enough to support a world-spanning giant. That the Barbie juggernaut did prosper would become evident in the fact that this symbol of consumerism became a symbol for the enormous American Baby Boom generation itself—even though the toy had not existed for the first half of the Boom and was, as a toy, marketed only to one sex of those post–Sputnik Boomers.[35]

The toy industry may have turned a blind eye to the irony in the situation. American manufacturers had faced an uphill battle until the 1860s, in trying to gain a foothold in their own country's toy business: for they faced overly stiff competition from overseas manufacturers, especially the "toy towns" of Germany. America subsequently saw the rise of her own toy towns, such as the ones in Winchendon, Massachusetts, and East Hampton, Connecticut. The internationally mass-produced toy's arrival, however, marked the beginning of the end for these minor capitols of American economic culture and manufacturing strength. The Age of the Masses encouraged conformity and uniformity, despite the heyday of personal individualism that would briefly and perhaps only apparently reign in the late 1960s and 1970s. Traditional diversity in toy-making, reflecting diverse childhood and parenthood needs and desires, had lost its center. The corporate planning office now held the gravitational center.

As mass-marketing and internationally distributed manufacturing grew in scale, the cynical manipulation of symbols purely for profit led to the ever-faster "change-over" affecting the symbolic items being offered to the public. Insofar as human meaning is created by cooperative group action, as George Herbert Mead observed, any such cultural dictation forces human meaning to suffer a loss. Groups have the flexibility to absorb ideas from inside or outside that have not arrived from communal sources; but they lack the energy to do so on a continuous basis and still rebound. If the group lacks time to find, or instill, human meaning within a symbol that has not developed naturally but has been imposed upon it, then it begins to operate in a void of significance. In this void it becomes a simple matter for the corporation to shove over the one symbol to be replaced by the next: for neither the old nor the new have any weight, socially or culturally. In the Age of the Masses it would become business as usual among some corporations to subsist by the constant maintenance and constant change of artificial symbols, ensuring a void of meaning so that a marketplace powered by disoriented consumerism might persist.

An End to the Modern Wonder Tale

The science-fantasy or science-fiction writers who "flourished" in the frequently published, poorly paying pulp-magazines of the 1950s had grown up in a literary atmosphere heavily influenced by such writers as Verne, Wells, Doyle, Burroughs, and A. Merritt, as well as by E.E. Smith, Ray Cummings, and the young John Campbell, Jr. They understood, viscerally, the tradition in which a tale's symbolic elements could rise to the foreground, to rule the narrative. Yet they understood, too, editorial demands for a more literate, more style-aware, and more character-generated approach to the wonder tale. The best among them felt the pull of their own literary hungers, and engaged in their own authentic struggles for artistry; and this, within this climate, seemed to confirm that Campbell was correct in saying that Character mattered, and that Idea mattered only if presented in the pressed and brushed-down garb of professional fiction. That the "pulps" aspired to be "slicks" agreed with many writers' aspirations.

The new science fiction stories, as "adult game fantasies," suited the changing times: for, as Brooks perceived, people were beginning to see "life not in terms of economic necessity but in terms of a game."[36]

These events altered the conditions within which the wonder tale as a literary form had flourished. After the 1957–58 satellite launches, a writer's ability to present "a string of roaring absurdities" by way of making a point, or of providing entertainment, faltered in the face of factual wonders—wonders that came wrapped in so many layers of technical accomplishment that factuality loomed larger than and dwarfed the non-technical imagination, and edged out any possibility that writers could enjoy the freedom they had explored, beforehand. Factuality displaced displacement, since the myths, as E.M. Forster much earlier had lamented, were drying up and blowing away. Rocketry and space travel were entering realms belonging to nonfiction and realism—as had the atom bomb and television a dozen

"And did the Waggoner ever come back?"
"Never, never. He loved, but drove away."

Never, Never. As polyethylene and vinyls replaced wood and cloth as toy-making materials, and hard plastic took over metal's role, toys at the end of the Modern century veered increasingly, in their appearance, from both traditional and characteristically Modern toys. Traditional toys especially seemed to be disappearing toward the sunset. Illustration by Alice B. Woodward, 1897 (from Edith M. King-Hall, *Adventures in Toyland*, ca. 1910).

years earlier—and as had radio, telephone, and telegraphy, and the automobile and the railroad locomotive, well before those. The achievement of global interconnection, by means of a globally shared physical symbol named Sputnik, meant that the provocative enticement of the future enclosure of humankind within its own technics, too, was losing its mystery. Western industrialized nations had created a technological sphere encompassing all the human lives within it. It became the outer clock that circled the smaller clock by which everyone kept time: for everyone lived within the outer clock, and upon the Earth-clock that formerly had been the sole sphere available for human activity. The human world had swallowed itself.

The wonder was diminishing, too, since this self-swallowing had entered the realm of fact—of naturalism. Huxley, Arthur Koestler, and Orwell had spoken so truly in the novels *Brave New World*, *Darkness at Noon*, *Coming Up for Air*, and *1984*, in all their different ways, that when society's self-enclosure came about, the wonder already had waned. The spectacle was a beep from a home-made apparatus. Earth itself, integrated as a whole into a human system, and seemingly within human grasp, was a toy—a ball, a globe, an automaton, a clock, a bomb: something to be tossed ahead, and into the future—

So that it might roll forever onward—

Unless, perhaps, it should be stopped by what lies ahead, and rebound.

Chapter Notes

Chapter One

1. Poe, 1983, p. 152: the poem "To One in Paradise" in its original version, in short story "The Visionary."
2. *Ibid.*, p. 1023: "The Thousand-and-Second Tale of Scheherazade."
3. Barzun, 1958, p. 334. Barzun quotes from the *Dictionary of Accepted Ideas*, published posthumously.
4. Ellis, 2009, Chapter 8.
5. EB, Vol. 3, p. 263. The *pila* was a small ball; the *paganica*, "a heavy ball stuffed with feathers;" and the *follis*, "a leather ball filled with air, the largest of the three." Interestingly, at one frontier of Roman influence, Scotland, the game that became golf began with "featheries." "Primitive explosive," p. 279.
6. Mumford 1970, p. 5. These visions came to dominate the West after Copernicus. The first vision, of the terrestrial New World, focused on the physical globe of the Earth and the lands being discovered and explored—especially the lands being called the New World, in the wake of Columbus's four journeys. The second vision, of the mechanical New World, arose from the realms of abstract thinking about technics and mechanical power, a realm that was opening to Western thinkers and experimenters in the same way, and during the same time, that the geographic world was opening to Western navigators and explorers. Mumford's description bears repeating: "When the active period of discovery and colonization was over and the promised land still lay below the horizon, much of the original faith and fervor was transferred from the exploitation of the indigenous 'New World' to that of the machine. But in fact these two different approaches to the New World—one aimed at natural resources to be discovered and appropriated, the other at mechanical power and artificial wealth, to be fabricated and profitably sold—had never from the beginning been far apart. Both impulses had sprung out of a militant medieval background, just as the ascetic, life-renouncing, orderly habits of early capitalism had sprung out of the medieval monastery."
7. Mumford, 1970, throughout.
8. Foley, 1962, p. 93.
9. EB, Vol. 1, p. 262. Vacuum tubes and electric light bulbs becoming commonplace presumably quelled further such speculations.
10. Holmes, 2010, p. 128.
11. EB, Vol. 1, p. 262; also Holmes, 2010, p. 128.
12. Jules-Verne, 1976, pp. 54, 57
13. EB, Vol. 1, pp. 266-7. The first ascent took place in Wolverhampton, followed by numerous more through 1866, with many being made from Sydenham Park, home to the New Crystal Palace. This ambitious schedule of launches undoubtedly helped make aeronautics seem an almost commonplace accomplishment. On June 25, 1868, an "aëronautical exhibition" opened at the New Crystal Palace (Columbian Arts Co., 1891, p. 367).
14. Pundita, its narrator, relates that when the first aeronaut "maintained the practicability of traversing the atmosphere in all directions, by merely ascending or descending until a favorable current was attained, he was scarcely hearkened to at all by his contemporaries, who looked upon him as merely an ingenious sort of madman, because the philosophers (?) of the day declared the thing impossible." Poe, 1984, p. 874. *See also* Holmes, 2010, pp. 146, 153, 156.
15. Jules-Verne, 1976, p. 55.
16. *Ibid.*, pp. 57-8.
17. Verne, 1978, p. 186. La Landelle was Gabriel de la Landelle.
18. Verne, 1958, pp. 13-5.
19. *Ibid.*, p. 12.
20. *The Compact Edition of the Oxford English Dictionary* (hereafter *OED*), 1971, p. 915.
21. United States Centennial Commission, 1876, pp. 109 and 111: the Excelsior Flint Glass Co. of Pittsburgh made "glass lamp chimneys, silvered glass reflectors"; the Excelsior School Furniture Manufacturing Co. of Cincinnati specialized in church furniture, and so may have not thought itself guilty of solecism. Official directories, of course, lacked room to comprehensively list all the trade-name products that appearing at fairs.
22. *OED, op. cit.*
23. Verne, 1978, p. 168.
24. Verne, 1958, pp. 21, 92-3.
25. *Ibid.*, p. 47.
26. Poe, 1984, p. 1001: "Note," to "The Unparalleled Adventure of One Hans Pfaall."
27. Bailey, 1972.
28. Brooks, 1957, p. 158, frames Mumford's understanding in this manner: "The notion of destruction involved for him the notion of renewal,

disintegration implied reintegration.... For him the resources of humankind were still inexhaustible, requiring only the sense of a new purpose and direction; and, with his feeling for the inner life, he was convinced that the problem of our time was to restore the lost respect for this. For Western man had forgotten it in his concentration on the improvement of the machine."

29. EB, vol. 10, p. 513.
30. Ellis, 2009, Chapter 8.
31. McClintock, 1961, p. 227: photograph.
32. *Ibid.*, p. 262.
33. *Ibid.*, p. 262: "sold well for so many years that Bradley had to make a new set of printing plates because real locomotives had changed so much." An undated catalog reproduction in Freeman, 1942, p. 290, shows "Sectional Railroad," which gave a child the chance to construct an eight-foot-long train. It came with extra pieces to vary it, including "an amusing smash-up scene." *For* W.S. Reed: p. 335.
34. Kouwenhoven, 1938, no. 41.
35. For example, in the Montgomery Ward & Co. catalog of 1889, in the two columns of animal-drawn "indestructible Malleable Iron Toys," fire-fighting equipment made up one-fourth of the selections, with a Fire Engine, a Hose Cart, and a Hook and Ladder Truck. The same catalog had a "Model Steam Fire Engine," which was a working steam toy. *See* Schroeder, 1971, pp. 30–1.
In its catalog for 1907, when transportation toys were still largely dominated by animal-drawn vehicles, the L.H. Mace & Co. advertised a full variety including "iron ice wagons," "iron carriages," "iron hansoms," "iron ox wagons" and "iron express wagons," among others. Of the slightly more than four pages devoted to animal-drawn floor toys, one full page was devoted to various sizes of either the "Iron Fire Engine," "Iron Hook and Ladder," and "Iron Fire Patrol." Twenty-three of the toys were fire-emergency vehicles, accounting for more than half the total of its animal-drawn toys. *See* Mace, 1907, pp. 37–41. Of the offerings from a new company that produced the "Hill Climber" toys, which employed a flywheel "motor," the 1907 line included only powered vehicles: autos, steam cruisers, and a locomotive. Of its dozen-plus toys, one was a Hook and Ladder, while another was a Fire Engine. In the category of "mechanical toys," which would have included spring-motor toys, the fire engines and hook and ladders made up a high percentage of the selections. *See* Mace, 1907, pp. 43, 101–2.
36. O'Brien, 1990, p. 16: pictured.
37. Freeman, 1942, p. 290: reproduced Milton Bradley Co. catalog page, undated.
38. EB, Vol. 1, p. 265. Nadar's extravagant cottage represented a forward-looking extrapolation from the earliest cars; and his thirteen voyagers, an optimistic expansion from the earliest space travelers, who were three in number—although none in that first instance were human.
Being the largest of its kind, the balloon was to contain over two hundred thousand cubic feet of gas. Beneath it a smaller balloon hung, designed to help prevent gas-loss during flight. The thirteen on board included the Princess de la Tour d'Auvergne and aeronauts Louis and Jules Godard. Nadar later exhibited his extravagant balloon and cabin at the New Crystal Palace and predicted that his *Géant* would be the last aerostatic balloon: for he expected future aeronautical vehicles would be driven by the principal of the screw. Despite *Le Géant*'s unimpressive showings, Nadar hoped to become a pioneer in that direction, as well.

39. *Ibid.*, pp. 262–3. This entry notes that "air-balloon" receives its name from the use of hydrogen, in 1911 still called "inflammable air." The "airships," as a consequence, were partly so-called not because of the medium through which they traveled, but because of their means for achieving buoyancy. Verne would strike a note similar to the one in this passage, in observing that French peasants had fired upon the first balloons they had seen, thinking them aerial monsters. *See* Verne, 1958, p. 121.
40. In a letter to Joseph Banks, December 1, 1783. Leonard Labaree and Whitfied Bell, Jr., eds., *Mr. Franklin, A Selection from his Personal Letters*. New Haven: Yale University Press, p. 56.
41. EB, Vol. 1, p. 263.
42. Parry-Crooke, 1981, p. 27. A 1906 catalog page shows these toys: "*Ballons en caoutchouc, dans un joli filet*"—rubber balls in pretty nets. The catalog shows the ball dangling in the net, as it might when held motionless in the child's hand, very much like an inverted image of an aerostatic balloon. Swung into the air straight upwards—as with the Moon-vehicle imagined by Fergusson's manservant Joe—it would have offered a right-side-up Charles-balloon image. On p. 58, reproduced from a 1910 catalog, is another example: "*Ballon caoutchouc avec filet aloes*." Similarly, p. 97, from 1913, and elsewhere.
43. Uglow, 2002, pp. 16–7, 372–3.
44. Poe, 1984, p. 951.
45. *Ibid.*, p. 747. The hoax errs, p. 745, putting the London-Weilburg journey in 1837, not 1836.
46. *Ibid.*, p. 743.
47. *Ibid.*, p. 745; Oxford University Press, 1953.
48. Poe, 1984, p. 745.
49. *Ibid.*, pp. 752, 753.
50. *Ibid.*, p. 743.
51. *Ibid.*, p. 883.
52. Holmes, 2010, p. 458.
53. Jaspers, 1957, p. 44.

Chapter Two

1. "Locksley Hall," lines 15–6.
2. Holmes, 1872, p. 358. The character "the Master" is speaking.
3. "Introduction," in *The Wonderful Wizard of Oz*.
4. Outcault, 1910.
5. Canada escaped British oversight just when its northwestern border was falling into North American hands, since Russia was ceding territory to the United States in an arrangement that seemed to justify the epithet, "Seward's Folly." If he did read the story, Frye must have been amused at Poe's suggestion of a future in which there would be not a North

and South America but rather "the Northern and Southern Kanadaw continents," in "Mellonta Tauta." *See* Poe, 1984, p. 879. By the time Frye was writing, a postwar meaning-shift had already occurred for the word "modern"—as a word but more importantly as a name. In at least one dictionary published just after World War II, "modern" remains identified as denoting only the period identified by historians as having followed the Renaissance. On the other hand, a book of word-origins published only a decade later, in 1958-59, which calls itself an *Etymological Dictionary of Modern English*, quite clearly addresses the English of the moment, not the English of the prior three centuries (Eric Partridge, 1959. *Origins: A Short Etymological Dictionary of Modern English*. New York: The Macmillan Company). "Modern" embraces a "contemporary" sense, in other words. The book, of which the 1959 version is a slightly revised edition of the original of 1958, is fittingly entitled, arriving as it did at the centenary of *On the Origin of Species*. Historian Geoffrey Barraclough's suggestion of "contemporary" as a way of describing this period of "transition," a period that also seemed to him already "post-modern," seems less satisfactory, from the present vantage-point.

6. McClintock, 1961, p. 220, 261. McLoughlin's version came slightly later, under the name "Whirligig of Life."

7. Barzun, 1958, p. xi.

8. Cross, 1899, p. xii. On the previous page, he notes, "in the language of science, he varies the type."

9. Holmes, 1872, p. 195. On p. 361, Holmes speaks of "the transition from old belief to a larger light and liberty," which may point the way toward understanding his observation. Thoughts by another, who was entering University College, London, in 1859, would yield to a similar mix of illumination and misinterpretation, and likewise would become inextricably intertwined with the fabric of Modern society. William Jevons, formulating his theory of utility by 1860, invested his understanding in the phrase that "value depends entirely upon utility" (Keynes, John Neville, 1911. "Jevons, William Stanley." EB, vol. 15, p. 361). His notions of *utility* and *value* would alter philosophy, while fertilizing economic thinking throughout the Modern years.

10. Kouwenhoven, 1938, no. 40. This flight was inspired by a flight of 1,150 miles made by John Wise, whom Verne's arrogant character Robur recalls, in 1886: "The boldest of your aeronauts, John Wise, although he has made an aerial voyage of twelve hundred miles above the American continent, has had to give up his project of crossing the Atlantic!" Verne, 1978, p. 171.

11. Poe, 1984, p. 878: "Mellonta Tauta." In a previous sentence the character notes, "Still a hundred or even two hundred miles an hour is slow traveling, after all."

12. Emerson, Jr., 1902, p. 1270. Writing of 1859, Emerson notes, "Great Britain at this crisis proposed a mutual disarmament. Louis Napoleon telegraphed to Cavour bidding him consent. Cavour, who saw himself at the culmination of all his intrigues, was so upset when this telegram came that his secretary feared that he would commit suicide. In bitterness of heart he telegraphed Sardinia's consent." Although Morse was one of several innovators in the development of electrical telegraphy, it was to him, in 1859, that the French Government of Louis Napoleon presented an award of 80,000 francs (p. 1286).

13. Wright, 1895: see chapters 11 and 12. On pp. 132-3, Wright gives reasons for regarding it as a "natural" division.

14. Kouwenhoven, 1938, no. 92. Of Pennsylvania: "By 1865 ... the state was producing three and a half million barrels, worth a quarter as much as the nation's wheat crop."

15. One witness reported never having seen so awkward a human being as the one upon the platform—and never having a first impression so completely overshadowed by the speaker's words and the mental workings evident behind them. William Dempster Hoard witnessed a Freeport debate between Lincoln and Senator Stephen A. Douglas in 1858. Hoard heard Lincoln again at the 1859 State Fair in Milwaukee, Wis. "His Milwaukee address ... was entirely free from politics, but it contained that same vein of prophecy concerning the future of the nation that had run through all his debates with Douglas." Hoard, who shared physical and personal traits with Lincoln, earned the epithet "The Lincoln of Wisconsin" (p. 25). In later years the phrase "strain of prophecy" would become firmly fixed to Lincoln by Edwin Markham, whose "Lincoln, the Man of the People," enjoyed great vogue (Rankin, George William, 1925. *William Dempster Hoard*. Fort Atkinson, Wisconsin: W.D. Hoard & Sons Company, p. 25-6, 30).

16. McClintock, 1961, p. 212, 257. According to O'Brien, 1990, p. 23, the former patent was the first American doll patent.

17. O'Brien, 1990, p. 22. McClintock, 1961, p. 453, lists Crosby, Nichols & Co., Boston, as beginning to make paper dolls and toy books around 1854.

18. McClintock, 1961, p. 151.

19. *Ibid.*, pp. 260-1.

20. *Ibid.*, pp. 258: by a teacher named August Smith, "aided by some female acquaintances"—presumably other teachers, or students.

21. Freeman, 1942, p. 177, showing patent illustrations. Similar toys likely already existed in Europe.

22. McClintock, 1961, p. 263.

23. *Ibid.*, p. 149: the Crandalls. In general, U.S. toy manufactures were located in the northern industrial belt.

24. "He bought some toys from Eastern manufacturers and imported others from his native Germany. He prospered so well that within a few years he had not only a good retail business but a substantial wholesale division based largely on his imports. Then came the war, increased tariffs, difficulties of transportation, and other troubles which, by 1864, reduced Meinecke's importations to almost nothing. He decided to start a factory of his own" (McClintock, 1961, p. 202). Once established in manufacturing, Meinecke's became a major concern. He was involved in the Centennial Exposition, as a member of the Wisconsin Board. *See* Philadelphia, 1876, p. 14.

25. O'Brien, 1990, p. 23.
26. McClintock, 1961, p. 201. *Also* O'Brien, 1990, p. 23.
27. McClintock, 1961, pp. 201–2.
28. *Ibid.*, p. 92. The name velocipede had been applied first to an English wheeled device patented in 1819—"the nothing of the day," as John Keats opined—which the rider, who was an adult and not a child, propelled by walking while astride it. Another name for the device was "swift walker." The name, in other words, shifted to designate a pedal-powered three-wheeler in subsequent decades.
29. Verne, 1965, p. 55.
30. Perhaps influencing Pyle's stories, a minor fashion for medievalism may have cropped up during this time, since Parker Brothers issued the game Chivalry in that same year, 1887, albeit to modest sales. Parker reintroduced it in 1927 as Camelot. *See* McClintock, 1961, p. 310 (pictured). Pyle's usage conforms with that of Hawthorne, for whom an "aerial wonder" was not a flying machine but Pegasus. In a different example, *Wonder Book of Bible Knowledge* (Anonymous, 1933) clearly employed the Romantic-Gothic usage—a thought which might have startled its publishers.
31. Cross, 1899, p. 281.
32. Frye, 1963, p. 74.
33. Cross, 1899, p. xv.
34. Frye, 1963, p. 53.
35. EB, vol. 28, p. 514; entry for Herbert George Wells. Also in Vol. 27, p. 1030, in the entry for Jules Verne, "fantastic story" appears again.
36. EB, Vol. 27, p. 1030.
37. Wells, 1934, pp. vii–ix.
38. Lovett and Hughes, 1932, p. 348 and elsewhere.
39. Appleton, 1925 (Don Sturdy), pp. 9, 141.
40. As in Bonner, 1913, with its *Wondership*.
41. Ash, 1977, p. 13.
42. As should be evident, the term "science fiction" falls short of the needs of these pages. When understood historically, many stories that clearly appear to be wonder tales, or participate in the wonder-tale tradition, are ones that are ignored or judged irrelevant to readers interested in "science fiction." Only a small fraction of Jules Verne's output, for instance, falls into the retrospective category of "science fiction." Yet in the early-middle years of the Modern, all Jules Verne novels were seen to offer "wonderlands"—in the authoritative view of a contemporary publication aimed expressly at children (*Youth's Companion* 60:43, Oct. 27, 1887, pp. 450–1). All his novels related to New Worlds idealism; and all, moreover, had a place within his scheme for literary world-conquest—for mapping the world fictionally. This literary scheme connected the entirety of his output, structurally, to the form he himself created.

Chapter Three

1. Lofting, 1956, pp. 17–8.
2. Hooker, Brian, 1915. *Poems*. Boston: Yale University Press, p. 4, "Ballade of the Dreamland Rose."
3. Barrie, 1965, p. 87.
4. King-Hall, 1910, p. 140.
5. Pyle, 1965, p. vi.
6. Beckford, 1986, p. 153.
7. John Croker, in 1818, in a review reprinted in Hunter, 1996, p. 189.
8. Wilson, 1931, p. 12; *and* Jules-Verne, 1976, p. 30: "it is certain that Verne read the first volume of *Tales* in the years following 1848."
9. Starkie, 1958, pp. 214–5, 221. Verne's own "Edgar Poe" would appear a dozen years later, in 1864.
10. *Ibid.*, p. 224.
11. Wilson, op. cit., p. 12.
12. Jules-Verne, 1976, p. 62.
13. Starkie, 1958, p. 296
14. From "Clarel"; F.O. Matthiesen, ed., 1950. *The Oxford Book of American Verse*. New York: Oxford University Press, p. 404.
15. Jules-Verne, 1976, p. 171.
16. Born, Franz, 1971. *Jules Verne: The Man Who Invented the Future*. New York: Scholastic. Of interest for its title and enthusiasm, not for biographical trustworthiness.
17. Wilson, 1931, p. 117.
18. Čapek, 1961, pp. 28–9.
19. Twain, 1961, p. 150.
20. *Ibid.*, p. 151
21. *Ibid.*, p. 151.
22. Mumford, 1970, p. 47. Kepler's work had particular influence upon Wells, whose Moon novel shows considerable debt to Kepler's Lunar society. *See* Chapter Twelve in the present work.
23. Kouwenhoven, 1938, no. 27.
24. Kunitz, Stanley J., and Howard Haycraft, eds., 1942. *Twentieth Century Authors: A Biographical Dictionary of Modern Literature*. New York: The H.W. Wilson Co., p. 1493.
25. Claude-Henri Saint-Simon (1760–1825) envisioned a society ruled by captains of industry, engineers, scientists, and artists. Likely due to his own experience, Verne saw the world as being led by the first three groups, with the last being left behind—as is distinctly the case in *Paris in the Twentieth Century*.

Chapter Four

1. Foley, 1962, p. 8.
2. Carroll, undated, p. 148.
3. McClintock, 1961, p. 94: quoting from an 1808 issue of *The New York Commercial Advertiser*.
4. Apparently *les Ombres Chinoses* first opened as shadow-theaters in the late 18th century. "Luminated toys" was another name (Freeman, 1942, p. 231). On p. 235, the Freemans reproduce an 1876 advertisement showing a magic lantern projecting from behind a screen, as in the shadowgraph and "phantasmagoria" manners. The way optical toys overlapped, or graded one into the other, finds an example here.
5. Graham, 1673–1751, also invented the mercurial pendulum and the "dead-beat escapement."

6. OED.
7. Culff, 1969, p. 63.
8. *Ibid.*, p. 63. Colza oil was a rapeseed oil.
9. *Ibid.*, p. 64.
10. *Ibid.*, pp. 64–7: Stevenson wrote the essay "A Penny Plain and Twopence Coloured" on the experience of growing up with the "giddy joy" of seeing the shop windows with Skelt toy theaters.
11. As noted, the paper doll quickly came into association with popular-audience magazines, which would be one of their most important means for dissemination: in 1859, through *Godey's Lady's Book*. See O'Brien, 1990, pp. 21–22. The term "paper-doll drama" appeared at least by the 1890s, appearing in Bangs, 1923 (1895), pp. 108–9, in reference to their being what "a great many modern writers do."
12. Holmes, 2010, p. 345: "on sale in Piccadilly, priced between six and twenty guineas."
13. Hobhouse, 1950, p. 87.
14. Uglow, 2002, p. 14: "Everywhere, people tried electric shocks on themselves and their friends."
15. Holmes, 2010, p. 17.
16. McClintock, 1961, p. 461.
17. Dunshee, Kenneth H., ed., 1947. "Toys on Parade," in *News from Home*, January, 8:1, p. 3. New York: The Home Insurance Company. Around 1800, too, Deming Jarves of Cape Cod began making doll dishes of glass. *See* McClintock, 1961, p. 457.
18. Innovations included an "oscillating axle" which the Crandalls applied to carriages. McClintock, 1961, pp. 147–8.
19. Dalrymple, 1991, p. 140.
20. McClintock, 1961, pp. 450–63; with some information from O'Brien, 1990, and other sources.
21. O'Brien, 1990, p. 17, shows an ark thought to be from 1850s Germany, with man and woman figures in addition to the paired animals, birds, and insects——beetles and butterflies. Since Dickens mentioned butterflies being included with these toys, 1800s arks may often have embraced these fragile invertebrates.
22. Although the author's copy is undated and lacks publisher information, it seems to have been given to a child in 1872. Pages cited: 5, 7, 10, 14, 20, 104.
23. Culff, 1969, p. 103: the photograph shows a lathed half-round of wood, part of which is sectioned into the rough forms of toy horses.
24. Poe, 1984, p. 449: "The Colloquy of Monos and Una." "Prophecy fiction" gained its footing, in America, in the 1900s. Although the word "prophetic" would see common application to both wonder stories and evangelical fiction, "prophecy" had connotations linking it to the Bible, and to the evangelical movement with its literalist readings of that venerable selection of visionary writings.
25. Barzun, 1958, p. 206.
26. McClintock, 1961, pp. 234 (pictured), 276–7.
27. *Ibid.*, p. 307 (pictured). The many who grew up with Monopoly will appreciate this game's squares which read, "Intemperance——Go to Rebuke," "Error——Go back to Humanity," and "Stubbornness——Go to Jealousy."
28. Van Dyne, 1911, pp. 35–6. "However eager her brother might be she had never yet allowed him to work a moment on a Sunday, and Steve deferred to her wishes in this regard."
29. Culff, 1969, p. 92: "roughly between the years 1820 and 1860."
30. Uglow, 2002, p. 96. After being appointed in 1757 as Mathematical Instrument Maker to Glasgow University, Watt opened a shop, first in the Saltmarket and later in the city center, selling instruments of both mathematical and musical natures, and goods in a variety that included toys. One item was his own version of a pantograph, a means for mechanically copying or transferring drawings. John Robison lived 1739–1805.
31. EB vol. 25, p. 818: noting of Watt, "His labours stand in natural sequence to those of Thomas Newcomen, and Newcomen's to those of Denis Papin and Thomas Savery. Savery's engine in its turn was the reduction to practical form of a contrivance which had long before been known as a scientific toy." While EB used the term "scientific toys," in Watt's time "philosophic" would have been understood.
32. Uglow, 2002, pp. 396–7: "It was often argued, and rightly, that patents held back other inventors. This was true of no one so much as Watt, who was ruthless in this respect. The umbrella patent of 1784, for example, contained a special clause laying claim to any use of steam on a wheeled carriage."
33. *Ibid.*, p. 397: "Watt's patent blocked Murdoch developing this any further." In the 1790s, Richard Trevithick took up the idea; and it happened to be in Redruth where Tevithick completed the first steam carriage for carrying passengers, in 1801. Murdoch had a tenuous literary connection, his father having been employed at James Boswell's Auchinleck estate.
34. EB v. 25, p. 888.
35. *Ibid.*, for "railway mania" of 1844——of which Stephenson disapproved.
36. Culff, 1969, p. 72, shows what may have been one of the first toys of the Rocket, slightly mislabeled as "Stevenson's." Other images on the page show a French locomotive said to have been introduced in England in 1840, and a German train of japanned tin plate, made "about 1840."
37. McClintock, 1961, pp. 92–3.
38. The *Rocket* would, in fact, continue to inspire new toys into the 1900s. In 1909 a new toy version was introduced with a brass boiler equipped with spirit lamp, whistle and safety valve. It pulled a coal tender, a cattle truck, and two passenger cars, to make a toy not quite a yard long, traveling on 1¾-inch gauge track. *See* Schroeder, 1971, p. 108: shown in a British catalog, from Bassett-Lowke, Ltd. The Moline, Ill., firm Strombeck-Becker included it in its historical train models, of wood, in the 1950s. This series enjoyed popularity.
39. O'Brien, 1990, p. 24, illustrated in color. O'Brien lists the toy as being from around 1885; the company apparently only continued until around 1880, however.
40. Sherman, 1914, p. 320: Sherman's words, not Dickens's.
41. *Ibid.*, p. 135: "The Signal-Man," first published in 1866. Its presence in this collection indicates that,

as a story, it enjoyed continuing currency among younger readers. The Keats poem is the sonnet addressed to Haydon.

42. EB vol. 4 p. 513. Contrary to Holmes, 2010, p. 445, Brewster was not the inventor. Apparently, as O'Brien, 1990, notes, p. 41, it "had probably originated in the Orient some time before that."

43. Holmes, 2010, pp. 450, 460.

44. EB vol. 15, p. 640. According to *The Concise Dictionary of National Biography* (Oxford University Press), Bradley d. 1732; birth year unknown.

45. EB vol. 4, p. 513; vol. 25, p. 898.

46. EB vol. 28, p. 583.

47. EB vol. 25, p. 900.

48. EB vol. 28, p. 583; Standage, 1998, pp. 33–5, 43–5. According to William Rose Benet (1960, *The Reader's Encyclopedia*; New York: Thomas Y. Crowell Co., p. 437), Joseph Glanville in his 1661 *The Vanity of Dogmatizing* "is thought to have anticipated the electric telegraph."

49. Hobhouse, 1950, p. 82.

50. EB vol. 25, 899.

51. Culff, 1969, pp. 105–7; Fraser, 1966, p. 122. Paris (1785–1856) became president of the Royal College of Surgeons in 1844. Both sources give the impression that Paris was president when he developed the toy.

52. Culff, 1969, pp. 104–7.

53. Shown in Targ, 1957, p. 199.

54. Reviewer John Croker wrote in *The Quarterly Review*, January 1818; reprinted in Hunter, 1996. See p. 188.

55. Parry-Crooke, 1981, p. 10. Interestingly, by 1913 such a toy was offered as "*Cinèmatographe enfantin*": *Ibid.*, p. 103.

56. Freeman, 1942, pp. 238–44.

57. *Ibid.*, pp. 238, 242–3. An advertising page, reproduced on p. 242, shows "comic slides," with five different comical figures; "natural history slides," with drawings of birds and animals; "nursery tale slides," with trios of images that called forth parts of children's stories; and others.

58. *Ibid.*, p. 245.

59. Culff, 1969, pp. 107, 109: quoting Baudelaire's essay "*Morale du joujou*," translated by Jonathan Mayne.

60. Verne, 1996, p. 70. Dickens's Signal-Man had kinship to Poe's chess-player——a human who appeared to viewers to be a machine——as well as to the figure Lewis Mumford would identify in the early astronauts: the lobotomized dwarf. This dwarf was the encapsulated man who trained his mind, expanded his human horizons, and then, due to his encapsulation, found his mind reduced to a vestigial organ, much as the appendix then was being seen to the medical establishment: present, but not in use. The Signal-Man is a displaced mind in the sense that his youthful exuberance——his animal expression, his own Id——caused him to be seen as unacceptable material for the system within which he was training. This youthful person, by non-machinelike behavior, ironically precipitated his own reduction to a cog. The chess-player comes in for discussion in Chapter Six.

61. Hobhouse, 1950, p. 84. "This was not by any means the first electric clock, but it was pretty ambitious for a time when the wiring of houses was half a century away. The pendulum of this clock was in the gallery with the other clocks; the mechanism was in the south transept; there were two dials on the balconies of the gallery at the extreme east and west of the building; and on the outside elevation of the south transept, two hands had been arranged as to use the twelve sectors of the arch as a huge clock face, the semi-circular shape being overcome by simply carrying each hand to an equal length on either side of its pivot."

Chapter Five

1. Hobhouse, 1950, p. 72.

2. Thomson, 1967, p. 335: "A Lady of Sorrow."

3. Foley, 1962, p. 20. "For centuries, 'Bring me a fairing' was a familiar request of the children of England, Holland and Russia, German, France and Italy, Belgium and Spain, and a dozen little countries now absorbed in the map of modern Europe."

4. Bleiler, 1970, p.33.

5. Irving, Washington, 1939, p. 198.

6. Verne, 1999, p. vi. The editor, Peter Costello, offers good arguments for the story having been written around 1870: "'The Humbug,' though his son Michel dated it from 1863, seems from internal evidence to have been written no earlier than 1869, two years after Verne himself had travelled to America on the *Great Eastern*, and made a trip up the Hudson, along the route given in the story.... This story of American enterprise owed much to the legendary figure of P.T. Barnum, but also the notorious Dr. Albert C. Koch, who had displayed a fake fossil sea-serpent in the 1840s, and the celebrated 'American Goliath,' the so-called Cardiff Giant, which caused a sensation in 1869–70." The story may owe a debt to Barnum for its title; for Barnum in 1865 published the book *Humbugs of the World*. Twain's "The Petrified Man," discussed in Chapter Three, appeared in 1862.

7. Verne, 1999, pp. 102–3.

8. Bruce, 1987, p. 132.

9. Joint Committee on Ceremonies, 1893, p. 17: "The Growth of Expositions."

10. *Ibid.*, p. 18. Figures vary, as to the building's size. In Columbian Arts Co., 1891, p. 364, for instance, the length is 1851 feet long.

11. Bruce, 1987, p. 133.

12. Hobhouse, 1950, p. 80.

13. Kime, Wayne R., 2003. *Fitz-James O'Brien: Selected Literary Journalism, 1852–1860.* Selinsgrove: Susquehanna University Press.

14. Hobhouse, 1950, pp. 169–173. The Queen wrote after the opening, "and my beloved husband the author of this 'Peace-Festival,' which united the industry of all nations of the earth" (p. 69).

15. Gosse, 1983, pp. 83, 88.

16. Thwaite, 2002, p. 183.

17. Preston, 1986, p. 12: "On opening night, a dinner was held for twenty-one people in the belly of one of the iguanodons. The invitations were sent on an

artificial pterodactyl wing, and the scientists at the dinner reportedly got so drunk that their boisterous singing could be heard across the entire park." Preston's "opening night" seems in error, since the dinner took place before that time.

See also the later Moon novel by Verne, discussed in Chapter Seven.

18. Columbian Arts Co., 1891, p. 366. The event recalled an oddly similar one in 1840, when John Herschel held a boisterous party within a different "relic of a past age"—William Herschel's giant forty-foot telescope, now being dismantled. "Relic" is historian Holmes's phrase, not Herschel's. See Holmes, 2010, p. 465.

19. McClintock, 1961, p. 70.
20. Ibid., p. 135.
21. McClintock, 1961, p. 135.
22. O'Brien, 1990, p. 22.
23. McClintock, 1961, p. 135: "According to a book on paper dolls published by Anson Randolph in 1856, a young miss in Boston in the 1830s or 1840s paid for her education by making paper dolls and selling them at the bookstore of Munroe & Francis."
24. As in the early scene with Mrs. Ramsay and James, in Virginia Woolf's *To the Lighthouse*.
25. Verne, 1999, p. 41.
26. Toys would have a similar effect of freezing scientific visualizations in place, even well after such visualizations had been superseded by others.
27. Thwaite, 2002, p. 183.
28. Merrill, 1924, pp. 123, 125. The notion of the subterranean, primeval ocean was commonly held, up to around 1835.
29. Verne, 1978, pp. 395, 397. This passage, with its Herschel-like acceptance of a universe without divine intervention, stands at some odds to the picture Verne presents of biological history, in symbolic terms, elsewhere in the novel. Since Verne's vision was humanistic in its focus, that he should have inconsistencies in his scientific vision (or should readily accept the inconsistencies in others' visions), seems not at all unusual.
30. EB v. 20, p. 681; v. 11, p. 300. Barker apparently developed the form at the suggestion of German architectural painter Breisig.
31. Freeman, 1942, p. 242.
32. McClintock, 1961, p. 262.
33. Parry-Crooke, 1981, p. 20: "Voyage en Afrique."
34. McClintock, 1961, p. 262. This was made even further like a tiny theater by the addition of "a sheaf of admission tickets, a showbill advertising the exhibition, and a brief descriptive lecture for the owner to read."
35. Freeman, 1942, p. 241.
36. According to the *OED*, soon after the word's coinage, magazine illustrations with odd or fantastic character appeared as "phantasmagoria." In Poe's "Usher" usages (1984, pp. 320, 325), the latter one distinctly conjures up the magic-lantern show: "One of the phantasmagoric conceptions of my friend, partaking not so rigidly of the spirit of abstraction, may be shadowed forth, although feebly, in words."

Lewis Carroll's ghost poem, "Phantasmagoria," came much later.

37. Thomson, 1967, p. 310. From "A Lady of Sorrow," published in 1867.
38. EB, vol. 20, p. 681, for panoramas; vol. 21, p. 346, for phantasmagoria. The latter is attributed to a Philipstal, perhaps Phillipthal.
39. Barzun, 1958, p. 134.
40. Sherman, 1914, p. 55.
41. EB, vol. 27, p. 283: of Trilobites: "despite the fact that their remains have not been found in rocks of the Mesozoic or Kainozoic epochs, it was conceived to be possible that living specimens might be dredged from the sea-floor during the exploration of the ocean depths undertaken by the 'Challenger' expedition. Needless to say this faint hope was not borne out by results." See vol. 5, pp. 807–9, for perspective on the *Challenger* expedition. That Verne continued out of step with evolutionary thinking would be revealed in later novels, as in a brief meditation from the late 1880s in which he reflects on the Bad Lands in the American West: "And in truth these Bad Lands are an immense ossuary where lie bleaching in the sun myriads of fragments of pachyderms, chelonians, and even, some would have us believe, fossil men, overwhelmed by unknown cataclysms ages and ages ago." See Verne, 1978, p. 200.
42. Holmes, 2010, p. 288: Humphry Davy's words.
43. Ibid., p. 54. Staged at Drury Lane.
44. Columbian Art Co., 1891, p. 368.
45. Bruce, 1987, p. 134.
46. Preston, 1986, p. 12–3.
47. Leidy, born in Philadelphia in 1823. Also a Philadelphia native, Cope was born in 1840.
48. Preston, 1986, p. 13. Laelaps would come to be renamed the Allosaurus.
49. Ibid., pp. 13–4. Preston suggests that Tweed found no way to profit from the dinosaur reconstructions, as rationale for his violent action. Tweed became state senator in 1868; his Tweed Ring fell before the efforts of Samuel J. Tilden and Thomas Nast in 1871. Sadly, Tweed accomplished enormous mischief in a short time.
50. McClintock, 1961, pp. 237, 280.
51. Poe, 1984, p. 964.
52. Verne, 1978, p. 194.
53. Ibid., p. 200. In a similar spirit, one can imagine the scene in Louisa May Alcott's *Little Men*, in which children create a "doomed village" that is entirely consumed, people and all, by fire (*see* Culff, 1969, p.71) as being the kind of "play" activity that allowed children to mature into the sort of adults that could participate imaginatively in the most cataclysmic wonder tales. The imagined cataclysm would exert a steady draw upon children's imagination. The author, in collecting toys, came upon a printing set from perhaps the 1940s, which included a small printed item. Letter by letter, the child had printed out a little placard: "FLASH FIRE BURNS UP ALL OF WILTON." Wilton was a village in western Wisconsin—and still is, despite the child's apocalyptic imagination.
54. Hobhouse, 1950, p. 82. Hobhouse considered

the figure, which contained 7,000 parts, an "entirely useless object."

55. Culff, 1969, p. 72, attributes picture-block development to the 1840s.

56. McClintock, 1961, p. 158–9.

57. Dalrymple, 1991, p. 109: photograph.

58. The Philadelphia publisher was Young and M'Culloch. Targ, 1957, p. 150.

59. McClintock, 1961, pp. 75–6: quoting May 7, 1785 issue. Similarly the Lilliput Bank designed by John Hall of Watertown, Massachusetts, and produced in cast iron by J. & E. Stevens, took its name from the diminutive stature of the figure it showed (O'Brien, 1990, p. 42).

60. Barlow, 1998, p. 14: an 1880 advertising drawing.

61. Verne, undated, p. 689: from (as it is named in this translation) *All Around the Moon*.

62. Roth, undated, p. 306.

63. *Ibid.*, p. 5: he states his affiliation at the end of his "Preface."

Chapter Six

1. Chapuis and Droz, 1958, p. 364.
2. McClintock, 1961, p. 257.
3. Ellis, 2009, Chapter 19.
4. Chapuis and Droz, 1958, p. 365: "Everywhere it aroused the liveliest curiosity, and its fame exceeded that of all genuine automata."
5. Poe, 1983, p. 273.
6. Fisher, 1990, p. 155: quoted. Brewster's perception contained echoes of Plato. Socrates, in *The Republic*, suggests that all that deceives may be said to enchant.
7. *Ibid.*, p. 79. Maurice J. Bennett, in "Art and Metaphysics in 'Hans Pfaall,'" quotes a review by Poe in the June 1835 *Southern Literary Messenger*.
8. EB v. 6, p. 947.
9. Brooks, 1957, p. 85, speaking of his childhood friend Frank (John Francis Stimson): "I remembered that when we were boys he defeated the turbaned automaton that played chess at the entrance of the Eden Musée in New York, a famous player behind his disguise who was supposed never to have been beaten."
10. Poe, 1983, p. 514.
11. *Ibid.*, pp. 516–7.
12. Because of the parallel between Pfaall's Rotterdam and Vondervotteimitiss, the "Lunarian" who appears above Rotterdam might be considered likewise an imp figure.
13. Poe, 1983, p. 221: in "King Pest the First."
14. Dalrymple, 1991, p. 40.
15. McClintock, 1961, p. 458; also 214, where the McClintocks note, "A complete one, made by Joseph Lyon & Company, is now in the Museum of the City of New York, in its original box. (There are also two at Essex Institute in Salem.) The doll is small, dressed in yellow silk with black lace, and has a *papier-mâché* head, cardboard body, and kid hands. It walks by means of a keywound mechanism inside the body." Richard O'Brien (1990, p. 35), on the other hand, says that the Morrison doll "was manufactured by New York's Martin and Runyan." Both assertions may well be accurate.

16. King, 1989, pp. 20–1: photograph. The variations, of course, may have been made by competitors.

17. McClintock, 1961, p. 215. Illustrated on p. 166. The McClintocks quote *The Scientific American*, December 16, 1868.

18. The Automatic Toy was a William F. Goodwin patent, in 1866; Toy Automaton was the name used on an 1863 patent for J.S. Brown and on another in 1873 for R.J. Clay. Sometime around 1870, Clay founded Automatic Toy Works in New York City, which produced important and popular toys including a creeping doll, a Scissors Grinder who sharpened scissors on a grindstone, and a lady at a sewing machine who "periodically lifted and scrutinized her work." Ives purchased Clay's business in the 1880s. *See* McClintock, 1961, pp. 161, 215, 288.

19. McClintock, 1961, p. 72. The name was apparently also spelled Pattison, or Paterson.

20. *Ibid.*, p. 88.

21. Boston, 1900. Even after the winnowing of companies that would take place by 1900, a directory would list four of the state's ten clock manufacturers as being based in Bristol, with one, E.N. Welch, actually in Forestville. Moreover, the state's clock-spring manufacturing centered there. These manufacturers were established by the time toymakers turned to mechanical toys, as indicated by the establishment in 1857 of the Wallace Barnes Company of Bristol, maker of small springs. *See* p. 2045: advertisement.

22. Brown may or may not have drawn directly upon New Britain manufacturing capacity. Richard O'Brien notes that Union Manufacturing Company of Clinton, Connecticut—located a fair distance away, on the same side of the Connecticut River, but down on Long Island Sound—supplied Brown with "large and small horses, in parts, men parts and ladies in parts" around 1856–61. O'Brien notes the Automatic Toy, but places it two years before Goodwin had obtained the relevant patent. *See* O'Brien, 1990, p. 18.

Carriage-making, with its long connection to toy making, had a strong presence in Connecticut, as in other New England states. A directory in 1900 would record there being six New Britain manufacturers in the carriage, coach, and sleigh category, with four in Bristol—with one of the latter, Thomas F. Smith, actually being in Forestville. The state even had specialists in "children's carriages," with the Bridgeport Baby Carriage and Rattan Manufacturing Company, while the North East Baby Carriage and Rattan Manufacturing Company had its factory in New Haven (*see* Boston, 1900). Although actual automobiles developed along different lines, the automaton-carriage combination stimulated many imaginations in the later 1800s.

23. O'Brien, 1990, p. 21: While identifying a "first" in the area of iron-casting seems chancy, O'Brien had considerable experience in researching the toy trade when he gave J. & E. Stevens pride of place. The Cromwell company apparently became the Joe

Stevens Company, since that name appears *in* Boston, 1900, p. 1624.

24. McClintock, 1961, p. 459.

25. O'Brien, 1990, p. 19.

26. McClintock, 1961, pp. 224, 257. Freeman, 1942, p. 359, shows images from a Hull & Stafford "Photographic Catalogue of Tin Toys." Freeman notes, "The stamped tin toy appears to have been produced almost simultaneously in Philadelphia by Francis, Field and Francis and in Connecticut by The American Toy Company and Hull and Stafford." The American Toy Co. was a "temporary selling organization," 1868–72, of Brown and Stevens (McClintock, p. 450).

27. McClintock, 1961, p. 287, cites listing from *The Connecticut Business Directory*, 1866, of Ives as basket manufacturer. O'Brien, 1990, p. 35, notes that Riley Ives, born 1808, established his metal-stamping business in the 1850s, and made buttons during the Civil War; afterwards he made whistles for the squeak toys being made by New York Rubber. Riley's son, Edward, born 1839, joined his father about 1860, according to O'Brien. Ives apparently did some work at the Blakeslee Carriage Shop in Plymouth, which would be still in operation in 1900 under the Enos Blakeslee name. McClintock, 1961, pp. 287–8; Boston, 1900, p. 1430.

28. Freeman, 1942, p. 246: showing advertisement. While the company goes unmentioned, the great number of hot-air toys suggests the involvement of a specialist, such as Ives.

29. Loncraine, 2009, p. 53. *In* Kouwenhoven, 1938: "vast Centennial Museum of living Mechanical Automata."

30. McClintock, p. 288: "Other inventive men of Bridgeport apparently had their toys manufactured by Ives, for the patent records of only three years show that toys were also devised by six other residents of that city."

31. O'Brien, 1990, p. 36.

32. King, 1989, p. 38.

33. O'Brien, 1990, p. 38. Ives Mfg. Co. in 1890 was located at 771 South Avenue, Bridgeport. *See* Boston, 1890, p. 1624.

34. C.F. Braitling, by 1900 (*see* Boston, 1900, p. 1624) was C.F. Braitling & Sons, 26 Cedar, Bridgeport. Later it was the Frederick K. Braitling Co., also the Fred K. Braitling Co. Bridgeport would continue as a toymaking center to the end of the Modern years. Besides Braitling, the town would have the New England Toy Manufacturing Company, a maker of fur-stuffed toys.

35. United States Centennial Commission, 1876, p. 128.

36. By 1873, J.A. Pierce was making mechanical and steam toys in that city. The amount of historical information lost in that fire may be indicated by the fact that Secor left an historical record of his dealings mainly because he switched to toymaking.

37. O'Brien, 1990, p. 37.

38. McClintock, 1961, p. 244: illustrated. The Ives connection may be conjectural, since the McClintocks use the word, "probably."

39. Bleiler, 1989, pp. 101–2.

40. *Ibid.*, p. 113. Steam automobiles were becoming common during this time. Ford saw one in 1876.

41. McClintock, 1961, p. 453.

42. Ellis, 2009, Chapters 8, "steam horses"; and 2.

43. *Ibid.*, Chapters 2, "wonderful"; and 7.

44. *Ibid.*, Chapters 14, "locomotive"; 20, "bomb-shell"; and 2, Colt's factory.

45. Wright, 1895, pp. 270–1.

46. Wright, 1895, p. 274.

47. Mumford, 1970, p. 10.

Chapter Seven

1. Poe, 1984, p. 1001: "Note," to "The Unparalleled Adventure of One Hans Pfaall." Poe also suggests the divided soul in "Pfaall," in Pfaall's comment on "a certain design with which either the devil or my better genius had inspired me." Poe, 1984, p. 957.

2. Verne, undated, p. 3: "Preface."

3. Anonymous, undated, p. 19.

4. Poe, 1984, p. 1000. "Note" by Poe to "The Unparalleled Adventure of One Hans Pfaall." The D'Avisson tale makes clear the connection between the Moon and an ideal state. In *L'Homme dans la lune*, a castaway on an island is "borne aloft by a multitude of wild swans (*ganzas*)," with the *ganzas* being native to the Moon, to which they periodically return. The tale's hero learns this by accident when taken there. "Here he finds, among other odd things, that the people enjoy extreme happiness; that they have no law; that they die without pain; that they are from ten to thirty feet in height; that they live five thousands years ... and that they can jump sixty feet high, when, being out of the gravitating influence, they fly about with fans."

5. Bleiler, 1970, p. 61.

6. Culff, 1969, pp. 109–10.

7. Goodfellow, pp. 16–7. The moral element has a minor presence—as in the "Ale House" square. The player landing there must "pay a Stake & Drink till his turn comes to throw again"—a minor and pleasurable penalty, in contrast to the "Prison" square, which stops a player while others advance toward game's end. Another version is shown *in* Culff, 1969, p. 111: "The New Game of Virtue Rewarded and Vice Punished," of 1818, "by T. Newton, Inventor of the New Game of the Mansion of Bliss," and published by William Darton, London. Interestingly, the game survived into the 1900s, at least in France, where the "*Jeu de l'Oie*" was sold as late as 1909–10, in a form closely similar to old ones in which the main playing area was in the form of the goose. *See* Parry-Crooke, 1981, p. 39, 51.

8. McClintock, p. 110. On pp. 344–5, the McClintocks make note of sailors bringing games from foreign parts to Salem.

9. Poe, 1984, pp. 951–3.

10. *Ibid.*, pp. 958–9.

11. *Ibid.*, p. 965.

12. *Ibid.*, p. 969.

13. *Ibid.*, pp. 975, 977.

14. Rich, 1992. Although it seems entirely likely that others than Poe came up with similar concepts

in the early 1800s, or earlier, instances have not come to the author's attention.

15. Poe, 1984, pp. 956, 958, 965.

16. Sharp, 1990. Sharp points out that seemingly supernatural elements in Poe's fiction frequently and perhaps always point to Poe's attempt to grapple with the scientific developments of the time, notably in the field of optics.

17. Jules-Verne, 1976, p. 62: quoting Verne's April, 1864, article "Edgar Poe" in *Musée des Familles.*

18. Verne, 1999, pp. 51, 60.

19. *Ibid.*, p. 54.

20. *Ibid.*, pp. 63–4.

21. *Ibid.*, p. 70.

22. *Ibid.*

23. Jules-Verne, 1976, p. 62: In his "Edgar Poe," Verne would point out "the materialistic side of these tales, in which the intervention of providence never makes itself felt. It would seem, indeed, that Poe rejects the possibility of that intervention and would fain explain all in terms of physical laws. "

24. Verne, undated, p. 4: "Preface," by Edward Roth.

25. Verne, 1999, p. 70.

26. Jules-Verne, 1976, p. 61.

27. Verne, 1999, p. 40.

28. Verne, undated, p. 554.

29. *Ibid.*, p. 547.

30. *Ibid.*, p. 549.

31. *Ibid.*, pp. 555, 561.

32. *Ibid.*, p. 575. The name of Maston is an interesting one, in terms of gigantism, evoking as it does the American prehistoric creature, the Mastodon. In *Houseboat on the Styx*, "mastodon" is used in a generic gigantic-creature sense, suggesting that usage to have become common. Since "mastodon" appeared in McGuffey's readers as a word to be learned, more people may have memorized its spelling than knew quite what its sounds designated. *See* Bangs, 1923, p. 149.

33. Roth, undated, p. 57.

34. Verne, undated, p. 557.

35. *Ibid.*, p. 574. The ancients also had entertained the notion of the mirror moon, as in Lucian's trip. Verne's cannon, in the short "*Un Voyage en ballon,*" which is intended for communicating with both Earth and Moon, might be a symbolic cousin to the notion.

36. *Ibid.*, pp. 622, 627.

37. Roth, undated, p. 170. America would, indeed, have an "Air Line" which would be a railroad.

38. Davy's work was completed by this time.

39. Verne, undated, p. 621, "feline;" p. 658, Noah's Ark. Verne also has a test-shot of a miniature projectile-vehicle, with a cat and squirrel as passengers; only the cat emerges.

40. *Ibid.*, p. 666.

41. *Ibid.*, p. 622. The "little pith figures which they sell for children's toys" might be rendered more literally as "little acrobats of elder-tree pith such as they give children for their amusement."

42. *Ibid.*, pp. 678, 699.

43. Jules-Verne, 1976, p. 61: quoting Verne's April 1864 article in *Musée des Familles.* As noted earlier in the chapter, the gas-cock's potential in toys had suggested itself to Bradley. Verne pursued this idea elsewhere, as in "Doctor Ox's Experiment."

44. A similar fate befalls the Gun Club's efforts in Verne's 1889 *Sans Dessus Dessous*, due to an error in ballistics calculations.

Chapter Eight

1. Verne, 1962, p. 45.

2. "The Land of Counterpane," in *A Child's Garden of Verses.*

3. Jules-Verne, 1976, p. 61.

4. In *Hard Times*, two years after *Bleak House*, Dickens offered a character who likewise seems to dwell on a superhuman level, almost invisibly to the reader. She does so through an exaggeration of a dissected-soul quality. Sissy Jupe embodies not merely the heart but the inerrant heart, whose sure-handed interventions guide the novel's resolution.

5. Keynes, John Neville, 1911. "Jevons, William Stanley." EB, vol. 15, p. 361.

6. Verne, 1981, p. 25. Elsewhere Verne reaffirms Conseil's usual inability to identify creatures.

7. Schroeder, 1971, p. 81, for instance, shows an 1894 version called The Brownie Ladder. "Finely lithographed in bright colors; presenting a ladder with Brownies climbing up and down. Two Brownies are provided, made of hardwood, which, when placed between nails at top of ladder, come wriggling down to the bottom in a most laughable manner."

8. Verne, 1976, p. 27.

9. In an example of enantodromia, in the Age of the Masses the "morpho" prefix, relating to fixed form, led to the intransitive verb "morph," a popular term arising, as it were, from cinematic, machine-assisted "animation," and referring to an unstable form that changes.

10. "In spite of having a name meaning 'Advice,' never gave any even when asked" (Verne, 1981, p. 24). Thus Conseil's fictional nature stands apart from the elder Gosse's historical nature.

11. Verne, 1977, pp. 98–100.

12. Verne, 1977, p. 349. Walter James Miller, the editor, comments on the oddity of the translator not having reverted to Poe's original text, rather than translating back into English the translation of Poe into French.

13. *Ibid.*, p. 352. A pre-echo, as it were, of the final utterance of another heavily shadowed figure from another novelist of the sea, Joseph Conrad. That story, too, relates to colonialism and slavery.

14. Poe, 1984, p. 432.

15. *Ibid.* As originally published the story lacked this opening quotation. *See* Poe, 1983, p. 685.

16. Verne, 1981, p. 98.

17. *Ibid.*, p. 22.

18. Stirn, 1990, p. 81. Not all fish-pond toys had this aspect. For instance, the French game *Joyeu Pecheurs* involved a box surface that appeared to be the upper surface of a lake or pond, with slits, into which the magnetic "hook" was to be lowered, to

catch fish, old boots, or bottles. *See* Parry-Crooke, 1981, p. 39.

19. Parry-Crooke, 1981, p. 11. It may be worth noting that such a toy would have involved a literal borrowing, if a child play-acted Nemo. Nemo never appears as a diver who descends from the world above the sea, but rather one who lives, breathes, and walks undersea from the *Nautilus*, much as others might from their houses.

20. Aldrich, 1942, p. 139. Charmingly, Captain Nutter brings it downstairs to perpetrate a hoax. Coincidently, this novel appeared in the same year as did Verne's submarine novel.

21. McClintock, 1961, p. 263.

22. Many, such as William Rose Benét, have described this novel as a satire, citing the attitude toward democracy expressed by the underground beings. The minimal humor with which this appears, however, fades before the fact that the attitude suits these beings, who are authoritarians.

23. Lytton, 1979, p. 28.

24. *Ibid.*, p. 43.

25. With his reed, however, Prometheus expressly was aiding humankind. Given the timing of the book's appearance, it seems unlikely that these rods were borrowings from Verne's electrical guns, in *20,000 Leagues*.

26. Bleiler, 1990, p. 93. "In Bulwer's manuscript version of the story the vril had supernatural elements that he later dropped. It was controlled by mesmeric passes, and it permitted communication with the dead."

27. Moorcock, 1976, includes the story.

28. Foley, 1962, pp. 62, 95. Foley notes the international fascination with Frederick the Great. He also notes having found an advertisement for toys in British-occupied New York City, in 1777. "The soldiers were undoubtedly dressed in British uniforms, for Hilpert and his associates had established such a well-organized business that they were making soldiers of many nationalities."

29. *Ibid.*, p. 65–6.

Chapter Nine

1. Holmes, 1872, p. 233.
2. Verne, 1978, p. 7.
3. Twain, 1962, p. 229: "The Turning-Point of My Life," from *What Is Man?*
4. Torrey, 1960, p. 195.
5. Dickens, 1935, pp. 23–4.
6. Verne, 1978, p. 4
7. *Ibid.*, p. 5. Passepartout is "mastered" by the clock—including his own pocket watch. His position might well be called inherited, as is his watch.
8. *Ibid.*, p. 4
9. *Ibid.*, p. 40.
10. *Ibid.*, p. 35
11. *Ibid.*, p. 60
12. *Ibid.*: "mathematically—he used the very word—arranged."
13. *Ibid.*, pp. 66–7; the orbital comparison also appears on p. 35.
14. *Ibid.*, p. 25.
15. *Ibid.*, p. 7. A character in the novel, in checking Fogg's statement about eighty days, lists distances between locations purely in terms of days, which add to eighty.
16. Poe, 1983, p. 731.
17. This element becomes a standard one within wonder stories—as, for instance, in Appleton, 1910, in which Tom Swift falls under suspicion of bank theft thanks to the efforts of the "bully," the boy-novel "imp" type of a non-Poe-esque sort.
18. Verne, 1978, p. 38.
19. *Ibid.*, p. 46.
20. McClintock, 1961, p. 263.
21. United States Centennial Commission, 1876, p. 321: Steiger seems to have been not a manufacturer but a jobber or retailer. Also p. 198: Bourgeois pére offered "colors without poison, for toys." Also p. 33: Education and Science. Also p. 21: "Buildings East of Belmont Avenue, and South of Fountain Avenue."
22. McClintock, 1961, p. 264.
23. Adams, 1931, p. 247.
24. Dickens, 1907, pp. 274–6, 279. Mrs. Smallweed's tendency recurs, on p. 278, when Mr. mentions "fifteen years," and she understands this as, "fifteen hundred pound." The following scene, interestingly, maintains references to play and toys, with Mrs. being a ninepin, the visitor Mr. George, a football, and Mr. Smallweed, a doll.
25. *Youth's Companion*, 1887, Oct. 27, 60:43, pp. 450–1. Youths were being exposed to a variety of stories of history and adventure, as well as fancy, in Frank Stockton's *Round About Rambles*—"Down in the earth, up in the air, through wonderful forests full of beasts strange and wise"—and in Robert Louis Stevenson's *Dr. Jekyll and Mr. Hyde* (pp. 450, 453).
26. Verne, 1978, p. 274. By this time realism had begun settling in regarding the challenges faced by "guidable" screw-propulsion balloons. As Verne amusingly relates, "In large covered halls their success was perfect. In a calm atmosphere they did very well. In a light wind of five or six yards a second they still moved. But nothing practical had been obtained. Against a miller's wind—nine yards a second—the machines had remained almost stationary. Against a fresh breeze—eleven yards a second—they would have advanced backwards. In a storm—twenty-seven to thirty-three yards a second—they would have been blown about like a feather. In a hurricane—sixty yards a second—they would have run the risk of being dashed to pieces. And in one of those cyclones which exceed a hundred yards a second not a fragment of them would have been left" (p. 166).
27. *Ibid.*, pp. 171, 279. On p. 186: "Bourcart, Le Bris, Kaufman, Smyth, Stringfellow, Prigent, Danjard, Pomés and De la Pauze, Moy, Pénaud, Jobert, Haureau de Villeneuve, Achenbach, Garapon, Duchesne, Danduran, Parisel, Dieuaide, Melkisff, Forlanini, Brearey, Tatin, Dandrieux, Edison, some with wings or screws, others with inclined planes, imagined, created, constructed, perfected, their flying machines.... This list may be a little long, but that will be forgiven, for it is necessary to give the various

steps in the ladder of aerial locomotion, on the top of which appeared Robur the Conqueror."

28. *Ibid.*, p. 189.

29. *Ibid.*, p. 194. Poe (1984, p. 878) suggested 150 m.p.h. for his "modern balloons" of "Mellonta Tauta." Verne's literal appropriation of the ocean-going clipper ship may seem more fully a symbolic leap, for some readers, than one made a dozen years later. In 1899, in *A Story of the Days to Come*, Wells presented a "flying-machine" that seems more fanciful than Robur's. Again it evokes a water-going vessel—not a coal-fueled behemoth but something akin to Tennyson's "magic sails": "At first it was a little oblong, faint and blue amidst the distant fleecy clouds; and then it grew swiftly large and white, and larger and whiter, until they could see the separate tiers of sails, each hundreds of feet wide, and the lank body they supported, and at last even the swinging seats of the passengers in a dotted row" (Wells, 1960, p. 199). These masts actually possess sails, for powering and directing the air-buoyant craft, much in the way sails power and direct water-buoyant ones. That Wells's imaginary craft also calls to mind the kite must have seemed natural to his contemporary readers, who probably participated in the then-recent rage for kite-flying and may well have flown kites themselves that had maritime associations, as did at least one with the name Sky-Clipper.

30. Bonner, 1913, p. 202.

31. William Rose Benét identifies Bly's name as coming from the Grundy and Solomon operetta *The Vicar of Bray*, 1882, and notes her having been influenced by Verne's novel. Benét, 1948. *The Reader's Encyclopedia*. New York: Thomas Y. Crowell Co., p. 122.

32. Malloy, 2000, p. 246: illustrated.

33. Joint Committee on Ceremonies, 1893, p. 3. This page shows this image, and also the official emblem, which is a circle with an image of the globe at its center. The American eagle sits atop it, while Columbus is shown directly underneath, as though an Atlas figure.

34. Joint Committee on Ceremonies, 1893, p. 263. W.A. Croffut's poem "The Prophecy" was read at the opening of the World's Columbian Exposition. The fair's proceedings appeared verbatim in newspapers.

35. This shift in roles, from captain-engineer to passenger or sightseer, put in symbolic terms the new life of convenience being held out as the desired end of social achievement. It represents the "divorce of labour from pleasure," in which "there is no continuity, only pastime" (Jaspers, 1958, p. 48). Fogg's character exemplified this with his world-circling games of whist.

36. Information and images for these games: in Malloy, 2000.

37. McClintock, 1961, p. 349.

38. O'Brien, 1990, p. 61.

39. McClintock, 1961, p. 349; *also* O'Brien, 1990, p. 61.

40. O'Brien, 1990, pp. 27, 38, 47.

41. Curiously, Coleridge, whom Poe admired, wrote in a letter: "There are three Suns recorded in Scripture—Joshua's, that stood still; Hezekiah's, that went backwards; and David's that went forth and hastened on his course." Quoted in Holmes, 2010, p. 292; letter written in 1803.

42. Frye, 1963, p. 73: the earlier noted "foreshortening of time."

43. Holmes, 2010, p. 466: quoting Herschel's "Elegy for the Old Forty-Foot," of 1840.

44. Poe, 1983, pp. 1025–6.

Chapter Ten

1. Adams, 1931, p. 465.
2. Stockton, 1892, pp. 1–2.
3. Verne, 1965, p. 35, 37.
4. Standard Oil Co., a business combination of Cleveland oil refineries, was nearing the height of its explosive growth—from 1870, when it was one of 250 refineries in the U.S., with its product comprising four percent of the nation's total, to 1877, when it would control a staggering 95 percent of oil refined in the States. Wealth being concentrated in the hands of the few was emerging as a clear demographic trend after the Civil War. *See* Coman, 1910, pp. 354–7.
5. Verne, 1999, p. 175.
6. Columbian Arts Co., 1891, p. 367.
7. Largest in world: Kouwenhoven, 1938, no. 169.
8. Grant and Emperor: Kouwenhoven, 1938, no. 170. Square footage of buildings: Joint Committee on Ceremonies, 1893, p. 21.
9. Kouwenhoven, 1938, no. 171; *and* Philadelphia, 1876, pp. 20–1, 198.
10. For many manufacturers the shift from human skilled labor to machine labor provided a source of pride. Among the many French exhibitors of clothing and fabric were Bacquet & Co., Boutenjeun, Robert Maxton & Co., J. Gaillard, and E. Davenierè, Jr., all companies of Saint-Pierre-les-Calais making "machine-made laces." In contrast, among the United States manufacturers was the Pawtucket Hair Cloth Co., offering "automatically woven hair cloths for upholstery," while Alex Smith & Sons Carpet Co. offered the products of their "power loom" (Philadelphia, 1876, p. 122). While Kursheedt & Co. of New York offered "embroideries, puffings, plaitings, and flutings, made on patented machines," (*Ibid.*, p. 126) on the whole in the area of fabric and clothing a process was underway in 1876 that would recur in different sectors of manufacturing—which was the replacement of the visibility of automation by its invisibility. Once machine involvement becomes more commonplace, it becomes an understood element, resulting in its going unstated. Other displays featured the imitation pearls and "imitation jewelry" and "imitation stones" being made in Paris. Similarly "imitation of precious stones and fancy cut stones" were offered by C. Cottier & Son of New York, among other "jewelers." A particular innovation for the time was "celluloid jewelry" (*Ibid.*: France, pp. 197–8; America, pp. 126–7; Celluloid Novelty Co., New York, made the "celluloid jewelry.") "Imitation leather" also was present, from H. Loewenberg of Charlottenburg, Germany (*Ibid.*, p. 203). The Canada Truss Factory of Montreal exhibited "artificial limbs," while A.A.

Marks of New York, with its "artificial limbs, india rubber hands and feet" was one of several New York and Philadelphia manufacturers of imitation limbs (*Ibid.*, pp. 135, 190). A variety of manufacturers were offering "artificial teeth," while James T. Davis of New York was offering "artificial human eyes," the offering, too, of L. Müller of Lauscha, Germany (*Ibid.*, p. 136; p. 205: Müller). Abundant mechanical prosthetics must have abounded at the fair, ranging from the everyday to the unusual. Some included the "invalid mechanical chair" by Roy & Co. of Montreal, p. 188; by William Hewett of Philadelphia, the "self-operating swing carriage for parks and lawns," and by H. Fisher of St. Louis, an "automatic swing," p. 114. Buffalo Decorating Co. of Buffalo, N.Y., offered "artificial ivy and autumn leaves," while Mrs. G.H. Smithers of New York offered "wax flowers and figures." From abroad other artificial flora arrived, with Edward Loth of Warsaw showing "basket of artificial flowers," while C.A. Burchardt and W. Boeck, both of Berlin, offered "artificial flowers and plants" and "artificial leaves." The practice may have had longer standing in Paris, whose L. Delivré, Auguste Goigly, Gosse-Perier, and L. Hiélard & Co. offered "artificial flowers" but whose A. Favier offered only "flowers and leaves" (*Ibid.*, p. 128, New York; p. 318, Warsaw; p. 204, Berlin; p. 198, Paris). Undoubtedly some products, too, employed such currently smart words simply for names, or to indicate the manufacturing process rather than the item itself, as in "Dobbins' electric soap," made by I.L. Cragin & Co., Philadelphia (*Ibid.*, p. 103).

11. United States Centennial Commission, 1876, p. 334; McClintock, 1961, 244 (a photo showing the "Songster" and its package); O'Brien, 1990, p. 38.

12. McClintock, 1961, pp. 287–8.

13. United States Centennial Commission, p. 129. "Recording banks" automatically tallied deposits. The company that seems to have been W.C. Goodwin's successor, C.D. Goodwin & Company, located at 70 Asylum Street, New Haven, in a 1900 directory, was listed as a specialist in mechanical toys.

Alongside other growing cities on the Connecticut coastline, New Haven would prove to be a minor toy-making center. A quarter-century after the Philadelphia Exposition, C.D. Goodwin would have a near neighbor in the New Haven Toy and Game Company, at 56 Brewster. Northeast along the coast was New London, with a toymaker named D.S. Merritt at 32 Williams. Southwest along the coast was Bridgeport, where the three toymaking companies were still thriving: C.F. Braitling & Sons, Columbia Instruction Company, and Ives. Yet farther to the southwest was South Norwalk, with the toymakers Austin & Craw.

14. McClintock, 1961, p. 287.

15. United States Centennial Commission, 1876, pp. 128–9.

16. *Ibid.*, pp. 198, 344–5.

17. *Ibid.*, 1876, p. 198; Cohumer & Collet also exhibited "children's and dolls' furniture." Likely other automata drew visitors to booths featuring items made by A. Dehors, Faivre, F. Jumeau, A. Loiseau, Maltète, and Radiguet. All these were Parisian.

18. *Ibid.*, p. 205, 349. From Nuremberg, in the "Bavarian Collective Exhibit of Toys and Small Wares," were G.J. Pabst, W. Hinrichsen, G.L. Eichner & Son, J.A. Issmayer, J. Norrmann, G. Helmbrecht, E. Schleuerpflug, J. Stief, Thomas Miller, J.P. Strobel, C. Baudenbacher, A. Kithil, L. Uebelacker, Mathew Hess, Schlenk & Lutzenberger, Gottfried Probst, Gebhard Ott, J. Schlegel, H. Sichling, and E. Plank. From Fürth, Gottlieb Hahn, Ziegele & Hauck, and Conrad Keller. From Erlangen, J.G. Fischer. From Bayreuth, Bettman & Kupfer and J.F.E. Stolze. Having individual exhibits were Cuno Dressel & Otto Sonneberg of Thuringia, with toys, dolls and slates; L. Schunemann of Magdeburg, with dolls; and J.D. Oehme & Sons of Grunhainichen, with toys. Other toys and related items would have appeared in the collective exhibits of "Nuremberg Mathematical Instrument Manufacturers" and "Black Forest Clock Manufacturers."

19. *Ibid.*, p. 355. Those offering "musical boxes" were Adank J. Jaques & Co., B.A. Brémond, Karrer & Co., and C. Paillard & Co.

20. McClintock, 1961, pp. 297–8, 336. The firm was originally Mason & Converse, until around 1883.

21. United States Centennial Commission, 1876, p. 205, Leipzig; p. 198, Paris. Brodin was grouped with other toy makers in the "Fancy Articles" area, not with makers of scientific instruments. Machinery Hall: p. 41.

22. Barlow, 1998, p. 60.

23. Malloy, 2000, p. 265.

24. United States Centennial Commission, 1876, p. 36.

25. *Ibid.*, pp. 321, 329, 343, 348.

26. *Ibid.*, p. 330. "Phantasmagoria:" John H. Schenck of New York, N.Y.

27. Adams, 1931, p. 330.

28. United States Centennial Commission, 1876, pp. 331–2.

29. Barraclough, 1967, pp. 64–5. "There was, without doubt, something febrile and inherently unstable about the 'gaudy empires spatchcocked together' in this way at this time .... It was nevertheless a stupendous movement, without parallel in history, which completely changed the shape of things to come." The movement would seem to have had firm roots in the 1700s. England, for instance, exerted itself to keep power looms and spinning jennies from being sent to America, in order to maintain its market there for finished goods, and to minimize the chances of the new U.S. becoming a competitor in the new mode of factory production. *See* Wright, 1895, p. 54 and elsewhere.

30. Barraclough, 1967, pp. 61–2, notes, "In 1876 not more than one-tenth of Africa was controlled by European powers ... by 1900 nine-tenths of the continent had been brought under European control."

31. *Ibid.*, p. 65.

32. Tennyson: "Locksley Hall" and "Locksley Hall Sixty Years After."

33. Verne symbolically links St. Louis's tomb and the volcano: for Servadac and his companions spot each from across darkened waters by their distant fire-gleams.

34. Knight, 1962, p. 23. The story appeared in Bierce's 1893 collection, *Can Such Things Be?*

35. McClintock, p. 341; illustrated pp. 300–1. The doll was priced $20 dressed; p. 343.

36. Described *in* Bleiler, 1990, p. 267.

37. McClintock, p. 246, shows an early version.

38. McClintock, pp. 248–9.

39. Villiers, 1982, p. xiv.

40. *Ibid.*, pp. x, xv.

41. Bleiler, E.F., 1989, p. 107.

42. Bleiler, 1990, pp. 615–7; *also* Clute and Nichols, 1993, p. 993: "Reade, Philip," by Everett F. Bleiler. *Electric Man* began as a serial in issue no. 588 of *The Boys of New York*, in November 1886.

43. Bleiler, 1990, pp. 547–8. Senarens's *The Steam Man of the Plains; or, the Terror of the West*, appeared in *The Boys of New York*, 28. Feb. to 24 April 1876. Dime novels were finding abundant outlets in weeklies. Ellis's *Steam Man of the Prairies*, retitled *The Huge Hunter*, had its reappearance near the beginning of this publishing trend. Through the late 1870s, the 1880s, and into the '90s, magazines including *The Nugget*, *Good News*, and *Frank Reade Library* offered wonder tales as regular features—exclusively so, in the last title. For more mature readers, the Frank. A. Munsey juvenile magazine *The Golden Argosy*, established in 1882, became *The Argosy* in 1888—with monthly issues averaging 135,000 words of adventure fiction (270). Under that and variant titles, it would prove the longest-lasting magazine to feature tales relating to New Worlds idealism. Although *Frank Reade* focused exclusively on boys'-technical-invention stories, *Argosy* published a full range of more mature tales that would lead to its being considered the first "pulp" magazine. *Argosy* and sister publication *All-Story* played a crucial role in making wonder tales typical fare for general readers in those middle years of the Modern—with their authors by the middle years including Howard R. Garis, George Griffith, and Garrett P. Serviss; and, later, Murray Leinster, Edgar Rice Burroughs, Ray Cummings, Ralph Milne Farley, Otis Adelbert Kline, and Abraham Merritt.

44. McClintock, 1961, p. 345. This practice may have started at or around the same time in toy-book publishing. An 1890 account, quoted in Freeman, 1942, p. 277, notes them being "done by children in their teens ... They sat around a table, each with a little pan of water-color, a partly colored copy as a guide, and a pile of printed sheets. One child would paint on the red, wherever it appeared on the copy, another followed, say with the yellow, and so on until the coloring was finished."

45. Facts concerning technological and scientific discoveries came into play as early as 1810, in English game Historical Pastimes, by John Harris. *See* Goodfellow, p. 32.

46. Foley, 1962, p. 86.

47. McClintock, 1961, p. 196. The headline "A New American Device for the Propaganda [*sic*] of Insanity in Great Britain" appeared in the *New York Herald*, when reprinting a story from London in May 1889.

48. Selchow & Righter, toymaker and jobber, represented Waverly Toy Works, and early after the game's release found it possible to meet local demand partially, and distant demand, barely. The McClintocks, 1961, discuss the Pigs in Clover phenomenon pp. 193–7, with illustrations pp. 116–7.

49. McClintock, 1961, p. 338–9. The company also made "tool chests, musical chimes, toy pianos, building blocks, toy animals (not only for Noah's Ark but for a railroad stock car), stilts, railroad trains with stations and villages, trolley cars, automobiles, and boats."

50. Dalrymple, 1991, pp. 128–9. An illustration shows a variety of early action books, including a *Robinson Crusoe*. Publication notes on abridged versions for children, published by Newbery (London) and Hugh Gaine (New York), appear *in* Targ, 1957, p. 150.

51. Dalrymple, 1991, p. 128.

Chapter Eleven

1. Joint Committee on Ceremonies, 1893, p. 206. At the inauguration of the Congress Auxiliary of the World's Columbian Exposition, 1893.

2. Baum, 1950s, pp. 147–8.

3. Bruce, 1987, p. 340, notes: "*The Journal of the Franklin Institute* observed in June 1876 that anyone with a smattering of science could understand the specimens of technology at the Crystal Palace of 1851, but that such matters had since become too complex for the average fairgoer to fathom."

4. *Ibid.*

5. Columbian Art Co., 1891, photograph opposite p. 197; on p. 56, a note that Washington Park was "far ahead" of other parks in its "flower plots and foliage painting." The city also had a new newspaper, the Chicago *Daily Globe*, which had been in operation since 1887. See *Ibid..*, p. 198.

6. *Ibid.*, pp. 202, 176.

7. Verne, 1965, p. 37.

8. Joint Committee on Ceremonies, 1893, pp. 8, 53. Cristobal Colon, the Duke of Veragua and a familial descendent of Columbus, appeared, and announced that the new "great Exhibition ... must serve to unite more closely the inhabitants of both Hemispheres by way of Commerce."

9. *Ibid.*, pp. 19–20.

10. Poe, 1984, p. 882. The narrator in "Mellonta Tauta" is looking back on Manhattan from the far future: "The entire area ... was, about eight hundred years ago, densely packed with houses, some of them twenty stories high; land (for some most unaccountable reason) being considered as especially precious just in this vicinity."

11. Columbian Arts Co., 1891, pp. 312–3. The description reads much like a wonder story, especially in its geographical elements, its touch of "orthodoxy," and its final sense of waking:

> There will be, a few feet above the street level, a handsome building which is to be the entrance to the caverns underneath, and also a café fitted with tables and fountains for soda and mineral waters. An eleva-

tor fitted with tiers of opera chairs, arranged as in a theater, and giving accommodations to one hundred persons, will connect the upper and lower regions. There will be a solid concrete or granite shaft about the elevator extending downward.

The visitors to the underground theater are to be given checks for seats in the huge elevator-car, and at stated intervals the door of the car will be closed and the elevator set in motion. It will shoot down past the gray rocks until it has reached a depth of 200 feet, where a stop will be made before the mouth of a huge cavern, and there before the eyes of the audience will be shown a coal-mine extending hundreds of feet away with dozens of miners working with pick and shovel by the light of miners' lamps worn on the hats. During the time the car is stopped a mine will be exploded and tons of coal thrown out by the force of the dynamite.

After full time has been given for seeing the practical workings of the coal-mine the elevator will again go on its downward trip. Another 200 feet and a second cavern will be shown, and as the car stops before the mouth there will be seen a view of snow-fields and icebergs, with fur-clothed Esquimaux in ice-sledges and others spearing walruses and seals. The bright glow of the aurora borealis will sweep up the northern heavens and the spectators will have a view of that wonder of the polar regions. Then 200 feet more descent, while the shaft above the car grows smaller and smaller until there is but a patch of light to mark where Chicago and its smoke are, and another cave will stretch out into the earth.

The third cave is to be a direct concession to Dr. Patton and his orthodoxy. It will be a scene from Dante's Inferno, and the gates of adamant and solid brass will be thrown wide open on invitation. There before the pools of burning sulphur, waiting for the sinners who died unrepentant, will be Mephistopheles and the smaller satans, attended by imps of darkness in fantastic red. It will be orthodox enough to suit the most orthodox.

The fourth stop, 200 feet below the last-named and 800 feet beneath the granite pavements of Chicago streets, there will be a cavern representing a submarine view. A sunken ship will be shown stranded on a coral bed and about it will be divers working in complete divers' suits. Fishes of all sorts will swim about before the entrance to the cave.

Just one more drop of 200 feet and the elevator will stop before a cavern 1,000 (feet) underground. It will be a cavern of dazzling brilliancy, with stalactites and stalagmites reflecting the light of hundreds of electric lights in globes of various colors. This will be the last stop, and here the passengers will alight and the elevator will start on its upward trip. At the tables, with which the cave is to be liberally provided, ice cream and cakes and various other refreshments will be served. The idea is to have the waiters and other attendants in costumes fitting the surroundings and indicating the great depth to which the visitor has been carried.

After those who have made the long descent have seen sufficient of the glories of the cavern and are ready to get up to earth again, they will be shown into a dimly lighted passage, two big folding-doors will suddenly fly open, and through the blinding flood of light that flows in will be seen passing teams and street-cars, and if all is quiet in the neighborhood a policeman may be seen standing on a street corner.

Instead of descending hundreds of feet into the earth the car containing the audience of one hundred persons has in reality gone down a distance of only ten feet and the lowest cavern is say five feet below the level of the street.

12. Columbian Arts Co., 1891, p. 313.
13. Handy, 1893, p. 195; *and* Joint Committee on Ceremonies, 1893, p. 42.
14. Handy, 1893, p. 195. Admission to panorama buildings was fifty cents—twice the cost of the Electric Scenic Theatre; *also* Joint Committee on Ceremonies, 1893, p. 43.
15. Columbian Art Co., 1891, *also* Banks, 1893, pp. 122, 128, 124. The Gettysburg panorama was executed in the original manner, to surround the viewer: "From a central elevation you view the contending armies in the full heat of strife." There was in Chicago a "Panorama of Niagara Falls" as late as 1891. *See* Columbian Art Co., 1891, p. 128; Banks, 1893, p. 128: "Situated at the corner of Wabash Avenue and Hubbard Court. This is the monster painting that had such a successful run in London, England, coming straight to this city from there. It was painted by the celebrated French artist, Paul Philippoteaux. It is fifty feet in height and 410 feet in circumference, while four tons of paint are spread on the canvas." In the same volume, however, the word is used in such a way that indicates a different kind of meaning-drift. On p. 56: "entrances to the park are gorgeous panoramas of tempered light, shifting shade and artistic blending of form and color." The phrase "monster painting" suggests how near "monster" remained to its source meaning, in being equivalent to "spectacular."
16. Joint Committee on Ceremonies, 1893, p. 41.
17. Columbian Arts Co., 1891, p. 313.
18. Joint Committee on Ceremonies, 1893, p. 259: "Opening the Exposition. The Ceremonies on May 1st, when President Cleveland Started the Machinery."
19. *Ibid.*, p. 261: "telegraphic key." On p. 266: "gold and ivory button." On p. 265: "and when you touch this magic key the ponderous machinery will start in its revolution."
20. *Ibid.*, p. 263. The sense of magic, of course, confirmed the widening gap between technological achievement and the public's ability to fathom it.
21. Columbian Art Co., 1891, p. 317.
22. Handy, 1893, p. 197.
23. Joint Committee on Ceremonies, 1893, p. 264, mentioning the selection. Wagner based his 1841 opera on the 1835 historical romance, *Rienzi, the Last of the Tribunes*, by Bulwer-Lytton.
24. Columbian Art Co., 1891, pp. 295–6, 314. *Also* Banks, 1893, p. 258: "In the matter of electric lighting, the World's Fair itself will be a great exhibition

ground." The court came to be called the Court of Honor.

25. Columbian Art Co., 1891, p. 295.
26. Smith, 1894, p. 5.
27. Banks, 1893, pp. 254–5.
28. Burnham, 1894, p. 179: "the glories of the Horticultural treasure house, surmounted by its illuminated crystal dome."
29. Handy, 1893, p. 196.
30. Columbian Art Co., 1891, p. 317; Handy, 1893, p. 196. The silent efficiency of these launches made a strong impression, as in Burnham, 1894, p. 179: "What wonder that a noiseless boat came gliding to his feet in answer to his wish to explore these distant, fairy vistas;" or p. 203: "electric launches passing and repassing silently and smoothly over the changing waves." This enhanced the dream-journey impression.
31. Handy, 1893, p. 196.
32. Joint Committee on Ceremonies, 1893, p. 59.
33. Ibid., p. 60.
34. Banks, 1893, p. 282.
35. Schwartz, 2009, pp. 100–1. In 1884 the Prohibition Party fielded for its presidential candidate John St. John, the governor who had succeeded in passing a prohibition amendment to the Kansas state constitution. St. John proved so effective a campaigner that his religious-based candidacy proved a spoiler for Republican hopes, helping Grover Cleveland into office. As Schwartz notes, "St. John received almost 150,000 votes, meaning the religious right effectively held sway over presidential politics for the very first time."
36. Smith, 1894, p. 6. The cultural relativism being promoted at the Anthropology building and Midway displays could have been understood as being in opposition to the idea of the ascendance of Christian belief. Ironically, many Midway performers were happy to perform for payment in "Chicago beer." Various sources note this. In Burnham, 1894, p. 239, one character says, "I gave him a dime or so to repeat the performance a sufficient number of times, and he was delighted, and kept saying 'Chicago beer.'" To this, another replies, "Yes ... They have to come to a Christian land for that." For these, perhaps, being "Chicagoed" had specific meaning. Exposition planners extended their appeal to rationality to religion, and scheduled a Parliament of Religions, which included not only such faiths as Catholicism, Judaism, Islam, Buddhism, Hinduism, and Protestant denominations, but also Theosophy. The idea of a unified or "world religion" would become anathema to fundamentalist Christians. For those interested in what Van Wyck Brooks would term "planetary mind" and Karl Jaspers would call "epochal consciousness," however, this seemed a pivotal event.
37. Smith, 1894, p. 17.
38. Banks, 1893, p. 243. Banks was given to this sort of phrasing, as on p. 279 he writes of the Fisheries Building having "the lilt and lightness of a fairy palace."
39. Joint Committee on Ceremonies, 1893, pp. 192–3. Also Handy, 1893, p. 196, where the name Vertical Revolving Wheel appears. Later in the book Ferris Wheel does appear. In Burnham's *Sweet Clover*, both Wheel and Ferris Wheel are used by characters.
40. Schwartz, 2009, pp. 229, 346.
41. Banks, 1893, p. 263.
42. Handy, 1893, p. 195.
43. Ibid., p. 196.
44. Stirn, 1990, pp. 65, 66. The balls measured 3½, 5, and 7 inches.
45. Columbian Art Co., 1891, pp. 330–1.
46. Handy, 1893.
47. Ibid., p. 254. At least two Canadian manufacturers exhibited: Edward Williams of Kentrille, Nova Scotia, showed checkerboards; J.A. Whelply & Co., unspecified toys.
48. Handy, 1893.
49. Stirn, 1990, p. 52. Manufacturer undiscovered.
50. Ibid., p. 76.
51. Ibid., pp. 52, 69 (trolley, 28-inch length), 80–1. On p. 88, Stirn shows Parker Brothers' World's Fair Game"and R. Bliss Mfg. Co.'s Game of the World's Columbian Exposition; and on p. 77, Columbian Base Ball Game. Molloy, 2000, p. 446, shows Chicago and the World's Columbian Exposition game by E.M. McLean.
52. Stirn, 1990, pp. 53, 58: mechanical toys. Columbia toys: pp. 60, 63, 71. As to the Columbus bank: "Place a coin in the slot at the feet of Columbus. Press the lever, and as the coin disappears an Indian chief suddenly leaps from his place of concealment in the log, extending the pipe of peace as Columbus salutes him." The Pig and Columbus Egg Bell Toy featured a pig in top hat and coat, with a "Chicago" banner around his middle. When the toy rolled forward, the pig attempted to upend the Columbus Egg at his front hooves, with the effort ringing a bell.
53. Enough so to apparently offer income to writers. "He might do as a great many modern writers do ... go in for the Paper-doll Drama. Cut the whole thing out with a pair of scissors." A fictional Artemis Ward says this, in Bangs, 1897, pp. 108–9.
54. Columbian Art Co., 1891, pp. 406, 410.
55. Stirn, 1990, p. 94.
56. Ibid., p. 92, 96–7.
57. Burnham, 1894, pp. 179, 181–2, 185, 215, 397–8.
58. Ibid., pp. 310, 245. Apparently the latter phrase had some currency. Burnham has a character qualify it: "'Barnumizing the Fair,' as they call it."
59. Ibid., p. 296. The phrase "arc-light moons" also appears, p. 183. Its earthly element was its encapsulation of travel around the globe, the Midway being, on p. 268, "the magic carpet in the Arabian Nights which transported its owner from one country to another."
60. Ibid., p. 206. Spoken by the character Gorham Page, in reference to the "wonderful" long-distance telephone.
61. Ibid., pp. 201, 263, 266. The phrase "gigantic steel web" in reference to the Wheel would have its echo much later in the Karl Jaspers phrase "titanic interlocking wheelwork," used in relation to humans becoming "little more than a part of the machinery."
62. Ibid., p. 137.

63. *Ibid.*, p. 154.
64. *Ibid.*, p. 201. Lovina Berry is often called Aunt Love. Her nickname is pertinent to the Galatea theme of the novel, as well as to the tale's romance nature. This passage also points in a wonder-tale direction, in its description of the Fair in terms of the divided soul.
65. *Ibid.*, p. 184–6. The speaker is again Van Tassel, as in the Galatea observation. He observes, pp. 184–5: "At the same moment the search light which had been upon the Quadriga sped to the angel above the pediment of the Agricultural Building. So light her poise, so strong her wings, so beneficent her outstretched arms, it seemed impossible in that mystical irradiation that she should not quit her lightly touched support and float downward to waiting mortals."
66. *Ibid.*, pp. 210, 225. On the former page she reflects on the "strange scenes in the miniature world" of the electric hatchery, and imagines the young chickens being produced as saying, "Who cares for mother now?" The fair offered other views of automation in motherhood, as in the display by Automatic Cradle Co. of Stevens Point, Wisconsin.
67. *Ibid.*, pp. 292, 376, elsewhere.
68. *Ibid.*, p. 351. The attraction of the Cadets to Fair-goers is mentioned several times, called "such a fad" on p. 356, and "cadet fever" on p. 360.
69. *Ibid.*, pp. 358–9.
70. *Ibid.*, p. 395: "Aunt Love was one of thousands whose complacent generalization of 'the heathen' received a blow." The East is represented in the life of Mildred Bryant by "a handsome coffee-colored Indian, who ... talked transcendental philosophy in the purest English."
71. *Ibid.*, pp. 188, 205.
72. *Ibid.*, pp. 204, 265.
73. *Ibid.*, pp. 201, 270–1, 279.
74. *Ibid.*, pp. 271, 282.
75. *Ibid.*, 1894, pp. 398, 402; the January 8 fire, pp. 405–10. To further bring an end to the matter, Chicago in 1894 lost much of its post-Exposition glow when brought to a standstill by the largest workers strike yet to hit U.S. industry. The strike began against one of the emblematic companies associated with Chicago and the Fair, Pullman's Palace Car Company. As had the Exposition, the strike's repercussions traveled around the nation. *See* Wright, 1895, pp. 313–7.
76. Loncraine, 2009, pp. 64, 86.
77. *Ibid.*, pp. 94–5.
78. *Ibid.*, pp. 166, 169.
79. Schwartz, 2009, p. 294.
80. Burnham, 1894, p. 311. Burnham's use of "king of the forest" suggests the phrase appeared in Hagenbeck's show-patter.
81. Baum's story for children, in other words, embodied the thought that just as emotions are to be found naturally within oneself, the senses of strength and direction are to be found, as well. The book gives expression, in a fanciful way, to the American myth of the "self-made man." In Greek, αυτοπαγης, or "autopages," meant self-made man: yet it also meant "cohering together" or "cohesive."

Baum's great American fairy tale proves to be a fable of self-realization.
82. Loncraine, 2009, p. 207.
83. *Ibid.*, p. 232.
84. Boston, 1900, pp. 1907, 1092, and 1374.
85. As an interesting side note, at the time of MGM's release of its film version of the Oz story, the mechanical-man aspect was recognized. At the gala launching of the film, the large, silver-clad figure on whose knee Edgar Bergen sat, hamming it up and pretending to be the metal being's ventriloquist dummy, was billed as the "robot," using the term that had become widely current by the late 1930s.
86. Baum, 1994, p. 73.
87. Baum was a Poe reader. Loncraine, 2009, p. 180.

Chapter Twelve

1. In "The Moon." Stevenson, 1916, p. 47.
2. Carroll, undated, p. 481.
3. Adams, 1931, p. 382. Power equipment proved to have an irresistible drawing force from the beginning of the international exhibitions. *From* Hobhouse, 1950, p. 72: "Steam ... There seemed no limits to its power. So that the huge oscillating masses of iron in the northern aisle drew greater crowds than all the treasures of the courts of fine arts."
4. A toy such as the 1922 Boys' Toy Watch and Chain ("Beautifully finished to imitate a gold watch. Real glass crystal. ... Merely turn stem and hands go round while watch ticks." In Spero, 1988, p. 33) would have especial power, having a motion that necessarily veered from "real" time, and that even so "worked." A stimulated imagination, in fact, meant the toy was "working."
5. Carrol, undated, pp. 456–7. All watches, as philosophic toys, could inspire such imaginings—especially when stopped or nonworking. Toy watches offered ever more spurs to the imagination, since the imagination was required for their "operation."
6. Wells, 1960, p. 270.
7. *Ibid.*, p. 314.
8. *Ibid.*, p. 313–4.
9. *Ibid.*, p. 322.
10. Torrey, 1960, p. 125.
11. Wollheim, 1948, pp. 8–9.
12. *Ibid.*, p. 9.
13. Poe, 1983, p. 137.
14. Poe, 1984, p. 192; Wollheim, 1948, pp. 144–5.
15. Baum, 1987, p. 115.
16. As in the 1792 *Description of the Geographical Clock*, noted in Chapter One; or in 1885 verse "The Sun Travels," in Stevenson's *A Child's Garden of Verses*.
17. Poe, 1983, pp. 141–2. Story printings after the first capitalized the word "eternity," which may have altered the word's context from physical philosophy to religious, for contemporary readers.
18. Wollheim, 1948, p. 143
19. *Ibid.*, pp. 205–6.
20. Wells, 1960, pp. 208–9.
21. *Ibid.*, p. 209.

22. *Ibid.*, p. 200.

23. Wingfield Stratford, quoted *in* Thomson, 1950, pp. 205–6.

24. Society denies the successful, conquering individual both his truthfulness and his ability to affect society's course. Conformity alone has impact, in this vision of the world. Poe's old man, isolated on his pinnacle of understanding and remembered ability, is the character of alienation, cut off from his own productive ability as effectively as would be the suffering souls perceived by Marx a few decades later, or by Sartre in the next century.

25. Markham helped deepen the national conversation about social consciousness by means of that smallest of social irritants, a poem. While a relatively minor work, his "The Man and the Hoe," inspired by a painting by Millet, changed minds and thereby society.

Chapter Thirteen

1. From "Clarel." F.O. Matthiesen, ed., 1950. *The Oxford Book of American Verse.* New York: Oxford University Press, p. 403.

2. Baum, 1911, p. 11.

3. Brooks, 1957, pp. 63–4.

4. Garis's characters include a black named Eradicate, who makes regular appearances in the Tom Swift novels. While still relying upon stereotypes, Garis seemed to distinguish between stage depictions of racial types and the types themselves, and avoided deploying the more pronounced, dismissive racism apparent in some books by other boys-novel writers. In other words, in these books he relies more upon the role-playing of the theatrical stock-character than upon racial stereotyping. This applies as much to "white" characters in Garis, as to those otherwise tinted. *See* Chapter Fourteen.

5. Hackett, 1945, pp. 12–3, 17. Bangs's *A House-Boat on the Styx*, 1896, and *The Pursuit of the House-Boat*, 1897; Barrie's *Sentimental Tommy*, 1896, and *Margaret Ogilvy* and again *Sentimental Tommy* in 1897.

6. Hackett, 1945, p. 21. She also notes C.N. and A.M. Williamson as specializing in "automobile romances."

7. Baum, 1997a, pp. 55–6, 147.

8. Bleiler, 1990, p. 265.

9. *Ibid.*, pp. 265–6.

10. Reynolds, 1916, p. 76.

11. Mumford, 1973, p. 358; *also* Mumford, 1970, p. 232.

12. Mumford, 1973, p. 353. On 352: "If any mind exhibited sensitive intellectual tentacles capable of probing the future, as radar probes space for signs of an oncoming body, it was the mind of Adams."

13. Frederick, 1940, p. 58.

14. Adams, 1931, p. 381.

15. Frederick, 1940, p. 56. In the popular mind, Mars remained the planet of the God of War, as in the sheet music for a "march and two step" named "A Signal from Mars" by E.T. Paull, published in 1911.

16. From "On a Tree Fallen Across the Road," which first appeared in 1923 volume *New Hampshire*. Its original composition might have arisen much prior, given its cutter-sled.

17. Thomson, 1950, pp. 187–8.

18. Burroughs, 1921, pp. 224–5. The passage has interest, too, for its awkwardly tumbling-forward sentences. They have the grace of being easily absorbed by the quickly reading eye, even if they lack the grace of correct structure. Conceivably Burroughs would have exerted less influence had he written "correct" sentences that might have slowed the story, or lessened its impact. Burroughs at this point enjoyed such extreme popularity as a novelist that likely he knew better than to meddle much with the basic materials and tools that had brought him success. Van Wyck Brooks, among others, has also noted how often great novels have been borne along by hasty writing.

19. Bleiler, 1990, gives first publication dates for this trio of novels and several other relevant ones: *Under the Moons of Mars*, as by Norman Bean, in *All-Story*, February-July 1912; *Tarzan of the Apes: All-Story*, October, 1912; *The Cave Girl*, *All-Story*, July-September, 1913; *The Eternal Lover*, in *All-Story*, March 7, 1914; *At the Earth's Core*, in *All-Story*, April 4–25, 1914; *Pellucidar*, in *All-Story-Cavalier*, May 1–29, 1915; *The Land That Time Forgot*, in *Blue Book*, August, 1918; *The People That Time Forgot*, in *Blue Book*, October, 1918; *Out of Time's Abyss*, in *Blue Book*, December, 1918; *Tarzan the Terrible*, in *Argosy-All-Story*, February 12 to March 26, 1921; *Tanar of Pellucidar*, in *Blue Book*, March-August, 1929; *Tarzan at the Earth's Core*, in *Blue Book*, September-March, 1929–30.

20. Reynolds, 1916, p. 75.

21. Adams, 1931, p. 493.

22. Reynolds, 1916, p. 75.

23. Barrier, 1999, p. 10.

24. *Ibid.*, p. 10: "the first American animator of consequence." Barrier notes Fisher's activity along the same lines. McCay also enjoyed success in the toy world. Early toys included cast-iron bell toys and Schoenhut roly-poly dolls. That E.I. Horsman's initiative with a Little Nemo doll was not out of the ordinary, another firm established by following suit. Strobel & Wilken Company began with dolls in 1864, the year before Horsman started in the business. Although established in Cincinnati, in 1882 it moved to the doll-making capitol of the country, New York City (McClintock, 1961, p. 349). There, Strobel & Wilken pursued the trade as a major doll distributor and apparently also manufacturer, although, like Ives before it, the company may simply have ordered dolls under its own name to be produced by other firms whose sole focus was on manufacturing. Around 1913 it produced a series of McCay dolls: Nemo, Flip, Imp, Primus and Dr. Pill (O'Brien, 1990, p. 61).

25. O'Brien, 1990, pp. 59–61, discusses the phenomenon.

26. Barlow, 1998, p. 136: reproduction page from Sears, Roebuck & Co., 1911.

27. Malloy, 2000, pp. 253–4: illustrated.

28. England, George Allan, 1926, February 25. *Lost from the Fleet*, "III. Away from the Ship." *The Youth's Companion* 100:8, p. 153.

29. Mace, 1907, p. 101.
30. Fraser, 1996, p. 195: "Obviously among mechanical toys at that period, aeroplanes had the same position then as space toys do now ... The aeroplane was definitely a toy which pointed towards the future."
31. *Ibid.*, p. 195, for both; also McClintock, 1961, 370. The latter toy was fastened to a string, to fly circles around the child—with that circle-of-flight design to become one of the typical ones for airplane toys for decades.
32. Barlow, 1998, p. 135: Sears, Roebuck & Co., 1911. Some flexibility in terms does occur. While the category is "Airships and Flying Machines," the "famous new model Biplane" appears under the title, "A Real Airship for $1.65." For point of reference, in 1911, new novels were typically priced less, around $1.30, and reprints, sometimes fifty cents (Hackett, 1945, p. 27). In other words, these foot-long toys ranked alongside the fancier toy automobiles and steam engines, and cost more than some adult diversions.
33. McClintock, 1961, p. 371. Baker made the Lee Toy Aeroplane. Nice was in Minneapolis; American, in New York City.
34. Moreland drew the pictures for Rueckheim Brothers & Epstein, a confection manufacturer that was following the initiative of fellow confection-maker Shotwell Manufacturing Company of Chicago, the maker of a popcorn treat called Checkers. Shotwell's packages included prizes as an incentive to buyers. Moreland's 1907 drawings appeared on two series of postcards to be obtained by sending to the company the cut-off box-sides from the popcorn-and-peanut confection. *See* White, 1997, p. 13.
35. Garis, 1910, p. 16; 1911, p. 4.
36. Young, 1911, p. 5.
37. Davidson, 1912, pp. 23, 37.
38. The British writer of wonder tales, Francis Harry Atkins, described an egg-shaped interplanetary craft in his 1909 *A Trip to Mars*, which Atkins called an "aerostat," although it sped between planets. *See* Bleiler, 1990, p. 23. Atkins wrote under the name Fenton Ash.
39. Barlow, 1998, p. 143: Sears, Roebuck page from 1914.
40. Dalrymple, 1991, pp. 96–7. The toymaker also produced dirigibles and the Zeppelin, issuing a great many of them with the markings "EPL I" or "EPL II," with "Lehmann" also in large letters—the flagships of the Lehmann aerial fleet. These metal toys, in several sizes, the child was to suspend on a string and then activate. A large, rear, celluloid propeller sent the ship forward—which meant in circles (King, 1989, p. 45). Unlike many other Lehmann toys, these were made without whimsical elements, and without unusual colors.
41. Bertoia, 1997, Oct. 10, p. 92, shows a selection of toy aircraft by Lehmann. The Mars and Jupiter balloons were apparently matched with another with Luna upon it, to judge from a Lehmann box shown here. These hot-air balloons had ropes that dropped down from the gondola; and at least the one box was marked "fesselballon," or captive balloon, meaning that they were balloons of the observational or signal sort—while evoking planets, at the same time.

Chapter Fourteen

1. Poe, 1984, p. 873: "Mellonta Tauta."
2. Bangs, 1923, pp. 146–47. "Iguanadon" is the book's spelling.
3. Bailey, 1919, p. 12–3.
4. O'Brien, 1990, p. 82.
5. That Austin Hall drew upon similar word-associations seems possible, for his "Dr. Robold" of 1919. In a style that seems somewhat influenced by telegraphy, Hall describes this character: "If it was not destiny, it was at least an accumulation of moment. In the heavy eye-glasses, the square, close-cut beard; and his uncompromising fact-seeking expression. Those who knew Dr. Robold are strong in the affirmation that he was the antithesis of all emotion. He was the sternest product of science: unbending, hardened by experiment, and caustic toward the frailness of human nature" (Hall, 1940, February, p. 8).
6. In 1923, E.V. Odle's *The Clockwork Man* featured a man from the future who was partly mechanical. *See* Bleiler, 1990, pp. 570–1.
7. Spengler, 1932, pp. 30–1.
8. Poe, 1984, p. 878.
9. Wollheim, 1948, p. 206.
10. *Ibid.*, p. 206.
11. Pascall, 1977, p. 14: the 1919 film *The Ghost of Slumber Mountain* "included many shots of prehistoric beasts. ... it enjoyed considerable financial and critical success."
12. *Ibid.*, p. 15. On p. 18: "it has been reported that for ... *The Lost World* every minute of animation that appeared on the screen required 960 separate movements of one or more models and he was lucky if 10 hours of work yielded 30 seconds of film."
13. *Ibid.*, p. 18.
14. Burnham, 1894, p. 271: "the rise and fall of the Sleeping Beauty's gentle breast was a marvel."
15. Conservative religious publishers, at least when the present author was a child in the 1960s, in pamphlets would hail the discovery of fossils that showed human footprints alongside a dinosaur's. The promotion of human-footprint fossils dated to 1822. The Rev. Frederick Rapp, head of the Harmonites sect, displayed a limestone slab found on the Mississippi banks at St. Louis. The geologist Henry Schoolcraft described the slab, and regarded the prints as authentic. By 1842, geologists largely discredited the find, and attributed it to aboriginal carving. (*See* Merrill, 1924, pp. 88–90.) Pointing to a folk-art origin rather than hoax may have been generous, on their part.
16. Tennessee law prohibited public-school teaching of theories contrary to the accepted interpretation of the biblical account of man's creation, in March 1925. John T. Scopes was tried in July 1925 for teaching Darwinian theory in a Dayton, Tenn., public school.
17. On the underside they bore identifications as

to type, such as "Brazilian Beetle." On the underside, too, children found a single, small wooden wheel. Drawing the toy backwards on a flat surface wound tight the hidden spring. The beetle then crawled forward, and because of its central wheel and rounded contour it tended to "crawl around" obstacles. Animate Toy included a "stunt circular" telling of "clever tricks" with these toys. It also sold them with game boards and game boxes, so that these "clever" beetles with their "slow, almost weird motion" became the players in such games as Bugatelle, Woozy Bug, Humbug, and Soccerbug. See Spero, 1988, p. 3, 11, and other pages. The games were grouped and packaged together under Bugville Games. Shufflebug was another, separately packaged game. The beetles were also sold with Cutup Toys, which added to their fanciful nature: for the "cutups" were little people— paper dolls—who rode upon or were pulled by the Bugs. Animate was located at 31 East 17th, New York City.

18. Gregory, 1922, pp. 22–3. "Balloons, Rubber," has twenty-three companies listed, including one that seems to have made nothing but: American Balloon Company, of New York.

19. Spero, 1988, p. 12.

20. For example, Pyralin Egg Shape Rattle, Spero, 1988, p. 5. The irony is in having a company famous for its explosives also being connected to the production of baby toys.

21. Gregory, 1922, p. 10.

22. Spero, 1988, p. 8: 1921, Electric Airplane, made of steel with "fine electric motor."

23. Ibid., p. 13.

24. Ibid., p. 29. A 1922 directory list of mechanical-toy manufacturers gives an idea of its prevalence: American Flyer Manufacturing Company of Chicago; American Toyland Creators of Newark; Animate Toy Company; Arcade Manufacturing Company; C.E. Bradley Corporation of Brattleboro, Vermont; Brighton Toy & Novelty Company of New Brighton, Pennsylvania; Morton E. Converse & Son Company; Crusader Products Company of Davenport, Iowa; A.B. Cummings of Attleboro, Massachusetts; Dayton Friction Toy Company, in Ohio; A.H. Franke Company of Manitowoc, Wisconsin; A.C. Gilbert Company of New Haven; Girard Model Works of New York; Hafner Manufacturing Company of Chicago; Kingsbury Manufacturing Company of Keene, New Hampshire; Klax Company of New Haven; Knapp Electric & Novelty Company of New York; Lindstrom Tool & Toy Manufacturing Company of Bridgeport, Connecticut; Lionel Corporation of New York; Moline Pressed Steel Company of East Moline, Illinois; Ohio Art Company, in Bryan; Pierce Manufacturing Company of Philadelphia; Schieble Toy & Novelty Company of Dayton; Leo Schlesinger & Company of New York; Smolens Novelty Company of Brooklyn; Structo Manufacturing Company of Freeport, Illinois; Thoswood Manufacturing Company of Chicago; Walbert Manufacturing; and Wolverine Supply & Manufacturing Company of Pittsburgh. That this list was incomplete was evident in its omitting Louis Marx, who had started producing toys on his own in 1921—and, more importantly for a 1922 list, in leaving out the name of Marx's former employer, Ferdinand Strauss, who had been in the mechanical-toy business for two decades with such success he was named the "Toy King." While Strauss would have difficulties in the 1920s, in 1923 he advertised the sale of well more than three million mechanical toys (O'Brien, 1990, p. 82: "3,600,000 mechanical toys in 1923"). By the later 1920s, Marx would be responsible for an increase in the already large numbers of mechanical toys being sold, adopting many of the toys formerly made by Strauss while introducing new ones, including a variety of "funny cars."

25. McCready, 1934, p. 82.

26. Spero, 1988, p. 49. The toy and the company would last together until at least 1934. McDowell used the "Mac Toys" name.

27. Ibid., p. 55. This toy appeared in several versions, with the globe-topped post being advertised in 1926. A l928 advertisement, shown in O'Brien, 1990, p. 106, identifies that year's version as Sky Bird Flyer. This kind of toy idea likely originated in Europe, in the various carousel toys and also in such toys as the "Aèrodrome course de ballons dirigeables et d'aèroplanes et helice mècanique." See Parry-Crooke, 1981, p. 38.

28. Goodfellow, 2002, p. 28: illustrated. Also Malloy, 2000, p. 273.

29. Spero, 1988, p. 49: in 1925. Manufacturer unknown. McDowell made a specialty of such games, having also made a Jungle Race.

30. John F. Dille Co., 326 West Madison Street, Chicago.

31. Among some children the experience proved an intense one: for it struck them at a tender age with a deluge of ideas. As Ray Bradbury said, "Buck Rogers hit me over the head when I was nine with the comic strips." Interview with Bradbury: www.tangentonline.com/interviews-Columnsmenu-166/1864-classic-ray-bradbury-interview.

32. White, 1997, pp. 33 and 63.

33. EB v. 11, p. 300.

34. Sources include OED, and Couch, 1959, p. 606.

35. OED, p. 163, puts it this way: "a toy consisting of fulminating powder and fine gravel wrapped in thin paper, which explodes when thrown on a hard surface." The author was surprised to find this definition. Children were still playing with these toys in the 1960s—made then with a BB, a single exploding cap, and small square of paper.

36. Barlow, 1998, p. 153.

37. Progress of the World, vol. 2, p. 69 photo. Publisher not noted, but presumably in Chicago.

38. Burroughs, 1934, pp. 21, 30

39. Ibid., pp. 30–2.

40. Ibid., p. 33.

41. Around this time The Conquest of Space by David Lasser appeared, touting the possibilities of rocketry; and a toy appeared with features that would become common in others that would have "rocket" in the name. Louis Marx introduced Speed King, a sixteen-inch, four-wheeled, open-cockpit race car. The body took the form of a narrowed dirigible, a

resemblance reinforced by the lateral-stabilizing fins to each side of the thinly tapering tail. While exhaust pipes were painted onto the body's sides, to make clear its race-car nature, the aerodynamic shape suggested that its proper medium for travel was not on earth but through air. Spero, 1988, p. 85, shows it in a 1932 advertisement. The Giant King Racer of 1930, shown on p. 74, in contrast had a boxier shape. The nose was a split-grille wedge, rather than the tapered cone of the Speed King. On p. 89, showing a 1933 page, the Mechanical Racer is shown with the same Speed King decorations, and described as having been "modeled after latest type racing cars." It is shown again unchanged on a 1934 page, p. 97. The later Speed King racer in plastic is unrelated except in general concept—although Renwal may well have borrowed the name, consciously or unconsciously.

42. Barlow, 1998, p. 250. At the same time, Marx was offering the Flying Zeppelin of "heavy metal construction," seventeen inches long, that would fly in circles when suspended from a string (p. 251).

43. Malloy, 2000, p. 281: illustrated. On p. 277: Another image of a four-finned dirigible appears in Bradley's 1938 Above the Clouds. On p. 273: Similarly, All-Fair's Zippy Zepps Air Game.

44. Words uttered by Passepartout. Verne, 1978, p. 22.

45. Malloy, 2000, p. 281.

46. Dawes, 1933, p. 121.

47. Claudy, 1933, p. i: prefatory note by managing editor George F. Pierrot.

48. Adams, 1931, p. 91

49. Čapek, 1961, p. 84. Poe's comment appears in "Scheherezade." Dickens called the crowd "a monster much dreaded," in *Tale of Two Cities* (Dickens, 1935, p. 165). As noted earlier, the mob's nature did alter.

50. Claudy, pp. 142, 161.

51. Adams, 1931, p. 91.

52. See www.oldwoodtoys.com/twistum.htm, for advertising images. The company seems to have been the same as the Atascadero Toy and Doll Factory, either changing its name to Twistum Toy Factory or using the latter in publicity. No. 81,Old Timer," measured 18 inches long, four inches high.

53. Murray & Fox, 1991, p. 30. Edward Savage designed these toys.

54. *Ibid.*, p. 31, shows the toy in a photograph. This example is painted primarily bright red, with blue on the head and feet.

55. Malloy, 2000, p. 283: illustrated.

56. As Brooks (1962, p. 86) observed, "A civilization that was ruled by business was no longer criticized, though it made America hated around the world. We were, in short, a Republican island on a socialistic planet, at odds with all mankind, and our literature seemed passively to accept this fate."

Chapter Fifteen

1. Wilson, 1965, p. 337.
2. Hall, 1940, p. 29.
3. Brooks, 1957, pp. 183–4.
4. "[T]he industrial revolution had created an enormous differential between the developed and the un-developed (or, as we would now say, the underdeveloped) parts of the world, and improved communications, technical innovations and new forms of business organization had increased immeasurably the possibilities of exploiting underdeveloped territories" (Barraclough, 1967, p. 69).

5. Barraclough, 1967, p. 70.

6. Dawes, 1933, p. 10. On p. 16: In the previous city administration another group, in 1923, had pursued the idea of a second Chicago Fair.

7. Dawes, 1933, p. 8.

8. *Ibid.*, p. 125.

9. *Ibid.*, p. 35: "Dioramas—pictures in three dimensions—are used in hundreds of displays at A Century of Progress Exposition. The foreground is modeled in true perspective to blend with a painted background." Curtis Lighting was responsible for lighting "all those weird animals in the World a Million Years Ago, and a lot of these dioramas that run through light effects from dawn to dusk and back to dawn again. They built and lighted the Clock of the Ages in the Hall of Science" ("Alice in Lightland," in Millar, 1933, p. 41).

10. Dawes, 1933, p. 187. The company was Messmore & Damon, Inc., a New York City company that specialized in automata: "Mechanical displays—animated figures of animals, clowns, etc." (Macready, 1934, p. 870). The firm was located at 404–408 West Twenty-Seventh.

11. Dawes, 1933, p. 106.

12. *Ibid.*, p. 186.

13. *Ibid.*, p. 188.

14. *Ibid.*, p. 188.

15. *Ibid.*, p. 183. Although unmarked as to manufacturer, the United States Playing Card Company, of Cincinnati, did offer an exhibit showing "playing cards and the history and development of card playing" in the Hall of Science, making it the probable manufacturer.

16. *Ibid.*, pp. 9, 42.

17. *Ibid.*, p. 43.

18. *Ibid.*, p. 69. Displayed in House of Tomorrow were such items as kitchen utensils manufactured by Polaware Company, tubular metal furnishings manufactured by Howell Company, and wood furniture manufactured by Tapp, DeWild and Wallace. The focus on futurity had a self-fulfilling aspect: for the mere fact of having so high-profile a display venue insured sales of items by these companies. All could boast, well into the future, of having helped complete the House of Tomorrow. House of Tomorrow was, oddly enough, one of two glass houses at the Exposition. Owens-Illinois Glass Company made (p. 70) "a building of glass blocks, with a central shaft fifty feet high. The glass blocks are many colored, semi-transparent, and approximately the size of the ordinary paving bricks."

19. Campbell, 1976, p. 2, in the story "The Last Evolution."

20. Howard, 1966, p. 51.

21. Dawes, 1933, pp. 173, 177.

22. *Ibid.*, p. 55; the italicized "live" at the end is original.

23. *Ibid.*, pp. 48, 77, 74, 37, in order of citations.
24. *Ibid.*, p. 37.
25. Millar, 1933, p. 33.
26. Dawes, 1933, p. 76.
27. Huxley, 1969, p. 50: "London's first scent and colour organ."
28. Millar, 1933, p. 41.
29. Dawes, 1933, pp. 74, 121.
30. Perhaps the Franco-Prussian War panorama. See EB v. 20, p. 681.
31. Millar, 1933, p. 33.
32. McCready, various years.
33. McCready, 1937, p. 276.
34. Sears, Roebuck emphasized the new mechanical movement in the toy that allowed the airplane to "loop the loop." Atop the skyscraper, a twenty-one-inch crossbeam had the "aeroplane," 6¾ inches long, and the "airship," 5½ inches long. See O'Brien, 1990, p. 106; *and* Spero, 1988, p. 62.
35. McCready, various years.
36. Dawes, 1933, p. 22. The passage continues: "'It would be incongruous to house exhibits showing man's progress in the past century in a Greek temple of the age of Pericles, or a Roman villa of the time of Hadrian,' said members of the architectural commission of the Exposition, all of whom are graduates of the École des Beaux Arts, home of the classical school. 'We are trying to show the world not what has happened in the past, because that has already been effectively done, but what is being done in the present, and what may happen in the future.'"
37. Dawes, 1933, pp. 23, 101.
38. *Ibid.*, p. 20.

Chapter Sixteen

1. Burroughs, 1934, p. 46-7.
2. Brooks, 1941, p. 16.
3. Mumford, 1970, pp. 204–5.
4. Phelps, Charles, 1898. *Register and Manual of the State of Connecticut*, 1898. Hartford: The Case, Lockwood & Brainard Co.
5. Twain, 1961, pp. 543-5, in "About All Kinds of Ships."
6. Brooks, 1957, p. 183, quoting Hendrik van Loon.
7. "You can't have quality in mass production. You don't want it because it lasts too long. So you substitute styling, which is a commercial swindle intended to produce artificial obsolescence," says a character in Raymond Chandler's *The Long Goodbye*. See 1922, New York: Vintage Books, p. 234.
8. Brooks, 1957., p. 187.
9. United States Centennial Commission, 1876, p. 202: "Joint Stock Co. for the Manufacture of Bronze Goods & Zinc Castings, Berlin. Chandelier of bronze, and zinc castings." P. 139: Miller & Krips.
10. O'Brien, 1990, p. 71.
11. A change in materials also indicated an ongoing change. Dowst first introduced toy cars with cast-metal tires. Zamac and other zinc alloys being employed in the die-casting business proved highly amenable to the needs of the toymaker, being capable of holding fine details and being inexpensive. In durability, however, it fell well short of its cast-iron antecedents. Zinc-alloy tires held up for mild play, but not the rough or repetitive play typical of childhood. In its 1933 catalog, Dowst offered some older toy autos with the metal-tire option. Yet alongside these it offered new versions with rubber tires—welcomed not only by children for their playtime durability but also by parents for their relative silence and reduced tendency to groove tabletop finishes or waxed floors.
12. Spero, 1988, p. 100.
13. *Ibid.*, p. 100. A small version without headlights was offered as the New Baby Streak-O-Lite Wagon, shown on p. 101. The Irish Mail was a lever-propelled ride-on toy, typically spare in appearance.
14. Streamline Railway is the name on the toy itself; the longer name was its catalog name in Sears, Roebuck. See Spero, 1988, p. 101.
15. McCready, 1937, p. 332 and others.
16. *Ibid.*, p. 316, 314. The term "floor train" refers to toys that had no tracks. Some wooden and then plastic ones lacked even wheels.
17. Hough, 1976, p. 85.
18. *Ibid.*, p. 86.
19. McCready, 1934, pp. 24–5.
20. The pioneering air-gun manufacturing scene is undoubtedly more complicated. There was, for instance, Eureka Manufacturing Co., in Boston, making air pistols in the 1870s. See United States Centennial Commission, 1876, p. 129.
21. Huxley, 1969, p. 146.
22. Hough, pp. 86–89.
23. *Playthings*, September, 1934, p. 28: Stephen Slesinger, Inc., advertisement.
24. McCready, 1934, pp. 273, 54, and others. See also "New Buck Rogers Booth Offers Many Sales Advantages," *Playthings*, September, 1935, p. 75.
25. *Ibid.*, p. 312 and others.
26. McCready, 1937, p. 326 and others.
27. *Ibid.*, p. 281 and others.
28. *Ibid.*, pp. 315–6, and others.
29. Hackett, 1945, p. 126, lists *Tarzan of the Apes* in her compilation "American Best Sellers 1880–1945," with sales of 750,000, although Burroughs makes no appearance in any specific year's bestseller list. By the 1940s more than 250 million copies of Tarzan books had been sold in fifty-six languages, according to Herzberg, 1962, p. 1115—who uses the phrase "tremendous hit" with reference to the movie.
30. *Playthings* magazine, June 1935, p. 18.
31. McCready, 1934, p. 316 and others. Similarly named but probably not meant to evoke "robot" was the Robuster child's exerciser, made by the A. Schoenhut Company of Philadelphia, and the Roc-A-Bot, a seesaw and merry-go-round "playground and juvenile exerciser," made by Heaney Laboratory, in Jackson Heights, Long Island.
32. Tumbusch, 1991, p. 26.
33. McCready, 1937, p. 319. These, however, seemed short-lived.
34. McCready, 1934, p. 320 and others. The former was a name applied to both a cast-iron auto

made by Arcade and "flying planes" made by Kingsbury, while the Golden Arrow was a Kingsbury toy racer. Similarly, the Silver Bullet was a toy auto made of aluminum by Buffalo Toy & Tool Works in upstate New York. Seeing similar use were Streak and Dash" Buffalo also made a Silver Dash aluminum auto. Several names and designs were borrowings from actual land-speed racers.

35. O'Brien, 1995, p. 593.

36. McCready, 1934, 1937, various pages. The listing in 1937, p. 319, of the Rocket steel coaster wagon by "Atlas Doll & Toy Co." may have been an error. There was an Atlas Toy Mfg. Co. at the time that made only soft toys. It may be worth noting that in the Sky Rocket name, which reflects the traditional firecracker rocket, the adjective "sky" may have seemed necessary, by this time, for clarity.

37. Automatic, located at 50 Pine Street, New York, specialized in mechanical toys of the early 1930s.

38. Not in 1939, as identified in some sources. Malloy, 2000, states "circa 1932," which appears too early.

39. Malloy, 2000, p. 302: photograph.

40. Ibid., p. 294: photograph.

41. Ibid., p. 290: photograph.

42. Wieland & Force, p. 50.

43. Ibid., p. 55.

44. Sheridan, 1973, p. 38.

45. Ibid., pp. 40, 42: this seemed to have prepared him for his career in political cartooning, which became his primary work at the end of the 1930s, for the *New York Sun*.

46. Stapledon, 1945, pp. 536, 540. The novel's narrator described this superhuman's prowess in this arena: "I will only say that, save for one universally adopted improvement in road-traffic appliances, he worked entirely in the field of household and personal labour-saving devices. The outstanding fact about John's career as an inventor was his knack of producing not merely occasional successes but a steady flow of 'best sellers.' Consequently to describe only a few minor achievements and interesting failures must give a very false impression of his genius. The reader must supplement this meagre report by means of his own imagination. Let him, in the act of using any of the more cunning and efficient little instruments of modern comfort, remind himself that this may well be one of the many 'gadgets' which were conceived by the urchin-superman in his subterranean lair."

47. Remotrol, 34 West 37th Street, New York City, was well-established by 1936. McCready, 1937, p. 131.

48. That this wave of popularity was comic-related seems indicated seems indicated by the fact that Tarzan licensing rights in the toy industry were being handled by Stephen Slesinger, who was handling a variety of comic characters. In 1937 other toys included Tarzan archery sets by The Archers and the Rollin Wilson Company, paint books and puzzles by Saalfield Publishing Company, school bags by United Leather Goods Co., and a target game by Movie-Jektor Co. Of a different sort of oddity from Remotrol's play sets was the offering from President Novelty & Jewelry Company: "Tarzan juvenile jewelry." See McCready, 1937. At least one mechanical Tarzan did appear, in the 1960s from Marusan—battery operated, with four actions. See Hultzman, 2002, p. 184.

49. The replacement occurred by the next year. See McCready, 1938.

50. McCready, various years. In 1941, Remotrol listed by name only the farm and ship sets. By 1944, catering to the times, Remotrol offeredFighting Ships in Motion. Although using metal in its toys, the company appears to have managed to continue manufacturing its line during the war years, although as was the case with other companies its toy production may have been partially sidelined by war-related contracts; its ability to meet store orders may not have been complete.

51. The firm remained at the same address, producing the same toys, through 1958 and later.

52. Wells, in Wollheim, 1948, p. 32.

53. "Tree Wrecks Piccard Strato-Balloon." *Modern Mechanix and Inventions* 13:3, January 1935, p. 46. The *Strato-Balloon* had its 1934 "take-off" from the airport in Detroit, Michigan, with the doctor and his wife, Jeanette, on board. The stratospheric journey proved successful in obtaining a cosmic-ray film record for Dr. Millikan at Cal Tech laboratories, although both balloon and gondola suffered damage in returning to Earth. The word "take-off" does appear in this account. The demise of similar spacecraft, of course, occurs fictionally in both Wells and Claudy.

54. Elam, 1957, p. 199.

55. Mumford, 1970, caption 14–15, "Encapsulated Man." Dr. Bruno Bettelheim described the autistic child.

56. Holmes, 1872, p. 357.

57. Loncraine, 2009, p. 287.

58. Barrier, 1999, p. 292. Intended primarily for children, Fleischer's film inspired a variety of new toys based on Swift's story, including a bank by the New York novelty-bank manufacturer Zell Products Company; paper dolls and books by Saalfield Publishing Company, of Akron; jointed wooden dolls by Ideal Novelty & Toy Company of New York City; rubber figures by Sun Rubber Company of Barberton, Ohio; molded gauze "false faces" and costumes of the movie's characters by Apon Novelty Company of Philadelphia; costumes by Collegeville Flag & Manufacturing Company, of Collegeville, Pennsylvania; and a wooden castle by Rich Manufacturing Co., of Clinton, Iowa. The toys that would have traditional "wonder toy" appeal, of an optical sort, were "Stereovues" of the Fleischer movie, made by Stereovue Corporation, of Long Island City (McCready, 1940, various pages: for all but Collegeville). O'Brien, 1990, p. 144, also mentions "a wooden boat, a tin sand pail, and a tin drum by Chein." J. Chein & Co., of New York City, was not listed by McCready, perhaps through oversight. In McCready, 1941, the companies are Saalfield, Sun, Collegeville, Ideal, and Apon. In 1942, only Ideal and Sun remain, of the list. Apparently only Sun Rubber continued offering

Gulliver's Travels toys farther into the war years, although they disappeared by 1944. That they survived on the manufacturer's lists was probably due more to intrinsic charm and appeal than to the movie or novel connection.

59. McCready, 1940, 1941, various pages.
60. O'Brien, 1990, p. 150.
61. Malloy, 2000, p. 281: illustrated.

Chapter Seventeen

1. Wilson, 1965, p. 337.
2. Orwell, 1961, p. 24.
3. King-Hall, 1910, pp. 69–70.
4. Poe, 1984, pp. 873–4, in "Mellonta Tauta."
5. Peterson, Roger Tory, 1949; tenth printing, 1957. *How To Know the Birds*. New York: Signet/New American Library, p. 111.
6. Lang, 1961, p. 39.
7. Molloy, 2000, p. 79; McCready, 1937, p. 329.
8. Brooks, 1941, p. 142.
9. Dillon-Beck was located at 103 Montgomery Avenue in Irvington, New Jersey, under Daniel C. Dillon, Jr., chairman, and John Beck, superintendent. New Jersey was proving a center for plastic manufacturers. In nearby Carlstadt, the Columbia Protektosite Company, already well established in the toy business, had done the molding work popular dime-store sellers during wartime: Bergen Toy and Novelty's's old-fashioned figures, depicting cowboys, Indians, circus animals, and World War I soldiers. Irvington's diminutive upstart, however, would be the one to introduce the best-selling postwar toy. To indicate their relative sizes, in 1947 Columbia Protektosite was running thirty injection machines, while Dillon-Beck was operating with four. Dillon-Beck employed one of the newer molding materials available, in the plastics industry: Lumarith, a formulation produced by Celanese Corporation of America, which was helping make injection-molding feasible for plastics. As a material, already by 1945, it took dyes in unlimited opaque colors, or could be molded into forms having a clear near-transparency.
10. This was made explicit in the promotional material for a later Dream Car, in 1953. The toy's box referred to the clear plastic bubble atop the car's body as a "bomber bubble."
11. By sometime in 1946, Dillon-Beck was using the Wannatoy name for its line of playthings. In the line, the focus on stylized and idealized vehicles continued.
12. Most 1940s Cars of the Future toys seem to have been made with cellulose acetate plastics. Though the technology existed to make acetates more resistant to heat and humidity, much ephemera, such as toys, were made from simpler formulations. They showed a tendency to warp, over time—if not already chipped, cracked or separated at the seams. This helps explain their relative obscurity, historically. As objects they tended not to survive. As dime-store items, moreover, they tended not to appear even in advertisements.
13. Other toy cars of the future, within a year of Dillon-Beck's release, came from Tuffy Toys, located at 8200 Harvard Avenue, Cleveland, Ohio, in 1946. Although it would become best known for small, mechanical, wheeled toys for diverting toddlers, it initially made toy autos, issuing them from until around 1951. Its streamlined auto, while also a two-door coupe with bubble top, emulated the teardrop shape more than did the Dillon-Beck toy: amply rounded to the front, tapering to the rear.

The Comet Speedster, another 1946 toy Car of the Future, took up considerably more space on the play floor, being fourteen and a half inches long, five wide, and four-and-a-half high. Unlike the Dillon-Beck and Tuffy Toys cars, the individual fenders were pronounced, although still smoothed into the overall streamlined form. Like the Tuffy Toys auto, the Comet Speedster had a teardrop shape, with the bubble top bluntly rounded toward the front, and the car's rear tapering to a thin trailing edge. This teardrop shape had resulted not from practical design considerations, but from the desire to imaginatively embody "speed" in a stationary, or essentially stationary, object. Besides suggesting the teardrop of falling raindrop, it mimicked a jet-wing cross-section. The Comet Speedster was made by Stack Plastics, located on the other side of the continent from the states that were so rich in plastics manufacturing, at 5835 W. Washington Boulevard, Culver City, California. The toy was exclusively a 1940s product, since the company continued in operation until at least 1948, although closing its doors by 1949. Yet another toy Car of the Future appearing in 1946 was the Plastic Rocket made by Plakie Toys of Youngstown, Ohio. Although its company name might be thought to derive somehow from "plastic," the company seems to have meant to evoke "play." It started only a few years earlier, as a maker of wooden toys for infants and children, making also "walkers" and "automobile baby hammocks." After war's end it added plastic toys, and probably thought it only natural to begin with the toy obviously successful in that material, the bubble-topped car. As was the Comet Speedster, the Plastic Rocket had distinct but streamlined fenders. Advertisements leave it unclear if this toy is a coupe, as are the others.

14. Orwell, 1961, pp. 5, 8.
15. *Ibid.*, pp. 5, 39, 42. A real plaything, a Snakes and Ladders game, appears in Winston Smith's memory, at a point too late to help him (p. 243). The "versificator" resonates with Thomas Love Peacock's notion, of more than a century prior: "our poetry is a kaleidoscope of false imagery." See Peacock, 1947, p. 172.
16. Peacock, 1947, p. 222; and Jaspers, 1957, p. 22.
17. Wilson, 1931, p. 284.
18. Schwartz, 2009, p. 309.
19. P. Schuyler Miller's "adult game fantasies" appeared in his review column "The Reference Library," *Astounding Science Fiction* 56:3, November 1955, p. 147. Valèry's comment, in Wilson, 1931, pp. 284–5.
20. The author came upon a more recent example of this while on a trip whose purposes was, in part, the visiting of the towns where toy factories

had once existed in northern Pennsylvania, which might be considered the cradle of American toy manufacturing. Although individual tinsmiths, turners, and hand-carvers had produced toys from Colonial times in the East of the country, Pennsylvania's ample resources and enterprising populace offered a combination that encouraged toy manufacture on a relatively large scale. Towns and villages with toy companies that exerted national influence were scattered in a chain across parts of the state, but especially in the north, where the Crandall family thrived and produced some of the nation's first nationwide fad-toys. Along that northern chain, which links towns such as Coudersport and Port Alleghany, one company began with such toys as electric motors, magnet sets, and Flicker Tops. Its history echoes others: established as Electric Toy Mfg. Co., 1908; became Marvel Toy Co., 1923; gutted by fire, 1913; became Smethport Specialty Co., 1931; made mica insulators for radio tubes in proximity fuses, and no toys, during World War II. Still in operation a century after its founding, the company was producing toys that employed magnets, but in ever-new configurations and designs. Whenever it would develop a new idea, as one of the few remaining companies that actually produced toys in the United States, it would find Chinese companies introducing closely similar toys soon thereafter. As a result, to survive, the company had to maintain a constant flow of changes and innovations.

21. U.S. Centennial Commission, 1876, p. 246.
22. Chapuis & Droz, 1958, pp. 161–3, 172. Bamboo would have been the wood involved.
23. Ministry of International Trade & Industry, 1956, p. 106.
24. *Ibid.*, p. 103.
25. *Ibid.*, pp. 103–4".
26. *Ibid.*, p. 104: "in recent years Japanese manufacturers are turning out toys of new mechanical devices and intricate mechanism on par in quality with German toys."
27. *Ibid.*, p. 103.
28. McReady, 1934, p. 25.
29. Rockwell, 1954, p. 129.
30. McCready, 1955. The companies responsible were Playtoy Industries, Thomas Manufacturing Company, Kaye Novelty Company, Gladen Enterprises, Viking Tailless Kite Company, and Newell Manufacturing Company, respectively.
31. McCready, 1959.
32. Verne, 1978, pp. 35, 66–7.
33. C.M. Kornbluth's trio of "The Altar at Midnight," *Takeoff*, and *Not This August* tap into this symbolic element. In "Altar" the satellite is the Moon itself, endowed with the same weapons of global domination as the artificial satellites of the other stories.
34. Gordon & Scheer, 1959, p. 59.
35. The author had an experience that underlined the power of this particular symbol. Some years ago he was hired to write a book upon the concept of the hundred "best" Baby Boom toys, with the idea being that a ranking of some sort would be imposed. After considerable deliberation, the author chose the number-one toy to be the Hassenfeld Brothers' Mr. Potato Head, for several reasons—notably that, in its initial form, it had actual interest as a toy that encouraged a great deal of creativity, and as a toy that appealed to both sexes—and to all ages, for that matter, in its beginning. It was also a toy that had been around for essentially the entire, unusually long period of the "generation," even though its form altered by the end. After the manuscript of this book was turned in, a contentious editorial meeting took place at the small publisher's offices, with the author's toy-ranking the cause. The author learned later how animated the meeting was, and its result: which was the insistence that the Top Ten be reorganized and changed, with it being essential that the Barbie doll be placed at number one. That most of these editors at the meeting who were making their various arguments were either extremely late Boom children or post-Boom had no bearing on their sense of authority in the matter. It made clear that Barbie dolls belated did, indeed, become symbolic of the generation. The higher-ups at the small publisher learned and objected to the idea of the editors contradicting the "expert"—too late, of course.
36. Brooks, 1941, p. 142.

Bibliography

Adams, Henry, 1931. *The Education of Henry Adams.* New York: The Modern Library.
Alcott, Louisa May, 1898. *Flower Fables.* Philadelphia: Henry Altemus Co.
_____. 1947. *Little Men.* New York: Grosset & Dunlap.
Aldredge, Edna M., and Jessie F. McKee, 1943. *The Timbertoes.* Chicago-Beckley-Cardy Co. Revised edition; originally 1932, The Harter Publishing Co.
Aldrich, Thomas Bailey, 1942. *The Story of a Bad Boy.* Cambridge: The Riverside Press, Houghton Mifflin Co. Introduction by C.J. Anderson. Originally 1870.
Alger, Horatio, Jr., 1990. *Ragged Dick.* New York: Signet Classic. Originally 1868. Introduction by Alan Trachtenberg.
_____. undated. *Herbert Carter's Legacy.* Chicago: M.A. Donohue & Co.
Anonymous, 1922. *Six Wonder Tales for Boys.* Racine: Whitman Publishing Co.
_____, 1933. *Wonder Book of Bible Knowledge.* New York and Nashville: Abingdon-Cokesbury Press.
Anonymous, undated. *Old Mother Goose: The Only Complete Collection.* Chicago: W.B. Conkey Co.
Appleton, Victor (Garis, Howard R.), 1910. *Tom Swift and His Airship.* New York: Grosset & Dunlap.
_____. 1911. *Tom Swift in the Caves of Ice.* New York: Grosset & Dunlap.
_____. 1915. *Tom Swift and His Aerial Warship.* New York: Grosset & Dunlap.
_____. 1925. *Don Sturdy in the Land of Volcanoes.* New York: Grosset & Dunlap.
_____. 1925. *Tom Swift and His Chest of Secrets.* New York: Grosset & Dunlap.
_____. 1927. *Tom Swift Circling the Globe.* New York: Grosset & Dunlap.
Appleton II, Victor, 1954. *Tom Swift and His Flying Lab.* New York: Grosset & Dunlap.
Arnold, Edwin L., 1964. *Gulliver of Mars.* New York: Ace Books. Introduction by Richard A. Lupoff. Edition contains no actual publication date. First published in 1905 as *Lieut. Gulliver Jones, His Vacation.*
Ash, Brian, ed., 1977. *The Visual Encyclopedia of Science Fiction.* New York: Harmony Books. First published in 1977 by Pan Books, London.
"Aunt Katie," undated, 1800s. *The Sunday Alphabet of Animals.* The well-worn copy in the author's possession was given to a Wisconsin child in 1872. Publisher unknown.
Bailey, J.O., 1972. *Pilgrims Through Space and Time: Trends and Patterns in Scientific and Utopian Fiction.* Westport, Connecticut: Greenwood Press. Reprinted from 1947 original.
Bailey, Temple, 1918. *The Tin Soldier.* New York: Grosset & Dunlap. Originally published by The Penn Publishing Co.
Bangs, John Kendrick, 1923. *A House-Boat on the Styx.* New York and London: Harper & Bros. Publishers. Originally 1895.
Banks, Charles Eugene, 1893. *The Artistic Guide to Chicago and the World's Columbian Exposition.* Chicago: R.S. Peale Co. *See also* Columbian Art Company.
Barlow, Ronald S., ed., 1998. *The Great American Antique Toy Bazaar 1879–1945.* El Cajon, California: Windmill Publishing Company.
Barraclough, Geoffrey, 1967. *An Introduction to Contemporary History.* Hammondsworth, Middlesex, England/Baltimore, Maryland: Penguin Books. Originally published 1964.
Barrie, James M., 1902. *Peter Pan in Kensington Gardens.* New York: Charles Scribner's Sons. 1920 printing; illustrated by Arthur Rackham.
_____ (or Anonymous), 1926. *The Story of Peter Pan.* New York: Charles E. Graham & Co. "Retold in story form from J.M. Barrie's Immortal Fairy Play." Illustrator not listed.
_____. 1965. *Peter Pan.* New York: Grosset & Dunlap, Tempo Books. Originally *Peter and Wendy*, 1911, based on the 1904 play.
Barrier, Michael, 1999. *Hollywood Cartoons: American Animation in Its Golden Age.* New York, Oxford: Oxford University Press.
Barzun, Jacques, 1958. *Darwin, Marx, Wagner.* Second edition. Garden City, New York: Doubleday Anchor Books.

Baum, L. Frank. *See also* Van Dyne, Edith.

_____. 1950s. *The Wizard of Oz/The New Wizard of Oz*. Indianapolis: The Bobbs-Merrill Co. (Or 1960s; has movie-photo endpapers.)

_____. 1987. *The Wonderful Wizard of Oz*. New York: HarperCollins Publishers. Illustrations by W.W. Denslow. Facsimile of 1900 original by George M. Hill Company.

_____. 1994. *Tik-Tok of Oz*. New York: Dover Publications. Semi-facsimile of 1914 original.

_____. 1997a. *The Master Key: An Electrical Fairy Tale*. New York: Books of Wonder. Originally published 1901.

_____. 1997b. *Mother Goose in Prose. A Selection of Storybook Land themes from Baum's first children's book*. Aberdeen, S.D.: Northern State University Press. Ed. and with intro. by Don Artz.

Beard, Lina, and Adelia B. Beard, 1910. *Little Folks' Handy Book*. New York: Charles Scribner's Sons.

Beckford, William, 1986. *In* Fairclough, 1986.

Bell, Eric Temple. *See* Taine, John.

Bellamy, Edward, 1946. *Looking Backward 2000–1887*. Cleveland, Ohio: World Publishing. Introduction by Paul Bellamy.

Bill Bertoia Auctions, 1997, October. *An Alpine Christmas Toy Sale*. Vineland, New Jersey: Bill Bertoia Auctions.

_____. 1998, March. *Ernest Trova and Robert Thurow Collections*. Vineland, New Jersey: Bill Bertoia Auctions.

_____. 1998, May. *The Stanley P. Sax Bank Collection*. Vineland, N.J.: Bill Bertoia Auctions.

Bleiler, E.F., 1960. "Introduction," in *Three Prophetic Novels of H.G. Wells*, edited by Bleiler. *See* Wells, 1960, for novels included.

_____. 1970. *Mother Goose's Melodies*. New York: Dover. Facsimile of 1833 Munroe and Francis edition, with introduction by Bleiler.

_____. 1989. "From the Newark Steam Man to Tom Swift." *Extrapolation* 30:2 (Summer), pp. 101–16.

_____. 1990. *Science-Fiction, the Early Years*. Kent, Ohio: The Kent State University Press.

Bleiler, Richard, 1989. "Forgotten Giant: A Brief History of Adventure Magazine." *Extrapolation* 30:4 (Winter), pp. 309–323.

Bonner, Richard, 1913. *The Boy Inventors' Flying Ship*. New York: Hurst & Company.

Boston, 1900. *The Greater Boston Business Directory and Register for 1900*. Boston: Sampson, Murdock & Co.

Briggs, Asa, 1972. *Victorian People*. Chicago: The University of Chicago Press.

Brinkley, Douglas, 2003. *Wheels for the World: Henry Ford, His Company, and a Century of Progress*. New York: Viking.

Brooks, Van Wyck, 1941. *Opinions of Oliver Allston*. New York: E.P. Dutton & Co.

_____. 1950. *New England: Indian Summer*. New York: E.P. Dutton & Co. Originally published 1940.

_____. 1953. *The Writer in America*. New York: E.P. Dutton & Co. Citations in the text are to the Avon edition of April 1964.

_____. 1957. *Days of the Phoenix: The Nineteen-Twenties I Remember*. New York: E.P. Dutton & Co.

_____. 1961. *From the Shadow of the Mountain: My Post-Meridian Years*. New York: E.P. Dutton & Co.

Bruce, Robert V., 1987. *The Launching of Modern American Science*. New York: Alfred A. Knopf.

Bulwer, Edward. *See* Lytton.

Burnham, Clara Loise, 1894. *Sweet Clover: A Romance of the White City*. New York: Grosset & Dunlap.

Burroughs, Edgar Rice, 1921. *Tarzan the Terrible*. New York: Grosset & Dunlap.

_____. 1923. *Pellucidar*. New York: Grosset & Dunlap. Originally 1915.

_____. 1934. *Pirates of Venus*. Tarzana, California: Edgar Rice Burroughs, Inc.

_____. 1963. *Tarzan of the Apes*. New York: Ballantine Books. Originally 1912.

Butler, Samuel, 1967. *Erewhon*. New York: Airmont Publishing Company. Introduction by Mary M. Threapleton.

Campbell, John W., Jr., 1976. *The Best of John W. Campbell*. Edited and with an introduction by Lester del Rey. New York: Ballantine Books.

Čapek, The Brothers, 1961. *R.U.R. & The Insect Play*. London: Oxford University Press. Karel Čapek's *R.U.R.* is translated by Paul Selver and adapted for the English stage by Nigel Playfair. *The Insect Play*, by the Brothers Čapek, is translated by Selver and adapted for stage by Playfair and Clifford Bax.

Carroll, Lewis, undated. *The Complete Works of Lewis Carrol*. New York: Random House, Modern Library.

Chapuis, Alfred, and Edmond Droz, 1958. *Automata: A Historical and Technological Study*. New York: Central Book Company. Translated by Alec Reid.

Christie's, 2007, March. *The Mike Williams TV Toy, Lead Figure and Game Collection*. London: Christie's South Kensington.

Claudy, Carl H., 1933. *The Mystery Men of Mars*. New York: Grosset & Dunlap.

Clute, John, and Peter Nicholls, 1995. *The Encyclopedia of Science Fiction*. New York: St. Martin's Griffin.

Collodi, C., 1932. *Pinocchio: The Adventures of a Marionette*. Boston: Ginn and Co. Translated by Walter S. Cramp and Sara E.H. Lockwood.

Columbian Art Company, 1891. *The Artistic Guide to Chicago and the World's Columbian Exposition*. Chicago: R.S. Peale Co. See also Banks, Charles Eugene.

Coman, Katherine, 1920. *The Industrial History of the United States, New and Revised Edition*. New York: The Macmillan Co. Earlier editions 1905, 1910.

Conklin, Groff, 1980. *Omnibus of Science Fiction*. New York: Bonanza Books. Reprint of 1952 edition.

Corbett, Elizabeth Burgoyne, 2014. *New Amazonia: A Foretaste of the Future*. Seattle: Aqueduct Press. Introduction by Alexis Lothian.

Côté, Jean Marc, and Isaac Asimov, 1986. *Futuredays: A Nineteenth-Century Vision of the Year 2000*. New York: Henry Holt and Co.

Couch, William T., editor-in chief, 1959. *Collier's Encyclopedia*. New York: P.F. Collier & Son Corporation.

Cousin Virginia, 1866. *The Kettle Club: Christmas Tales for Children*. Boston: Nichols and Noyes.

Cox, Palmer, ca. 1890s. *Brownies and Other Stories*. Chicago: M.A. Donahue & Co. Illustrated by Cox; "the stories told in prose by E. Veale, the Fair Tale Authoress."

Cross, Wilbur L., 1899. *The Development of the English Novel*. New York: The Macmillan Company.

Culff, Robert, 1969. *The World of Toys*. London: The Hamlyn Publishing Group.

Dalrymple, Marya, ed., 1991. *American Country Toys and Games*. Richmond, Virginia: Time-Life Books.

Davidson, Edith B., 1912. *The Bunnikins-Bunnies and the Moon King*. Boston: Little, Brown, and Company.

Dawes, Rufus C., et al., 1933. *A Century of Progress International Exposition: Official Guide Book of the Fair*. Chicago: A Century of Progress Administration.

Dickens, Charles, 1907. *Bleak House*. London: J.M. Dent & Sons. Introduction by G.K. Chesterton. 1949 printing.

_____. 1935. *A Tale of Two Cities*. New York: The Modern Library.

_____. 1983. *The Complete Ghost Stories of Charles Dickens*. New York: Franklin Watts. Edited by Peter Haining.

Disney, Walt, 1936. *Mickey Mouse in Pigmy Land*. Racine, Wisconsin: Whitman Publishing Co.

Dodgson, Charles. *See* Carroll, Lewis.

EB. *See* Encyclopaedia Britannica Company.

Elam, Richard M., Jr., 1957. *Teen-Age Super Science Stories* (The Teen-age Library). New York: Grosset & Dunlap. Illustrated by Frank E. Vaughn.

Ellis, Edward S., 2009. *The Huge Hunter, or, The Steam Man of the Prairies*. Project Gutenberg. The present author has cited by chapter, not page.

Emerson, Edwin, Jr., 1902. *A History of the Nineteenth Century Year by Year, Volume Three*. New York: P.F. Collier and Son.

The Encyclopaedia Britannica Company, 1911. *The Encyclopaedia Britannica, Eleventh Edition*. New York: The Encyclopaedia Britannica Company.

Fairclough, Peter, ed., 1986. *Three Gothic Novels*. London: Penguin Books. Introduction by Mario Praz. Includes Horace Walpole's *The Castle of Otranto* (1765; 1798 final revision text), William Beckford's *Vathek* (1786), and Mary Shelley's *Frankenstein* (1818; 1831 final revision text).

Fisher, Benjamin Franklin, IV, ed., 1990. *Poe and His Times: The Artist and His Milieu*. Baltimore: The Edgar Allan Poe Society.

Fisher, Bud, 1929. *Mutt and Jeff, Book 14*. New York: Cupples & Leon Company.

Fiske, John, 1912. *The Destiny of Man, Viewed in the Light of his Origin*. Boston and New York: Houghton Mifflin Co. Originally 1884.

Foley, Dan, 1962. *Toys Through the Ages*. Philadelphia: Chilton Books.

Fontany, Elena, 1934. *Other Worlds Than This*. Chicago: Follett Publishing Co. Revised from original 1930 edition. Illustrations by John Dukes McKee.

Forster, E.M., 1976. *The Celestial Omnibus and Other Stories*. New York: Vintage Books.

Fraser, Antonia, 1996. *A History of Toys*. Frankfurt-am-Main, Germany: George Weidenfeld and Nicolson.

Frederick, J. George, 1940. "The Planet Juggler." *Famous Fantastic Mysteries*, 1:6, March 1940, pp. 42–68. Original copyright 1908, The Frank A. Munsey Company, for this story.

Freeman, Mary Wilkins. *See* Solomon, Barbara H.

Freeman, Ruth and Larry, 1942. *Cavalcade of Toys*. New York: Century House.

Frye, Northrop, 1963. *Fables of Identity: Studies in Poetic Mythology*. New York, Burlingame: Harcourt, Brace & World, A Harbinger Book.

_____. 1967. *The Modern Century*. Toronto: Oxford University Press.

Gallagher, William C., 2005. *Modern Toys from Japan, 1940s-1980s*. Atglen, Pennsylvania: Schiffer Publishing.

Garis, Howard R. *See* Appleton, Victor.

Gernsback, Hugo, 1958. *Ralph 124C 41+*. New York: Crest Books/Fawcett World Library. Foreword by Fletcher Pratt.

Goldman, Eric F., 1960. *The Crucial Decade—and After: America, 1945–1960*. New York: Vintage Books. An enlarged edition of The Crucial Decade: America, 1945–1955, of 1956.

Goodfellow, Caroline, 2002. *Games & Puzzles*. Hertfordshire, England: Eagle Editions.

Gordon, Theodore J., and Julian Scheer, 1959. *First into Outer Space*. New York: St. Martin's Press.

Gosse, Edmund, 1983. *Father and Son*. Middlesex/New York: Penguin Books. Originally 1907.

Grahame, Kenneth, 1898. *Dream Days*. Garden City, New York: Garden City Publishing Co., The Sun Dial Library.

Gregory, Walter D., ed., 1922, April. *Hardware Buyers Directory*. New York: Iron Age Publishing Co.

Gribben, Crawford, 2009. *Writing the Rapture: Prophecy Fiction in Evangelical America*. New York and Oxford: Oxford University Press.

Hackett, Alice Payne, 1945. *Fifty Years of Best Sellers 1895–1945*. New York: R.R. Bowker Co.

Haining, Peter, ed., 1976. *The Fantastic Pulps*. New York: Vintage Books.

Hall, Austin, 1939. "Almost Immortal." *Famous Fantastic Mysteries,* 1:2, November 1939, pp. 82–108. Originally published 1916. The story can also be found in *Magazine of Horror,* 3:1 (No. 13), Summer 1966, pp. 83–122.

_____. 1940. "The Man Who Saved the Earth," *Famous Fantastic Mysteries,* 1:5, February 1940, pp. 6–32. Originally published 1919.

Handy, Moses P., ed., 1893. *The Official Directory of the World's Columbian Exposition, May 1st to October 30th, 1893.* Chicago: W.B. Conkey Co.

Harris, Alice, 1905. *Eugene Field Reader.* New York: Charles Scribner's Sons. Illustrated; artists unknown.

Hawthorne, Nathaniel, undated. *A Wonder Book for Girls and Boys.* Philadelphia: Henry Altemus Co.

Haycraft, Howard, 1941. *Murder for Pleasure: The Life and Times of the Detective Story.* New York: D. Appleton-Century Company.

Herlocher, Dawn, 1999. *Doll Makers & Marks: A Guide to Identification.* Norfolk, Virginia: Antique Trader Books.

Herzberg, Max J., 1962. *The Reader's Encyclopedia of American Literature.* New York: Thomas Y. Crowell Co.

Hobhouse, Christopher, 1950. *1851 and the Crystal Palace.* London: John Murray. Introduction by Osbert Lancaster. Revised edition; originally published 1937.

Holmes, Oliver Wendell, 1872. *The Poet at the Breakfast-Table.* Boston: James R. Osgood & Co.

Holmes, Richard, 2010. *The Age of Wonder.* New York: Vintage Books.

Hough, Cass S., 1976. *It's a Daisy!* Rogers, Arkansas: Daisy Division, Victor Comptometer Corporation.

Howard, Robert E., 1966. "Valley of the Lost," in *Magazine of Horror,* 3:1 (no. 13), pp. 36–55. Apparently first written around 1934.

Howells, William Dean, 1957. *A Traveler from Altruria.* New York: Sagamore Press. Introduction by Howard Mumford Jones.

Hultzman, Don, 1998. *Collector's Guide to Battery Toys.* Paducah, Kentucky: Collector Books. Second edition, 2002.

Hunter, J. Paul, ed., 1996. *Mary Shelley, Frankenstein*: A Norton Critical Edition. New York: W.W. Norton & Co.

Huxley, Aldous, 1969. *Brave New World.* New York: Perennial Classic, Harper & Row.

Irving, Washington, 1939. *The Sketch Book of Geoffrey Crayon, Gent.* New York: The Heritage Press.

Jaspers, Karl, 1957. *Man in the Modern Age.* Garden City, New York: Doubleday & Co.

Jewett, Sarah Orne. *See* Solomon, Barbara H.

Johnson Smith & Co., 1935. *Our Latest Catalogue of Surprising Novelties, Puzzles, Tricks, Joke Goods, Useful Articles, Etc.* (Catalog No. 139). Racine, Wisconsin: Johnson Smith & Company.

Joint Committee on Ceremonies, 1893. *Memorial Volume. Dedicatory and Opening Ceremonies of the World's Columbian Exposition.* Chicago: Stone, Kastler & Painter.

Jonnes, Jill, 2010. *Eiffel's Tower.* New York: Penguin Books.

Jules-Verne, Jean, 1976. *Jules Verne, a Biography.* Taplinger Publishing: New York.

"Just Right" Authors and Artists, 1927. Merry Christmas Stories: Good Cheer Tales from "Just Right" Editions. Chicago: Albert Whitman & Co.

Kaufmann & Fabry Company, 1934. *Official Pictures of the 1934 World's Fair.* Chicago: A Century of Progress/ McNeely Printing Company.

Kermode, Frank, 1967. *The Sense of an Ending.* New York: Oxford University Press.

Ketterer, David, 1974. *New Worlds for Old.* Garden City, New York: Anchor Press, Doubleday.

King, Constance, 1989. *Metal Toys & Automata.* Secaucus, New Jersey: Chartwell Books.

King-Hall, Edith, ca. 1910. *Adventures in Toyland.* London: Blackie & Son. Illustrated by Alice B. Woodward. Originally 1897.

Klein, Raymond R., 1993. *Greenberg's Guide to Tootsietoys 1945–1969.* Waukesha, Wisconsin: Greenberg Book Division, Kalmbach Publishing Company.

Knight, Damon, 1962. *A Century of Science Fiction.* New York: Dell Publishing Co.

Kornbluth, C.M., 1952. *Takeoff.* Garden City, New York: Doubleday.

_____. 1955. *Not This August.* Garden City, N.Y.: Doubleday.

_____. 1997. *His Share of Glory: The Complete Short Science Fiction of C.M. Kornbluth.* Framingham, Mass.: The NESFA Press. Edited by Timothy P. Szczesuil.

Kouwenhoven, John A., 1938. *Adventures of America 1857–1900.* New York: Harper & Brothers. The book, ordered chronologically, goes without pagination. Rather than impose page numbers the present author has simply cited author and date.

Kuhns, William, 1969. *Environmental Man.* New York: Harper & Row.

L-W Book Sales, ed., 1994. *Collectors Encyclopedia: Toys, Banks.* Gas City, Indiana: L-W Book Sales.

Lang, Andrew, ed., 1965. *The Blue Fairy Book.* New York: Dover Publications. Unabridged edition of original 1889 edition of Longmans, Green, and Co.

Lang, Daniel, 1961. *From Hiroshima to the Moon.* New York: Dell Publishing Co., Laurel Edition.

Leonard, Jonathan Norton, 1954. *Flight into Space.* New York: New American Library.

Leopard, Dave, 1994. *Rubber Toy Vehicles.* West Columbia, South Carolina: Wentworth Printing Corporation.

Ley, Willy, 1958. *Rockets, Missiles, and Space Travel: Revised Edition.* New York: The Viking Press. Revised and enlarged edition, otherwise the sixth printing of the Revised Edition first published in 1957. The third printing of the Revised Edition, in 1957, was the first to include data on Sputnik. Before the Revised Edition, the book was published originally in June 1951, and went through six printings.

Lofting, Hugh, 1956. *Doctor Doolittle in the Moon*. Philadelphia & New York: J.B. Lippincott Co. Original copyright 1928.

Loncraine, Rebecca, 2009. *The Real Wizard of Oz*. New York: Gotham Books.

London, Jack, 1963. *The Call of the Wild*. New York: Grosset & Dunlap. Originally 1904.

Lovett, Robert Morss, and Helen Sard Hughes, 1932. *The History of the Novel in England*. Boston: Houghton Mifflin Co.

Lytton, Lord Edward Bulwer, 1979. *The Coming Race*. Santa Barbara, California: Woodbridge Press Publishing Co. Introduction by John Weeks.

Malloy, Alex G., 2000. *American Games: Comprehensive Collector's Guide*. Iola, Wisconsin: Antique Trader Books.

McClintock, Inez and Marshall, 1961. *Toys in America*. Washington, D.C.: Public Affairs Press.

McCready Publishing Co., various years. *Playthings Directory*. New York: McCready Publishing Co.

McLoughlin Bros, 1973. *Catalog of McLoughlin Bros*. Reproduction by Antique Toy Collectors of America.

Mead, George Herbert, 1964. *George Herbert Mead on Social Psychology*. Chicago: The University of Chicago Press. Anselm Strauss, ed. and author of an introduction. Second edition; first published in 1956 as *The Social Psychology of George Herbert Mead*.

Merrill, George P., 1924. *The First One Hundred Years of American Geology*. New Haven: Yale University Press.

Milhous, Katherine, 1943. *Corporal Keeperupper*. New York: Charles Scribner's Sons.

Millar, Ronald, 1933. *Official World's Fair Weekly: Week Ending July 29*. Chicago: The Cuneo Press.

Ministry of International Trade & Industry, Japanese Government, 1956. *Japanese Trade Guide*. Tokyo: The Jiji Press.

Moorcock, Michael, ed., 1976. *Before Armageddon: An Anthology of Victorian and Edwardian Fiction Published Before 1914*. London: Wyndham Publications, A Star Book. Originally published 1975.

Morgan, Leon, 1933. *The World a Million Years Ago*. Chicago: Magill-Weinsheimer Co. Illustrated by H.G. Arbo.

Mumford, Lewis, 1967. *The Myth of the Machine*. New York: Harcourt, Brace & World.

_____. 1970. *The Myth of the Machine: The Pentagon of Power*. New York: Harcourt Brace Jovanovich.

_____. 1973. *Interpretations and Forecasts*. New York: Harcourt, Brace Jovanovich.

Murray, John J., and Bruce R. Fox, 1991. *Fisher-Price 1931–1963: A Historical, Rarity, Value Guide*. Florence, Alabama: Books Americana.

Northrop, Henry Davenport, 1890. *Jord, Hav og Himmel*. Chicago: Waverly Publishing Co.

O'Brien, Karen, 2008. *O'Brien's Collecting Toys*. 12th Edition. Iola, Wisconsin: Krause Publications. This O'Brien is no relation to Richard O'Brien, though a capable successor editor to several of the latter's *Collecting* volumes.

O'Brien, Richard, 1990. *The Story of American Toys*. New York: Abbeville Press.

_____. 1994. *Collecting Toys Cars & Trucks, No. 1: Identification and Value Guide*. Florence, Alabama: Books Americana.

_____. 1995. *Collecting Toys, No. 7: A Collector's Identification & Value Guide*. Florence, Alabama: Books Americana.

_____. 1997. *Collecting American-Made Toy Soldiers: Identification and Value Guide*. Third edition. Florence, Alabama: Books Americana.

_____. 1997. *Collecting Foreign-Made Toy Soldiers: Identification and Value Guide*. Iola, Wisconsin: Krause Publications.

_____. 1997. *Collecting Toys Cars & Trucks: Identification and Value Guide*. Second edition. Iola, Wisconsin: Krause Publications.

Orwell, George, 1961. *1984*. New York: New American Library of World Literature, Signet Classics.

Outcault, R.F., 1910. *My Resolutions: Buster Brown*. Chicago: Outcault Advertising Co. Also bears a 1906 copyright for Frederic A. Stokes Co.; unpaginated.

Oxford University Press, 1953. *The Dictionary of National Biography* (Concise, Part 1). London: Oxford University Press.

Page, Thomas Nelson, 1918. *Tommy Trot's Visit to Santa Claus*. New York: Charles Scribner's Sons. Includes "A Captured Santa Claus." Originally 1891.

Parry-Crooke, Charlotte, ed., 1981. *Toys, Dolls, Games: Paris 1903–1914*. London: Denys Ingram Publishers.

Pascall, Jeremy, 1977. *The King Kong Story*. Secaucus, New Jersey: Chartwell Books.

Peacock, Thomas Love, 1947. *Nightmare Abbey* and *Crotchet Castle*. London: Hamish Hamilton. Originally published 1818 and 1831. Introduction by J.B. Priestley.

Poe, Edgar Allan, 1983. *The Unabridged Edgar Allan Poe*. Tam Mossman, ed. Philadelphia: Running Press.

_____. 1984. *Poetry and Tales*. Patrick F. Quinn, ed. New York: The Library of America.

Preston, Douglas J., 1986. *Dinosaurs in the Attic: An Excursion into the American Museum of Natural History*. New York: Ballantine Books.

Pringle, David, 1987. *Imaginary People*. New York: World Almanac.

Progressive, undated but ca. 1953. *Toys: Christmas, Halloween Goods*. Los Angeles: Progressive Wholesalers, Inc.

Pyle, Howard, 1965. *The Wonder Clock, or Four & Twenty Marvelous Tales, Being One for Each Hour of the Day.* New York: Dover Publications. Originally 1887.
Rackham, Arthur, ed., 1987. *The Arthur Rackham Fairy Book.* New York: Crown Publishers, Weathervane Books.
Remak, Joachim, 1967. *The Origins of World War I, 1871–1914.* Hinsdale, Illinois: The Dryden Press.
Reynolds, Francis J., et al., eds., 1916. *The Story of The Great War.* New York: P.F. Collier & Son.
Rich, Mark, 1992. "De la Terre a l'Ecosphere: Science Fiction, Space-ships and Ecology." *Actes du Quatrieme Colloque International de Science-Fiction de Nice.* Nice, France: Centre d'Etude de la Metaphore; pp. 373–382. French translation "De la Terre a l'Ecosphere: science-fiction, vaisseaux spatiaux et Ècologie," pp. 383–393.
_____. 2000. *100 Greatest Baby Boomer Toys.* Iola, Wisconsin: Krause Publications.
_____. 2001, July. "Buck Rogers Stuff: Notes Toward an Oblique History of Science Fiction, Toys, and Society." *Science Fiction Chronicle* 22:7, pp. 34–38.
_____. 2001. *Toys A to Z.* Iola, Wisconsin: Krause Publications.
_____. 2002 [September]. "James Thomson (1814–1882)." *Critical Survey of Poetry, Second Revised Edition.* Pasadena, Calif.: Salem Press.
_____. 2005. *Warman's 101 Greatest Baby Boomer Toys.* Iola, Wisconsin: Krause Publications.
_____. 2009. "Introduction." *In* Verne, 2009.
_____. 2010. *C.M. Kornbluth: Life and Works of a Science Fiction Visionary.* Jefferson, N.C.: McFarland & Co.
Rockwell, Carey, 1954. *The Revolt on Venus: A Tom Corbett Space Cadet Adventure.* New York: Grosset & Dunlap. "Willy Ley, Technical Adviser."
Roth, Edward, undated. *The Space Novels of Jules Verne: From the Earth to the Moon; All Around the Moon.* Translated and with a preface by Edward Roth. New York: Dover Publications. The introduction bears an 1874 date. While this is a "translation," the insertions and stylistic efflorescences of Roth make this akin to an American variation on the theme provided by Verne's original text. Despite his ostensible enthusiasm for the works of Verne, Roth himself, p. 5, reveals his hope that he has "improved" Verne.
Schroeder, Joseph J., Jr., ed., 1971. *The Wonderful World of Toys, Games & Dolls 1860–1930.* Northfield, Illinois: DBI Books.
Schwartz, Evan I., 2009. *Finding Oz: How L. Frank Baum Discovered the Great American Story.* Boston: Houghton Mifflin Harcourt.
Sharp, Roberta, 1990. "Poe's Chapters on 'Natural Magic.'" *In* Fisher, 1990, pp. 154–166.
Shea, James J., and Charles Mercer, 1960. *It's All in the Game.* New York: G.P. Putnam's Sons.
Shelley, Mary, 1996. See Hunter, 1996.
Sheridan, Martin, 1973. *Classic Comics & Their Creators: Life Stories of American Cartoonists from the Golden Age.* Arcadia, California: Post-Era Books. Reprint of original 1942 printing of Comics and Their Creators.
Sherman, Harold M., 1931. *The Land of Monsters.* New York: Grosset & Dunlap.
Smith, H.S., 1894, April 2. *The Magic City, A Portfolio of Original Photographic Views of the Great World's Fair.* Historical Fine Art Series, 1:12. Philadelphia: Historical Publishing Co.
Smith, Ron, and William C. Gallagher, 2004. *The Big Book of Tin Toy Cars: Passenger, Sports, and Concept Vehicles*; two volumes. Atglen, Pennsylvania: Schiffer Publishing.
Solomon, Barbara H., ed. *Short Fiction of Sarah Orne Jewett and Mary Wilkins Freeman.* New York: New American Library, Meridian Classic, 1987.
Spero, James, 1988. *Collectible Toys and Games of the Twenties and Thirties from Sears, Roebuck and Co. Catalogs.* New York: Dover Publications.
Stapledon, Olaf, 1945. *Odd John. In* Wollheim, 1945: page citations are to this text. Stapledon's book originally appeared in America in 1935, New York: E.P. Dutton & Company; and 1935, London: Methuen & Company.
_____. 1968. *Last and First Men & Star Maker.* New York: Dover Publications. Unabridged reprinting of the 1931 edition of *Last and First Men* and 1937 edition of *Star Maker.*
Starkie, Enid, 1958. *Baudelaire.* Norfolk, Connecticut: New Directions.
Stevenson, Robert Louis, 1916. *A Child's Garden of Verses.* New York: Charles Scribner's Sons. Illustrated by Florence Edith Storer. Originally 1885.
Stirn, Carl P., 1990. *Turn-of-the-Century Dolls, Toys and Games: The Complete Illustrated Carl P. Stirn Catalog from 1893.* New York: Dover Publications. Published in association with the Henry Ford Museum & Greenfield Village, Dearborn, Michigan. Introduction by Mary Lynn Stevens Heininger.
Stockton, Frank R. 1892. *The Clocks of Rondaine, and Other Stories.* New York: Charles Scribner's Sons.
Taine, John, 1934. *Before the Dawn.* Baltimore: The Williams & Wilkins Co. Also reprinted in Wollheim, 1945.
Targ, William, ed., 1957. *Bibliophile in the Nursery: A Bookman's Treasury of Collector's Lore on Old and Rare Children's Books.* Cleveland: The World Publishing Co. Thomson, David, 1950. *England in the Nineteenth Century (1815–1914).* London: Penguin Books.
Thomson (B.V.), James, 1967. *The Speedy Extinction of Evil and Misery.* William David Schaefer, ed. Berkeley and Los Angeles: University of California Press.
Thwaite, Ann, 2002. *Glimpses of the Wonderful: The Life of Philip Henry Gosse.* London: Faber & Faber.
Torrey, Norman L., 1960. *Les Philosophes.* New York: Capricorn Books.
Toy Manufacturers of the U.S.A., 1947. *How to Sell Toys: A Sales Manual for Toys and Playthings.* New York: Toy Mfrs. of the U.S.A.
Tropp, Martin, 1976. *Mary Shelley's Monster.* Houghton Mifflin: Boston.

Bibliography

Tumbusch, Tom, 1991. *Tomart's Price Guide to Radio Premiums and Cereal Box Collectibles*. Radnor, Pennsylvania: Wallace-Homestead Book Co.
Twain, Mark, 1961. *The Complete Humorous Sketches and Tales of Mark Twain*. Charles Neider, ed. Garden City, N.Y.: Doubleday & Co.
_____. 1962. *Great Short Works of Mark Twain*. New York: Harper & Row/Perennial Classics.
Uglow, Jenny, 2002. *The Lunar Men: The Friends Who Made the Future, 1730–1810*. London: Faber & Faber.
United States Centennial Commission, 1876. *International Exhibition, 1876, Official Catalogue*. Second and revised edition. Philadelphia: John R. Nagle & Co.
Van Dyne, Edith (Baum, L. Frank), 1911. *The Flying Girl*. Chicago: The Reilly & Britton Co.
_____. 1912. *The Flying Girl and Her Chum*. Chicago: The Reilly & Britton Co.
_____. 1917. *Mary Louise Solves a Mystery*. Chicago: Reilly & Lee.
Verne, Jules, 1906. *Hector Servadac*. New York: Charles Scribner's Sons.
_____. 1958. *Five Weeks in a Balloon*. Westport, Connecticut: Associated Booksellers. A "Fitzroy" edition, with introduction by I.O. Evans.
_____. 1965. *Propeller Island*. London: Panther Books.
_____. 1977. *The Annotated Jules Verne: Twenty Thousand Leagues Under the Sea*. Walter James Miller, editor. New York: New American Library.
_____. 1978. *The Best of Jules Verne*. Edited and with an introduction by Alan K. Russell. Secaucus, New Jersey: Castle Books. This compendium includes the 1874 George M. Towle translation of *Around the World in Eighty Days*; the first English translation of *The Clipper of the Clouds* (*Robur le Conquèrant*, 1886), by Sampson Low, of 1887; and the 1872 translation by Griffith and Farran of *Journey to the Centre of the Earth*. It also includes Marie A. Belloc's "Jules Verne at Home," originally published in the February 1895 *The Strand*.
_____. 1981. *20,000 Leagues Under the Sea*. Translated by Anthony Bonner; introduction by Ray Bradbury. New York: Bantam Books. Originally published 1962.
_____. 1996. *Paris in the Twentieth Century*, Richard Howard, translator. Introduction by Eugen Weber. New York: Random House.
_____. 1999. *The Eternal Adam and Other Stories*. Selected and with an introduction by Peter Costello. London: Orion Publishing Group. This includes the short memoir "Recollections of Childhood and Youth," and stories "The First Ships of the Mexican Navy," "A Drama in the Air," "Master Zacharius," "The Humbug," "Dr. Ox's Experiment," "An Ideal City," "Dr. Trifulgas," and "Gil Braltar." Three stories in which Michel Verne had a hand also appear: "In the Twenty-Ninth Century," "An Express of the Future," and "The Eternal Adam."
_____. 2007. *Lighthouse at the End of the World*. Lincoln: University of Nebraska Press. Translated and introduced by William Butcher.
_____. 2009. *A Journey to the Center of the Earth*. Vancouver, British Columbia: Engage Books. Introduction by Mark Rich.
_____. Undated A. *The Omnibus Jules Verne*. Philadelphia and New York: J.B. Lippincott Company. No editor listed; novels include *Around the World in Eighty Days*, *From the Earth to the Moon and a Trip Around It*, *Twenty Thousand Leagues Under the Sea*, and *The Blockade Runners*. The translation of *Earth to the Moon* might be the 1873 English translation by L. Mercier and E.C. King of *From the Earth to the Moon Direct in 97 Hours 20 Minutes; and a Trip Around It*. The translation seems fairly faithful.
_____. Undated B. Verne, Jules, undated. *A Special Correspondent (Claudius Bombarnec)*. Akron, Ohio: The New Werner Company. "The Best Books Series."
_____. *See also* Roth, Edward.
Villiers de l'Isle-Adam, Jean Marie, 1982. *Tomorrow's Eve*. Robert Martin Adams, translator. Urbana: University of Illinois Press. The writer's full name was Jean Marie Mathias Philippe Auguste Villiers de l'Isle-Adam.
Walpole, Horace, 1986. *See* Fairclough, 1986.
Wells, H.G., 1934. *Seven Famous Novels*. Garden City, N.Y.: Garden City Publishing Co. With preface by Wells.
_____. 1945. *The First Men in the Moon*. See Wollheim, 1945. Citations in the text are to that 1945 reprint. Originally published 1901, London: A.P. Watt & Son.
_____. 1960. *Three Prophetic Novels*. E.F. Bleiler, ed. New York: Dover Publications. In this useful collection, the edition of *When the Sleeper Wakes* follows the 1899 Harper first edition; *A Story of the Days To Come* follows the 1899 version that appeared in *Tales of Space and Time*; and *The Time Machine* follows the 1895 Heinemann edition, with the addition of a scene from the original serial version in *National Review*, omitted from subsequent book versions. Bleiler provides a useful introduction.
_____. *see also* Wollheim.
White, Larry, 1997. *Cracker Jack Toys*. Atglen, Penn.: Schiffer Publishing.
Wieland, James, and Edward Force, 1980. *Tootsietoys: World's First Diecast Models*. Osceola, Wisconsin: Motorbooks International.
Williams, A.C., Company, 1934. *Toys, House Furnishing Specialties and Hardware, Fifty-First Edition*. Revenna, Ohio: The A.C. Williams Co. The catalog has no date. The pages reprinted in L-W Book Sales, 1994, identify the catalog as 1934, however. Style developments reflected in the catalog would seem to confirm this.
Williams, Rosalind, 1990. *Notes on the Underground: An Essay on Technology, Society, and the Imagination*. Cambridge, Mass.: The MIT Press.

Wilson, Edmund, 1931. *Axel's Castle: A Study in the Imaginative Literature of 1870 to 1930.* New York: Charles Scribner's Sons.

_____. 1965. *The Bit Between My Teeth.* New York: Farrar, Straus and Giroux.

Wollheim, Donald A., ed., 1948. *The Portable Novels of Science.* New York: The Viking Press. Includes, besides introductory notes by Wollheim: *The First Men in the Moon,* by H.G. Wells; *Before the Dawn,* by John Taine; *The Shadow Out of Time,* by H.P. Lovecraft; and *Odd John,* by Olaf Stapledon.

Wright, Carroll D., 1895. *The Industrial Evolution of the United States.* Meadville, Pennsylvania, and New York: Flood and Vincent.

Wyss, Johann David, undated. *The Swiss Family Robinson.* Garden City, N.Y.: Junior Deluxe Editions.

Young, Clarence, 1911. *The Motor Boys Over the Rockies, or A Mystery of the Air.* New York: Cupples & Leon Company. (This particular Motor Boys adventure was apparently not by Garis.)

Index

Numbers in **_bold italics_** indicate pages with illustrations

A. Schoenhut Co. *175*, ***187***, 188, 300*n*24, 304*ch*16*n*31
Aberdeen, North Dakota 163
absurdism 11, 16, 31, 43, 73, 94, 96
A.C. Williams Co. 12, ***13***, 50
acoucryptophone 58
acrobat toy 65, 110, 114; Crandall's 135
Adams, Henry 131, 137, 140, 168, 181, 183–4, 186, 198, 217–8, 220–1, 300*n*12
Addams, Jane 177
Adventures in Toyland 44, ***51***, ***87***, ***280***
The Adventures of Captain Gulliver 82
aerial toy 5, 6, 11, 15, 23, 140, 191, 196; *see also* fire balloon
"aero" prefix 240
Aerona Balloon 193
aeronaut 8, 14–5, 159, 212, 284*n*38
aeronef 16, 21, 34, 42, 132–3; *see also* airship
aeroplane 179, 192, 212, 215, 240, 301*n*30; toy ***190***–1, 209, 301*n*30–3, 302*n*27, 304*ch*15*n*34
Aeroplane Race Game (McDowell) 209–10
Aeroplane Race Game (Wolverine) ***199***
aerostat 5, 6, 9, 15, 33, 34, 62, 98, 100, 132, 140, 159, 301*n*38; *see also* balloon
Africa 9, 43, 82, 270
Agassiz, Louis 120
Age of the Masses 2, 234, 278–9, 292*n*9
A.H. Andrews & Co. 140
A.I. Root Co. 232–3
air rifle 244
Air Wonder Stories 27
Airflow 240–1
Airline Pursuit ***263***
"The Airlords of Han" 21

airplane 100, 179, 196, 212, 223, 251, 261; toy 209–10, 215, 232, ***239***, 251, 262, ***264***, 301*n*31, 302*n*22, 304*n*34, 302*n*22; *see also* aeroplane; monoplane
airship 100–1, 141, ***191***, 236; figural 189, 193; inversion for spaceship 250–1; toy 209, ***209***, 301*n*40; *see also* Zeppelin
Ajeeb 85, 129
Aladdin 157–8, 161
Albert of Saxony 5
Alcott, Louisa May 86, 289*n*53
Aldrich, Thomas Bailey 119
Alexander Doll Co. 230
Alger, Horatio 176
Alice in Lightland 231
Alice's Adventures in Wonderland 40, 46, 204
All-Fair 134, 210
All Metal Products Co. 239; *see also* Wyandotte Toys
All-Story 183, 185, 296*n*43, 300*n*19
Allen, A.M. 145
Alley Oop 219, ***232***
Althof, Bergmann & Co. 139
aluminum toy 263
Amazing Stories 27, 207, 210, 228, 248
American Aeroplane Mfg. Co. 191
American Balloon Co. 302*n*18
American Boy Magazine 216
American Fire Department 13
American Flyer 241, 302*n*24; *see also* Gilbert, A.C.
American Indian 91–2, 220
American Mechanical Toy Co. (Dayton, Ohio) 154, 190
American Mechanical Toy Co. (New York City) 139
American Model Builder 154, 190
American National Co. 250
The American Songster 91

American Toy Co. 291*n*26
American Toy Watch Co. 88
American West 91
Amundsen, Roald 189
Animals in Motion 255
Animate Toy Co. 208, ***213***, 301–2*n*17, 302*n*24
animated picture 46–7
Animateur 59
animation 25, 59–61, 84, 106, 205, 229, 231; in film 186–7, 205, 247–8
Anning, Mary 70, 207
antediluvian 72, 120
anthropology 157, 223
antigravity *see* gravity, anti-
ape, giant *see* gorilla
Apon Novelty Co. 305*n*58
Appleton, Victor 27, 44, 174, 220, 247–8, 259; *see also* Garis, Howard
Appleton, Victor II 81
aquarium 67–8, 117–8, 157
Aquarium 67
arcade 66, 258
Arcade Mfg. Co. 241, 302*n*24, 304–5*n*24
Argosy 182, 296*n*43
Aristotle 72
Arkwright, Richard 56
"Armageddon, 2419 A.D." 210
Arnold, Edwin 40
Around the Moon 110–11
around-the-world book 161; game 133–4, 199, 209–10, 215–6, 255, 272–3
Around the World in Eighty Days 125–30, 133, 142–4, 181, 248; film 273; game and play set 273
Arronax, Professor 113–6, 119
Art Deco *see* "Deco" styling
the artificial 25, 46, 59, 107, 138, 146, 154, 230, 233–4, 294*n*10; as all-embracing 234; city 162–3; flowers 132, 294–5*n*10; man 85,

317

126, 162; manufacturers of, at Centennial 294–5n10; stone 137; worker 200
Ash, Fenton 193, 301n38; see also Atkins, Francis Henry
Asimov, Isaac 40
Astor, John Jacob 180, 186
"Astounding News by Express, via Norfolk!" 26–7; see also "The Balloon-Hoax"
Astounding Science Fiction 28, 37, 259, 306n19
Astounding Stories of Super Science 28, 259
astronaut 256–8
astronomy 4, 18, 41, 120, 140, 143, 153, 272
At the Earth's Core 185, 300n19
Atherton, Gertrude 180
Atkins, Francis Henry 179, 301n38; see also Ash, Fenton
Atlantic Ocean 16, 41, 71
Atlas Steel & Mfg. Co. 250, 205n36
atom bomb 38, 183, 263, 265, 280; atomic destruction 274
atomic energy 264
"atomic" toy 272, 277
Austin & Craw 295n13
Austria 20, 59, 65–6, 85, 122
Authors game 23
Auto-Bike Co. 232
Auto Magic Picture Gun 232
"auto" prefix 232
Auto Speedway 232
Auto-Wheel Coaster Co. 232
Autocraft Co. 232
the automatic 138, 166, 206, 229–31; usage shift 208
Automatic Bird Target 232
Automatic Cradle Co. 299n66
Automatic Railway 138
Automatic Recording Safe Co. 231
Automatic Rubber Co. 231
Automatic Toy 88–9, 290n18, 290n22
Automatic Toy Corp. 231, 251
Automatic Toy Works 145–6, 290n18, 305n37
Automatic Waltzer 89
automation 61; achieving totality 217, 233; in daily life 138, 153, 231, 252, 264; disappearing 208–9, 229–31, 233, 294n10; of light 231, 233; public acceptance 56; of travel 128, 130, 147
automatism 25, 42, 43, 66, 138, 155–6, 201, 234, 252; consolidation into 232; diversionary 92–3, 139
automaton 4, 17–8, 86; false 84–5, 166; film as 205–6; global 128, 133, 272–3, 281; human 93, 107–8, 113–4, 125–30, 273; machine 18, 42, 46, 47 58, 84–6, 89–93, 103–4, 120–1, 129, 144–7, 165; machine as woman 145–7; musical 58, 85, 90–1, 138–9; toy 24, 25, 87–8, 130, 138–40, 145, 161, 208, 230, 249, 290n18; see also celestial sphere; earth; mechanical toy
The Automaton 87–8
automobile 179, 181, 232, 236–7, 239, 240, 280; amusement-park *278*; old-fashioned toy 272; toy ***195*–196, *238***, 240–1, 254, 265, ***275***, 296n49; see also Car of the Future
automobile romance 181, 300n6
Autoperipatetikos 88, 164, 290n15
Les Aventures de Capitaine Hatteras 20
Les Aventures de Gordon Pym 25, 32
Axel's vision 74–6, 78, 117, 120, 231

B. Haas, Jr. & Co. 139
Babbage, Charles 57–84
Baby Boom 268, 279, 307n35
baby walker 232
Bach, J.S. 105
bagatelle 250
Bailey, Temple 197, 254
Baker Toy Aeroplane Mfg. Co. 191, 301n33
Baldwin, Matthias W. 55–6
ball 3, 4, 5, 10, 50, 106, 108, 110, 119, 159, 208, 255, 283n5; cannonball 106–8, 110–11; Earth as 181, 281
Ballads and Other Poems 7
balloon 10, 21, 207; aerostatic 6–9, 14–5; captive 159, 301n41; figural 140, 203; to the Moon 9, 97, 99–100, 102–3; rubber 208, 246, 302n18; stratospheric 251, 255–6, 275; toy 4, 5, 15, 33, 62, 140, 165, 196, 208, 272; see also fire balloon
"The Balloon-Hoax" 16
Balzac, Honoré 6
Bangs, John Kendrick 43, 53, 180, 187, 197, 253, 287n11
bank (toy) 50, 135, 249, 290; architectural 160, 232; character 231, 246, 305, 246, 305n58; mechanical 80, 160–1, 249, 298, 295n13
banking 108–9, 126, 128, 131, 220, 264; see also business
Banks, Joseph 78, 284
Barbicane, Impey 106–7, 110, 113, 200
Barbie doll 278–9, 307n35

Barker, Robert 75–6
Barney & Berry 159
Barney Google 252
Barnum, P.T. 65, 70, 89, 223, 288n6; "Barnumizing" 162, 189, 298n58; fictional 53, 197
Barnum Museum 82
Barraclough, Geoffrey 141, 223
Barrie, James M. 29, 36, 180, 187, 199, 300n5
Barth & Wagner 139
"Bartholomew baby" 54; see also St. Bartholomew Fair
Barzun, Jacques 20, 44
bathysphere 255–6
battery *iv*, 48–9, 132
battery-operated see electrical toy
"The Battle of Dorking" 122–3
Baudelaire, Charles Pierre 19, 25, 27, 30–2, 42, 60, 67, 147
Baum, Lyman Frank 19, 23, 26, 36, 40, 54, 152, 163–7, 170, 172, 174, 179–81, 199, 205, 246, 259
Bavaria 134, 139, 198, 295n18
Beadle's Pocket Library 147
Beckford, William 30
The Begum's Fortune 178
Belcher, J. 70
Belgium 59, 66
Bell, Alexander Graham 138, 141
bell toy 49, 80, 135, ***160*–161**, 298n52
Bellamy, Edward 40, 153, 163, 180, 184, 210, 236
"La Belle au Bois Dormante" 39
"The Bells" 13
Benét, William Rose 293ch8n22, 294n31
Bennett, Alma 218
Bergen, Edgar 299n85
Bergen Toy & Novelty 262, 306n9
Berlin, Germany 66, 140
"Beton" see Bergen Toy & Novelty
Bettelheim, Bruno 305n55
Bevin Bros. 49
Beyond the Planet Earth 258
Biblical history see providential world-view
Biblical tale 26, 52–3, 179
bicycle 140, 241
Bierce, Ambrose 87, 144–5, 179
Big Brother 267
Billiken 243
biology 20, 72–3, 272
The Black Indies 35, 178
Blackwoods magazine 122
Blake, William 93
Blakeslee, Cornelius 89
Blakeslee, Enos 291n27
Blakeslee Carriage Shop 291n27
Blanchard, Jean-Pierre 6

Blavatsky, Helena 163
Bleak House 23, 131–2, 175, 223, 293*ch*9*n*24
Bleriot 196
Blish, James 8
blocks, alphabet 23, **47**, 49, 82, 130; construction 82, 296*n*49; nesting **175**; picture 82, 160
Blondie Goes to Leisureland **253**
Blown-Up Fort 12
Blue Fairy Book 163
Bluebird racer 241
Bly, Nellie 133–4, 149, 247
boat: electrical 157, 298*n*30; electrical toy 160; mechanical toy **90**, 118–9, 145; overturned 237; toy 65, 196, 262, 296*n*49, 305*n*58; *see also* steamboat
Bontems, B. 139
Boston, Massachusetts 70, 130, 138, 140; *Daily Advertiser* 181
bouleversement 183–4, 211
Boulton, Matthew 15, 55
Bouton, C.M. 77
box toy *see* play set
boy inventor 91–2, 147, 253, 305*n*46
Boyle, Charles 47
The Boys of New York 147, 296*n*43
Bozo the Clown 270
Bradbury, Ray 40, 302*n*31
Bradley, Milton 23, 130
Bradley, Richard 58
Braitling, C.F. 90, 291*n*34; & Sons 295*n*13
Brave New World 217, 231, 280
Brazil 138
Brewster, David 57–8, 84–5, 125
Brinkman, Milt 242, 244
Britains 249
British Association for the Advancement of Science 6, 57
British North America Act 19
Brodin *fils* 140
Brontosaurus 169, 187, 206–7, **225**, 234; toy 218–9, 303*n*52
Brooks, Van Wyck 179–80, 182, 197, 222, 235, 237, 265, 280, 283*n*28, 290*n*9, 298*n*36, 300*n*18, 303*n*56
Brown, George W. 89–90, 138
Brown, John 22
Brown, J.S. 290*n*18
Brownies 204, 292*n*7
Browning, Robert 31
Browning, Elizabeth Barrett 31
Brunel, Isambard 16, 64, 66
Bryan, William Jennings 207, 224
bubble 119, 256; enclosure 265–6; pipe 119; wand 119
Bubble Gun **258**
Buck Rogers 40, 62, 210, 232, 239, **243**–8, 259; as adjective 241–2, 247; Battlecruiser 252; Caster Set 249; Flash Blast Attack Ship 252; game 245; phenomenon 246–9, 302*n*31; promotion **242**, 244–5; Rocket Ship Battlecruiser 252; Rocket Ship Fleet 246; Space Ranger Kit **273**; spaceship 239, **243**, 250–2; 25th Century Rocket Pistol 245, 263; 25th Century Rocket Ship 245; Venus Duo-Destroyer 252
Buck Rogers in the 25th Century 210, 254
Bucket, Mr. 113, 175
Buckland, William 57
Buddy "L" Mfg. Co. 241, 249
Buddy "L" Toys 262
Buffalo Bill 248
Buffalo Toy & Tool Works 304–5*n*34
bullet 108, 110–11
The Bunnikins-Bunnies and the Moon King 193
Bunyan, John 60
burial alive 85, 113
Burnham, Clara 162–4, 202, 298*n*36, 298*n*39
Burnham, Daniel 154
Burnham and Root 154
Burroughs, Edgar Rice 40, 180–1, 185–6, 199, 206, 215–6, 235, 246, 248, 279, 296*n*43, 300*n*18, 304*ch*16*n*29; novels in *All-Story* and *Blue Book* 300*n*19
Bushnell, E.W. 50
business 11, 93, 121, 131, 147, 181–2, 220, 223, 236, 264, 303*n*56; advertising 181–2; as a machine 126; *see also* banking; industry
Buster Brown 187, 248
Butler, Samuel 179
Byron, Lord 53

Cabell, James Branch 180
The Cabinet of Chemical Wonders 132
Cadaco, Ltd. 249
California 38, 164; Oakland 249; *see also* San Francisco
Calkins, Dick 244, 254
The Call of the Wild 185, 210
Calvinism 51, 63–4, 68, 154, 157, 263
camera lucida 60; obscura 106; photographic 177
Campbell, John W., Jr. 28, 228, 259, 279
Canada 19, 98, 270, 284*n*5, 298*n*47
candy 65, 123–4; *see also* Cracker Jack; gingerbread

cannon 106–10, 292*n*35
cap-exploding bomb 187, 214, 302*n*35; cane 196; gun 24, 196; torpedo 214
Čapek, Karl 37, 180, 199–201, 203, 207, 217, 249
Car of the Future 239, 254, 265–6, 306*n*9–13
Cardiff Giant 288*n*6
carriage making 49, 50, 129, 290*n*22
carriage, toy 88, **175**
Carroll, Lewis 1, 26, 40, 44, 46, 48, 168–9, 204, 289*n*36; *see also* Dodgson, Charles
Carter, John 185, 199, 246–7, 246–7
cartoon character 62, 186–7
cartooning 186, 204
Cass, N.D. 262
The Castle of Otranto 29
casting outfit 248–9
catastrophe 10–2, 17–8, 43, 52, 72, 206, 263; aerial 11, 105, 284*n*39; by artificial agency 201; bridge 12, 21, 22; celestial 112, 143–4; cosmic 183; by explosion 12, 43, 92, 119, 181; by fire 12–3, 85, 289*n*53; by human agency 15; as redemption 9–11, 18, 44, 91–2; by superhuman agency 120–1; symbolic 17; by waking 188; by water 12, 43, 91, 116; *see also* Earth, in cataclysm
catastrophism 12, 69, 73–4, 120, 207, 289*n*41
Catholicism 72–3, 103–4, 115, 125, 143
the "Cave Man" 186, 206–7, 223, 231; toy 271
Cavor 171–2, 200, 216, 255–6
CBS 267
C.D. Goodwin & Co. 295*n*13
celestial sphere 4, 17, 41–2, 84, 86–7, 128, 153, 168, 173
celluloid 159, 196, 208, 265, 269–70
Centennial Exposition 8, 90, 130, 138–41, 146, 152–3, 155, 157, 159–60, 174, 269; Machinery Hall 138, 140; Singer Sewing Machine Building 138
centralization 142, 181, 234, 254, 262
A Century of Progress Exposition 134, 217–8, 224–31, 233–4, 240, 247, 249, 259, 267; Alice in Lightland 231, 303*n*9; Clock of the Ages 224, 227, 303*n*9; Dairy Building 231; Earth-in-swirl logo **225**, 239, 242; Electrical Building 229–

31; Embryological and Prehistoric Show 226; Enchanted Island 226–7, 230; evolutionary theme 224; General Motors Building 231; Gorilla Villa 226; Hall of Progress 226; Hall of Science 224, 230; Home and Industrial Arts 228; House of Tomorrow 228, 303*n*15; Petroleum Industries Exhibit 229; Sinclair Dinosaur Exhibit **225–6**; Sky-Ride 215–6, 231; Travel and Transport Building 230; The World a Million Years Ago **224**–6, 231, 303*n*9
ceramic toy 269
H.M.S. *Challenger* 78, 186, 289*n*41
Challenger, Professor 186, 205, 223
Chandler, Raymond 304*n*7
Chandler Mfg. Co. 194
character, fictional *see* dissected soul; stock character; type character
Charageat, E. 138
Charles, Jacques Alexandre César 15, 34, 158
Charles, William 70
The Checkered Game of Life 23, 147
Chemcraft 245
chemistry 13, 30, 48, 57, 132
Chesney, George Tomkyns 122–3, 170, 219
chess 49, 84, 145, 290*n*9
Chess-Player *see* "Maelzel's Chess Player"
Chesterton, G.K. 180
Chicago 22, 69, 90, 140–1, 164, 192, 211, 223–4, 241, 245–6, 249; Adler Planetarium 227; Epstein's Dime Museum 155; Great Fire 90, 153; Jackson Park 157, 225; Masonic Temple 154, 160; Museum of Science and Industry 224–5; panoramas 155, 297*n*15; Washington Park 153; *see also* Century of Progress; Columbian Exposition
Chicago Roller Skate Co. 241
A Child's Garden of Verses 36, 43–4, 112, 123, 168, 254
China 4, 20, 21
Chinese shades 46, 76
Christmas 18, 99, **175**, 266; Father 99; ornament 241; secular shift 105
A Christmas Carol 41
Chromatrope 60, 76
Cinderella 131
Cinderella's Chariot and Chime 54

cinema 36–8, 178, 186, 199, 205–7, 248–9, 259, 267–8; silent film 34, 205–6, 248
Cinq Semaines en Ballon 7–11, 38, 44, 103, 106, 115
circumnavigation 41, 125–30, 133–4, 273
circus 151, 188–9, 196
"The City in the Sea" 43, 116
The City of New York 21
Civil War 22–4, 50, 92, 107, 123
"Clarel" 152
Clark & Sowden 118
Classical influence 7, 38, 88, 115, 164, 233, 304*n*36
Claudius Bombarnac 134
Claudy, Carl H. 174, 180, 216–8, 220, 247, 305*n*53
Clavilux 231
Clay, R.J. 290*n*18
Clemens, Samuel 38–9, 79, 179–80, 236; *see also* Twain, Mark
Cleveland, Grover 155–6, 159, 298*n*35
The Clipper of the Clouds 132–3, **148–9**, 176, 190
clock 4–5, 41–2, 61, 67, 84, 86, 113, 137, 139, 153, 165, 170, 281l; around the 130–1; as a being 46, 103, **104**, 105, 110, 170–1; destruction 86, 103, 130; educational or moral 130–1; electric 288*n*61; of the future 172; game 135; the geographical 4–5, 78, 128–9; fantasy 25, 105, 143; for a heart 103, 165–6; inaccurate 130, 137; "Lunar" and "Solar" 140; as mechanical diversion 137; of the past 76 224; railway as 130; regulator 86–7, 111, 125; sectional 288*n*61; society as 126; stoppage 103, 116, 131, 143; tower 41, 86, 111, 137, 140; toy 130–1, 135–6, 168; *see also* Earth; time; watch
clockmaker 67, 84, 87, 89, 103, 138–9, 166
"The Clocks of Rondaine" 137
clockwork 11, 88–90, 110, 132, 145, 147, 160, 166; *see also* spring motor
Cohen, Harold 147, 180
Coleridge, Samuel Taylor 39, 294*n*41
Collegeville Flag & Mfg. Co. 305*n*58
Collodi, C. 86
"The Colloquy of Monos and Una" 76
Colon, Christobal 159, 296*n*8
colonization 53, 66, 141–3, 223, 277; outer-space 258, 274, 276
Colt, Samuel 66, 92
Columbia, South Carolina 231

Columbia Instruction Co. 90, 295*n*13
Columbian Exposition 134, 152–64, 170, 181, 224, 234; Administration Building 156, 160; Anthropology Building 163, 298*n*36; "Columbia" goddess statue 158–9, 184; Electric Fountain 156; Electric Intramural Railway 157; Electric Scenic Theater 155; Electricity Building 156, 161, 163; electricity theme 155–7; Ferris Wheel 158, 160, 162, 215–6, 298*n*39; Fisheries or Aquarial Building 157; game 160; Hagenbeck's animals, 164, 299*n*80; Horticultural Building 156–7; Machinery Hall, 156, 158; as Magic City 155–6, 158; Manufactures Building 156–7, 161; Midway Plaisance 155, 157–60, 162, 298*n*36; Moorish Palace, 158, 160, 163, 205; Parliament of Religions 162, 177, 298*n*36; toy 159–61, 298*n*52; Women's Building 159
comedy 10
comet 142–3, **192**
comic book 38, 256
comic strip *see* newspaper, cartoon
comical *see* toy, comical
The Coming Race 35, 119–20, 174
Coming Up for Air 280
communication: with the dead 121; faster 122; instantaneous 156; video 210; *see also* global communication; telegraph; telephone; television
composition (toy material) 23, 101, 262
Comus 84
Conan Doyle, Arthur 180, 185–6, 205, 279
concept car 62
concertina 58
conformity 264–5, 267, 270, 278–9, 300*ch*12*n*24
Conkey, W.B. 95
Connecticut 50, 138, 147, 153, 244; Ansonia 138; Berlin 88–9, 139; Bridgeport 89–90, 290*n*22, 295*n*13; Bristol 50, 89, 290*n*21; Clinton 290*n*22; Connecticut River Valley 88, 290*n*22; Cromwell 49, 80, 89, 290*n*23; Durham 89; East Hampton 49, 54, 279; Forestville 89, 290*n*21; Hartford 92; Hartford County 89; Litchfield County 89, 138; Menlo Park 139; Meriden 139; New Britain 88–9, 139, 290*n*22; New Hart-

ford 50; New Haven 138–9, 290*n*22, 295*n*13; New London 295*n*13; Plymouth 89; South Norwalk 295*n*13; Thomaston 138; Waterbury 138; Winchester 138
A Connecticut Yankee in King Arthur's Court 153
conquest of space
Conrad, Joseph 292*n*13
Conseil 113–5, 117, 119, 292*n*10
Consolidated Electric Storage Co. 160
construction toy 196
consumerism 264, 278; disoriented 279
convenience 240, 264
"The Conversation of Eiros and Charmion" 76
Converse, Morton E. 139, 149, 158, 159, 302*n*24
Cook, James 78, 134
Cooke, William Fothergill 58
Cope, Edward Drinker 79
Copernicus 4, 41
Corbett, Elizabeth Burgogne 131
Corbett, Tom 271–2
Corcoran Mfg. Co. 240
Corliss, George 138
Cornwall 55
Corporal Keeperupper 254
Cossus 133
costume **242**, 246, 257, 259, 305*n*58; disguise 113; mask 259
Cousin Virginia 105
Cox, Gideon 49
Cox, Palmer 204
Cracker Jack Co. 212, 301*n*34; Bears 191–2
Craftsman Outfits 248–9
Crandall, Asa 49
Crandall, Benjamin Potter 49
Crandall, Charles M. 6, 20, 50, 82, 135, 140, 148–9, 270, 306–7*n*20
Crandall, Jesse 23, 98
Cream of Wheat 249
Cretaceous Reptiles of the United States 79
Crimean War 122
Critique of Political Economy 20
Croffut, W.A. 156, 294*n*34
croquet 140
Crosby, Nichols & Co. 70
cryptography 58
Crystal Palace Exhibition 8, 25, 49, 58, 66–7, 72, 79, 81–2, 118, 152–4, 157, 215–6, 233–4, 258; Shepherd's electric clock 61, 288*n*61; see also New Crystal Palace
Crystal Palace (New York) 25, 79–80
Cubism 230

Cummings, Ray 279, 296*n*43
Curie, Marie 183
Curie, Pierre 183
Curtis Lighting 231, 303*n*9
Cuvier, Baron Georges 12, 70, 72–3, 120
Cyclorama 155

Daedalum 59
Daguerre, Jacques 77
Daisy Mfg. Co. 244–6, 263, 304*n*20
d'Amécourt, Ponton 6, 11, 133
Dare Devil Flyer 215, 232
Darkness at Noon 280
Darrow, Clarence 223
Dart Board Equipment Co. 259
Darwin, Charles 20–2, 30–1, 71–4, 120, 200, 207, 248, 255, 258, 272; see also evolutionism; natural selection; *On the Origin of Species*
Darwin, Erasmus 255
Darwinian revolution 20–1, 80
Davenport, Iowa 21
Davidson, Edith B. 193
Davis, George R. 156
d'Avisson, Monsieur 96, 291*n*4
Dayton, Tennessee 301*n*16
Dayton Friction Toy Co. 302*n*24
Davy, Humphry 48, 78
De la Terre à la Lune 94, 106; see also *From the Earth to the Moon*
Debain & Co. 139
DeBeck, William 252
de Bergerac, Cyrano 96–7, 99
decalcomania 161
Decamps 146
"Deco" styling 224, 237, 239, 251, 259, 262, 265
decomposed movement 60–1
Dederick, Zadoc P. 91
Defoe, Daniel 151, 200
Deism 17, 31, 47, 128
Delcassé, Theophile 123
de Mechel, Chrètien 84
demystification 32, 84–5
Denslow, W.W. 163
de Rozier, Jean-François Pilâtre 6, 15
Descartes, René 41
"A Descent into the Maelström" 30, 113, 116, 120; see also maelstrom tale
A Description of the Geographical Clock 4
detective 113, 129–30, 174, 180–1
determinism 21, 33, 41, 47, 153, 169, 228–9
de Vaucanson, Jacques 84, 87
"The Devil in the Belfry" 25, 31, 86, 93, 103, 129
d'Holbach, Baron 125

"The Diamond Lens" 25
Dickens, Charles 1, 7, 23, 31, 41, 48, 56–7, 93, 113, 126, 131–2, 170, 175, 177–8, 200, 254, 287*n*21, 303*n*49
Dickinson & Thayer 50
die-cast toy 240, 250
Dille, John Flint 210, 244
Dillon-Beck Mfg. Co. 265, **266**, 306*n*9, 306*n*11, 306*n*13
dime novel 11, 91–3, 180, 185, 202, 207, 296*n*43
Dimetrodon 225
dinosaur 119–20, 185,186–7, 224–6, 272; automated 225–6, 233; film 187, 205–7, 223; toy 62, 72, 218–9, 271
The Dinosaur and the Missing Link 187, 205
Dinosauria 25, 53, 57, 69, 72–3, 83
diorama 77, 155, 223, 225, 227, 229–30, 303*n*9
dirigible see airship
Dirks, Rudolph 187
Disney, Walt 248, 259; phenomenon 249
disintegration 116, 121
Dispensational Christianity 120–1
displacement 39, 95–6
dissected map or picture 11–2, 82
dissected soul or protagonist 9–10, 18, 42, 109, 111, 113–5, 119, 143, 219–20, 268; see also catastrophe, as redemption; sectional character
diver 116, 118–9, 256–7; toy 118–9, **229**, **257**
The Diver 118–9
Dizzy Dino 218
Dr. Jeckyl and Mr. Hyde 293*ch*9*n*25
Dodge & Myer 91
Dodgson, Charles 179–80; see also Carroll, Lewis
doll 50, 53–4, 65, 90, 118, 131, 140, 167, 262, 285*n*16, 295*n*17–8; automated 87–9; character 188, 196, 246, 300*n*24, 305*n*58; fashion 278; furniture 49, 295*n*17; house 240, 262; talking 145, 188; trunk 150; velocipede-riding 88–9, 145, 161, 270; walking 87–9; see also paper doll
Don Sturdy in the Land of Volcanoes 189
Donnelly & Sons, R.R. 226
doppelganger 113
Douglas, Stephen A. 22
Dowst, Samuel 240
Dowst Brothers Co. 240–1, 304*n*11

Index

Dowst Mfg. Co. 239–40, 246, 250–2
"A Drama in the Air" 105; *see also* "Un Voyage en ballon"
Dream Days 4
dream-journey *see* sleep-journey
"A Dream of Armageddon" 198
dream of flight *see* romance of flight
drum 65, 149–50, *175*, 267
Dublin, Ireland 153
Duchamp, Marcel 238–9
The Duck 84
"The Duel" 104
Dufour, A.M. 226
Dunin, Count 82
"The Dupe of a Realist" 182
Dupin, character 112–3, 174–5
Du Pont 208
dwarf 19, 86–7, 102, 170–1; within the machine 85–6, 116, 166–7, 181, 205, 288n60; in relation to technics 82–4, 86, 91
Dyer family 48
Dyke, Samuel C. 135
dystopian vision 180, 222

E. Henderson & Co. 50
Eagles, Israel C. 91
Earth 17, 25, 41, 73, 75, 82, 140, 171, 256, 272; in cataclysm 8, 17, 26, 76, 181, 217; as clock 4–5, 26, 128, 133, 135, 172–3, 280; in Colombia's hand 158–9, 184; descent into 73–6, 78, 106, 119–20, 154, 173, 185 225; within enclosure 67, 110, 158, 258, 273, 277, 280; encompassed by machinery 134, 181, 198, 201, 234; figural 133–4; free of the Sun 184; functional equivalent to 102; hollow 185; miniaturized 102, 109, 134, 258; Mother 258, 274–5; as organism 128, 258; shrinkage 16, 41, 67, 78, 82, 110–11, 125, 128, 135, 141–3, 158–9, 171, 209–10, 277
East Hampton Bell Co. 49
ecosphere 102, 109, 258
Edison, Thomas 138–9, 141, 145, 259; fictional 147, 182, 191, 218
Edison, Thomas, Jr. 147, 191, 218
Edison Co. 205
Edison Talking Doll 145, 149
education 19, 20, 23, 27, 57, 67, 88, 115, 119, 130, 146, 155, 217, 220, 289
educational game 71, 80, 146–9; toy 4–5, 23–4, *47*, 51, 59, 71, 110, 130–1, 144, 150 248
Edward K. Tryon Co. 246
E.E. Fairchild Corp. 210, 251
egg, symbolic 98, 109, 179, 258,

274, 301n38; toy **160**, 298n52, 302n38
Eidotrope 60
1851 and the Crystal Palace 66
Einson-Freeman Co. 246
Electric Airplane 209
Electric Game Co. 232
The Electric Man 147
Electric Questioner 48
Electric Thriller 48
Electric Toy Mfg. Co. 306–7n20
Electrical Car 139
electrical motor 160–1
electrical toy *48*, 49, 160; battery-operated **274–5**
electricity 25, 48–9, 57–8, 60
"Elegy in a Country Churchyard" 57, 186, 207
Eliot, T.S. 35, 77
The Elixir of Hate 198
Ellis, Edward Sylvester 3, 11, 84, 91, 147, 179, 296n43
Eloffe & Co. 140
the Eloi 202–3
Embossing Co. 233
emergency vehicle toy 14, 284n35; *see also* fire-fighting toy
Encyclopaedia Brittanica 27
Encyclopedists 31, 114, 125
England 11, 15, 18, 24, 25, 29–31, 47, 54–5, 58–9, 64–7, 70, 73–4, 77–8, 87, 105–6, 122, 141, 151, 178, 198, 219, 263; Birmingham 15–6, 66; Cambridge 58; Manchester 114; Portsmouth 78; *see also* London
England, George Allan 180, 189–90, 198
Enton, Harry 147
encapsulated living space 14–5; *see also* technical envelopment
environmental suit 256–8; *see also* diver
Ernest Schotte & Co. 140
Estes, E.B. 50
Estes & Sons, E.B. 159
ethnology 157–8, 162
Eugene Field Reader 104
eugenics 142
Eureka 31
Eureka Mfg. Co. 304n20
Europe 64–6, 70, 84, 97, 146, 270
l'Eve future 146–7
"evolutionary human" 203–4
evolutionary theory 19–21, 72–3, 157, 223; catastrophic 120; viewpoint 186; *see also* natural selection
evolutionism 21, 63, 122, 169, 203, 217–8, 221, 223, 272
excelsior 7, 10, 18, 21
Excelsior 7–8, 233
Experimenter Publishing 27

exposition, industrial 65, 138, 155; international 25, 66, 169, 259; national 65–6; *see also* Centennial Exposition; A Century of Progress; Columbian Exposition; Crystal Palace, 1851; New York World's Fair; Paris Exposition; Vienna International Exhibition
Expression Blocks 82
Extinct Mammalian Fauna of Dakota and Nebraska 80
extinction 73–4, 78, 120, 272; human 18, 64, 120, 201; *see also* relict population
extraterrestrial being *81*, 107–8, 172–3, 203–4, 256; being as a toy 249, 271; conquest 276; experience **143**, **202**, 256; *see also* outer space

F. & R. Lockwood Co. 49
fable 38
Factitious Spider 255
factory 22, 65, 92, 122, 147–50, 278, 295n29; fictional 200–1; scientific 92–3, 273
fairing 54, 64, 70, 159, 227, 288n3
fairy tale 19, 26, 39, 47, 59, 82, 94–5, 98, 113, 117, 120, 131, 135, 151, 163, 170, 187, 259
Faivre
"The Fall of the House of Usher" 43, 76, 78, 289n36
Famous Fantastic Mysteries 182
fandango 139, 158–60
fantasy 28, 96
fantoccini 46, 59
Faraday, Michael 59
Farley, Ralph Milne 296n43
fashion 236, 253; doll 278, 307n35
Father and Son 67–8
Fergusson, Dr. Samuel 7–9, 106, 239, 247, 251
Field, Eugene 104
film *see* cinema
fire balloon 5, 15, 33, 140
Fire Cracker Pistol 24
fire-fighting toy 12–4, 62
fire mill 56–7; *see also* locomotive
firework 4, 15
The First Men in the Moon 170–3, 181, 203–4, 216, 218, 255
Fish Pond ***117–8***, 292ch8n18
Fisher, Bud 186, 205, 237
Fisher-Price Co. 218–9
Fiske, John 203
Five Weeks in a Balloon see *Cinq Semaines en Ballon*
flashlight 246
Flaubert, Gustave 3

Fleischer, Max 259
Flexible Flyer **263**
The Flying Girl 44, 54, 179
flying machine 132–3, 140, 191, 294*n*29
Flying Saucer Rattle **265**
Flying Top 23
Fogg, Phileas 125–30, 133–5, 158, 170–1, 200, 216, 247, 255, 273–4, 294*n*35
Foley, Dan 4, 46
Fontany, Elena 81, 99, 202, 212
For the Flag 183
Ford Motor Co. 239
foreshortening *see* space, foreshortening; time, foreshortening
Forster, E.M. 280
fossil 38, 57, 64, 69–71, 73
Fowler Fly Fan Co. 139
Foxy Grandpa 187–8
France 5, 11, 15, 20, 22, 25, 27, 31, 59, 64, 67, 70–75, 122, 125, 137, 139, 141, 143, 145–6, 177, 191, 198, 213, 238, 294–5*n*10; Annonay 5; Champ de Mars 15, 153; Lyons 5; Nantes 103; *see also* Paris
Francis, Field & Francis 13, 49, 291*n*26
Franco-Prussian War 122
Frank, Waldo 222
Frank Reade Library 296*n*43
Frankenstein, or The Modern Prometheus 30, 171; "the Being" 59, 113, 175, 200–1, 205; as cinema 37
Franklin, Benjamin 15
Frederick, Justus George 180–4, 198, 248
Frederick the Great 123, 125
Freeman, Mary Wilkins 54
friction toy 245
Froebel 51
From the Earth to the Moon 94, 106–11, 158, 166, 170, 205, 234, 258
Frost, Robert 93, 184
Frye, Northrop 19, 26–7, 39, 77, 95–6, 143, 278, 284–5*n*5
Fuller, Alice W. 145
Fulton, Robert 3, 67, 75, 95–6, 119, 213
Fundamentalism 177, 217, 223
Futrelle, Jacques 180
the future 17, 25, 40, 63, 93, 121, 137, 152–3, 172–3, 222, 224, 247–8, 253, 262, 266, 271, 274, 280; looking back to present 17; in retreat 262–3, 277; space travel as 82; symbolic futurity 190, 203, 239; versus current setting 247–8
Futurism 239

the futuristic 243, 246–7, 254, 262, 268; anti- 267

Galatea 161, 299*n*64
game 23, 49, 50, 71, 117–8, 127, 133–4, 138, 147–8, 159, 209–10, 215–6, 245–6, 273; life becoming 280; literature as 267–8, 280, 306*n*19; marble 148–9; of moral education 98, 147, 291*n*7; spiral 97–8, 147; *see also* croquet; educational game; whist
A Game of Christian Endeavor 54
The Game of Speculation 140
Game of the Golden Goose 97
The Game of the World Flyers 210
Garis, Howard R. 27–8, 101, 180–1, 189, 192, 220, 296*n*43, 300*n*4
Garton Toy Co. 241, 250
Gavioli, C. 139
Le Géant 14–5, 106, 284*n*38
Geneva, Switzerland 103
genocide 121, 277
geographical diversion 155–7
geology 20, 25, 72–4, 79, 169, 173
George W. Brown & Co. 89
Germany 39, 49, 51, 59, 70, 77, 87, 109, 122–3, 134, 141, 151, 194, 197–8, 202, 215, 217, 233, 240, 263, 269, 276, 278, 279, 294–5*n*10; Brandenburg 195; Dachau 202; Dresden 202; Frankfort 160; Leipzig 140; Magdeburg, Germany 77; Nuremburg 81, 123, 139, 160, 295*n*18; Rodach 139; *see also* Berlin
Gernsback, Hugo 27–8, 180, 207–8, 210, 243, 247–8, 259
Gertie 187
The Ghost of Slumber Mountain 301*n*11
ghost tale 41
giant 81–2
Giffard, Henri 21
gigantism 25, 106–7, 117, 137–8, 142, 157–8, 162, 205–6, 223, 233, 259, 271; "Brobdignagian" 162–3
Gilbert, A.C. 271, 302*n*24; *see also* American Flyer
Gimbel's 242
gingerbread 65, 70; *see also* candy
G.L. Wild & Bro. 139
Glanville, Joseph 288*n*48
Glasgow, Scotland 54
global communication 21–2, 109, 128, 13, 140–2, 181, 277; enclosure 258; integration 21–2, 25,

128; machinery 263; militarism 182–3, 277; simultaneity 181–3; travel 21–2; unification 108–9, 142, 181–4, 209, 234, 272, 279–80
globe iv, 4–5, 41, 110, 140, 158, 184, 193, 210, 281; balloon as 105, 159; floral 153; as playball 159; spinning 134, 136, 162–3, 181; tin 161, **127**, 272; *see also* earth, shrinkage
Globe Co. 250
Godey's Lady's Book 23, 71, 287*n*11
Godwin, Mary Wollstonecraft *see* Shelley, Mary
"The Gold-Bug" 41, 113
Goldberg, Reuben Lucius 252
golden age: science fiction 28; toys, America 54, 135; toys, England 54
Golden Argosy 296*n*43
Golden Arrow 250, 304–5*n*34
Gong Bell Mfg. Co. 54, 250
Good News 147, 296*n*43
Goodrich, Chauncey 89
Goodwin, W.C. 88–9, 138
Goodwin, William F. 290*n*18, 290*n*22
goose, symbolic 95, 97–8, **98**, 291*n*4
gorilla 222–3, 226, 272; Giant 226–7
Gosse, Edmund 67–8
Gosse, Philip Henry 67–8, 71, 118
Gotham Presed Steel Corp. 241, 250
Gothic novel *see* wonder tale, Gothic
gradualism 69
Graf Zeppelin 210, 215; toy 215, 301*n*40, 303*n*42–3; *see also* airship
Graham, George 47
Grahame, Kenneth 4, 180
Grant, Ulysses S. 138
Graustark 180
gravity anti- 171, 210, 256; low **143**, 185, **202**, 212; on Mars 246; -power in toys 46
Gray, Elisha 141
Gray, Thomas 57, 186, 207
Great Depression 223, 234, 237, 239–40, 247, 259
S.S. *Great Eastern* 21, 25, 64, 288*n*6
The Great Exposition see Crystal Palace Exhibition
Green, Charles 16
Green, J.K. 48
Greiner, Ludwig 23, 50
Grey Iron Casting Co. 246
Griffith, George 296*n*43

Groof 6
Gropper Mfg. Co. 246
Growth of a Century 149
Gruelle, Johnny 180
Gulliver, Lemuel 82, 91, 245
Gulliver's Travels 35, 82, 187; movie 259; movie toys 305n58
The Gumps 243
Gunsmoke 277
gyroscope 165, 194, 213

Hackett, Alice Payne 181
Hadrosaurus 79
Haeckel, Ernst 203, 229
Haggard, H. Rider 163, 180, 185
Hailman, Mrs. E.N. 159
Hale, Edward Everett 179
Hall, Austin 180, 222, 301n5
Hall, John 290n59
Hamilton, Alexander 24
Hamlin, Vince 219
"Hans Pfaall" *see* "The Unparalleled Adventure of One Hans Pfaall"
"Hans Phaall — A Tale" 16
Happy Hooligan 187
Hard Times 1, 254, 292n4
Hardwigg, Professor 73, 143, 186, 271
Harpers Ferry, Virginia 22
Harris, Alice 104
Harvard University 7, 120, 164
Hattersley, Robert 50
Hawaii 155
Hawkins, Benjamin Waterhouse 69–72, 74, 79–80
Hawkins, G.H. 88
Hawsky, Adalbert 140
Hawthorne, Nathaniel 38, 77
Heaney Laboratory 304ch16n31
Hector Servadac **9**, 142, **143**, 144, 176, 185
helicopter 11, 267
helmet 116, 118–9, 256–8
Hemingway, Ernest 268
hermetic life-enclosure 98, 102, 116
Herschel, John 47, 289n18
Herschel, William 18, 47, 289n18
Hersey, Joseph H. 50
Hetzel, Pierre-Jules 6, 20, 44, 73, 105–6, 121, 176
Heywood Bros. 49
Hi-Flier Mfg. Co. 241
Hill, S.L. 23
Hill-Climber **175**, 284n35
Hilpert, Andreas 123, 293n28
Histoires Extraordinaires 25
Histoires Grotesques et Sérieuses 31–2
historical materialism 63, 72
historical novel 180
Historoscope 76

The History and Adventures of Little Henry 70
History of British Fossil Reptiles 70
Hitler, Adolf 41, 202, 261
hoax 16, 38–9, 65, 85, 102, 112, 301n15
Hobbes 85, 126
hobby 252
hobbyhorse 49–50, 64
Hobhouse, Christopher 64, 66
Hodgson, Orlando 48
Hodgson & Co. 48
Hoffman, E.T.A. 145
Hoge Mfg. Co. 232
Holland 40, 125, 198; Amsterdam 148
Hollond, Ellen Julia 23
Hollond, Robert 16, 23
Hollywood 259
Holmes, Oliver Wendell 21, 125, 258
home-casting *see* casting outfit
L'Homme machine 125
Hood, J.V. 226
Hooker, Brian 29
"Hop-Frog: or, The Eight Chained Ourang-Outangs" 86–7, 91
Horner, William George 59
horror tale 31, 122, 217, 274
horse: automaton 84; toy 58, 65, 135, 165, 248, 255, 287n23, 290n22; race 188, 255; steam 91, 291n42; *see also* hobbyhorse
horse-drawn toy 12–13, **14**, 55, 145, 160, 284n35
Horsman, E.I. 300n24
hot-air toy 5, 89–90
Hough, Cass 244
The Hound of the Baskervilles 180
House of Tomorrow
The Houseboat on the Styx 43, 53, 253, 292n32, 300n5
household toy 61, 88–9, 196, 262
How a Mosquito Operates 186
How to Know the Birds 264
Howard, Robert E. 228
Howdy Doody 270
Howells, William Dean 174, 177, 200
Hubley Mfg. Co. 240
The Huge Hunter 147
Hull & Stafford 89, 291n26
Hull & Wright 89
humanism 18, 142, 177–8
humanoid 37
"The Humbug" 65, 288n6
Humbug 302n17
humbuggery 152, 162, 164, 167
Humpty Dumpty Circus 188
Hunt, Edward A. 91
Hunterian Collection 70

Hurst Gyroscope **194**
Hutton, James x, 69, 74, 120, 173
Huxley, Aldous 180, 217, 231, 245, 280
Huxley, T.H. 40, 248

Icthyosaurus 64, **68**, 70
"An Ideal City" 138
Ideal Magic Lantern & Polyopticon 132
Ideal Novelty & Toy Co. 259, 305n58
Iguanodon **69**, 79, 197, 288–9n17
Illinois 22, 146; Dekatur 241; East Moline 249; Freeport 241; Moline 241; *see also* Chicago
immortality 120, 180
the imp 86, 111, 129–30, 290n12
"The imp of the Perverse" 86
In Memoriam 31, 173
"An Independent Thinker" 54
India 20
Indiana Indianapolis 48, 194; Kokomo, 241; Washington 240
The Industrial Evolution of the United States 21
industry 11, 64–5, 83, 93, 109–10, 121, 126, 131, 137, 141, 184, 202–3, 220, 223, 239, 264, 272, 276; automation 22, 61; consolidation 149, 280; development in United States 22; militarization 141; symbolized in an individual 141, 259; wartime conscription 262; *see also* business; exposition
interchangeable parts 61
"interiorism" 233–4; *see also* technical life-enclosure
inventor 65, 90, 247; *see also* boy inventor
invisibility 113, 170, 261
The Invisible Man 170
Ireland 88, 153
Ireland, Archbishop 152
Irish Mail 241
The Iron Heel 198
iron toy 12, 13, 24, 50, 80, 147, 160–1, 187, 232, 263, 284n35
Irving, Washington 24, 40–1, 65
Isis Revealed: A Master Key 163
island: artificial 137; figural 128, 193, 200; shipwreck tale 53, 78
The Island of Doctor Moreau 170, 176, 218
"The Island of the Fay" 128
Italy 3, 97
Ives, Edward Riley 89, 291n27
Ives, S.B. 98, 147
Ives, W. 98, 147
Ives, Blakeslee & Co. 89–90, 135, 138, 145, 290n18, 295n13
Ives, Blakeslee & Williams 159
Ives Mfg. Co. 291n33

J. & E. Stevens & Co. 24, 49, 80, 89, 290n59, 290n23
J. Chein & Co. 246, 305n58
"Jack and the Beanstalk" 98
jack-in-the-box 106
"Jack the Giant-Killer" 132, 161
jackstones 196, 246
Jacob, Joseph 50
James, Henry 32
James H. Hawes Mfg. Co. 50
Jameson, J.H. 48
Japan 19, 21, 101, 258, 268–70, 274; Kyoto 268; Tokyo 269–70
Jaspers, Karl 18, 267, 294n35, 298n36, 298n61
Jeep 262, 266
Jevons, William Stanley 114, 285n9
Jewels for Playthings 262
J.L. Hudson Co. 242–3
John F. Dille Co. 246, 250
Johnson, J. 24
Jonah and the Whale 53–4; toy 54
Jord, Hav og Himmel 68–9
Joseph Lyon & Co. 88, 290n15
A Journey to the Centre of the Earth 35, 68, 74–6, 78–9, 114, 117, 120–1, 185
Joyce, James 268
Jules Verne: The Man Who Invented the Future 33
jumping frog story (Twain) 39
jumping jack 65, 91
Juvet, L.P. 140

kaleidophone 58
kaleidoscope 57, 161, 163, 267, 306n15
Kansas 267, 298n35
Das Kapital 19–20
Katzenjammer Kids 187
Kaufmann & Fabry Co. 226
KDP Co. 258
Keats, John 57, 286n28
Keck, Fred 228
Kellogg's 242
Kepler 4, 39, 41, 172–3, 286n22
The Kettle Club 105
Kilgore Mfg. 262
Kinder-Garten Alphabet and Building Blocks 130
kindergarten 23, 130, 159, 264
King Features Syndicate 246
King-Hall, Edith 29, 44, 51, 87, 106, 261, 280
King Kong 222–3, 226, 234, 248, 259
King's College 58
Kingsbury Mfg. Co. 240–1, 304–5n34
Kingsley, Charles 69, 72
Kingston Products 241
Kipling, Rudyard 122, 170, 180

kite 140, 190, 241, 246, 272, 194, 307, 241, 294n29
Kline, Otis Adelbert 180, 296n43
Knapp Electric & Novelty Co. 48, 302n24
Knight, Charles R. 206
knucklebones 81
Koch, Albert C. 288n6
Koestler, Arthur 280
Kornbluth, Cyril 2, 40, 277, 307n33
Kuhnel, Paul 140

labor 13, 56–7, 60, 92, 184, 220, 299n75; buried proletariat 202–3; child 92–3, 131; factory 37, 93, 249; mechanized 165–6, 200, 202, 294n10; superceded 166, 201; women's 92–3
labor-saving device 252–4, 305n46
Labyrinthodont 70
lacquerware 269
ladder of progress *see* progress
"A Lady of Sorrow" 20
Laelaps 79
Lamarckian theory 79, 203
Lambert 195
La Mettrie, Julien Offroy de 125
Lana, Francis 5
The Land of Monsters 27, 219
"The Land of Nod" 43–4
la Landelle, Gabriel de 6, 11, 133
Lang, Andrew 163
Lang, Fritz 37, 248
Langdon, William 50
Lasser, David 302n41
the Last Man 201, 267
Lavoisier, Antoine 5
Lear, Edward 45
Lee-Tex Rubber Products 246
Lee Toy Aeroplane 301n33
Legrand, William 113
Lehmann, Ernst Paul 195–6, 198, 301n40–1
Leidy, Joseph 79–80
Leinster, Murray 296n43
Leo Schlesinger Co. 135, 302n24
Let's Go Shopping 264
Letters on Natural Magic 84
Lewis, C.S. 35, 43
L.H. Mace & Co. 190, 192, 284n35
La Liberté de Penser 31
Liedenbrock, Professor 73–4
Lieutenant Gulliver Jones, His Vacation 40
Life (Gosse) 71
life-support 14–5, 256–8; *see also* technical envelopment
light: artificial 25; automated 155–6; search- 156, 262
lighthouse 57

Lilliput Bank 290n59
Lilliputian 82, 197, 245
"Lily Bell and Thistledown" 86
Lincoln, Abraham 22, 23, 30, 115, 201, 285n15
Lincoln Zephyr 241
Lind, Jenny 65
Lindberg, Charles 200, 212
Lindstrom Tool & Toy Co. 250
lines of motion 237–9, 241, 259, 265
Linnean classification 114–5
lion **13**, 164, **167**, 270, 299n80
literal appropriation 98, **99**, 100–2, 110, 121, 133, 142–3, 148, 189, 192–3, 203, 212–3, 255
lithography 70, 80, 82; chromolithography 147
Little Buckeye Magic Lantern 60
Little Nemo in Slumberland 186–8, 205, 243, 300n24, 300n24
Little Orphan Annie 188; Travel Game **219**
"Little Thumb" 113
Lloyd, Alford 67, 69
Lloyd, Robert 48
Locke 51
Lockwood, Brooks & Co. 141
locomotive 21, 55–6, 91, 280; figural 56, 91, 133–4, 184, 223, 239; toy 56, 89, 130, 132, 138, **139**, **167**, **193**, 287n36; *see also* railroad train; railway
Lofting, Hugh 108, 180
London 35, 56, 65, 75, 77, 109, 152, 223, 234, 263; Egyptian Hall 129; Hyde Park 66; Islington 65; Smithfield 65; Stoke Newington 30; Sydenham Park 67–72, 74, 109, 283n14; Vauxhall Gardens 16
London, Jack 180, 185, 198
London Cries 59
Longfellow, Henry Wadsworth 7
Looking Backwards 40, 153
Lorry, Jarvis 88, 126, 130
Los Alamos, New Mexico 41
U.S.N. *Los Angeles* 252
Lost from the Fleet 189–90
The Lost World 185; as film 205–7, 218, 223, 234, 248, 301n12
Louis Marx & Co. **198**, 210, 215, 232, 245–6, 268, 271, 302n24, 302n41; play sets 271
Louis Williams & Co. 244
Louis XVIII 15
Louvrié 6
Love, Bessie 218
"The Love Song of J. Alfred Prufrock" 77
Lovecraft, Howard Philips 180, 256
Lowe, Calincourt 21
Lowe, N.M. 140

Lowell, James Russell 31, 172
Lucian 97, 99, 292*n*35
Luddite 53, 56
Lutz & Sheinkman 245
Lyell, Charles 69
Lytton, Edward Bulwer 35, 119, 123, 167, 180, 186, 203, 297*n*23

Mac Toys *see* McDowell Mfg. Co.
machine 11, 125–6, 138, 158; as alive 11, 103–5, 165–7; determining human action 85, 88, 93, 126, 256–7; extraterrestrial 172; as hoax 85, 102, 166–7; human 113, 230; labor 120–1, 294*n*10; mega- 257, 260; military 162, 198; of Modern society 115; of money 126; "pure" 84, 201; reduction to 93, 165, 170, 201; state 217; *see also* clock; dwarf within the machine; marvelous machine; world-machine
machine-dependency *see* technical envelopment
Macy's 135, 245
maelstrom tale 115–7, 119–23, 176, 218, 220, 300*ch*12*n*24
Maelzel, Leonard 84
"Maelzel's Chess-Player" 84–7, 103, 112–3, 129, 166, 205, 288*n*60
Le Magasin d'Education et de Rècrèation 20
magazine 8, 14, 24, 67, 71, 104, 122, 147, 175, 184–5, 206–8, 216, 240, 249, 287*n*11, 288*n*36; electrical 153, 207–8, 210–2; "pseudo-scientifics" 259; *see also* pulp magazine
Maggie Magnetic, Inc. 277–8
Magic Camera 60
Magic City 224; *see also* A Century of Progress; Columbian Exposition
Magic Farmyard 255
magic key 156, **227**, 297*n*19; *see also* master key
magic lantern 46, 59, 60, 76, **77**, 132, 161, 196, 244, 286*ch*4*n*4
magic set 244
magic wand 120
The Magician 84
magnetic toy 118, 255, 306–7*n*20
Maillardet 84
La Maison à Vapeur 254
Mallarmé, Stéphane 32, 147
mammoth 64, 163, 225, 228
The Man in Lower Ten 180
"The Man That Was Used Up" 30
"The Man Who Could Work Miracles" 170
Mandel Toy Co. 211

Mann, Horace 92
Mansion of Happiness 98, 147
maps 140
marbles 24, 135, 148, 246
"The Marching Morons" 40–1
marionette 46, 59, 84, 230, 244
Markham, Edwin 177, 300*ch*12*n*25
Mars 40, 81, 184–5, 192–3, 196, 198, 216–8, 246, 255; god 198–9, 300*n*15, 301*n*38
Martian **81**, 185, 216–8, 242
Marusan 305*n*48
Marvel Toy Co. 306–7*n*20
marvelous machine 2, 10, 15–7, 38, 43, 84–5, 119, 121, 188, 260, 268; destruction of 10–2, 15, 17–8, 43–4, 85, 92, 96, 116; *see also* catastrophe; dissected soul; technical envelopment
Marx, Karl 77, 201, 300*ch*12*n*24
Marxism 222, 261
Maryland: Baltimore 65, 250; Hagerstown 245
Maskelyne and Cooke 129
Mason, Monck 15–6
Mason & Converse 295*n*20
mass audience 206, 212
mass culture 249, 270
mass-production 122, 135, 138, 147, 149–50, 159, 199–201, 203, 217–8, 261, 266, 270–1, 304*n*7; international 278–9; and mass-marketing 195, 271, 279; technological supremacy through 186
mass violence 254
Massachusetts 50, 92; Gardner 49; Granville 149; Hadley 50; Holyoke 232; Leominster 12; Salem 50, 147, 291*n*8; South Hingham 49–50; Springfield 159; Winchendon 139, 149, 279; Worthington 50; *see also* Boston
the masses 56, 93, 200, 261
master key 130, 163; *see also* magic key
The Master Key 181, 246
"Master Zacharias" 73, 103–5, 107, 110–11
Mastodon 74, 79, 292*n*32
materialism 20–1, 44, 72, 93, 96, 101, 106–7, 125, 147, 201, 217, 220, 259; fictional 96, 103, 120; Nature-perception in opposition to 258
Mather, A.C. 160
Mattel 278–9
"May-Day Ode" 67
Maynard Tape Primer 24
McCay, Winsor 186–8, 205, 237–8, 300*n*24; character toys 300*n*24

McClintock, Marshall and Inez 12, 135
McCormick, Cyrus 22, 66
McCutcheon, George Barr 180, 187
McDougall, Walt 164
McDowell Mfg. Co. 209–10, 302*n*26, 302*n*29
McGinty Surprise Watch **161**
McKee, John Dukes 81, 99, 202, 212
McLean, E.M. 298*n*51
McLoughlin Bros. 117–8, 133–4, 161, 189
McReady Publishing Co. 24, 232
Mead, George Herbert 279
mechanical, bank 80; being 104–5; entertainment 205; picture 161; speed 55; uniformity 41, 53, 59, 62; world picture 41; zoo 230
Mechanical Flying Ships 190, 192
Mechanical Organette 132
mechanical toy 11, 24, 49, 84, **87**, 88–91, 132, 135, 138–9, 145–6, 150, 158–61, 195, 198–9, 209, 231, 269–70, 302–3*n*41; "comical" 187; 1922 manufacturers 302*n*24
mechanical world-view 4, 17–8; *see also* materialism; New Worlds idealism; progress
Megalosaurus 53, 69–70, 223
Megatherium 74, 169
Meggendorfer, Lothar 151
Meinecke, Adolph 23, 198, 285*n*24
Méliès, Georges 37
"Mellonta Tauta" 6, 17, 21, 144, 154, 197, 202, 235–6, 261, 265, 283*n*14, 285*n*5, 294*n*29, 296*n*10, 301*n*1, 306*n*4
melodrama 10–1, 34, 36–7, 41–3, 47, 91, 142, 164, 171, 199, 216, 247, 259, 267–8; stage 34–5, 164, 206; movie 259
Melville, Herman 32, 152, 179
Menippus 97
Merriam Mfg. Co. 89
Merril, Judith 28
Merritt, Abraham 180, 279, 296*n*43
Merritt, D.S. 295*n*13
merry-go-round 65
"Mesmeric Revelation" 31
mesmerism 30, 121
Mesozoic 78, 224, 226, 233, 289*n*41, 271
metal casting 245
Metalcraft Corp. 215, 251
Metro-Goldwyn-Mayer 259, 299*n*85
Metropolis 37, 248

Mexico 270
Michael Strogoff 132
Michigan 146; Detroit 242, 305n53; Plymouth 244; Wyandotte 239
Mickey Mouse 231, 259
Mickey Mouse in Pigmy Land **245**
"Micromegas" 81
microphone 142, 244
microscope 25, 132
middle class 54, 56–7, 71, 87, 93
Midgetoy 250
Milhouse, Katherine 254
Miller, P. Schuyler 37, 268, 306n19
Miller & Krips 240
Milne, Robert Duncan 179
Milton, John 114
Milton Bradley Co. 11–3, 20, 23, 59, 76, 118–9, 130–1, 133, 136, 155, 191, 215, 219, 241, 259, 303n43
Minamoto Trading Co. 274–5
Minerva Toy Co. 264
minikin 81–3, 106, 159, **244**, 254, 259, 271; see also Lilliputian
Mirrorscope 60
missile-launching truck 277
Mississippi River 21
Mitchell, S.A. 140
Modern Century 19–26, 234, 284–5n5
Modern Electronics 208
Modern Plastic Toys
Modern Toys (company) 269
Moline Pressed Steel Co. 302n24; see also Buddy "L" Mfg. Co.
monoplane **99**, 101, **200**, 212–3
monster 69, 72, 74, 79, 103, 109
monstrum horrendum 103, 105, 170
Montgolfier, Jacques Étienne 5, 15
Montgolfier, Joseph Michel 5, 15
Montgolfier balloon 5, 15, 34, 251; toy **6**, 34, 140
Montgomery, Dave 164
Montgomery Ward & Co. 135
moon 94, 234, 256, 258; journey 9, 29, 94–5, 97–**99**, 100–102, 106–10, 158, 170–2, 181, 193, 212; journey game 251; man in the **99**, **108**; symbolizing futurity 172–3, 203
Morand & Tourneur 139
Moreland, B.E. 191–2, 301n34
Morgan, Leon 226
Morlocks 170, 202, 210
Morrison, Enoch Rice 88, 290n15
Morse, Samuel F.B. 22, 38
Mosasaurus 70

Mother Goose **95**, 98
motor, gasoline 101–2
Motor Boys 101, 181, 192
The Motor Boys in the Clouds 192
The Motor Boys Over the Rockies 192
Motor Race **195**
"motormania" 181
movie see cinema
Movie-Jektor Co. 245, 305n48
movie projector, juvenile 244
moving sidewalk 137, 157, 225, 227
"Moxon's Master" 145
"Ms. Found in a Bottle" 170, 172–3, 185
Multiple Products Corp. 271
Mumford, Lewis ix, 1, 4, 10, 18, 41–2, 93, 167, 183, 235, 257, 283–4n28, 288n60
Munsey, Frank A. 296n43
"The Murders in the Rue Morgue" 113
Murdoch, William 55, 287n33
Musée de Familles 104
museum 30, 70, 115, 155, 163, 169, 206
music box 91, 139, 295n19; see also automaton, musical; toy, musical
Mutt and Jeff 188, 208, 237–8
Muybridge, Eadweard 60
My Lord 55
Myriopticon 76
Mysterious Island 132
The Mystery Men of Mars 216–8, 255
Mystery Plane **239**, 262
mystery play 70
mythological tale 26, 38, 95, 113; as underpinning 39, 95–6

Nadar, Félix Tournachon 6, 11, 14–6, 106, 108, 284n38
Napoleon I 213
Napoleon III 122
"The Narrative of Arthur Gordon Pym" 116, 185
Nashville, Tennessee 244
Nassau balloon 16
nationalism 85, 121, 141–2, 146, 172
natural philosophy 4, 30, 31, 36, 41, 57, 60, 70–2, 95–7, 115
natural selection 20–1, 72–3, 203, 207, 248, 301n16; "survival of the fittest" 21
naturalism 36–7, 172, 174–6, 6 178, 180, 210, 268, 280
nature 17; conquest of 92
Nautilus 67, 119, 213; fictional submarine 43, 114–6, 121, 131, 214, 234
navigator 41–3, 171

Nebraska Bad Lands 81
Negro Preacher 145–6
Neill, John R. 259
Nelson, Thomas Page 44
Nemo, Captain 43, 115–7, 119, 121, 134, 200, 214, 293ch8n19
neon 224
Nevada 38–9
New Crystal Palace 25, 53, 67–70, 72, 85, 138, 174, 223–4, 284n38; see also Crystal Palace Exhibition
New England 80, 88–9, 146
New England Toy Co. 88
New England Toy Mfg. Co. 291n34
New Hampshire Keene 240; Marlborough 50
New Haven Clock Co. 90
New Haven Toy & Game Co. 295n13
New Improved Scamp Wagon 240
New Jersey 25, 306n9; Haddonfield 79; Irvington 259, 265; Jersey City Heights 140; Menlo Park 139, 141; Newark 91, 141, 266; Red Bank 91
New Orleans, Louisiana 50
New Worlds fatalism 123
New Worlds idealism 1, 4, 10, 18, 20, 26, 30, 32, 39, 41–2, 44, 51, 61–2, 96–7, 122, 126, 140–2, 153, 161, 180, 210, 283n6, 286n42; subservience to 10, 41–3, 53
New York 3, 7, 23, 25, 50, 60, 67, 147; Albany 50, 65; Brooklyn 226, 246, 264; Chittenango 163; East Aurora 218; Glen's Falls 140; Jackson Heights; Long Island City 246; Manhattan 17, 255; North Tonawanda 232; Rochester 210, 246; Staten Island 231; Waverly 148; Williamsburg 23
New York City 17, 24, 46, 49, 50, 56, 65, 70, 79, 82, 88–9, 130, 133, 139–41, 149, 153, 159–60, 164, 186, 231, 241, 244–5, 265; Armory 238; Central Park 79–80, 83; Eden Musée 85, 290n9; Fifth Avenue Building 244; Hotel McAlpin 244; Lenox Lyceum 145; Tammany Hall 80, 83
New York *Ledger* 84
New York Rubber Co. 159, 291n27
New York Sun 16
New York World's Fair 259
The New Yorker 264
Newark Indian Rubber Mfg. Co. 50

Newark Mask Co. 259
newspaper 13–4, 22, 38–9, 70, 105–6, 249, 263; cartoon 186–7, 210, 232, 242, 246–8, 259; syndicate 210; as a timepiece 130
Newton and Thomson 49
The Nic Projector Corp. 241
Nice, H.J. 191, 301*n*33
1984 267, 280
N.N. Hill Brass Co. 54
Noachian flood 52–3, 74, 120–1, 143; journey 51–2, 63, 111, 275; post–Noachian world 121, 272; pre-Noachian world 121, 272
Noah's Ark 51–4, 254, 287*n*21, 296*n*49; figural 67, 111
Noble & Cooley 149
Noma Electric 262
North Dakota 163
North Pole 16; *see also* romance of polar discovery
Northrop, Henry Davenport 68–9
Northwestern Products 246
Not This August 277, 307*n*33
Les Nouvelles Histoires Extraordinaires 25
novelty 62, 65, 138
Nowlan, Philip Francis 40, 180, 210, 244, 254
nuclear power 183
The Nugget Library 147, 296*n*43
Nuremberg scale 123
nursery rhyme 65, 95, 97–8, 131, 145

Oberammergau 51
O'Brien, Fitz-James 25, 67, 179
O'Brien, Richard 198
O'Brien, Willis 187, 205–7, 222–3
obsolescence 62, 236, 268, 278, 304*n*7; human 201
The Ocean 67
Odd John 44, 253, 305*n*46
"Ode on Intimations of Immortality" 96
Odle, E.V. 301*n*6
Oehme & Sons, J.D.
Og, Son of Fire 232
Ohio 12, 50, 146; Chagrin Falls 12; Cincinnati 232; Cleveland 149; Dayton 175; Medina 233; Ravenna 12; South Akron 135; Toledo 50, 241, 250
Ohio Art Co. 198, 302*n*24
Old Ironsides 56
The Old Mother Goose 95
"Old West" toy 262, 277
Oliver Twist 48
Omai 78, 134
Omphalos
On Liberty 20
On the Connexion of the Physical Sciences 18

On the Origin of Species 20–1, 73, 203, 272
Opium War 21
Opper, Frederick Burr 187
optical diversion 46, 74–8, 106, 155–6, **177**, 205–6, 286*ch*4*n*4; illusion 30, 163, 231, 263; toy 8, 20, 25, 46, 57–62, 76–7, 160–1, 205, 286*ch*4*n*4, 305*n*58, 305*n*58
optics 30, 56, 292*ch*7*n*16
orrery 47, 110, 140, 256; figural 144
Orwell, George 261, 267, 280
Other Worlds Than This 81, 99, 202, 212
Out of the Silent Planet 35, 43
Outcault, Richard Felton 187
outer space 248, 256; undersea borrowing 256; *see also* extraterrestrial; space
outfit *see* play set
Ovid 161
Owen, Richard 69–74, 79
Owen, Robert 30
"The Owl and the Pussycat" 45
Ozma of Oz 166

paedomorphosis 203–4
Paladin 277
paleontology 69, 71–3, 79, 83, 169
Palmerston, Viscount 19
panorama 74–**75**, 76–7, 115, 155, 163, 206, 231, 297*n*15; moving 225; toy 76, 160
pantomime 78, 161
paper doll 23, 48, 70–1, 88, 151, 161, 165, 285*n*17, 287*n*11, 289*n*23, 301–2*n*17, 305*n*58; drama 48, 161, 287*n*11, 298*n*53, 287*n*11, 298*n*53
paper toy 47–8, 70–1, 119, 140, 150–1, 165, 262, 269
Papin, Denis
Paris 10, 25, 65–6, 77, 87, 138, 140, 144, 146, 295*n*17; basin 74
Paris, John Ayrton 58
Paris Exposition 19, 153, 156–7
Paris in the Twentieth Century 44, 121, 176, 247, 286*ch*3*n*25
Park, Mungo 43
Parker, George S. 147, 153
Parker Brothers 118, 133–4, 159, 216, 251, 259, 272, 286*n*30, 298*n*51
The Parlour Magazine of the Literature of All Nations 67
Passepartout, Jean 126, 128–30, 293, 303
Patent Soap Bubble Toy 119
Patterson, Edward 88
Paxton, Joseph 66–7, 72
Paya 90

Peabody, Elizabeth 130
Peale, Charles Willson 55, 79
Peale, Franklin 55
Peale Museum 55, 163
Pellucidar 185, 300*n*19
Penaud 191
Pennsylvania 23, 50, 56, 80, 130, 146–7, 306–7*n*20; Attleborough 50; Cambridgeboro 159; Covington 49–50; Lancaster 240; Montrose 82; Mount Joy 246; Pittsburgh 199, 209, 241; Titusville 22; Towanda 50; *see also* Philadelphia
penny toy 49, 65, 110
Permian Coal Measures 70
Perrault, Charles 39, 113
Perry, Commodore 21
Peter Coddle at the New World's Fair 216
"Peter Klaus" 39–40
Peter Pan **36**, 43, 220
Peterson, Roger Tory 264
"The Petrified Man" 38–9
petroleum 22
pewter toy 50, 159
phantasmagoria 75–7, 81, 289*n*36; as a clock 140
Phelps & Bartholomew 138
Phenakistiscope 59
Philadelphia 4, 12, 15, 49, 50, 55–6, 65, 79, 82–3, 90, 138, 140–1, 160, 163, 246; Academy of Natural Sciences 79; Fairmount Park 138, 153; Philosophical Society 15; *see also* Centennial Exposition
Phillipthal, M. 76
philosophical toy 8, 25, 33, 41, 55, 57–61, 71, 106, 132, 287*n*30–1; *see also* scientific toy
phonograph 145, 149
photography 6, 15, 62, 106, 132, 157, 177; stop-motion 205–6
Pia, Peter 50, 159
piano 147, 34, 58, 139; automaton 138–9; toy 187, 296, 296*n*49
Picasso 230
Piccard, Jean 255–6, 305*n*53
Piccard, Jeanette 255–6, 305*n*53
Pierce, Franklin 79
Pierce, J.A. 291*n*36
Pigs in Clover 148–9, 270, 296*n*48
Pilgrim's Progress 60
Pinocchio 86, 254
Pirates of Venus 215
"The Pit and the Pendulum" 18
Pittonacio, Signor 103–4, 125, 170–1, 254
Plakie Toys 306*n*13
"The Planet Juggler" **182**, 183–4, 199, 248

Index

planetary mind 182
Plank, Ernst 160
plastic 262, 265–6, 271, 280, 304*n*16, 306*n*9–13; manufacturer 306*n*9–13
Plateau, Joseph 59
Plato 10, 72, 164, 290*n*6
play 4, 131–2, 170, *177*; -acting 92, 119, 164; guided 131; imaginative 4, 12, 33, 34, 63, 105, 244, 254, 271, 299*n*4; realism in 244; and social change 13, 61; as symbolic act 4, 5, 13, 15; -time 131; with time 131
play set 52, 69, 244–5, 248, 254–5, 262, 271; conflict-oriented 271
play suit *see* costume
Playfair, John 69
playing cards 227, 303*n*15
Playthings Magazine 24, 232, 242–3
Plesiosaurus 68, 70
Poe, Edgar Allan 3, 13, 16–8, 21–5, 27, 29–31, 35, 41, 53, 57–8, 70, 75–6, 81, 94, 104, 106, 108, 110, 115–7, 119–20, 123, 128–30, 154, 166–7, 169–73, 176, 178–9, 181, 185, 197, 207–8, 235–6; and Baudelaire 25, 27, 30–2; black humor 31, 36; celestial disaster 17, 53, 76, 112, 217; clock fantasy 25, 86; and his contemporaries 30–1; demystification 84–5; and the Gothic impulse 29–31; influence on Verne 6–7, 9–10, 17, 29, 31–2, 113, 116, 128–9; machine-enveloped soul 18, 84–7, 181, 201, 233–4; and natural philosophy 30, 57; ratiocinative hero 7, 41, 112–3, 174–5; ratiocinative process 30–1; rational world-view 31; space fantasy 16–7, 81, 96–100; and symbolism 30–2, 96; time-travel tale 25, 129, 135–6, 169; and the wonder tale 10, 16–8, 29–30, 39, 173; *see also* dwarf in the machine; the imp; maelstrom tale; *monstrum horrendum*
polar exploration *see* romance of polar discovery
Pollock, B. 48
polyethylene 280
Pop-Up Kritters 218–9
Popeye 246, 259
Porter Chemical Co. 245–6
Portugal 66
positivism 7–8, 11, 27, 32, 42, 63, 96, 103, 106–7, 115, 125–6, 170, 185, 201, 207, 248, 260, 274
Praxinoscope 59–60

"pre–Adamite" 68, 79
Prehistoric Animal Show 225
prehistoric creature 20, 25, 64–5, 69–74, 79, 180, 205–7, 223, 225, 227, 271–2, 301*n*11; toy 69; *see also* "cave man"; dinosaur; *Dinosauria*
Prehistoric Times 271
Priestly, Joseph 5
the "primitive" 78, 180, 184–6, 223, 227; noble savage 247; recrudescence of 185; regression to 186, 222, 228–9
primitivism, anachronistic 206, 223, 232, *219*, 271
A Princess of Mars 40, 185, 198
Principles of Geology 69
progress 18, 21, 96, 138, 147, 169, 184, 203, 207, 217–8, 239, 248, 253; ladder of 207, 223, 293–4*n*27; leading to the primitive 184, 186; parade of 207, 228, 271; *see also* positivism
Progress (toy) 56, 132, 235
Prohibition Party 157, 298*n*35
projector 59–60, 77
Prometheus 120
propeller 24
Propeller Island 61, 137–8, 153
prophecy novel 53, 287*n*24
Protoceratops **226**
providence 44, 74, 104–6, 116–7, 143, 200; authorial 44, 78–9, 176
providential world-view 4, 8, 17, 30, 32, 44, 71–4, 120
Prussia 122–3, 125
Psycho (automaton) 129
psychology 30
Pterodactyl 64, 69–70, 74, 206, 225, 288–9*n*17
Pterosaur 72
Ptolemy 41
Pullman Railplane 241
pulp magazine 27–8, 37, 40, 147, 207–8, 217, 228–9, 247, 256, 259, 279, 296
puppet 46, 85, 151
Punch 66
Puritan worldview 64, 71–2, 136, 147, 164, 239; *see also* Calvinism
puzzle, picture 160, 246; *see also* dissected map/picture
Pyle, Howard 26, 29, 286*n*30
Pym *see* "The Narrative of Arthur Gordon Pym"

Queen Victoria 70
Queen Victoria's Diamond Jubilee *see* Crystal Palace Exhibition
Queer Visitors from the Marvelous Land of Oz 164

R. Bliss & Co. 50, 298*n*51
race 120–2, 142; blackface tradition 220; "Indian" depiction 92, 220; prejudice 217; stereotyping 92, 180, 220, 300*n*4
Race to the Moon 251
radar 263; toy 262
radio 165, 231–2, 242, 249, 257, 259, 262, 267–8, 277, 280; game 210
Radio Flyer 240–1
Radio Play Co. of America 165
radium 183
railroad train 241, 296*n*49; *see also* locomotive
railroads: Illinois Central 226; Liverpool & Manchester 55; Miniature 230; New York, New Haven & Hartford 236; Stockton & Darlington 55
railway 11–3, 21, 55, 130, 138, 140, 146, 235–6, 278; electric toy 160, 196; elevated 12; fireman 13; mechanical toy 161
Ralph 124C 41+ 208, 248
Rapaport Bros. 245–6, 248–9
ratiocination 7, 31–2, 85, 111–2, 135, 166
"The Raven" 119, 174
ray, disintigrator 210; gun 210, 243, 262
Reade, Frank, Jr. 147
realism 10, 28, 37, 95–6, 101, 142, 174–8, 206, 260, 262, 267–8, 280; pseudo- 95–7, 268; sentimental 267; "stupid" 278; *see also* naturalism; type character
Redington, John 48
Redruth, Cornwall 55
regression, social or human 63; *see also* the "primitive"
relict population 73–4, 78, 117, 119–20, 185–6, 206
religious feast day 64–5
religious toy *see* game of moral education; Sunday doll; Sunday toy
remote control 58, 66, 119–20, 141, 167, 254–5, 267, **274–5**; terror 277
Remotrol Co. 255, 305*n*48, 305*n*50
Renaissance 97
Revue de Paris 31
Reynaud, Emile 59
Rhode Island Hokington 49; Providence 50, 88
Rich Mfg. Co. 305*n*58
Rinehart, Mary Roberts 180
Ring, E.T. 50
Riou 114
"Rip van Winkle" 40–1, 131, 161

"Robin Hood" 161
Robinson, L. 50
Robinson Crusoe 35, 143, 151, 161, 187, 296n50
Robison, John 54
robot 167; in *Buck Rogers* **243**, 249; in Čapek 37; in Claudy 217–8; Japanese toy 270, **274**, **275**; and remote control 254; Sears, Roebuck 230–1; shifting designation 249; toy 249, 304n31
Robotball 249
Robotennis 249
Robotoy 249
Robur 132–4, 148, 200, 247, 276
Robur le Conquérant 147; see also *The Clipper of the Clouds*
"Rock-A-Bot"
rocket 56, **192**, 215–7, 250, 263, 274, 277; German V2 276
rocket: juvenile auto 250; ride-on toy 251; wagon 250
The Rocket 7, 55, 56; toy 56–7, 235, 287n36, 287n38
Rocket Pistol see Buck Rogers 25th Century Rocket Pistol
Rocket Racer: by Gong Bell 250; by Marx 251; by Wyandotte 250
rocket ship 250–1, 259, 276; see also spaceship
Rocket Shot 250
rocketry 280
Roget, Peter Mark 59
Rollin Wilson Co. 305n48
Rolly Dolly **175**, **187**
romance, literary 26–7, 34
romance: of flight 15, 190; of geographical conquest 16–7, 25, 133; of polar discovery 16, 30, 154, 189–90; of speed 16–7, 24, 56, 150; of speed evoked 236–7; of speed's end 235–6
Romanticism 7, 26, 32, 53
Roney, Benjamin T. 50
Root, John 154, 232
Rosenfeld, Paul 222
Roth, Edward 83, 94, 108
Rotterdam 16
Rousseau, Jean-Jacques 10–1, 42, 86, 122, 170, 203, 217
Rowley, John 47
Roy Toy Co. 232
Royal College of Surgeons 70
Royal Game of Goose 97
Royal Geographical Society 7
Royal Society 57, 114
rubber stamp **243**, 246
rubber toy 50, 80, 108, 110, 159, 161, 208, **229**, 246, 284n42
"Rube Goldberg device" 252–3
Rueckheim Bros. & Epstein 301n34

R.U.R. 37, 199–201, 203, 208, 217
Russia 66, 141, 258, 264, 277–8

S. & J. Fuller 70
Saalfield Publishing Co. 246, 305n48, 305n58
Sackman Bros. Co. 245–6
Sadler, James 6
Sail-Me Co. 241
St. Bartholomew Fair 64–5
St. George's dragon 70
St. Louis, Missouri 246, 251
St. Nicholas 99, 148
Saint-Simon, Claude-Henri de Rouvroy, Comte de 125, 218, 286ch3n25
saint's day 64–5
Samson-United Corp. 246
Samuel Gabriel Sons & Co. 241, 264, 272
San Francisco 186, 244; *Bulletin* 38
Sand, George 6
Santa Claus **100–1**, 161, **192**
Sardinia 66
Sarg, Tony 230
Sartre 36, 300ch12n24
satellite: artificial 109–11, 264, 272, 274, 277, 280, 307n33; as clock 280; communication 109, 277, 292n35; figural 273–4; as threat 307n33; toy 277–8
Le Scaphandrier 118–9
Scarecrow 152, 164–5, 172, 227
Schedler, Joseph 140
Schillitz, Carl 160
Schoenner, Jean 160
Schoolcraft, Henry 301n15
Schultze, Carl E. 187
Schurz, Mrs. Carl 23
Schwartz, David S. 226
science 4, 11, 207; vanities of 103; see also natural philosophy
science fantasy 2, 28, 96, 275, 277
science fiction 2, 28, 37–8, 96, 259, 268, 275, 277, 286n42
Science Fiction 28
Science Fiction Chronicle ix
Science Wonder Quarterly 27
Science Wonder Stories 27
scientific expedition
scientific toy 33, 68–9, 118; see also philosophic toy
scientification 2, 27–8, 208, 243, 247, 259
scientism 27–8, 36, 44, 106, 122, 203, 206, 247, 259–60, 271–2
scientist ii, iv, 57, 126
scooter **238**
Scopes, John T. 301n16
Scopes Monkey Trial 207
Scotland 25, 43, 55, 69–70; Edinburgh 70, 75

Sears, Roebuck 191, 209, 241; Building 233; Robot 230
Secor, Jerome B. 90–1, 138, 244
sectional characters 38, 43–4, 91, 96, 114, 142, 164–7, 174, 176, 206, 216, 247, 259; see also dissected soul
Seiss Mfg. Co. 241
Selenites 107–8, 172–3, 203–4
self-enclosed environment see hermetic life-enclosure
Senarens, Luis P. 147, 180, 296n43
the sense of wonder 37, 102
Serviss, Garrett P. 180, 296n43
Seth Thomas 138
The Seven Arts 222
sewing machine 90, 138
shadowgraph 46, 76, 286ch4n4
Shakespeare 200
Shaw, George Bernard 163
Sheboygan Coaster & Wagon Works 250
Shelley, Mary 30, 53, 59, 103, 170, 175, 179, 200, 205, 207
Shelley, Percy Bysshe 53, 59
Sherman, Harold M. 27, 219
Shikki-shosha 268
Shipman, Charles 49
Ships in Motion 255
shoofly 23, **98**
Shotwell Mfg. Co. 301n34
Side Show 252
"A Signal from Mars" 198–9, 300n15
"The Signal Man" 57, 61, 93, 126, 184, 200, 288n60
Silliman, Benjamin 74
Silver Arrow 250, 304–5n34
Silvie and Bruno 1, 44, 48, 168–9
Simon's Sons, E. 246, 259
"Sinbad the Sailor" 132
Sinclair, Upton 178
Sinclair Refining Co. 225–6
singing bird 90–1, 138–9, 160
Six Wonder Tales for Boys 26
skates 159, 241
Skelt family 48
Ski-Scraper blocks 233
Sky-Hy blocks 233
Sky Rocket, by various manufacturers 250, 305n36
skyrocket 56, 215, 250, 252, 258
skyscraper 17, 234; as spaceship inspiration 251; toy 232
Skyscraper Game 251
sled **192**, 241
slavery 66, 85, 115, 121, 141–2, 201–3, 217
sleep-journey 2, **36**, 39, 40–4, 74–6, 119, 137–8, 153, 180, 185–6, 188, 199, 205, 247, 260
"Sleeping Beauty" 39–40, 161, 205, 301n14

sleigh 909, **100–1**
Smashed Up Locomotive 11–2, 60, 284n33
Smethport Specialty Co. 306–7n20
Smith, Edward Elmer 180, 279
Smithfield Fair 54
Smith's Comic Electric Telegraph 58, **66**
Smyth, John 214
Snow, Leonard 50
Snow White 259
S.O. Barnum & Son 50
soap 65
Social Darwinism 142
socialism 125, 180, 202–3
society: ant 121, 123, 126, 203; bee 261; in crisis 122; "primitive" 223; superior 119, 120–1; totalitarian 121
sociology 21
Solar System 143–4, 276; *see also* orrery
Somerville, Mary 18
Somnium 39
song of ideas 35, 43–4, 119, 143, 176
"A Sonnet — To Science" 96, 207
space, annihilating 162, 181; figural foreshortening 144, 155; toy 242–4, 247, 263, 272, **274**, 277; travel 10, 14–5, 35, 82, 102, 216, 275, 280, 284n38; travel as time travel 272; *see also* outer space
"spaceman" 256–7, **274**
spaceship 239, **243**, 262; *see also* Buck Rogers; *The First Men in the Moon*; *From the Earth to the Moon*; rocket ship; "The Unparalleled Adventure of One Hans Pfaall"
spacesuit *see* environmental suit
Spain 66, 90
spectacle 8–10, 12–6, 32, 36, 43, 55, 70, 75, 98, 101, 117–8, 132, 135, 142, 151, 155–9, 231, 280
spectacle toy 11–14
spectator 15
speculative fiction 2, 37
speed 21, 212–6; evoked 236, 238–9, 241, 265, 306n12; to the future 237, 252; in games 210, 236, 259; high 17, 81, 133, 235–6; land 56, 128, 241, 304–5n34; mechanical 55–6, 93, 235; in optical automation 60, 206; and progress 128; toward stasis 17, 235–6, 265; in toys 24, **238**, **239**, 24–1, **266**, 306n12; uniformity 267
Speed King: by Marx 250–1, 302–3n41; by Renwal 302–3n41

Spencer, Herbert 21, 122, 203, 223
Spengler, Oswald 201
sporting goods 246
spring motor 16, 89, 145, 159–60; *see also* clockwork
Sputnik 37–8, 62, **276**, 277, 279–80; toy 277–8
Stack Plastics 306n13
Stahlwood Toy Mfg. Co. 265
Stalin, Joseph 261
Standard Oil 137, 294n4
Stanley, Henry Morton 82
Stanley Toy Co. 277
Stapledon, Olaf 44, 180, 253, 305n46
Starr, Frederick 223
steam engine 54–5, 91, 138, 152; toy 24, 44 47, 48, 89, 91, 132, 135, 160–1, 196, 272
Steam King 91
The Steam Man 91–3, 141, 166, 200, 254; fictional 91–2, 146–7, 249
The Steam Man of the Plains 296n43
The Steam Man of the Prairies 84, 91–2, 249, 296n43
steam power 12–3, 56, 64, 135
steamboat 3, 12, 21, 127, 236; toy 49, 135
Steiger, E. 130
Stein, Gertrude 222
Steinbeck, John 178
Stellar Publishing 27
Stephens Products Co. 232
Stephenson, George 55–6
Stephenson, Robert 55, 64, 66
stereoscope 58, 62, 246
Stereovue Corporation 305n58
Stevens, Elisha 89
Stevens & Brown 56, 89–91, 291n26
Stevenson, Robert Louis 36, 43–5, 48, 112, 123, 168, 180, 217, 254, 293ch9n25
Stirn, Carl P. 160–1
stock character 10, 37, 42, 91, 142, 147, 171, 220, 247, 300n4
Stockton, Frank R. 43, 137, 179, 293ch9n25
Stone, Fred 164
The Story of a Bad Boy 119
The Story of Peter Pan 37
Strat-O-Flier 241
Stratemeyer, Edward 180–1, 220
stratigraphy 73–4
Strato-Balloon 255–6, 305n53
Stratosphere (Whitman and Parker Bros.) 251
Strauss, Ferdinand 198, 302n24
Streak-O-Lite 240–1, 304n13
Streamline 241
Streamliner 241

streamlining 236, **237–8**, 240, 262, 265–6
Street & Smith 147
streetcar 139, 160, 241, 296n49
Strobel & Wilken 300n24
Stroboscopic Disc 59
Strombeck-Becker Mfg. Co. 241
the sublime 35
submarine 43, 67, 114–6, 122, 213, 248, 263; toy 119; toy, electric 160
submergence 117–8, 121–2, 256–7; in automated system 88, 116, 184, 133–4
subterranean journey 35, 68, 74–6, 78–9, 114, 117, 119–20
"A Succession of Sundays" 25, 129–30, 135–6, 169
Suez Canal 21
Sun Rubber Co. 305n58
The Sunday Alphabet of Animals 51–2
Sunday doll 54, 105
Sunday school equipment 130
Sunday toy 50–4, 64
Super-Jector 246
"super" prefix 10, 246–7
superhuman 113, 115–7, 120–1, 133, 141, 174–5, 180, 184–6, 217, 220, 305n46; comical 246–7; "magazine superman" 175, 184, 246; through technics 246–7
Superior Type Co. 243, 246
Superjax 246
Superman wood toy 259
Superman Speed Game 259
supernatural worldview 31, 36, 38; *see also* providential worldview
Surrealism 10
Sweden 65, 70
Sweet Clover: A Romance of the White City 162–4
Swift, Jonathan 35, 305n58
Swinburne, Charles Algernon 32
Swiss Family Robinson 62, 78–9, 161, 200, 258
Switzerland 66, 139, 155; *see also* Geneva
symbolic appropriation 26, 94–6, 100–1, 120, 143, 174, 203, 243
symbolic expansion 105
symbolic melodrama 32–3, 38; *see also* wonder tale, modern
symbolic reality 33
symbolic values 95
symbolism 19–20, 26, 30, 32, 146–7, 163, 177, 268
symbolized technics 34

T-N Co. 275
Tabolewsky, Mrs. A.J. 159–60
Tahiti 78, 134
Takeoff 277, 307n33

"A Tale of the Days To Come" 35, 176, 202, 228, 294n29
A Tale of Two Cities 88, 126, 303n49
tall-tale 38, 91, 113
"Tammany Bank" 80
Tarzan 246, 246–8, 255, 300n19, 304ch16n29, 305n48; Jungle Set 255; movie 248; toy 255, 305n48
Tarzan Jungle 255
Tarzan of the Apes 40, 185, 248, 300n19, 304ch16n29
Tarzan the Terrible 185
taxonomy 114–5, 120
Taylor, Bayard 31
Taylor Tot **237**
technical envelopment 10–1, 17–8, 56–7, 61, 63, 67, 85–6, 102, 109, 113, 115–6, 172–3, 181, 184, 201, 232, 234, 255, 256–7, 280; in a toy **161**; *see also* dwarf within the machine; environmental suit
technological globalism 277
technological idealism 11; *see also* positivism
telegraphy 22, 38, 58, 66, 133, 140–2, 148, 156, 165, 181, 183, 280, 285n12; automatic 58, 138; toy 244; wireless 181; wireless toy **211**
telephone 142, 165, 173, 280
telescope *iv*, 8, 108
television 62, 257, 267–8, 277, 280; advertising 271; -related toy 277
"The Tell-Tale Heart" 86
Temple, Henry John 19
Tenniel, John 204
Tennyson, Alfred Lord 19, 30, 31, 142, 173
terrarium 258
Tesla, fictional 182
Thackeray, W.M. 67
Thaeter, Jean 160
thaumatrope 58–9
Thaumotropical Amusement 59
theater 10, 25, 111, 154–5, 165, 178, 186–7, 199, 205–6, 220, 229, 230, 267; machinery 10; movie- 205, 207; *see also* paper doll drama; toy theater
Theatre Pictoresque & Méchanique 46
Thomas Mfg. Corp. 266, 207n30
Thompson, Ruth Plumley 180
Thomson, James, "B.V." 20, 27, 64, 76–7, 179
Thornecraft 241
"Three Sundays in a Week" *see* "A Succession of Sundays"
Thrilling Wonder Stories 37
Tik-Tok 166, 200, 249, 254

The Tik-Tok Man of Oz 166
Tim-Mee Toys 271
time: and business 88, 126, 130–1; foreshortening 77, 131, 143–4; geological 20, 72, 224, 272; Greenwich 129; quickening 77; reversal 11–2, 74–6, 135, 168, 227; seeing across disjunct 135–6, 272; shrinkage 169; simultaneity 129–30, 135–6, 169, 172–3, 181; slowing 116, 131; in stratigraphy 74; suspended 116, 131, 172, 210; thirteen o'clock 86, 131, 267; travel 25, 40–1, 74–6, 129–30, 135, 169, 186, 210; *see also* clock stoppage; earth as clock
Time Globe 140
The Time Machine 169–71, 202
the Time Traveler 169–70, 210
The Tin Soldier 197, 254
tin toy 12–3, 18, 49–50, 80, 88, **90**, 91, 110, 123, **127**, 130, 134–5, 139, 147, 161, 198, 269, 274, 305n58
Tin Woodman 164–6, 171–2, 249, 254; as robot 299n85
tinsmith 88–9, 166
tinware 88–9
"To Haydon" 57
"To the North Pole by Airship" 189
Tom Swift 44, 81, 181, 218, 220, 248
Tom Swift and His Air-Ship 101, **191**, 192
Tom Swift and His Flying Lab 81
Tom Swift and His Motor-Boat 101
Tom Swift and His Motor-Cycle 101
Tom Swift in the Caves of Ice 189
Tommy Trot's Visit to Santa Claus 36, 44
Toonin—A Real Radio Game 210
Tootsietoy 239, 252
top: flying 23; spinning 65, 131–2, 134, 306–7n20; *see also* gyroscope
torpedo 213, **214**, 215, 250, 276; toy 214
Torpedo Flying Machine 214
Le Tour du monde en quatre-vingt jours 126; *see also* Around the World in Eighty Days
Tower, William S. 49
toy: American 20; animal 89, 196, 254–5, 262, 306n9; bestseller 12; book 50, 70, 130, **150**–1, 161, 196, 212; branded 65; carriage 88; comical 186–88, 198, 208, 214, 242,

245–7, 288n57, 305n48; cowboy and Indian 262, 271, 306n9; department 135, **242**, 246; factory 12, 59, 61, 62, 87, 279; fad 15, 55, 123, 140, 148–9, 270; as "fancy good" 15–6, 49, 132; farm 254–5, 262; floor vs. track 55, **193**, 304n16; geographical 47, 51,; gun 24, 138, 161, 196, 262, 267, 272, 304n20; import to America 23–4, 46, 268–70, 279; industry 242–4, 267, 279; licensed 167, 231, 245–6, 248–52, 255, 259, 271; manufacture 11, 14, 47, 49, 50, 52, 54, 69, 82, 87–8, 268–9, 272; military 262, 271; mirror 165, 255; as model 16, 33, 54–5, 62; modern symbolic 61–3, 88, 196; musical 246, 278, 296n49; nostalgia 263, 277; parachute 161; promotional *iv*, 65, 165, 240, 244, 249, **273**; representing cultural change 13–4, 62; soldier 23, 52, 81, 123, 198, 202, 217, 248, 254, 262, 306n9; standards **24**, 130; theater 8, 10, 47–49, 76, 151, 161, 165, 187, 196, 286ch4n4, 287n10, 289n34; traditional 14, 50, 54, 61, 63, 80–1, **175**, 196, 209, 249, 254, 262, 280; train 89; and violence 4, 15, 24, 51, 119, 123, 254; in wartime 23, 209, 262–3
Toy Automaton 88, 290n18
Toy Center, or Toy Building 244
Toy Clock Dial 130–1, 135–6
Toy Fair 244–6
"toy men" 243–4, 249
Toy Mfrs. of the U.S.A. 198, 244, 270
Toy Town Shopping Center 264
Traffic Jam Game 241
Train, Arthur 180
transatlantic cable 22
Transcontinental Rocket Ship **250**
transformation book **150**
Transparent Man 233
A Traveler from Altruria 174
Treasure Island 45
Trevithick, Richard 286n33
Triceratops 206, 225
tricycle 196, **238**, 241
"The Tricycle of the Future" 43
Trilobite 78
Tristan and Isolde 20
Trojan, Inc. 246
trolley car *see* streetcar
Truffy 139
Truro, Cornwall 55

Index

Tsiolkovsky, Konstantin 258, 275, 277
Tuffy Toys 306*n*13
Tussaud, Madame 126
Twain, Mark 36, 38, 39, 125, 163; *see also* Clemens, Samuel
Tweed, William "Boss" 80, 289*n*49
Twenty Thousand Leagues Under the Sea 18, 48, 112–6, 122, 132, 142, 247–8, 293*ch*8*n*25; film 272
Twisted Tales 252
Twistum Toy Factory 218, 303*n*52
type character 142, 171, 174, 176
typewriter 196
Tyrannosaurus Rex 272

Under the Moons of Mars 40, 185, 300*n*19; *see also A Princess of Mars*
An Underground Theater 154–5, 296–7*n*11
uniformitarianism 69–70
Union Mfg. Co. 290*n*22
Unique Arts Mfg. Co. 198
United States 20, 23, 58, 65–6, 70, 74, 79, 92, 137–8, 141, 145–6, 198, 259; architecture 154, 224, 233, 239, 304*n*36; economy 22, 149, 159, 224; industrial development 22
universal life-apparatus 18; *see also* technical envelopment
"The Unparalleled Adventure of One Hans Pfaall" 16–7, 81, 102–3, 109, 116, 176, 291*n*1, 291*n*4
utopian tale 119, 121
utopian vision 21, 40, 222, 234, 265

Valéry, Paul-Ambroise 35, 267–8
"Valley of the Lost" 228
van Dyne, Edith 44, 179; *see also* Baum, L. Frank
Vathek 30
velocipede 24, **129**, 196, 286*n*28; clockwork 89–90
Venus 272
verisimilitude 9–10, 16, 32, 39, 94, 96, 106, 145, 256
Vermont Novelty Works 24
Verne, Honorine 5
Verne, Jules 5–11, 14, 17–8, 20, 25–33, 35–8, 40, 42, 44, 48, 61, 65, 68, 81, 83, 100, 103–6, 112–21, 125–30, 132, 134, 142, 158, 170–2, 174, 176, 178–81, 183, 185–6, 190, 199–201, 205–8, 225, 234, 247–8, 251, 254, 258–9, 272–4, 277, 286*n*42, 293*ch*9*n*26; clock fantasy 103–5; and evolutionary theory 73–4, 120, 289*n*29, 289*n*41; on Poe 32, 96, 105, 113; *see also* dissected soul; Earth, descent into; Earth, shrinkage; marvelous machine; sectional character; wonder tale, modern
Victoria: in Poe 16, 17, 35; in Verne 9, 10, 35, 106, 115
La Vie Moderne 147
Vienna World International Exhibition 90
Une Ville flottante see Propeller Island
Villers de l'Isle-Adams, Mathias 146–7
vinyl toy 278, 280
vision, backward 74–6, 78, 117, 227–8; forward 227–8
vivarium *see* aquarium; terrarium
volcano 68, 143, 206, 295*n*33
Voltaire 81
von Bismarck, Otto 122–4
Vondervotteimitiss 93, 105, 113, 290*n*12
von Humboldt, Baron 20
von Kempelen, Baron 84–5
von Stampfer, Simon 59
von Zeppelin, Ferdinand 141
Voyage au Centre de la Terre 20; *see also A Journey to the Centre of the Earth*
Le Voyage dans la Lune 37
Un Voyage en ballon 105–6, 292*n*35
Voyages extraordinaires 32
Vril-ya *see The Coming Race*
Vulcan locomotive 132

Wagner, Richard 20, 147, 156
Wagnerism 21
wagon, coaster 240–1, 246, 250
Walbert Mfg. Co. 198, 302*n*24
Walpole, Horace 29–30
Walt Disney Enterprises 248–9
Wannatoy see Dillon-Beck Mfg. Co.
war 24, 186, 236, 262; between worlds 111, 183–4; fictional 92, 122, 199, 201; influencing toys 24; surrogate for 236; technological 122
The War of the Worlds 122, 170, 198
Warner, N.S. 90
Washington, George 149
Washington, D.C. 65, 139
watch 93, 103, 125, 129, 139–40, 144, 146, 171; toy 84, 86, 88, 93, 161, 168–9, 299*n*4–5
Water Pistol 244–5
Watt, James 54–5, 67, 287*n*30–3
Waverly Toy Works 148, 296*n*48
The Well-Tempered Clavier 105
Wells, Herbert George 26–7, 35–8, 40, 61, 96, 122, 163, 169–78, 180, 198, 202, 208, 210, 216, 220, 228, 248, 259, 279, 305*n*53
West, Julian 210
West, William 48
Western Auto Stores 238
Westinghouse 253
Wheatstone, Charles 58
Wheel-O 277
wheel toy 13, 24, 49, 161, 262
When the Sleeper Wakes 40, 44, 170, 202
"When the Speed Comes" 93
"Whirl" name 241
whist 127–30, 134, 136, 273, 294, 294*n*35
whistle 65, 89, 91–2, 291*n*27
Whitall, Henry 140
White, Samuel S. 141
"The White City" *see* Columbian Exposition
White City Ferris Wheel **154**
Whitehead, Robert 213
Whitman Publishing Co. 245, 251
"A Wife Manufactured to Order" 145
Wilcox, James 15
Wilde, Oscar 163
Willard, Frances 157
William I 122
"William Wilson" 113
Willys *see* Jeep
Wilson, Edmund 32, 35, 222, 261
The Wind in the Willows 102
Winter, Milo 100
Wisconsin 23, 146; Milwaukee 23; Racine 226, 245; Sheboygan 241, 250
The Wizard gyroscope top 165
The Wizard of Oz: movie-based game 259; movie version 259, 267; stage version 164, 267; *see also The Wonderful Wizard of Oz*
Wolfe, Bob 245
Wolverine Supply & Mfg. Co. 195, 198–9, 241, 302*n*24
Woman's Rights Advocate 145–6
women's suffrage 177, 184
A Wonder-Book for Girls and Boys 38
The Wonder Clock 26
Wonder Stories 27–8, 37
wonder tale 10, 15, 17–9, 24–9, 32–3, 38, 54, 93, 98, 146, 154–5, 161, 172, 178–81, 188, 207–8, 271–2, 274, 279, 280; in comics 164, 186–8, 210; Gothic 28–31, 35–7, 41–2, 44, 59, 97–8, 113, 117, 121–2, 145, 170, 199, 217; in

film 36–7, 186–7, 205–7, 259; and the future 248; as *jeu d'esprit* 17, 135, 169; modern 34–8, 43–4, 94–5, 98, 117, 131, 151, 170, 173–7, 248, 259, 268; philosophic 34, 39, 95; as prophesy 11, 17, 101; Romantic 38; on stage 37, 40; of "super-science" 248; *see also* marvelous machine; science fiction; scientifiction; sectional character

The Wonderful Game of Oz 259

The Wonderful Wizard of Oz 152, 163–7, 170, 205, 267; silent film 205; Oz playthings 64, 67; Oz series 181

wonderland 26, 132, 157, 188, 286n42

"The Wondersmith" 25

wood toy 11–2, 49–52, 80, 123, 139, 149, 151, 159, 188, 259, 262, 269, **280**

Woodward, Alice B. 51, 87, 106, 280

Woolf, Virginia 268, 289n24

Wordsworth, William 7, 96

world-clock *see* clock, geographical

The World Flyers Around the World Flight Air Race 134

world-machine 43, 172–3, 180, 183, 204, 214, 263, 274

The World of Tomorrow *see* New York World's Fair

World Travel set 255

World War I 38, 186, 198, 231, 262, 269

World War II 14, 37–8, 262–3, 268–9, 277

World Without Color 272

World's Fair 65–6, 137, 155; Panorama 160; *see also* Exposition, International

The World's Noah's Ark 161

Wright, George F. 152–3

Wright, Orville 63, 191, 196

Wright, Wilbur 63, 191, 196

Wright Aeroplane *190*

W.S. Reed Toy Co. 12

Wyandotte Toys 215, 262

Wyss, Johann Rudolph 53–4, 78–9, 170, 178

Yale University 164

Yeats, William Butler 32, 268

The Yellow Kid 187–8, 214, 243, 248

Young, Clarence 180

Youth's Companion 132, 189

Zell Products Co. 305n58

"Zephyr" name 241

zeppelin *see Graf Zeppelin*

zinc toy *see* die-cast toy

Zip Zip Shooter 231

Zippy Zepps Air Game 303n43

Zoetrope, or Wheel of Life 59–60; as generic designation 161

Zola, Émil 177

zoology 67, 72, 78–9, 114

Zoomer the Robot **275**

www.ingramcontent.com/pod-product-compliance
Ingram Content Group UK Ltd.
Pitfield, Milton Keynes, MK11 3LW, UK
UKHW051850210426
5322IPUK00025B/653